SEXUALITIES

IDENTITIES, BEHAVIORS, AND SOCIETY

EDITED BY

Michael S. Kimmel
Rebecca F. Plante

New York   Oxford
OXFORD UNIVERSITY PRESS
2004

Oxford University Press

Oxford   New York
Auckland   Bangkok   Buenos Aires   Cape Town   Chennai
Dar es Salaam   Delhi   Hong Kong   Istanbul   Karachi   Kolkata
Kuala Lumpur   Madrid   Melbourne   Mexico City   Mumbai
Nairobi   São Paulo   Shanghai   Taipei   Tokyo   Toronto

Published by Oxford University Press, Inc.
198 Madison Avenue, New York, New York, 10016
http://www.oup-usa.org

Oxford is a registered trademark of Oxford University Press

Library of Congress Cataloging-in-Publication Data

Sexualities: identities, behaviors, and society / edited by Michael S. Kimmel,
Rebecca F. Plante.
      p. cm.
   Includes index.
   ISBN 978-0-19-515760-4
      1. Sex. 2. Sex (Psychology) 3. Sexual orientation. 4. Sex crimes. I. Kimmel,
Michael S. II. Plante, Rebecca F.
HQ21.S47514 2004
306.7—dc22

                                                                      2003060969

Printed in the United States of America
on acid-free pape

FOR GRANDMOTHER AND GRANDFATHER
—RFP

FOR JOHN GAGNON
—MSK

CONTENTS

INTRODUCTION

Coitus can scarcely be said to take place in a vacuum; although of itself it appears a biological and physical activity, it is set so deeply within the larger context of human affairs that it serves as a charged microcosm of the variety of attitudes and values to which culture subscribes. Among other things, it may serve as a model of sexual politics on an individual or personal place.

—*Kate Millett,* Sexual Politics (1970)

At this moment, you might be asking yourself what a topic like sex is doing in a social science course. Isn't sex something to be kept private? It certainly does not seem like something to talk about in school! Won't studying sex demystify it? Or, worse, isn't studying sex an invitation to experiment, making it politically volatile? And if we do study sexuality, shouldn't we do so in the natural science, since sex is a matter of biology and reproduction?

Well, obviously, the answer is "no" because you're already here in a class devoted to the study of sexuality. Biology is certainly an appropriate domain through which one can examine various facets of our sexualities. But the thesis underlying this book is that what we do sexually, and what we think about what we do sexually, are as much a product of our interactions with each other and with our cultural assumptions about sexuality as sexuality is about drives and biological imperatives to reproduce.

I

The book is about the social construction of sexualities. We believe that, rather than being the simple product of natural "urges" or "drives," human sexualities are also shaped and constructed in social contexts. Hence there is a considerable range of sexual variations in our own society and even more variation if we look across time and place at sexual attitudes and behaviors.

As sociologist John Gagnon put it in *Human Sexualities* (1977):

In any given society, at any given moment in its history, people become sexual in the same way they become everything else. Without much reflection, they pick up directions from their social environment. They acquire and assemble meanings, skills and values from the people around them. Their critical choices are often made by going along and drifting. People learn when they are quite young a few of the things they are expected to be, and continue slowly to accumulate a belief in who they are and ought to be throughout the rest of childhood, adolescence and adulthood. Sexual conduct is learned in the same ways and through the same processes; it is acquired and assembled in human interaction, judged and performed in specific cultural and historical worlds. (p. 2)

Sexual behavior is, in this sense, no different from all the other behaviors in our lives. We learn it from the people and institutions and ideas around us, and assemble it into a coherent narrative.

That's also why we use the word "sexual*ies*" in our title and in our work. There is no singular model for how people have sex, why, where, how often, or even with whom. There is an enormous range of responses to "how often" people "should" have sex, and what types of sex they should have, and with whom they should have it. There are even debates about what constitutes "sex" in the first place. Does oral sex count? What about "everything but"? Do other cultures have "technical virgins"?

The sexual aspect of life is both personal and social. Nothing in our lives is more personal. It's rare that we actually, honestly, talk about our sexual lives. And often it seems that the more universal the sexual behavior is, the more secretive and private we are about it. Take masturbation, for example, which surveys indicate is the single most common sexual behavior in the United States. When was the last time you had a frank heart-to-heart talk with a friend about what you think about when you masturbate? And yet nothing we do is more social than sex in that we learn what it is, how to do it, and what to feel when we are doing it from a wide array of clues we find in our culture—bits of shared information, misinformation, and even disinformation (lies other people tell us about sex).

Sex is also political, as the feminist movement and the gay and lesbian movements have demonstrated. Some of the most widely discussed social issues in recent months involve the politicization and "public-ness" of discussions about sexuality. What does it mean that we can consume so many images of sex so readily in videos, on the Internet, in movies or magazines? And sexual behavior sometimes involves force; it often involves negotiation, power differences, and ethics.

Our task, then, is a large one: to examine the psychological, social, ethical, and political dimensions of our sexual lives. We want to look at both identities and behaviors and see the ways in which they fit together—or the ways in which they do not.

II

To accomplish our task, we approach sex like any other subject of the social sciences and ask specific questions of what we know and what we think we know. What evidence is used to demonstrate various claims about sexuality? What is the logic of the argument being made? Does it make sense? What are matters of opinion and what are matters of scientifically based knowledge? To address such matters requires that we set some boundaries, so we will consider only the contemporary United States, although we will do so in comparative and historical perspective.

The book is divided into ten chapters, and we hope that these can form the foundation for a full semester's course.

Chapters One and Two provide some examples of the ways in which we have come to think about sexualities in the social sciences. First we look at some classic statements, then some contemporary ones, that define the boundaries of contemporary sexual discussion and set the agenda for other inquiries.

Chapters Three, Four, and Five explore the ways in which we become sexual and the ways in which we begin to develop sexual identities, both heterosexual and homosexual. Where do we get our sexual identities? Why are some people gay and most straight?

Chapter Six expands the discussion to include sexual behaviors and identities that are often considered problematic or "deviant." What are the dynamics of consensual S/M scenes? Why do some people use props?

Chapters Eight and Nine examine the commodification of sex. Sex is not only something one "does," it's also something that one can buy and sell in a marketplace—either in real flesh-and-blood people (prostitution, sex tourism, sex trafficking) or in fantasies (like pornography). What effects does this form of sexual consumerism have on our sexual identities and behaviors?

Chapter Nine explores the intersections of sexualities and violence, especially those activities in which sex is the means by which other ends are achieved. What are the factors that make for relatively rape-prone or rape-free cultures—or college campuses?

And, finally, in Chapter Ten, we question how to teach the next generation about sex. Are we even to teach them at all?

III

All books have arguments; no text is purely objective. If anyone ever tells you that they're just presenting the facts without editorializing, they're either lying or naïve. And nowhere is this more evident than when discussing sexuality.

We make a few arguments throughout this book. First, we believe that the remarkably rich diversity of sexual activities, identities, and behaviors is something that ought to be acknowledged. There are many ways to be sexual—we humans are an amazingly creative species compared to other mammals. (Ever watch dogs mate? They're not especially inventive about it. It's unlikely that Fido and Rover will ever collaborate on the puppy version of the *Kama Sutra*.) And, while we don't subscribe to a simple endorsement of all sexual activities being created equal, we do believe that when two adults consent to mutual pleasure, moral predisposition should yield to wonder.

This leads to a second argument: People's sexual experiences and expressions don't fall tidily into neat little compartments. Although a wide variety of moral codes—religions, secular ethical systems—have declared that some sexualities are "normal" and others are "unnatural," nature itself doesn't see things that way. Same-sex and opposite-sex behaviors are found among virtually every species on the planet. Some couples mate for life; others for a moment. Some are fully faithful; others as promiscuous as the proverbial rabbit. Some find a vital, active, predatory "him" pursuing a sweet young passive damsel; others find females actively seeking to mate with as many suitors as possible in a very brief time period.

What is considered "normal" is a political decision, as cultures decide which behaviors to include and which to exclude from the menu of regulated sexual activities. It is political because what is declared to be "normal" is really what is "normative"—that is, whatever is prescribed by any particular culture at any particular time. To say that certain sexual behaviors are normative is not to say they are not "normal" of course; they are just as normal as those that are excluded. We only seek to acknowledge that social processes are at work in rendering those behaviors and identities normal or not. "There can be no such thing as natural behavior," wrote the anthropologist Marcel Mauss. "Nothing is more essentially transmitted by a social process of learning than sexual behavior."

We make yet another argument: More sexual information is, in the long run, better for us as individuals, as sexual partners, and as a culture. There is no evidence whatsoever, for example, that increased sexual information leads to increased sexual behavior: If there were such evidence, this would be by far the most popular course in the history of the university! In fact, there is some evidence that increased sexual information may lead to a slight decrease in sexual activity. Before you go looking for the "drop" slip to get out of the course, though, there is some other evidence that you might consider. Increased sexual information decidedly does lead to safer sex—fewer STDs, fewer unwanted pregnancies, and fewer cases of sexual assault. Whether it leads to "better" sex we leave for you to determine.

Third, and most important theoretically, we believe the evidence indicates that the great sexual divide in our culture is not between homosexuals and heterosexuals, but between women and men. "She" may make love "just like a woman," as Bob Dylan famously sang, but "he" would make love just like a man. Though we often think sexual orientation is the great dividing line in our sexual expression—if one is gay or straight one knows all one needs to know about their sexualities—the evidence points decidedly the other way, toward an understanding that gender, not sexual orientation, is the dividing line along which sexual expression, desire, and experience are organized. Gay men and straight men think and act in sexually similar ways, as do lesbians and straight women. In that sense, sexually speaking, gay men and lesbians are gender conformists. Lesbians and straight women have "feminine" sex; gay men and straight men have "masculine" sex—in their expression, cognition, and representation.

IV

Our sexual world is dramatically different from the world of our parents' and grandparents' generations. For one thing, there have been many changes in the technologies of sex, from pills that prevent pregnancies to those that promise to increase sexual functioning, as well as medical breakthroughs that have increased sexual functioning, longevity, and health.

Another change is that we now expect to engage in sexual activities throughout our lives. Not so long ago, perhaps at the end of the last century, most people over fifty probably had sex less than once a year, if that. Few, if any, people could have imagined their grandparents having sex, let alone their parents.

And sex is both safer and more dangerous than ever. The dramatic spread of STDs, especially HIV, among young people has been alarming. Approximately one quarter of the 15 million new STD cases diagnosed each year in the United States are teenagers. The most common of these—chlamydia, genital herpes, and HIV—were unheard of as recently as 1960.

Sex is also increasingly public, both in terms of the proliferation of sex in our culture and the visibility of different sexualities. Not so very long ago, those whose sexual identity was non-normative—gay or lesbian, bisexual, or transgender—or whose sexual behaviors fell outside of the mainstream—such as S/M or what used to be called "paraphilia" (use of sex toys and erotic objects)—were forced to conceal themselves in closets of shame and fear.

Today, thanks to the social movements of the 1960s—the women's movement and the gay and lesbian movement specifically—those whose identities are non-normative are increasingly visible, both politically and culturally. Gays and lesbians have become organized political forces, so that even the Log Cabin Club, an organization for gay and lesbian Republicans, exerts political clout in the Republican Party. And every major city boasts sex shops that rival the catalogs of various online suppliers to every sexual taste imaginable—and some you've probably never even imagined!

Today, one can see the most graphically sexual images with the click of a mouse and sex is used to sell everything from shampoo or deodorant to industrial equipment and personal technologies. At times it seems as though we are surrounded by sexual images, that we are drowning in a sea of unbridled sexuality. Except, that is, in schools, where today's students are actually learning *less* about sexuality than they were a couple of decades ago.

In fact, it is this combination of the proliferation of sexuality all over the culture and the absence of any real sustained honest conversation about it that motivated us to begin to teach courses on human sexualities and to decide to bring together in this book the best articles we could find that will enable you to begin that conversation yourselves.

In editing this book, we have had two aims. First, we hope that our book will expand your intellectual understanding and your general sociological sophistication. Second, we hope that you will find the exploration of this subject to be a rewarding personal experience, one that leads to a reexamination of your own experience, values, beliefs, and assumptions.

ACKNOWLEDGMENTS

This book arose from our search for an ideal human sexualities text for sociology and women's studies classes. The readings here are inspired by the ideas we initially worked through with our first "Sexuality and Society" students, in separate courses at the University of New Hampshire and SUNY at Stony Brook. We thank our students and the many others who have helped this book come to fruition.

Rebecca Plante acknowledges: First I must acknowledge 14 years of good mentoring, inspiring intellectual interchanges, and solid friendship of my coeditor, Michael S. Kimmel. I have benefited in untold ways from Michael's unwavering support. Much of my work on the book came during my years at Wittenberg University in Springfield, Ohio. Many thanks are due to the Sociology Department, especially Keith Doubt, for photocopying assistance, student aides, and clerical help (especially Robin Heil). My student aides, Gillian Taylor and Jamie Shampine, were invaluable in their pursuit of provocative articles and permissions of information. Thomas Library staff—especially Karen Balliet—provided timely OhioLink books and journal articles. Also thanks to the Sociology Department at Ithaca College—especially Vikki Hammond—for help with the final manuscript details. Finally, warm professional thanks for laughs and careful readings to editors Sean Mahoney and Peter Labella, as well as the production and design staffs at Oxford.

My friends and family have provided much-appreciated love, comfort and support. My parents have been profoundly supportive of everything I have done. I owe my intellectual curiosity to them and to my maternal grandparents, to whom my work is dedicated. The academic lifestyle (i.e., moving regularly) has enabled me to make fantastic friends all over the country. Suzanne, Ken, and Arlaine have heard most of my joys and frustrations since 2000; thanks for friendship, meals, and shopping. Annie, Alaina, Jen W., Ruthie, Katie, Abbe, Valerie, and Trent are shining stars. For long-term love and faith: Chris in Georgia (who first told me I could do a book on sex!), ORT, John, Kenny, Synth, Jeff, Cheryl, Tonya and Ignacio, Aaron, Talin, Eric, Christina, Matt, Ezinna, Schmitt, Angus, Leslie, Alan, MEOw, RayRay, and my beloved (Red)Rob. And Brody is the best friend I ever could have dreamed of, the best person I have ever known, and the best keeper-of-my-sanity. I owe you big.

Michael Kimmel acknowledges: It's a pleasure to acknowledge a 14-year collaboration with Rebecca, who has always been as much a colleague as student. As a young sexuality scholar, she is peerless. I have benefited so much from my students in my sexuality courses at

Stony Brook, who often challenge the flat platitudes of statistical research. And I was fortunate to teach in the same department as John Gagnon, perhaps the pre-eminent sexuality researcher of our era. Our conversations over many meals and countless commutes were inspiring, even if all our joint projects did not come to fruition. What work we did, we did well. I thank Cathy Greenblat also for that collaboration and friendship, and for her efforts to right a listing ship.

My friends and family are the foundation from which all my work is built. They know how much I love them. For twenty years or so, I've had running conversations about sex with Marty Duberman, Michael Kaufman, and Lillian Rubin—conversations that have pushed around my assumptions more than any others. For ten of those years, Marty Levine and I carried that conversation into the public arena, writing and lecturing together about gay and straight masculinity. I miss him still.

I feel enormously lucky to have landed at Oxford University Press, where I've continued my longtime friendship with my editor Peter Labella, and have been so fortunate to work with Sean Mahoney, Robert Miller, Elyse Dubin, Mary Beth Jarrad, and Catherine Lively. They remind me that the relationship between writer and publisher need not be class warfare (except on the softball field).

As always, it's Amy and Zachary around whom my world turns.

"Sex is one of the nine great mysteries of life," Henry Miller once wrote. "The other eight are unimportant." We hope that we have collected works that will enable readers to think critically about sex, but without losing its mystery. To shed light is not always to reduce heat.

Michael S. Kimmel
Rebecca F. Plante

SEXUALITIES

PART ONE

INTRODUCTION TO SEXUALITIES

CHAPTER ONE

CLASSICAL INQUIRIES

Human beings have been fascinated by sexuality since the beginning of our species. After all, both Darwinian evolution and the Bible begin with sex—reproductive adaptations to changing environmental conditions or the sinful temptation of desire of God's first man. But the study of sexuality and its role in human affairs expanded dramatically at the turn of the twentieth century in Europe, when inquiries into sexuality were linked to questions about the modern self, sexual orientations, and gender identity.

Though Sigmund Freud was not the first to pose such questions, his writings are perhaps the most influential starting point, because he posed them in a way that has galvanized sexual theorizing ever since. Freud made four claims that are of interest to us here. First, he argued that sexual energy was the life force, and that all human activity was driven by libido, a highly sexualized energy. Second, he argued that gender was the organizing principle of sexuality—males and females differed dramatically in their sexual desires and expressions. Third, Freud argued that sexual identity was not a "given" but was the result of an arduous process of organizing one's "appropriate" (same gender) models for identification and desire. And, since this was not given in nature but was the result of socialization within the family, something could go wrong and a boy could end up identifying with his mother, or a girl with her father, which would lead to erotic attraction to the same sex. Thus, homosexuality was a "gender" problem—a problem of boys who identified as feminine and girls who identified as masculine. These ideas are still with us today in various forms, especially in the stereotypes of gay men as effeminate and lesbians as masculine.

While Freud focused mostly on the perils of "normal" development, his contemporaries, notably Havelock Ellis and Richard von Krafft-Ebing, were preoccupied with what happened when things went wrong. Krafft-Ebing first labeled the behaviors of "sadism" and "masochism," while Ellis created a sort of pleasantly sensual utopia as his vision of sexual freedom.

The suppression of sexual inquiry in Germany in the middle of the twentieth century (books and articles about sexuality were destroyed because many researchers were Jewish or homosexual) shifted sexual exploration from Europe to the United States. In 1948, Alfred Kinsey published the book *Sexual Behavior in the Human Male,* to be followed five years later by *Sexual Behavior in the Human Female.* Based on extensive and explicit interviews with several thousand American men and women, Kinsey's straightforward scientific approach (he was interested only in behavior, not in attitudes) gave a shocking and sensational portrait of American sexuality. That Kinsey only studied certain Americans did not seem to bother him much, and he assumed that what his subjects did was what other "human" males and females were doing. Actually, Kinsey's research samples were neither representative nor random, and he often drew from populations of prostitutes, convicted criminals, and university students (all of whom have higher rates of sexual activity), among others.

Nonetheless, Kinsey's books created a sensation, and a popular book written from Kinsey's dry scientific tomes was an instant best-seller. Among his most shocking findings were that Americans had far more sex than pundits seemed to think and that nearly 40 percent of all males had had at least one homosexual encounter to orgasm (although the overwhelming majority of these were in single-sex venues like religious seminaries, prisons, the military, the Boy Scouts, or single-sex summer camp or school).

Now that the sexual aspect of life seemed to have become so visible, others rushed in to help us do it better. William Masters and Virginia Johnson began their career monitoring the physiological experience of sex and orgasm, but ended up as therapists instructing people on how to do it "better." Their many books, including *Human Sexual Response,* sold millions of copies, as did many other sex advice books of the era.

In the social sciences, though, perhaps the most important theoretical breakthrough in thinking about sexuality came from sociologists John Gagnon and William Simon. Collaborators with Kinsey on the last volume of his studies, Gagnon and Simon made sexual behavior as comprehensible as any other culturally organized behavior. Nothing mysterious—just the product of a wide variety of socio-sexual ideas, assumptions, and beliefs that are organized by us into "scripts" that we follow to organize the who, what, where, when, and why of our sexual lives.

1.1 FEMININITY[1]

Sigmund Freud

Both sexes seem to pass through the early phases of libidinal development in the same manner. It might have been expected that in girls there would already have been some lag in aggressiveness in the sadistic anal phase, but such is not the case. Analysis of children's play has shown our women analysts that the aggressive impulses of little girls leave nothing to be desired in the way of abundance and violence. With their entry into the phallic phase the differences between the sexes are completely eclipsed by their agreements. We are now obliged to recognize that the little girl is a little man. In boys, as we know, this phase is marked by the fact that they have learnt how to derive pleasurable sensations from their small penis and connect its excited state with their ideas of sexual intercourse. Little girls do the same thing with their still smaller clitoris. It seems that with them all their masturbatory acts are carried out on this penis-equivalent, and that the truly feminine vagina is still undiscovered by both sexes. It is true that there are a few isolated reports of early vaginal sensations as well, but it could not be easy to distinguish these from sensations in the anus or vestibulum; in any case they cannot play a great part. We are entitled to keep to our view that in the phallic phase of girls the clitoris is the leading erotogenic zone. But it is not, of course, going to remain so. With the change to femininity the clitoris should wholly or in part hand over its sensitivity, and at the same time its importance, to the vagina. This would be one of the two tasks which a woman has to perform in the course of her development, whereas the more fortunate man has only to continue at the time of his sexual maturity the activity that he has previously carried out at the period of the early efflorescence of his sexuality.

We shall return to the part played by the clitoris; let us now turn to the second task with which a girl's development is burdened. A boy's mother is the first object of his love, and she remains so too during the formation of his Oedipus complex and, in essence, all through his life. For a girl too her first object must be her mother (and the figures of wet nurses and foster mothers that merge into her). The first object-cathexes occur in attachment to the satisfaction of the major and simple vital needs, and the circumstances of the care of children are the same for both sexes. But in the Oedipus situation the girl's father has become her love object, and we expect that in the normal course of development she will find her way from this paternal object to her final choice of an object. In the course of time, therefore, a girl has to change her erotogenic zone and her object—both of which a boy retains. The question then arises of how this happens: in particular, how does a girl pass from her mother to an attachment to her father? or, in other words, how does she pass from her masculine phase to the feminine one to which she is biologically destined?

It would be a solution of ideal simplicity if we could suppose that from a particular age onwards the elementary influence of the mutual attraction between the sexes makes itself felt and impels the small woman towards men, while the same law allows the boy to continue with his mother. We might suppose in addition that in this the children are following the pointer given them by the sexual preference of their parents. But we are not going to find things so easy; we scarcely know whether we are to believe seriously in the power of which poets talk so much and with such enthusiasm but which cannot be further dissected analytically. We have found an answer of quite another sort by means of laborious investigations, the material for which at least was easy to arrive at. For you must know that the number of women who remain till a late age tenderly dependent on a paternal object, or indeed on their real father, is very great. We have established some surprising facts about these women with an intense attachment of long duration to their father. We knew, of course, that there had been a preliminary stage of attachment to the mother, but we did not know that it could be so rich in content and so long lasting, and could leave behind so many opportunities for fixations and dispositions. During this time the girl's father is only a troublesome rival; in some cases the attachment to her mother lasts beyond the fourth year of life. Almost everything that we find later in her relation to her father was already present in this earlier attachment and has been transferred subsequently on to her father. In short, we get an impression that we cannot understand women unless we appreciate this phase of their pre-Oedipus attachment to their mother.

We shall be glad, then, to know the nature of the girl's libidinal relations to her mother. The answer is that they are of very many different kinds. Since they persist through all three phases of infantile sexuality, they also take on the characteristics of the different phases and express themselves by oral, sadistic anal and phallic wishes. These wishes represent active as well as passive impulses; if we relate them to the differentiation of the sexes which is to appear later—though we should avoid doing so as far as possible—we may call them masculine and feminine. Besides this, they are completely ambivalent, both affectionate and of a hostile and aggressive nature. The latter often only come to light after being changed into anxiety ideas. It is not always easy to point to a formulation of these early sexual wishes; what is most clearly expressed is a wish to get the mother with child and the corresponding wish to bear her a child—both belonging to the phallic period and sufficiently surprising, but established beyond doubt by analytic observation. The attractiveness of these investigations lies in the surprising detailed findings which they bring us. Thus, for instance, we discover the fear of being murdered or poisoned, which may later form the core of a paranoic illness, already present in this pre-Oedipus period, in relation to the mother. Or another case: you will recall an interesting episode in the history of analytic research which caused me many distressing hours. In the period in which the main interest was directed to discovering infantile sexual traumas, almost all my women patients told me that they had been seduced by their father. I was driven to recognize in the end that these reports were untrue and so came to understand that hysterical symptoms are derived from fantasies and not from real occurrences. It was only later that I was able to recognize in this fantasy of being seduced by the father the expression of the typical Oedipus complex in women. And now we find the fantasy of seduction once more in the pre-Oedipus prehistory of girls; but the seducer is regularly the mother. Here, however, the fantasy touches the ground of reality, for it was really the mother who by her activities over the child's bodily hygiene inevitably stimulated, and perhaps even roused for the first time, pleasurable sensations in her genitals.[2]

I have no doubt you are ready to suspect that this portrayal of the abundance and strength of a little girl's sexual relations with her mother is very much overdrawn. After all, one has opportunities of seeing little girls and notices nothing of the sort. But the objection is not to the point. Enough can be seen in the children if one knows how to look. And besides, you should consider how little of its sexual wishes a child can bring to pre-conscious expression or communicate at all. Accordingly we are only within our rights if we study the residues and consequences of this emotional world in retrospect, in people in whom these processes of development had attained a specially clear and even excessive degree of expansion. Pathology has always done us the service of making discernible by isolation and exaggeration conditions which would remain concealed in a normal state. And since our investigations have been carried out on people who were by no means seriously abnormal, I think we should regard their outcome as deserving belief.

We will now turn our interest on to the single question of what it is that brings this powerful attachment of the girl to her mother to an end. This, as we know, is its usual fate: it is destined to make room for an attachment to her father. Here we come upon a fact which is a pointer to our further advance. This step in development does not involve only a simple change of object. The turning away from the mother is accompanied by hostility; the attachment to the mother ends in hate. A hate of that kind may become very striking and last all through life; it may be carefully overcompensated later on; as a rule one part of it is overcome while another part persists. Events of later years naturally influence this greatly. We will restrict ourselves, however, to studying it at the time at which the girl turns to her father and to enquiring into the motives for it. We are then given a long list of accusations and grievances against the mother which are supposed to justify the child's hostile feelings; they are of varying validity which we shall not fail to examine. A number of them are obvious rationalizations and the true sources of enmity remain to be found. I hope you will be interested if on this occasion I take you through all the details of a psycho-analytic investigation.

The reproach against the mother which goes back furthest is that she gave the child too little milk—which is construed against her as lack of love. Now there is some justification for this reproach in our families. Mothers often have insufficient nourishment to give their children and are content to suckle them for a few months, for half or three-quarters of a year. Among primitive peoples children are fed at their mother's breast for two or three years. The figure of the wet nurse who suckles the child is as a rule merged into the mother; when this has not happened, the reproach is turned into another one—that the nurse, who fed the child so willingly, was sent away by the mother too early. But whatever the true state of affairs may have been, it is impossible that the child's reproach can be justified as often as it is met with. It seems, rather, that the child's avidity for its earliest nourishment is altogether insatiable, that it never gets over the pain of losing its mother's breast. I should not be surprised if the analysis of a primitive child, who could still suck at its mother's breast when it was already able to run about and talk, were to bring the same reproach to light. The fear of being poisoned is also probably connected with the withdrawal of the breast. Poison is nourishment that makes one ill. Perhaps children trace back their early illnesses too to this frustration. A fair amount of intellectual education is a prerequisite for believing in chance; primitive people and uneducated ones, and no doubt children as well, are able to assign a ground for everything that happens. Perhaps originally it was a reason on animistic lines. Even today in some strata of our population no one can die without having been killed by someone else—preferably by the doctor. And the regular reaction of a neurotic to the death of someone closely connected with him is to put the blame on himself for having caused the death.

The next accusation against the child's mother flares up when the next baby appears in the nursery. If possible the connection with oral frustration is preserved: the mother could not or would not give the child any more milk because she needed the nourishment for the new arrival. In cases in which the two children are so close in age that lactation is prejudiced by the second pregnancy, this reproach acquires a real basis, and it is a remarkable fact that a child, even with an age difference of only 11 months, is not too young to take notice of what is happening. But what the child grudges the unwanted intruder and rival is not only the suckling but all the other signs of maternal care. It feels that it has been dethroned, despoiled, prejudiced in its rights; it casts a jealous hatred upon the new baby and develops a grievance against the faithless mother which often finds expression in a disagreeable change in its behavior. It becomes "naughty," perhaps, irritable and disobedient and goes back on the advances it has made towards controlling its excretions. All of this has been very long familiar and is accepted as self-evident; but we rarely form a correct idea of the strength of these jealous impulses, of the tenacity with which they persist and of the magnitude of their influence on later development. Especially as this jealousy is constantly receiving fresh nourishment in the later years of childhood and the whole shock is repeated with the birth of each new brother or sister. Nor does it make much difference if the child happens to remain the mother's preferred favorite. A child's demands for love are immoderate, they make exclusive claims and tolerate no sharing.

An abundant source of a child's hostility to its mother is provided by its multifarious sexual wishes, which alter according to the phase of the libido and which cannot for the most part be satisfied. The strongest of these frustrations occur at the phallic period, if the mother forbids pleasurable activity with the genitals—often with severe threats and every sign of displeasure—activity to which, after all, she herself had introduced the child. One would think these were reasons enough to account for a girl's turning away from her mother. One would judge, if so, that the estrangement follows inevitably from the nature of children's sexuality, from the immoderate character of their demand for love and the impossibility of ful-

filling their sexual wishes. It might be thought indeed that this first love-relation of the child's is doomed to dissolution for the very reason that it is the first, for these early object-cathexes are regularly ambivalent to a high degree. A powerful tendency to aggressiveness is always present beside a powerful love, and the more passionately a child loves its object, the more sensitive does it become to disappointments and frustrations from that object; and in the end the love must succumb to the accumulated hostility. Or the idea that there is an original ambivalence such as this in erotic cathexes may be rejected, and it may be pointed out that it is the special nature of the mother-child relation that leads, with equal inevitability, to the destruction of the child's love; for even the mildest upbringing cannot avoid using compulsion and introducing restrictions, and any such intervention in the child's liberty must provoke as a reaction an inclination to rebelliousness and aggressiveness. A discussion of these possibilities might, I think, be most interesting; but an objection suddenly emerges which forces our interest in another direction. All these factors—the slights, the disappointments in love, the jealousy, the seduction followed by prohibition—are, after all, also in operation in the relation of a *boy* to his mother and are yet unable to alienate him from the maternal object. Unless we can find something that is specific for girls and is not present or not in the same way present in boys, we shall not have explained the termination of the attachment of girls to their mother.

I believe we have found this specific factor, and indeed where we expected to find it, even though in a surprising form. Where we expected to find it, I say, for it lies in the castration complex. After all, the anatomical distinction [between the sexes] must express itself in psychical consequences. It was, however, a surprise to learn from analyses that girls hold their mother responsible for their lack of a penis and do not forgive her for their being thus put at a disadvantage.

As you hear, then, we ascribe a castration complex to women as well. And for good reasons, though its content cannot be the same as with boys. In the latter the castration complex arises after they have learnt from the sight of the female genitals that the organ which they value so highly need not necessarily accompany the body. At this the boy recalls to mind the threats he brought on himself by his doings with that organ, he begins to give credence to them and falls under the influence of fear of castration, which will be the most powerful motive force in his subsequent development. The castration complex of girls is also started by the sight of the genitals of the other sex. They at once notice the difference and, it must be admitted, its significance too. They feel seriously wronged, often declare that they want to "have something like it too," and fall a victim to "envy for the penis," which will leave ineradicable traces on their development and the formation of their character and which will not be surmounted in even the most favorable cases without a severe expenditure of psychical energy. The girl's recognition of the fact of her being without a penis does not by any means imply that she submits to the fact easily. On the contrary, she continues to hold on for a long time to the wish to get something like it herself and she believes in that possibility for improbably long years; and analysis can show that, at a period when knowledge of reality has long since rejected the fulfillment of the wish as unattainable, it persists in the unconscious and retains a considerable cathexis of energy. The wish to get the longed-for penis eventually in spite of everything may contribute to the motives that drive a mature woman to analysis, and what she may reasonably expect from analysis—a capacity, for instance, to carry on an intellectual profession—may often be recognized as a sublimated modification of this repressed wish.

One cannot very well doubt the importance of envy for the penis. You may take it as an instance of male injustice if I assert that envy and jealousy play an even greater part in the mental life of women than of men. It is not that I think these characteristics are absent in men or that I think they have no other roots in women than envy for the penis; but I am inclined to attribute their greater amount in women to this latter influence. Some analysts, however, have shown an inclination to depreciate the importance of this first installment of penis envy in the phallic phase. They are of opinion that what we find of this attitude in women is in the main a secondary structure which has come about on the occasion of later conflicts by regression to this early infantile impulse. This, however, is a general problem of depth psychology. In many pathological—or even un-usual—instinctual attitudes (for instance, in all sexual perversions) the question arises of how much of their strength is to be attributed to early infantile fixations and how much to the influence of later experiences and developments. In such cases it is almost always a matter of complemental series such as we put forward in our discussion of the aetiology of the neuroses. Both factors play a part in varying amounts in the causation; a less on the one side is balanced by a more on the other. The infantile factor sets the pattern in all cases but does not always determine the issue, though it often does. Precisely in the case of penis envy I should argue decidedly in favor of the preponderance of the infantile factor.

The discovery that she is castrated is a turning point in a girl's growth. Three possible lines of development start from it: one leads to sexual inhibition or to neurosis, the second to change of character in the sense of a masculinity complex, the third, finally, to normal femininity. We have learnt a fair amount, though not everything, about all three.

The essential content of the first is as follows: the little girl has hitherto lived in a masculine way, has been able to get pleasure by the excitation of her clitoris and has brought this activity into relation with her sexual wishes directed towards her mother, which are often active ones; now, owing to the influence of her penis-envy, she loses her enjoyment in her phallic sexuality. Her self-love is mortified by the comparison with the boy's far superior equipment and in consequence she renounces her masturbatory satisfaction from her clitoris, repudiates her love for her mother and at the same time not infrequently represses a good part of her sexual trends in general. No doubt her turning away from her mother does not occur all at once, for to begin with the girl regards her castration as an individual misfortune, and only gradually extends it to other females and finally to her mother as well. Her love was directed to her *phallic* mother; with the discovery that her mother is castrated it becomes possible to drop her as an object, so that the motives for hostility, which have long been accumulating, gain the upper hand. This means, therefore, that as a result of the discovery of women's lack of a penis they are debased in value for girls just as they are for boys and later perhaps for men.

You all know the immense ætiological importance attributed by our neurotic patients to their masturbation. They make it responsible for all their troubles and we have the greatest difficulty in persuading them that they are mistaken. In fact, however, we ought to admit to them that they are right, for masturbation is the executive agent of infantile sexuality, from the faulty development of which they are indeed suffering. But what neurotics mostly blame is the masturbation of the period of puberty; they have mostly forgotten that of early infancy, which is what is really in question. I wish I might have an opportunity some time of explaining to you at length how important all the factual details of early masturbation become for the individual's subsequent neurosis or character: whether or not it was discovered, how the parents struggled against it or permitted it, or whether he succeeded in suppressing it himself. All of this leaves permanent traces on his development. But I am on the whole glad that I need not do this. It would be a hard and tedious task and at the end of it you would put me in an embarrassing situation by quite certainly asking me to give you some practical advice as to how a parent or educator should deal with the masturbation of small children.[3] From the development of girls, which is what my present lecture is concerned with, I can give you the example of a child herself trying to get free from masturbating. She does not always succeed in this. If envy for the penis has provoked a powerful impulse against clitoridal masturbation but this nevertheless refuses to give way, a violent struggle for liberation ensues in which the girl, as it were, herself takes over the role of her deposed mother and gives expression to her entire dissatisfaction with her inferior clitoris in her efforts against obtaining satisfaction from it. Many years later, when her masturbatory activity has long since been suppressed, an interest still persists which we must interpret as a defense against a temptation that is still dreaded. It manifests itself in the emergence of sympathy for those to whom similar difficulties are attributed, it plays a part as a motive in contracting a marriage and, indeed, it may determine the choice of a husband or lover. Disposing of early infantile masturbation is truly no easy or indifferent business.

Along with the abandonment of clitoridal masturbation a certain amount of activity is renounced. Pas-

sivity now has the upper hand, and the girl's turning to her father is accomplished principally with the help of passive instinctual impulses. You can see that a wave of development like this, which clears the phallic activity out of the way, smooths the ground for femininity. If too much is not lost in the course of it through repression, this femininity may turn out to be normal. The wish with which the girl turns to her father is no doubt originally the wish for the penis which her mother has refused her and which she now expects from her father. The feminine situation is only established, however, if the wish for a penis is replaced by one for a baby, if, that is, a baby takes the place of a penis in accordance with an ancient symbolic equivalence. It has not escaped us that the girl has wished for a baby earlier, in the undisturbed phallic phase: that, of course, was the meaning of her playing with dolls. But that play was not in fact an expression of her femininity; it served as an identification with her mother with the intention of substituting activity for passivity. *She* was playing the part of her mother and the doll was herself: now she could do with the baby everything that her mother used to do with her. Not until the emergence of the wish for a penis does the doll-baby become a baby from the girl's father, and thereafter the aim of the most powerful feminine wish. Her happiness is great if later on this wish for a baby finds fulfillment in reality, and quite especially so if the baby is a little boy who brings the longed-for penis with him. Often enough in her combined picture of "a baby from her father" the emphasis is laid on the baby and her father left unstressed. In this way the ancient masculine wish for the possession of a penis is still faintly visible through the femininity now achieved. But perhaps we ought rather to recognize this wish for a penis as being *par excellence* a feminine one.

With the transference of the wish for a penis-baby on to her father, the girl has entered the situation of the Oedipus complex. Her hostility to her mother, which did not need to be freshly created, is now greatly intensified, for she becomes the girl's rival, who receives from her father everything that she desires from him. For a long time the girl's Oedipus complex concealed her pre-Oedipus attachment to her mother from our view, though it is nevertheless so important and leaves such lasting fixations behind it. For girls the Oedipus situation is the outcome of a long and difficult development; it is a kind of preliminary solution, a position of rest which is not soon abandoned, especially as the beginning of the latency period is not far distant. And we are now struck by a difference between the two sexes, which is probably momentous, in regard to the relation of the Oedipus complex to the castration complex. In a boy the Oedipus complex, in which he desires his mother and would like to get rid of his father as being a rival, develops naturally from the phase of his phallic sexuality. The threat of castration compels him, however, to give up that attitude. Under the impression of the danger of losing his penis, the Oedipus complex is abandoned, repressed and, in the most normal cases, entirely destroyed, and a severe super-ego is set up as its heir. What happens with a girl is almost the opposite. The castration complex prepares for the Oedipus complex instead of destroying it; the girl is driven out of her attachment to her mother through the influence of her envy for the penis and she enters the Oedipus situation as though into a haven of refuge. In the absence of fear of castration the chief motive is lacking which leads boys to surmount the Oedipus complex. Girls remain in it for an indeterminate length of time; they demolish it late and, even so, incompletely. In these circumstances the formation of the super-ego must suffer; it cannot attain the strength and independence which give it its cultural significance, and feminists are not pleased when we point out to them the effects of this factor upon the average feminine character.

To go back a little. We mentioned as the second possible reaction to the discovery of female castration the development of a powerful masculinity complex. By this we mean that the girl refuses, as it were, to recognize the unwelcome fact and, defiantly rebellious, even exaggerates her previous masculinity, clings to her clitoridal activity and takes refuge in an identification with her phallic mother or her father. What can it be that decides in favor of this outcome? We can only suppose that it is a constitutional factor, a greater amount of activity, such as is ordinarily characteristic of a male. However that may be, the essence of this process is that at this point in devel-

opment the wave of passivity is avoided which opens the way to the turn towards femininity. The extreme achievement of such a masculinity complex would appear to be the influencing of the choice of an object in the sense of manifest homosexuality. Analytic experience teaches us, to be sure, that female homosexuality is seldom or never a direct continuation of infantile masculinity. Even for a girl of this kind it seems necessary that she should take her father as an object for some time and enter the Oedipus situation. But afterwards, as a result of her inevitable disappointments from her father, she is driven to regress into her early masculinity complex. The significance of these disappointments must not be exaggerated; a girl who is destined to become feminine is not spared them, though they do not have the same effect. The predominance of the constitutional factor seems indisputable; but the two phases in the development of female homosexuality are well mirrored in the practices of homosexuals, who play the parts of mother and baby with each other as often and as clearly as those of husband and wife.

NOTES

1. [This lecture is mainly based on two earlier papers: "Some Psychical Consequences of the Anatomical Distinction between the Sexes" (1925*j*) and "Female Sexuality" (1931*b*). The last section, however, dealing with women in adult life, contains new material. Freud returned to the subject once again in Chapter VII of the posthumous *Outline of Psycho-Analysis* (1940*a* [1938]).]

2. [In his early discussions of the aetiology of hysteria Freud often mentioned seduction by adults as among its commonest causes (see, for instance, the second paper on the neuropsychoses of defense (1896*b*), *Standard Ed.*, **3**, 164, and "The Aetiology of Hysteria" (1896*c*), ibid., 208). But nowhere in these early publications did he specifically inculpate the girl's father. Indeed, in some additional footnotes written in 1924 for the *Gesammelte Schriften* reprint of *Studies on Hysteria*, he admitted to having on two occasions suppressed the fact of the father's responsibility (see *Standard Ed.*, **2**, 134 *n*, and 170 *n.*). He made this quite clear, however, in the letter to Fliess of September 21, 1897 (Freud, 1950*a*, Letter 69), in which he first expressed his skepticism about these stories told by his patients. His first published admission of his mistake was given several years later in a hint in the second of the *Three Essays* (1905*d*), *Standard Ed.*, **7**, 190, but a much fuller account of the position followed in his contribution on the aetiology of the neuroses to

a volume by Löwenfeld (1906a), ibid., **7**, 274–5. Later on he gave two accounts of the effects that this discovery of his mistake had on his own mind—in his "History of the Psycho-Analytic Movement" (1914d), ibid., **14**, 17–18 and in his *Autobiographical Study* (1925d), ibid., **20**, 33–5. The further discovery which is described in the present paragraph of the text

had already been indicated in the paper on "Female Sexuality" (1931b), ibid., **21**, 238.]

3. [Freud's fullest discussion of masturbation was in his contribution to a symposium on the subject in the Vienna Psycho-Analytical Society (1912f), *Standard Ed.*, **12**, 241 ff., where a number of other references are given.]

1.2 A System of Psychology of Sexual life

Richard von Krafft-Ebing

Woman far surpasses man in the natural psychology of love, partly because evolution and training have made love her proper element, and partly because she is animated by more refined feelings.

Even the best of breeding concedes to man that he looks upon woman mainly as a means by which to satisfy the cravings of his natural instinct, though it confines him only to the woman of his choice. Thus civilisation establishes a binding social contract which is called marriage, and grants by legal statutes protection and support to the wife and her issue.

It is important, and on account of certain pathological manifestations (to be referred to later on) indispensable, to examine into those psychological events which draw man and woman into that close union which concentrates the fulness of affection upon the beloved one only to the exclusion of all other persons of the same sex.

If one could demonstrate design in the processes of nature—adaptation cannot be denied them—then the fact of fascination by one person of the opposite sex with indifference towards all others, as it occurs between true and happy lovers, would appear as a wonderful provision to ensure monogamy for the promotion of its object.

The scientific observer finds in this loving bond of hearts by no means simply a mystery of souls, but

he can refer it nearly always to certain physical or mental peculiarities by which the attracting power is qualified.

Hence the words FETICH and FETICHISM. The word fetich signifies an object, or parts or attributes of objects, which by virtue of association to sentiment, personality, or absorbing ideas, exert a charm (the Portuguese "fetisso") or at least produce a peculiar individual impression which is in no wise connected with the external appearance of the sign, symbol or fetich.[1]

The individual valuation of the fetich extending even to unreasoning enthusiasm is called *fetichism*. This interesting psychological phenomenon may be explained by an empirical law of association, *i.e.*, the relation existing between the notion itself and the parts thereof which are essentially active in the production of pleasurable emotions. It is most commonly found in *religious* and *erotic* spheres. *Religious* fetichism finds its original motive in the delusion that its object, *i.e.*, the idol, is not a mere symbol, but possesses divine attributes, and ascribes to it peculiar wonder-working (relics) or protective (amulets) virtues.

Erotic fetichism makes an idol of physical or mental qualities of a person or even merely of objects used by that person, etc., because they awaken mighty

---

From *Psychopathia Sexualis*, by Richard von Krafft-Ebing.

associations with the beloved person, thus originating strong emotions of sexual pleasure. Analogies with religious fetichism are always discernible; for, in the latter, the most insignificant objects (hair, nails, bones, etc.) become at times fetiches which produce feelings of delight and even ecstasy.

The germ of sexual love is probably to be found in the individual charm (fetich) with which persons of opposite sex sway each other.

The case is simple enough when the sight of a person of the opposite sex occurs simultaneously with sexual excitement, whereby the latter is intensified.

Emotional and optical impressions combine and are so deeply embedded in the mind that a recurring sensation awakens the visual memory and causes renewed sexual excitement, even orgasm and pollution (often only in dreams), in which case the physical appearance acts as a fetich.

Binet, inter alia, contends that mere peculiarities, whether physical or mental, may have the effect of the fetich, if their perception coincides with sexual emotion.

Experience shows that chance controls in a large measure this mental association, that the nature of the fetich varies with the personality of the individual, thus arousing the oddest sympathies or antipathies.

These physiological facts of fetichism often account for the affections that suddenly arise between man and woman, the preference of a certain person to all others of the same sex. Since the fetich assumes the form of a distinctive mark it is clear that its effect can only be of an individual character. Being accentuated by the strongest feelings of pleasure, it follows, that existing faults in the beloved are overlooked ("Love is blind") and an infatuation is produced which appears incomprehensible or silly to others. Thus it happens that the devoted lover who worships and invests his love with qualities which in reality do not exist, is looked upon by others simply as mad. Thus love exhibits itself now as a mere passion, now as a pronounced psychical anomaly which attains what seemed impossible, renders the ugly beautiful, the profane sublime, and obliterates all consciousness of existing duties towards others.

Tarde ("Archives de l'Anthropologie Criminelle," vol. v., No. 30) argues that the type of this fetich (ism) varies with persons as well as with nations, but that the ideal of beauty remains the same among civilised peoples of the same era.

Binet has more thoroughly analysed and studied this *fetichism of love.*

From it springs the particular choice for slender or plump forms, for blondes or brunettes, for particular form or colour of the eyes, tone of the voice, odour of the hair or body (even artificial perfume), shape of the hand, foot or ear, etc., which constitute the individual charm, the first link in a complicated chain of mental processes, all converging in that one focus, love, *i.e.,* the physical and mental possession of the beloved.

This fact establishes the existence of *physiological* fetichism.

Without showing a pathological condition the fetich may exercise its power so long as its leading qualities represent the integral parts, and so long as the love engendered by it comprises the entire mental and physical personality.

"Normal love appears to us as a symphony of tones *Max Dessoir* (pseudonym Ludwig Brunn)[2] in an article "The Fetichism of Love," cleverly says:—

"Normal love appears to us as a symphony of tones of all kinds. It is roused by the most varied agencies. It is, so to speak, polytheistic. Fetichism recognises only the tone-colour of a single instrument; it issues forth from a single motive; it is monotheistic."

Even moderate thought will carry the conviction that the term real love (so often misused) can only apply where the entire person of the beloved becomes the physical and mental object of veneration.

Of course, there is always a sensual element in love, *i.e.,* the desire to enjoy the full possession of the beloved object, and, in union with it, to fulfil the laws of nature.

But where the body of the beloved person is made the sole object of love, or if sexual pleasure only is sought without regard to the communion of soul and mind, true love does not exist. Neither is it found among the disciples of Plato, who love the soul only and despise sexual enjoyment. In the one case the body is the fetich, in the other the soul, and love is fetichism.

Instances such as these represent simply transitions to pathological fetichism.

This assumption is enhanced by another criterion of true love, *viz.,* the mental satisfaction derived from the sexual act.[3]

A striking phenomenon in fetichism is that among the many things which may serve as fetiches there are some which gain that significance more commonly than others; for instance, the HAIR, the HAND, the FOOT of woman, or the expression of the EYE. This is important in the pathology of fetichism.

Woman certainly seems to be more or less conscious of these facts. For she devotes great attention to her hair and often spends an unreasonable amount of time and money upon its cultivation. How carefully the mother looks after her little daughter's hair! What an important part the hairdresser plays! The falling out of the hair causes despair to many a young lady. The author remembers the case of a vain woman who fell into melancholia on account of this trouble, and finally committed suicide. A favourite subject of conversation among ladies is *coiffures.* They are envious of each other's luxuriant tresses.

Beautiful hair is a mighty fetich with many men. In the legend of the Lorelei, who lured men to destruction, the "golden hair" which she combs with a golden comb appears as a fetich. Frequently the *hand* or the *foot* possesses an attractiveness no less powerful; but in these instances masochistic and sadistic feelings often—though not always—assist in determining the peculiar kind of fetich.

By a transference through association of ideas, *gloves* or *shoes* obtain the significance of a fetich.

Max Dessoir (op. cit.) points out that among the customs of the middle ages drinking from the shoe of a beautiful woman (still to be found in Poland) played a remarkable part in gallantry and homage. The shoe also plays an important *rôle* in the legend of Aschenbrödel.

The *expression of the eye* is particularly important as a means of kindling the spark of love. A neuropathic eye frequently affects persons of either sex as a fetich. "Madame, vos beaux yeux me font mourir d'amour." (*Molière*).

There are many examples showing that *odours* of the body become fetiches.

This fact is taken advantage of in the "Ars amandi" by woman either consciously or unconsciously. Ruth sought to attract Boaz by perfuming herself. The *demimonde* of ancient and modern times is noted for its lavish use of strong scents. *Jäger,* in his "Discovery of the Soul," calls attention to many olfactory sympathies.

Cases are known where men have married ugly women solely because their personal odours were exceedingly pleasing.

Binet makes it probable that the voice also may act as a fetich.

Belot in his novel "Les baigneuses de Trouville" makes the same assertion. *Binet* thinks that many marriages with singers are due to the fetich of their voices. He also observes that among the singing birds the voice has the same sexual significance as odours among the quadrupeds. The birds allure by their song, and the male that sings most beautifully is joined at night by the charmed mate.

The pathological facts of masochism and sadism show that mental peculiarities may also act as fetiches but in a wider sense.

Thus the fact of idiosyncrasies is explained, and the old proverb "*De gustibus* non est disputandum" retains its force.

With regard to fetichism in woman, science must at least for the present time be content with mere conjectures. This much seems to be certain, that being a physiological factor, its effects are analogous to those in men, *i.e.,* producing sexual sympathies towards persons of the same sex.

Details will come to our knowledge only when medical women enter into the study of this subject.

We may take it for granted that the physical as well as the mental qualities of man assume the form of the female fetich. In most cases, no doubt, physical attributes in the male exercise this power without regard to the existence of conscious sensuality. On the other hand it will be found that the mental superiority of man constitutes the attractive power where physical beauty is wanting. In the upper "strata" of society this is more apparent, even if we disregard the enormous influence exercised by "blue blood" and high breeding. The possibility that superior intellectual development favours advancement in social position, and opens the way to a brilliant career, does not seem to weigh heavily in the balance of judgment.

The fetichism of body and mind is of importance in progeneration; it favours the selection of the fittest and the transmission of physical and mental virtues.

Generally speaking the following masculine qualities impose on woman, *viz.,* physical strength, courage, nobility of mind, chivalry, self-confidence, even self-assertion, insolence, bravado, and a conscious show of mastery over the weaker sex.

A "Don Juan" impresses many women and elicits admiration, for he establishes the proof of his virile powers, although the inexperienced maiden can in no wise suspect the many risks of lues and chronic urethritis she runs from a marital union with this otherwise interesting rake.

The successful actor, musician, or vocal artiste, the circus rider, the athlete, and even the criminal, often fascinate the bread and butter miss as well as the maturer woman. At any rate women rave over them, and inundate them with love letters.

It is a well-known fact that the female heart has predominant weakness for military uniforms, that of the cavalry-man ever having the preference.

The hair of man, especially the beard, the emblem of virility, the secondary symbol of generative power—is a predominant fetich with woman. In the measure in which women bestow special care upon the cultivation of their hair, men who seek to attract and please women, cultivate the elegant growth of the beard, and especially that of the moustache.

The eye as well as the voice exert the same charm. Singers of renown easily touch woman's heart. They are overwhelmed with love letters and offers of marriage. Tenors have a decided advantage.

Binet (*op. cit.*) refers to an observation of this character made by *Dumas* in his novel "La maison du vent". A woman who falls in love with a tenor-voice loses her virtue.

The author has thus far not succeeded in obtaining facts with regard to pathological fetichism in woman.

NOTES

1. *Cf. Max Müller* who derives the word fetich etymologically from *factitius, i.e.,* artificial, insignificant.

2. "Deutsches Montagsblatt," Berlin, 20, 8, 80.

3. *Magnan's* "spinal cérébral postérieur" who finds gratification with any sort of woman, is only animated by lust. Meretricious love that is purchased cannot be genuine (*Mantegazza*). Whoever coined the adage: "Sublata lucerna nullum discrimen inter feminas," was a cynic, indeed. The power to perform love's act is by no means a guarantee of the noblest enjoyment of love.

There are urnings who are potent for women—men who do not love their wives, but are nevertheless able to perform the marital "duty". In the majority of these cases even lustful pleasure is absent; for it is simply an onanistic act rendered possible by the aid of imagination which substitutes another beloved being. This deception may, indeed, superinduce sexual pleasure, but, rudimentary gratification as it is, it can only arise from a psychic trick, just as in solitary onanism voluptuous satisfaction is obtained chiefly with the assistance of fancy. As a matter of fact that degree of orgasm which completes the lustful act is entirely dependent upon the intervention of fancy.

Where psychic impediments exist (such as indifference, disgust, aversion, fear of contagion or impregnation, etc.) the feeling of sexual gratification seems to be wanting altogether.

1.3 ANALYSIS OF THE SEXUAL IMPULSE

Havelock Ellis

The conjunction of the sexes is seen to be an end only to be obtained with much struggle; the difficulty of achieving sexual erethism in both sexes, the difficulty of so stimulating such erethism in the female that her instinctive coyness is overcome, these difficulties the best and most vigorous males, those most adapted in other respects to carry on the race, may most easily overcome. [. . .]

Force is the foundation of virility, and its psychic manifestation is courage. In the struggle for life violence is the first virtue. The modesty of women—in its primordial form consisting in physical resistance, active or passive, to the assaults of the male—aided selection by putting to the test man's most important quality, force. Thus it is that when choosing among rivals for her favors a woman attributes value to violence. [. . .]

The relation of love to pain is one of the most difficult problems, and yet one of the most fundamental, in the whole range of sexual psychology. Why is it that love inflicts, and even seeks to inflict, pain? Why is it that love suffers pain, and even seeks to suffer it? In answering that question, it seems to me, we have to take an apparently circuitous route, sometimes going beyond the ostensible limits of sex altogether; but if we can succeed in answering it we shall have come very near one of the great mysteries of love. At the same time we shall have made clear the normal basis on which rest the extreme aberrations of love.

The chief key to the relationship of love to pain is to be found by returning to the consideration of the essential phenomena of courtship in the animal world generally. Courtship is a play, a game; even its combats are often, to a large extent, mock-combats; but the process behind it is one of terrible earnestness, and the play may at any moment become deadly. Court-ship tends to involve a mock-combat between males for the possession of the female which may at any time become a real combat; it is a pursuit of the female by the male which may at any time become a kind of persecution; so that, as Colin Scott remarks, "Courting may be looked upon as a refined and delicate form of combat." The note of courtship, more especially among mammals, is very easily forced, and as soon as we force it we reach pain. The intimate and inevitable association in the animal world of combat—of the fighting and hunting impulses—with the process of courtship alone suffices to bring love into close connection with pain.

Among mammals the male wins the female very largely by the display of force. The infliction of pain must inevitably be a frequent indirect result of the exertion of power. It is even more than this; the infliction of pain by the male on the female may itself be a gratification of the impulse to exert force. This tendency has always to be held in check, for it is of the essence of courtship that the male should win the female, and she can only be won by the promise of pleasure. The tendency of the male to inflict pain must be restrained, so far as the female is concerned, by the consideration of what is pleasing to her. Yet, the more carefully we study the essential elements of courtship, the clearer it becomes that, playful as these manifestations may seem on the surface, in every direction they are verging on pain. It is so among animals generally; it is so in man among savages.

At the outset, then, the impulse to inflict pain is brought into courtship, and at the same time rendered a pleasurable idea to the female, because with primitive man, as well as among his immediate ancestors, the victor in love has been the bravest and strongest rather than the most beautiful or the most skillful.

Until he can fight he is not reckoned a man and he cannot hope to win a woman. Among the African Masai a man is not supposed to marry until he has blooded his spear, and in a very different part of the world, among the Dyaks of Borneo, there can be little doubt that the chief incentive to head-hunting is the desire to please the woman, the possession of a head decapitated by himself being an excellent way of winning a maiden's favor. [...] Here, indeed, we have the source of that love of cruelty which some have found so marked in women. This is a phase of courtship which helps us to understand how it is that, as we shall see, the idea of pain, having become associated with sexual emotion, may be pleasurable to women.

Thus, in order to understand the connection between love and pain, we have once more to return to the consideration, under a somewhat new aspect, of the fundamental elements in the sexual impulse. In discussing the "Evolution of Modesty" we found that the primary part of the female in courtship is the playful, yet serious, assumption of the role of a hunted animal who lures on the pursuer, not with the object of escaping, but with the object of being finally caught. In considering the "Analysis of the Sexual Impulse" we found that the primary part of the male in courtship is by the display of his energy and skill to capture the female or to arouse in her an emotional condition which leads her to surrender herself to him, this process itself at the same time heightening his own excitement. In the playing of these two different parts is attained in both male and female that charging of nervous energy, that degree of vascular tumescence necessary for adequate discharge and detumescence in an explosion by which sperm-cells and germ-cells are brought together for the propagation of the race. We are now concerned with the necessary interplay of the differing male and female roles in courtship, and with the accidental emotional by-products. Both male and female are instinctively seeking the same end of sexual union at the moment of highest excitement. There cannot, therefore, be real conflict. But there is the semblance of a conflict, an apparent clash of aim, an appearance of cruelty. Moreover,—and this is a significant moment in the process from our present point of view,—when there are rivals for the possession of

one female there is always a possibility of actual combat, so tending to introduce an element of real violence, of undisguised cruelty, which the male inflicts on his rival and which the female views with satisfaction and delight in the prowess of the successful claimant. Here we are brought close to the zoölogical root of the connection between love and pain. [...]

This association between love and pain still persists even among the most normal civilized men and women possessing well-developed sexual impulses. The masculine tendency to delight in domination, the feminine tendency to delight in submission, still maintain the ancient traditions when the male animal pursued the female. The phenomena of "marriage by capture," in its real and its simulated forms, have been traced to various causes. But it has to be remembered that these causes could only have been operative in the presence of a favorable emotional aptitude, constituted by the zoölogical history of our race and still traceable even to-day. To exert power, as psychologists well recognize, is one of our most primary impulses, and it always tends to be manifested in the attitude of a man toward the woman he loves.

It might be possible to maintain that the primitive element of more or less latent cruelty in courtship tends to be more rather than less marked in civilized man. In civilization the opportunity of dissipating the surplus energy of the courtship process by inflicting pain on rivals usually has to be inhibited; thus the woman to be wooed tends to become the recipient of the whole of this energy, both in its pleasure-giving and its pain-giving aspects. Moreover, the natural process of courtship, as it exists among animals and usually among the lower human races, tends to become disguised and distorted in civilization, as well by economic conditions as by conventional social conditions and even ethical prescription. It becomes forgotten that the woman's pleasure is an essential element in the process of courtship. A woman is often reduced to seek a man for the sake of maintenance; she is taught that pleasure is sinful or shameful, that sex-matters are disgusting, and that it is a woman's duty, and also her best policy, to be in subjection to her husband. Thus, various external checks which normally inhibit any passing over of masculine sexual energy into cruelty are liable to be removed.

We have to admit that a certain pleasure in manifesting his power over a woman by inflicting pain upon her is an outcome and survival of the primitive process of courtship, and an almost or quite normal constituent of the sexual impulse in man. But it must be at once added that in the normal well-balanced and well-conditioned man this constituent of the sexual impulse, when present, is always held in check. When the normal man inflicts, or feels the impulse to inflict, some degree of physical pain on the woman he loves he can scarcely be said to be moved by cruelty. He feels, more or less obscurely, that the pain he inflicts, or desires to inflict, is really a part of his love, and that, moreover, it is not really resented by the woman on whom it is exercised. His feeling is by no means always according to knowledge, but it has to be taken into account as an essential part of his emotional state. The physical force, the teasing and bullying, which he may be moved to exert under the stress of sexual excitement, are, he usually more or less unconsciously persuades himself, not really unwelcome to the object of his love. Moreover, we have to bear in mind the fact—a very significant fact from more than one point of view—that the normal manifestations of a woman's sexual pleasure are exceedingly like those of pain. "The outward expressions of pain," as a lady very truly writes, "—tears, cries, etc.,—which are laid stress on to prove the cruelty of the person who inflicts it, are not so different from those of a woman in the ecstasy of passion, when she implores the man to desist, though that is really the last thing she desires." If a man is convinced that he is causing real and unmitigated pain, he becomes repentant at once. If this is not the case he must either be regarded as a radically abnormal person or as carried away by passion to a point of temporary insanity. [. . .]

We thus see that there are here two separate groups of feelings: one, in the masculine line, which delights in displaying force and often inflicts pain or the simulacrum of pain; the other, in the feminine line, which delights in submitting to that force, and even finds pleasure in a slight amount of pain, or the idea of pain, when associated with the experiences of love. We see, also, that these two groups of feelings are complementary. Within the limits consistent with normal and healthy life, what men are impelled to give

women love to receive. So that we need not unduly deprecate the "cruelty" of men within these limits, nor unduly commiserate the women who are subjected to it. [. . .]

There is certainly one purely natural sexual difference of a fundamental character, which lies at the basis of whatever truth may be in the assertion that women are not susceptible of sexual emotion. As may be seen when considering the phenomena of modesty, the part played by the female in courtship throughout Nature is usually different from that played by the male, and is, in some respects, a more difficult and complex part. Except when the male fails to play his part properly, she is usually comparatively passive; in the proper playing of her part she has to appear to shun the male, to flee from his approaches—even actually to repel them.

Courtship resembles very closely, indeed, a drama or game; and the aggressiveness of the male, the coyness of the female, are alike unconsciously assumed in order to bring about in the most effectual manner the ultimate union of the sexes. The seeming reluctance of the female is not intended to inhibit sexual activity either in the male or in herself, but to increase it in both. The passivity of the female, therefore, is not a real, but only an apparent, passivity, and this holds true of our own species as much as of the lower animals. [. . .]

There is another characteristic of great significance by which the sexual impulse in women differs from that in men: the widely unlike character of the physical mechanism involved in the process of coitus. Considering how obvious this difference is, it is strange that its fundamental importance should so often be underrated. In man the process of tumescence and detumescence is simple. In women it is complex. In man we have the more or less spontaneously erectile penis, which needs but very simple conditions to secure the ejaculation which brings relief. In women we have in the clitoris a corresponding apparatus on a small scale, but behind this has developed a much more extensive mechanism, which also demands satisfaction, and requires for that satisfaction the presence of various conditions that are almost antagonistic. Naturally the more complex mechanism is the more easily disturbed. It is the difference, roughly speaking, between a lock and a key. This analogy is far from indicating all the difficulties involved. We have to imagine a lock that not only requires a key to fit it, but should only be entered at the right moment, and, under the best conditions, can only become adjusted to the key by considerable use. The fact that the man takes the more active part in coitus has increased these difficulties; the woman is too often taught to believe that the whole function is low and impure, only to be submitted to at her husband's will and for his sake, and the man has no proper knowledge of the mechanism involved and the best way of dealing with it. The grossest brutality thus may be, and not infrequently is, exercised in all innocence by an ignorant husband who simply believes that he is performing his "marital duties." For a woman to exercise this physical brutality on a man is with difficulty possible; a man's pleasurable excitement is usually the necessary condition of the woman's sexual gratification. But the reverse is not the case, and if the man is sufficiently ignorant or sufficiently coarse-grained to be satisfied with the woman's submission, he may easily become to her, in all innocence, a cause of torture.

To the man coitus must be in some slight degree pleasurable or it cannot take place at all. To the woman the same act which, under some circumstances, in the desire it arouses and the satisfaction it imparts, will cause the whole universe to shrivel into nothingness, under other circumstances will be a source of anguish, physical and mental. This is so to some extent even in the presence of the right and fit man. There can be no doubt whatever that the mucus which is so profusely poured out over the external sexual organs in woman during the excitement of sexual desire has for its end the lubrication of the parts and the facilitation of the passage of the intromittent organ. The most casual inspection of the cold, contracted, dry vulva in its usual aspect and the same when distended, hot, and moist, suffices to show which condition is and which is not that ready for intercourse, and until the proper condition is reached it is certain that coitus should not be attempted.

The varying sensitiveness of the female parts again offers difficulties. Sexual relations in women are, at the onset, almost inevitably painful; and to

some extent the same experience may be repeated at every act of coitus. Ordinary tactile sensibility in the female genito-urinary region is notably obtuse, but at the beginning of the sexual act there is normally a hyperaesthesia which may be painful or pleasurable, as excitement culminates passing into a seeming anaesthesia, which even craves for rough contact; so that in sexual excitement a woman normally displays in quick succession that same quality of sensibility to superficial pressure and insensibility to deep pressure which the hysterical woman exhibits simultaneously.

Thus we see that a highly important practical result follows from the greater complexity of the sexual apparatus in women and the greater difficulty with which it is aroused. In coitus the orgasm tends to occur more slowly in women than in men. It may easily happen that the whole process of detumescence is completed in the man before it has begun in his partner, who is left either cold or unsatisfied.

It is thus a result of the complexity of the sexual mechanism in women that the whole attitude of a woman toward the sexual relationship is liable to be affected disastrously by the husband's lack of skill or consideration in initiating her into this intimate mystery. Normally the stage of apparent repulsion and passivity, often associated with great sensitiveness, physical and moral, passes into one of active participation and aid in the consummation of the sexual act. But if, from whatever cause, there is partial arrest on the woman's side of this evolution in the process of courtship, if her submission is merely a mental and deliberate act of will, and not an instinctive and impulsive participation, there is a necessary failure of sexual relief and gratification. When we find that a woman displays a certain degree of indifference in sexual relationships, and a failure of complete gratification, we have to recognize that the fault may possibly lie, not in her, but in the defective skill of a lover who has not known how to play successfully the complex and subtle game of courtship. Sexual coldness due to the shock and suffering of the wedding-night is a phenomenon that is far too frequent. Hence it is that many women may never experience sexual gratification and relief, through no defect on their part, but through the failure of the husband to understand the lover's part. We make a false analogy when we compare the courtship of animals exclusively with our own courtships before marriage. Courtship, properly understood, is the process whereby both the male and the female are brought into that state of sexual tumescence which is a more or less necessary condition for sexual intercourse. The play of courtship cannot, therefore, be considered to be definitely brought to an end by the ceremony of marriage; it may more properly be regarded as the natural preliminary to every act of coitus. [. . .]

There is a further important difference, though intimately related to some of these differences already mentioned, between the sexual impulse in women and in men. In women it is at once larger and more diffused. In men the sexual impulse is, as it were, focused to a single point. This is necessarily so, for the whole of the essentially necessary part of the male in the process of human procreation is confined to the ejaculation of semen into the vagina. But in women, mainly owing to the fact that women are the child-bearers, in place of one primary sexual center and one primary erogenous region, there are at least three such sexual centers and erogenous regions: the clitoris (corresponding to the penis), the vaginal passage up to the womb, and the nipple. In both sexes there are other secondary and reflex centers, but there is good reason for believing that these are more numerous and more wide-spread in women than in men. [. . .]

This great diffusion of the sexual impulse and emotions in women is as visible on the psychic as on the physical side. A woman can find sexual satisfaction in a great number of ways that do not include the sexual act proper, and in a great number of ways that apparently are not physical at all, simply because their physical basis is diffused or is to be found in one of the outlying sexual zones. [. . .]

In conclusion it may be worth while to sum up the main points brought out in this brief discussion of a very large question. We have seen that there are two streams of opinion regarding the relative strength of the sexual impulse in men and women: one tending to regard it as greater in men, the other as greater in women. We have concluded that, since a large body of facts may be brought forward to support either view, we may fairly hold that, roughly speaking, the distribution of the sexual impulse between the two sexes is fairly balanced.

We have, however, further seen that the phenomena are in reality too complex to be settled by the usual crude method of attempting to discover quantitative differences in the sexual impulse. We more nearly get to the bottom of the question by a more analytic method, breaking up our mass of facts into groups. In this way we find that there are certain well-marked characteristics by which the sexual impulse in women differs from the same impulse in men: 1. It shows greater apparent passivity. 2. It is more complex, less apt to appear spontaneously, and more often needing to be aroused, while the sexual orgasm develops more slowly than in men. 3. It tends to become stronger after sexual relationships are established. 4. The threshold of excess is less easily reached than in men. 5. The sexual sphere is larger and more diffused. 6. There is a more marked tendency to periodicity in the spontaneous manifestations of sexual desire. 7. Largely as a result of these characteristics, the sexual impulse shows a greater range of variation in women than in men, both as between woman and woman and in the same woman at different periods.

1.4 LEARNING TO MASTURBATE

Alfred Kinsey, Wardell Pomeroy, and Clyde Martin

SELF-DISCOVERY

Most of the females in our sample had discovered how to masturbate as a result of their exploration of their own genitalia. Since the child's experience from the day it is born has shown it that satisfactions may be secured from the tactile stimulation of various parts of its body, one might expect that all children would sooner or later discover, quite on their own, that the greatest satisfactions may be obtained from such genital stimulation as masturbation might afford.

A considerable portion of the masturbation which we have found among infants and young pre-adolescent girls in our sample appears to have been self-discovered. Some 70 per cent of the older pre-adolescent girls who had begun to masturbate before adolescence also appear to have discovered the possibilities through their own exploration.[1] Although some of the adults who were the sources of our information had probably forgotten the part which other children and even adults played in inspiring their early experimentation, some 58 per cent of the females who had begun masturbation between eleven and twenty years of age reported that their activity had been self-discovered.[2] The figures were lower for the lower educational levels, and higher for the college and graduate school groups, but they were not particularly different in the several generations covered by the sample.

Interestingly enough, many of the older individuals who did not begin to masturbate until they were well along in their twenties or thirties, and even in their forties and fifties, were still discovering the possibilities of such activity through their own exploration.[3] This provides striking evidence of the ignorance which is frequent among females of sexual activities which are outside of their own experience, even though they may be common in the population as

a whole. Some 28 per cent of the boys in our sample had discovered masturbation on their own, but 75 per cent of them had heard about masturbation, 40 per cent of them had actually observed it, and 9 per cent had been masturbated by other males before they began their own activities. It is obvious that neither younger girls nor older women discuss their sexual experience in the open way that males do.

Not a few of the females in the sample had learned that masturbation occurred among males long before they learned that it was possible among females.

Among the females in the sample who had not begun masturbating until after age thirty, 19 per cent had not heard of it before they began their own masturbation. However, 27 per cent of the graduate school group, from whom the professional counselors of youth most often come, had not known that masturbation was possible in the female until they discovered it in the course of their own experimentation after they were past thirty years of age. Since most of the males had begun masturbating before they became adolescent or soon after the onset of adolescence, most of them knew about masturbation and had actually been masturbating for ten or twenty years before some of their mothers and teachers ever learned that there was such a phenomenon.

Some females had masturbated for some years before they learned that the activity in which they had been engaged had any sexual connotation and constituted what is known as masturbation.[4]

Verbal and Printed Sources

Approximately 43 per cent of those females in the sample who had ever masturbated, had learned that such a thing was possible from information acquired through verbal and/or printed sources.[5] This was the

---

second most important source of first knowledge for those who had begun masturbation by age twenty. It was the most important source, surpassed by no other, for those who had begun masturbation after that age. In this regard, there were no significant differences between the generations born in the four decades covered by the sample. On the other hand, 75 per cent of the males in our sample had acquired their first information about masturbation from verbal and/or printed sources, but chiefly from verbal sources. The females in the sample had more often obtained their information from books—chiefly from moral and sex education literature, and from religious lectures which were designed to discourage masturbation.[6]

Most of the females in the sample had begun to masturbate soon after they had learned that such a thing was possible, but some of them had waited months and even years after they learned of masturbation before they began their own activity. Males who hear of masturbation rarely delay their actual experimentation.

Petting Experience

The females in the sample had begun masturbation as a result of their petting or pre-coital experience with males in approximately 12 per cent of the cases.[7] There were very few males who had not known of masturbation before they ever engaged in heterosexual petting. Some of the females, even though they had had males manipulate their genitalia and bring them to orgasm in the course of a petting relationship, had not realized that self-manipulation could effect similar results. Although extensive heterosexual petting is somewhat more frequent in the younger generation, it seems to have provided an introduction to masturbation among older generations, forty years ago, fully as often as it does for the younger generation today.

Observation

Observing other persons in masturbatory activities was the chief inspiration for the beginning of masturbation for only about 11 per cent of the females in the sample.[8] Such observation was the source of inspiration for the initial experimentation of some 40 per cent of the males. There appear to have been no changes in the importance of such observation over the last four decades.

The direct observation of masturbation is most often possible during pre-adolescent or early adolescent years. Not infrequently girls observe boys rather than other girls in masturbation, and subsequently explore their own capacities. There were even cases of older women who had found the initial stimulus for their masturbatory activities in their observation of infants and young pre-adolescent girls.

Homosexual Experience

About 3 per cent of the females in the sample had begun their masturbation as a result of their homosexual contacts in pre-adolescent, adolescent, or more adult years.[9] In a few instances it was a nurse, housemaid, or female relative who had provided the first experience for the child. It was 9 per cent of the boys in the sample who had learned of masturbation through their homosexual experience.

RELATION TO AGE AND MARITAL STATUS

In our sample, masturbation had occurred among females of every group, from infancy to old age.

Among Children

We have records of 67 infants and small girls three years of age or younger who were observed in masturbation, or who as adults recalled that they had masturbated at that age. We have one record of a seven-month-old infant and records of 5 infants under one year of age who were observed in masturbation.[10] There were undoubtedly many more females who engaged in true masturbatory activities when they were young; but it has been impossible to calculate incidence figures from the available records.

Our records, however, include specific and repeated observations on several children whose responses were unmistakably erotic. We have records of 23 girls three years old or younger who reached orgasm in self-masturbation. There are more records of small girls than there are of small boys masturbating to orgasm at such an early age. It requires some experience and some development of muscular coordinations to effect the rhythmic manual movements on which masturbation depends, and the small boy does not so often manage to achieve that end. Some 19 per cent of the girls had masturbated prior to adolescence.

Accumulative Incidence

About 62 per cent of all the females in the sample had masturbated at some time in the course of their lives.[11] About 58 per cent had masturbated at some time to the point of orgasm. The 4 to 6 per cent which had masturbated without reaching orgasm was chiefly a group of females who had made only single or desultory and infrequent trials of their capacities, for nearly all of those who had seriously experimented soon learned to reach orgasm. The discussion in the present chapter is, therefore, confined (except in a few places expressly noted) to females whose masturbation had proceeded to the point of orgasm.

The incidences for those who had masturbated to the point of orgasm were 4 per cent by seven years of age, 12 per cent by twelve (which is the average age at which adolescence begins), and 15 per cent by age thirteen (which is the average age at which menstruation first occurs).[12] The incidence curves for both experience and orgasm then rose more or less continuously from adolescence until age 35. The curves still continued to rise but more slowly after that, and there were still some females who began to masturbate for the first time after age forty. The steady development of the curves had not been affected by the ages at which the females had married.

Active Incidence

Although 58 per cent of the females in our sample were masturbating to orgasm at some time in their lives, it was a much smaller percentage which had masturbated within any particular year or period of years. Because of the considerable discontinuity of most of the masturbatory histories, it is probable that not more than a fifth—20 per cent—of the females were masturbating within any particular year. It was perhaps 75 per cent of the single males and 30 per cent

of the married males who were masturbating in any one year.

The active incidences of masturbation were lowest in the younger groups, and highest in the older groups of females. In the younger groups, as few as 20 per cent of the females were masturbating, while as many as 58 per cent of some of the older groups were having experience within a single five-year period.[13] There may have been several explanations of these higher incidences of masturbation among the older females: (1) There may have been an actual increase in erotic responsiveness at the older ages. (2) The availability of socio-sexual outlets had been reduced at older ages, and this may have forced an increasing number of females to masturbate. (3) There was often a reduction of inhibitions among the older females. (4) The older females, having had more experience in petting and coitus, had learned, thereby, that similar satisfactions are obtainable through self-masturbation.

This increase in the incidence of masturbation among the older females sharply contrasts with the record for the single males where the active incidences reach their peak (88 per cent) in the mid-teens, and drop steadily from there into old age.[14]

The active incidences of masturbation to orgasm among the single females (ranging from 20 to 54 per cent) were somewhat higher than they were (23 to 36 per cent) among the corresponding married groups. Many of those who had depended on this outlet before marriage had stopped masturbating when marital coitus became available. On the other hand, there were some females who had not begun masturbating until after they had learned from their pre-coital petting experience in marriage that self-stimulation could also bring sexual satisfaction. Some women who fail to reach orgasm in coitus are then stimulated manually by their husbands, or they masturbate themselves until they reach orgasm. Some of the married females, on the other hand, confine their masturbation to periods when their husbands are away from home.

Frequency to Orgasm

The average (active median and active mean) frequencies of masturbation were remarkably uniform among most of the groups of single females, from age twenty to the oldest age group in the sample. The average frequencies among the married females and the previously married females were similarly uniform in most of the age groups in the sample. The frequencies of the married females were only a bit lower than the frequencies among the single females and among those who had been previously married.

Among the single females who were actually masturbating (the active sample), the average (median) individual was reaching orgasm about once in every two and a half to three weeks (between 0.3 and 0.4 per week). Among the married females the frequencies averaged about once in a month (0.2 per week).[15] Between the ages of sixteen and fifty among the single females, and between the ages of twenty-one and fifty-five among the married and previously married females, there had been only slight changes in the active median frequencies of masturbation. We shall find that this is more or less true of the frequencies of several other types of female activity and of the total sexual outlet of single females. This is one of the most remarkable aspects of female sexuality, and one which most sharply distinguishes it from the sexuality of the male. Hormonal factors may be involved.

NOTES

1. The self-discovery of masturbation has been noted by many writers, including: Forel acc. Back 1910:112. Moll 1912:171. Hirschfeld 1916:122. Krafft-Ebing (Moll ed.) 1924:80. Rohleder in Stern 1927:283. Hoyer 1929:223. Hutton 1937:76.

2. Other American studies show similar percentages learning to masturbate through self-discovery: Hamilton 1929:427 (65 per cent; records the circumstances). Davis 1929:109–110, 161 (51 per cent; records the circumstances). Dickinson and Beam 1931:350 (the majority). Landis and Bolles 1942:21 (69 per cent).

3. Davis 1929:161 also mentions this late self-discovery in over a third of her married females who had started masturbation after age 14.

4. For additional records of the female masturbating even to orgasm without realizing the sexual nature of the activity, see: Hirschfeld 1916:130. Meagher 1929:74. Davis 1929:400. Kelly 1930:174. Meagher and Jelliffe 1936:76.

5. Learning from verbal and printed sources is also recorded in: Adler 1911:98, 101, 105. Achilles 1923:45 (about 50 per cent). Hellmann acc. Weissenberg 1924b:211 (friends, 35 per cent; literature, 16 per cent). Schbankov acc. Weissenberg 1924a:14 (servants, 13 per cent; literature and shows, 31 per

cent). Golossowker acc. Weissenberg 1925:175 (friends, 39 per cent; literature, 10 per cent). Gurewitsch and Grosser 1929:528 (friends, 51 per cent; literature, 16 per cent). Davis 1929:109, 161 (30 per cent). Hamilton 1929:426 (25 per cent). Dickinson and Beam 1931:350. Landis and Bolles 1942:21 (15 per cent).

6. Religious books as inspiration for masturbating are also cited in: Moraglia 1897:9. For the Bible and classics as sources, see: Wulffen 1913:257. G. S. Hall and Brill acc. Meagher and Jelliffe 1936:75 deny that serious books have such an influence, but our data do not support them.

7. Hamilton 1929:426 found 18 per cent of his females reported masturbation which originated in petting, but did not distinguish between heterosexual and homosexual petting. Davis 1929:110 reported that 3 per cent of the unmarried females started masturbation from petting.

8. Masturbation originating from imitation of others is recorded in: Hamilton 1929:426 (6 per cent).

9. Homosexual relationships as the origin of masturbation are also noted in: Adler 1911:101. Krafft-Ebing (Moll ed.) 1924:501. Davis 1929:110. Hamilton 1929:426.

10. Similar cases of definitely erotic performances in masturbation in very young girls are reported by: Townsend 1896:186–189 (5 cases under 1 year of age). Moll 1909:52–53; 1912:57–58. Talmey 1910:92–93 (one 9 months, acc. Jacobi, and several 3-year-old girls). Stekel 1920:34; 1950:72 (at 4 years). Hirschsprung acc. Rohleder 1921:66 (at 4, 13, 18 months). Blache (1877) acc. Rohleder 1921:68 (at 17 months). Kraft acc. Rohleder 1921:66 (at 11 months). Krafft-Ebing 1922:55–56 (at 2, 3, 4 years). Krafft-Ebing (Moll ed.) 1924:81 (at 18 months). Riolan 1927:73 (at 3 years). Hodann 1929:28. Friedjung and Hetzer acc. Bühler 1931:616–617 (6, 11, 16 months). West acc. Havelock Ellis 1936 (II,1): 155 (6–9 months). Spitz 1949:95 (rocking and genital play observed in over half of 248 children under one year of age). Levine 1951:118–121 ("typical orgasms even prior to the age of three"—sex not specified). Tactile stimulation, some of it genital but some of it less specifically sexual, is reported in Levy 1928:889. Dillon 1934:165–166. Koch 1935:145. Hattwick 1937:347.

11. American data are also in: Davis 1929:98, 153 (65 per cent of single females; 52 per cent of all women; based, however, on an erroneous assumption that none began masturbation after marriage). Hamilton 1929:427 (74 per cent). Dickinson and Beam 1931:172 (49 per cent); 349 (41 per cent). Dickinson and Beam 1934:460 (76 per cent). Strakosch 1934:37 (66 per cent). Landis et al. 1940:59 (54 per cent). Dearborn 1952:51 (75–80 per cent). These American figures are very close to our own. The wide variation in accumulative incidence figures given by European authors depends for the most part on the fact that they are estimates, or data based on the select samples which go to clinics.

12. Previous studies on masturbation show ages for beginning which are close to our own. See: Hamilton 1929:427 (15 per cent before adolescence). Davis 1929:106, 115 (12 per cent

with orgasm by fourteen years of age). Ackerson 1931:224 (14 per cent by age 12). Harvey 1932a:98 (15 per cent by age 12 as the median of previous studies). Landis and Bolles 1942:21 (20 per cent by adolescence).

13. Published figures which appear to be active incidence figures, whether with or without orgasm, are in: Achilles 1923:50. Schbankov acc. Weissenberg 1924a:13. Hellmann acc. Weissenberg 1924b:211. Golossowker acc. Weissenberg 1925:175. Gurewitsch and Grosser 1929:525. Davis 1929: 102–103. Hamilton 1929:425. Strakosch 1934:35–39. Landis and Bolles 1942:21. The higher incidence of masturbation among older females, whether single or married, is also noted

in: Krafft-Ebing (Moll ed.) 1924:566. Hamilton 1929:439 (56 per cent for older married females). Davis 1929:100 (20 per cent at ages 22–27 rising to 39 per cent by ages 37–42, single females, active incidence at age of reporting). Hutton 1937:77.

14. For incidences and frequencies of male masturbation, see: Kinsey, Pomeroy, and Martin 1948:218–262 and elsewhere.

15. For other data on the frequency of masturbation, see: Davis 1929:122–123 (failed to categorize her data). Hamilton 1929:435–436 (for married females, a median frequency of less than once per month). Landis et al. 1940:288 (median frequency of 1 to 2 times a month, in 122 females).

1.5 THE SEXUAL RESPONSE CYCLE

William H. Masters and Virginia E. Johnson

In 1954 an investigation of the anatomy and physiology of human sexual response was initiated within the framework of the Department of Obstetrics and Gynecology of Washington University School of Medicine. A closely coordinated clinical-research program in problems of human sexual inadequacy was instituted in 1959. Since January, 1964, these programs have been continued under the auspices of the Reproductive Biology Research Foundation. During the past decade the anatomy of human response to sexual stimuli has been established, and such physiologic variables as intensity and duration of individual reaction patterns have been observed and recorded. . . .

Kinsey and co-workers published a monumental compilation of statistics reflecting patterns of sexual behavior in this country from 1938 to 1952. These reports of human sexual practices obtained by techniques of direct interrogation offer an invaluable baseline of sociologic information. Future evaluation of the work may reveal its greatest contribution to be that of opening the previously closed doors of our culture to definitive investigation of human sexual response.

Although the Kinsey work has become a landmark of sociologic investigation, it was not designed to

interpret physiologic or psychologic response to sexual stimulation. These fundamentals of human sexual behavior cannot be established until two questions are answered: What physical reactions develop as the human male and female respond to effective sexual stimulation? Why do men and women behave as they do when responding to effective sexual stimulation? If human sexual inadequacy ever is to be treated successfully, the medical and behavioral professions must provide answers to these basic questions. The current study of human sexual response has been designed to create a foundation of basic scientific information from which definitive answers can be developed to these multifaceted problems.

The techniques of defining and describing the gross physical changes which develop during the human male's and female's sexual response cycles have been primarily those of direct observation and physical measurement. Since the integrity of human observation for specific detail varies significantly, regardless of the observer's training and considered objectivity, reliability of reporting has been supported by many of the accepted techniques of physiologic measurement and the frequent use of color cinematographic recording in all phases of the sexual response cycle.

A more concise picture of physiologic reaction to sexual stimuli may be presented by dividing the human male's and female's cycles of sexual response into four separate phases. Progressively, the four phases are: (1) the excitement phase; (2) the plateau phase; (3) the orgasmic phase; and (4) the resolution phase. This arbitrary four-part division of the sexual response cycle provides an effective framework for detailed description of physiologic variants in sexual reaction, some of which are frequently so transient in character as to appear in only one phase of the total orgasmic cycle.

Only one sexual response pattern has been diagrammed for the human male. Admittedly, there are many identifiable variations in the male sexual reaction. However, since these variants are usually related to duration rather than intensity of response, multiple diagrams would be more repetitive than informative. Comparably, three different sexual response patterns have been diagrammed for the human female. It should be emphasized that these patterns are simplifications of those most frequently observed and are only representative of the infinite variety in female sexual response. Here, intensity as well as duration of response are factors that must be considered when evaluating sexual reaction in the human female.

The first or excitement phase of the human cycle of sexual response develops from any source of somatogenic or psychogenic stimulation. The stimulative factor is of major import in establishing sufficient increment of sexual tension to extend the cycle. If the stimulation remains adequate to individual demand, the intensity of response usually increases rapidly. In this manner the excitement phase is accelerated or shortened. If the stimulative approach is physically or psychologically objectionable, or is interrupted, the excitement phase may be prolonged greatly or even aborted. This first segment and the final segment (resolution phase) consume most of the time expended in the complete cycle of human sexual response.

From excitement phase the human male or female enters the second or plateau phase of the sexual cycle, if effective sexual stimulation is continued. In this phase sexual tensions are intensified and subsequently reach the extreme level from which the individual ultimately may move to orgasm. The duration of the plateau phase is largely dependent upon the effectiveness of the stimuli employed, combined with the factor of individual drive for culmination of sex tension increment. If either stimuli or the drive is inadequate or if all stimuli are withdrawn, the individual will not achieve orgasmic release and will drop slowly from plateau-phase tension levels into an excessively prolonged resolution phase.

The orgasmic phase is limited to those few seconds during which the vasoconcentration and myotonia developed from sexual stimuli are released. This involuntary climax is reached at any level that represents maximum sexual tension increment for the particular occasion. Subjective (sensual) awareness of orgasm is pelvic in focus, specifically concentrated in the clitoral body, vagina, and uterus of the female and in the penis, prostate, and seminal vesicles of the male. Total-body involvement in the response to sexual tensions, although physiologically well-defined, is experienced subjectively on the basis of individual reaction patterns. There is great variation in both the intensity and the duration of female orgasmic experience, while the male tends to follow standard patterns of ejaculatory reaction with less individual variation.

The human male and female resolve from the height of their orgasmic expressions into the last or resolution phase of the sexual cycle. This involuntary period of tension loss develops as a reverse reaction pattern that returns the individual through plateau and excitement levels to an unstimulated state. Women have the response potential of returning to another orgasmic experience from any point in the resolution phase if they submit to the reapplication of effective stimulation. This facility for multiple orgasmic expression is evident particularly if reversal is instituted at plateau tension level. For the man the resolution phase includes a superimposed refractory period which may extend during the involutionary phase as far as a lower excitement level of response. Effective restimulation to higher levels of sexual tension is possible only upon termination of this refractory period. With few exceptions, the physiologic ability of the male to respond to restimulation is much slower than that of the female.

Physiologic residuals of sexual tension usually are dissipated slowly in both the male and female unless an overwhelming orgasmic release has been experienced. Total involution is completed only after all manner of sexual stimuli have been withdrawn.

It always should be borne in mind that there is wide individual variation in the duration and intensity of every specific physiologic response to sexual stimulation. Those that occur early in the response cycle and continue without interruption during several phases are obvious (penile erection or vaginal lubrication). However, some physiologic reactions are fleeting in character and may be confined to one particular phase of the cycle. Examples are the plateau-phase color changes of the minor labia in the female and the coronal engorgement of the penis in the male.

In brief, the division of the human male's or female's cycle of sexual response into four specific phases admittedly is inadequate for evaluation of finite psychogenic aspects of elevated sexual tensions. However, the establishment of this purely arbitrary design provides anatomic structuring and assures inclusion and correct placement of specifics of physiologic response within the sequential continuum of human response to effective sexual stimulation.

The basic physiologic responses of the human body to sexual stimulation are twofold in character. The primary reaction to sexual stimuli is widespread vasocongestion, and the secondary response is a generalized increase in muscle tension. The vasocongestion may be either superficial or deep in distribution, and the myotonia reflected by voluntary or involuntary muscle contractions. The more severe vasocongestive and myotonic reactions are confined to plateau and orgasmic phases of the sexual cycle. . . .

The widespread problems of human sexual inadequacy will not be attacked effectively by either medical or behavioral personnel until more definitive information is accumulated. Such data only will become available as the mores of our society come to accept objective research in human sexuality. . . .

THE RESEARCH POPULATION

The initial selection of individuals for study in the investigation of human sexual response was made from the prostitute population. This socially isolated group was regarded as knowledgeable, cooperative, and available for study. Availability was the determining factor during the initial stages of the program. It was presumed, at that time, that study subjects from more conservative segments of the general population would not be available (a presumption which later was proved to be entirely false).

For the first twenty months of the program, a total of 118 female and 27 male prostitutes contributed their sociosexual, occupational, and medical histories to the investigation. Ultimately, a small number of the total group (8 women and 3 men) were selected for anatomic and physiologic study. The criteria for selection were obvious intelligence, diverse experience in prostitution, ability to vocalize effectively, and, of course, a consistently high degree of availability and cooperation.

Suggestions by this select group of techniques for support and control of the human male and female in situations of direct sexual response proved invaluable. They described many methods for elevating or controlling sexual tensions and demonstrated innumerable variations in stimulative technique. Ultimately many of these techniques have been found to have direct application in therapy of male and female sexual inadequacy and have been integrated into the clinical research program. This small group also served as laboratory-study subjects during the trial-and-error periods required initially to devise and to establish the investigative techniques subsequently employed throughout the study.

The interrogative material and experimental results derived from the prostitute population have not been included in the material being presented. Two factors influenced this decision: (1) The migratory tendencies of this population discouraged the recording of individual study-subject response patterns over extended periods of time, and (2) the varying degrees of pathology of the reproductive organs usually present in this population precluded the possibility of establishing a secure baseline of anatomic normalcy. Faced with the experimental necessity of developing a group of study subjects whose reproductive viscera could be related to baselines of anatomic normalcy and from whom long-range cooperation was possible, volunteers were sought from relatively selected social, intellectual, and economic backgrounds.

The study-subject population as finally constituted for this investigation has been established from selected segments of a metropolitan community. More specifically, it has been developed primarily from and sustained by the academic community associated with a large university-hospital complex. The concentration of study subjects from upper socioeconomic and intellectual strata provided by this major source of supply has not been offset by a statistically significant number of lower-range family units obtained from out-patient clinic sources.

There have been other sources of subject recruitment. A number of family units, initially presenting clinical problems either of sexual inadequacy or conceptive inadequacy, subsequently became a part of the study-subject population. They provide a wide range of sociogeographic and educational backgrounds. In recent years as knowledge of the work in progress spread locally, volunteers of all ages came from all social strata, and from a wide variety of educational backgrounds. . . .

A total of 382 women have cooperated actively with the investigation. The age range of female study subjects is from 18 to 78 years. As might be expected, most of them (321 women, or 84 percent) were in the 18–40-year age bracket, with the largest concentration of active participants in the 21–30-year age group (182, or 47.6 percent). . . .

While to date the majority of the study-subject population has been female, 312 males have cooperated with the program on at least one occasion. Their ages have ranged from 21 to 89 years. The majority of cooperative male study subjects (231, or 74 percent) were 21 to 40 years of age, with the largest number of active participants in the 21–30-age group (120, or 38.5 percent). . . .

Of major import is the unique opportunity created by the research environment to observe, to record, and to evaluate the patterns of physiologic and psychologic response to effective sexual stimulation in a small, arbitrarily selected segment of male and female society to a degree never possible previously in medical or behavioral environment. Rather than material returned from interviews or questionnaires being the lone source from which to draw conclusions concerning human sexual behavior, the material in the chapters oriented to clinical reaction has been drawn from direct observation of sexual response—interviews in depth of behavioral content, discussions of the individual's sexual response patterns, laboratory recording and analysis of reactive patterns, and so on. . . .

Finally, and possibly most important, is the information gleaned from eleven years of opportunity to work directly with the human male and female responding to effective sexual stimulation. It constantly should be borne in mind that the primary research interest has been concentrated quite literally upon what men and women do in response to effective sexual stimulation, and why they do it, rather than on what people say they do or even think their sexual reactions and experiences might be.

Further, modes or means of sexual stimulation will be described without reservation at this point and not constantly referred to in the body of the text. Recorded and observed sexual activity of study subjects has included, at various times, manual and mechanical manipulation, natural coition with the female partner in supine, superior, or knee-chest position and, for many female study subjects, artificial coition in supine and knee-chest positions. No study subject has been able to fantasy to orgasm under observation.

The artificial coital equipment was created by radiophysicists. The penises are plastic and were developed with the same optics as plate glass. Cold-light illumination allows observation and recording without distortion. The equipment can be adjusted for physical variations in size, weight, and vaginal development. The rate and depth of penile thrust is initiated and controlled completely by the responding individual. As tension elevates, rapidity and depth of thrust are increased voluntarily, paralleling subjective demand. The equipment is powered electrically.

Orientation to this equipment obviously was necessary for study subjects with established coital and/or automanipulative experience. The orientation periods provided opportunities for evaluating subjective fantasy and conditioning processes employed by study subjects for sex tension increment.

In view of the artificial nature of the equipment, legitimate issue may be raised with the integrity of observed reaction patterns. Suffice it to say that intravaginal physiologic response corresponds in every way with previously established reaction patterns observed and recorded during hundreds of cycles in response to automanipulation. . . .

Once selected as study subjects, males and females were exposed to a controlled orientation program before assuming active participation as members of the research population. Detailed medical, social, and sexual histories were obtained from each study subject by both male and female interrogators. The technique of dual-sexed interrogation was designed to satisfy two purposes. First was the necessity to orient a prospective study subject to the fact of bisexual supervision of all investigative procedures, and second was the demand for security of factual reporting. Material of sexual connotation has been elicited from study subjects more effectively and accurately by interview teams with both sexes represented than by single-sexed interrogation. The exposure to the prostitute population emphasized the advantages of this technique. History-taking also served secondarily as a step in preparation for active participation in the program. It acquainted the study subject with the investigative personnel and established in his or her mind the investigators' nonjudgmental attitudes and their authoritative roles.

The next step in the orientation program was to demand that potential study subjects undergo physical examinations to rule out any gross pathology, particularly of the reproductive organs.

The individuals considering active cooperation with the program then were exposed to the research quarters. All equipment was exhibited and its function explained to the uninitiated. Sexual activity first was encouraged in privacy in the research quarters and then continued with the investigative team present, until the study subjects were quite at ease in their artificial surroundings. No attempt was made to record reactions or introduce other members of the research personnel to the reacting unit, until the study subjects felt secure in their surroundings and confident of their ability to perform. They rapidly gained confidence in their ability to respond successfully while subjected to a variety of recording techniques. Finally, this period of training established a sense of security in the integrity of the research interest and in the absolute anonymity embodied in the program.

Once total confidence was attained, the study subjects were directed to the particular phase of the overall program in which their cooperation was considered to be of greatest value. These areas have included the specific and long-continued recording of anatomic and physiologic response to effective sexual stimulation, pregnancy sexuality, geriatric sexuality, etc. Frequently, one recording session for a family unit was sufficient to demonstrate conclusively the anatomic variations and physiologic reactions that will be described in this text. In other instances family units have been immersed in multiple facets of the investigative program and have cooperated actively for many years.

1.6 THE SOCIAL ORIGINS OF SEXUAL DEVELOPMENT

John H. Gagnon and William Simon

THE SEXUAL TRADITION

The most important set of images for sex or eroticism in the modern West, either for scientists or in conventional educated speech, derives from the language of psychoanalysis. It would be difficult to overstate the coercive power of Freud's innovative verbal reformulations of a whole range of early conceptualizations about the role of sexuality in its biological, personal, and societal contexts. In an important sense Freud remains the superego of nearly all researchers into the sexual, since we must in some measure either conform to or rebel against his body of ideas. As with most great innovators, Freud began with the available set of contemporary ideas that were part of the heritage of the eighteenth and nineteenth centuries. It is difficult for those in the 1970s, for whom Freud is received wisdom and whose conservative postures are now most evident and emphasized, to recognize his role as a radical theorist of sexuality as well as representing a force for sociopolitical liberalism. The emphasis on the instinctual basis for the experience of the sexual and the universality of man's sexual experience, though possibly wrong in fact and theory, served to introduce a great change in sexual values at the turn of the century. Perhaps more important, by asserting the universality of the human experience, Freud significantly helped erode the dubious anthropology that imperial Europe used to describe its colonial subjects. The Freudian codification provided for modern, educated, Western man a set of verbal categories through which he might describe his internal states, explain the origins of his sexual proclivities, describe his own and others' motives, and ultimately reanalyze literature, histories, and societies as well as individual lives. The cultural assimilation of much of psychoanalytic theory, especially on a popular level, resides in its essential continuity with popular wisdom about the instinctive nature of sexuality. This version of sexuality as an innate and dangerous instinct is shared not only by the man in the street, but also by psychological theorists deeply opposed to Freudian thought, as well as by sociologists whose rejection of analytic theory is nearly total. Hence the language of Kingsley Davis:

> The development and maintenance of a stable competitive order with respect to sex is extremely difficult because sexual desire itself is inherently unstable and anarchic. Erotic relations are subject to constant danger—a change of whim, a loss of interest, a third party, a misunderstanding. Competition for the same sexual object inflames passions, and stirs conflicts; failure injures ones self-esteem. The intertwining of sex and society is a fertile ground for paranoia, for homicide and suicide.[1]

The seventeenth-century political image of the individual against the state is translated by the Romantic tradition into a contest between the individual and his culture. The Hobbesian contest between natural instinct and imposed constraint was moved by Freud (as well as many other post-Romantic innovators) from the arena of the state, power conflicts, and the social contract to the arena of the mind, sexuality, and the parent-child contract. The sexual instinct presses against cultural controls, pleasure contests with reality, as the sociocultural forces in the form of parents (Leviathan writ small) block, shape, and organize the sexual drive and convert it from lust to love, from societal destruction to social service.

This tradition is surely present in Freud with his emphasis on a drive model of development, a libidinal thrust that sequentially organizes intra- and extrapsychic life as well as the very meaning of the parts of the body. This direct relation between the external signs of physiological events and necessary motiva-

---

tional and cognitive states is a given for nearly all students of sexual behavior, whose frequent error is to confuse the outcomes of sexual learning with their apparent origins.

The Freudian or Kinseyian traditions share the prevailing image of the sexual drive as a basic biological mandate that presses against and must be controlled by the cultural and social matrix. This drive reduction model of sexual behavior as mediated by cultural and social controls is preeminent in "sexological" literature. Explanations of sexual behavior that flow from this model are relatively simple. The sex drive is thought to exist at some constant level in any cohort of the population, with rising and falling levels in the individual's life cycle. It presses for expression, and in the absence of controls, which exist either in laws and mores or in appropriate internalized repressions learned in early socialization, there will be outbreaks of "abnormal sexual activity." In the more primitive versions of this drive theory, there is a remarkable congruence between the potentiating mechanisms for specifically sexual and generally sinful behavior. The organism is inherently sexual (sinful) and its behavior is controlled by the presence of inhibitory training and channeling, internalized injunctions, and the absence of temptation. If these mechanisms fail, there will certainly be sexual misconduct (sin). More sophisticated models can be found in functional theories in sociology or in revisionist psychoanalytic models, but fundamental to each is a drive reduction notion that sees sex as having necessary collective and individual consequences because of its biological origins.

What is truly innovative about Freud's thought is not his utilization of prior constructs about sexuality and the nature of man, but his placement of these ideas about sexuality at the center of human concerns, beginning in infancy, an essential to normal human development. As Erik Erikson has observed, prior to Freud, "sexology" tended to see sexuality as suddenly appearing with the onset of adolescence.[2] From Erikson's point of view, Freud's discovery of infantile and childhood expressions of sexuality was a crucial part of his contribution. Libido—the generation of psychosexual energies—was viewed after Freud as a fundamental element of the human experience from its

very inception, beginning at the latest with birth and possibly prior to birth. Libido was conceived as something essential to the organism, representing a kind of constitutional factor with which forms of social life at all levels of sociocultural organization and development, as well as personality structure at each point in the individual life cycle, had to cope.

In Freud's view the human infant and child behaved in ways that were intrinsically sexual and these early behaviors remained in effective and influential continuity with later forms of psychosexual development.[3] Implicit in this view was the assumption that the relations between available sexual energies and emergent motives and attachments would be complex but direct. In some aspects of psychoanalytic thinking, both adolescent and adult sexuality were viewed as being in some measure a reenactment of sexual commitments developed, learned, or acquired during infancy and childhood.[4]

From the vantage point of the late twentieth century, it is apparent that this point of view presents both an epistemological and a sociolinguistic problem. Freud's descriptive language for sexuality was the language of adults describing their current and childhood "sexual" experience (as transmuted through psychoanalytic interviews), which was then imposed upon the "apparent" behavior and "assumed" responses, feelings, and cognitions of infants and children. Acts and feelings are described as sexual, not because of the child's sense of the experience, but because of the meanings attached to those acts by adult observers or interpreters whose only available language is that of adult sexual experience.

It is important to note here the extraordinary difficulties of all developmental research in getting accurate data and also that research on infancy and childhood through adulthood faces a problem which most of the psychoanalytic literature obscures. Part of the problem is faulty recall, some of which is locatable in the problem of inaccurate memories, but another source of error is located in the existentalist insight that instead of the past determining the character of the present, the present significantly reshapes the past as we reconstruct our biographies in an effort to bring them into greater congruence with our current identities, roles, situations, and available vocabularies. Indeed, the role of the analyst in providing an alternative self-conception for patients by creating a new vocabulary of motives is central to the therapeutic impulse and opposed to the gathering of accurate information about the past.

The other major problem of data quality control results from attempting to gather data either from children who are, because of their stage of development, ill-equipped to report on their internal states or from adults who were asked to report about periods in their life when complex vocabularies for internal states did not exist for them.[5] How can the researcher determine what is being felt or thought when the researcher is confronted with organisms whose restricted language skills may preclude certain feelings and thoughts? The child in this situation possesses internal states that in a verbal sense are meaningless and that will begin to be named and organized only during later development. The adult loses access to that inchoate period of his own experience by learning new ways of attributing meaning to experiences. The organism cannot hold onto both sets of experiences at once. Indeed, this may be the central meaning of development, that the acquisition of new categories for experience erase the past. Opie and Opie report that adolescents quickly forget childhood games. How much more quickly do we forget earlier and more diffuse experiences?[6]

The assumption of an identity between perception based upon a adult terminology for the description of a child's behavior and the meaning of that behavior for the child must be treated with extreme caution. The dilemma is in distinguishing between the sources of specific actions, gestures, and bodily movements and the ways in which they are labeled as sexual at various stages of development. For the infant touching his penis, the activity cannot be sexual in the same sense as adult masturbation but is merely a diffusely pleasurable activity, like many other activities. Only through maturing and learning these adult labels for his experience and activity can the child come to masturbate in the adult sense of that word. The complexity of adult masturbation as an act is enormous, requiring the close coordination of physical, psychological, and social resources, all of which change dynamically after puberty. It is through the developmental process of converting external labels into internal capacities

for naming that activities become more precisely defined and linked to a structure of sociocultural expectations and needs that define what is sexual. The naive external observer of this behavior often imputes to the child the complex set of motivational states that are generally associated (often wrongly) with physically homologous adult activities.

In the Freudian schema, this gap between observer and observed, between the language of adult experience and the lived experience of the child is bridged by locating an instinctual sexual energy source within the infant. The child is seen as possessed of certain emergent sexual characteristics that express themselves regardless of parental action systems. These actions of the child are viewed as being rooted in the constitutional nature of the organism. Consequent upon this primitive Freudian position is an over generalized presumption that all contacts with or stimulation of the end organs of the infant have a protosexual or completely sexual meaning.

To suggest that infant or childhood experience, even that which is identified as genital, is prototypical of or determines adult patterns is to credit the biological organism with more wisdom than we normally do in other areas where the biological and sociocultural intersect. Undeniably, what we conventionally describe as sexual behavior is rooted in biological capacities and processes, but no more than other forms of behavior. Admitting the existence of a biological substrate for sex in no way allows a greater degree of biological determinism than is true of other areas of corresponding intersection. Indeed, the reverse is more likely to be true: the sexual area may be precisely that realm wherein the superordinate position of the sociocultural over the biological level is most complete.[7]

The unproven assumption in psychoanalytic theory (and much conventional wisdom) of the "power" of the psychosexual drive as a fixed biological attribute may prove to be the major obstacle to the understanding of psychosexual development. In its more specific psychoanalytic formulation, we find little evidence to suggest that such a "drive" need find expression in specific sexual acts or categories of sexual acts.[8] Similarly, we must call into question the even more dubious assumption that there are innate sexual capacities or specific experiences that tend to translate immediately into a kind of universal wisdom, that sexuality possesses a magical ability allowing biological drives to seek direct expression in psychosocial and social ways that we do not expect in other biologically rooted behaviors. This assumption can be seen in the psychoanalytic literature, for example, in which the child who views the "primal scene" is seen on some primitive level as intuiting its sexual character. Also, the term *latency,* in its usage by psychoanalytic theorists, suggests a period of integration by the child of prior intrinsically sexual experiences and reactions; on this level, adolescence is reduced to little more than the management or organization on a manifest level of the commitments and styles already prefigured, if not preformed, in infancy and childhood experience.

In contradistinction to this tradition, we have adopted the view that the point at which the individual begins to respond in intrinsically sexual ways, particularly in terms of socially available or defined outlets and objects, reflects a discontinuity with previous "sexual experience" (however that might be defined). Further, at this point in the developmental process, both seemingly sexual and seemingly nonsexual elements "contend" for influence in complex ways that in no respect assure priority for experiences that are apparently sexual in character and occur earlier in the life cycle.

Essential to our perspective is the assumption that with the beginnings of adolescence—and with the increasing acknowledgement by the surrounding social world of an individual's sexual capacity—many novel factors come into play, and an overemphasis upon a search for continuity with infant and childhood experiences may be dangerously misleading. In particular, it may be a costly mistake to be overimpressed with preadolescent behaviors that appear to be manifestly sexual. In general, it is possible that much of the power of sexuality may be a function of the fact that it has been defined as powerful or dangerous. But this overenriched conception of sexual behavior (to the degree that it is possessed by any individual) must largely follow upon considerable training in an adult language that includes an overdetermined conception of sexuality. Thus it does not necessarily follow that the untrained infant or child

will respond as powerfully or as complexly to his own seemingly sexual behaviors as an adult observer.

We must also question the prevailing image of the sexual component in human experience as that of an intense drive stemming from the biological substratum that constrains the individual to seek sexual gratification either directly or indirectly. This is clearly present in the Freudian tradition. A similar position is observable in more sociological writings. This is apparent, for example, in the thinking of sociologists for whom sex is also a high intensity, societal constant that must be properly channeled lest it find expression in behaviors which threaten the maintenance of collective life.[9]

Our sense of the available data suggests a somewhat different picture of human sexuality, one of generally lower levels of intensity or, at least, greater variability in intensity. There are numerous social situations in which the reduction and even elimination of sexual activity is managed by greatly disparate populations of biologically normal males and females with little evidence of corollary or compensatory intensification in other spheres of life.[10] It is possible that, given the historical nature of human societies, we are victim to the needs of earlier social orders. For earlier societies it may not have been a need to constrain severely the powerful sexual impulse in order to maintain social stability or limit inherently antisocial force, but rather a matter of having to invent an importance for sexuality. This would not only assure a high level of reproductive activity but also provide socially available rewards unlimited by natural resources, rewards that promote conforming behavior in sectors of social life far more important than the sexual. Part of the legacy of Freud is that we have all become adept at seeking out the sexual ingredient in many forms of nonsexual behavior and symbolism. We are suggesting what is in essence the insight of Kenneth Burke: it is just as plausible to examine sexual behavior for its capacity to express and serve nonsexual motives as the reverse.[11]

A major flaw in the psychoanalytic tradition is that psychosexual development, while a universal component in the human experience, certainly does not occur with universal modalities. Even ignoring the striking forms of cross-cultural variability, we can observe striking differences within our own population, differences that appear to require not a unitary description of psychosexual development but descriptions of different developmental processes characterizing different segments of the population.[12] The most evident of these are the large number of important differences between observable male and female patterns of sexual behavior.[13] This particular difference may in some respects be partly attributable to the role played by the biological substratum. We have to account not only for the gross physiological differences and the different roles in the reproductive process that follow from these physiological differences, but must also consider differences in hormone functions at particular ages.[14] However, while our knowledge of many of the salient physiological and physiochemical processes involved is far from complete, there is still little immediate justification for asserting a direct casual link between these processes and specific differential patterns of sexual development observed in our society. The work of Masters and Johnson, for example, clearly points to far greater orgasmic capacities on the part of females than males; however, their concept of orgasm as a physiological process would hardly be a basis for accurately predicting rates of sexual behavior.[15] Similarly, within each sex, important distinctions must be made for various socioeconomic status groups whose patterns of sexual development will vary considerably, more impressively for males than for females.[16] And with reference to socioeconomic status differences, the link to the biological level appears even more tenuous, unless one is willing to invoke the relatively unfashionable conceptual equipment of Social Darwinism. These differences, then, not only suggest the importance of sociocultural elements and social structure, but also stand as a warning against too uncritical an acceptance of unqualified generalizations about psychosexual development.

SCRIPTS AND THE ATTRIBUTION OF MEANING

The term *script* might properly be invoked to describe virtually all human behavior in the sense that there is very little that can in a full measure be called spontaneous. Ironically, the current vogue of using "encounter groups" to facilitate "spontaneous" behavior can be defined as learning the appropriate script for spontaneous behavior. Indeed, the sense of the *internal rehearsal* consistent with both psychoanalytic and symbolic interactionist theory suggests just such scripting of all but the most routinized behavior.

It is the result of our collective blindness to or ineptitude in locating and defining these scripts that has allowed the prepotence of a biological mandate in the explanation of sexual behavior. (This possibly occurs precisely because the notion of such a biological mandate is a common element within the sexual scripts of Western societies.) Without the proper elements of a script that defines the situation, names the actors, and plots the behavior, nothing sexual is likely to happen. One can easily conceive of numerous social situations in which all or almost all of the ingredients of a sexual event are present but that remain nonsexual in that not even sexual arousal occurs. Thus, combining such elements as desire, privacy, and a physically attractive person of the appropriate sex, the probability of something sexual happening will, under normal circumstances, remain exceedingly small until either one or both actors organize these behaviors into an appropriate script.

Elements of such scripting occur across many aspects of the sexual situation. Scripts are involved in learning the meaning of internal states, organizing the sequences of specifically sexual acts, decoding novel situations, setting the limits on sexual responses, and linking meanings from nonsexual aspects of life to specifically sexual experience. These would at first seem only to be versions of the old sociological saw that nothing occurs internally that does not occur in the external social world. But it is more than this in two ways. Using this model the process of sexual learning can be specified without depending on nonbehavioral elements, and doing this reorders the sources of meaning for phenomena and the ways in which we think about the sexual experience.

This can be exemplified even more dramatically. Take an ordinary middle-class male, detach him from his regular social location, and place him for some business or professional reason in a large, relatively anonymous hotel. One might even endow him with an interest in sexual adventure. Upon returning to the hotel at night, he opens his hotel door and there in the shaft of light from the hall-way, he observes a nearly nude, extremely attractive female. One may assume that his initial reaction will *not* be one of sexual arousal. A few men—the slightly more paranoid—might begin to cast about for signs of their wife's lawyer or a private detective. Most, however, would simply beat a hasty and profoundly embarrassed retreat. Even back in the hall and with a moment's reflection to establish the correctness of the room number, the next impulse would still *not* be one of sexual arousal or activity but most probably a trip to the lobby to seek clarification—via the affectively neutral telephone. What is lacking in this situation is an effective sexual script that would allow him to define the female as a potentially erotic actor (the mere fact of her being attractive or nearly nude is not sufficient) and the situation as potentially sexual. If these two definitional elements did exist, much of what might follow can be predicted with fair accuracy. But without such a script, little by way of sexual activity or even sexual arousal will transpire.

Our use of the term *script* with reference to the sexual has two major dimensions. One deals with the external, the interpersonal—the script as the organization of mutually shared conventions that allows two or more actors to participate in a complex act involving mutual dependence. The second deals with the internal, the intrapsychic, the motivational elements that produce arousal or at least a commitment to the activity.

At the level of convention is that large class of gestures, both verbal and nonverbal, that are mutually accessible. Routinized language, the sequence of petting behaviors among adolescents and adults, the conventional styles establishing sexual willingness are all parts of culturally shared, external routines. These are the strategies involved in the "doing" of sex, concrete and continuous elements of what a culture agrees is sexual. They are assembled, learned over time, reflecting—as will be clear in subsequent chapters—general patterns of stages of development. This relatively stylized behavior, however, tells us little of the meaning it has for its participants. The same sequence of acts may have different meanings for both different pairs of actors or the participants in the same act. This is the

world where sexual activity can be expressive of love or rage, the will to power or the will to self-degradation, where the behavioral is experienced through the symbolic.

On the level of internal experience, it is apparent from the work of Schachter and others that the meaning attributed to many states of physiological arousal depends upon the situation in which they are experienced.[17] In this way, meaning is attributed to the interior of the body by many of the same rules as it is to an exterior experience, depending on a vocabulary of motives that makes the biological into a meaningful psychological experience. This phenomena is well understood in research in drug effects, with the meaning of the drug experience being dependent on mood, situation of use, prior history of the user, and the like, rather than what is spuriously referred to as the drug effect. This is apparent in the effects of all of the so-called mind-altering drugs including marijuana. The differing reports on the internal effects of LSD-25 lysergic acid (good trips, psychomimetic experiences, paranoid trips, art nouveau hallucinations, meetings with God) seem more attributable to the person-situation effect than to the drug. This is observable in young adolescents when they are required to learn what the feelings they have with reference to early post-pubertal sexual arousal "mean." Events variously categorized as anxiety, nausea, fear are reported which are later finally categorized as (or dismissed, even though they still occur) sexual excitement. A vast number of physiological events get reported to the central nervous system, but of this number only a small proportion are attended to in any single moment. (How many persons, for instance, experience their toes curl or the anal sphincter twitch at the moment of orgasm?) It is this small proportion that is recognized as the internal correlates or internal "meanings" of the experience. In this case, the meaning is a consensual experience with various elements brought together to be the appropriate behaviors that will elicit the internal correlates or consequences of the external behaviors.

Scripting also occurs not only in the making of meaningful interior states, but in providing the ordering of bodily activities that will release these internal biological states. Here scripts are the mechanisms through which biological events can be potentiated. An example from the adult world is most apt in revealing this process. If one examines the assembly of events that are the physical elements of the current script in the United States for adolescent or adult heterosexual behavior that leads to coitus, it is clear that there is a progression from hugging and kissing, to petting above the waist, to hand-genital contacts (sometimes mouth-genital contacts) and finally to coitus. There is some variation about these acts in timing (both in order and duration), but roughly this is—at the physical level—what normal heterosexual activity is. Prior to or in the course of this sequence of physical acts, sexual arousal occurs, and in some cases orgasm results for one or both of the two persons involved. What is misleading in this physical description is that it sounds as if one were rubbing two sticks together to produce fire; that is, if only enough body heat is generated, orgasm occurs. However, orgasm is not only a physical event, but also the outcome of a combination of both biological and, more importantly, social psychological factors. Unless the two people involved recognize that the physical events outlined are sexual and are embedded in a sexual situation, there will not be the potentiation of the physiological concomitants that Masters and Johnson have demonstrated as necessary in the production of sexual excitement and the orgasmic cycle.[18] The social meaning given to the physical acts releases biological events. Most of the physical acts described in the foregoing sexual sequence occur in many other situations—the palpation of the breast for cancer, the gynecological examination, the insertion of tampons, mouth-to-mouth resuscitation—all involve homologous physical events. But the social situation and the actors are not defined as sexual or potentially sexual, and the introduction of a sexual element is seen as a violation of the expected social arrangements. The social-psychological meaning of sexual events must be learned because they supply the channels through which biology is expressed. In some cases, the system of naming must exist for the event to occur; in others, portions of the event that are biologically necessary are never observed in the psychological field of the participating persons.

The term *script* (or *scripted behavior*) immediately suggests the dramatic, which is appropriate; but it also suggests the conventional dramatic narrative form, which more often than not is inappropriate. The latter tendency is reinforced by our most general conception of the sex act itself, which is seen as a dramatic event with continuous cumulative action. This is suggested, for example, by the language of Masters and Johnson—"arousal, plateau, climax, and resolution"—a conception resembling somewhat an Aristotelian notion of the dramatic or the design for a nineteenth-century symphony. However, the sources of arousal, passion or excitement (the recognition of a sexual possibility), as well as the way the event is experienced (if, indeed, an event follows), derive from a complicated set of layered symbolic meanings that are not only difficult to comprehend from the observed behavior, but also may not be shared by the participants. Even where there is minimal sharing of elements of a script by persons acting toward each other (which, while not necessary, clearly facilitates execution of the acts with mutual satisfaction), they may be organized in different ways and invoked at different times.

The same overt gesture may have both a different meaning and/or play a different role in organizing the sexual "performance." The identical gesture undertaken during sexual activity may be read by one participant with a content that might resemble that of Sade or Sacher-Mosoch, while the other participant reads content from *Love Story*.

Elements entering into the performance may be both relatively remote to the erotic (or what is conventionally defined as remote to the erotic), as well as the immediately and intrinsically erotic. Moreover, the logic of organization may more closely follow the nonnarrative qualities of modern poetry, the surrealistic tradition, or the theater of the absurd than conventional narrative modes. The sexual provides us with a situation where the mere invocation of some powerfully organizing metaphor links behavior to whole universes of meaning; a situation where the power of a metaphorically enriched gesture, act, characteristic, object, or posture cannot be determined by the relative frequency with which it occurs; such organizing metaphors need only be suggested for their effects to be realized.

An example of this may be seen in Jerzy N. Kosinski's novel *Steps*,[19] where our nameless hero finds himself looking down upon a fellow office worker (female) whom he has long desired sexually and who is in a posture of unrestrained sexual accessibility. Though it is a moment he has long desired, he finds himself unable to become aroused. He then recalls the moment of his initial sexual interest; a moment in which, while watching her in the act of filing papers with uplifted arms, he catches a fleeing glimpse of her bra. This trivial image, originally arousing, remains arousing and our hero goes on to complete the act. It is that image (and what it links to) that both names her as an erotic object in terms of his sense of the erotic and names also what he is about to do to her. Though the image need only be briefly suggested (both in its origins and subsequent utilization), and though it may remain unknown to the behaviorist observer, it becomes critical to the performance. Its meanings could be multiple. For example, that the sexual becomes erotically enriched when it is hidden, latent, denied, or when it is essentially violative (deriving from unintended exposure). It also legitimates the appropriate name for the behavior. Consider the possible "labels" our hero could have invoked that could have been applied to the behavior, each with its own powerful and powerfully distinct associations—making love, making out, fucking, screwing, humping, doing, raping.

The erotic component we can assume is minimally necessary if sexual activity is to occur; that is its very importance. (A dramatic exception, of course, are many women whose participation in sexual activity has often—historically, possibly more often than not—had little to do with their own sense of the erotic.) On the other hand, a preoccupation with the erotic may reach obsessive proportions without overt sexual behavior necessarily following. Thus, like the biological component, it can be described as simultaneously being of critical importance and also insufficient by itself to be either fully descriptive or predictive of actual sexual careers.

While the importance of the erotic can be asserted, it may be the most difficult to elaborate, as a concern for the erotic—the acquisition of sexual culture—is possibly the least well understood or attended aspect of sexual behavior. We know very little about how it is acquired or, for that matter, the ways in which it influences both our sexual and nonsexual lives. Persistence of concepts such as libido or the sex drive obviate need for this knowledge. For those who hold these or comparable positions, the body is frequently seen as being both wise and articulate; recognizing and speaking a compelling language. Still others have assumed, in too unexamined a way, a direct link between collective sexual cultures and private sexual cultures, despite the fact that for many what is collectively defined as erotic may not be associated with sexual response or that much that the collectivity defines as non- or even anti-erotic may become part of the private sexual culture of a given individual; for example, various kinds of full and partial fetishisms. As a result, much of the research on responses to erotic materials often begins with the dubious assumption that experimental stimuli are recognizable in terms of a conventional social definition.[20]

One thing that is clear is that for contemporary society erotic imagery or metaphors are for the most part discontinuously or only latently a part of the images or metaphors of nonsexual identity or social life. (The exceptions are those social roles that are specifically assumed to have a "known" erotic aspect, such as the prostitute, the homosexual, the stewardess, or the divorcee, all of whom we tend to see as either fully erotic or unusually erotic to the point where we have difficulty seeing them in anything but erotic terms.) Thus, for conventional actors in relatively conventional settings, the invocation of the erotic, necessary for sexual arousal, frequently requires a series of rituals of transformation before the participants or the setting license (as it were) the sexual moment. For example, much of precoital petting or foreplay may serve less as facilitators of a physiological process, than as elements in a ritual drama that allow one or both actors to rename themselves, their partners, as well as various parts of the body in terms of the "special" purpose. The intrusion of nonerotic, manifest meanings to images—that is, parts of the body or other role commitments of one or another of the actors is experienced as disruptive of sexual interest or capacity, if only because such commitments are rarely predictive of sexual role needs. For most, as a consequence, the sexual flourishes best in a sheltered and, in some sense, isolated universe, a landscape denuded of all but the most relevant aspects of identity.

At the same time, the larger part of identity and sense of the rest of social life frequently intrude in an indirect way. The elaboration of the erotic or its direct expression is often constrained by an anticipation of an anticipated return to that larger social role, that more continuous sense of self. For some this may involve merely the insulation of silence; for others, symbolic reinterpretation and condensation—for example, an intensity of pressure that allows the actor to represent by that gesture either passion (or the message that uncharacteristic behavior is thereby explained), or love and affection (that the actor is the same as he or she is in their more conventional mode of relating), or sadistic aggression (illuminating a complicated fantasy rehearsed and experienced sufficiently that the gesture successfully evokes most of the emotional density generated by a long and frequently complicated scenario).

Beyond the very general level, however, little can be said. Important questions dealing not only with origins but careers have yet to be even examined provisionally. Where do such images come from? In terms of what sexual and nonsexual experiences do their meanings change? Is there need for elaboration? These, and many more, are the questions that we may have to examine before sexual activity, which all too often can be described as a "dumb-show" for its participants, becomes something other than a dumb-show for behavioral science.

NOTES

1. Kingsley Davis, "Sexual Behavior," in *Contemporary Social Problems* eds. R. K. Merton and R. Nishet (New York: Harcourt Brace Jovanovich, 1971), p. 317.

2. E. H. Erikson, *Childhood and Society,* 2nd ed. (New York: Norton, 1963).

3. Sigmund Freud, "Three Essays on Sexuality," *Complete Psychological Works,* vol. 7 (London: Hogarth, 1953), pp. 135–245. Also, E. Jones, "Freud's Conception of Libido," in *Human Sexual Behavior: A Book of Readings,* ed. Bernhardt Lieberman (New York: John Wiley & Sons, Inc., 1971), pp.

42–60; P. Chodoff, "Critique of Freud's Theory of Infantile Sexuality," *American Journal of Psychiatry* 123 (1966): 507–18.

4. Sigmund Freud, *A General Introduction to Psychoanalysis* (New York: Liveright, 1935), pp. 283–84.

5. E. Schachtel, *Metamorphosis* (New York: Basic Books, 1959).

6. There is a body of evidence that among young children there is a large amount of game and folklore material that is rapidly forgotten after puberty. A certain amount of this material is sexual, but the folklorists who work with children usually fail to keep records of this, or if they do so, do not publish it. An interesting aspect of this material is its eternal character—that is, it is passed on from generation to generation. For example, children in England are currently singing a recognizable variant of a song about Bonaparte popular in the early nineteenth century. See Iona Opie and Peter Opie, *The Lore and Language of School Children* (London: Oxford Press, 1959), pp. 98–99.

7. Even on the level of organismic needs and gratification, the linking of these to the sexual or protosexual may be too limited, too simple. Robert White has argued cogently that during infancy and early childhood an emergent commitment to "competence" may rival sensual expressions of the pleasure principle in organizing the young organism's activities, as the child "sacrifices" immediate sensual gratification in order to develop and experience his or her own competence. See "Psychosexual Development and Competence," *The Nebraska Symposium on Motivation* (Lincoln, University of Nebraska Press, 1960).

8. Frank A. Beach, "Characteristics of Masculine 'Sex Drive'," *The Nebraska Symposium on Motivation* (Lincoln: University of Nebraska Press, 1956).

9. E. Durkheim, *Suicide* (Glencoe, Ill. The Free Press, 1951).

10. J. H. Gagnon and W. Simon, "The Social Meaning of Prison Homosexuality," *Federal Probation,* 1968.

11. K. Burke, *Permanence and Change* (New York: New Republic, Inc., 1935).

12. C. F. Ford and F. A. Beach, *Patterns of Sexual Behavior* (New York: Harper, 1951).

13. E. Maccoby, ed., *The Development of Sex Differences* (Stanford: Stanford University Press, 1966).

14. D. A. Hamburg and D. T. Lunde, "Sex Hormones in the Development of Sex Differences in Human Behavior," in Maccoby, *The Development of Sex Differences,* pp. 1–24; W. R. Young, R. Goy, and C. Phoenix, "Hormones and Sexual Behavior," *Science* 143 (1964): 212–18.

15. W. H. Masters and V. E. Johnson, *Human Sexual Response* (Boston: Little, Brown and Co., 1966).

16. A. C. Kinsey et al., *Sexual Behavior in the Human Male* (Philadelphia: W. B. Saunders Co., 1948).

17. Stanley Schachter, "The Interaction of Cognitive and Emotional Determinants of Emotional State," in *Advances in Experimental Social Psychology,* vol. 1, ed. Leonard Berkowitz (New York: Academic Press, 1964), pp. 49–80. That similar processes of control over the autonomic nervous system also exist and can be operantly conditioned is demonstrated by Neal Miller, "Learning of Visceral and Glandular Responses," *Science* 163 (January 31, 1969): 434–45. Work on increasing "vol-

untary" control of sexual responses (e.g., penile erection) is beginning only at the present moment.

18. Masters and Johnson, *Human Sexual Response.*

19. Jerzy N. Kosinski, *Steps* (New York: Random House, 1968).

20. Masters and Johnson, *Human Sexual Response.*

—— CHAPTER TWO ——

CONTEMPORARY INTERROGATIONS

Classical studies of sexuality focused on how we got to be sexual in the first place, what we did sexually, and what was normal and what was not. Contemporary inquiries question all three of these, further complicating the questions we raise and making the search for easy answers virtually impossible.

In the 1990s, John Gagnon was part of a research team at the University of Chicago that undertook a more comprehensive survey of American's sexual behavior than had ever been done in our history, outdoing the Kinsey study in both reach and scope. The team found that Americans had less sex than we had previously thought and the most surprising finding was that Kinsey's original estimates of homosexuality were dramatically inflated. The results of the new survey indicated that only about 4–5 percent of American men and about 1–2 percent of American women identified as homosexual.

These findings caused a significant controversy. Some thought the numbers were low because people were far more circumspect than researchers thought and likely to be dishonest in conversations with sex researchers. Others found the numbers too high and the dissemination of information about sex to be an invitation to perversion.

But most contemporary discussion about sex research has been about the criteria that the researchers used—and the limits of that type of research in the first place. Jonathan Katz makes clear that the terms "homosexual" and "heterosexual" used as nouns to describe discrete and identifiable identities (not as adjectives describing behaviors) is as recent as the turn of the last century, so applying them to historical cases may be inaccurate. Biologist Anne Fausto-Sterling suggests that a simple binary model of two sexes fails to adequately capture the full range of humans as biological creatures, with dramatic implications for sexualities. And Suzanne Kessler makes it clear that it is often doctors, not individuals, who decide biological sex based on their assumptions of what would make a person happiest. What you see is not always what you are, or will become.

Leonore Tiefer in one selection, and Julia Ericksen and Sally Steffen in another, get inside the famous sex surveys of the twentieth century, offering powerful critiques both of what was included and what was left out.

2.1 THE FIVE SEXES
Why Male and Female Are Not Enough

Anne Fausto-Sterling

In 1843 Levi Suydam, a twenty-three-year-old resident of Salisbury, Connecticut, asked the town board of selectmen to validate his right to vote as a Whig in a hotly contested local election. The request raised a flurry of objections from the opposition party, for reasons that must be rare in the annals of American democracy: it was said that Suydam was more female than male and thus (some eighty years before suffrage was extended to women) could not be allowed to cast a ballot. To settle the dispute a physician, one William James Barry, was brought in to examine Suydam. And, presumably upon encountering a phallus, the good doctor declared the prospective voter male. With Suydam safely in their column the Whigs won the election by a majority of one.

Barry's diagnosis, however, turned out to be somewhat premature. Within a few days he discovered that, phallus notwithstanding, Suydam menstruated regularly and had a vaginal opening. Both his/her physique and his/her mental predispositions were more complex than was first suspected. S/he had narrow shoulders and broad hips and felt occasional sexual yearnings for women. Suydam's "feminine propensities, such as a fondness for gay colors, for pieces of calico, comparing and placing them together, and an aversion for bodily labor, and an inability to perform the same, were remarked by many," Barry later wrote. It is not clear whether Suydam lost or retained the vote, or whether the election results were reversed.

Western culture is deeply committed to the idea that there are only two sexes. Even language refuses other possibilities; thus to write about Levi Suydam I have had to invent conventions—S/he and his/her—to denote someone who is clearly neither male nor female or who is perhaps both sexes at once. Legally, too, every adult is either man or woman, and the dif-ference, of course, is not trivial. For Suydam it meant the franchise; today it means being available for, or exempt from, draft registration, as well as being subject, in various ways, to a number of laws governing marriage, the family and human intimacy. In many parts of the United States, for instance, two people legally registered as men cannot have sexual relations without violating anti-sodomy statutes.

But if the state and the legal system have an interest in maintaining a two-party sexual system, they are in defiance of nature. For biologically speaking, there are many gradations running from female to male; and depending on how one calls the shots, one can argue that along that spectrum lie at least five sexes—and perhaps even more.

For some time medical investigators have recognized the concept of the intersexual body. But the standard medical literature uses the term *intersex* as a catch-all for three major subgroups with some mixture of male and female characteristics: the so-called true hermaphrodites, whom I call herms, who possess one testis and one ovary the (sperm- and egg-producing vessels, or gonads); the male pseudohermaphrodites (the "merms"), who have testes and some aspects of the female genitalia but no ovaries; and the female pseudohermaphrodites the ("ferms"), who have ovaries and some aspects of the male genitalia but lack testes. Each of those categories is in itself complex; the percentage of male and female characteristics, for instance, can vary enormously among members of the same subgroup. Moreover, the inner lives of the people in each subgroup—their special needs and their problems, attractions and repulsions—have gone unexplored by science. But on the basis of what is known about them I suggest that the three inter-sexes, herm, merm and ferm, deserve to be considered additional sexes each in its own right. Indeed, I would

---

argue further that sex is a vast, infinitely malleable continuum that defies the constraints of even five categories.

Not surprisingly, it is extremely difficult to estimate the frequency of intersexuality, much less the frequency of each of the three additional sexes: it is not the sort of information one volunteers on a job application. The psychologist John Money of Johns Hopkins University, a specialist in the study of congenital sexual-organ defects, suggests intersexuals may constitute as many as 4 percent of births. As I point out to my students at Brown University, in a student body of about 6,000 that fraction, if correct, implies there may be as many as 240 intersexuals on campus—surely enough to form a minority caucus of some kind.

In reality though, few such students would make it as far as Brown in sexually diverse form. Recent advances in physiology and surgical technology now enable physicians to catch most intersexuals at the moment of birth. Almost at once such infants are entered into a program of hormonal and surgical management so that they can slip quietly into society as "normal" heterosexual males or females. I emphasize that the motive is in no way conspiratorial. The aims of the policy are genuinely humanitarian, reflecting the wish that people be able to "fit in" both physically and psychologically. In the medical community, however, the assumptions behind that wish—that there be only two sexes, that heterosexuality alone is normal, that there is one true model of psychological health—have gone virtually unexamined.

The word *hermaphrodite* comes from the Greek names Hermes, variously known as the messenger of the gods, the patron of music, the controller of dreams or the protector of livestock, and Aphrodite, the goddess of sexual love and beauty. According to Greek mythology, those two gods parented Hermaphroditus, who at age fifteen became half male and half female when his body fused with the body of a nymph he fell in love with. In some true hermaphrodites the testis and the ovary grow separately but bilaterally; in others they grow together within the same organ, forming an ovo-testis. Not infrequently, at least one of the gonads functions quite well, producing either sperm cells or eggs, as well as functional levels of the sex

hormones—androgens or estrogens. Although in theory it might be possible for a true hermaphrodite to become both father and mother to a child, in practice the appropriate ducts and tubes are not configured so that egg and sperm can meet.

In contrast with the true hermaphrodites, the pseudo-hermaphrodites possess two gonads of the same kind along with the usual male (XY) or female (XX) chromosomal makeup. But their external genitalia and secondary sex characteristics do not match their chromosomes. Thus merms have testes and XY chromosomes, yet they also have a vagina and a clitoris, and at puberty they often develop breasts. They do not menstruate, however. Ferms have ovaries, two X chromosomes and sometimes a uterus, but they also have at least partly masculine external genitalia. Without medical intervention they can develop beards, deep voices and adult-size penises.

No classification scheme could more than suggest the variety of sexual anatomy encountered in clinical practice. In 1969, for example, two French investigators, Paul Guinet of the Endocrine Clinic in Lyons and Jacques Decourt of the Endocrine Clinic in Paris, described ninety-eight cases of true hermaphroditism—again, signifying people with both ovarian and testicular tissue—solely according to the appearance of the external genitalia and the accompanying ducts. In some cases the people exhibited strongly feminine development. They had separate openings for the vagina and the urethra, a cleft vulva defined by both the large and the small labia, or vaginal lips, and at puberty they developed breasts and usually began to menstruate. It was the oversize and sexually alert clitoris, which threatened sometimes at puberty to grow into a penis, that usually impelled them to seek medical attention. Members of another group also had breasts and a feminine body type, and they menstruated. But their labia were at least partly fused, forming an incomplete scrotum. The phallus (here an embryological term for a structure that during usual development goes on to form either a clitoris or a penis) was between 1.5 and 2.8 inches long; nevertheless, they urinated through a urethra that opened into or near the vagina.

By far the most frequent form of true hermaphrodite encountered by Guinet and Decourt—55 percent—appeared to have a more masculine physique.

In such people the urethra runs either through or near the phallus, which looks more like a penis than a clitoris. Any menstrual blood exits periodically during urination. But in spite of the relatively male appearance of the genitalia, breasts appear at puberty. It is possible that a sample larger than ninety-eight so-called true hermaphrodites would yield even more contrasts and subtleties. Suffice it to say that the varieties are so diverse that it is possible to know which parts are present and what is attached to what only after exploratory surgery.

The embryological origins of human hermaphrodites clearly fit what is known about male and female sexual development. The embryonic gonad generally chooses early in development to follow either a male or a female sexual pathway; for the ovo-testis, however, that choice is fudged. Similarly, the embryonic phallus most often ends up as a clitoris or a penis, but the existence of intermediate states comes as no surprise to the embryologist. There are also uro-genital swellings in the embryo that usually either stay open and become the vaginal labia or fuse and become a scrotum. In some hermaphrodites, though, the choice of opening or closing is ambivalent. Finally, all mammalian embryos have structures that can become the female uterus and the fallopian tubes, as well as structures that can become part of the male sperm-transport system. Typically either the male or the female set of those primordial genital organs degenerates, and the remaining structures achieve their sex-appropriate future. In hermaphrodites both sets of organs develop to varying degrees.

Intersexuality itself is old news. Hermaphrodites, for instance, are often featured in stories about human origins. Early biblical scholars believed Adam began life as a hermaphrodite and later divided into two people—a male and a female—after falling from grace. According to Plato there once were three sexes—male, female and hermaphrodite—but the third sex was lost with time.

Both the Talmud and the Tosefta, the Jewish books of law, list extensive regulations for people of mixed sex. The Tosefta expressly forbids hermaphrodites to inherit their fathers' estates (like daughters), to seclude themselves with women (like sons) or to shave (like men). When hermaphrodites menstruate they must be isolated from men (like women); they are disqualified from serving as witnesses or as priests (like women), but the laws of pederasty apply to them.

In Europe a pattern emerged by the end of the Middle Ages that, in a sense, has lasted to the present day: hermaphrodites were compelled to choose an established gender role and stick with it. The penalty for transgression was often death. Thus in the 1600s a Scottish hermaphrodite living as a woman was buried alive after impregnating his/her master's daughter.

For questions of inheritance, legitimacy, paternity, succession to title and eligibility for certain professions to be determined, modern Anglo-Saxon legal systems require that newborns be registered as either male or female. In the U.S. today sex determination is governed by state laws. Illinois permits adults to change the sex recorded on their birth certificates should a physician attest to having performed the appropriate surgery. The New York Academy of Medicine, on the other hand, has taken an opposite view. In spite of surgical alterations of the external genitalia, the academy argued in 1966, the chromosomal sex remains the same. By that measure, a person's wish to conceal his or her original sex cannot outweigh the public interest in protection against fraud.

During this century the medical community has completed what the legal world began—the complete erasure of any form of embodied sex that does not conform to a male-female, heterosexual pattern. Ironically, a more sophisticated knowledge of the complexity of sexual systems has led to the repression of such intricacy.

In 1937 the urologist Hugh H. Young of Johns Hopkins University published a volume titled *Genital Abnormalities, Hermaphroditism and Related Adrenal Diseases*. The book is remarkable for its erudition, scientific insight and open-mindedness. In it Young drew together a wealth of carefully documented case histories to demonstrate and study the medical treatment of such "accidents of birth." Young did not pass judgment on the people he studied, nor did he attempt to coerce into treatment those intersexuals who rejected that option. And he showed unusual even-handedness in referring to those people who had had sexual experiences as both men and women as "practicing hermaphrodites."

One of Young's more interesting cases was a hermaphrodite named Emma who had grown up as a female. Emma had both a penis-size clitoris and a vagina, which made it possible for him/her to have "normal" heterosexual sex with both men and women. As a teenager Emma had had sex with a number of girls to whom s/he was deeply attracted; but at the age of nineteen s/he had married a man. Unfortunately, he had given Emma little sexual pleasure (though *he* had had no complaints), and so throughout that marriage and subsequent ones Emma had kept girlfriends on the side. With some frequency s/he had pleasurable sex with them. Young describes his subject as appearing "to be quite content and even happy." In conversation Emma occasionally told him of his/her wish to be a man, a circumstance Young said would be relatively easy to bring about. But Emma's reply strikes a heroic blow for self-interest:

> Would you have to remove that vagina? I don't know about that because that's my meal ticket. If you did that, I would have to quit my husband and go to work, so I think I'll keep it and stay as I am. My husband supports me well, and even though I don't have any sexual pleasure with him, I do have lots with my girlfriends.

Yet even as Young was illuminating intersexuality with the light of scientific reason, he was beginning its suppression. For his book is also an extended treatise on the most modern surgical and hormonal methods of changing intersexuals into either males or females. Young may have differed from his successors in being less judgmental and controlling of the patients and their families, but he nonetheless supplied the foundation on which current intervention practices were built.

By 1969, when the English physicians Christopher J. Dewhurst and Ronald R. Gordon wrote *The Intersexual Disorders,* medical and surgical approaches to intersexuality had neared a state of rigid uniformity. It is hardly surprising that such a hardening of opinion took place in the era of the feminine mystique—of the post-Second World War flight to the suburbs and the strict division of family roles according to sex. That the medical consensus was not quite universal (or perhaps that it seemed poised to break apart again) can be gleaned from the near-hysterical tone of Dewhurst and Gordon's book, which contrasts markedly with the calm reason of Young's founding work. Consider their opening description of an intersexual newborn:

> One can only attempt to imagine the anguish of the parents. That a newborn should have a deformity . . . [affecting] so fundamental an issue as the very sex of the child . . . is a tragic event which immediately conjures up visions of a hopeless psychological misfit doomed to live always as a sexual freak in loneliness and frustration.

Dewhurst and Gordon warned that such a miserable fate would, indeed, be a baby's lot should the case be improperly managed; "but fortunately," they wrote, "with correct management the outlook is infinitely better than the poor parents—emotionally stunned by the event—or indeed anyone without special knowledge could ever imagine."

Scientific dogma has held fast to the assumption that without medical care hermaphrodites are doomed to a life of misery. Yet there are few empirical studies to back up that assumption, and some of the same research gathered to build a case for medical treatment contradicts it. Francies Benton, another of Young's practicing hermaphrodites, "had not worried over his condition, did not wish to be changed, and was enjoying life." The same could be said of Emma, the opportunistic hausfrau. Even Dewhurst and Gordon, adamant about the psychological importance of treating intersexuals at the infant stage, acknowledged great success in "changing the sex" of older patients. They reported on twenty cases of children reclassified into a different sex after the supposedly critical age of eighteen months. They asserted that all the reclassifications were "successful," and they wondered then whether reregistration could be "recommended more readily than [had] been suggested so far."

The treatment of intersexuality in this century provides a clear example of what the French historian Michel Foucault has called biopower. The knowledge developed in biochemistry, embryology, endocrinology, psychology and surgery has enabled physicians to control the very sex of the human body. The multiple contradictions in that kind of power call for some scrutiny. On the one hand, the medical "management" of intersexuality certainly developed as part of an attempt to free people from perceived psychological pain (though whether the pain was the patient's, the parents' of the physician's is unclear). And if one accepts the assumption that in a sex-divided culture people can realize their greatest potential for happiness and productivity only if they are sure they belong to one of only two acknowledged sexes, modern medicine has been extremely successful.

On the other hand, the same medical accomplishments can be read not as progress but as a mode of discipline. Hermaphrodites have unruly bodies. They do not fall naturally into a binary classification; only a surgical shoehorn can put them there. But why should we care if a "woman," defined as one who has breasts, a vagina, a uterus and ovaries and who menstruates, also has a clitoris large enough to penetrate the vagina of another woman? Why should we care if there are people whose biological equipment enables them to have sex "naturally" with both men and women? The answers seem to lie in a cultural need to maintain clear distinctions between the sexes. Society mandates the control of intersexual bodies because they blur and bridge the great divide. Inasmuch as hermaphrodites literally embody both sexes, they challenge traditional beliefs about sexual difference: they possess the irritating ability to live sometimes as one sex and sometimes the other, and they raise the specter of homosexuality.

But what if things were altogether different? Imagine a world in which the same knowledge that has enabled medicine to intervene in the management of intersexual patients has been placed at the service of multiple sexualities. Imagine that the sexes have multiplied beyond currently imaginable limits. It would have to be a world of shared powers. Patient and physician, parent and child, male and female, heterosexual and homosexual—all those oppositions and others would have to be dissolved as sources of division. A new ethic of medical treatment would arise, one that would permit ambiguity in a culture that had overcome sexual division. The central mission of medical treatment would be to preserve life. Thus hermaphrodites would be concerned primarily not about whether they can conform to society but

about whether they might develop potentially life-threatening conditions—hernias, gonadal tumors, salt imbalance caused by adrenal malfunction—that sometimes accompany hermaphroditic development. In my ideal world medical intervention for intersexuals would take place only rarely before the age of reason; subsequent treatment would be a cooperative venture between physician, patient and other advisers trained in issues of gender multiplicity.

I do not pretend that the transition to my utopia would be smooth. Sex, even the supposedly "normal," heterosexual kind, continues to cause untold anxieties in Western society. And certainly a culture that has yet to come to grips—religiously and, in some states, legally—with the ancient and relatively uncomplicated reality of homosexual love will not readily embrace intersexuality. No doubt the most troublesome arena by far would be the rearing of children. Parents, at least since the Victorian era, have fretted, sometimes to the point of outright denial, over the fact that their children are sexual beings.

All that and more amply explains why intersexual children are generally squeezed into one of the two prevailing sexual categories. But what would be the psychological consequences of taking the alternative road—raising children as unabashed intersexuals? On the surface that tack seems fraught with peril. What, for example, would happen to the intersexual child amid the unrelenting cruelty of the school yard? When the time came to shower in gym class, what horrors and humiliations would await the intersexual as his/her anatomy was displayed in all its nontraditional glory? In whose gym class would s/he register to begin with? What bathroom would s/he use? And how on earth would Mom and Dad help shepherd him/her through the mine field of puberty?

In the past thirty years those questions have been ignored, as the scientific community has, with remarkable unanimity, avoided contemplating the alternative route of unimpeded intersexuality. But modern investigators tend to overlook a substantial body of case histories, most of them compiled between 1930 and 1960, before surgical intervention became rampant. Almost without exception, those reports describe children who grew up knowing they were intersexual (though they did not advertise it) and adjusted to their unusual status. Some of the studies are richly detailed—described at the level of gym-class showering (which most intersexuals avoided without incident); in any event, there is not a psychotic or a suicide in the lot.

Still, the nuances of socialization among intersexuals cry out for more sophisticated analysis. Clearly, before my vision of sexual multiplicity can be realized, the first openly intersexual children and their parents will have to be brave pioneers who will bear the brunt of society's growing pains. But in the long view—though it could take generations to achieve—the prize might be a society in which sexuality is something to be celebrated for its subtleties and not something to be feared or ridiculed.

2.2 "HOMOSEXUAL" AND "HETEROSEXUAL"
Questioning the Terms

Jonathan Ned Katz

In the late 1970s and early 1980s, as I researched a second book on homosexual American history, I was astonished to discover that the now common, unquestioned bifurcation of people, their emotions and acts, into "homosexual" and "heterosexual" was a recent manufacture.

The terms "homosexual" and "heterosexual," I learned, were coined by a writer (not a medical doctor), Karl Maria Kertbeny, and are first known to have been used by him in a private letter of May 6, 1868, to Karl Heinrich Ulrichs, another pioneering sex reformer. Kertbeny first publicly used the term "homosexual" in 1869, in a petition against the German law criminalizing "unnatural fornication." The label homosexual was then appropriated by late nineteenth-century medical men as a way of naming, condemning, and asserting their own proprietary rights over a group then parading into sight in the bars, dance halls, and streets of Europe's and America's larger cities.

At the same time, the label heterosexual was also appropriated by doctors as a word for the erotic intercourse of men with women. But since such intercourse was not necessarily reproductive, the word "heterosexual," well into the twentieth century, continued to signify a bad, immoral relation.

The words "homosexual" and "heterosexual," I learned, were first printed in an American publication, a medical journal, in May 1892, raising a new and interesting question: How were the intimacies of the sexes categorized in April, and, of course, earlier? In their debut appearance, I noticed, the terms "heterosexual" and "homosexual" defined two kinds of sexual perversion, judged according to a procreative standard. A list of "Sexual perversions proper" included "Psychical hermaphroditism or heterosexuals." A note explained that "heterosexuals" were persons in whom occur "inclinations to both sexes," as well as inclinations "to abnormal methods of gratification."

Only gradually, I began to realize, did American medical publications agree that the word "heterosexual" referred to a "normal" male-female eroticism. In 1901, a Philadelphia medical dictionary was still defining "heterosexuality" as "Abnormal or perverted appetite toward the opposite sex." In 1910 Havelock Ellis was still protesting that we "have no simple, precise, natural word" for the "normal sexual love" of the sexes. As late as 1923, I discovered, the authoritative Merriam-Webster dictionary was still defining "heterosexual" as a medical term meaning "Morbid sexual passion for one of the opposite sex."

Only in the first quarter of the twentieth century, I finally realized, did heterosexuality's doctor advocates succeed in constructing and distributing it as a signifier of sexuality's Standard Brand. Their regularization of eros paralleled contemporary attempts to standardize masculinity and femininity, intelligence and manufacturing. The doctors' heterosexual category proclaimed a new erotic separatism, a novel sex orthodoxy, that forcefully segregated sex "normals" from sex "perverts," and set "hetero" over "homo" in a hierarchy of superior and inferior eroticisms. But only gradually did the idea that there were such creatures as heterosexuals and homosexuals emerge from the narrow realm of medical discourse to become a popular, commonplace notion.

Upon historical examination we find that "homosexual" and "heterosexual," the terms we moderns take for granted, are fairly recent creations. Though presented to us as words marking an eternal fact of nature, the terms "heterosexual" and "homosexual" constitute a normative sexual ethic, a sexual-political ideology, and one historically specific way of categorizing the relationships of the sexes.

The terms "heterosexual" and "homosexual," I suggest, also arise out of and help maintain a historically specific way of socially ordering gender and eroticism. "Heterosexual" and "homosexual" refer to groups, identities, and even behaviors and experiences that are time-limited, specifically modern phenomena, contingent on a peculiar institutional structuring of masculinity, femininity, and lust.

Many researchers now commonly agree that sexual and gender categories, erotic identities, communities, meanings, and institutions are historical and change over time. But even theorists of the social construction of sex have continued to posit an ahistorical "homosexual behavior." For example, a historian from whom I have learned a great deal refers to the distinction "between homosexual behavior, which is universal, and a homosexual identity, which is historically specific." But only the most mechanistic, biologistic idea of "behavior" permits this distinction between a universal behavior and historical identity.

Even as we labor to historicize sexuality and gender, many historians continue to assume that, whatever a behavior was called in its own time, we now know its real name and character: That behavior was *really homosexual, heterosexual, or bisexual.* Our epistemological hubris and ontological chutzpah prevent us from understanding the varieties of sexuality and gender within their own social structure and time.

If sexual behavior is more than just a conjunction of organs, if it is always shaped by the particular system within which it functions, and if it always includes a mix of socially defined feelings and meanings, behavior is just as historically relative and constructed as identity.

Don't get me wrong. Some sexual acts similar to those performed in New York last night were no doubt performed in New Amsterdam in the early colonial American era. But that early colonial sexual behavior was enmeshed within a different economy. So profound is the historically specific character of sexual behavior that only with the loosest accuracy can we speak of sodomy in the early colonies and "sodomy" in present-day New York as "the same thing." In another example, to speak of "heterosexual behavior" as occurring universally is to apply one term to a great variety of activities produced within a great variety of sexual and gender systems.

Radical social constructionists, myself among them, posit the historical relativity of sexual behaviors, as well as of identities, meanings, categories, groups, and institutions. Such relativity theory is no longer particularly radical when applied to the changing historical emotions and institutions of "the family," for example. But it remains subversive when applied to erotic and gender history, for it challenges our stubborn, ingrained idea of an essential, eternal heterosexuality and homosexuality.

It is particularly unsettling, I think, to speak of heterosexual history, for that history challenges our usual, implicit, deterministic assumption that heterosexuality is fixed, timeless, biological, synonymous with the conjunction of female and male organs and acts. To the contrary, I argue, heterosexuality (like homosexuality) has an unheralded, various past, and an open, undetermined future. To paraphrase Karl Marx, women and men make their own sexual and affectional history. But they do not make this history just as they please. They make it under circumstances given by the past and altered by their political activity and organization, and their vision of a valued future. Erotic and gender relationships are always under construction and reconstruction within specific historical settings.

In the last sentence, let us note, I fall back into a mode of speech suggesting the existence of some essential, universal eroticism and gender always being reconstructed. Such is the power over our minds of essentialist thought that I know no way to avoid it. But the move away from a history of homosexuality and heterosexuality to a history of eroticism and gender does, I think, empower a pragmatic, strategic conceptual advance, allowing us to ask new questions.

When, for example, we stop positing the Eternal Homosexual, we are encouraged to ask how men in early and mid-nineteenth-century New York City structured their erotic relations with men, what thoughts, judgments, and physical acts of theirs we can find evidence of, and what words they used about those relations.

My social constructionist hypothesis does not, by the way, suggest that heterosexual or homosexual feelings are less real, profound, or legitimate because they are socially constructed, simply that they are not omnipresent, not a biological fate.

In order, then, to understand the historical diversity of the sexes' relations, I challenge researchers to suspend temporarily, at least, our usual universalizing heterosexual/homosexual hypothesis. If we stop projecting those categories on societies in which they did not operate, we can open our eyes to the historical varieties of gender, affection, and eroticism past.

2.3 Asking Questions About Sex

Julia Eriksen and Sally Steffen

During the twentieth century, experts following in the footsteps of Freud and Ellis espoused increasingly liberal views of sexuality and, like Ellis, sought to liberate sexuality from societal repression. Foucault viewed this twentieth-century espousal of sexual liberty as an endless discussion that, rather than creating actual liberation, increased concern about sexual normality while changing the definition of normal. There were other contributors to this discussion as well. Individuals and institutions concerned with the general welfare, including the government, public health officials, the media, and social scientists, continued to worry that private acts threatened public safety.

All those providing sexual advice viewed the family as the bedrock of social stability and the gendered couple as its foundation. For them, women and men occupied separate spheres of control. Men's assertive personalities, symbolized in their role in sexual intercourse, were ideally suited to run public life, while women were keepers of the private sphere who provided sustenance, sexual and otherwise, to those who ran the world. Over the century, despite significant modifications of these assumptions, the gendered nature of private sexual behavior remained central. Likewise, a pervasive sense that sexuality is so inherently unstable and irrational that society must be ever vigilant kept experts busy proffering advice. This fear that private behavior could affect public well-being fed repeated panics about such issues as venereal disease, teenage pregnancy, and indiscriminate sex, while it fostered an interest in expert counsel.

The first sexologists relied on their own insights supplemented by clinical records to document the dangers of sexual excess. In the twentieth century this task fell to social scientists. Since the Progressive era, American social scientists have viewed their disciplines as capable of furthering human progress by alleviating such panic. They approached this task using scientific methods, in particular statistical methods. In each time of sexual crisis they perceived an urgent need for information. Yet they did not collect data with the scientific disinterest they imagined. Instead, their assumption that men and women differed from each other sexually dictated the form of their questions about the nation's social and sexual health. Believing that solutions start with the facts, the experts produced their urgently needed data through a filter of gendered sexuality.

Given the long-standing American belief that numbers provide factual representations of the world, surveys are an obvious source of information.[1] Since sex is an arena in which what others do is unclear, actual information about sexual behavior had two ready-made audiences: experts concerned that private behavior had a negative impact on public order, and individuals anxious to use hard evidence to evaluate and regulate their own behavior. Since 1892, when the biology student Clelia Mosher started asking upper-middle-class married women whether they liked intercourse, how often they had intercourse, and how often they wanted to have intercourse[2]—information she never had the courage to publish—researchers have asked hundreds of thousands of people about their sexual behavior and *have* published their findings for others to read.

This intense scrutiny created a window into the sexual lives of ordinary women and men that exposed private behavior to professional interpretation. Experts relayed this information to the public in reports and press releases. They evaluated the meaning of the data for what men and women should do, what they should like to do, and what they should fear doing. They not only reported what they believed to be the facts but helped create these facts in line with their own ideological positions, particularly their beliefs about gender. These facts, in turn, helped create sexual practices in two ways. First, reports about what others were doing suggested to readers that they should model their behavior on those who appeared to represent them. Second, surveys evaluated the behav-

ior of those in the surveys, and this also provided lessons to readers. Thus even reports that accurately described aspects of the behavior of a particular group at a particular time created behavior by acting as guides or warnings to others. Since the most consistent assumption on which the surveys rested was of a gendered sexuality, albeit a changing one, surveys helped sustain a vision of sexuality as innately contained within masculinity and femininity.

The potential impact of such revelations is the reason those who disagree with results find it necessary to discredit them. Since the meanings attributed to the data have political implications beyond the facts, those who conduct sex surveys feel pressure to meet certain social needs. Investigators do not operate in a cultural vacuum. They approach their research holding beliefs about what is normal and what they expect to find, beliefs shaped by their personal experiences and desires, by their social circumstances, and by the findings of earlier researchers. Furthermore, when survey results become public, readers may change their sexual behavior as a result of finding out what others "like them" do, and researchers find themselves influencing what they had merely hoped to record.

Survey researchers, sensitive to charges of subjectivity, claim that as scientists using modern survey methods they can eliminate the effects of the expectations and biases they bring to their research. They concede that, without the advantage of modern techniques, early researchers were less objective, but they insist that today's methodology can take care of such problems. Asking questions of persons one at a time and aggregating the answers appears to reveal reality. Such scientific surveys seem the perfect way to amass information about a variety of social problems—venereal disease, divorce, teen pregnancy, for example—in order to develop informed public policies aimed at alleviating their ill effects.

Modern survey practice evolved throughout the twentieth century but came into its own after the Second World War.[3] Nowadays, letting prior hypotheses influence outcomes is decried as poor technique and a betrayal of the fundamental principles of science. Researchers view the scientific method as demanding hypotheses, or at least research questions, which they test in ways that do not influence the outcome.

Although there has been little acknowledgment that the choice of research topic inevitably represents a point of view, four phases of the survey process have been the subjects of methodological studies intended to achieve this goal of objectivity. These are decisions about whom to interview; methods of data collection, including interviewer training; content and structure of the interview schedule; and the analysis of data.

Early researchers did not understand either the importance of interviewing all segments of the target population or that researchers who chose which respondents to interview might influence the results. They consciously surveyed "the better part of the middle class," or those who were "not pathological mentally or physically," in order to present the best possible case for their arguments.[4] The use of random sampling in surveys, a technique that ensures that each person in the target population has an equal, or a known, probability of being selected, developed in the 1930s. In this method, researchers completely remove themselves from decisions about which persons to interview. By 1940 the U.S. Bureau of the Census had adopted random sampling for its monthly survey of employment and unemployment.[5]

While sampling techniques changed survey research, sex researchers were slow to adopt these superior methods. Alfred Kinsey, who undertook his survey when modern sampling was in its infancy, did not believe random sampling was possible in sex surveys, and many subsequent sex surveyors followed his example. Kinsey believed that people contacted at random would refuse to answer personal questions. Instead, he selected respondents himself. Unlike his predecessors, Kinsey understood that all segments of the population should be included, so he went to great lengths to represent all sexual tastes. Unfortunately, in his determination to be inclusive, he most likely overestimated less common sexual activities such as same-gender sexual behavior.

Since the 1980s this avoidance of random sampling has ended. A number of recent sexual behavior surveys, for example the Battelle survey, have successfully used random sampling techniques to select respondents. While a 100 percent response rate is unlikely in a random sample, and nonrespondents can bias the results, the use of this method of selecting respondents has improved the reliability of the data immeasurably.

The history of interviewing in sex surveys is more complex, and many issues remain unresolved. From the beginning some researchers insisted on using face-to-face interviews on the grounds that this would create the intimacy and trust necessary for respondents to reveal their sexual secrets. But they did not understand the problems involved when researchers personally conducted the interviews. Gilbert Hamilton, who surveyed the sexual adjustment of married couples in New York in the late 1920s, did all the interviewing himself and imposed his own notions of intimacy and trust idiosyncratically. Commenting that his interviewing technique produced frequent "weeping and trips to the toilet," he maintained scientific objectivity by noting all such occurrences and by tying "the subject's chair to the wall in order to forestall the tendency that most persons have to draw closer to the recipient of confidences as these become more intimate."[6] Kinsey also was too early to understand the importance of using professional interviewers, of keeping the hypotheses from interviewers, and of training interviewers to ask sensitive questions.

By 1955, when the sociologist Ronald Freedman conducted the first national survey of married women's contraceptive practices, he and his colleagues used properly trained and monitored interviewers; and techniques have further improved since then.[7] Today investigators make well-informed decisions on whether to have interviewers ask the questions or to ask them in other ways, such as by computer. Interviewers receive extensive training and are held to rigorous standards. Researchers study the impact of interviewer traits like gender and race on different respondents. From the beginning some researchers avoided interviews. Instead, they designed self-administered questionnaires for respondents to fill out and return. This method assures respondents of confidentiality and increases their willingness to disclose sexual secrets. But it produces lower response rates and creates problems for respondents who have difficulty reading.

All surveys, regardless of interview method, require some type of questionnaire. Because the researcher holding the hypothesis selects, words, and orders the questions, questionnaire design is particularly vulnerable to researcher bias. In the early years of sex surveys, surveyors did not understand the problem, and, in order to protect themselves from respondent outrage, wrote reassurances that the sexual acts respondents were being asked to describe were normal. Katharine Davis's 1920 mail-in survey of the sexual experiences of middle-class women included a long prefatory statement to her questions on masturbation communicating the opinion—shared by other progressive thinkers in her day—that, in spite of condemnation, masturbation was not harmful for women. Indeed, some experts, she said, maintained that it was "a normal stage in the development of the sex nature and must be passed through if sexual development is to be complete."[8]

Davis expected to find that many women masturbated, and not surprisingly she found this. In modern questionnaires, such reassurance—which may push a respondent in the direction of a particular response—rarely appears. Before the survey takes place, pretesting helps achieve clear, nondirective questions. Careful wording and ordering of questions produce more accurate responses. It is more difficult to examine the effect of turning abstract concepts into terms that respondents can understand, or to ascertain what a respondent might reasonably remember. Even here, however, research has made progress. For example, one source of variation in estimates of the size of the gay population is the questions asked. Not only does asking the gender of respondents' sexual partners produce different results than asking respondents if they are homosexual, bisexual, or heterosexual, but the specific wording of the question makes a difference. It is hard to compare the findings of the Battelle researchers with those of Kinsey because of the differences in the questions.

During the final phase, data analysis, bias was endemic but often unrecognized in early surveys. Indeed, obtaining impartial data and analyzing them in a manner unfettered by the investigator's agenda was not always the aim. Max Exner, who in 1913 embarked on one of the earliest sex surveys, stated that "we are in urgent need of facts which would enable us to speak with reasonable definiteness" about the need for sex education as a way of curbing young

men's excessive sexual desires.[9] Although draped in scientific garb, Exner's questions and analysis reveal that for him the survey was not a tool to discover information. He used it to support his preexisting "knowledge" that learning about sex from the street led to unhygienic sexual practices.

Over time, with increasingly rigorous survey methods, such obviously prejudiced practices ceased. Researchers even began to realize that their unconscious biases could influence the outcome. With more sophisticated data analysis techniques, researchers could be more certain of their conclusions and less able to shape them to satisfy an agenda. Yet they remained largely oblivious of the fact that the questions they ask of the data reveal a point of view. The Battelle researchers insisted that the furor over their reported incidence of male homosexuality was misplaced. This, they said, was not the main target of their research, and they did not have sufficient data for accuracy. But they revealed this result in a carefully orchestrated manner that seemed designed to maximize publicity.

Throughout the century, survey researchers interested in sexual behavior viewed their results as improvements on earlier findings. Indeed, this brief description of survey practice suggests that a history of surveys of sexual behavior should be a history of the growing sophistication of researchers and the increasing certainty of their conclusions. In order for this to be the case, two conditions would have to hold. First, researchers would have to be neutral observers of sexual behavior, an unlikely proposition in a world where no one escapes pressure to monitor personal sexual standards and desires. Second, sexual behavior would have to be independent of history and culture. In such a case, questions such as the proportion of gays in the population would be technical, not political or historically specific questions.

In fact, while survey improvements have produced more accurate reflections of historical moments, surveys do not divulge universal truths, only those relative to their time and place. Furthermore, even with the best intentions, researchers have managed their surveys in such a way as to produce findings reflecting their own beliefs about gender and normality and their concerns about the dangers of sex research. Responsible researchers adopted techniques to neutralize the effect of their biases, but their very choice of research topics assumed a certain view of sexuality. When, in 1992, the research team quoted in the epigraph to this chapter finally received funds for a large national survey of American adults, they used the latest survey techniques. Yet they conducted their research in a climate in which sexual coupling, especially with strangers, was perceived as potentially fatal. Their concern over "promiscuity" colored all aspects of the survey.[10]

In addition to researchers and respondents, two other groups had an impact on what information surveys revealed: those who funded surveys and those who interpreted the results for larger audiences. At first sex surveys were commissioned by private organizations interested in promoting a particular point of view. In later years the federal government took over much of the funding. Those who dispensed federal dollars also had a point of view to promote, although they did so in a less directive manner.

In the early years, researchers not only controlled who respondents were and what their answers meant; they also controlled the dissemination of results to other experts and the general public. As more sources of dissemination appeared, it became difficult to exert such control. Once the media began reporting the results of surveys, their goals differed widely from those of the researchers, who often found their results presented in a distorted manner. The Battelle researchers experienced this. They used the media to promote their survey, but they quickly lost control of the debate. As discussion raged over the percentage of men who were gay, the rest of the results, including those of most interest to the researchers, almost disappeared from view.

Do these limits and problems mean we can learn little from surveys of sexual behavior? On the contrary, such surveys teach us a great deal about sexuality in America, about the beliefs that have shaped sexual behavior, and about the concerns that have driven researchers to ask questions. They show the changes in these concerns and in assumptions about sexuality. Tracing these changes reveals the history of sexuality in the twentieth century. Furthermore, as survey practice improved, the ensuing descriptions of sexual practice not only provided a behavioral control but provided comfort and encouraged people to act on their desires.

We tell this story in the belief that sexuality is not a trait with which individuals are born but a crucial aspect of identity that is socially created. Researchers often assumed that sexuality was innate and that their task was to reveal what already existed. In contrast, we believe that the assumptions driving the research helped create the sexuality the research revealed. Researchers' assumptions were the product of the larger society, of the researchers' positions within that society, and of the findings of their predecessors. While the culture changed over time and researchers did not occupy identical social or professional positions, two factors remained almost constant. First, researchers shared general beliefs in the existence of innate differences between men and women and viewed such differences as the basis of sexual attraction. Second, most researchers were men and viewed the world through the eyes of male privilege. They assumed a straightforward male sexuality while puzzling over "the problem of female sexuality." In this, their major concern was that women should satisfy men's needs. Female sexual pleasure was increasingly viewed as a way to make men happy and families secure. It was not until the 1980s, when women began to undertake sex surveys, that the focus began shifting to female pleasure as a woman's concern.

Researchers believed that women become aroused slowly and through love, while men experience constant arousal. These beliefs influenced surveys and were so powerful that researchers did not always know how to handle contrary findings. For example, the few women surveyors in the early decades described a strong female sex drive, more similar to than different from men's.[11] Yet even as male experts reported these women's results they ignored the voices behind them, choosing instead to reinterpret findings to fit conventional assumptions. Furthermore, these assumptions about gender and sexuality differed according to respondents' race, class, and age. Middle-class adults received the most attention because of beliefs that only they had the time or education to achieve sexual bliss. Only during periods of crisis when sexuality became a symbol for concern about other social changes did groups other than the white middle class become the targets of sex research.

Part of the reason for caution over whom to interview involved researchers' need to justify sex surveys while protecting themselves from charges of prurience. Those undertaking sex surveys found them to be a dangerous enterprise. Sex talk, with its forbidden overtones, was often embarrassing because it was exciting. Doing the research involved invading a private sphere. This affected the nature of the research questions and the explanations given for asking them. Surveyors rarely justified sex surveys on the grounds of interest. Instead, they used the urgent social problems of the day as an explanation for their questions. Their justifications had implications for the collection of data, for the questions asked, and for what constituted knowledge. Discomfort over sex talk, even in scientific guise, made sex surveys more vulnerable to personal pressures at every stage of the survey process.

Researchers in many areas claim their results are definitive, but these claims have a particular cast in sex research because worries about criticism often lead to overstatement of the reliability of conclusions. In reaction to the claims of conservative opponents like Senator Jesse Helms that "most Americans resent even being asked to answer questions about how often they engage in sex, with whom, their preferences for sexual partners, and which sex act they prefer,"[12] researchers tended to downplay the methodological and theoretical challenges of their research. In such a climate they were loath to consider the impact of their research on behavior. They tried to convince skeptical audiences that asking questions about sex was easy and the results were trustworthy. Paradoxically, this need for certainty created resistance to research on the methodology of sex surveys, since such research requires an acknowledgment of uncertainty. It also made researchers hesitant to share their experiences with other researchers, which, in turn, slowed the accumulation of knowledge on which to build. This made researchers vulnerable to attack on methodological grounds even from those whose objections were actually political.

Nevertheless, the history of sexual behavior surveys remains a history of the optimism of researchers and of the enlightenment of readers. Living in a culture in which no topic has been considered too difficult or too private for scientific inquiry, and believing that knowledge would further human progress, sur-

veyors saw themselves as pioneers venturing where others dared not go and doing so without fear of personal consequences. Their goal was to delve into the most secret and shame-laden human behavior, and to reveal it for all to see in the hope that the truth would liberate people from ignorance and stigma. In recent years many writers about sexuality have agreed with Foucault's argument that talk about sex does not liberate sex but is merely another way of controlling it. Researchers had a limited understanding of how they shaped the results of surveys. But they showed courage in following their beliefs that social stability is best served by exposing practice rather than by hiding it. Their work reveals an important thread of cultural and sexual history in the twentieth century.

NOTES

1. Bruce Voeller, "Some Uses and Abuses of the Kinsey Scale," in David P. McWhirter, Stephanie A. Sanders, and June Machover Reinisch, eds., *Homosexuality/Heterosexuality* (New York: Oxford University Press, 1990).

2. Interview with Robert Knight, May 24, 1993.

3. John O. G. Billy et al., "The Sexual Behavior of Men in the United States," *Family Planning Perspectives* 25, no. 2 (March/April 1993).

4. John D'Emilio, *Sexual Politics, Sexual Communities* (Chicago: University of Chicago Press, 1983).

5. Thomas Laqueur, *Making Sex* (Cambridge, Mass.: Harvard University Press, 1990).

6. Michel Foucault, *The History of Sexuality,* vol. 1 (New York: Random House, 1978).

7. Richard von Krafft-Ebing, *Psychopathia Sexualis* (New York: Physicians and Surgeons Book Co., 1931).

8. John D'Emilio and Estelle B. Freedman, *Intimate Matters: A History of Sexuality in America* (New York: Harper and Row, 1988).

9. Havelock Ellis, *Studies in the Psychology of Sex* (1899; New York: Random House, 1942).

10. Patricia Cline Cohen, *A Calculating People* (Chicago: University of Chicago Press, 1982).

11. James MaHood and Kristine Wenburg, *The Mosher Survey* (New York: Arno, 1980).

12. Bernard Lecuyer and Anthony R. Oberschall, "The Early History of Social Research: Postscript: Research in the United States at the Turn of the Century," in *International Encyclopedia of Statistics,* ed. William H. Kruskal and Judith M. Tanur (New York: Free Press, 1978).

2.4 Historical, Scientific, Clinical, and Feminist Criticisms of "The Human Sexual Response Cycle" Model

Leonore Tiefer

> The sexuality that is measured is taken to be the definition of sexuality itself.
>
> —*Lionel Trilling*

The Human Sexual Response Cycle Metaphor: A Universal Machine Without a Motor

The idea of the the human sexual response cycle (HSRC) by that name was initially introduced by William Masters and Virginia Johnson (1966) to describe the sequence of physiological changes they observed and measured during laboratory-performed sexual activities such as masturbation and coitus. The goal of their research was to answer the question: "What physical reactions develop as the human male and female respond to effective sexual stimulation?" (Masters and Johnson, 1966, p. 4). Although they coined terms for their four stages, it appears that the metaphor of "the" overall sexual "cycle" was assumed from the very outset. They wrote: "A more concise picture of physiologic reaction to sexual stimuli may be presented by dividing *the human male's and female's cycles* of sexual response into four separate phases. . . . This arbitrary four-part division of *the sexual response cycle* provides an effective framework for detailed description of physiological variants in sexual reaction" (p. 4, emphasis added).

The cycle metaphor indicates that Masters and Johnson envisioned sexual response from the start as a built-in, orderly sequence of events that would tend to repeat itself. The idea of a four-stage cycle brings to mind examples such as the four seasons of the annual calendar or the four-stroke internal combustion engine. Whether the cycle is designed by human agency or "nature," once begun it cycles independently of its origins, perhaps with some variability, but without reorganization or added stages, and the same cycle applies to everyone.

The idea of a sexual response cycle has some history, although its precursors focused heavily on an element omitted from the HSRC—the idea of sexual drive. In his intellectual history of modern sexology, Paul Robinson (1976) saw the origin of Masters and Johnson's four-stage HSRC in Havelock Ellis's theme of "tumescence and detumescence."[1]

But the language of tumescence and detumescence was popular even prior to Ellis. In his analysis of Freud's theory of the libido, Frank Sulloway (1979) discussed nineteenth-century German and Austrian sexological ideas in circulation while Freud was writing. Sulloway pointed out that many sexological terms associated with Freud, such as *libido* and *erotogenic zones,* were in widespread use in European medical writings by the turn of the century, and he credited Albert Moll (then "possibly the best-known authority on sexual pathology in all of Europe" though "an obscure figure today") with originating a theory of two sexual drives—one of attraction and the other of detumescence (Sulloway, 1979, p. 302).

It is significant that, despite this long heritage of sexologic theorizing about sexual "energy," Masters and Johnson's model of sexual response did not include initiating components. Their omission of sexual drive, libido, desire, passion, and the like would return to haunt clinical sexology in the 1970s. Actually, in avoiding discussion of sexual drive, Masters and Johnson were following a trend peculiar to sexologists (in contrast to psychiatrists and psychoanalysts) during the twentieth century. Perhaps because of the history of elaborate but vague nineteenth-century writings, perhaps because of the subjective connotations to *desire,* talk of sex drive seemed to cause nothing but confusion for modern sexual scientists interested in operational definitions. Kinsey used the term only in passing, and meant by it "sexual capacity," the capacity to respond to stimulation with physical arousal (e.g., Kinsey, Pomeroy, Martin, and Gebhard, 1953, p. 102). Sexologists could compare individuals and groups in terms of this hypothetical internal mechanism, capacity, by looking at their frequencies of sexual behavior, thresholds for response, and so on with no reference to internal experience.

Frank Beach (1956), writing during the time Masters and Johnson were beginning their physiological observations, argued that talking about sex *drive* is usually circular and unproductive and approvingly noted that even Kinsey "equates sexual drive with frequency of orgasm." Beach suggested that sexual *drive* had nothing to do with "genuine biological or tissue needs" and that the concept should be replaced by sexual *appetite,* which is "a product of experience, . . . [with] little or no relation to biological or physiological needs" (Beach, 1956, p. 4). Although the concept of appetite never caught on in sexology, the recent rediscovery of "desire" indicates that ignoring the issue of initiation of sexual behaviors did not solve the problem.

By omitting the concept of drive from their model, Masters and Johnson eliminated an element of sexuality that is notoriously variable within populations and succeeded in proposing a universal model seemingly without much variability. In what I think is the only reference to sexual drive in their text, Masters and Johnson indicated their belief that the sexual response cycle was actually an inborn drive to orgasm: "The cycle of sexual response, with orgasm as the ultimate point in progression, generally is believed to develop from a drive of biologic origin deeply integrated into the condition of human existence" (Masters and Johnson, 1966, p. 127). The cycle of sexual response, then, reflects the operation of an inborn program, like the workings of a mechanical clock. As long as the "effec-

tive sexual stimulation" (i.e., energy source) continues, the cycle proceeds through its set sequence.

SCIENTIFIC CRITICISMS OF THE HSRC MODEL

Masters and Johnson proposed a universal model for sexual response. At no point did they talk of "a" human sexual response cycle, but only of "the" human sexual response cycle. The critique of the HSRC model begins with a discussion of the generalizability of Masters and Johnson's research results. Analysis of their work shows that the existence of the HSRC was assumed before the research began and that this assumption guided subject selection and research methods.

Subject Selection Biases: Orgasm with Coital and Masturbatory Experience

In a passage buried four pages from the end of their text, Masters and Johnson revealed that for their research they had established "a *requirement* that there be a positive history of masturbatory and coital orgasmic experience before any study subject [could be] accepted into the program" (Masters and Johnson, 1966, p. 311, emphasis added). This requirement in and of itself would seem to invalidate any notion that the HSRC is universal. It indicates that Masters and Johnson's research was designed to identify physiological functions of subjects who had experienced *particular,* preselected sexual responses. That is, rather than the HSRC being the best-fit model chosen to accommodate the results of their research, the HSRC actually guided the selection of subjects for the research.

Two popularizations of Masters and Johnson's physiological research commented on this element of subject selection but disregarded its implications for HSRC generalizability:

> Men and women unable to respond sexually and to reach orgasm were also weeded out. Since this was to be a study of sexual responses, those unable to respond could contribute little to it. (Brecher and Brecher, 1966, p. 54)

> If you are going to find out what happens, obviously you must work with those to whom it happens. (Lehrman, 1970, p. 170)

"Unable to respond"? If you want to study human singing behaviors, do you only select international recording artists? One could just as easily argue that there are many sexually active and sexually responsive men and women who do not regularly experience orgasm during masturbation and/or coitus whose patterns of physiological arousal and subjective pleasure were deliberately excluded from the sample. No research was undertaken to investigate "human" sexual physiology and subjectivity, only to measure the responses of an easily orgasmic sample. The "discovery" of the HSRC was a self-fulfilling prophecy, with the research subjects selected so as to compress diversity. The HSRC cannot be universalized to the general population.

The apparently identical performance requirements for male and female research subjects masked the bias of real-world gender differences in masturbatory experience. Masters and Johnson began their physiological research in 1954. In 1953, the Kinsey group had reported that only "58 percent of the females" in their sample had been "masturbating to orgasm at some time in their lives" (Kinsey, Pomeroy, Martin, and Gebhard, 1953, p. 143). Married women, the predominant subjects in Masters and Johnson's research, had even lower masturbatory frequencies than divorced or single women. This contrasts with the 92 percent incidence of men with masturbatory experience reported by the same researchers (Kinsey, Pomeroy, and Martin, 1948, p. 339). Masters and Johnson had to find men and women with similar sexual patterns despite having been raised in dissimilar sociosexual worlds. Obviously, because of this requirement the women research participants were less representative than the men.

Subject Selection Biases: Class Differences

Just as Masters and Johnson chose subjects with certain types of sexual experiences, they deliberately chose subjects who did not represent a cross-section of socioeconomic backgrounds. They wrote: "As discussed, the sample was weighted *purposely* toward higher than average intelligence levels and socioeconomic backgrounds. *Further selectivity* was established . . . to determine willingness to participate, fa-

cility of sexual responsiveness, and ability to communicate finite details of sexual reaction" Masters and Johnson, 1966, p. 12, emphasis added). Masters and Johnson's popularizers disparaged the possible bias introduced by this selectivity with such comments as, "The higher than average educational level of the women volunteers is hardly likely to affect the acidity of their vaginal fluids" (Brecher and Brecher, 1966, p. 60).

But one cannot simply dismiss possible class differences in physiology with an assertion that there are none. *Could* differences in social location affect the physiology of sexuality? The irony of assuming that physiology is universal and therefore that class differences make no difference is that no one conducts research that asks the question.

In fact, Kinsey and his colleagues had shown wide differences between members (especially males) of different socioeconomic classes with regard to incidence and prevalence of masturbation, premarital sexual activities, petting (including breast stimulation), sex with prostitutes, positions used in intercourse, oral-genital sex, and even nocturnal emissions. For example, "There are 10 to 12 times as frequent nocturnal emissions among males of the upper educational classes as there are among males of the lower classes" (Kinsey, Pomeroy, and Martin, 1948, p. 345). Kinsey noted, "It is particularly interesting to find that there are [great] differences between educational levels in regard to nocturnal emissions—a type of sexual outlet which one might suppose would represent involuntary behavior" (p. 343). Given this finding, doesn't it seem possible, even likely, that numerous physiological details might indeed relate to differences in sexual habits? Kinsey also mentioned class differences in latency to male orgasm (p. 580). The more the variation in physiological details among subjects from different socioeconomic backgrounds, the less the HSRC is appropriate as a universal norm.

Subject Selection Biases: Sexual Enthusiasm

Masters and Johnson concluded their physiological research text as follows: "Through the years of research exposure, the one factor in sexuality that consistently has been present among members of the study-subject population has been a basic interest in and desire for effectiveness of sexual performance. *This one factor may represent the major area of difference between the research study subjects and the general population*" (Masters and Johnson, 1966, p. 315, emphasis added).

Masters and Johnson do not explain what they mean by their comment that "the general population" might not share the enthusiasm for sexual performance of their research subjects and do not speculate at all on the possible impact of this comment on the generalizability of their results. Whereas at first it may seem reasonable to assume that everyone has "a basic interest in and desire for effectiveness of sexual performance," on closer examination the phrase "*effectiveness* of sexual *performance*" seems not so much to characterize everyone as to identify devotees of a particular sexual style.

We get some small idea of Masters and Johnson's research subjects from the four profiles given in Chapter 19 of *Human Sexual Response* (1966). These profiled subjects were selected by the authors from the 382 women and 312 men who participated in their study. The two women described had masturbated regularly (beginning at ages ten and fifteen, respectively), had begun having intercourse in adolescence (at ages fifteen and seventeen), and were almost always orgasmic and occasionally multiorgasmic in the laboratory. For the first woman, twenty-six and currently unmarried, it was explicitly stated that "sexual activity [was] a major factor in [her] life" (Masters and Johnson, 1966, p. 304) and that she became a research subject because of "financial demand and sexual tension" (p. 305). No comparable information was given about the second woman, who was thirty-one and married, but she and her husband had "stated categorically" that they had "found [research participation] of significant importance in their marriage" (p. 307).

The unmarried male subject, age twenty-seven, was described as having had adolescent onset of masturbation, petting, and heterosexual intercourse as well as four reported homosexual experiences at different points in his life. The married man, age thirty-four, had had little sexual experience until age twenty-five. He and his wife of six years had joined the research pro-

gram "hoping to acquire knowledge to enhance the sexual component of their marriage" (Masters and Johnson, 1966, p. 311). The researchers noted, "[His] wife has stated repeatedly that subsequent to [research project] participation her husband has been infinitely more effective both in stimulating and satisfying her sexual tensions. He in turn finds her sexually responsive without reservation. Her freedom and security of response are particularly pleasing to him" (p. 311).

Every discussion of sex research methodology emphasizes the effects of volunteer bias and bemoans the reliance on samples of convenience that characterizes its research literature (e.g., Green and Wiener, 1980). Masters and Johnson make no attempt to compare their research subjects with any other research sample, saying, "There are no established norms for male and female sexuality in our society . . . [and] there is no scale with which to measure or evaluate the sexuality of the male and female study-subject population" (Masters and Johnson, 1966, p. 302). Although there may not be "norms," there are other sex research surveys of attitudes and behavior. For example, volunteers for sex research are usually shown to be more liberal in their attitudes than socioeconomically comparable nonvolunteer groups (Hoch, Safir, Peres, and Shepher, 1981; Clement, 1990).

How might the sample's interest in "effective sexual performance" have affected Masters and Johnson's research and their description of the HSRC? The answer relates both to the consequences of ego-investment in sexual performance and to the impact of specialization in a sexual style focused on orgasm, and we don't know what such consequences might be. I cannot specify the effect of this sexually skewed sample any more than I could guess what might be the consequences for research on singing of only studying stars of the Metropolitan Opera. The point is that the subject group was exceptional, and only by *assuming* HSRC universality can we generalize its results to others.

Experimenter Bias in the Sexuality Laboratory

Masters and Johnson made no secret of the fact that subjects volunteering for their research underwent a period of adjustment, or a "controlled orientation program," as they called it (Masters and Johnson, 1966,

p. 22). This "period of training" helped the subjects "gain confidence in their ability to respond successfully while subjected to a variety of recording devices" (p. 23). Such a training period provided an opportunity for numerous kinds of "experimenter biases," as they are known in social psychology research, wherein the expectations of the experimenters are communicated to the subjects and have an effect on their behavior (Rosenthal, 1966). The fact that Masters and Johnson repeatedly referred to episodes of sexual activity with orgasm as "successes" and those without orgasm or without rigid erection or rapid ejaculation as "failures" (e.g., Masters and Johnson, 1966, p. 313) makes it seem highly likely that their performance standards were communicated to their subjects. Moreover, they were candid about their role as sex therapists for their subjects: "When female orgasmic or male ejaculatory failures develop in the laboratory, the *situation is discussed* immediately. Once the individual has been *reassured, suggestions* are made for improvement of future performance" (p. 314, emphasis added).

Another example of the tutelage provided is given in the quotation from the thirty-four-year-old man described in Chapter 19 of their book. He and his wife had entered the program hoping to obtain sexual instruction and seemed to have received all they expected and more. Masters and Johnson appeared to be unaware of any incompatibility between the roles of research subject and student or patient. Again, this reveals their preexisting standards for sexual response and their interest in measuring in the laboratory only sexual patterning consisting of erections, orgasms, ejaculations, whole-body physical arousal, and so on, that is, that which they already defined as sexual response.

In addition to overt instruction and feedback, social psychology alerts us to the role of covert cues. Research has shown that volunteer subjects often are more sensitive to experimenters' covert cues than are nonvolunteers (Rosenthal and Rosnow, 1969). One could speculate that sex research volunteers characterized by a "desire for effective sexual performance" may well be especially attentive to covert as well as overt indications that they are performing as expected in the eyes of the white-coated researchers.

The Bias of "Effective" Sexual Stimulation

As mentioned near the beginning of this chapter, Masters and Johnson set out to answer the question, "What physical reactions develop as the human male and female respond to effective sexual stimulation?" (Masters and Johnson, 1966, p. 4). What is "effective" sexual stimulation? In fact, I think this is a key question in deconstructing the HSRC. Masters and Johnson stated, "It constantly should be borne in mind that the primary research interest has been concentrated quite literally upon what men and women do in response to effective sexual stimulation" (p. 20).

The *intended* emphasis in this sentence, I believe, is that the authors' "primary" interest was not in euphemism, and not in vague generality, but in the "literal" physical reactions people experience during sexual activity. I think the *actual* emphasis of the sentence, however, is that the authors were interested in only one type of sexual response, that which people experience in reaction to a particular type of stimulation. Such a perspective would be akin to vision researchers only being interested in optic system responses to lights of certain wavelengths, say, red and yellow, or movement physiologists only being interested in physical function during certain activities, such as running.

In each of the book's chapters devoted to the physical reactions of a particular organ or group of organs (e.g., clitoris, penis, uterus, respiratory system), Masters and Johnson began by stating their intention to look at the responses to "effective sexual stimulation." But where is that specific type of stimulation described? Although the phrase appears dozens of times in the text, it is not in the glossary or the index, and no definition or description can be found. The reader must discover that *"effective sexual stimulation" is that stimulation which facilitates a response that conforms to the HSRC.* This conclusion is inferred from observations such as the following, taken from the section on labia minora responses in the chapter on "female external genitalia": "Many women have progressed well into plateau-phase levels of sexual response, had the effective stimulative techniques withdrawn, and been unable to achieve orgasmic-phase tension release. . . . When an obviously effective means of sexual stimulation is withdrawn and orgasmic-phase release is not achieved, the minor-labial coloration will fade rapidly" (Masters and Johnson, 1966, p. 41).

Effective stimulation is that stimulation which facilitates "progress" from one stage of the HSRC to the next, particularly that which facilitates orgasm. Any stimulation resulting in responses other than greater physiological excitation and orgasm is defined by exclusion as "ineffective" and is not of interest to these authors.

This emphasis on "effective stimulation" sets up a tautology comparable to that resulting from biased subject selection. The HSRC cannot be a scientific *discovery* if the acknowledged "primary research interest" was to study stimulation defined as that which facilitates the HSRC. Again, the HSRC, "with orgasm as the ultimate point in progression" (Masters and Johnson, 1966, p. 127), preordained the results.

CLINICAL CRITICISMS OF THE HSRC MODEL

The HSRC model has had a profound impact on clinical sexology through its role as the centerpiece of contemporary diagnostic nomenclature. In this section, I will first discuss how contemporary nomenclature came to rely on the HSRC model and then describe what I see as several deleterious consequences.

HSRC and the DSM Classification of Sexual Disorders

I have elsewhere detailed the development of sexual dysfunction nosology in the four sequential editions of the American Psychiatric Association's *Diagnostic and Statistical Manual of Mental Disorders* (*DSM*) (Tiefer, 1992). Over a period of thirty-five years, the nosology evolved from not listing sexual dysfunctions at all (APA, 1952, or *DSM-I*) to listing them as symptoms of psychosomatic disorders (APA, 1968, or *DSM-II*), as a subcategory of psychosexual disorders (APA, 1980, or *DSM-III*), and as a subcategory of sexual disorders (APA, 1987, or *DSM-III-R*).

The relation of this nosology to the HSRC language can be seen in the introduction to the section on sexual dysfunctions (identical in both *DSM-III* and *DSM-III-R*):[2]

> The *essential feature* is inhibition in the appetitive or psychophysiological changes that characterize *the complete sexual response cycle*. The complete sexual response cycle can be divided into the following phases: 1. Appetitive. This consists of fantasies about sexual activity and a desire to have sexual activity. 2. Excitement. This consists of a subjective sense of sexual pleasure and accompanying physiological changes. . . . 3. Orgasm. This consists of a peaking of sexual pleasure, with release of sexual tension and rhythmic contraction of the perineal muscles and pelvic reproductive organs. . . . 4. Resolution. This consists of a sense of general relaxation, well-being, and muscular relaxation. (APA, 1987, pp. 290–291, emphasis added)

In fact, this cycle is not identical to Masters and Johnson's HSRC (although it, too, uses the universalizing language of "the" sexual response cycle). The first, or appetitive, phase was added when sexologists confronted clinical problems having to do with sexual disinterest. In their second book (1970), Masters and Johnson loosely used their HSRC physiological research to generate a list of sexual dysfunctions: premature ejaculation, ejaculatory incompetence, orgasmic dysfunction (women's), vaginismus, and dyspareunia (men's and women's). These were put forth as deviations from the HSRC that research had revealed as the norm. By the late 1970s, however, clinicians were describing a syndrome of sexual disinterest that did not fit into the accepted response cycle. Helen Singer Kaplan argued that a "separate phase [sexual desire] which had previously been neglected, must be added for conceptual completeness and clinical effectiveness" (Kaplan, 1979, p. xviii). *DSM-III* and *DSM-III-R* then merged the original HSRC with the norm of sexual desire to generate "the complete response cycle" presented above.

Clearly, the idea and much of the language of the nosology derived from Masters and Johnson's work, and in fact they are cited in the *DSM* footnotes as the primary source. Is it appropriate to use the HSRC to generate a clinical standard of normality? Is it appropriate to enshrine the HSRC as the standard of human sexuality such that deviations from it become the essential feature of abnormality?

Let us briefly examine how sexual problems are linked to mental disorders in the *DSM* and how the HSRC was used in the sexuality section. The definition of mental disorder offered in *DSM-III* specifies:

> In *DSM-III* each of the mental disorders is conceptualized as a clinically significant behavioral or psychological syndrome or pattern that occurs in an individual and that is typically associated with either a painful symptom (distress) or impairment in one or more areas of function (disability). In addition, there is an inference that there is a behavioral, psychological or biological dysfunction. (APA, 1980, p. 6)

In an article introducing the new classification scheme to the psychiatric profession, the APA task force explained their decisions. With regard to sexual dysfunctions, the task force members had concluded that "inability to experience *the normative sexual response cycle* [emphasis added] represented a *disability* in *the important area* of sexual functioning, whether or not the individual was distressed by the symptom" (Spitzer, Williams, and Skodol, 1980, pp. 153–154). That is, deviation from the now-normative sexual response cycle was to be considered a disorder even if the person had no complaints.

The diagnostic classification system clearly assumed that the HSRC was a universal bedrock of sexuality. Yet I have shown that it was a self-fulfilling result of Masters and Johnson's methodological decisions rather than a scientific discovery. It was the result of a priori assumptions rather than empirical research. Arguably, a clinical standard requires a greater demonstration of health impact and universal applicability than that offered by Masters and Johnson's research.

In fact, it is likely the case that the *DSM* authors adopted the HSRC model because it was useful and convenient. Professional and political factors that probably facilitated the adoption include professional needs within psychiatry to move away from a neurosis disorder model to a more concrete and empirical model, legitimacy needs within the new specialty of sex therapy, and the interests of feminists in progressive sexual standards for women (Tiefer, 1992b).

Thus, the enshrinement of the HSRC and its upgraded versions as the centerpiece of sexual dysfunction nomenclature in *DSM-III* and *DSM-III-R* is not scientifically reliable and represents a triumph of politics and professionalism.

Sexuality as the Performances of Fragmented Body Parts

One deleterious clinical consequence of the utilization of the HSRC model as the sexual norm has been increased focus on segmented psychophysiological functioning. Just for example, consider the following disorder descriptions, which appear in *DSM-III-R:*

1. "partial or complete failure to attain or maintain the lubrication-swelling response of sexual excitement [Female Arousal Disorder]"
2. "involuntary spasm of the musculature of the outer third of the vagina that interferes with coitus [Vaginismus]"
3. "inability to reach orgasm in the vagina [Inhibited Male Orgasm]"

In the current nosology, the body as a whole is never mentioned but instead has become a fragmented collection of parts that pop in and out at different points in the performance sequence. This compartmentalization lends itself to mechanical imagery, to framing sexuality as the smooth operation and integration of complex machines, and to seeing problems of sexuality as "machines in disrepair" that need to be evaluated by high-technology part-healers (Soble, 1987). If there is a sexual problem, check each component systematically to detect the component out of commission. Overall satisfaction (which is mentioned nowhere in the nosology) is assumed to be a result of perfect parts-functioning. Recall that subjective distress is not even required for diagnosis, just objective indication of deviation from the HSRC.

This model promotes the idea that sexual disorder can be defined as deviation from "normal" as indicated by medical test results. A bit of thought, however, will show that identifying proper norms for these types of measurements is a tricky matter. How rigid is rigid? How quick is premature? How delayed is delayed? The answers to these questions are more a product of expectations, cultural standards, and particular partner than they are of objective measurement. And yet a series of complex and often invasive genital measurements are already being routinely used in evaluations of erectile dysfunction (Krane, Goldstein, and DeTejada, 1989). Norms for many of the tests are more often provided by medical technology manufacturers than by scientific research, and measurements on nonpatient samples are often lacking. Despite calls for caution in use and interpretation, the use of sexuality measurement technology continues to escalate (Burris, Banks, and Sherins, 1989; Kirkeby, Andersen, and Poulson, 1989; Schiavi, 1988; Sharlip, 1989).

This example illustrates a general medical trend: While reliance on tests and technology for objective information is increasing, reliance on patients' individualized standards and subjective reports of illness is decreasing (Osherson and AmaraSingham, 1981). The end result may be, as Lionel Trilling (1950) worried in a review of the first Kinsey report, that "the sexuality that is measured is taken to be the definition of sexuality itself" (p. 223). Although it seems only common sense and good clinical practice to want to "rule out" medical causes prior to initiating a course of psychotherapeutic or couple treatment for sexual complaints, such "ruling out" has become a growth industry rather than an adjunct to psychological and couple-oriented history-taking. Moreover, there is a growing risk of iatrogenic disorders being induced during the extensive "ruling out" procedures.

The HSRC has contributed significantly to the idea of sexuality as proper parts-functioning. Masters and Johnson's original research can hardly be faulted for studying individual physiological components to answer the question, "What physical reactions develop as the human male and female respond to effective sexual stimulation?" But once the physiological aspects became solidified into a universal, normative sequence known as "the" HSRC, the stage was set for clinical preoccupation with parts-functioning. Despite Masters and Johnson's avowed interest in sexuality as communication, intimacy, self-expression, and mutual pleasuring, their clinical ideas were ultimately mechanical (Masters and Johnson, 1975).

Exclusive Genital (i.e., Reproductive) Focus for Sexuality

"Hypoactive sexual desire" is the only sexual dysfunction in the *DSM-III-R* defined without regard to the genital organs. "Sexual aversion," for example, is specifically identified as aversion *to the genitals*. The other sexual dysfunctions are defined in terms of *genital* pain, spasm, dryness, deflation, uncontrolled responses, delayed responses, too-brief responses, or absent responses. The *DSM* locates the boundary between normal and abnormal (or between healthy and unhealthy) sexual function exclusively on genital performances.

"Genitals" are those organs involved in acts of generation, or biological reproduction. Although the *DSM* does not explicitly endorse reproduction as the primary purpose of sexual activity, the genital focus of the sexual dysfunction nosology implies such a priority. The only sexual acts mentioned are coitus, [vaginal] penetration, sexual intercourse, and noncoital clitoral stimulation. Only one is not a heterosexual coital act. Masturbation is only mentioned as a "form of stimulation." Full *genital performance during heterosexual intercourse is the essence of sexual functioning,* which excludes and demotes nongenital possibilities for pleasure and expression. Involvement or noninvolvement of the nongenital body becomes incidental, of interest only as it impacts on genital responses identified in the nosology.

Actually, the HSRC is a whole-body response, and Masters and Johnson were as interested in the physiology of "extragenital" responses as genital ones. Yet the stages of the HSRC as reflected in heart rate or breast changes did not make it into the *DSM*s. As Masters and Johnson transformed their physiological cycle into a clinical cycle, they privileged a reproductive purpose for sexuality by focusing on the genitals. It would seem that once they turned their interest to sexual problems rather than sexual process, their focus shifted to *sexuality as outcome.*

There is no section on diagnosis in Masters and Johnson's second, clinical, book (1970), no definition of normal sexuality, and no hint of how the particular list of erectile, orgasmic, and other genitally focused disorders was derived. The authors merely described their treatments of "the specific varieties of sexual dysfunction that serve as presenting complaints of patients referred" (Masters and Johnson, 1970, p. 91). But surely this explanation cannot be the whole story. Why did they exclude problems like "inability to relax, . . . attraction to partner other than mate, . . . partner chooses inconvenient time, . . . too little tenderness" or others of the sort later labeled "sexual difficulties" (Frank, Anderson, and Rubinstein, 1978)? Why did they exclude problems like "partner is only interested in orgasm, . . . partner can't kiss, . . . partner is too hasty, . . . partner has no sense of romance," or others of the sort identified in surveys of women (Hite, 1976)?

In fact, the list of disorders proposed by Masters and Johnson seems like a list devised by Freudians who, based on their developmental stage theory of sexuality, define genital sexuality as the sine qua non of sexual maturity. Despite the whole-body focus of the HSRC physiology research, the clinical interest of its authors in proper genital performance as the essence of normal sexuality indicates their adherence to an earlier tradition. The vast spectrum of sexual possibility is narrowed to genital, that is, to reproductive performance.

Symptom Reversal as the Measure of Sex Therapy Success

A final undesirable clinical consequence of the HSRC and its evolution in the *DSM* is the limitation it imposes on the evaluation of therapy success. Once sexual disturbances are defined as specific malperformances within "the" sexual response cycle, evaluation of treatment effectiveness narrows to symptom reversal.

But the use of symptom reversal as the major or only measure of success contrasts with sex therapy as actually taught and practiced (Hawton, 1985). Typical practice focuses on individual and relationship satisfaction and includes elements such as education, permission-giving, attitude change, anxiety reduction, improved communication, and intervention in destructive sex roles and life-styles (LoPiccolo, 1977). A recent extensive survey of 289 sex therapy providers in private practice reinforced the statement that "much of sex therapy actually was nonsexual in nature" and confirmed that therapy focuses on communication skills,

individual issues, and the "nonsexual relationship" (Kilmann et al., 1986).

Follow-up studies measuring satisfaction with therapy and changes in sexual, psychological, and interpersonal issues show varying patterns of improvement, perhaps because therapists tend to heedlessly lump together cases with the "same" symptom. It is erroneous to assume that couples and their experience of sex therapy are at all homogeneous, despite their assignment to specific and discrete diagnostic categories based on the HSRC. Citing his own "painful experience" (Bancroft, 1989, p. 489) with unreplicable results of studies comparing different forms of treatment, John Bancroft suggested that there is significant prognostic variability among individuals and couples even within diagnostic categories. He concluded, "It may be that there is no alternative to defining various aspects of the sexual relationship, e.g., sexual response, communication, enjoyment, etc. and assessing each separately" (p. 497).

It might be thought that using symptom reversal as the measure of success is easier than evaluating multiple issues of relationship satisfaction, but this is not true, since *any* measure of human satisfaction needs to be subtle. That is, it is indeed easy to measure "success" with objective technologies that evaluate whether a prosthesis successfully inflates or an injection successfully produces erectile rigidity of a certain degree. When evaluating the human success of physical treatments, however, researchers invariably introduce complex subjective elements. The questions they select, the way they ask the questions, and their interpretations of the answers are all subjective (Tiefer, Pedersen, and Melman, 1988). In evaluating patients' satisfaction with penile implant treatment, asking the patients whether they would have prosthesis surgery again produces different results from evaluating postoperative satisfaction with sexual frequency, the internal feeling of the prosthesis during sex, anxieties about the indwelling prosthesis, changes in relationship quality, and so on.

The present diagnostic nomenclature, based on the genitally focused HSRC, results in evaluation of treatment success exclusively in terms of symptom reversal and ignores the complex sociopsychological context of sexual performance and experience. The neat four-stage model, the seemingly clean clinical typology, all result in neat and clean evaluation research—which turns out to relate only partially to real people's experiences.

FEMINIST CRITICISMS OF THE HSRC MODEL

Paul Robinson (1976) and Janice Irvine (1990) have discussed at length how Masters and Johnson deliberately made choices throughout *Human Sexual Response* and *Human Sexual Inadequacy* to emphasize male-female sexual similarities. The most fundamental similarity, of course, was that men and women had identical HSRCs. The diagnostic nomenclature continues this emphasis by basing the whole idea of sexual dysfunction on the gender-neutral HSRC and by scrupulously assigning equal numbers and parallel dysfunctions to men and women. (Desire disorders are not specified as to gender; other dysfunctions include one arousal disorder for each gender, one inhibited orgasm disorder for each gender, premature ejaculation for men and vaginismus for women, and dyspareunia, which is defined as "recurrent or persistent genital pain in either a male or a female.")

Yet, is the HSRC really gender-neutral? Along with other feminists, I have argued that the HSRC model of sexuality, and its elaboration and application in clinical work, favors men's sexual interests over those of women (e.g., Tiefer, 1988). Some have argued that sex role socialization introduces fundamental gender differences and inequalities into adult sexual experience that cannot be set aside by a model that simply proclaims male and female sexuality as fundamentally the same (Stock, 1984). I have argued that the HSRC, with its alleged gender equity, disguises and trivializes *social* reality, that is, gender inequality (Tiefer, 1990a) and thus makes it all the harder for women to become sexually equal in fact.

Let's look briefly at some of these gender differences in the real world. First, to oversimplify many cultural variations on this theme, men and women are raised with different sets of sexual values—men toward varied experience and physical gratification, women toward intimacy and emotional communion (Gagnon, 1977; Gagnon, 1979; Gagnon and Simon,

1969; Simon and Gagnon, 1986). By focusing on the physical aspects of sexuality and ignoring the rest, the HSRC favors men's value training over women's. Second, men's greater experience with masturbation encourages them toward a genital focus in sexuality, whereas women learn to avoid acting on genital urges because of the threat of lost social respect. With its genital focus, the HSRC favors men's training over women's. As has been mentioned earlier, by requiring experience and comfort with masturbation to orgasm as a criterion for all participants, the selection of research subjects for *Human Sexual Response* looked gender-neutral but in fact led to an unrepresentative sampling of women participants.

Third, the whole issue of "effective sexual stimulation" needs to be addressed from a feminist perspective. As we have seen, the HSRC model was based on a particular kind of sexual activity, that with "effective sexual stimulation." Socioeconomic subordination, threats of pregnancy, fear of male violence, and society's double standard reduce women's power in heterosexual relationships and militate against women's sexual knowledge, sexual assertiveness, and sexual candor (Snitow, Stansell, and Thompson, 1983; Vance, 1984). Under such circumstances, it seems likely that "effective sexual stimulation" in the laboratory or at home favors what men prefer.

The HSRC assumes that men and women have and want the same kind of sexuality since physiological research suggests that in some ways, and under selected test conditions, we are built the same. Yet social realities dictate that we are not all the same sexually—not in our socially shaped wishes, in our sexual self-development, or in our interpersonal sexual meanings. Many different studies—from questionnaires distributed by feminist organizations to interviews of self-defined happily married couples, from popular magazine surveys to social psychologists' meta-analyses of relationship research—show that women rate affection and emotional communication as more important than orgasm in a sexual relationship (Hite, 1987; Frank, Anderson, and Rubinstein, 1978; Tavris and Sadd, 1977; Peplau and Gordon, 1985). Given this evidence, it denies women's voices entirely to continue to insist that sexuality is best represented by the universal "cycle of sexual response, with orgasm as the ultimate point in progression" (Masters and Johnson, 1966, p. 127).

Masters and Johnson's comparisons of the sexual techniques used by heterosexual and homosexual couples can be seen to support the claim that "effective sexual stimulation" simply means what men prefer. Here are examples of the contrasts:

> The sexual behavior of the married couples was far more performance-oriented. . . . Preoccupation with orgasmic attainment was expressed time and again by heterosexual men and women during interrogation after each testing session. . . . [By contrast] the committed homosexual couples *took their time* in sexual interaction in the laboratory. . . . In committed heterosexual couples' interaction, the male's sexual approach to the female, . . . rarely more than 30 seconds to a minute, were spent holding close or caressing the total body area before the breasts and/or genitals were directly stimulated. This was considerably shorter than the corresponding time interval observed in homosexual couples. (Masters and Johnson, 1979, pp. 64–65, 66)

After describing various techniques of breast stimulation, the authors reported that heterosexual women enjoyed it much less than lesbians but that "all the [heterosexual] women thought that breast play was very important in their husband's arousal" (p. 67). The authors repeatedly emphasized that the differences between lesbian and heterosexual techniques were greater than between heterosexual and male homosexual techniques.[3]

The enshrinement of the HSRC in the *DSM* diagnostic nomenclature represented the ultimate in context-stripping, as far as women's sexuality is concerned. To speak merely of desire, arousal, and orgasm as constitutive of sexuality and ignore relationships and women's psychosocial development is to ignore women's experiences of exploitation, harassment, and abuse and to deny women's social limitations. To reduce sexuality to the biological specifically disadvantages women, feminists argue, because women as a class are disadvantaged by *social* sexual reality (Laws, 1990; Hubbard, 1990; Birke, 1986).

Finally, the biological reductionism of the HSRC and the *DSM* is subtly conveyed by their persistent use of the terms *males* and *females* rather than *men* and *women*. There are no men and no women in the latest edition of the diagnostic nomenclature, only males and females and vaginas and so forth. In *Human Sexual Response,* men and women appear in the text from time to time, but only males and females make it to the chapter headings, and a rough count of a few pages here and there in the text reveals a 7:1 use of the general animal kingdom terms over the specifically human ones. A feminist deconstruction of the HSRC and of contemporary perspectives on sexuality could do worse than begin by noticing and interpreting how the choice of vocabulary signals the intention to ignore culture.

CONCLUSION

I have argued in this chapter that the human sexual response cycle (HSRC) model of sexuality is flawed from scientific, clinical, and feminist points of view. Popularized primarily because clinicians and researchers needed norms that were both objective and universal, the model is actually neither objective nor universal. It imposes a false biological uniformity on sexuality that does not support the human uses and meanings of sexual potential. The most exciting work in sex therapy evolves toward systems analyses and interventions that combine psychophysiological sophistication with respect for individual and couple diversity (e.g., Verhulst and Heiman, 1988). Subjective dissatisfactions are seen more as relative dyssynchronies between individuals or between elements of culturally based sexual scripts than as malfunctions of some universal sexual essence.

Defining the essence of sexuality as a specific sequence of physiological changes promotes biological reductionism. Biological reductionism not only separates genital sexual performance from personalities, relationships, conduct, context, and values but also overvalues the former at the expense of the latter. As Abraham Maslow (1966) emphasized, studying parts may be easier than studying people, but what do you understand when you're through? Deconstructing and desacralizing the HSRC should help sex research unhook itself from the albatross of biological reductionism.

NOTES

1. Robinson suggests that Masters and Johnson's "scheme of four phases" is "irrelevant" and "merely creates the impression of scientific precision where none exists" (Robinson, 1976, p. 130). The reader is referred to his dissection of the model's stages.

2. The same introduction persists in the just-released *DSM-IV* (APA, 1994). See Chapter 10, note 1, for further information about *DSM-IV*.

3. Again, it must be emphasized that subject selection plays a large role, as acknowledged by Masters and Johnson: "Study subjects were selected because they were specifically facile in sexual response.... The carefully selected homosexual and heterosexual study subjects employed in the Institute's research programs must not be considered representative of a cross-section of sexually adult men and women in our culture" (Masters and Johnson, 1979, pp. 61–62).

REFERENCES

American Psychiatric Association. (1980). *Diagnostic and statistical manual of mental disorders, 3rd ed.* Washington, DC: APA.

American Psychiatric Association. (1987). *Diagnostic and statistical manual of mental disorders, 3rd ed rev.* Washington, DC: APA.

Bancroft, J. (1989). *Human sexuality and its problems (2nd ed.).* Edinburgh: Churchill Livingstone.

Beach, F. A. (1956). Characteristics of masculine "sex drive." In M. R. Jones (Ed.), *Nebraska symposium on motivation,* (pp. 1–32). Lincoln: University of Nebraska Press.

Birke, L. (1986). *Women, feminism and biology.* New York: Methuen.

Brecher, R., & Brecher, E. (Eds.), (1966). *An analysis of human sexual response.* New York: Signet.

Burris, A. S., Banks, S. M., & Sherins, R. J. (1989). Quantitative assessment of nocturnal penile tumescence and rigidity in normal men using a home monitor. *Journal of Andrology, 10,* 492–497.

Clement, U. (1990). Surveys of heterosexual behavior. *Annual Review of Sex Research, 1,* 45–74.

Frank, E., Anderson, C., & Rubinstein, D. (1978). Frequency of sexual dysfunction in "normal" couples. *New England Journal of Medicine, 299,* 111–115.

Gagnon, J. H. (1977). Human Sexualities. Glenview, ILL.: Scott, Foresman.

Gagnon, J. H. (1979). The interaction of gender roles and sexual conduct. In H. A. Katchadourian (Ed.), *Human sexuality: A developmental perspective,* (pp. 225–245). Berkeley: University of California Press.

Gagnon, J. H., & Simon, W. (1969). Sex education and human development. In P. J. Fink & V. O. Hammet (Eds.), *Sexual function and dysfunction,* (pp. 113–126). Philadelphia: F. A. Davis.

Green, R., & Wiener, J. (1980). *Methodology in sex research.* DHHS Report No. 80–1502. Washington, DC: US Government Printing Office.

Hite, S. (1976). *The Hite report.* New York: Macmillan.

Hoch, Z., Safir, M., Peres, Y., & Shepher, J. (1981). An evaluation of sexual performance: Comparison between sexually dysfunctional and functional couples. *Journal of Sex and Marital Therapy, 7,* 195–206.

Hubbard, R. (1990). *The politics of women's biology.* New Brunswick: Rutgers University Press.

Irvine, J. M. (1990). *Disorders of desire: Sex and gender in modern American sexology.* Philadelphia: Temple University Press.

Kaplan, H. S. (1979). *Disorders of sexual desire.* New York: Brunner/Mazel.

Kilmann, P. R., Boland, J. P., Norton, S. P., Davidson, E., & Caid, C. (1986). Perspectives of Sex Therapy Outcome: A survey of AASECT providers. *Journal of Sex and Marital Therapy, 12,* 116–138.

Kinsey, A. C., Pomeroy, W. B., & Martin, C. E. (1948). *Sexual behavior in the human male.* Philadelphia: W. B. Saunders Co.

Kinsey, A. C., Pomeroy, W. B., Martin, C. E., & Gebhard, P. H. (1953). *Sexual behavior in the human female.* Philadelphia: W. B. Saunders Co.

Kirkeby, H. J., Andersen, A. J., & Poulsen, E. U. (1989). Nocturnal penile tumescence and rigidity: Translation of data obtained from normal males. *International Journal of Impotence Research, 1,* 115–125.

Krane, R. J., Goldstein, I., & DeTejada, I. S. (1989). Impotence. *New England Journal of Medicine 321,* 1648–1659.

Laws, S. (1990). *Issues of blood: The politics of menstruation.* New York: Columbia University Press.

LoPiccolo, J. (1977). The professionalization of sex therapy: Issues and problems. *Society, 14,* 60–68.

Lehrman, N. (1970). *Masters and Johnson explained.* Chicago: Playboy Press.

Maslow, A. H. (1966). *The psychology of science.* New York: Harper and Row.

Masters, W. H., & Johnson, V. E. (1966). *Human sexual response.* Boston: Little, Brown.

Masters, W. H., & Johnson, V. E. (1970). *Human sexual inadequacy.* Boston: Little, Brown.

Masters, W. H., & Johnson, V. E. (1975). *The pleasure bond.* Boston: Little, Brown.

Masters, W. H., & Johnson, V. E. (1979). *Homosexuality in perspective.* Boston: Little, Brown.

Osherson, S. D., & AmaraSingham, L. (1981). The machine metaphor in medicine. In E. G. Mishler, L. AmaraSingham, S. T. Hauser, R. Liem, S. D. Osherson, & N. E. Waxler.

(Eds.), *Social contexts of health, illness and patient care,* (pp. 218–249). Cambridge: Cambridge University Press.

Peplau, L. A., & Gordon, S. L. (1985). Women and men in love: Gender differences in close heterosexual relationships. In V. E. O'Leary, R. K. Unger, & B. S. Wallston (Eds.), *Women, gender and social psychology,* (pp. 257–291). Hillsdale, NJ: Lawrence Erlbaum Associates.

Robinson, P. (1976). *The modernization of sex.* New York: Harper and Row.

Rosenthal, R. (1966). *Experimenter effects in behavioral research.* New York: Appleton-Century-Crofts.

Rosenthal, R., & Rosnow, R. L. (1969). The volunteer subject. In R. Rosenthal, & R. L. Rosnow (Eds.), *Artifact in behavioral research.* New York: Academic Press.

Schiavi, R. C. (1988). Nocturnal penile tumescence in the evaluation of erectile disorders: A critical review. Journal of Sex and Marital Therapy, 14, 83–97.

Sharlip, I. (1989). Editorial. *International Journal of Impotence Research, 1,* 67–69.

Simon, W., & Gagnon, J. H. (1986). Sexual scripts: Permanence and change. *Archives of Sexual Behavior, 15,* 97–120.

Snitow, A., Stansell, C., & Thompson, S. (1983). *Powers of desire: The politics of sexuality.* New York: Monthly Review Press.

Soble, A. (1987). Philosophy, medicine and healthy sexuality. In E. E. Shelp (Ed.), *Sexuality and medicine, vol. I: Conceptual roots,* (pp. 111–138). Dordrecht Holland): D. Reidel Publishing Co.

Spitzer, R. L., Williams, J. B. W., & Skodol, A. E. (1980). DSM-III: The major achievements and an overview. *American Journal of Psychiatry, 137,* 151–164.

Stock, W. (1984). Sex roles and sexual dysfunction. In C. S. Widom (Ed.), *Sex roles and psychopathology.* New York: Plenum Press

Sulloway, F. J. (1979). *Freud: Biologist of the mind.* New York: Basic Books.

Tavris, C., & Sadd, S. (1977). *The Redbook report on female sexuality.* New York: Delacorte Press.

_____ . Social constructionism and the study of human sexuality. In P. Shaver & C. Hendrick (Eds.), *Sex and gender,* (pp. 70–94). Beverly Hills, CA.: Sage.

Tiefer, L. (1988). A feminist critique of the sexual dysfunction nomenclature. *Women and therapy, 7,* 5–21.

Tiefer, L. (1990a). *Sexual biology and the symbolism of the natural.* Paper delivered at International Academy of Sex Research, Sigtuna, Sweden (August).

_____ . (1990b, August). *Gender and meaning in the the DSM-III and DSM-IIIR sexual dysfunctions.* Paper delivered at American Psychological Association, Boston.

Tiefer, L. (1992) Critique of the DSM-IIIR nosology of sexual dysfunctions. *Psychiatric Medicine, 10,* 227–245.

Tiefer, L., Pedersen, B., & Melman, A. (1988). Psychosocial follow-up of penile prosthesis implant patients and partners. *Journal of Sex and Marital Therapy, 14,* 184–201.

Trilling, L. (1950). The Kinsey Report. In L. Trilling (Ed.), *The liberal imagination: Essays on literature and society.* Garden City, NY: Doubleday Anchor.

Vance, C. S. (Ed.), (1984). *Pleasure and danger: Exploring female sexuality.* Boston: Routledge and Kegan Paul.

Verhulst, J., & Heiman, J. R. (1988). A systems perspective on sexual desire. In S. R. Leiblum & R. C. Rosen (Eds.), *Sexual desire disorders,* pp. 243–267). New York: Guilford Press.

2.5 CREATING GOOD-LOOKING GENITALS IN THE SERVICE OF GENDER

Suzanne Kessler

In previous research, I have studied the management of intersexed infants. Through interviews with psychiatric endocrinologists, urologists, and surgeons, as well as reading the management literature, I came to some understanding of how physicians normalize the intersexed condition for the parents. For example, physicians imply that it is not the gender of the child that is ambiguous, but rather the genitals. I analyzed the physicians' gender-assignment decisions and drew some conclusions about cultural factors that influenced those decisions. A major criterion for assigning "male" is the length of the infant's penis and the future ability of that penis to fill a vagina. Finally, in that earlier work, I argued that neither physicians nor parents of the intersexed infant emerged from that experience with a greater understanding of the social construction of gender.

After my article was published I received a letter from an intersexed woman who had read it. I had written, in passing, that there is virtually no information about the handling of intersexuality from the viewpoint of the intersexed individual. She had two main things to say to me. First, she agreed with me that the voice of the intersexed is missing from the professional literature. And second, I had taken for granted too much of what the physicians had told me about the success of the surgery. Somehow, by concentrating on the social decision making and the management issues, I had glossed the whole surgical enterprise, and assumed that while cultural aspects were problematic, technical aspects were not. She begged to differ with me. Her letter precipitated a lengthy correspondence, and I have since corresponded and talked with other intersexuals. I have also talked with parents of newly diagnosed infants, and read about a hundred letters from parents of intersexed infants. In addition, I have plowed through the surgical literature, much like an anthropologist in foreign territory, armed with some knowledge of terminology, but not sharing the taken-for-granted convictions that genital surgery is either necessary or successful. I realized that I was dumb to such issues as what genitals are supposed to look like and how genitals are supposed to function. And the professional literature is written in such a way as to capitalize on this ignorance. Yet this dumbness had proven to be an advantage in helping me see what is between the lines, although those on the front lines of genital surgery would just say I was dumb.

What you need to know about gender assignment is that when a baby is born with ambiguous genitals, a chromosomal test is done. If the baby is XX, then the phallic tissue is reduced in size, labia are made, and a vagina is eventually created if there is none. If the baby is XY, a decision is made about whether the phallic tissue is large enough, or will be large enough if given hormonal treatment, to be a "good" penis. If

"yes," then surgery is done to "improve" the phallus and testicles. If "no," then surgery is done to create a clitoris and labia. About 10 percent of intersexed infants are assigned to the male gender, the remaining are assigned to be female. I'll be talking primarily about female genitals, especially the clitoris, the vagina, and the labia.

I will begin with the question of how physicians know when they are confronted with ambiguous genitals. In reading the medical literature, I extracted the following kinds of quotations. Ambiguous genitals are described, I would have to say, ambiguously:

> Their external genitals look much more like a clitoris and a labia than a penis or a scrotum.[1]
> The tip should be the expected size for the patient's age.[2]
> The size of an enlarged clitoris cannot be stated in exact measurements.[3]

Maybe I was asking the wrong question. Maybe I should ask what normal genitals look like and then I will be able to recognize abnormal ones. At birth the normal clitoris is supposed to be up to 1 centimeter long, and the normal penis between 2.5 and 4.5 centimeters. And then we've got these enlarged clitorises with the intersexed conditions that are between 1.5 and 4. I guess you are just not allowed to have a genital that is between 1 centimeter and 2.5. The genital boundaries have to be considerably separated, which is kind of interesting. I am not sure what that means.

The measurements depend on how something is measured: whether you are measuring the relaxed phallus, the stretched one, the erect one. Ambiguity or decisiveness is at least partially determined by factors such as who is looking why they are looking, and how hard they are looking. There is considerable vagueness, suggesting that when one encounters a "problem" genital one will know it. Although there are a few studies that report precise measurements of genital size, shape, and location, I can't imagine surgeons standing at the table, as someone has just given birth, with a ruler in hand comparing what's there with some kind of chart, looking back and forth. I've taken some examples from the medical literature reflecting the language of genital surgeons about large clitorises: "imperfect," "defective," "malformation," "anatomic derangements," "deformed," "major clitoral over-growth," "obtrusive," "grossly enlarged," "ungainly masculine enlargement," "offending shaft," "embarrassing," "offensive," "incompatible with satisfactory feminine presentation or adjustment," "disfiguring," "troublesome," "challenging to a feminine cosmetic result."

These descriptors suggest not only that there is a size and malformation problem, but there is an aesthetic one as well, experienced as a moral violation. The language is emotional. Physician-researchers seem personally outraged. The early items on the list suggest that the large clitoris is imperfect and ugly. The later items suggest more of a personal affront. From the perspective of the viewer, the clitoris is portrayed as offending and embarrassing. Who, exactly, is offended and embarrassed, and why? A comment from an intersexed adult woman about her childhood is relevant: "I experienced the behavior of virtually everyone towards me as absolutely dishonest and embarrassing." What's interesting is that she didn't say she experienced the organ as embarrassing, even though she was not operated on until she was eight. Objects in the world, even non-normative objects, are not embarrassing. People's reactions to them are. Perhaps the last item on the list says it best: the clitoris is "challenging."

My favorite quote of all the reading I've done is "The annals of medical history bulge with strange cases of enlarged clitorises."[4]

What about the language used to describe the micro-phallus, the small penis? I've found that it is not emotional. It is not particularly pejorative. Some common descriptors for the small penis are "short," "buried," "anomalous." There is usually some discussion about whether the micro-phallus is normally proportioned or whether it has a feminine stigmata. Descriptions of the micro-penis, however, are tied quite explicitly to gender role. Here are more quotes:

Is the size of the phallus adequate to support a male sex assignment?[5]

A ten-year-old boy with a small penis was given testosterone ointment, "after which"—I don't know whether it was momentarily or it took a while—"after which he reaffirmed his allegiance to things masculine."[6]

After B's 15th birthday, her penis developed erections. She produced ejaculations and she found herself feeling a sexual interest in girls.[7]

Clearly, once the penis is large enough to support masculinity, with or without extra hormones, everyone will be more comfortable. Once that penis starts to work, it will direct the owner, even if she is a girl, toward a sexual interest in girls.

There is considerably less discussion of how the labia ought to look than how the clitoris ought to. Labial variation is permissible. The labia majora don't have to completely cover the minora. Minor fusion of the labia is acceptable. And it is all right if the prepuce adheres to the clitoris. Here is a quotation from a 1930s marriage manual:

In some women the inner lips protrude somewhat. The inner lips meet at their upper ends, and when separated, are approximately in the form of the wishbone of a hen, approximately two inches at width.[8]

Then there is the "Hottentot apron." "In all the women of the Bushman, in South Africa, and in some of the Hottentot women (according to one early textbook), "the labia minora hang halfway down to the knees."[9] There were women with this condition or (beautification) who went on tour in Europe and were exposed to people. They lay down and people came and looked at them.

I want to relate this very briefly to female genital mutilation today, one rationale for which is that the labia are considered unsightly and unclean, and if they are not excised they will dangle between the legs and may threaten the penis.[10]

Does the average person have any idea what genitals should look like? Would the average person permit more variation than the average surgeon? Imagine a set of criteria pictures by which someone's genitals would be judged: "How much does the clitoris protrude from the labia?" I located one study of what women know about their sex organs.[11] Women were asked to draw both their internal and external sex organs, and the outer and inner lips of the external genitalia were in fact seldom drawn. So women actually didn't draw labia when they were asked to draw the female genitals. It is, perhaps, more interesting that in this group of women only 41 percent drew the clitoris. One of my students is interviewing surgeons who do genital reconstruction for women who have had genital cancers. One physician told her, "There is usually only a labia majora made by the surgeon, because people are not that sophisticated. They don't require a labia minora, and they are much more difficult to construct. You can fool most of the people most of the time."

Perhaps the labia are so poorly conceptualized because their function is obscure. A nineteenth-century medical text clarifies the function of the labia.

> The labia majora protect the deeper parts. They lead the male organ to them and serve as buffers during coitus. The function of the labia minora is to ensure a more perfect adaptation and act as an irritant for the nerves of the male member at the same time that their own nerves are acted on.[12]

So one wonders who the female genitals belong to. Some 1930s marriage manuals show the same blatant heterosexism in their descriptions of the vagina. There was one picture of the female sex organs, separated into what the author called the "working parts" and the "sensation providing parts."[13] The "working parts" were the fallopian tubes, the womb, the ovary, and the vagina. (I guess the work they do is reproductive work), and the "sensation providing parts" were the clitoris and the labia. The vagina is from the Latin word meaning "sheath": the male sex organ fits into it like a sword into a sheath.

In a 1906 text, a diagrammatic section of the median plane of the female genital organs includes the end of the penis.[14] There is no clitoris. The caption describes the drawing as the "internally more important part of the female sexual apparatus."

More modern scientific literature also blends appearance and function, albeit with more subtlety. Here's a representative description of the clitoris:

> The clitoris is not essential for *adequate sexual function* and sexual *gratification,* but its preservation would seem to be desirable if achieved while maintaining *satisfactory appearance* and function. Yet the clitoris clearly has a relation to erotic stimulation and to sexual gratification and its presence is desirable even in patients with intersexed anomalies if that presence does not interfere with *cosmetic, psychological, social and sexual adjustment.*[15]

The emphases are mine. I have some questions. What is meant by "adequate sexual function"? Is that the same thing as "gratification"? If not, what is "gratification"? Are either of them the same as orgasm? Who would this be desirable for? The patient? The doctor? The natural state of things? And what is a "satisfactory appearance"? How are the four different "adjustments" listed at the end ranked? Is that order accidental?

Before I talk about surgeries on intersexed genitals, I want to summarize what I think are the surgeons' beliefs about female genitals (although never stated, they are important because they underlie surgical practices): The most important thing about the clitoris is that it be small. The labia might just as well not exist. And the vagina is basically just an adjunct to the penis. (I'll provide more support for that statement later.) In Western culture there are no female genitals. (All this should be contrasted with the view of the cultures in Africa and the Middle East that are performing clitorectomies, where clearly the female genitals are very striking and powerful and dangerous, and no matter what their size, they need to be gotten rid of.)

Here is a brief description of some clitoral surgeries. Clitorectomy, which was the earliest, is also called clitoridectomy, or amputation. In the argument for doing a complete clitorectomy, which is sometimes still done today, it has been said that it is not good to have any halfway measures because doing it halfway, removing only the exposed portion, would "allow the bulk of the clitoral shaft to remain and such tissue can become turgid and painful."[16] The technique of "clitoral recession," developed in 1961 by John Lattimer at Columbia Presbyterian, was an operation to reduce or cover the enlarged clitoris without removing it. I thought it interesting that it is acceptable to have a large clitoris as long as it is covered.

Then there is clitoral reduction, which is a technique developed in 1970 by Judson Randolph to preserve more of the erectile tissue. He wrote in a letter (1993), "I came to the conclusion that sparing the clitoris would be more physiologic and more appropriate." One intersexed woman says that half a dozen intersex surgeons she spoke with were uniformly ignorant of the Randolph technique, and the Lattimer technique is the most common and is still used at

Columbia Presbyterian today. As far I could tell, from my reading of the literature, there is no size criteria or medical criteria by which one would choose one technique over another.

In reading through the medical literature, I have noted something about the language used to discuss the surgery. It is described as "necessary" not because anyone, or any one profession, has deemed it so, but because the genital itself requires the improvement. Here are some quotations:

> Given that the clitoris must be reduced, what is the best way to do it?[17]
>
> When the female sex is assigned, an operation on the clitoris, together with other necessary procedures to modify the genitalia, becomes necessary for the establishment of proper psychological and social adjustment.[18]
>
> The size of an enlarged clitoris demanding clitorectomy cannot be stated in exact measurements.[19]

We have this sense that the clitoris is "demanding," maybe with placards or something, to be reduced. Where does the clitoris get its right to demand reduction? Why, from "Nature." And now that we know that the large clitoris is an affront to "Nature," it is understandable why the language used to describe it is so emotional.

I had some questions when I began reading the literature. How good is the surgery that is performed on the intersexed? How much scarring results from the clitoral reductions, recessions, or creations? Does this affect the ability to experience orgasm? Does it cause irritation or pain? How credible is the appearance? How functional is the vagina? Is it long enough? Wide enough? Does it lubricate enough? How credible is its appearance? Does the vagina scar and tend to close, requiring further surgeries? If so, is this because the surgical techniques themselves are imperfect, or because of patient noncompliance?

I reviewed eleven follow-up studies, published between 1961 and 1992, on intersex surgery. Some of the studies were conducted by the surgeons who developed the techniques, Lattimer and Randolph, assessing the effects of their own surgery; other studies were comparisons of different surgical techniques.

It is not always easy extracting from the studies exactly what criteria were used to measure success. Sometimes the language is so vague as to be mystifying. "The surgery yielded an acceptable appearance and, in most instances, satisfactory sexual adjustment leading to an improved psychologic base."[20] Acceptable to whom? Satisfactory in what sense? Improved from what? Compared to what?

Some follow-up studies give more specific criteria.[21] I have grouped the criteria according to categories in the order that I believe is important to physicians. Despite all the discussion about enlarged clitorises, most studies consider that the intersexed patient has been successfully treated if her vagina size and functioning are good. "Vaginoplasty" is the term used to refer to surgery to create a vagina that wasn't there, or to correct an "imperfect" vagina. There are a number of different techniques used on intersexed girls, most of which have been developed on transsexuals. This surgery is also done on women with genital cancers. Vaginoplasty on the intersexed used to be done in early childhood, shortly after clitoral surgery, which is usually performed within the first year. Now vaginoplasties are often delayed until puberty, after the body has finished growing and when the child is old enough to do all the things she has to do to keep the vagina from closing up. It is a quite complicated, tedious procedure. Delaying the surgery is presumably also in the service of reducing the amount of dense scarring. One father of an intersexed child told me he wanted vaginoplasty on his baby daughter delayed as long as possible.

The size of the vagina is related to whether it is used successfully in intercourse. It is sometimes unclear who is evaluating "unsuccessful" attempts at vaginal intercourse. Studies that are explicit about evaluating the vagina suggest that the results are far from perfect. In one study fifteen of twenty-three women who had vaginal reconstruction during infancy had functionally inadequate vaginas.[22]

When vaginoplasty for transsexuals is discussed in the literature, sexual intercourse is described as "useful" in keeping the vagina open, thereby contributing to a successful surgical outcome, as though the whole point is a successful surgical outcome. A specific heterosexual sex activity is seen as useful for the purpose of creating and maintaining a particular anatomy—a new take on anatomy as destiny. You're destined to have the anatomy. You don't want a vagina so you can be functionally heterosexual; you function heterosexually so you can have a vagina. In that sense, plastic dilators are as good as penises.

Based on my reading of vagina measurements, I would say that transsexuals are getting bigger vaginas than adult women. An adult female virgin nontranssexual's vagina is three and a half to four and three-fourths inches, and transsexuals are getting vaginas up to seven and an eighth inches. I don't know if anyone wants to protest that. I guess if you are paying that much "ya gotta get a big one."

A surgeon who does genital reconstruction of women with genital cancer said,

> If you can give a patient a functioning vagina, you have accomplished what Eve set out to accomplish. Without a vagina a woman is not normal. It's like having a nose. You can breathe fine without a nose, but you look funny without a nose. The women don't feel normal. I don't think it is very important whether it is ever used.

When asked whether there was consensus in the field about this, he said, "I haven't sat down with other plastic surgeons and discussed it. I am not aware of any psychological studies." Does his answer about not needing to use the vagina suggest that he is not being heterosexist? Or does his requirement of the vagina for complete femaleness reflect what a heterosexual man means by "complete woman" in terms of his own self-interest: the vagina should be there if it is ever needed?

The second criterion is the aesthetics of the anatomy, which is rated by the surgeons. I haven't come across any reference to patients being asked how satisfied they were with the way their genitals look. One researcher says, "Gross appearance of the external genitalia was acceptable, although on close examination the lack of the clitoris was obvious."[23] Having no clitoris is described as an "acceptable appearance." Another researcher evaluated anatomy,

rating it as "excellent," "satisfactory," or "unsatisfactory," but he didn't give the criteria by which he judged it.[24] Others suggested that appearance is "unsatisfactory" if the glans is positioned too high or if there is persistent prominent size.

The third criterion is discomfort: "No prepubital girl," according to one study, "expressed any discomfort of the clitoris or described troublesome erections."[25] I wonder exactly who would be troubled by these erections, and what was troubling about them. Other researchers mention frequent erections and constant irritation and pain.

Some researchers, who are apparently unwilling to ask their patients direct questions, display their naïveté when they describe why erotic response can't be directly assessed. Thus one study reports, "some patients, of marriageable age, are still single, and any relevant conclusion regarding the erotic response of the glans is hard to determine."[26] I guess unless you're married, there would be no way to test whether your genitals were working or not. From a follow-up study of transsexuals' surgery, the researcher makes reference to male-to-female transsexuals having the "sensation of orgasm."[27] That phrase is in quotes in the original article. Is there a difference between an orgasm and merely the "sensation" of an orgasm? I found that in other articles, too, erotic response is described as having the "sensation of an orgasm." I suspect that isn't quite an orgasm yet.

The fourth criterion is the occurrence of complications, such as "cysts" or "fistulas." This is rated by the surgeons, and there is very little discussion of this. One gets the *sense* that the surgical procedures are pretty good in avoiding such complications. This is in striking contrast to the result of mutilations performed under unsterile conditions in Africa.

The final criteria are marriage and pregnancy. As evidence of the success of the surgical technique, one researcher cites the case of a twenty-one-year-old intersexed woman who was married and was in the final month of her second pregnancy.[28] Another mentions two women from the sample who were married.[29] Although marriage and pregnancy are not referred to in every intersex follow-up study, the emphasis on the vagina suggests that the ultimate test of the vagina is a successful marriage and eventually a pregnancy. In other words, heterosexuality.

NOTES

1. Jared Diamond, "Turning A Man," *Discover,* June 1992, 71–77.

2. John K. Lattimer, "Relocation and Recession of the Enlarged Clitoris with Preservation of the Glans: An Alternative to Amputation," *Journal of Urology* 86, 1 (1961): 113–16.

3. Robert E. Gross, Judson Randolph, and John F. Crigler, Jr., "Clitorectomy for Sexual Abnormalities: Indications and Technique," *Surgery,* February 1966, 300–308.

4. L. T. Woodward, *Sophisticated Sex Techniques in Marriage* (New York: Lancer Books, 1968).

5. Kurt Newman, Judson Randolph, and Kathryn Anderson, "The Surgical Management of Infants and Children with Ambiguous Genitalia," *Ann. Surg.* 215, 6 (June 1992): 644–53.

6. Frank Hinman, Jr., "Microphallus: Characteristics and Choice of Treatment from a Study of Twenty Cases," *Journal of Urology* 107 (March 1972): 499–505.

7. Diamond (n. 1 above).

8. M. J. Exner, *The Sexual Side of Marriage* (New York: W. W. Norton, 1932).

9. Henry J. Garriques, *A Textbook of the Diseases of Women* (Philadelphia: W. B. Saunders, 1894).

10. J. Ruminjo, "Circumcision in Women," *East African Medical Journal,* September 1992, 477–78.

11. Lucille Hollander Blum, "Darkness in an Enlightened Era: Women's Drawings of their Sexual Organs," *Psychological Reports* 42 (1978): 867–73.

12. Garriques (n. 9 above).

13. Helena Wright, *The Sex Factor in Marriage* (New York: Vanguard Press, 1931).

14. August Forel and C. F. Marshall, *The Sexual Question* (Brooklyn: Physicians and Surgeons Book Co., 1906).

15. Judson G. Randolph and Wellington Hung, "Reduction Clitoroplasty in Females with Hypertrophied Clitoris," *Journal of Pediatric Surgery* 5, 2 April 1970): 224–31.

16. Gross, Randolph, and Crigler (n. 3 above).

17. Lattimer (n. 2 above).

18. H. Kumar, J. H. Kiefer, I. E. Rosenthal, and S. S. Clark, "Clitoroplasty: Experience during a Nineteen-Year Period," *Journal of Urology* 111 (1974): 81–84.

19. Gross, Randolph, and Crigler (n. 3 above).

20. Judson Randolph, Wellington Hung, and Mary Colainni Rathlev, "Clitoroplasty for Females Born with Ambiguous Genitalia: A Long-Term Study of Thirty-seven Patients," *Journal of Pediatric Surgery* 16, 6 (December 1981): 882–87.

21. A. Sotiropoulos, A. Morishima, Y. Homsy, and J. K. Lattimer, "Long-Term Assessment of Genital Reconstruction in Female Pseudohermaphrodites," *Journal of Urology* 115 (May 1976): 599–601; Lawrence E. Allen, B. E. Hardy, and B. M. Churchill, "The Surgical Management of the Enlarged Clitoris," *Journal of Urology* 128 (August 1982): 351–54; F.M.E. Skijper, H. J. van der Kamp, H. Brandenburg, S.M.P.F. de Muinck Keizer-Schrama, S.L.A. Drop, and J. C. Molendaar, "Evaluation of Psychosexual Development of Young Women with Congenital Adrenal Hyperplasia: A Pilot Study," *Journal of Sex Education and Therapy* 18, 3 (1992): 200–207.

22. Allen, Hardy, and Churchill (n. 21 above).

23. Sotiropoulos, et al. (n. 21 above).

24. Randolph, Hung, and Colainni Rathlev (n. 20 above).

25. Randolph, Hung, and Colainni Rathlev (n. 20 above).

26. Kumar et al. (n. 18 above).

27. Sara Perovic, "Male to Female Surgery: A New Contribution to Operative Techniques," *Plastic and Reconstructive Surgery* 91, 4 (April 1993): 708–9.

28. Allen, Hardy, and Churchill (n. 21 above).

29. Rose M. Mulaikai, Claude J. Migeon, and John A. Rock, "Fertility Rates in Female Patients with Congenital Adrenal Hyperplasia Due to 21-Hydroxylase Deficiency," *New England Journal of Medicine* 316, 4 (January 1987): 178–82.

PART TWO

SEXUAL
IDENTITIES

CHAPTER THREE

BECOMING SEXUAL

We *become* sexual. We learn how to have sex, whom to desire, what to do, and why. And we begin to learn this in childhood, as we start to make sense of the cavalcade of messages we receive and transmit to others. In this section, we examine some of the ways in which people learn how to be sexual and begin to develop their own sexual identities.

We may make our own sexualities, but we don't do it alone. The larger social context of sexual socialization provides us with the institutional and cultural arena in which we create our sexualities. Four cultural themes collide into the frameworks we use.

First, we live in a culture that positively screams sexuality. Everywhere we look there is sex—images, representations, jokes, conversations. What we learn is that sexuality is *really* important and we had better "do" it right.

Second, we live in a sexual culture that shrouds sexuality in secrecy and shame. Religion, secular moralities, general cultural disgust with the associated effluvia of our bodies "down there" all combine to make sex seem dirty and shameful, as well as delightful and ecstatic. No matter how much you might protest that you love sex and love your own and other human bodies, no one in this culture has a sexuality that is completely unfettered from these moral and ethnical pronouncements. (If you don't believe it, think about the last time you had a casual conversation with a friend or a parent about what feels good when you masturbate, something that virtually everyone does and virtually no one discusses honestly.)

Third, we live in a culture of dramatic gender inequality, in which girls and women are discriminated against, have their bodies and sexuality used against them, and are often denied access to their sexual desires.

Fourth, we live in a culture in which sexual identity itself is the basis for inequality—as gay men, lesbians, bisexuals, transgendered people, and even those who practice marginalized sexual activities are marginalized, labeled deviant, and the subject of scorn, derision, violence, and discrimination. To desire the "wrong" person, to enjoy the "wrong" behavior, may be risking your life.

The essays in this section address these themes. Barrie Thorne and Zella Luria explore how gender and sexuality are part of children's play—and how that play reproduces the sorts of sexual and gender hierarchies we find among adults. And Anthony Smith and colleagues describe how our masturbatory experiences reflect and construct our developing sexual selves.

Deborah Tolman, Ritch Savin-Williams, and Connie Chan all explore the claiming of sexual identity and behavior among groups where such a conversation takes place on the margins—because of gender, ethnicity, race sexuality, or a combination of all of them. How can those whose sexualities are problematized—invisible, hypervisible, impermissible—claim healthy sexual identities?

3.1 SEXUALITY AND GENDER IN CHILDREN'S DAILY WORLDS*

Barrie Thorne and Zella Luria

The ambiguities of "sex"—a word used to refer to biological sex, to cultural gender, and also to sexuality—contain a series of complicated questions. Although our cultural understandings often merge these three domains, they can be separated analytically; their interrelationships lie at the core of the social organization of sex and gender.[1] In this paper we focus on the domains of gender and sexuality as they are organized and experienced among elementary school children, especially nine to eleven year-olds. This analysis helps illuminate age-based variations and transitions in the organization of sexuality and gender.

We use "gender" to refer to cultural and social phenomena—divisions of labor, activity, and identity which are associated with but not fully determined by biological sex. The core of sexuality, as we use it here, is desire and arousal. Desire and arousal are shaped by and associated with socially learned activities and meanings which Gagnon and Simon (1973) call "sexual scripts." Sexual scripts—defining who does what, with whom, when, how, and what it means—are related to the adult society's view of gender (Miller and Simon, 1981).

In our culture, gender and sexuality are deeply intertwined, especially for adults; "woman/man," and especially, "femininity/masculinity" are categories loaded with heterosexual meanings. Erotic orientation and gender are not as closely linked in our culture's definitions of children. Although there is greater acknowledgement of childhood sexuality than in the past, we continue—often after quoting Freud to the contrary—to define children as innocent, vulnerable, and in need of protection from adult sexual knowledge and practice.[2]

Children are not, of course, asexual. They experience arousal, and they sometimes engage in practices (even some leading to orgasm) that adults call "sexual" (Kinsey et al., 1948, 1953). Some children learn and use sexual words at a relatively young age, and, as we will describe later, they draw on sexual meanings (although not necessarily adult understandings) in constructing their social worlds. But special taboos and tensions surround the feelings and language of sexuality in childhood. In our culture we limit the "fully sexual" (sexual acts tied to accepted adult meanings) to adolescence and adulthood. Among children any explicitly sexual activity, beyond ill-defined crushes, is treated as culturally deviant.

Nine to eleven year-old children are beginning the transition from the gender system of childhood to that of adolescence. They are largely defined (and define themselves) as children, but they are on the verge of sexual maturity, cultural adolescence, and a gender system organized around the institution of heterosex-

---

From *Social Problems* 33(3): 176–90. Copyright © 1986 University of California Press. Reprinted by permission of The Society for the Study of Social Problems.

* We presented this paper at the 1985 annual meetings of the American Sociological Association in Washington, DC, and, in an earlier version, in a 1983 lecture series on female sexuality sponsored by the Stanford University Center for Research on Women. We would like to acknowledge helpful comments from Eleanor W. Herzog, Linda Hughes, Cathy Reback, Patricia A. Adler, Peter Adler, Gary Alan Fine, and Sue K. Hammersmith.

uality. Their experiences help illuminate complex and shifting relationships between sexuality and gender.

First we explore the segregated gender arrangements of middle childhood as contexts for learning adolescent and adult sexual scirpts. We then turn from their separate worlds to relations *between* boys and girls, and examine how fourth and fifth grade children use sexual idioms to mark gender boundaries. Separate gender groups and ritualized, asymmetric relations between girls and boys lay the groundwork for the more overtly sexual scripts of adolescence.

METHODS AND SOURCES OF DATA

Our data are drawn from observations of children in elementary school playgrounds, classrooms, hallways, and lunchrooms. All of the schools went up through sixth grade. One of us (Thorne) was a participant-observer for eight months in a largely white, working-class elementary school in California, a school with about 500 students (5 percent black, 20 percent Chicana/o, and 75 percent white). She also observed for three months in a Michigan elementary school with around 400, largely working-class students (8 percent black, 12 percent Chicana/o, and 80 percent white). Playground observations included all ages, but emphasized fourth and fifth graders. The other author (Luria) observed for one-and-a-half academic years in a middle-class, suburban Massachusetts public school and in an upper-middle-class private school in the Boston area. Both schools had about 275 students—17 percent black and 83 percent white—in the fourth through sixth grades.[3] A separate Massachusetts sample of 27 fourth and fifth graders was interviewed to ascertain children's knowledge of what boys and girls "should do" and know. We have combined our data for this paper.

Throughout our fieldwork we tried to observe children in situations where they were under less adult supervision and control and hence more likely construct their own activities and social relations. Although we could not pass as children, we did try to separate ourselves from the adult authority systems of the schools. We essentially tried to hang out—watching, talking, and sometimes playing with the children. We interacted freely with the children and sometimes elicited their understanding of ongoing situations. On a number of occasions, we each observed significant breaking of school rules, a backhanded compliment to our trustworthiness, if not our invisibility.[4]

Elementary schools may not seem to be the most fruitful contexts for gathering information about sexuality. Indeed, had we observed the same children in more informal and private settings, such as in neighborhoods or summer camps, we probably would have observed more extensive sexual talk and behavior (as did Fine, 1980, in an ethnographic study of preadolescent boys on Little League baseball teams).

On the other hand, children spend a great deal of time in schools, and they often construct their own interactions within the structure of adult-controlled school days. The presence of teachers and aides gave us many opportunities to observe children guarding their more secret lives from potential interference from adults, and to see children and adults negotiating sexual meanings.[5] Furthermore, the dynamics of gender separation and integration are especially vivid in densely-populated school settings.

The social categories of observers have no simple bearing on the process of research, but the fact that we are women may well have affected what we saw and how we interpreted it. Our gender enhanced access to groups of girls, but the more public nature of boys' groups made them generally easier to observe. Age may mute the effects of gender; just as very young boys may go into women's bathrooms, so, by virtue of age, adult women may cross ritual boundaries separating groups of boys from groups of girls. We both found it easier to see and articulate the social relations of boys than those of girls, a skew also evident in the literature. Having grown up as girls, we may have had less detachment from their interactions. In addition, until recently, more research had been done on groups of boys than on groups of girls, and categories for description and analysis have come more from male than female experience.

THE DAILY SEPARATION OF GIRLS AND BOYS

Gender segregation—the separation of girls and boys in friendships and casual encounters—is central to daily life in elementary schools. A series of snapshots taken in varied school settings would reveal extensive spatial separation between girls and boys. When they choose seats, select companions for work or play, or arrange themselves in line, elementary school children frequently cluster into same-sex groups. At lunchtime, boys and girls often sit separately and talk matter-of-factly about "girls' tables" and "boys' tables." Playgrounds have gendered spaces: boys control some areas and activities, such as large playing fields and basketball courts; and girls control smaller enclaves like jungle-gym areas and concrete spaces for hopscotch or jumprope. Extensive gender segregation in everyday encounters and in friendships has been found in many other studies of elementary- and middle-school children (e.g., Best, 1983; Eder and Hallinan, 1978; Lockheed, 1985). Gender segregation in elementary and middle schools has been found to account for more segregation than race (Schofield, 1982).

Gender segregation is not total. Snapshots of school settings would also reveal some groups with a fairly even mix of boys and girls, especially in games like kickball, dodgeball, and handball, and in classroom and playground activities organized by adults. Some girls frequently play with boys, integrating their groups in a token way, and a few boys, especially in the lower grades, play with groups of girls.

The amount of gender segregation varies not only by situation, but also by school. For example, quantitative inventories in the Massachusetts schools indicated that in the private, upper-middle class school, 65 percent of playground clusters were same-gender, compared with 80 percent in the matched, middle-class public school.[6] Social class may help account for the difference, but so may school culture; the private

school had initiated large group games, like one called "Ghost," which were not typed by gender. The extent of adult supervision also makes a difference. In general, there is more gender segregation when children are freer to construct their own activities.[7]

Gender arrangements in elementary schools have a "with-then-apart" structure (a term coined by Goffman, 1977). In any playground, cafeteria, or classroom, there are mixed-gender, as well as same-gender groups. Mixed-gender groups, and patterns of activity and solidarity which draw boys and girls together, need closer attention (see Thorne, 1986). On the other hand, children so often separate themselves by gender—ritualizing boundaries between girls and boys, and talking about them as separate "teams" or "sides"—that they create bounded spaces and relationships in which somewhat different subcultures are sustained. In some respects, then, boys and girls occupy separate worlds.

Most of the research on gender and children's social relations emphasizes patterns of separation, contrasting the social organization and cultures of girls' groups with those of boys (e.g., see Best, 1983; Eder, 1985; Eder and Hallinan, 1978; Goodwin, 1980a; Lever, 1976; Maccoby and Jacklin, 1974; Maltz and Borker, 1983; Savin-Williams, 1976; Waldrop and Halverson, 1975).[8] In brief summary: Boys tend to interact in larger and more publically-visible groups; they more often play outdoors, and their activities take up more space than those of girls. Boys engage in more physically aggressive play and fighting; their social relations tend to be overtly hierarchical and competitive. Organized sports are both a central activity and a major metaphor among boys; they use a language of "teams" and "captains" even when not engaged in sports.

Girls more often interact in smaller groups or friendship pairs, organized in shifting alliances. Compared with boys, they more often engage in turn-taking activities like jumprope and doing tricks on the bars, and they less often play organized sports. While boys use a rhetoric of contests and teams, girls describe their relations using language which stresses cooperation and "being nice." But the rhetorics of either group should not be taken for the full reality. Girls *do* engage in conflict, although it tends to take more indirect forms than the direct insults and challenges more often found in interactions among boys, and between girls and boys. In a study of disputes among children in a black working-class neighborhood, Goodwin (1980b) found that girls more often talked about the offenses of other girls in their absence. Hughes (1983; 1985) found that groups of third and fourth grade girls playing four-square used a rhetoric of "friends" and "nice" to justify, rather than avoid, competitive exchanges, and to construct complex large-group activity. This recent research is important in providing a more complex portrayal of girls' interactions—their patterns of competition and conflict, as well as cooperation.

Informal, gender segregated groups are powerful contexts for learning. Children may be especially attentive to one another when they are outside of adult surveillance and in situations not formally defined as ones of teaching and learning. Peers and friends are especially valued because they never seem to teach, or, as one child defined "friend": "they never tell you to wash your hands" (Rubin, 1973).

In the Massachusetts public school, when children asked her purpose, the observer said she was watching how children taught one another things through the rules of games. After incredulous stares, one boy easily turned this bizarre statement into a playground joke: "*She* thinks we teach each other something!" For children in solid positions inside gender segregated peer groups, such learning may appear seamless and almost invisible, associated with free choice and pleasure. Excluded children probably have fewer doubts about the teaching of peers.

Because of time spent and emotions invested in gender-differentiated worlds, girls and boys have somewhat different environments for learning. Gender-differentiated social relations and subcultures may teach distinctive patterns of talk (Maltz and Borker, 1983) and forms of prosocial and antisocial behavior (Maccoby, 1985). Our focus is on how the gender-specific contexts of middle and late childhood may help shape the sexual scripts—the social rela-

tions and meanings associated with desire—of adolescent boys and girls.

INTERACTION AMONG BOYS

In daily patterns of talk and play, boys in all-male groups often build towards heightened and intense moments, moments one can describe in terms of group arousal with excited emotions. This especially happens when boys violate rules. In a Massachusetts fifth grade, four boys played a game called "Flak" which one of them had invented. The game took place on a $8^1/_2'' \times 11''$ piece of paper with drawings of spaceships with guns on each of the corners. The airspace in the middle of the paper was covered by short lines representing metal flak. The purpose of the game was to shoot down all opponents by using one's hand as a gun while making shooting noises. The danger was that one's shots could ricochet off the flak, destroying one's spaceship. The random straying of flak was such that there was no way—if the game was played honestly—to survive one's own shots. Boys playing the game evolved implicit (never stated) rules about cheating: Cheating was permitted up to about one-fourth the distance to an opponent's corner, then the others could complain that flak would stop a player, but not before. At the instigation of the observer, the boys enthusiastically taught the game to the brightest girl in the class, who found the game "boring" and "crazy." The excitement the boys associated with the game was lost on her; she did not remark on the cheating.

Dirty words are a focus of rules, and rule breaking, in elementary schools. Both girls and boys know dirty words, but flaunting of the words and risking punishment for their use was more frequent in boys' than in girls' groups in all the schools we studied. In the middle-class Massachusetts public school, both male and female teachers punished ballplayers for frequent cries of "Shit" and "You fucked it up." But teachers were not present after lunch and before school, when most group-directed play took place. A female paraprofessional, who alone managed almost 150 children on the playground, never intervened to stop bad language in play; the male gym teacher who occasionally appeared on the field at after-lunch recess always did. Boys resumed dirty talk immediately after he passed them. Dirty talk is a stable part of the repertoire of boys' groups (also see Fine, 1980). Such talk defines their groups as, at least in part, outside the reach of the school's discipline.

Some of the dirty talk may be explicitly sexual, as it was in the Massachusetts public school when a group of five fifth-grade boys played a game called "Mad Lib" (also described in Luria, 1983). The game consisted of a paragraph (in this case, a section of a textbook discussing the U.S. Constitution) with key words deleted, to be filled in by the players. Making the paragraph absurd and violating rules to create excitement seemed to be the goal of the game. The boys clearly knew that their intentions were "dirty": they requested the field observer not to watch the game. Instead the observer negotiated a post-game interrogation on the rules of the game. The boys had completed the sentence, "The _____ was ratified in _____ in 1788," with "The *shit* was ratified in *Cuntville* in 1788."

The boys reacted with disbelief when the adult woman observer read the entire paragraph aloud, with no judgment, only requesting correction of pronunciation. The next day, in a gesture which connected rule violation to the interests of the male group, one of the boys asked the observer, "Hey lady, did ya watch the Celtics' game last night?" Sports, dirty words, and testing the limits are part of what boys teach boys how to do. The assumption seems to be: dirty words, sports interest and knowledge, and transgression of politeness are closely connected.

Rule Transgression: Comparing Girls' and Boys' Groups

Rule transgression in *public* is exciting to boys in their groups. Boys' groups are attentive to potential consequences of transgression, but, compared with girls, groups of boys appear to be greater risk-takers. Adults tending and teaching children do not often undertake discipline of an entire boys' group; the adults might lose out and they cannot risk that. Girls are more likely to affirm the reasonableness of rules, and, when it occurs, rule-breaking by girls is smaller

scale. This may be related to the smaller size of girls' groups and to adults' readiness to use rules on girls who seem to believe in them. It is dubious if an isolated pair of boys (a pair is the modal size of girls' groups) could get away with the rule-breaking that characterizes the larger male group. A boy may not have power, but a boys' *group* does. Teachers avoid disciplining whole groups of boys, partly for fear of seeming unfair. Boys rarely identify those who proposed direct transgressions and, when confronted, they claim (singly), "I didn't start it; why should I be punished?"

Boys are visibly excited when they break rules together—they are flushed as they play, they wipe their hands on their jeans, some of them look guilty. The Mad Lib game described above not only violates rules, it also evokes sexual meanings within an all-male group. Arousal is not purely individual; in this case, it is shared by the group. Farts and cunts—words used in the game—are part of a forbidden, undressed, sexual universe evoked in the presence of four other boys. The audience for the excitement is the gender-segregated peer group, where each boy increases the excitement by adding still a "worse" word. All of this takes place in a game ("rules") context, and hence with anonymity despite the close-up contact of the game.

While we never observed girls playing a Mad Lib game of this sort, some of our female students recall playing the game in grade school but giving it up after being caught by teachers, or out of fear of being caught. Both boys and girls may acquire knowledge of the game, but boys repeatedly perform it because their gender groups give support for transgression.

These instances all suggest that boys experience a shared, arousing context for transgression, with sustained gender group support for rule-breaking. Girls' groups may engage in rule-breaking, but the gender group's support for repeated public transgression is far less certain. The smaller size of girls' gender groupings in comparison with those of boys, and girls' greater susceptibility to rules and social control by teachers, make girls' groups easier to control. Boys' larger groups give each transgressor a degree of anonymity. Anonymity—which means less probability of detection and punishment—enhances the contagious excitement of rule-breaking.

The higher rates of contagious excitement, transgression, and limit-testing in boys' groups means that when they are excited, boys are often "playing" to male audiences. The public nature of such excitement forges bonds among boys. This kind of bonding is also evident when boys play team sports, and when they act aggressively toward marginal or isolated boys. Such aggression is both physical and verbal (taunts like "sissy," "fag," or "mental"). Sharing a target of aggression may be another source of arousal for groups of boys.[9]

The Tie to Sexuality in Males

When Gagnon and Simon (1973) argued that there are gender-differentiated sexual scripts in adolescence, they implied what our observations suggest: the gender arrangements and subcultures of middle childhood prepare the way for the sexual scripts of adolescence. Fifth and sixth grade boys share pornography, in the form of soft-core magazines like *Playboy* and *Penthouse,* with great care to avoid confiscation. Like the Mad Lib games with their forbidden content, soft-core magazines are also shared in all-male contexts, providing explicit knowledge about what is considered sexually arousing and about attitudes and fantasies. Since pornography is typically forbidden for children in both schools and families, this secret sharing occurs in a context of rule-breaking.

While many theorists since Freud have stressed the importance of boys loosening ties and identification with females (as mother surrogates), few theorists have questioned why "communally-aroused" males do not uniformly bond sexually to other males. If the male groups of fifth and sixth grade are the forerunners of the "frankly" heterosexual gender groups of the junior and high school years, what keeps these early groups from open homosexual expression? Scripting in same-gender peer groups may, in fact, be more about gender than about sexual orientation. Boys, who will later view themselves as having homosexual or heterosexual preferences, are learning patterns of masculinity. The answer may also lie in the teaching of homophobia.

By the fourth grade, children, especially boys, have begun to use homophobic labels—"fag," "faggot," "queer"—as terms of insult, especially for mar-

ginal boys. They draw upon sexual allusions (often not fully understood, except for their negative and contaminating import) to reaffirm male hierarchies and patterns of exclusion. As "fag" talk increases, relaxed and cuddling patterns of touch decrease among boys. Kindergarten and first-grade boys touch one another frequently and with ease, with arms around shoulders, hugs, and holding hands. By fifth grade, touch among boys becomes more constrained, gradually shifting to mock violence and the use of poking, shoving, and ritual gestures like "giving five" (flat hand slaps) to express bonding. The tough surface of boys' friendships is no longer like the gentle touching of girls in friendship.

"Fag talk," pornography, and the rules for segregation from girls create a separate, forbidden, and arousing area of life among boys. Group teasing for suspected crushes (which we discuss later) heightens the importance of the ambiguous opening toward the institutionalized heterosexuality of adolescence. The underside of this phenomenon is the beginning of homosexual relationships by some 11- and 12-year-old males and the rule-violating fantasy of early male masturbation (Bell et al., 1981; Kinsey et al., 1948). Fag talk helps keep homosexual experiments quiet and heightens the import of the lessons of pornography and gender segregation. Homoeroticism and homophobia coexist, often in tension, in male peer groups of middle childhood, and in some later adolescent and adult male groups. Our hunch is that the high *arousal* of the peer group may provide much of the cuing for the homophobic control. For males, navigating the onset of masturbation and social sexuality is another example of handling rule violations. Miller and Simon (1981) point out that violating rules is felt to impart excitement and an almost moral fervor to early sexual events.

INTERACTION AMONG GIRLS

In contrast with the larger, hierarchical organization of groups of boys, fourth- and fifth-grade girls more often organize themselves in pairs of "best friends" linked in shifting coalitions. These pairs are not "marriages"; the pattern is more one of dyads moving into triads, since girls often participate in two or more pairs at one time. This may result in quite complex social networks. Girls often talk about who is friends with or "likes" whom; they continually negotiate the parameters of friendships.

For example, in the California school, Chris, a fifth-grade girl, frequently said that Kathryn was her "best friend." Kathryn didn't proclaim the friendship as often; she also played and talked a lot with Judy.[10] After watching Kathryn talk to Judy during a transition period in the classroom, Chris went over, took Kathryn aside, and said with an accusing tone, "You talk to Judy more than me." Kathryn responded defensively, "I talk to you as much as I talk to Judy."

In talking about their relationships with one another, girls use a language of "friends," "nice," and "mean." They talk about who is most and least "liked," which anticipates the concern about "popularity" found among junior high and high school girls (Eder, 1985). Since relationships sometimes break off, girls hedge bets by structuring networks of potential friends. The activity of constructing and breaking dyads is often carried out through talk with third parties. Some of these processes are evident in a sequence recorded in a Massachusetts school:

> The fifth-grade girls, Flo and Pauline, spoke of themselves as "best friends," while Flo said she was "sort of friends" with Doris. When a lengthy illness kept Pauline out of school, Flo spent more time with Doris. One day Doris abruptly broke off her friendship with Flo and began criticizing her to other girls. Flo, who felt very badly, went around asking others in their network, "What did I do? Why is Doris being so mean? Why is she telling everyone not to play with me?"

On school playgrounds girls are less likely than boys to organize themselves into team sports. They more often engage in small-scale, turn-taking kinds of play. When they jump rope or play on the bars, they take turns performing and watching others perform in stylized movements which may involve considerable skill. Sometimes girls work out group choreographies, counting and jumping rope in unison, or swinging around the bars. In other synchronized body rituals, clusters of fifth- and sixth-grade girls practice cheerleading routines or dance steps. In interactions with

one another, girls often use relaxed gestures of physical intimacy, moving bodies in harmony, coming close in space, and reciprocating cuddly touches.[11] We should add that girls also poke and grab, pin one another from behind, and use hand-slap rituals like "giving five," although less frequently than boys.

When the teacher of a combined fourth- and fifth-grade classroom in the California school pitted girls against boys for spelling and math contests, there were vivid gender group differences in the use of touch, space, and movement. During the contests the girls sat close together on desk tops, their arms and shoulders touching. Occasionally a gesture, such as a push or a lean way to one side, would move like a wave through their line. When one of them got a right answer, she would walk along the row of girls, "giving five" before returning to her place. The boys mostly stood along the other side of the classroom, leaning against desks; their bodies didn't touch except for "giving five" when one of them got a right answer.

In other gestures of intimacy, which one rarely sees among boys, girls stroke or comb their friends' hair. They notice and comment on one another's physical appearance such as haircuts or clothes. Best friends monitor one another's emotions. They share secrets and become mutually vulnerable through self-disclosure, with an implicit demand that the expression of one's inadequacy will induce the friend to disclose a related inadequacy. In contrast, disclosure of weakness among boys is far more likely to be exposed to others through joking or horsing around.

Implications for Sexuality

Compared with boys, girls are more focused on constructing intimacy and talking about one-to-one relationships. Their smaller and more personal groups provide less protective anonymity than the larger groups of boys. Bonding thorough mutual self-disclosure, especially through disclosure of vulnerability, and breaking off friendships by "acting mean," teach the creation, sustaining, and ending of emotionally intimate relations. Girls' preoccupation with who is friends with whom, and their monitoring of cues of "nice" and "mean," liking and disliking, teach them strategies for forming and leaving personal relationships. In their interactions girls show knowledge of motivational rules for dyads and insight into both outer and inner realities of social relationships. Occasionally, girls indicate that they see boys as lacking such "obvious" knowledge.

Girls' greater interest in verbally sorting out relationships was evident during an incident in the Massachusetts public school. The fifth-grade boys often insulted John, a socially isolated boy who was not good at sports. On one such occasion during gym class, Bill, a high status boy, angrily yelled "creep" and "mental" when John fumbled the ball. The teacher stopped the game and asked the class to discuss the incident. Both boys and girls vigorously talked about "words that kill," with Bill saying he was sorry for what he said, that he had lost control in the excitement of the game. The girls kept asking, "How could anyone do that?" The boys kept returning to, "When you get excited, you do things you don't mean." Both girls and boys understood and verbalized the dilemma, but after the group discussion the boys dropped the topic. The girls continued to converse, with one repeatedly asking, "How could Bill be so stupid? Didn't he know how he'd make John feel?"

When talking with one another, girls use dirty words much less often than boys do. The shared arousal and bonding among boys which we think occurs around public rule-breaking has as its counterpart the far less frequent giggling sessions of girls, usually in groups larger than three. The giggling often centers on carefully guarded topics, sometimes, although not always, about boys.

The sexually related discourse of girls focuses less on dirty words than on themes of romance. In the Michigan school, first- and second-grade girls often jumped rope to rhymes about romance. A favorite was, "Down in the Valley Where the Green Grass Grows," a saga of heterosexual romance which, with the name of the jumper and a boy of her choice filled in, concludes: ". . . along came Jason, and kissed her on the cheek . . . first comes love, then comes marriage, then along comes Cindy with a baby carriage." In the Michigan and California schools, fourth- and fifth-grade girls talked privately about crushes and about which boys were "cute," as shown in the following incident recorded in the lunchroom of the Michigan school:

> The girls and boys from one of the fourth-grade classes sat at separate tables. Three of the girls talked as they peered at a nearby table of fifth-grade boys, "Look behind you," one said. "Ooh," said the other two. "That boy's named Todd." "I know where my favorite guy is . . . there," another gestured with her head while her friends looked.

In the Massachusetts private school, fifth-grade girls plotted about how to get particular boy-girl pairs together.

As Gagnon and Simon (1973) have suggested, two strands of sexuality are differently emphasized among adolescent girls and boys. Girls emphasize and learn about the emotional and romantic before the explicitly sexual. The sequence for boys is the reverse; commitment to sexual acts precedes commitment to emotion-laden, intimate relationships and the rhetoric of romantic love. Dating and courtship, Gagon and Simon suggest, are processes in which each sex teaches the other what each wants and expects. The exchange, as they point out, does not always go smoothly. Indeed, in heterosexual relationships among older adults, tension often persists between the scripts (and felt needs) of women and of men (Chodorow, 1978; Rubin, 1983).

Other patterns initially learned in the girls' groups of middle childhood later may be worked into more explicitly sexual scripts. In all the schools we studied, emphasis on appearance increased over the course of fifth grade, and symbols of cultural adolescence—lip gloss (kept hidden in desks and clandestinely passed from girl to girl), hairbrushes, and long-tailed combs—began to appear. However, the girls who first began to use these teen artifacts were not necessarily the ones who showed physical signs of puberty. In the California school, fourth- and fifth-grade girls talked about who was prettiest and confessed feelings of being ugly. Girls remark on their own and others' appearance long before they talk about issues of attractiveness to boys. The concern with appearance, and the pattern of performing and being watched, may be integrated into sexual expression later.

CHILDREN'S SEXUAL MEANINGS AND THE CONSTRUCTION OF GENDER ARRANGEMENTS

Girls and boys, who spend considerable time in gender-separate groups, learn different patterns of interaction which, we have argued, lay the groundwork for the sexual scripts of adolescence and adulthood. However, sexuality is not simply delayed until adolescence. Children engage in sexual practices—kissing, erotic forms of touch, masturbation, and sometimes intercourse (see Constantine and Martinson, 1981; Finkelhor, 1979). As school-based observers, we saw only a few overt sexual activities among children, mostly incidents of public, cross-gender kissing, surrounded by teasing, chasing, and laughter.

In elementary school life the overtly sexual is mostly a matter of words, labels, and charged rituals of play. In identifying this behavior as "sexual," we are cautious about imposing adult perspectives. When children say words like "fag" or "fuck," they rarely share adult meanings, as was apparent in their use of "fag" essentially as a synonym for "nerd" and as an epithet occasionally applied to girls as well as to boys.

Although their sexual knowledge is fragmentary and different from that of adults, children learn early on that certain words and gestures are forbidden and charged with special meaning. Adults and children jointly construct the domain considered to be "sexual." For example, both adults and children know and sometimes enforce taboos against the use of dirty words in school, as shown in an incident in the library of the California school:

> "Miss Smith, Donny is being a bad boy, he's being nasty, he's looking up sex," a fourth-grade girl told the teacher as they stood near the card catalogue. "No I'm not, I'm looking up sunset," Donny said defensively.

Heterosexual Teasing and the Importance of Third Parties

The special loading of sexual words and gestures makes them useful for accomplishing nonsexual purposes. Sexual idioms provide a major resource which children draw upon as they construct and maintain gender segregation. Through the years of elementary school, children use with increasing frequency heterosexual idioms—claims that a particular girl or boy "likes," "has a crush on," or is "goin with" someone from the other gender group. Unlike alternative, non-gendered terms for affiliation ("friends," "playmates"), heterosexual idioms imply that interaction between girls and boys has sexual overtones. Children rarely use sexual language to describe within-gender interaction. From an early age, the erotic is prescriptively heterosexual, and male (but, significantly, much less female) homophobic.

Children's language for heterosexual relationships consists of a very few, often repeated, and sticky words. In a context of teasing, the charge that a particular boy "likes" a particular girl (or vice versa) may be hurled like an insult. The difficulty children have in countering such accusations was evident in a conversation between the observer and a group of third-grade girls in the lunchroom of the Michigan school:

> Susan asked me what I was doing, and I said I was observing the things children do and play. Nicole volunteered, "I like running, boys chase all the girls. See Tim over there? Judy chases him all around the school. She likes him." Judy, sitting across the table, quickly responded, "I hate him. I like him for a friend." "Tim loves Judy," Nicole said in a loud, sing-song voice.

Sexual and romantic teasing marks social hierarchies. The most popular children and the pariahs—the lowest status, excluded children—are most frequently mentioned as targets of "liking." Linking someone with a pariah suggests shared contamination and is an especially vicious tease.

When a girl or boy publicly says that she or he "likes" someone or has a boyfriend or girlfriend, that person defines the romantic situation and is less susceptible to teasing than those targeted by someone else. Crushes may be secretly revealed to friends, a mark of intimacy, especially among girls. The entrusted may then go public with the secret ("Wendy likes John"), which may be experienced as betrayal, but which also may be a way of testing the romantic waters. Such leaks, like those of government officials, can be denied or acted upon by the original source of information.

Third parties—witnesses and kibbitzers—are central to the structure of heterosexual teasing. The teasing constructs dyads (very few of them actively "couples"), but within the control of larger gender groups. Several of the white fifth graders in the Michigan and California schools and some of the black students in the Massachusetts schools occasionally went on dates, which were much discussed around the schools. Same-gender groups provide launching pads, staging grounds, and retreats for heterosexual couples, both real and imagined. Messengers and emissaries go between groups, indicating who likes whom and checking out romantic interest. By the time "couples" actually get together (if they do at all), the groups and their messengers have provided a network of constructed meanings, a kind of agenda for the pair. As we have argued, gender-divided peer groups sustain different meanings of the sexual. They also regulate heterosexual behavior by helping to define the emerging sexual scripts of adolescence (who "likes" whom, who might "go with" whom, what it means to be a couple).

In the California and Michigan schools, when children reported news from the playground to an adult observer, they defined two types of activities as especially newsworthy: physical fights (who fought with and beat up whom), and who "liked," had a crush on, or was "goin with" whom. Like fights, purported romantic liaisons (e.g., "Frank likes Bonnie") are matters of public notice and of widespread rumor and teasing. The charge of "liking" or having a "girlfriend" or "boyfriend" may be constructed from very small clues—for example, that Frank sat down by or talked with Bonnie, or that he chose her as a partner in PE.

When a girl or boy consistently initiates talk or play with someone of the other gender group, she or he risks being teased. This risk is so severe that close friendships between boys and girls that are formed and maintained in other places like neighborhoods or church sometimes go underground during the school day.[12] Heterosexual meanings, which one might think would unite boys and girls, in fact may keep them apart. Children use heterosexual teasing to maintain and police boundaries between "the girls" and "the boys," defined as separate groups.

Heterosexually Charged Rituals

Boundaries between boys and girls are also emphasized and maintained by heterosexually charged rituals like cross-sex chasing.[13] Formal games of tag and informal episodes of chasing punctuate life on playgrounds. The informal episodes usually open with a provocation—taunts like "You can't get me!" or "Slobber monster!," bodily pokes, or the grabbing of possessions like a hat or scarf. The person who is provoked may ignore the taunt or poke, handle it verbally ("leave me alone!"), or respond by chasing. After a chasing sequence, which may end after a short run or a pummeling, the chaser and chased may switch roles.

Chasing has a gendered structure. When boys chase one another, they often end up wrestling or in mock fights. When girls chase girls, they less often wrestle one another to the ground. Unless organized as a formal game like "freeze tag," same-gender chasing goes unnamed and usually undiscussed. But children set apart cross-gender chasing with special names—"girls chase the boys"; "boys chase the girls"; "the chase"; "chasers"; "chase and kiss" "kiss-chase"; "kissers and chasers"; "kiss or kill"—and with animated talk about the activity. The names vary by region and school, but inevitably contain both gender and sexual meanings.[14]

When boys and girls chase one another, they become, by definition, separate teams. Gender terms override individual identities, especially for the other team: "Help, a girl's chasin' me!"; "C'mon Sarah, let's get that boy"; "Tony, help save me from the girls." Individuals may call for help from, or offer help to, others of their gender. In acts of treason, they may also grab someone of their gender and turn them over to the opposing team, as when, in the Michigan school, Ryan grabbed Billy from behind, wrestled him to the ground, and then called, "Hey girls, get 'im."

Names like "chase and kiss" mark the sexual meanings of cross-gender chasing. The threat of kissing—most often girls threatening to kiss boys—is a ritualized form of provocation. Teachers and aides are often amused by this form of play among children in the lower grades; they are more perturbed by cross-gender chasing among fifth- and sixth-graders, perhaps because at those ages some girls "have their development" (breasts make sexual meanings seem more consequential), and because of the more elaborate patterns of touch and touch avoidance in chasing rituals among older children. The principal of one Michigan school forbade the sixth-graders from playing "pom-pom," a complicated chasing game, because it entailed "inappropriate touch."

Cross-gender chasing is sometimes structured around rituals of pollution, such as "cooties," where individuals or groups are treated as contaminating or carrying "germs." Children have rituals for transferring cooties (usually touching someone else and shouting "You've got cooties!"), for immunization (e.g., writing "CV" for "cootie vaccination" on their arms), and for eliminating cooties (e.g., saying "no gives" or using "cootie catchers" made of folded paper [described in Knapp and Knapp, 1976]). Boys may transmit cooties, but cooties usually originate with girls. One version of cooties played in Michigan is called "girl stain"; the fourth-graders whom Karkau (1973) describes used the phrase, "girl touch." Although cooties is framed as play, the import may be serious. Female pariahs—the ultimate school untouchables by virtue of gender and some added stigma such as being overweight or from a very poor family—are sometimes called "cootie queens" or "cootie girls." Conversely, we have never heard or read about "cootie kings" or "cootie boys."

In these cross-gender rituals girls are defined as sexual. Boys sometimes threaten to kiss girls, but it is girls' kisses and touch which are deemed especially contaminating. Girls more often use the threat of kissing to tease boys and to make them run away, as in this example recorded among fourth-graders on the playground of the California school:

> Smiling and laughing, Lisa and Jill pulled a fourth-grade boy along by his hands, while a group of girls sitting on the jungle-gym called out, "Kiss him, kiss him." Grabbing at his hair, Lisa said to Jill, "Wanna kiss Jonathan?" Jonathan got away, and the girls chased after him. "Jill's gonna kiss your hair," Lisa yelled.

The use of kisses as a threat is doubled-edged, since the power comes from the threat of pollution. A girl who frequently uses this threat may be stigmatized as a "kisser."

Gender-marked rituals of teasing, chasing, and pollution heighten the boundaries between boys and girls. They also convey assumptions which get worked into later sexual scripts: (1) that girls and boys are members of distinctive, opposing, and sometimes antagonistic groups; (2) that cross-gender contact is potentially sexual and contaminating, fraught with both pleasure and danger; and (3) that girls are more sexually-defined (and polluting) than boys.

These meanings are not always evoked. Girls and boys sometimes interact in relaxed ways, and gender is not always salient in their encounters (see Thorne, 1986). But sexual meanings, embedded in patterns of teasing and ritualized play, help maintain gender divisions; they enhance social distance, asymmetry, and antagonism between girls and boys. These patterns may persist in the sexual scripts of adolescence.

CONCLUSION

Social scientists have often viewed the heterosexual dating rituals of adolescence—when girls and boys "finally" get together—as the concluding stage after the separate, presumably non-sexual, boys' and girls' groups that are so prevalent in childhood. We urge a closer look at the organization of sexuality and of gender in middle and late childhood. The gender-divided social worlds of children are not totally asexual. And same-gender groups have continuing import in the more overtly sexual scripts of adolescence and adulthood.

From an early age "the sexual" is prescriptively heterosexual and male homophobic. Children draw on sexual meanings to maintain gender segregation—to make cross-gender interaction risky and to mark and ritualize boundaries between "the boys" and "the girls." In their separate gender groups, girls and boys learn somewhat different patterns of bonding—boys sharing the arousal of group rule-breaking; girls emphasizing the construction of intimacy, and themes of romance. Coming to adolescent sexual intimacy from different and asymmetric gender subcultures, girls and boys bring somewhat different needs, capacities, and types of knowledge.

It is obvious that heterosexual acts require some form of cross-gender interaction. Among early adolescents, social support for such interaction comes from separate girls' and boys' groups that construct couples through talk and teasing long before dating is prevalent. Girls' and boys' groups do not measure with the same ruler; they promote different sexual meanings. An argument may be made that the audiences (those who share our measures) remain same-gender peer groups later as well as early in life. Perhaps our culture's concern with the question of the sex of the sexual partner has obscured how much our sexual life is tied to group gender arrangements. Gender segregation and its effects on the narrowing of the audiences to which we play are not limited to childhood. The social supports for gender segregation—in work and other institutions—are lifelong. Their effects extend into the organization of gender and of sexuality in later life.

Transitions not only involve continuity, but also disjuncture and loss. By the sixth and seventh grades, culturally-defined heterosexual rituals (like "goin with") have begun to replace the more relaxed and non-sexualized contact found between some girls and boys at earlier ages. Adult women who were "tomboys" often speak of adolescence as a painful time when they were pushed away from comfortable participation in boys' activities. Other adult women say they experienced entry into adolescent rituals of heterosexual dating as a time of loss, when intense, even erotic ties with other girls were altered and even suppressed (Rich, 1980).

With the shift to adolescence, heterosexual encounters assume more importance. They may alter relations in same-gender groups. For example, Janet Schofield (1982) reports that for sixth- and seventh-grade children in a middle school, the popularity of girls with other girls was affected by their popularity with boys, while boys' status with other boys did not depend on their relations with girls.

As it is defined in this culture, entry into adolescence entails the assumption of sexuality as a core of identity. How, in the shift away from the less sexual definitions of gender in childhood, does sexuality become seen and experienced as an intrinsic "personal" characteristic? How are different sexualities constructed? Analysis of the somewhat separate systems of gender and sexuality, with attention to

changes over the life course, may begin to provide answers to such questions.

Notes

1. Physiological psychologists define "sex" as the structures and functions (dimorphisms) of biological *maleness* and *femaleness*. They define "sexuality" as the social meanings that are attached to sex—i.e., masculinity, femininity, learned stimuli for sexual arousal. By these definitions, sexuality includes the *social* meanings that transform males and females to boys and girls, men and women—that is, "gender." Sexuality also includes the learning of the wide range of stimuli (virtually everything beyond direct genital touch) that produce sexual arousal (see Luria and Rose, 1979). Depending on one's definitions, this paper deals with two aspects of what physiological psychologists call sexuality: gender *and* learned aspects of sexual arousal and sexual meanings, or what most sociologists call gender and sexuality (learned arousal/social meanings). Writing for a sociological audience, we—a sociologist and a psychologist—have chosen the latter language and conceptualization. Our usage is clarified in the body of the paper.

2. In the western world, this definition is made possible by the physical separation of the sexual life of adults from the everyday life of children, a privilege not extended to families who inhabit one room in much of the rest of the world.

3. In this paper, we have set out to trace general patterns in age-based relationships between sexuality and gender. We have not, except incidentally, explored possible variations by region, social class, and race or ethnicity. All of these dimensions should be more fully addressed. For example, our data suggest that the transition to adolescent sexual scripts begins earlier in working-class than in middle-class or upper-middle-class schools. However, the transition began earlier in the Massachusetts, upper-middle-class private school than in the more middle-class public school. The relation of class, type of school, and age of transition to adolescent sexual scripts is obviously complex.

4. On the special challenges of fieldwork with children, see Fine and Glassner (1979) and Mandell (1985).

5. We will discuss the joint construction of "dirty words" later.

6. All playground clusters were counted, regardless of activity; such an inventory characterizes groups of children, rather than individuals. This may overrate the "quality" of cross-gender activity when, for example, a single girl integrates a soccer game, or when one boy chases a large group of girls (both types of groups, as well as those with more even gender ratios, were counted as mixed-gender).

7. In the private Massachusetts school, which had less gender segregation, children could stay indoors after lunch. Thus, they were more often under adult supervision than the public

school children who, during the noontime recess, were all on the playground without adults organizing their activity.

8. In this paper we also use a comparative strategy, emphasizing the occasions when girls and boys are apart, and the ways they mark and ritualize gender boundaries. A full analysis would also stress the occasions of "with": pressures for gender integration, occasions when gender is muted in salience, the dynamics of mixed-gender groups, and the ways that girls and boys *share* culture (including the particular activities and meanings associated with being in fourth or fifth grade). A full analysis would also examine variations among girls and among boys: specific groups and networks; the vantage points of those at the margins as well as at the center of same-gender groups; and the experiences of those who frequently join the groups and activities of the other gender.

9. For a related analysis of bonding among adult men, see Lyman (Forthcoming).

10. All names in this paper are fictitious.

11. These patterns accord with other studies of gender differentiation in the use of space and touch; see Henley, 1977. We noticed a pattern which distinguishes touch among children from patterns adults use to mark status. In adult hierarchies, subordinates tend to avoid initiating touch to dominate (Henley, 1977). But, in a sort of courting gesture, subordinate children (both girls and boys) often initiate touch to more dominant or popular children of the same gender. Refusing these bids for acceptance or liking, the more popular sometimes shake away such touch they also may verbally refuse physical contact ("Don't do that, it bothers me"). These gestures are powerful markers of social position.

12. This is especially a risk for lower status children. Those of top status run less risk in crossing the gender divide.

13. See Thorne (1986) for more extended analysis of the marking and crossing of gender boundaries among children.

14. This form of play is briefly analyzed in Best (1983), Finnan (1982), and Sluckin (1981).

REFERENCES

Bell, Alan T., Martin S. Weinberg, and Sue K. Hammsersmith. 1981. Sexual Preference: Its Development in Men and Women. Bloomington: Indiana University Press.

Best, Raphaela. 1983. We've All Got Scars. Bloomington: Indiana University Press.

Chodorow, Nancy. 1978. The Reproduction of Mothering. Berkeley: University of California Press.

Constantine, Larry L. and Floyd M. Martinson. 1981. Children and Sex. Boston: Little, Brown.

Eder, Donna. 1985. "The cycle of popularity: interpersonal relations among female adolescents." Sociology of Education 58:154–65.

Eder, Donna and Maureen T. Hallinan. 1978. "Sex differences in children's friendships." American Sociological Review 43:237–50.

Fine, Gary Alan. 1980. "The natural history of preadolescent male friendship groups." Pp. 293–320 in Hugh C. Foot, Antony J. Chapman and Jean R. Smith (eds.), Friendship and Social Relations in Children. New York: Wiley.

Fine, Gary Alan and Barry Glassner. 1979. "Participant observation with children: promise and problems." Urban Life 8:153–74.

Finkelhor, David. 1979. Sexually Victimized Children. New York: Free Press.

Finnan, Christine R. 1982. "The ethnography of children's spontaneous play." Pp. 358–80 in George Spindler (ed.), Doing the Ethnography of Schooling. New York: Holt, Rinehart & Winston.

Gagnon, John H. and William Simon. 1973. Sexual Conduct. Chicago: Aldine.

Goffman, Erving. 1977. "The arrangement between the sexes." Theory and Society 4:301–36.

Goodwin, Marjorie Harness. 1980a. "Directive-response speech sequences in girls' and boys' task activities." Pp. 157–73 in Sally McConnell-Ginet, Ruth Borker, and Nelly Furman (eds.), Women and Language in Literature and Society. New York: Praeger.

———. 1980b. "'He-said-she-said': formal cultural procedures for the construction of a gossip dispute activity." American Ethnologist 7:674–95.

Henley, Nancy. 1977. Body Politics. Englewood, NJ: Prentice-Hall.

Hughes, Linda A. 1983. Beyond the Rules of the Game: Girls' Gaming at a Friends' School. Unpublished Ph.D. dissertation, University of Pennsylvania Graduate School of Education.

———. 1985. "The study of children's gaming." In Brian Sutton-Smith, Jay Mechling and Thomas Johnson (eds.), A Handbook of Children's Folklore. Washington, DC: Smithsonian.

Karkau, Kevin. 1973. "Sexism in the fourth grade." Pittsburgh: KNOW, Inc.

Kinsey, Alfred C., Wardell B. Pomeroy, and Clyde E. Martin. 1948. Sexual Behavior in the Human Male. Philadelphia: Saunders.

Kinsey, Alfred C., Wardell B. Pomeroy, Clyde E. Martin, and Paul H. Gebhard. 1953. Sexual Behavior in the Human Female. Philadelphia: Saunders.

Knapp, Mary and Herbert Knapp. 1976. One Potato, Two Potato. New York: W.W. Norton.

Lever, Janet. 1976. "Sex differences in the games children play." Social Problems 23:478–87.

Lockheed, Marlaine E. 1985. "Sex equity in classroom organization and climate." Pp. 189–217 in Susan S. Klein (ed.), Handbook for Achieving Sex Equity Through Education. Baltimore, MD: Johns Hopkins University Press.

Luria, Zella. 1983. "Sexual fantasy and pornography: two cases of girls brought up with pornography." Archives of Sexual Behavior 11:395–404.

Luria, Zella and Mitchel D. Rose. 1979. The Psychology of Human Sexuality. New York: Wiley.

Lyman, Peter. 1987. "The fraternal bond as a joking relationship." In Michael Kimmel (ed.), Changing Men. Beverly coming Hills, CA: Sage.

Maccoby, Eleanor. 1985. "Social groupings in childhood: their relationship to prosocial and antisocial behavior in boys and girls." Pp. 263–84 in Dan Olweas, Jack Block, and Marian Radke-Yarrow (eds.), Development of Antisocial and Prosocial Behavior. San Diego, CA: Academic Press.

Maccoby, Eleanor and Carol Jacklin. 1974. The Psychology of Sex Differences. Stanford, CA: Stanford University Press.

Maltz, Daniel N. and Ruth A. Borker. 1983. "A cultural approach to male-female miscommunication." Pp. 195–216 in John J. Gumperz (ed.), Language and Social Identity. New York: Cambridge University Press.

Mandell, Nancy. 1985. "The research role in observational fieldwork with preschool children." Paper presented at annual meetings of Eastern Sociological Association.

Miller, Patricia Y. and William Simon. 1981. "The development of sexuality in adolescence." Pp. 383–407 in Joseph Adelson (ed.), Handbook of Adolescent Psychology. New York: Wiley.

Rich, Adrienne. 1980. "Compulsory heterosexuality and lesbian existence." Signs 5:631–60.

Rubin, Lillian. 1983. Intimate Strangers. New York: Harper and Row.

Rubin, Zick. 1973. Liking and Loving. New York: Holt.

Savin-Williams, Richard C. 1976. "An ethological study of dominance formation and maintenance in a group of human adolescents." Child Development 47:972–79.

Schofield, Janet. 1982. Black and White in School. New York: Praeger.

Sluckin, Andy. 1981. Growing Up in the Playground. London: Routledge & Kegan Paul.

Thorne, Barrie. 1986. "Girls and boys together . . . but mostly apart: gender arrangements in elementary schools." Pp. 167–84 in Willard W. Hartup and Zick Rubin (eds.), Relationships and Development. Hillsdale, NJ: Lawrence Erlbaum.

Waldrop, Mary F. and Charles F. Halverson. 1975. "Intensive and extensive peer behavior: longitudinal and cross-sectional analysis." Child Development 46:16–19.

3.2 DOING DESIRE
Adolescent Girls' Struggles for/with Sexuality

Deborah L. Tolman

> In order to perpetuate itself, every oppression must corrupt or distort those various sources of power within the culture of the oppressed that can provide energy for change. For women, this has meant suppression of the erotic as a considered source of power and information within our lives. (Lorde 1984, 53)

Recent research suggests that adolescence is the crucial moment in the development of psychological disempowerment for many women (e.g., Brown and Gilligan 1992; Gilligan 1990). As they enter adolescence, many girls may lose an ability to speak about what they know, see, feel, and experience evident in childhood as they come under cultural pressure to be "nice girls" and ultimately "good women" in adolescence. When their bodies take on women's contours, girls begin to be seen as sexual, and sexuality becomes an aspect of adolescent girls' lives; yet "nice" girls and "good" women are not supposed to be sexual outside of heterosexual, monogamous marriage (Tolman

From Gender & Society 8(3): 324–42. Copyright © 1994 by Sage Publications, Inc. Reprinted by permission of Sage Publications, Inc.

1991). Many girls experience a "crisis of connection," a relational dilemma of how to be oneself and stay in relationships with others who may not want to know the truth of girls' experiences (Gilligan 1989). In studies of adolescent girls' development, many girls have demonstrated the ironic tendency to silence their own thoughts and feelings for the sake of relationships, when what they think and feel threatens to be disruptive (Brown and Gilligan 1992). At adolescence, the energy needed for resistance to crushing conventions of femininity often begins to get siphoned off for the purpose of maintaining cultural standards that stand between women and their empowerment. Focusing explicitly on embodied desire, Tolman and Debold (1993) observed similar patterns in the process of girls learning to look at, rather than experience, themselves, to know themselves from the perspective of men, thereby losing touch with their own bodily feelings and desires. It is at this moment in their development that many women will start to experience and develop ways of responding to their own sexual feelings. Given these realities, what are adolescent girls' experiences of sexual desire? How do girls enter their sexual lives and learn to negotiate or respond to their sexuality?

Despite the real gains that feminism and the sexual revolution achieved in securing women's reproductive rights and increasing women's sexual liberation (Rubin 1990), the tactics of silencing and denigrating women's sexual desire are deeply entrenched in this patriarchal society (Brown 1991). The Madonna/whore dichotomy is alternately virulent and subtle in the cultures of adolescents (Lees 1986; Tolman 1992). Sex education curricula name male adolescent sexual desire; girls are taught to recognize and to keep a lid on the sexual desire of boys but not taught to acknowledge or even to recognize their own sexual feelings (Fine 1988; Tolman 1991). The few feminist empirical studies of girls' sexuality suggest that sexual desire is a complicated, important experience for adolescent girls about which little is known. In an ethnographic study, Fine noticed that adolescent girls' sexuality was acknowledged by adults in school, but in terms that denied the sexual subjectivity of girls; this "missing discourse of desire" was, however, not always absent from the ways girls themselves spoke about their sexual experiences (Fine 1988). Rather than being "educated," girls' bodies are suppressed under surveillance and silenced in the schools (see also Lesko 1988). Although Fine ably conveys the existence of girls' discourse of desire, she does not articulate that discourse. Thompson collected 400 girls' narratives about sexuality, romance, contraception and pregnancy (Thompson 1984, 1990) in which girls' desire seems frequently absent or not relevant to the terms of their sexual relationships. The minority of girls who spoke of sexual pleasure voiced more sexual agency than girls whose experiences were devoid of pleasure. Within the context of girls' psychological development, Fine's and Thompson's work underscore the need to understand what girls' experiences of their sexual desire are like.

A psychological analysis of this experience for girls can contribute an understanding of both the possibilities and limits for sexual freedom for women in the current social climate. By identifying how the culture has become anchored in the interior of women's lives—an interior that is birthed through living in the exterior of material conditions and relationships—this approach can keep distinct women's psychological responses to sexual oppression and also the sources of that oppression. This distinction is necessary for avoiding the trap of blaming women for the ways our minds and bodies have become constrained.

METHODOLOGICAL DISCUSSION
Sample and Data Collection

To examine this subject, I interviewed 30 girls who were juniors in an urban and a suburban public high school ($n = 28$) or members of a gay and lesbian youth group ($n = 2$). They were 16.5 years old on average and randomly selected. The girls in the larger study are a heterogeneous group, representing different races and ethnic backgrounds (Black, including Haitian and African American; Latina, including Puerto Rican and Colombian; Euro-American, including Eastern and Western European), religions (Catholic, Jewish, and Protestant), and sexual experiences. With the exception of one Puerto Rican girl, all of the girls from the suburban school were Euro-American; the racial/ethnic diversity in the sample is represented by the urban school. Interviews with school personnel confirmed that the student population of the urban school was almost exclusively poor or working class and the students in the suburban school were middle and upper-middle class. This information is important in that my focus is on how girls' social environments shape their understanding of their sexuality. The fact that girls who live in the urban area experience the visibility of and discourse about violence, danger and the consequences of unprotected sex, and that the suburban girls live in a community that offers a veneer of safety and stability, informs their experiences of sexuality. Awareness of these features of the social contexts in which these girls are developing is essential for listening to and understanding their narratives about sexual experiences.

The data were collected in one-on-one, semistructured clinical interviews (Brown and Gilligan 1992). This method of interviewing consists of following a structured interview protocol that does not direct specific probes but elicits narratives. The interviewer listens carefully to a girl, taking in her voice, and responding with questions that will enable the girl to clarify her story and know she is being heard. In these interviews, I asked girls direct questions about desire to elicit descriptions and narratives. Most of the young women wove their concerns about danger into the narratives they told.

Analytic Strategy

To analyze these narratives, I used the Listening Guide—an interpretive methodology that joins hermeneutics and feminist standpoint epistemology (Brown et al. 1991). It is a voice-centered, relational method by which a researcher becomes a listener, taking in the voice of a girl, developing an interpretation of her experience. Through multiple readings of the same text, this method makes audible the "polyphonic and complex" nature of voice and experience (Brown and Gilligan 1992, 15). Both speaker and listener are recognized as individuals who bring thoughts and feelings to the text, acknowledging the necessary subjectivity of both participants. Self-consciously embedded in a standpoint acknowledging that patriarchal culture silences and obscures women's experiences, the method is explicitly psychological and feminist in pro-

viding the listener with an organized way to respond to the coded or indirect language of girls and women, especially regarding topics such as sexuality that girls and women are not supposed to speak of. This method leaves a trail of evidence for the listener's interpretation, and thus leaves room for other interpretations by other listeners consistent with the epistemological stance that there is multiple meaning in such stories. I present *a* way to understand the stories these young women chose to tell me, our story as I have heard and understood it. Therefore, in the interpretations that follow I include my responses, those of an adult woman, to these girls' words, providing information about girls' experiences of sexual desire much like countertransference informs psychotherapy.

Adolescent Girls' Experiences of Sexual Desire

The first layer of the complexity of girls' experiences of their sexual desire was revealed initially in determining whether or not they felt sexual feelings. A majority of these girls (two-thirds) said unequivocally that they experienced sexual desire; in them I heard a clear and powerful way of speaking about the experience of feeling desire that was explicitly relational and also embodied. Only three of the girls said they did not experience sexual feelings, describing silent bodies and an absence of or intense confusion about romantic or sexual relationships. The remaining girls evidenced confusion or spoke in confusing ways about their own sexual feelings. Such confusion can be understood as a psychic solution to sexual feelings that arise in a culture that denigrates, suppresses, and heightens the dangers of girls' sexuality and in which contradictory messages about women's sexuality abound.

For the girls who said they experienced sexual desire, I turned my attention to how they said they responded to their sexual feelings. What characterized their responses was a sense of struggle; the question of "doing desire"—that is, what to do when they felt sexual desire—was not straightforward for any of them. While speaking of the power of their embodied feelings, the girls in this sample described the difficulties that their sexual feelings posed, being aware of both the potential for pleasure and the threat of danger that their desire holds for them. The struggle took different shapes for different girls, with some notable patterns emerging. Among the urban girls, the focus was on how to stay safe from bodily harm, in and out of the context of relational or social consequences, whereas among the suburban girls the most pronounced issue was how to maintain a sense of themselves as "good" and "normal" girls (Tolman 1992). In this article, I will offer portraits of three girls. By focusing on three girls in depth, I can balance an approach to "variance" with the kind of case study presentation that enables me to illustrate both similarities and differences in how girls in the larger sample spoke about their sexual feelings. These three girls represent different sexual preferences—one heterosexual, one bisexual, and one lesbian.[1] I have chosen to forefront the difference of sexual preference because it has been for some women a source of empowerment and a route to community; it has also been a source of divisiveness among feminists. Through this approach, I can illustrate *both* the similarities and differences in their experiences of sexual desire, which are nested in their individual experiences as well as their social contexts. Although there are many other demarcations that differentiate these girls—social class, race, religion, sexual experience—and this is not the most pervasive difference in this sample,[2] sexual preference calls attention to the kinds of relationships in which girls are experiencing or exploring their sexual desire and which take meaning from gender arrangements and from both the presence and absence of institutionalization (Fine 1988; Friend 1993). Because any woman whose sexuality is not directly circumscribed by heterosexual, monogamous marriage is rendered deviant in our society, all adolescent girls bear suspicion regarding their sexuality, which sexual preference highlights. In addition, questions of identity are heightened at adolescence.

Rochelle Doing Desire

Rochelle is a tall, larger, African American girl who is heterosexual. Her small, sweet voice and shy smile are a startling contrast to her large body, clothed in white spandex the day of our interview. She lives in an urban area where violence is embedded in the fabric of everyday life. She speaks about her sexual experience with a detailed knowledge of how her sexuality is shaped, silenced, denigrated, and possible in relation-

ships with young men. As a sophomore, she thought she "had to get a boyfriend" and became "eager" for a sexual relationship. As she describes her first experience of sexual intercourse, she describes a traditional framing of male-female relationships:

> I felt as though I had to conform to everything he said that, you know, things that a girl and a guy were supposed to do, so like, when the sex came, like, I did it without thinking, like, I wish I would have waited . . . we started kissing and all that stuff and it just happened. And when I got, went home, I was like, I was shocked, I was like, why did I do that? I wish I wouldn't a did it.

Did you want to do it?

> Not really. Not really. I just did it because, maybe because he wanted it, and I was always like tryin' to please him and like, he was real mean, mean to me, now that I think about it. I was like kind of stupid, cause like I did everything for him and he just treated me like I was nothing and I just thought I had just to stay with him because I needed a boyfriend so bad to make my life complete but like now it's different.

Rochelle's own sexual desire is absent in her story of defloration—in fact, she seems to be missing altogether. In a virtual caricature of dominant cultural conventions of femininity, Rochelle connects her disappearance at the moment of sex—"it just happened"—to her attempts to fulfill the cultural guidelines for how to "make [her] life complete." She has sex because "he wanted it," a response that holds no place for whether or not she feels desire. In reflecting on this arrangement, Rochelle now feels she was "stupid . . . to do everything for him" and in her current relationship, things are "different." As she explains: "I don't take as much as I did with the first guy, cause like, if he's doin' stuff that I don't like, I tell him, I'll go, I don't like this and I think you shouldn't do it and we compromise, you know. I don't think I can just let him treat me bad and stuff."

During the interview, I begin to notice that desire is not a main plot line in Rochelle's stories about her sexual experiences, especially in her intimate relationships. When I ask her about her experiences of sexual pleasure and sexual desire, she voices contradictions. On one hand, as the interview unfolds, she is more and more clear that she does not enjoy sex: "I don't like sex" quickly becomes "I hate sex . . . I don't really have pleasure." On the other hand, she explains that

> there are certain times when I really really really enjoy it, but then, that's like, not a majority of the times, it's only sometimes, once in a while . . . if I was to have sex once a month, then I would enjoy it . . . if I like go a long period of time without havin' it then, it's really good to me, cause it's like, I haven't had something for a long time and I miss it. It's like, say I don't eat cake a lot, but say, like every two months, I had some cake, then it would be real good to me, so that's like the same thing.

Rochelle conveys a careful knowledge of her body's hunger, her need for tension as an aspect of her sexual pleasure, but her voiced dislike of sex suggests that she does not feel she has much say over when and how she engages in sexual activity.

In describing her experiences with sexuality, I am overwhelmed at how frequently Rochelle says that she "was scared." She is keenly aware of the many consequences that feeling and responding to her sexual desire could have. She is scared of being talked about and getting an undeserved reputation: "I was always scared that if I did that (had sexual intercourse) I would be portrayed as, you know, something bad." Even having sex within the confines of a relationship, which has been described by some girls as a safe haven for their sexuality (Rubin 1990; Tolman 1992), makes her vulnerable; she "could've had a bad reputation, but luckily he wasn't like that"; he did not choose to tell other boys (who then tell girls) about their sexual activity. Thinking she had a sexually transmitted disease was scary. Because she had been faithful to her boyfriend, having such a disease would mean having to know that her boyfriend cheated on her and would also make her vulnerable to false accusations of promiscuity from him. Her concern about the kind of woman she may be taken for is embedded in her fear of using contraception: "When you get birth control pills, people automatically think you're having sex every night and that's not true." Being thought of as sexually insatiable or out of control is a fear that many girls voice (Tolman 1992); this may be intensified for African American girls, who are creat-

ing a sexual identity in a dominant cultural context that stereotypes Black women as alternately asexual and hypersexual (Spillers 1984).

Rochelle's history provides other sources of fear. After her boyfriend "flattened [her] face, " when she realized she no longer wanted to be with him and broke off the relationship, she learned that her own desire may lead to male violence. Rochelle confided to me that she has had an abortion, suffering such intense sadness, guilt, and anxiety in the wake of it that, were she to become pregnant again, she would have the baby. For Rochelle, the risk of getting pregnant puts her education at risk, because she will have to sacrifice going to college. This goal is tied to security for her; she wants to "have something of my own before I get a husband, you know, so if he ever tries leavin' me, I have my own money." Given this wall of fears, I am not surprised when Rochelle describes a time when simply feeling desire made her "so scared that I started to cry." Feeling her constant and pervasive fear, I began to find it hard to imagine how she can feel any other feelings, including sexual ones.

I was thus caught off guard when I asked Rochelle directly if she has felt desire and she told me that she does experience sexual desire; however, she explained "most of the time, I'm by myself when I do." She launched, in breathless tones, into a story about an experience of her own sexual desire just the previous night:

> Last night, I had this crank call. . . . At first I thought it was my boyfriend, cause he likes to play around, you know. But I was sitting there talking, you know, and thinking of him and then I found out it's not him, it was so crazy weird, so I hang the phone up and he called back, he called back and called back. And then I couldn't sleep, I just had this feeling that, I wanted to have sex so so bad. It was like three o'clock in the morning. And I didn't sleep the rest of the night. And like, I called my boyfriend and I was tellin' him, and he was like, what do you want me to do, Rochelle, I'm sleeping! [Laughs.] I was like, okay, okay, well I'll talk to you later, bye. And then, like, I don't know, I just wanted to, and like, I kept tossin' and turnin'. And I'm trying to think who it was, who was callin' me, cause like, it's always the same guy who always crank calls me, he says he knows me. It's kinda scary. . . . I can't sleep, I'm like, I just think

about it, like, oh I wanna have sex so bad, you know, it's like a fever, drugs, something like that. Like last night, I don't know, I think if I woulda had the car and stuff, I probably woulda left the house. And went over to his house, you know. But I couldn't, cause I was babysitting.

When I told her that it sounds a little frightening but it sounds like there's something exciting about it, she smiled and leaned forward, exclaiming, "Yeah! It's like sorta arousing." I was struck by the intensity of her sexual feelings and also by the fact that she is alone and essentially assured of remaining alone due to the late hour and her responsibilities. By being alone, not subject to observation or physical, social, emotional, or material vulnerability, Rochelle experienced the turbulent feelings that are awakened by this call in her body. Rochelle's desire has not been obliterated by her fear; desire and fear both reverberate through her psyche. But she is not completely alone in this experience of desire, for her feelings occur in response to another person, whom she at first suspects is her boyfriend speaking from a safe distance, conveying the relational contours of her sexual desire. Her wish to bring her desire into her relationship, voiced in her response of calling her boyfriend, is in conflict with her fear of what might happen if she did pursue her wish—getting pregnant and having a baby, a consequence that Rochelle is desperate to avoid.

I am struck by her awareness of both the pleasure and danger in this experience and how she works the contradiction without dissociating from her own strong feelings. There is a brilliance and also a sadness in the logic her body and psyche have played out in the face of her experiences with sexuality and relationships. The psychological solution to the dilemma that desire means for her, of feeling sexual desire only when she cannot respond as she says she would like to, arises from her focus on these conflicts as personal experiences, which she suffers and solves privately. By identifying and solving the dilemma in this way, Rochelle is diminished, as is the possibility of her developing a critique of these conflicts as not just personal problems but as social inequities that emerge in her personal relationships and on her body. Without this perspective, Rochelle is less likely to become empowered through her own desire to identify that the

ways in which she must curtail herself and be curtailed by others are socially constructed, suspect, and in need of change.

Megan Doing Desire

Megan, a small, freckled, perky Euro-American, is dressed in baggy sweats, comfortable, unassuming, and counterpointed by her lively engagement in our interview.[3] She identifies herself as "being bisexual" and belongs to a gay youth group; she lives in a city in which wealth and housing projects coexist. Megan speaks of knowing she is feeling sexual desire for boys because she has "kind of just this feeling, you know? Just this feeling inside my body." She explains: "My vagina starts to kinda like act up and it kinda like quivers and stuff, and like I'll get like tingles and and, you can just feel your hormones (laughing) doing something weird, and you just, you get happy and you just get, you know, restimulated kind of and it's just, and Oh! Oh!" and "Your nerves feel good." Megan speaks about her sexual desire in two distinct ways, one for boys and one for girls. In our interview, she speaks most frequently about her sexual feelings in relation to boys. The power of her own desire and her doubt about her ability to control herself frighten her: "It scares me when I'm involved in a sexual situation and I just wanna go further and further and cause it just, and it scares me that, well, I have control, but if I even just let myself not have control, you know? . . . I'd have sex and I can't do that." Megan knows that girls who lose control over their desire like that can be called "sluts" and ostracized.

When asked to speak about an experience of sexual desire, Megan chooses to describe the safety of a heterosexual, monogamous relationship. She tells me how she feels when a boyfriend was "feeling me up"; not only is she aware of and articulate about his bodily reactions and her own, she narrates the relational synergy between her own desire and his:

> I just wanted to go on, you know? Like I could feel his penis, you know, 'cause we'd kinda lied down you know, and, you just really get so into it and intense and, you just wanna, well you just kinda keep wanting to go on or something, but it just feels good. . . . His penis being on my leg made, you know, it hit a nerve or something, it did something

because it just made me start to get more horny or whatever, you know, it just made me want to do more things and stuff. I don't know how, I can't, it's hard for me to describe exactly how I felt, you know like, (intake of breath) . . . when he gets more excited then he starts to do things and you can kind of feel his pleasure and then you start to get more excited.

With this young man, Megan knows her feelings of sexual desire to be "intense, " to have a momentum of their own, and to be pleasurable. Using the concrete information of his erection, she describes the relational contours of her own embodied sexual desire, a desire that she is clear is her own and located in her body but that also arises in response to his excitement.

Although able to speak clearly in describing a specific experience she has had with her desire, I hear confusion seep into her voice when she notices that her feelings contradict or challenge societal messages about girls and sexuality:

It's so confusing, 'cause you have to like say no, you have to be the one to say no, but why should you be the one to, cause I mean maybe you're enjoying it and you shouldn't have to say no or anything. But if you don't, maybe the guy'll just keep going and going, and you can't do that, because then you would be a slut. There's so [much] like, you know, stuff that you have to deal with and I don't know, just I keep losing my thought.

Although she knows the logic offered by society— that she must "say no" to keep him from "going and going," which will make her "a slut"—Megan identifies what is missing from that logic, that "maybe you're"—she, the girl—"the one who is enjoying it." The fact that she may be experiencing sexual desire makes the scripted response—to silence his body— dizzying. Because she does feel her own desire and can identify the potential of her own pleasure, Megan asks the next logical question, the question that can lead to outrage, critique, and empowerment: "Why should you have to be the one to [say no]?" But Megan also gives voice to why sustaining the question is difficult; she knows that if she does not conform, if she does not "say no"—both to him and to herself—then she may be called a slut, which could lead to denigration and isolation. Megan is caught in the contradiction between the reality of her sexual feelings in her

body and the absence of her sexual feelings in the cultural script for adolescent girls' sexuality. Her confusion is an understandable response to this untenable and unfair choice: a connection with herself, her body, and sexual pleasure or a connection with the social world.

Megan is an avid reader of the dominant culture. Not only has she observed the ways that messages about girls' sexuality leave out or condemn her embodied feelings for boys, she is also keenly aware of the pervasiveness of cultural norms and images that demand heterosexuality:

Every teen magazine you look at is like, guy this, how to get a date, guys, guys, guys, guys, guys. So you're constantly faced with I have to have a boyfriend, I have to have a boyfriend, you know, even if you don't have a boyfriend, just [have] a fling, you know, you just want to kiss a guy or something. I've had that mentality for so long.

In this description of compulsory heterosexuality (Rich 1983), Megan captures the pressure she feels to have a boyfriend and how she experiences the insistence of this demand, which is ironically in conflict with the mandate to say no when with a boy. She is aware of how her psyche has been shaped into a "mentality" requiring any sexual or relational interests to be heterosexual, which does not corroborate how she feels. Compulsory heterosexuality comes between Megan and her feelings, making her vulnerable to a dissociation of her "feelings" under this pressure.

Although she calls herself bisexual, Megan does not describe her sexual feelings for girls very much in this interview. In fact, she becomes so confused that at one point she says she is not sure if her feelings for girls are sexual:

I mean, I'll see a girl I really really like, you know, because I think she's so beautiful, and I might, I don't know. I'm so confused. . . . But there's, you know, that same mentality as me liking a guy if he's really cute, I'm like, oh my God, you know, he's so cute. If I see a woman that I like, a girl, it's just like wow, she's so pretty, you know. See I can picture like hugging a girl; I just can't picture the sex, or anything, so, there's something being blocked.

Megan links her confusion with her awareness of the absence of images of lesbian sexuality in the spoken or imagistic lexicon of the culture, counterpointing the pervasiveness of heterosexual imagery all around her. Megan suggests that another reason that she might feel "confused" about her feelings for girls is a lack of sexual experience. Megan knows she is feeling sexual desire when she can identify feelings in her own body—when her "vagina acts up"—and these feelings occur for her in the context of a sexual relationship, when she can feel the other person's desire. Because she has never been in a situation with a girl that would allow this embodied sexual response, she posits a connection between her lack of sexual experience with girls and her confusion.

Yet she has been in a situation where she was "close to" a girl and narrates how she does not let her body speak:

> There was this one girl that I had kinda liked from school, and it was like really weird 'cause she's really popular and everything. And we were sitting next to each other during the movie and, kind of her leg was on my leg and I was like, wow, you know, and that was, I think that's like the first time that I've ever felt like sexual pleasure for a girl. But it's so impossible, I think I just like block it out, I mean, it could never happen. . . . I just can't know what I'm feeling. . . .
>
> I probably first mentally just say no, don't feel it, you know, maybe. But I never start to feel, I don't know. It's so confusing. 'Cause finally it's all right for me to like a girl, you know? Before it was like, you know, the two times that I really, that it was just really obvious that I liked them a lot, I had to keep saying no no no no, you know, I just would not let myself. I just hated myself for it, and this year now that I'm talking about it, now I can start to think about it.

Megan both narrates and interprets her dissociation from her embodied sexual feelings and describes the disciplinary stance of her mind over her body in how she "mentally" silences her body by saying "no," preempting her embodied response. Without her body's feelings, her embodied knowledge, Megan feels confused. If she runs interference with her own sexual feelings by silencing her body, making it impossible for her to feel her desire for girls, then she can avoid the problems she knows will inevitably

arise if she feels sexual feelings she "can't know"— compulsory heterosexuality and homophobia combine to render this knowledge problematic for her. Fearing rejection, Megan keeps herself from feelings that could lead to disappointment, embarrassment, or frustration, leaving her safe in some ways, yet also psychologically vulnerable.

Echoing dominant cultural constructions of sexual desire, Megan links her desire for girls with feelings of fear: "I've had crushes on some girls . . . you can picture yourself kissing a guy but then if you like a girl a lot and then you picture yourself kissing her, it's just like, I can't, you know, oh my God, no (laughs), you know it's like scary . . . it's society . . . you never would think of, you know, it's natural to kiss a girl." Megan's fear about her desire for girls is different from the fears associated with her desire for boys; whereas being too sexual with boys brings the stigma of being called a "slut," Megan fears "society" and being thought of as "unnatural" when it comes to her feelings for girls. Given what she knows about the heterosexual culture in which she is immersed—the pressure she feels to be interested in "guys" and also given what she knows about homophobia—there is an inherent logic in Megan's confused response to her feelings for girls.

Melissa Doing Desire

Melissa, dressed in a flowing gypsy skirt, white skin pale against the lively colors she wears, is clear about her sexual desire for girls, referring to herself as "lesbian"; she is also a member of a gay/lesbian youth group. In speaking of her desire, Melissa names not only powerful feelings of "being excited" and "wanting," but also more contained feelings; she has "like little crushes on like millions of people and I mean, it's enough for me." Living in a world defined as heterosexual, Melissa finds that "little crushes" have to suffice, given a lack of opportunity for sexual exploration or relationship: "I don't know very many people my age that are even bisexual or lesbians . . . so I pretty much stick to that, like, being hugely infatuated with straight people. Which can get a little touchy at times . . . realistically, I can't like get too ambitious, because that would just not be realistic."

At the forefront of how Melissa describes her desire is her awareness that her sexual feelings make her vulnerable to harm. Whereas the heterosexual girls in this study link their vulnerability to the outcomes of responding to their desire—pregnancy, disease, or getting a bad reputation—Melissa is aware that even the existence of her sexual desire for girls can lead to anger or violence if others know of it: "Well I'm really lucky that like nothing bad has happened or no one's gotten mad at me so far, that, by telling people about them, hasn't gotten me into more trouble than, it has, I mean, little things but not like, anything really awful. I think about that and I think it, sometimes, I mean, it could be more dangerous." In response to this threat of violence, Melissa attempts to restrain her own desire: "Whenever I start, I feel like I can't help looking at someone for more than a few seconds, and I keep, and I feel like I have to make myself not, stare at them or something." Another strategy is to express her desire covertly by being physically affectionate with other girls, a behavior that is common and acceptable; by keeping her sexuality secret, she can "hang all over [girls] and stuff and they wouldn't even think that I meant anything by it." I am not surprised that Melissa associates feeling sexual desire with frustration; she explains that she "find(s) it safer to just think about the person than what I wanna do, because if I think about that too much and I can't do it, then that'll just frustrate me," leading her to try to intervene in her feelings by "just think[ing] about the person" rather than about the more sexual things she "want(s) to do." In this way, Melissa may jeopardize her ability to know her sexual desire and, in focusing on containing what society has named improper feelings, minimize or exorcise her empowerment to expose that construction as problematic and unjust.

My questions about girls' sexual desire connect deeply with Melissa's own questions about herself; she is in her first intimate relationship, and this interview proves an opportunity to explore and clarify painful twinges of doubt that she had begun to have about it. This relationship began on the initiative of the other girl, with whom she had been very close, rather than out of any sexual feelings on Melissa's part. In fact, Melissa was surprised when her friend had expressed a sexual interest, because she had not "been thinking that" about this close friend. After a history of having to hold back her sexual desire, of feeling "frustrated" and being "hugely infatuated with straight people," rather than having the chance to explore her sexuality, Melissa's response to this potential relationship was that she "should take advantage of this situation." As the interview progresses, Melissa begins to question whether she is sexually attracted to this girl or "it's just sort of like I just wanted something like this for so long that I'm just taking advantage of the situation."

When I ask Melissa questions about the role of her body in her experience of sexual desire, her confusion at first intensifies:

Is that [your body] part of what feels like it might be missing?

(eight-second pause) It's not, well, sometimes, I mean I don't know how, what I feel all the time. It's hard like, because I mean I'm so confused about this. And it's hard like when it's actually happening to be like, ok, now how do I feel right now? How do I feel right now? How am I gonna feel about this? . . . I don't know, 'cause I don't know what to expect, and I haven't been with anyone else so I don't know what's supposed to happen. So, I mean I'm pretty confused.

The way she speaks about monitoring her body suggests that she is searching for bodily feelings, making me wonder what, if anything, she felt. I discern what she does not say directly; that her body was silent in these sexual experiences. Her hunger for a relationship is palpable: "I really wanted someone really badly, I think, I was getting really sick of being by myself. . . . I would be like God, I really need someone." The desperation in her voice, and the sexual frustration she describes, suggest that her "want" and "need" are distinctly sexual as well as relational.

One reason that Melissa seems to be confused is that she felt a strong desire to be "mothered," her own mother having died last year. In trying to distinguish her different desires in this interview, Melissa began to distinguish erotic feelings from another kind of wanting she also experienced: she said that "it's more of like but I kind of feel like it's really more of like a maternal thing, that I really want her to take care of me and I just wanna touch someone and I just really like the feeling of just how I mean I like, when I'm with her and touching her and stuff. A lot, but it's not necessarily a sexual thing at this point." In contrast to her feelings for her girlfriend, Melissa describes feeling sexually attracted to another girl. In so doing, Melissa clarifies what is missing in these first sexual adventures, enabling her to know what had bothered her about her relationship with her girlfriend:

> I don't really think I'm getting that much pleasure, from her, it's just, I mean it's almost like I'm getting experience, and I'm sort of having fun, it's not even that exciting, and that's why I think I don't really like her . . . because my friend asked me this the other day, well, I mean does it get, I mean when you're with her does it get really, I don't remember the word she used, but just really, like what was the word she used? But I guess she meant just like, exciting [laughing]. But it doesn't, to me. It's weird, because I can't really say that, I mean I can't think of like a time when I was really excited and it was like really, sexual pleasure, for me, because I don't think it's really like that. I mean not that I think that this isn't good because, I don't know, I mean, I like it, but I mean I think I have to, sort of realize that I'm not that much attracted to her, personally.

Wanting both a relationship and sexual pleasure, a chance to explore closeness and her sexual curiosity, and discovering that this relationship leaves out her sexual desire, Melissa laments her silent body: "I sort of expect or hope or whatever that there would be some kind of more excited feeling just from feeling sexually stimulated or whatever. I would hope that there would be more of a feeling than I've gotten so far." Knowing consciously what she "knows" about the absence of her sexual feelings in this relationship has left her with a relational conflict of large proportions for her: "I'm not that attracted to her and I don't know if I should tell her that. Or if I should just kind of pretend I am and try to . . . anyway" I ask her how she would go about doing that—pretending that she is. She replies, "I don't think I could pretend it for too long." Not being able to "pretend" to have feelings that she knows she wants as part of an intimate relationship, Melissa faces a

dilemma of desire that may leave her feeling isolated and lonely or even fraudulent.

ADOLESCENT GIRLS' SEXUAL DESIRE AND THE POSSIBILITIES OF EMPOWERMENT

All of the girls in this study who said they felt sexual desire expressed conflict when describing their responses to their sexual feelings—conflict between their embodied sexual feelings and their perceptions of how those feelings are, in one way or another, anathema or problematic within the social and relational contexts of their lives. Their experiences of sexual desire are strong and pleasurable, yet they speak very often not of the power of desire but of how their desire may get them into trouble. These girls are beginning to voice the internalized oppression of their women's bodies; they knew and spoke about, in explicit or more indirect ways, the pressure they felt to silence their desire, to dissociate from those bodies in which they inescapably live. Larger societal forces of social control in the form of compulsory heterosexuality (Rich 1983), the policing of girls' bodies through school codes (Lesko 1988), and media images play a clear part in forcing this silence and dissociation. Specific relational dynamics, such as concern about a reputation that can easily be besmirched by other girls and by boys, fear of male violence in intimate relationships, and fear of violent repercussion of violating norms of heterosexuality are also audible in these girls' voices.

To be able to know their sexual feelings, to listen when their bodies speak about themselves and about their relationships, might enable these and other girls to identify and know more clearly the sources of oppression that press on their full personhood and their capacity for knowledge, joy, and connection. Living in the margins of a heterosexual society, the bisexual and lesbian girls voice an awareness of these forces as formative of the experiences of their bodies and relationships; the heterosexual girls are less clear and less critical about the ways that dominant constructions of their sexuality impinge on their embodied and relational worlds. Even when they are aware that societal ambivalence and fears are being played out on their minds and bodies, they do not speak of a need for collective action, or even the possibility of engaging in such activities. More often, they speak of the danger of speaking about desire at all. By dousing desire with fear and confusion, or simple, "uncomplicated" denial, silence, and dissociation, the girls in this study make individual psychological moves whereby they distance or disconnect themselves from discomfort and danger. Although disciplining their bodies and curbing their desire is a very logical and understandable way to stay physically, socially, and emotionally safe, it also heightens the chance that girls and women may lose track of the fact that an inequitable social system, and not a necessary situation, renders women's sexual desire a source of danger, rather than one of pleasure and power in their lives. In "not knowing" desire, girls and women are at risk for not knowing that there is nothing wrong with having sexual feelings and responding to them in ways that bring joy and agency.

Virtually every girl in the larger study told me that no woman had ever talked to her about sexual desire and pleasure "like this"—in depth, listening to her speak about her own experiences, responding when she asked questions about how to masturbate, how to have cunnilingus, what sex is like after marriage. In the words of Rubin: "The ethos of privacy and silence about our personal sexual experience makes it easy to rationalize the refusal to speak [to adolescents]" (1990, 83; Segal 1993). Thompson (1990) found that daughters of women who had talked with them about pleasure and desire told narratives about first intercourse that were informed by pleasure and agency. The recurrent strategy the girls in my study describe of keeping their desire under wraps as a way to protect themselves also keeps girls out of authentic relationships with other girls and women. It is within these relationships that the empowerment of women can develop and be nurtured through shared experiences of both oppression and power, in which collectively articulated critiques are carved out and voiced. Such knowledge of how a patriarchal society systematically keeps girls and women from their own desire can instigate demand and agency for social change. By not talking about sexual desire with each other or with women, a source for empowerment is lost. There is a

symbiotic interplay between desire and empowerment: to be empowered to desire one needs a critical perspective, and that critical perspective will be extended and sustained through knowing and experiencing the possibilities of desire and healthy embodied living. Each of these girls illustrates the phenomenon observed in the larger study—the difficulty for girls in having or sustaining a critical perspective on the culture's silencing of their sexual desire. They are denied full access to the power of their own desire and to structural supports for that access.

Common threads of fear and joy, pleasure and danger, weave through the narratives about sexual desire in this study, exemplified by the three portraits. Girls have the right to be informed that gaining pleasure and a strong sense of self and power through their bodies does not make them bad or unworthy. The experiences of these and other adolescent girls illustrate why girls deserve to be educated about their sexual desire. Thompson concludes that "to take possession of sexuality in the wake of the anti-erotic sexist socialization that remains the majority experience, most teenage girls need an erotic education" (1990, 406). Girls need to be educated about the duality of their sexuality, to have safe contexts in which they can explore both danger and desire (Fine 1988) and to consider why their desire is so dangerous and how they can become active participants in their own redemption. Girls can be empowered to know and act on their own desire, a different educational direction than the simplistic strategies for avoiding boys' desire that they are offered. The "just say no" curriculum obscures the larger social inequities being played out on girls' bodies in heterosexual relationships and is not relevant for girls who feel sexual feelings for girls. Even adults who are willing or able to acknowledge that girls experience sexual feelings worry that knowing about their own sexual desire will place girls in danger (Segal 1993). But keeping girls in the dark about their power to choose based on their own feelings fails to keep them any safer from these dangers. Girls who trust their minds and bodies may experience a stronger sense of self, entitlement, and empowerment that could enhance their ability to make safe decisions. One approach to educating girls is for women to speak to them about the vicissitudes of sexual desire—which means that women must let themselves speak and know their own sexual feelings, as well as the pleasures and dangers associated with women's sexuality and the solutions that we have wrought to the dilemma of desire: how to balance the realities of pleasure and danger in women's sexuality.

Asking these girls to speak about sexual desire, and listening and responding to their answers and also to their questions, proved to be an effective way to interrupt the standard "dire consequences" discourse adults usually employ when speaking at all to girls about their sexuality. Knowing and speaking about the ways in which their sexuality continues to be unfairly constrained may interrupt the appearance of social equity that many adolescent girls (especially white, middle-class young women) naively and trustingly believe, thus leading them to reject feminism as unnecessary and mean-spirited and not relevant to their lives. As we know from the consciousness-raising activities that characterized the initial years of second-wave feminism, listening to the words of other girls and women can make it possible for girls to know and voice their experiences, their justified confusion and fears, their curiosities. Through such relationships, we help ourselves and each other to live in our different female bodies with an awareness of danger, but also with a desire to feel the power of the erotic, to fine-tune our bodies and our psyches to what Audre Lorde has called the "yes within ourselves" (Lorde 1984, 54).

NOTES

1. The bisexual girl and the lesbian girl were members of a gay/lesbian youth group and identify themselves using these categories. As is typical for members of privileged groups for whom membership is a given, the girls who feel sexual desire for boys and not for girls (about which they were asked explicitly) do not use the term "heterosexual" to describe themselves. Although I am aware of the debate surrounding the use of these categories and labels to delimit women's (and men's) experience, because my interpretive practice is informed by the ways society makes meaning of girls' sexuality, the categories that float in the culture as ways of describing the girls are relevant to my analysis. In addition, the bisexual and lesbian girls in this study are deeply aware of compulsory heterosexuality and its impact on their lives.

2. Of the 30 girls in this sample, 27 speak of a desire for boys and not for girls. This pattern was ascertained by who appeared in their desire narratives and also by their response to

direct questions about sexual feelings for girls, designed explicitly to interrupt the hegemony of heterosexuality. Two of the 30 girls described sexual desire for both boys and girls and one girl described sexual desire for girls and not for boys.

3. Parts of this analysis appear in Tolman (1994).

REFERENCES

Brown, L. 1991. Telling a girl's life: Self authorization as a form of resistance. In *Women, girls and psychotherapy: Reframing resistance,* edited by C. Gilligan, A. Rogers, and D. Tolman. New York: Haworth.

Brown, L., E. Debold, M. Tappan, and C. Gilligan. 1991. Reading narratives of conflict for self and moral voice: A relational method. In *Handbook of moral behavior and development: Theory, research, and application,* edited by W. Kurtines and J. Gewirtz. Hillsdale, NJ: Lawrence Erlbaum.

Brown, L., and C. Gilligan. 1992. *Meeting at the crossroads: Women's psychology and girls' development.* Cambridge, MA: Harvard University Press.

Fine, Michelle. 1988. Sexuality, schooling and adolescent females: The missing discourse of desire. *Harvard Educational Review* 58:29–53.

Friend, Richard. 1993. Choices, not closets. In *Beyond silenced voices,* edited by M. Fine and L. Weis. New York: State University of New York Press.

Gilligan, Carol. 1989. Teaching Shakespeare's sister. In *Making connections: The relational world of adolescent girls at Emma Willard School,* edited by C. Gilligan, N. Lyons, and T. Hamner. Cambridge, MA: Harvard University Press.

———. 1990. Joining the resistance: Psychology, politics, girls and women. *Michigan Quarterly Review* 29:501–36.

Lees, Susan. 1986. *Losing out: Sexuality and adolescent girls.* London: Hutchinson.

Lesko, Nancy. 1988. The curriculum of the body: Lessons from a Catholic high school. In *Becoming feminine: The politics of popular culture,* edited by L. Roman. Philadelphia: Falmer.

Lorde, Audre. 1984. The uses of the erotic as power. In *Sister outsider: Essays and speeches.* Freedom, CA: Crossing Press.

Miller, Jean Baker. 1976. *Towards a new psychology of woman.* Boston: Beacon Press.

Rich, Adrienne. 1983. Compulsory heterosexuality and lesbian existence. In *Powers of desire: The politics of sexuality,* edited by A. Snitow, C. Stansell, and S. Thompson. New York: Monthly Review Press.

Rubin, Lillian. 1990. *Erotic wars: What happened to the sexual revolution?* New York: Harper-Collins.

Segal, Lynne. 1993. Introduction. In *Sex exposed: Sexuality and the pornography debate,* edited by L. Segal and M. McIntosh. New Brunswick, NJ: Rutgers University Press.

Spillers, Hortense. 1984. Interstices: A small drama of words. In *Pleasure and danger: Exploring female sexuality,* edited by C. Vance. Boston: Routledge and Kegan Paul.

Thompson, Sharon. 1984. Search for tomorrow: On feminism and the reconstruction of teen romance. In *Pleasure and danger: Exploring female sexuality,* edited by C. Vance. Boston: Routledge and Kegan Paul.

———. 1990. Putting a big thing in a little hole: Teenage girls' accounts of sexual initiation. *Journal of Sex Research* 27:341–61.

Tolman, Deborah L. 1991. Adolescent girls, women and sexuality: Discerning dilemmas of desire. *Women girls and psychotherapy: Reframing resistance,* edited by C. Gilligan, A. Rogers, and D. Tolman. New York: Haworth.

———. 1992. Voicing the body: A psychological study of adolescent girls' sexual desire. Unpublished dissertation, Harvard University.

———. 1994. Daring to desire: Culture and the bodies of adolescent girls. In *Sexual cultures: Adolescents, communities and the construction of identity,* edited by J. Irvine. Philadelphia: Temple University Press.

Tolman, Deborah, and Elizabeth Debold. 1993. Conflicts of body and image: Female adolescents, desire, and the no-body. In *Feminist treatment and therapy of eating disorders,* edited by M. Katzman, P. Fallon, and S. Wooley. New York: Guilford.

3.3 HIGH SCHOOLERS' MASTURBATORY PRACTICES
Their Relationship to Sexual Intercourse and Personal Characteristics

Anthony M. A. Smith, Doreen A. Rosenthal, and Heidi Reichler

Masturbation, defined as any deliberate self-stimulation which brings sexual arousal, not necessarily to climax or orgasm (Sparrow, 1994), is a common yet little discussed aspect of human sexuality. The lack of interest in this topic among researchers may stem in part from the belief that exploration of this intimate behaviour is too difficult and too invasive given social norms around sexual privacy. There is also the lingering perception in Western society that masturbation is a shameful and problematic activity in spite of the fact that many cultures accept this sexual practice as a normal part of human sexuality.

Kinsey and his colleagues were among the first to document masturbatory practices. They found that most men and 62% of women reported that they had masturbated at some point in their lifetimes (Kinsey, Pomeroy, & Martin, 1948; Kinsey, Pomeroy, Martin, & Gebhard, 1953) although methodological concerns about the Kinsey studies restrict the generalisability of those findings. Studies subsequently have focussed on how many people masturbate, how often, and how they learned to do so, and most have been based on American college students (Arafat & Cotton, 1974; Leiblum, Rosen, Platt, Cross, & Black, 1993; Mi-

chael, Gagnon, Laumann, & Kolata, 1994). The number of individuals who have ever masturbated varies considerably, and most studies have shown a significant gender difference with more men (between 80% and 93%) than women (between 46% and 72%) engaging in this behaviour. Masturbation begins early and by early teens most of those who report having ever masturbated have already done so (Arafat & Cotton, 1974; Green, 1985; Leitenberg, Detzer, & Srebnik, 1993).

Turning to the question of how young people learned about masturbation, a consistent picture emerges. Most men and women first become aware of masturbation through self-discovery, with friends being the next major learning source (Arafat & Cotton, 1974; Green, 1985; Leitenberg, et al., 1993) although Green found that female respondents were more likely than males to report learning about masturbation from parents, books, magazines, and sex education in schools, and significantly less likely to learn through either self-discovery or from peers.

Studies of younger adolescents confirm that masturbation is relatively common among this group and that boys engage in this practice more than girls

(Knoth, Boyd, & Singer, 1988; Sorensen, 1973). Sorensen found that girls began masturbating at an earlier age than boys and, of those who masturbated, most girls had begun before the age of 13 years and most boys had begun by age 14 years.

The limited examination of masturbation described thus far sheds little light on the role of this practice in subsequent sexual activity and on the personal characteristics of young people who engage, frequently or otherwise, in masturbation. Few studies have addressed the link between masturbation and other sexual activities and whether masturbation is an early step on the path to sexual intercourse. There is some evidence to suggest that masturbation is unrelated to other sexual behaviours. Davidson and Moore (1994) found no differences between college age women who masturbated and those who did not with regard to age of first sexual intercourse. In a more comprehensive examination of the relationship between masturbation and other sexual behaviours, Leitenberg, et al. (1993) found that preadolescent or early adolescent masturbation was unrelated to later sexual behaviour including experience of intercourse, frequency of intercourse, number of sexual partners, age of initiation of intercourse, length of relationships with a sexual partner, or sexual adjustment.

Arafat and Cotton (1974) found that almost half of their college sample reported that masturbation ceased when they had regular sexual activity with a partner, suggesting that for some young people masturbation is superceded as a sexual practice when relational sexual activity begins. This raises the question of whether masturbation is a precursor to more satisfying relational sexual practices so that, when these are available, masturbatory activity ceases or diminishes (a 'replacement' model) or whether this activity is maintained alongside other sexual practices (a 'supplementation' model).

Among younger adolescents (Sorensen, 1973) the relationships between intercourse and masturbation differed from those reported by college students. Having ever masturbated was less common among virgins (34%) than among nonvirgins (62%). Of the nonvirgins, boys who had had sexual intercourse in the last month masturbated less than those who had not had intercourse in that time. This difference was not pres-

ent among girls. These latter findings suggest that for boys, but not girls, a replacement model prevails with sexual intercourse replacing masturbation as a preferred sexual practice.

While we have very little information about the role of masturbation in the sexual development of young people, we have none about the personal characteristics of the masturbating teenager. As masturbation is usually a solitary practice, we might hypothesise that young people who have low self-esteem or who perceive themselves to be physically less developed than their peers may be inclined to engage in these practices in lieu of sexual behaviours which require a partner. Given the strong proscriptions about premarital sexual activity among some religions, young people who maintain strong religious beliefs may regard masturbation as an unacceptable practice; or they may consider masturbation to be an acceptable alternative to intercourse.

Also, there is now considerable evidence to indicate that young people whose parents communicate about sex are less likely to engage in sexual intercourse (Lewis, 1973) and have fewer sexual partners (Treboux & Busch-Rossnagel, 1990). Moreover, adolescents' perceptions of parental attitudes have been found to influence their sexual behaviours (Miller, McCoy, Olson, & Wallace, 1986; Moore & Rosenthal, 1991). To our knowledge, no study has focussed on parents' influence on young people's masturbatory practices. It could be hypothesised that the delay in other sexual practices associated with parental influence may also be observed with respect to masturbation. Alternatively, young people whose parents provide models of sexuality which are characterised by openness and enjoyment may be more likely to engage in masturbatory activity through the destigmatisation of such practices.

The aims of the current study were threefold. First, we wanted to describe the masturbatory practices of a sample of young Australian adolescents, including the proportion who had ever masturbated, the age at which they began, how frequently they masturbated, and how or where they learned about masturbation. The second aim was to examine the relationship between masturbation (including the age at which young people first masturbated and their frequency of masturbation) and sexual intercourse. Finally, we investigated the correlates of masturbatory practices, specifically the contribution of personal characteristics and parental modelling of sexuality.

METHOD

Respondents

Participants were drawn from years 10 and 11 (modal ages 15 years and 16 years, respectively) at four coeducational high schools in metropolitan Melbourne. The sample numbered 248 girls and 188 boys. Most were Australian-born, of English-speaking background, and drawn from middle-class families.

Procedure

Ethics approval was obtained from the university and informed consent was sought from parents of all students enrolled in years 10 and 11 at the four schools. Of 1507 students, 745 consent forms were returned and, of these, 708 parents and students (95% of those who returned the forms) agreed to participate. However, 121 students were absent on the day and 37 questionnaires were returned largely incomplete. Complete data for the analyses reported in this paper were available for 436 of the 550 students who completed the questionnaire. Students completed an anonymous self-administered questionnaire during class time.

Measures

We report here the measures used in the examination of masturbatory experience which were collected as part of a larger study of young people's sexual and social health. The questions on masturbation asked respondents whether they had ever masturbated and, if so, where they learned about masturbation, the age at which they first masturbated, and their frequency of masturbating in the past month. The response choices for how they learned about masturbation were self-taught, friends, books or magazines, parents, videos, siblings or relations, or other. These were subsequently collapsed into three categories for analysis, self-taught, friends/parents/siblings/relations, and books/

magazines/videos. The response choices for estimating frequency of masturbation in the *past month* were 'not at all,' 'once or twice,' 'once or twice a week,' 'three or four times a week,' 'once a day,' 'more than once a day.'

Personal characteristics were self-rated physical maturity, sexual experience, sexual self-esteem in relation to themselves and to partners, and religiosity. Self-rated physical maturity was assessed with respect to same-sex peers of the same age as 'less mature than most,' 'about the same as most,' or 'more mature than most.' There were two measures of sexual self-esteem, taken from previously developed scales (Rosenthal, Moore, & Flynn, 1990). Sexual self-esteem with respect to oneself was assessed through a 6-item scale which included items such as "I feel comfortable with my sexuality" and "I feel good about my sexual behaviour." Sexual self-esteem with respect to one's partners was assessed through a 10-item scale which included items such as "Intimate partners have found (or would find) me sexually satisfying" and "I don't think I could be comfortable in a sexual situation." Response categories for both scales were 'strongly disagree' (scored as 1), 'disagree' (2), 'agree' (3), and 'strongly agree' (4). Scores were computed as the mean of the responses when subjects had completed at least four of the six items relating to sexual self-esteem with respect to oneself and six of the ten items relating to sexual self-esteem with respect to one's partners.

A scale of parental modelling of sexuality was developed for this study and assessed with six items which included 'My parents openly discuss issues about sexuality with me,' 'My parents have told me that sexuality is a normal and natural part of life,' 'It is clear to me that my parents still enjoy their sex life,' Responses were rated on a 4-point scale from 1 (strongly disagree) to 4 (strongly agree) and scores were computed as the mean where subjects had completed at least four of the six items. The scale had good internal consistency (Cronbach alpha = 0.74). Religiosity was assessed through the single item 'My religious beliefs provide the guidelines by which I conduct my life' with a 7-point response ranging from 'not at all true' to 'definitely true.' Sexual experience was summarised through two items whether the respondents had ever had sexual intercourse and, of those who had, whether they had had intercourse in the previous month.

RESULTS

Ever Having Masturbated

Boys were significantly more likely to report having masturbated than were girls ($\chi_1^2 = 11.7$, $p < .001$), a difference apparent at each age (Table 3.3.1). The incidence of having masturbated increased strongly with age (trend $\chi_1^2 = 13.1$, $p < .001$) for both sexes. By age 16, having masturbated was a practice for most boys in this sample.

Most respondents (71% of boys and 75% of girls) stated that they taught themselves about masturbation. A smaller number (14% of boys and 16% of girls) had learned about masturbation through books, magazines, and videos and a similar number of male respondents (15%) though not females (7%) nominated friends, siblings, and relations as sources of information.

Comparisons of those who reported ever having masturbated and those who did not are shown in Table 3.3.2. Ever having masturbated was associated with scores on both measures of sexual self-esteem. Those who reported having masturbated scored higher on sexual self-esteem with respect to oneself and one's partners ($F_{1,435} = 9.5$, $p < .01$ and $F_{1,435} = 17.2$, $p < .001$, respectively). Scores on religiosity were unrelated to reporting masturbation but more sex-positive parental modelling was ($F_{1,435} = 4.5$, $p < .05$). Self-rated physi-

cal maturity was associated with reporting having masturbated ($\chi_2^2 = 8.2$, $p < .05$), with those rating their maturity as less than their peers being less likely to report having masturbated. Having reported sexual intercourse was unrelated to reporting masturbation.

Logistic regression analysis was used to determine which of the personal characteristics made an independent contribution to whether respondents reported ever having masturbated. Ever having masturbated was significantly associated with age, self-reported parental modelling, sex, and scores on the measures of sexual self-esteem with respect to partners but not with religiosity, sexual self-esteem with respect to oneself, or engaging in sexual intercourse. Reporting masturbation was strongly associated with increasing age [odds ratio = 1.56 (95% CI 1.19–2.03), $\chi_1^2 = 10.6$, $p < .01$], and boys were approximately twice as likely as girls to report having masturbated [odds ratio = 2.0 (95% CI 1.33–3.03), $\chi_1^2 = 11.1$, $p < .001$]. Reporting masturbation was associated with higher scores on parental modelling [odds ratio = 1.46 (95% CI

Table 3.3.1 Percentage of Students Reporting Ever Having Masturbated*

	Boys		**Girls**	
Age, yr.	**Total *n***	**%**	**Total *n***	**%**
15	58	50.0	78	32.1
16	91	58.2	115	41.7
17	34	67.1	52	59.8
18	5	100.0	3	66.7

*Percentages are derived from responses of 436 respondents from a total of 1507 approached.

Table 3.3.2 Comparison of Those Respondents Who Have Ever/Never Masturbated

	Never Masturbated ($n = 214$)		**Ever Masturbated** ($n = 222$)	
Measure	**M**	**SD**	**M**	**SD**
Personal Characteristics				
Sexual Self-esteem (self)	2.12	0.42	2.24	0.40
Sexual Self-esteem (partner)	1.91	0.46	2.09	0.43
Religiosity	1.01	1.72	1.14	1.71
Parental Modelling	1.54	0.58	1.66	0.59
Physical Maturity Relative to Peers, %				
Less	9.9		19.6	
About the Same	82.4		73.4	
More	7.7		7.0	
Sexual Activity				
Virgin	73.0		64.5	
Nonvirgin, but no sex in last month	14.4		17.3	
Sex in last month	12.6		18.2	

1.03–2.07), $\chi_1^2 = 4.6$, $p < .05$] and sexual self-esteem with respect to partners [odds ratio = 1.97 (95% CI 1.25–3.10), $\chi_1^2 = 8.5$, $p < .01$].

Age at Initiation of Masturbation

The reported age of initiation of masturbation was similar for boys and girls in this sample, with the majority beginning between the ages of 12 and 14 years (Table 3.3.3). There was no association between age at initiation of masturbation and current age, sex, scores on the measures of sexual self-esteem with respect to oneself and partners, parental modelling, or religiosity. Self-rated physical maturity was associated with age at initiation of masturbation ($F_{2,194} = 3.4$, $p < .05$), with those reporting being either more or less mature than their peers initiating masturbation earlier (less mature, mean age at initiation 12.8 ± 1.9 years, about as mature 13.2 ± 1.5, more mature 12.2 ± 1.5). Post hoc testing did not show that any of the mean ages differed significantly. Reporting sexual intercourse was unrelated to age at initiation of masturbation.

Of the 76 young people who had experienced both masturbation and sexual intercourse, the age of initiation of both behaviours was available for 61. There was no significant Pearson correlation ($r = .03$) between the age of initiation of masturbation and the age of initiation of sexual intercourse.

Table 3.3.3 Age of Initiation (%) and Frequency of Masturbation in the Previous Month (%) For Respondents Who Reported Having Ever Masturbated

Age at Initiation (yr.)	Boys $n = 98$	Girls $n = 97$
<10	6.1	12.4
11	6.1	9.3
12	16.3	18.6
13	29.6	14.4
14	25.5	20.6
15	11.2	19.6
16	5.1	5.2
Frequency	$n = 110$	$n = 104$
Infrequent	39.1	72.1
Occasional	22.7	19.2
Frequent	38.2	8.7

Linear regression analysis of the age at initiation of masturbation indicated that only reports of being physically more mature than one's peers was associated with an earlier age at initiation.

Frequency of Masturbation

For the analysis of frequency of masturbation, data were restricted to those respondents who reported ever having masturbated. Frequency of masturbation in the previous month was coded as infrequent (never, once, or twice), occasional (once or twice a week), or frequent (three or more times a week).

Boys and girls reported significantly different patterns of the frequency of masturbation in the previous month ($\chi_2^2 = 30.4$, $p < .001$) (Table 3.3.3). Nearly three-quarters of the girls reported that they masturbated infrequently in the last month, compared to 39% of boys. Over-all, girls masturbated less frequently than their male peers.

Age was associated with reported frequency of masturbation ($F_{2,213} = 4.3$, $p < .05$), and post hoc testing indicated that those who masturbated infrequently in the previous month were older than those who masturbated frequently but not those who masturbated occasionally (16.2 ± 0.81 years versus 15.8 ± 0.7 and 15.9 ± 0.81, respectively). Frequency of masturbation was not associated with scores on either measure of sexual self-esteem, self-rated maturity, or religiosity but was significantly associated with parental modelling ($F_{2,213} = 5.4$, $p < .01$). Those who masturbated frequently reported lower parental modelling than did those who masturbated infrequently or occasionally (1.5 ± 0.5 vs $1.7 \pm .06$ and 1.8 ± 0.5, respectively).

There was no significant association between having reported sexual intercourse in the previous month and frequency of masturbation ($p = .27$). However, those who had sexual intercourse in the previous month were less likely to report masturbating occasionally or frequently (15.4% and 17.9%) than those who had not had sexual intercourse in the previous month (22.3% and 25.1%, respectively).

Logistic regression analysis was used to examine differences between those who had masturbated frequently in the previous month versus those who had not. Boys were more than six times more likely than girls to have masturbated frequently in the previous month [odds ratio = 6.64 (95% CI 3.00–14.66), χ_1^2 = 21.9, $p < .001$] and those who were younger were more likely to have masturbated frequently in the previous month [odds ratio = 0.61 (95% CI 0.39–0.95), $\chi_1^2 = 4.91$, $p < .05$]. No other variables proved significant.

DISCUSSION

The data presented here are derived from 436 subjects of a total of 1507 who were approached. The relatively low response rate may indicate that the results have been heavily swayed by a self-selection bias. However, as no information is available on the nonrespondents the extent and nature of such bias remains unknown. Regardless, the results of this study should be generalised with caution.

The proportion of adolescents who reported ever having masturbated in this study is consistent with those in other studies (Arafat & Cotton, 1974; Leiblum, et al., 1993). Similarly, gender differences reported previously are supported here (Leiblum, et al., 1993; Michael, et al., 1994), although there were no differences in age of initiation of masturbation as has been observed in some studies (Green, 1985; Sorensen, 1973) but not others (Leitenberg, et al., 1993). Of those who masturbated, boys did so considerably more frequently than did girls (approximately six times).

Contrary to Sorensen (1973), we found no relationship between either ever having masturbated or the frequency of masturbation and engaging in sexual intercourse. We are unable to resolve the question of masturbation being 'replaced' or 'supplemented' by sexual intercourse. In part, this may be due to the relatively small number of young people in this study who had engaged in both masturbation and sexual intercourse. Also, it is possible that intercourse may not have been frequent enough to constitute a viable 'replacement' for masturbation.

Turning to the correlates of masturbation, there was a complex relationship between respondents' reports of personal characteristics, parent behaviour, and masturbatory practices. Scores on measures of sexual self-esteem had only limited links with reported masturbatory practices. Neither measure of

self-esteem correlated significantly with reported age of initiation or frequency of masturbation and, although scores on both measures of self-esteem correlated significantly with reporting masturbation, only scores on sexual self-esteem with respect to one's partner made a unique contribution to reports of ever having masturbated.

Scores on the measure of parental modelling of sexuality had significant associations with reports of both ever having masturbated and frequency of masturbation. Thus there was support for our contention that young people whose parents provide models of sexuality which are positive are more likely to report having masturbated. However, the relationship between scores on the measure of parental modelling and reported masturbation is clearly complex as masturbating frequently (as opposed to infrequently or occasionally) was associated with lower scores on the measure of parental modelling. In part the apparent complexity may be a statistical artefact arising from examining only those young people who reported masturbation, a group with a higher mean and restricted range of scores on the measure of parental modelling.

It is also, in the present study, impossible to determine whether these associations reflect a relationship between masturbation and parental modelling or, instead, a relationship between modelling and the likelihood of reporting masturbation. Clearly, the apparently complex relationships between the environment within which sexuality is discussed and displayed by parents and the masturbatory practices of young people deserve further study.

As with parental modelling, the relationship between masturbatory practices and physical maturity is complex. As we hypothesised, young people who rated their physical maturity as less than that of their peers were more likely to have masturbated. However, earlier initiation of masturbation was associated with being either more or less mature than one's peers, thus suggesting the potential contribution of both biological and social factors.

Masturbation remains the most significant source of orgasmic sexual pleasure for young people. While the promotion of masturbation remains controversial, masturbation is a physically safe sexual practice that

becomes an integral component of the sexual repertoire of most adults (see, for example, Michael, et al.,
1994) and may well play a role in the ability to establish mature intimate relationships. The present study
has demonstrated the complexity of factors associated
with masturbation and the importance of some personal characteristics and aspects of family context.
Undoubtedly, there remain other significant contributors to young people's masturbatory practices and the
ways in which these practices are viewed by young
people themselves and by others. These social and
contextual factors need to be explored to describe
fully and understand this very important component
of young people's sexual experience.

REFERENCES

Arafat, I. S., & Cotton, W. L. (1974) Masturbation practices of
males and females. *Journal of Sex Research,* 10, 293–307.

Davidson, J. K., & Moore, N. B. (1994) Masturbation and premarital sexual intercourse among college women: making
choices for sexual fulfillment. *Journal of Sex and Marital
Therapy,* 20, 178–199.

Green, V. (1985) Experiential factors in childhood and adolescent sexual behavior: family interaction and previous sexual
experiences. *Journal of Sex Research,* 21, 157–182.

Kinsey, A. C., Pomeroy, W. B., & Martin, C. E. (1948) *Sexual
behavior in the human male.* Philadelphia, PA: Saunders.

Kinsey, A. C., Pomeroy, W. B., Martin, C. E., & Gebhard, P. H.
(1953) *Sexual behaviour in the human female.* Philadelphia,
PA: Saunders.

Knoth, R., Boyd, K., & Singer, B. (1988) Empirical tests of sexual selection theory: predictions of sex differences in onset,
intensity, and time course of sexual arousal. *Journal of Sex
Research,* 24, 73–89.

Leiblum, S. R., Rosen, R. C., Platt, M., Cross, R. J., & Black, C.
(1993) Sexual attitudes and behaviour of a cross-sectional
sample of United States medical students: effects of gender,
age and year of study. *Journal of Sex Education and Therapy,*
19, 235–245.

Leitenberg, H., Detzer, M. J., & Srebnik, D. (1993) Gender differences in masturbation and the relation of masturbation
experience in preadolescence and/or early adolescence to
sexual behavior and sexual adjustment in young adulthood.
Archives of Sexual Behavior, 22, 87–98.

Lewis, R. A. (1973) Parents and peers: socialisation agents in
the coital behavior of young adults. *Journal of Sex Research,*
2, 156–170.

Michael, R. T., Gagnon, J. H., Laumann, E. O., & Kolata, G.
(1994) *Sex in America.* London: Little, Brown.

Miller, B. C., McCoy, J. K., Olson, T. D., & Wallace, C. M.
(1986) Parental discipline and control attempts in relation to
adolescent sexual attitudes and behavior. *Journal of Marriage and the Family,* 48, 503–512.

Moore, S. M., & Rosenthal, D. A. (1991) Adolescents' perceptions of parents' and peers' attitudes to sex and sexual risk-
taking. *Journal of Community and Applied Social Psychology,* 1, 189–200.

Rosenthal, D., Moore, S., & Flynn, I. (1990) Adolescent self-
efficacy, self-esteem and sexual risk-taking. *Journal of Community and Applied Social Psychology,* 1, 77–88.

Sorensen, R. C. (1973) *Adolescent sexuality in contemporary
America.* New York: World.

Sparrow, M. (1994) Masturbation and safer sex: clinical, historical and social issues. *Venereology,* 7, 164–169.

Treboux, D., & Busch-Rossnagel, N. A. (1990) Social network
influences on adolescent sexual attitudes and behaviors.
Journal of Adolescent Research, 5, 175–189.

3.4 ASIAN-AMERICAN ADOLESCENTS
Issues in the Expression of Sexuality

Connie S. Chan

As a group that is bicultural and bilingual to varying degrees, Asian-American teenagers confront a sometimes conflicting and confusing set of social and cultural values from their own ethnic and familial origins and from their exposure to the mainstream American culture. How do they make sense of these cues and these values? How do they experience their sexuality, and what models do they follow in developing their sense of themselves as sexual beings? My discussion of these factors is based upon a review of the research literature in this area and upon my own clinical experience of many years with Asian-American teenagers and families, all of whom would be considered "normative nonclinical populations." The individuals and families with whom I worked were outpatients in a community health center or participants in an Asian students' support-discussion group at a local high school in the Boston area.

First, consider that the term "Asians" covers a very heterogeneous group, with over thirty separate and distinct ethnic groups, each with its own values, language, customs, behaviors, and traditions. For my purposes here, Asian or Asian-American culture entails a certain degree of generalization across the Asian cultural factors that arise from a commonly shared, broadly based culture best defined as East Asian culture, inclusive of the ethnic groups of Chinese, Japanese, Korean, and Vietnamese (constituting the population with whom I worked on a clinical basis), and from the common experience that native-born Asian-Americans and immigrants alike share as individuals of Asian descent in the United States. This experience has a history of racism characterized by a host of exclusionary laws that institutionalized the prejudice against Asians. There were laws that prohibited Asians from becoming American citizens, laws that did not allow them to own land, antimiscegenation laws that outlawed marriage between Asians and whites, and immigration laws that limited the number of Asians who were allowed into the United States.

This "shared" Asian-American experience of prejudice also reflects the tendency of the majority of non-Asians not to distinguish between the Asian subgroups and to treat all Asian-Americans in the same manner without regard to individual and ethnic group differences. Although actual individual experiences of Asians in America are diverse and varied, from recent immigrants or refugees to fourth-generation American citizens, many Americans cannot distinguish between similar Asiatic physical appearances. As a result, most Asians in America, regardless of individual and group differences, may experience similar reactions from American society. At the same time, the personal assimilation and acculturation backgrounds of Asian-Americans are unique and very much influenced by their individual and familial experiences. Thus, it is imperative to consider individual differences in acculturation, assimilation, and language, as well as socioeconomic factors, when counseling or teaching Asian-Americans. It is necessary to understand Asian-American individuals within the context of each individual's specific ethnic, sociocultural, and historical background.

With these considerations in mind, the research literature provides some foundation in understanding the concept of sexuality for Asian-Americans. Alice Tsui points out that any open discussion of sexuality is unusual, since sexuality is a very sensitive subject.[1] Even among one's closest friends, a discussion about sexuality is considered to be awkward and highly embarrassing at best, and at worst, strictly taboo.

This extreme discomfort with open and direct discussion of sexuality is sometimes misconstrued as *asexuality* or as an extreme repression of sexual interest on the part of Asians. Both perceptions, though common, are incorrect. Most East Asian cultures are neither asexual nor extremely repressed in their views of sexuality. There is a long history of Chinese and Japanese erotica, both in literature and in art, as well as documentation of private expressions of sexuality and sexual interest in personal journals and letters. However, what is presented publicly is very different from what is presented in private.

The distinction between the public and the private selves is an important concept in most Asian cultures. The public self is that which conforms to gendered and familial role expectations, behaves in a manner in accordance with social norms, and seeks to avoid actions that would bring shame not only upon oneself but also upon one's family. Sexuality would rarely be expressed in the context of one's public self. Only within the context of the private self can such a subject find easy expression. The private self is never seen by anyone other than one's most intimate family and friends (in some cases, a person may choose never to reveal a private self to anyone). The dichotomous nature of the public and the private selves is much more distinct than in Western cultures, where there is far more fluidity between the two.

The relevance of this public-private self split within Asian culture is not only that there is very little public expression of sexuality but also that the private expressions of sexuality may take on different forms for Asians than would be the norm in Western culture. One example of this would be in sexual and erotic behavior, which may be expressed privately and in far more indirect ways. Many such behaviors might be misperceived as nonsexual by Westerners unaccustomed to subtle nuances such as a change in the register of voices of two people having a conversation, the minimal physical contact of a hand brushing against the other person, language patterns that might reflect affection but are indiscernible to the casual observer. And casual observers are not only non-Asians but also young Asian-American children and adolescents who may not see any obvious sexual behavior from their parents and other adults. This lack of models for sex-

ual and erotic behavior may leave Asian-American adolescents searching for ways to express their sexual feelings by observing non-Asian peers, watching movies and television shows, and seeking out sexually explicit pictures and stories in magazines.

Most of the Asian cultures also pride themselves on their sense of propriety and good manners. Sexuality exists but is rarely allowed open expression, since the control of individual sexual gratification and expression is considered to be necessary for the survival of a cultural system where individual needs, which are secondary to familial and community needs, are suppressed. Repression of sexual desire is expected because one is not allowed to indulge individual needs that might bring shame or dishonor to the family. Historically, to express one's sexuality and desire for sexual activity openly would undermine the tradition of arranged marriages based upon social class. In addition, any open expression of sexuality outside of marriage is strictly forbidden and would bring great shame not only upon the individual but, more important, upon the family and even one's clan and community.

These restrictions upon the public and open expression of sexuality should not be mistaken, however, as a denial of one's sexuality by Asians. As Tsui noted, on the contrary, sexuality is to be taken as a very normal part of life and a very integral part of existence.[2] Though given little attention (like one gives very little attention to the normal breathing process), an individual's sexuality is expected to "stay healthy." Any clinical dysfunction is often seen as the individual's personal responsibility and a source of great shame.

Although this perception of sexuality as a "very normal part of life" seems to be in contradiction to the reported sexually conservative behavior among Asian-Americans, the two views are actually compatible. Research on Asian-American sexual behavior, though sparse, describes conservative sexual behavior. P. I. Erickson and D. S. Moore termed Asian views and expressions of sexuality "sexual conservatism," reporting that Asian-Americans were significantly less likely to talk about sex than were whites, Hispanics, or Blacks.[3] Although open discussion of sexuality may be unusual for Asian-Americans, its absence may affect a teenager's perceptions of his or her own sexuality in various ways. One view is that sexual conservatism among traditional Asians is caused by strong familial dynamics and by the strict behavioral restrictions of Asian cultures, as noted by Chun Hoon on Chinese-American culture and by H. Hirayama and K. K. Hirayama on Japanese-American culture.[4] In their study of the sexual practices of Asian-American heterosexual young adults, Susan Cochran, Vickie Mays, and Laurie Leung cite the Hirayamas:

> Within much of traditional Asian cultures, social order and control of emotions and feelings are highly valued. An outward display of strong emotions is not viewed favorably [Hirayama and Hirayama, "The Sexuality of Japanese Americans"]. In contrast to the Western concept of individualism, Asian cultures stress group or family unity and cohesiveness. The children are taught to depend on the family and to have the utmost respect for their parents (filial piety). This restrictiveness may give the family a greater degree of control over their teenage and adult children. As a result, sexual expression and behavior of children may to a greater extent be influenced by familial values.[5]

Furthermore, Cochran and her colleagues assert that conservatism in the outward expression of one's sexuality should not be confused with the absence of HIV-related risk behavior. Although traditional Asian cultural values such as strong disapproval of marital infidelity, noted by H. T. Christensen, and a tendency toward sexually conservative behavior, defined by Erickson and Moore, may help to reduce behavioral risk for HIV, there are other indications that Asian-American youth engage in high-risk sexual practices in the same percentages as non-Asian youth.[6] In the study by Cochran and her colleagues, Asian-American college students, when questioned about the private expression of their sexuality, reported sexual behaviors, such as sexual intercourse without use of a condom, in the same prevalence as the non-Asian population sample. They also found no difference between native-born and immigrant Asian-American students in their practice of sexual behaviors that would transmit HIV should it be present. This information is useful when considering the kinds of educa-

tional outreach that should be used when targeting Asian communities for AIDS education.

In some traditional East Asian cultures, such as Japan and China, expressions of sexuality are constrained so as not to disrupt the established social order, but sexuality is nevertheless viewed as a normal, private aspect of life.

The roots of sexual conservatism are not based upon a philosophical rejection of the body (in favor of reason and intellect) or upon religious morality, as in Western culture, but are founded upon the traditional Asian values of familial unity. The family and social pressure that can be exerted upon young people to conform to such behaviors is generally very effective.

What happens when Asian-American teenagers are also exposed to mainstream American cultural values that place far greater emphasis upon open expressions of sexuality and sexual behavior? How do adolescents in this position make sense of the conflicting value systems and learn to express their own sexuality?

One common assumption is that Asian-American teenagers and young adults are less sexually active than their non-Asian-American peers. There is some evidence, both clinical and in the research literature, that this perception is accurate. In their study of 153 single, heterosexual Asian-American college students eighteen to twenty-five years old, Cochran, Mays, and Leung found that 47 percent of their sample population were sexually active, a rate that statistically was significantly lower than among the other 480 white (72 percent sexually active), Black (84 percent), and Hispanic (59 percent) young adults surveyed.[7] This 47 percent figure is also lower than the national estimates for white teenagers, where between 54 and 57 percent of nineteen-year-olds are estimated to be sexually active. Given that the sample used by Cochran and her colleagues was an even older one, between eighteen and twenty-five years of age, the 47 percent figure indicates that Asian-American college students are less sexually active than their white, Black, and Hispanic peers.

Clinical experience with Asian-American teenagers supports this research finding of less sexual activity among both genders. Specific cultural factors may play a role in explaining why Asian-American teenagers are less sexually active than are their non-Asian peers. One explanation is that Asians have stricter family expectations to refrain from being sexually active and less pressure from their peers to be sexually active. In my adolescent discussion groups, Asian-born teenage boys (fifteen to eighteen) commonly reported that they felt there were explicit demands from their parents to refrain from sexual activity. They noted that non-Asian boys at school joked and talked about having sex, but within their own Asian peer group they knew there was the explicit expectation that couples do not engage in sexual intercourse unless engaged to be married or "very seriously" involved. The cultural expectation is that sexual activity should be pursued only within the context of emotional intimacy.

For Asian-American teenage girls, the importance of emotional intimacy was even more salient. Girls reported little interest in sexual activity of any kind without what they considered serious emotional attachment and commitment in a long-term relationship. Until they were convinced of the existence of such commitment, they attempted to avoid sexual activity in their relationships. Moreover, Asian-American adolescent girls expressed the strong desire to avoid and downplay expressions of their sexuality in any form. This would include the external, or physical appearance—conservative dress, minimal use of makeup, nonsexual body language—as well as the interpersonal: preferring not to be alone with boys, limiting sexual expression to kissing, or holding hands rather than what they termed "petting and making out."

In addition, adolescent Asian-American girls struggle with their own version of meeting the idealized American female concept of beauty. My 1985 study of thirty Asian-American teenage girls found that they were less satisfied with their physical looks than were their non-Asian peers.[8] They reported that they were shorter and smaller, had smaller breasts, and were less physically strong than their white, Black, and Hispanic classmates. Their lack of satisfaction with their body image is reflected in their sense of self, since their scores on self-esteem scales were also lower than the standardized norms for teenage girls. The girls (all immigrants with an average mean of five years in the United States) also reported feeling more "vulnerable" in the social environment in the United States; they felt that they had to learn to adapt to new social standards and expectations while still fulfilling their parents' expectations.

Given that social control of the expression of sexuality comes from three primary sources—that is, the family (including parents, grandparents, and older siblings), the adolescents' peer group, and the social environment—Asian-American adolescents may be faced with juggling conflicting expectations. The greater the influence of traditional Asian culture on each of these three factors, the more constrained an Asian-American teenager will feel in terms of open expression of sexuality.

Within traditional Asian families, parents play the dominant role in the adolescents' understanding of what would be considered appropriate expressions of sexuality. Although open and frank discussion of these issues with parents is unusual, Asian-American teenagers consistently report that they receive strong and direct messages if their appearance or behavior is considered by their parents to be too overtly sexual. The messages that these Asian-American teenagers receive from their parents may not be very different from those from non-Asian parents; however, there is a greater risk faced by Asian-American teens if they do not follow prescribed behavioral, cultural, and gendered role expectations of appropriate sexual behavior. The consequences of breaking such expectations tend to be much more severe than in non-Asian-American families. Any deviation from the range of acceptable behaviors not only would result in punishment but also would be accompanied by expressions of disappointment and a strong sense of shame from family members.

An Asian-American adolescent who transgresses in the realm of sexual activity (such as being "caught" kissing, necking, or petting in a car; having premarital sex; engaging in homosexual physical contact; getting pregnant or getting a girl pregnant) would expect to be punished and would likely internalize much of the disappointment and shame expressed by family members. This internalization could include, but not be limited to, a sense of shame, feelings of guilt, a sense of having let the family down, loss of self-esteem, and feelings of depression. Symptoms are often psychosomatic, including physical ailments, irritability, lack of concentration, pulling back from emotional attachments, and a withdrawal of interest in things that are usually pleasurable. Many of these symptoms are classic symptoms of depression, and Asian-American teenagers frequently exhibit signs of depression when struggling with the conflict between their desires to express their sexuality and a culture that restricts such expression. Western counselors and therapists frequently misunderstand this internalization of guilt and shame and the accompanying symptoms as an overreaction to familial disappointment or to one's own rigid superego (conscience). However, within the context of Asian-American culture, reactions of this type are not uncommon. In particular, first- and second-generation Asian-American teenagers who feel an extra burden of meeting their family's expectations of the American dream often are caught in these transitional cultural norms. Given their parents' sacrifices to immigrate to this new land, teenagers who are the first and second generation of their families in this country often feel a greater burden to meet their families' expectations and feel guilt if unable to live up to those demands. They experience the pressures of maintaining the mother culture *and* assimilating into the American culture. When those cultural-familial expectations clash, the transitional generation faces the difficult task of integrating conflicting values. During the teenage years, the struggle often focuses on sexuality and its expression. The manifestation of this struggle may not be apparent, and frequently sexuality is not even in the picture. It requires sensitivity and awareness on the part of educators, counselors, and youth workers involved with Asian-American adolescents to draw out the underlying issues around sexuality to determine the role it may be playing in a teenager's life.

Lee, sixteen, a Chinese-American immigrant whose family moved to this country when he was ten, is an example of an adolescent whose struggle with sexuality was initially hidden. Referred for psychotherapy by his teachers, Lee's apparent problem was that he was having difficulties in school: after two years of excellent academic achievement, Lee's grades had plummeted. His teachers reported that he seemed to be trying as hard as before but that the quality of his work was now very poor. When they con-

fronted him with these problems, Lee maintained that he was fine and that he did not understand why he was now doing so poorly on his tests and papers. Lee's parents accompanied him to our first clinical session, saying that they supported his psychotherapy work with me. Their view of the problem was that Lee had somehow gotten "stuck" in his thinking and needed some help to move him past this stage. They believed that he was working hard but felt that he was not being efficient or productive. No emotional issues were addressed; Lee's parents asserted that he seemed as stable and as content as always and that he had always been a happy, outgoing child.

Initially, Lee resisted opening up in our treatment sessions. He denied any emotional concerns and attributed his poor academic work to the increasing difficulty of the material as he entered his junior year in high school and to the much stiffer competition for grades. While there was some truth in his analysis, it seemed clear that there was something more that was troubling Lee and affecting his ability to perform in school. He was not expressing any emotions, negative or positive, in treatment sessions. His affect was quite flat, and he seemed to have a resigned (although not depressed) attitude toward life.

During the initial phase of psychotherapy, lasting about two months, Lee was compliant, but unresponsive in sharing any feelings, and I began to question whether I would be able to make a meaningful connection with him. It was not until I suggested that our sessions were not fruitful and that perhaps he might try something else that Lee decided to confide in me and express some personal concerns. While avoiding eye contact and in a very soft voice, Lee described how he had been agonizing over what he termed a "sexual encounter" with a cousin and how his anguish had caused him to be preoccupied for the past three months. As the story of how he and his sixteen-year-old female cousin had engaged in "heavy kissing and fondling" on two occasions unfolded, Lee became more and more agitated in his behavior. He paced around the room, unable to contain his anxiety about what he termed his greatest fear: the consequences if his parents were to find out. Lee assumed all responsibility for his sexual behavior and felt extremely guilt-ridden. He was terrified that either his cousin's family or his own family would find out what they had done. As a result of his strong fears, he had told his cousin that he could no longer see her, even though he liked her very much. Lee then admitted that his feelings of guilt and his fear of being caught had caused him so much anxiety that he could no longer concentrate on his studies, which had once been a source of pride to him and his family. Now he lacked self-confidence and was filled with despair, having lost the hope that he would ever be happy again until he was old enough to live his own life separate from his family.

Given the lack of direct communication about sexuality within most Asian-American families and even between teenage peers, Lee's reaction is neither uncommon nor an overreaction. The expectations can be so rigidly defined and the stakes so high if an adolescent should "falter" that the internalized guilt and shame can frequently lead to unrecognized symptoms of depression or loss of self-esteem or both. The therapist's role in this situation is first to let the Asian-American teenager know that he or she is understood (by the therapist) and that he or she is facing a difficult situation. Then I would explore the various messages about sexual pleasure and behavior that the teenager might be receiving from parents, peers, and his or her own internal impulses, and the messages from American society. Lee described how these conflicting messages told him to restrain his sexual impulses at the same time it told him to be an assertive teenager and to express his sexuality. No wonder he was in such turmoil. When the reality of the conflict was presented to Lee and he was able to recognize the bind he was in, he also could grasp the concept that some of his dilemma was externally based upon different cultural expectations. He began to understand that while he did have responsibility for his actions, his feelings were acceptable, and he could find ways of balancing his needs within his familial-social context. Given this knowledge, Lee could then achieve an understanding of why he had felt pulled in different directions and how he could learn to resolve these issues. Although it was still a struggle and Lee experienced further anguish around his feelings for his cousin and the expectations of his family, Lee was eventually able to negotiate his way through this obstacle course of sexual desire and find acceptable expressions of sexuality. However, not until he was older and more emotionally independent from his family did Lee feel comfortable with his sexuality and with sexual behavior.

While Asian-American adolescents must still take responsibility for their choices and for their actions, the understanding that external factors do impinge upon their ability to meet differing cultural-peer expectations can help them in their decision making. This understanding helps teenagers to recognize that there is nothing wrong with them individually, that their personal needs are not inappropriate, but that they can be caught in an intersection where varying expectations of their sexual behavior clash. It is when they do achieve this recognition of the conflicting messages that they can learn to make informed choices and to anticipate the kinds of reactions they might have to the expressions of sexuality that they choose.

One such choice might be to engage in homosexual or bisexual activity. Given the traditional Asian cultural restrictions against open (public) expression of sexuality, to identify oneself as being lesbian, gay, or bisexual would make public a private expression of sexuality and thus be out of character with traditional Asian cultural values. Indeed, identification of *any* sexual identity (whether homosexual, heterosexual, or bisexual) may be unacceptable in traditional Asian cultures that allow only a private expression of sexuality. As a result, there is a common perception that there are proportionately fewer Asian and Asian-American openly lesbian, gay, and bisexual individuals than in the non-Asian population. Whether that perception is numerically accurate is unknown, but if it is, it is plausibly explained by prohibitions against public expressions of sexual orientation. It can also be argued that an individual with an Asian-American ethnic identity who comes out as openly lesbian, gay, or bisexual would have a stronger identification with American or Western cultural influences, since Asian cultures value keeping one's sexuality a private matter. My 1989 study of lesbian and gay Asian-Americans supports this concept, showing that both Asian-American lesbians and gay men preferred to be affirmed for both aspects of their identity.[9] If forced to choose to identify more strongly with either the homosexual or Asian-American community, respondents tended to identify more closely with the homosexual community. Although they felt marginalized and somewhat stereotyped within the homosexual community, they reported feeling even more invisible and invalidated for being homosexual within the Asian-American community.

Ironically, the restrictions upon open expression of sexuality may actually create less of a dichotomization of heterosexual versus homosexual behavior as well as less of a rigidly defined sexual-orientation identity within Asian cultures. Instead, with the importance of the concept of private expression of sexuality, there could be more allowance of fluidity within a sexual-behavior continuum, without the necessity for any definition or declaration of sexual orientation or sexual identity.

The impact of this fluidity of identity on Asian-American teenagers' development of sexuality and sexual identity is unclear. Asian-American adolescents, regardless of gender, report that their parents never directly address the issue of homosexuality or bisexuality with them. However, the teenagers are exposed to both positive and negative images of openly lesbian, gay, and bisexual people in American society. Given this far greater awareness, Asian-American teenagers might experience relatively greater flexibility in their private explorations of sexuality but still have the restrictions upon their public expressions of sexuality. Within the private self, homosexual activity may carry weight equal to heterosexual activity—after all, it is *sexual behavior* that must be expressed privately—and, ironically, may be perceived as not carrying as strong a stigma as within Western culture. This concept of fluidity of sexual behavior does not necessarily mean that Asian cultures are less homophobic or that homosexuality is more tolerated within Asian communities, because any public expression or definition of homosexuality is considered taboo. However, private expressions of sexual behavior, whether heterosexual or homosexual, may be more acceptable as long as they remain private and undefined or unidentified publicly. It is only within the realm of the private self that the fluidity of sexuality can exist within Asian cultures.

Asian-American lesbians and gay men have reported that parents frequently have as much diffi-culty acknowledging that their daughters or sons are sexually active in any way as acknowledging that they are lesbian or gay. For some families of Asian-American lesbians and gay men, the issue of engaging in homosexual behavior may be avoided by parents who focus on the taboo of the public expression of sexuality and expend energy in condemning sexual activity and the expression of one's sexual desires.

A case in my 1992 study might clarify this point:

Sachiko, 32, is a Japanese American lesbian who came out to her family shortly after becoming sexually active. Refusing to accept or even discuss her identity as a lesbian, her parents were extremely upset that she was sexually active in any way and declared that she would never be fit to be married or to be a real part of her family again. No matter how she tried to explain her sexual orientation or identity as a lesbian to her parents, they refused to acknowledge that Sachiko was anything but a sexually active unmarried woman. By affirming her own identity, Sachiko was perceived by her parents as having willingly brought considerable shame upon her family. The family forbade her to disclose her lesbian identity to others. Sachiko, however, refused to remain closeted.[10]

Asian-American adolescents confront a variety of messages concerning their sexuality and face many restrictions on what is acceptable private and public sexual behavior. The traditional Asian cultural influence places a greater demand to restrict open expression of sexuality, while mainstream American culture exerts pressure to be more individualistic, to be more openly sexual and expressive. Yet concurrently, American culture places greater emphasis upon choosing either a homosexual or a heterosexual orientation, while the private expression of sexuality in Asian culture may allow for greater fluidity and movement between a continuum of sexual expression. Asian-American teenagers make sense of these many messages and develop their own sense of themselves as sexual beings in individual ways, finding their unique balance between Asian and American cultural influences. As with any identity development, sexual identity development is an ever-changing, fluid concept that will integrate different aspects of both cultures over an individual's life span. For adolescents, the pressure of parental approval may loom largest and play the biggest role in determining their expressions of sexuality, but as they become adults, Asian-American teens may develop their own sense of sexuality that is less tied to their cultural-familial influences and is more reflective of their bicultural social environment.

NOTES

1. Alice Tsui, "Psychotherapeutic Considerations in Sexual Counseling for Asian Immigrants," *Psychotherapy* 22 (1985): 357–62.

2. Ibid., 358.

3. P. I. Erickson and D. S. Moore, "Sexual Activity, Birth Control Use, and Attitudes Among High School Students from Three Minority Groups" (Paper presented at the 1986 meeting of the American Public Health Association, Las Vegas).

4. Lowell Chun-Hoon, "Jade Snow Wong and the Fate of the Chinese-American Identity," *Amerasia* 1 (1971): 52–63; H. Hirayama and K. K. Hirayama, "The Sexuality of Japanese Americans," *Journal of Social Work and Human Sexuality* 4 (1986): 83.

5. Susan D. Cochran, Vickie M. Mays, and Laurie Leung, "Sexual Practices of Heterosexual Asian-American Young Adults: Implications for Risk of HIV Infection," *Archives of Sexual Behavior* 20, no. 4 (1991): 381–91.

6. H. T. Christensen, "Attitudes Toward Marital Infidelity: A Nine-Culture Sampling of University Student Opinion," *Journal of Comparative Family Studies* 4: 197–214; Erickson and Moore, "Sexual Activity."

7. Cochran, Mays, and Leung, "Sexual Practices," 383.

8. Connie S. Chan, "Self-esteem and Body Image of Asian American Adolescent Girls," *Journal of the Asian American Psychological Association* 4 (1985): 24–25.

9. Connie S. Chan, "Issues of Identity Development Among Asian American Lesbians and Gay Men," *Journal of Counseling and Development* 68 (1989): 16–20.

10. Connie S. Chan, "Cultural Considerations in Counseling Asian American Lesbians and Gay Men," in *Counseling Gay Men and Lesbians: Journey to the End of the Rainbow*, ed. Sari H. Dworkin and Fernando Gutierrez (Alexandria, Va.: American Association for Counseling and Development, 1992), 122.

3.5 DATING AND ROMANTIC RELATIONSHIPS AMONG GAY, LESBIAN, AND BISEXUAL YOUTHS

Ritch C. Savin-Williams[1]

THE IMPORTANCE OF DATING AND ROMANCE

According to Scarf (1987), the developmental significance of an intimate relationship is to help us "contact archaic, dimly perceived and yet powerfully meaningful aspects of our inner selves" (p. 79). We desire closeness within the context of a trusting, intimate relationship. Attachment theory posits that humans are prewired for loving and developing strongly felt emotional attachments (Bowlby, 1973). When established, we experience safety, security, and nurturance.

Early attachments, including those in infancy, are thought to circumscribe an internal blueprint that profoundly affects future relationships, such as the establishment of intimate friendships and romances in adolescence and adulthood (Hazan & Shaver, 1987).

Developmentally, dating is a means by which romantic relationships are practiced, pursued, and established. It serves a number of important functions, such as entertainment, recreation, and socialization, that assist participants in developing appropriate means of interacting. It also enhances peer group status and facilitates the selection of a mate (Skipper &

Nass, 1966). Adolescents who are most confident in their dating abilities begin dating during early adolescence, date frequently, are satisfied with their dating, and are most likely to become involved in a "committed" dating relationship (Herold, 1979).

The establishment of romantic relationships is important for youths regardless of sexual orientation. Isay (1989) noted that falling in love was a critical factor in helping his gay clients feel comfortable with their gay identity and that "the self-affirming value of a mutual relationship over time cannot be overemphasized" (p. 50). Clinician Browning (1987) regarded lesbian love relationships as an opportunity to enhance

> . . . the development of the individual's adult identity by validating her personhood, reinforcing that she deserves to receive and give love. A relationship can also be a source of tremendous emotional support as the woman explores her goals, values, and relationship to the world. (p. 51)

Because dating experience increases the likelihood that an intimate romantic relationship will evolve, the absence of this opportunity may have long-term repercussions. Malyon (1981) noted some of the reverberations:

> For example, their most charged sexual desires are usually seen as perverted, and their deepest feelings of psychological attachment are regarded as unacceptable. This social disapproval interferes with the preintimacy involvement that fosters the evolution of maturity and self-respect in the domain of object relations. (p. 326)

CULTURE'S DEVALUATION OF SAME-SEX RELATIONSHIPS

Relatively speaking, our culture is far more willing to turn a blind eye to sexual than to romantic relationships among same-sex adolescent partners. Same-sex activity may appear "temporary," an experiment, a phase, or a perverted source of fun. But falling in love with someone of the same gender and maintaining a sustained emotional involvement with that person implies an irreversible deviancy at worst and a bad decision at best. In our homes, schools, religious institutions, and media, we teach that intense relationships

after early adolescence among members of the same sex "should" raise the concern of good parents, good friends, and good teachers. One result is that youths of all sexual orientations may become frightened of developing close friendships with same-sex peers. They fear that these friendships will be viewed as sexually intimate.

It is hardly surprising that a sexual-minority adolescent can easily become "the loneliest person . . . in the typical high school of today" (Norton, 1976, p. 376).

> For the homosexual-identified student, high school is often a lonely place where, from every vantage point, there are couples: couples holding hands as they enter school; couples dissolving into an endless wet kiss between school bells; couples exchanging rings with ephemeral vows of devotion and love. (Sears, 1991, pp. 326–327)

The separation of a youth's homoerotic passion from the socially sanctioned act of heterosexual dating can generate self-doubt, anger, and resentment, and can ultimately retard or distort the development of interpersonal intimacy during the adolescent years. Thus, many youths never consider same-sex dating to be a reasonable option, except in their fantasies. Scientific and clinical writings that ignore same-sex romance and dating among youth contribute to this conspiracy of silence. Sexual-minority youth struggle with issues of identity and intimacy because important impediments rooted in our cultural values and attitudes deter them from dating those they love and instead mandate that they date those they cannot love.

EMPIRICAL STUDIES OF SAME-SEX ROMANTIC RELATIONSHIPS AMONG YOUTH

Until the last several years same-sex relationships among sexual-minority youths were seldom recognized in the empirical, scientific literature. With the recent visibility of gay, bisexual, and lesbian youths in the culture at large, social and behavioral scientists are beginning to conduct research focusing on various developmental processes of such youths, including their sexuality and intimacy.

Bisexual, lesbian, and gay youths, whether in Detroit, Minneapolis, Pennsylvania, New York, or the Netherlands, report that they desire to have long-lasting, committed same-sex romantic relationships in their future (D'Augelli, 1991; Harry & DeVall, 1978; Remafedi, 1987a; Sanders, 1980; Savin-Williams, 1990). According to Silverstein (1981), establishing a romantic relationship with a same-sex partner helps one to feel "chosen," to resolve issues of sexual identity, and to feel more complete. Indeed, those who are in a long-term love relationship generally have high levels of self-esteem and self-acceptance.[2]

Although there are few published studies of teens that focus primarily on their same-sex dating or romantic relationships, there are suggestive data that debunk the myth in our culture that gays, lesbians, and bisexuals neither want nor maintain steady, loving same-sex relationships. In two studies of gay and bisexual male youths, same-sex relationships are regarded as highly desirable. Among 29 Minnesota youths, 10 had a steady male partner at the time of the interview, 11 had been in a same-sex relationship, and, most tellingly, all but 2 hoped for a steady male partner in their future (Remafedi, 1987a, 1987b). For these youths, many of whom were living independently with friends or on the street, being in a long-term relationship was considered to be an ideal state. With a college-age sample of 61 males, D'Augelli (1991) reported similar results. One half of his sample was "partnered," and their most troubling mental health concern was termination of a close relationship, ranking just ahead of telling parents about their homosexuality.

The difficulty, however, is to maintain a visible same-sex romance in high school. Sears (1991) interviewed 36 Southern late adolescent and young adult lesbians, gays, and bisexuals. He discovered that although nearly everyone had heterosexually dated in high school, very few dated a member of the same sex during that time. Because of concerns about secrecy and the lack of social support, most same-sex romances involved little emotional commitment and were of short duration. None were overt.

Research with over 300 gay, bisexual, and lesbian youths between the ages of 14 and 23 years (Savin-Williams, 1990) supports the finding that sexual-minority youths have romantic relationships during adolescence and young adulthood. Almost 90% of the females and two thirds of the males reported that they have had a romantic relationship. Of the total number of romances listed, 60% were with same-sex partners. The male youths were slightly more likely than lesbian and bisexual female youths to begin their romantic career with a same-sex, rather than an opposite-sex, partner.

In the same study, the lesbians and bisexual females who had a high proportion of same-sex romances were most likely to be "out" to others. However, their self-esteem level was essentially the same as those who had a high percentage of heterosexual relationships. If she began same-sex dating early, during adolescence, then a lesbian or bisexual female also tended to be in a current relationship and to experience long-lasting romances. Gay and bisexual male youths who had a large percentage of adolescent romantic relationships with boys had high self-esteem. They were more likely to be publicly "out" to friends and family if they had had a large number of romances. Boys who initiated same-sex romances at an early age were more likely to report that they have had long-term and multiple same-sex relationships.

The findings from these studies are admittedly sparse and do not provide the depth and insight that are needed to help us better understand the experience of being in a same-sex romantic relationship. They do illustrate that youths have same-sex romances while in high school. Where there is desire, some youths will find a way. Sexually active same-sex friendships may evolve into romantic relationships (Savin-Williams, 1995), and those most publicly out are most likely to have had adolescent same-sex romances. Certainly, most lesbian, gay, and bisexual youths value the importance of a same-sex, lifelong, committed relationship in their adult years.

Perhaps the primary issue is not the absence of same-sex romances during adolescence, but the hidden nature of the romances. They are seldom recognized and rarely supported or celebrated. The research data offer little information regarding the psychological impact of not being involved in a same-sex romantic relationship or of having to hide such a relationship when it exists. For this, one must turn to stories of the personal struggles of adolescents.

PERSONAL STRUGGLES

Youths who have same-sex romances during their adolescence face a severe struggle to have these relationships acknowledged and supported. Gibson (1989) noted the troubling contradictions:

> The first romantic involvements of lesbian and gay male youth are a source of great joy to them in affirming their sexual identity, providing them with support, and assuring them that they too can experience love. However, society places extreme hardships on these relationships that make them difficult to establish and maintain. (pp. 3–130)

The 11-year-old male narrator in Picano's (1985) novel, *Ambidextrous,* had his first sexual encounter with the Flaherty sisters. It was sex, acceptability, and enjoyment, but it was not love. Love and sex, romance and friendship would come into his life when he was 14 years old—not with a girl but with Ricky.

> I joined him and we began kissing sitting up, then wrapped our arms around each other and slowly floated down to the bedspread in a kiss that seemed to last forever and to merge us completely into each other so that we were pilot and co-pilot zooming lightning swift through the lower atmosphere, high as a meteorite. (Picano, 1985, p. 88)

He and Ricky wanted to live together, but they were torn apart by their parents and life circumstances, plunging them "into an instant and near total grief that all Ricky's soothing words and kisses couldn't completely assuage" (p. 98). The narrator's romance with Ricky was perceived by family and friends as merely an adolescent chumship. The intensity of the sex, the affectionate feelings, and the emotional arousal clearly label this as a romantic relationship, a critical marker in the narrator's young life.

A significant number of youths, perhaps those feeling most insecure regarding their sexual identity, may fantasize about being sexually intimate with a same-sex partner but have little hope that it could in fact become a reality. One youth, Lawrence, reported this feeling in his coming-out story.

> While growing up, love was something I watched other people experience and enjoy. . . . The countless men I secretly loved and fantasized about were only in private, empty dreams in which love was never

returned. I seemed to be the only person in the world with no need for love and companionship. . . . Throughout high school and college I had no way to meet people of the same sex and sexual orientation. These were more years of isolation and secrecy. I saw what other guys my age did, listened to what they said and how they felt. I was expected to be part of a world with which I had nothing in common. (Curtis, 1988, pp. 109–110)

A young lesbian, Diane, recalled that "love of women was never a possibility that I even realized could be. You loved your mother and your aunts, and you had girl-friends for a while. Someday, though, you would always meet a man" (Stanley & Wolfe, 1980, p. 47). Girls dated boys and not other girls. Because she did not want to date boys, she did not date.

Another youth knew he had homoerotic attractions, but he never fathomed that they could be expressed to the boy that he most admired, his high school soccer teammate. It took alcohol and the right situation.

> I knew I was checking out the guys in the shower after soccer practice. This scared the shit out of me. Like everyone else I was lookin' through *Playboys* only I was searchin' for the pricks beside the naked women. I thought of myself as hetero who had the urge for males. I fought it, said it was a phase. And then it happened.
>
> Derek was my best friend. After soccer practice the fall of our junior year we celebrated both making the "A" team by getting really drunk. We were just fooling around and suddenly our pants were off and our pricks were in the hands of the other. I was so scared I stayed out of school for three days but we kept being friends and nothing was said until a year later when I came out to everyone and he came up to me with these tears and asked if he made me homosexual. (Savin-Williams, 1995)

It is never easy for youths to directly confront the mores of peers whose values and attitudes are routinely supported by the culture. Nearly all youths know implicitly the rules of socially appropriate behavior and the consequences of nonconformity. This single, most influential barrier to same-sex dating, the threat posed by peers, can have severe repercussions. The penalty for crossing the line of "normalcy" can result in emotional and physical pain.

PEER HARASSMENT AS A BARRIER TO DATING

In a paper addressed to school personnel concerning high school students' attitudes toward homosexuality, Price (1982) concluded, "Adolescents can be very cruel to others who are different, who do not conform to the expectations of the peer group" (p. 472). Very little has changed in the last decade. For example, 17-year-old actor Ryan Phillippe worried about the consequences on his family and friends if he played a gay teen on ABC's soap opera "One Life to Live" (Gable, 1992, p. 3D). David Ruffin, 19, of Ferndale, Michigan, explained why he boycotted his high school senior prom: "The kids could tell I was different from them, and I think I was different because I was gay. And when you're dealing with young people, different means not cool" (Bruni, 1992, p. 10A).

Unlike heterosexual dating, little social advantage, such as peer popularity or acceptance, is gained by holding hands and kissing a same-sex peer in school hallways, shopping malls, or synagogues. Lies are spun to protect secrets and to avoid peer harassment. One lesbian youth, Kim, felt that she had to be an actress around her friends. She lied to friends by creating "Andrew" when she was dating "Andrea" over the weekend (Bruni, 1992).

To avoid harassment, sexual minority adolescents may monitor their interpersonal interactions. They may wonder, "Am I standing too close?" or "Do I appear too happy to see him(her)?" (Anderson, 1987). Hetrick and Martin (1987) found that youths are often apprehensive to show "friendship for a friend of the same sex for fear of being misunderstood or giving away their secretly held sexual orientation" (p. 31). If erotic desires become aroused and threaten expression, youths may seek to terminate same-sex friendships rather than risk revealing their secret. For many adolescents, especially bisexual youths, relationships with the other sex may be easier to develop. The appeal of such relationships is that the youths will be viewed by peers as heterosexual, thus peer acceptance will be enhanced and the threat of harassment and rejection will be reduced. The result is that some sexual-minority youths feel inherently "fake" and they therefore retreat from becoming intimate with others.

Although they may meet the implicit and explicit demands of their culture, it is at a cost—their sense of authenticity.

FAKING IT: HETEROSEXUAL SEX AND DATING

Retrospective data from gay, bisexual, and lesbian adults reveal the extent to which heterosexual dating and sex are commonplace during the adolescent and young adult years (see Bell & Weinberg, 1978; Gundlach & Riess, 1968; Saghir & Robins, 1973; Schafer, 1976; Spada, 1979; Troiden & Goode, 1980; Weinberg & Williams, 1974). These might be one-night stands, brief romances, or long-term relationships. Across various studies, nearly two thirds of gay men and three quarters of lesbians report having had heterosexual sex in their past. Motivations include fun, curiosity, denial of homoerotic feelings, and pressure to conform to society's insistence on heterosexual norms and behaviors. Even though heterosexual sex often results in a low level of sexual gratification, it is deemed a necessary sacrifice to meet the expectations of peers and, by extension, receive their approval. Only later, as adults, when they have the opportunity to compare these heterosexual relationships with same-sex ones do they fully realize that which they had missed during their younger years.

Several studies with lesbian, bisexual, and gay adolescents document the extent to which they are sexually involved with opposite-sex partners. In five samples of gay and bisexual male youths, over one half reported that they have had heterosexual experiences (Herdt & Boxer, 1993; Remafedi, 1987a, 1987b; Roesler & Deisher, 1972; Savin-Williams, 1990; Sears, 1991). Few, however, had *extensive* sexual contact with females, even among those who began heterosexual sex at an early age. Sex with one or two girls was usually considered "quite enough." Not infrequently these girls were best friends who expressed a romantic or sexual interest in the gay boys. The male youths liked the girls, but they preferred friendships rather than sexual relations. One youth expressed this dilemma:

> She was a year older and we had been friends for a long time before beginning dating. It was a date with

the full thing: dinner, theater, alcohol, making out, sex. At her house and I think we both came during intercourse. I was disappointed because it was such hard work—not physically I mean but emotionally. Later on in my masturbation my fantasies were never of her. We did it once more in high school and then once more when we were in college. I labeled it love but not sexual love. I really wanted them to occur together. It all ended when I labeled myself gay. (Savin-Williams, 1995)

An even greater percentage of lesbian and bisexual female adolescents engaged in heterosexual sexual experiences—2 of every 3 in one study (Herdt & Boxer, 1993), 3 of every 4 in a second (Sears, 1991), and 8 of 10 in a third (Savin-Williams, 1990). Heterosexual activity began as early as second grade and as late as senior year in high school. Few of these girls, however, had extensive sex with boys—usually with two or three boys within the context of dating. Eighteen-year-old Kimba noted that she went through a heterosexual stage,

. . . trying to figure out what was so great about guys sexually. I still don't understand. I guess that, for straights, it is like it is for me when I am with a woman. . . . I experimented in whatever ways I thought would make a difference, but it was no go. My closest friends are guys; there is caring and closeness between us. (Heron, 1983, p. 82)

Georgina also tried to follow a heterosexual script:

In sixth and seventh grades you start wearing makeup, you start getting your hair cut, you start liking boys—you start thinking about letting them 'French kiss' you. I did all those major things. But, I still didn't feel very satisfied with myself. I remember I never really wanted to be intimate with any guy. I always wanted to be their best friend. (Sears, 1991, p. 327)

One young lesbian, Lisa, found herself "having sex with boys to prove I wasn't gay. Maybe I was even trying to prove it to myself I didn't enjoy having sex with boys" (Heron, 1983, p. 76). These three lesbian youths forfeited a sense of authenticity, intimacy, and love because they were taught that emotional intimacy can only be achieved with members of the other sex.

The reasons sexual-minority adolescents gave in research studies as to why they engaged in heterosex-

ual sex were similar to those reported in retrospective studies by adults. The youths needed to test whether their heterosexual attractions were as strong as their homoerotic ones—thus attempting to disconfirm their homosexuality—and to mask their homosexuality so as to win peer- and self-acceptance and to avoid peer rejection. Many youths in these studies believed that they could not really know whether they were lesbian, gay, bisexual, or heterosexual without first experiencing heterosexual sex. For many, however, heterosexual activities consisted of sex without feelings that they tried to enjoy without much success (Herdt & Boxer, 1993). Heterosexual sex felt unnatural because it lacked the desired emotional intensity.

One young gay youth reported:

We'd been dating for three months. I was 15 and she, a year or so older. We had petted previously and so she planned this event. We attempted intercourse in her barn, but I was too nervous and I think she was on the rag. I didn't feel good afterwards because it was not successful. We did it every week for a month or so. It was fun but it wasn't a big deal. But then I did not have a great lust or drive. Just comfortable. This was just normal I guess. It gave me something to do to tell the other guys who were always bragging. (Savin-Williams, 1995)

Similarly, Kimberly always had a steady heterosexual relationship: "It was like I was just going through the motions. It was expected of me, so I did it. I'd kiss him or embrace him but it was like I was just there. He was probably enjoying it, but I wasn't" (Sears, 1991, p. 327).

Jacob, an African American adolescent (Sears, 1991), dated the prettiest girls in his school in order to maintain his image: "It was more like President Reagan entertaining heads of state. It's expected of you when you're in a certain position" (pp. 126–127). Another Southern male youth, Grant, used "group dates" to reinforce his heterosexual image. Rumors that he was gay were squelched because his jock friends came to his defense: "He's not a fag. He has a girlfriend" (Sears, 1991, p. 328).

These and other personal stories of youths vividly recount the use of heterosexual sex and dating as a cover for an emerging same-sex or bisexual identity. Dating provides opportunities to temporarily "pass" as straight until the meaning of homoerotic feelings are resolved or youths find a safe haven to be lesbian or gay. Heterosexual sex and dating may be less pleasurable than same-sex encounters, but many sexual-minority youths feel that the former are the only safe, acceptable options.

IMPEDIMENTS AND CONSEQUENCES

The difficulties inherent in dating same-sex partners during adolescence are monumental. First is the fundamental difficulty of finding a suitable partner. The vast majority of lesbian, bisexual, and gay youths are closeted, not out to themselves, let alone to others. A second barrier, reviewed earlier in this chapter, is the consequences of same-sex dating, such as verbal and physical harassment from peers. A third impediment is the lack of public recognition or "celebration" of those who are romantically involved with a member of the same gender. Thus, same-sex dating remains hidden and mysterious, something that is either ridiculed, condemned, or ignored.

The consequences of an exclusively heterosexually oriented atmosphere in the peer social world can be severe and enduring. An adolescent may feel isolated and socially excluded from the world of peers. Sex with others of the same gender may be associated exclusively with anonymous, guilt-ridden encounters, handicapping the ability to develop healthy intimate relationships in adulthood. Denied the opportunity for romantic involvement with someone of the same sex, a youth may suffer impaired self-esteem that reinforces the belief that one is unworthy of love, affection, and intimacy. One youth, Rick, even doubted his ability to love:

> When I started my senior year, I was still unclear about my sexuality. I had dated women with increasing frequency, but never felt love for any of them. I discovered that I could perform sexually with a woman, but heterosexual experiences were not satisfying emotionally. I felt neither love nor emotional oneness with women. Indeed, I had concluded that I was incapable of human love. (Heron, 1983, pp. 95–96)

If youths are to take advantage of opportunities to explore their erotic sexuality, it is sometimes, at least

for males, confined to clandestine sexual encounters, void of romance, affection, and intimacy but replete with misgivings, anonymity, and guilt.

> Ted was 21 and me, 16. It was New Year's Eve and it was a swimming pool party at my rich friend's house. Not sure why Ted was there but he really came on to me, even putting his arm around me in front of everyone. He'd been drinking. I wasn't ready for that but I liked it. Real nervous. New Year's Day, every time Ted looked at me I looked away because I thought it was obvious that we had had sex. I know I was an asshole and probably hurt him. It did clarify things for me. It didn't feel like I was cheating on [my girlfriend] Beth because the sex felt so different, so right. (Savin-Williams, 1995)

A gay youth may have genital contact with another boy without ever kissing him because to do so would be too meaningful. Remafedi (1990) found this escape from intimacy to be very damaging: "Without appropriate opportunities for peer dating and socialization, gay youth frequently eschew intimacy altogether and resort to transient and anonymous sexual encounters with adults" (p. 1173). One consequence is the increased risk for contracting sexually transmitted diseases, including HIV. This is particularly risky for youths who turn to prostitution to meet their intimacy needs (Coleman, 1989).

When youths eventually match their erotic and intimacy needs, they may be surprised with the results. This was Jacob's experience (Sears, 1991) when he fell in love with Warren, an African American senior who also sang in the choir. Sex quickly evolved into "an emotional thing." Jacob explained: "He got to the point of telling me he loved me. That was the first time anybody ever said anything like that. It was kind of hard to believe that *even after sex* there are really feelings" (p. 127).

Equally common, however, especially among closeted youths, is that lesbian, bisexual, and gay teens may experience a poverty of intimacy in their lives and considerable social and emotional isolation. One youth, Grant, enjoyed occasional sex with a star football player, but he was devastated by the subsequent exclusion the athlete meted out to him: "We would see each other and barely speak but after school we'd see each other a lot. He had his image that he had to keep up and, since it was rumored that I was gay, he didn't want to get a close identity with me" (Sears, 1991, p. 330).

Largely because of negative peer prohibitions and the lack of social support and recognition, same-sex romances that are initiated have difficulty flourishing. Irwin met Benji in the eighth grade and was immediately attracted to him (Sears, 1991). They shared interests in music and academics and enjoyed long conversations, playing music, and riding in the countryside. Eventually, their attractions for each other were expressed and a romantic, sexual relationship began. Although Irwin was in love with Benji, their relationship soon ended because it was no match for the social pressures and personal goals that conflicted with Irwin being in a same-sex relationship.

Georgina's relationship with Kay began dramatically with intense feelings that were at times ambivalent for both of them. At one point she overheard Kay praying, "Dear Lord, forgive me for the way I am" (Sears, 1991, p. 333). Georgina's parents demanded that she end her "friendship" with Kay. Georgina told classmates they were just "good friends" and began dating boys as a cover. Despite her love for Kay, the relationship ended when Georgina's boyfriend told her that no one liked her because she hung around "that dyke, Kay." In retrospect, Georgina wished: "If everybody would have accepted everybody, I would have stayed with Kay" (p. 334).

Given this situation, lesbian, bisexual, and gay youths in same-sex relationships may place unreasonable and ultimately destructive demands on each other. For example, they may expect that the relationship will resolve all fears of loneliness and isolation and validate all aspects of their personal identity (Browning, 1987).

A Success Story

A vivid account of how a same-sex romantic relationship can empower a youth is depicted in the seminal autobiography of Aaron Fricke (1981), *Reflections of a Rock Lobster*. He fell in love with a classmate, Paul.

> With Paul's help, I started to challenge all the prejudice I had encountered during $16^{1}/_{2}$ years of life. Sure, it was scary to think that half my classmates

might hate me if they knew my secret, but from Paul's example I knew it was possible to one day be strong and face them without apprehension. (p. 44)

Through Paul, Aaron became more resilient and self-confident.

> His strengths were my strengths. . . . I realized that my feelings for him were unlike anything I had felt before. The sense of camaraderie was familiar from other friendships; the deep spiritual love I felt for Paul was new. So was the openness, the sense of communication with another. (p. 45)

Life gained significance. He wrote poems. He planned a future. He learned to express both kindness and strength. Aaron was in love, with another boy.

But no guidelines or models existed on how best to express these feelings.

> Heterosexuals learn early in life what behavior is expected of them. They get practice in their early teens having crushes, talking to their friends about their feelings, going on first dates and to chaperoned parties, and figuring out their feelings. Paul and I hadn't gotten all that practice; our relationship was formed without much of a model to base it on. It was the first time either of us had been in love like this and we spent much of our time just figuring out what that meant for us. (p. 46)

Eventually, after a court case that received national attention, Aaron won the right to take Paul to the senior prom as his date. This victory was relatively minor compared to the self-respect, authenticity, and pride in being gay that their relationship won for each of them.

Final Reflections

As a clinical and developmental psychologist, I find it disheartening to observe our culture ignoring and condemning sexual-minority youth. One consequence is that myths and stereotypes are perpetuated that interfere with or prevent youths from developing intimate same-sex relationships with those to whom they are erotically and emotionally attracted. Separating passion from affection, engaging in sex with strangers in impersonal and sometimes unsafe places, and finding alienation rather than intimacy in those relationships are not conducive to psychological health. In one study the most common reason given for initial suicide attempts by lesbians and gay men was relationship problems (Bell & Weinberg, 1978).

A youth's limited ability to meet other bisexual, lesbian, and gay adolescents compounds a sense of isolation and alienation. Crushes may develop on "unknowing friends, teachers, and peers. These are often cases of unrequited love with the youth never revealing their true feelings" (Gibson, 1989, pp. 3–131).

Sexual-minority youths need the validation of those around them as they attempt to develop a personal integrity and to discover those similar to themselves. How long can gay, bisexual, and lesbian adolescents maintain their charades before they encounter difficulty separating the pretensions from the realities? Many "use" heterosexual dating to blind themselves and others. By so doing they attempt to disconfirm to themselves the growing encroachment of their homoerotic attractions while escaping derogatory name calling and gaining peer status and prestige. The incidence of heterosexual sex and relationships in the adolescence of gay men and lesbians attests to these desires.

Future generations of adolescents will no doubt find it easier to establish same-sex relationships. This is due in part to the dramatic increase in the visibility that adult same-sex relationships have received during the last few years. Domestic partnership ordinances in several cities and counties, victories for spousal equivalency rights in businesses, court cases addressing adoption by lesbian couples and challenges to marriage laws by several male couples, the dramatic story of the life partnership of Karen Thompson and Sharon Kowalski, and the "marriage" of former Mr. Universe Bob Paris to male Supermodel Rod Jackson raise public awareness of same-sex romantic relationships. Even Ann Landers (1992) is spreading the word. In a recent column, an 18-year-old gay teen from Santa Barbara requested that girls quit hitting on him because, as he explained, "I have a very special friend who is a student at the local university . . . and [we] are very happy with each other" (p. 2B).

A decade after Aaron Fricke fought for and won the right to take his boyfriend to the prom, a dozen lesbian, gay, and bisexual youths in the Detroit-Ann Arbor area arranged to have their own prom. Most felt excluded from the traditional high school prom, which they considered "a final, bitter postscript to painful years of feeling left out" (Bruni, 1992, p. 10A). Seventeen-year-old Brenda said, "I want to feel rich for one moment. I want to feel all glamorous, just for one night" (Bruni, 1992, p. 10A). Going to the "Fantasy" prom was a celebration that created a sense of pride, a connection with other sexual-minority teens, and a chance to dance—"two girls together, unguarded and unashamed, in the middle of a room filled with teenagers just like them" (Bruni, 1992, p. 10A). One year later, I attended this prom with my life partner and the number of youths in attendance had increased sixfold.

We need to listen to youths such as Aaron, Diane, Sadie, Georgina, and Picano's narrator, to hear their concerns, insights, and solutions. Most of all, we need to end the invisibility of same-sex romantic relationships. It is easily within our power to enhance the well-being of millions of youths, including "Billy Joe," a character in a famous Bobbie Gentry song. If Billy Joe had seen an option to a heterosexual life style, he might have considered an alternative to ending his life by jumping off the Tallahatchie Bridge.

NOTES

1. Portions of this chapter were previously presented in Savin-Williams (1994).

2. The casual pathway, however, is unclear (Savin-Williams, 1990). That is, being in a same-sex romance may build positive self-regard, but it may also be true that those with high self-esteem are more likely to form love relationships and to stay in them.

REFERENCES

Anderson, D. (1987). Family and peer relations of gay adolescents. In S. C. Geinstein (Ed.), *Adolescent psychiatry: Developmental and clinical studies: Vol. 14* (pp. 162–178). Chicago: The University of Chicago Press.

Bell, A. P., & Weinberg, M. S. (1978). *Homosexualities: A study of diversity among men and women.* New York: Simon & Schuster.

Bowlby, J. (1973). *Attachment and loss: Vol. 2. Separation.* New York: Basic Books.

Browning, C. (1987). Therapeutic issues and intervention strategies with young adult lesbian client: A developmental approach. *Journal of Homosexuality, 14,* 45–52.

Bruni, F. (1992, May 22). A prom night of their own to dance, laugh, reminisce. *Detroit Free Press,* pp. 1A, 10A.

Coleman, E. (1989). The development of male prostitution activity among gay and bisexual adolescents. *Journal of Homosexuality, 17,* 131–149.

Curtis, W. (Ed.). (1988). *Revelations: A collection of gay male coming out stories.* Boston: Alyson.

D'Augelli, A. R. (1991). Gay men in college: Identity processes and adaptations. *Journal of College Student Development, 32,* 140–146.

Fricke, A. (1981). *Reflections of a rock lobster: A story about growing up gay.* Boston: Alyson.

Gable, D. (1992, June 2). "Life" story looks at roots of homophobia. *USA Today,* p. 3D.

Gibson, P. (1989). Gay male and lesbian youth suicide. In M. R. Feinleib (Ed.), *Report of the secretary's task force on youth suicide, Vol. 3: Prevention and interventions in youth suicide (3-110-3-142).* Rockville, MD: U.S. Department of Health and Human Services.

Gundlach, R. H., & Riess, B. F. (1968). Self and sexual identity in the female: A study of female homosexuals. In B. F. Riess (Ed.), *New directions in mental health* (pp. 205–231). New York: Grunet Stratton.

Harry, J., & DeVall, W. B. (1978). *The social organization of gay males.* New York: Praeger.

Hazan, C., & Shaver, P. (1987). Romantic love conceptualized as an attachment process. *Journal of Personality and Social Psychology, 52,* 511–524.

Herdt, G., & Boxer, A. (1993). *Children of horizons: How gay and lesbian teens are leading a new way out of the closet.* Boston: Beacon.

Herold, E. S. (1979). Variables influencing the dating adjustment of university students. *Journal of Youth and Adolescence, 8,* 73–79.

Heron, A. (Ed.). (1983). *One teenager in ten.* Boston: Alyson.

Hetrick, E. S., & Martin, A. D. (1987). Developmental issues and their resolution for gay and lesbian adolescents. *Journal of Homosexuality, 14,* 25–44.

Isay, R. A. (1989). *Being homosexual: Gay men and their development.* New York: Avon.

Landers, A. (1992, May 26). Gay teen tired of advances from sexually aggressive girls. *Detroit Free Press,* p. 2B.

Malyon, A. K. (1981). The homosexual adolescent. Developmental issues and social bias. *Child Welfare, 60,* 321–330.

Norton, J. L. (1976). The homosexual and counseling. *Personnel and Guidance Jourgnal, 54,* 374–377.

Picano, F. (1985). *Ambidextrous.* New York: Penguin.

Price, J. H. (1982). High school students' attitudes toward homosexuality. *Journal of School Health, 52,* 469–474.

Remafedi, G. (1987a). Adolescent homosexuality: Psychosocial and medical implications. *Pediatrics, 79,* 331–337.

Remafedi, G. (1987b). Male homosexuality: The adolescent's perspective. *Pediatrics, 79,* 326–330.

Remafedi, G. (1990). Fundamental issues in the care of homosexual youth. *Adolescent Medicine, 74,* 1169–1179.

Roesler, T., & Deisher, R. (1972). Youthful male homosexuality. *Journal of the American Medical Association, 219,* 1018–1023.

Saghir, M. T., & Robins, E. (1973). *Male and female homosexuality.* Baltimore: Williams & Willins.

Sanders, G. (1980). Homosexualities in the Netherlands. *Alternative Lifestyles, 3,* 278–311.

Savin-Williams, R. C. (1990). *Gay and lesbian youth: Expressions of identity.* New York: Hemisphere.

Savin-Williams, R. C. (1994). Dating those you can't love and loving those you can't date. In R. Montemayor, G. R. Adams, & T. P. Gullotta (Eds.), *Personal relationships during adolescence: Vol. 6. Advances in adolescent development* (pp. 196–215). Newbury Park, CA: Sage.

Savin-Williams, R. C. (1995). *Sex and sexual identity among gay and bisexual males.* Manuscript in preparation, Cornell University, Ithaca, NY.

Scarf, M. (1987). *Intimate partners: Patterns in love and marriage.* New York: Random House.

Schafer, S. (1976). Sexual and social problems of lesbians. *Journal of Sex Research, 12,* 50–69.

Sears, J. T. (1991). *Growing up gay in the South: Race, gender, and journeys of the spirit.* New York: Harrington Park Press.

Silverstein, C. (1981). *Man to man: Gay couples in America.* New York: William Morrow.

Skipper, J. K., Jr., & Nass, G. (1966). Dating behavior: A framework for analysis and an illustration. *Journal of Marriage and the Family, 27,* 412–420.

Spada, J. (1979). *The Spada report: The newest survey of gay male sexuality.* New York: New American Library.

Stanley, J. P., & Wolfe, S. J. (Eds.). (1980). *The coming out stories.* New York: Persephone.

Troiden, R. R., & Goode, E. (1980). Variables related to the acquisition of a gay identity. *Journal of Homosexuality, 5,* 383–392.

Weinberg, M., & Williams, C. J. (1974). *Male homosexuals: Their problems and adaptations.* New York: Penguin.

CHAPTER FOUR

SEXUAL IDENTITIES AND SEXUAL BEHAVIORS

The sexualities that we begin to develop as children are elaborated and amplified as we become sexual adults. And the same processes of assembling and sorting through sexual information are the processes we use as adults. The same four themes—proliferation of sexual images, sexual shame and guilt, gender inequality, and sexual inequality—form the basis of adult sexual behavior.

Lillie Ransom explores the intersection of religious values and sexual activity—one from a survey of college-age virgins and the other from the point of view of a black Christian woman. On the other side of the continuum, Eleanor Maticka-Tyndale and colleagues examine the most casual of casual sex: "hooking up" during spring break. And Sumie Okazaki details the intersection of ethnicity and sexuality.

The essay by this book's editors explores the ways in which gender provides the basis for our sexual fantasies: how we are gender conformists, even in our dreams.

M. Rochlin's clever questionnaire makes clear the ways that daily life reproduces inequalities based on sexuality.

4.1 THE GENDER OF DESIRE
The Sexual Fantasies of Women and Men

Michael S. Kimmel and Rebecca F. Plante

My sex fantasy is pretty straightforward: having sex with a porno star. All out, no holds barred, continuous sex with someone who obviously knows what she's doing. It doesn't really have to be in any specific place, and scenery isn't too important. Sorry to all of you who are into the scenery thing. [man]

It's having sex on the beach. Very romantic setting, very sweet, caring experience. The 'sociological' part would be, I guess, that it includes being 'the woman' i.e., being carried, not being the 'aggressor', rather, being passive. [woman]

I've always had the fantasy of having sex with three or more beautiful blonde babes. It would take

place on a huge waterbed in a big white room overlooking the ocean. Lesbian activity would be fine. I would try to please them at the same time (up to four) two hands, mouth, and groin and they would try to please me. One on top with the others massaging and kissing my body. Two women pleasing each other orally would be a nice enhancement. Oh yes, beforehand we would cover each other in Huskers "corn" oil and no condoms would be used. [man]

Not have a favorite fantasy "scene", more just an overwhelming feeling of tenderness and complete emotional unity between myself and my partner/husband. Loving actions that lead to sex (never really fantasize about the act), i.e., kissing (hand, arm, body), massage, being on an island (Caribbean) with no distractions. Or perhaps spontaneity in location: not in the bedroom on the bed. [woman]

These are actual sexual fantasies from a sample of nearly 350 sexual fantasies collected from undergraduates at several universities during the past decade. Gender differences are visible in every aspect of these sexual fantasies—from language to sexual activities, in both content and form. Sexual fantasies can be viewed as illustrations of socially constructed gender differences and of the landscape of intrapsychic sexuality. In fantasies, we may see more about gendered conceptualizations of sexuality than if we look at actual sexual conduct, which often involves culturally expected gendered compromises.

The most basic element in the social construction of sexualities is gender. In both sexual fantasies and sexual conduct, men and women imagine and enact different sexual scripts, the culturally articulated blueprints we use to shape "appropriate" sexual conduct (Gagnon & Simon, 1973). Sexual scripts also help to confirm gender identities, consequently expressed in both fantasies and conduct.

Contrary to earlier studies of sexuality, researchers now understand fantasy to be a "normal" component of sexual experience (Kaplan, 1974; Masters & Johnson, 1966, 1970). Sexual fantasy has assumed an increasingly salient place in sexualities research, so that it is now understood that:

> Sexual fantasy is hypothesized to have links to the cognitive, affective, and behavioral systems as erotic fantasies can contain factual information, affective reactions, and lead to overt responses. Sexual fantasies can also serve as the stimulus leading to physiological arousal, the subsequent cognitive and affective evaluation, and ultimately, overt behavior. In short, sexual fantasies may be the driving force for human sexuality (Chick & Gold, 1988, p. 62).

Some researchers even claim that sexual fantasy "provides a clearer picture of male and female sexual natures than does the study of sexual action" (Ellis & Symons, 1990, p. 551). As evidenced by their phrase "male and female sexual natures," Ellis and Symons offer a sociobiological analysis of fantasy, arguing that fantasies are rooted in evolutionary, sex-based strategies.

But how do we begin to conceptualize and operationalize possible connections between fantasies and (inter)actions? And are there sociological explanations for gender (not sex) differences? Using respondent-written fantasies, we explore gender differences in active and passive language, sexual and sensual content, and emotional and romantic imagery. We propose some sociostructural explanations for the differences we document, and discuss some links between fantasies and behaviors.

METHODS AND DATA COLLECTION

For this research, we collected 340 usable responses (249 women and 91 men) to an open-ended question about sexual fantasies. Usable responses were defined as: only one fantasy mentioned, with sex of the respondent clearly indicated. We simply asked respondents to write a sexual fantasy that they consistently found arousing, perhaps the one they thought about most often. We gave no instructions about whether or how to specify details of the fantasy; respondents were free to be as descriptive or vague as they wished. Also, respondents may have provided masturbatory or coital fantasies, or daydreams, as we did not specify. The open-ended design enabled us to obtain fantasies expressed in the language, tone, and descriptive depth that each respondent chose. We collected these fantasies in seven social science classes at two colleges and one public university in suburban Long Island, New York. The lack of representation in this sample, along with other methodological considerations, is extensively discussed later.

Respondents were assured of the anonymity and confidentiality of their responses. If respondents did not wish to participate for any reason, we asked them to state something to the effect of 'I do not wish to participate'; some did so and also explained why. These were collected along with the fantasies. In all, nine men (7%) and 46 women (18.5%) did not wish to participate. After analyzing the fantasies a researcher returned to each class and discussed methods, findings, and how to sociologically interpret the results.

We were particularly interested in four themes in the collected fantasies:

1. narrative description: the use of language, linguistic explicitness vs. vagueness, use of slang;

2. emotional description: relationship of affective behaviors to sexual behaviors, explicitness of emotional/intimate feelings;

3. sensual imagery: scene setting, use of props, level of nonsexual detail, geographical and temporal settings; and

4. sexual imagery: elaborateness, specificity, and vagueness of sexual activities.

In men's fantasies, we expected to find more explicit discussion of sexual conduct, vague or unspecified emotional content, little sensual imagery and romance, and diverse sexual imaginations. In women's fantasies, we expected to find vague or unspecified descriptions of sexual conduct, detailed emotional connections with partners, descriptive sensual imagery and romantic content and less diverse sexual imaginations.

We also expected to find that men's fantasies, compared with women's, employed more "active" language. For example, except when specifically describing sexual or mental submission to a partner, we expected men to use language like, "I took off her clothes." We expected women to use language like, "He took off my clothes," unless explicitly describing a fantasy of dominance.

While our primary analysis is qualitative, the fantasies were also quantitatively content analyzed using a simple coding scheme and gamma, a measure of association and order in dichotomous variables (see Table 4.1.1). We coded each fantasy based on presence or absence of 33 variables, including partner

Table 4.1.1 Gamma and Descriptive Statistics

Variable Name	Gamma	% of men mentioning	% of women mentioning
Partner Type:			
significant other	0.6596	15.38	46.99
famous person	−0.6243	6.59	1.61
taboo person	−0.3047	12.09	6.83
multiple partners	−0.7522	40.66	8.84
"mr(mrs) right"	0.6732	3.3	14.86
Fantasy Dimensions:			
Romance/romantic	0.6911	7.69	31.33
emotions/emotional	0.6208	10.99	34.54
place mentioned	0.3108	24.18	37.75
time/moment specified	0.5071	45.05	71.49
time described	0.4896	16.48	36.55
sensual props?	0.031	17.58	28.51
intercourse occurred	−0.3039	78.02	65.46
fellatio occurred	−0.5714	12.09	3.61
masturbation occurred	−0.4303	7.69	3.21
lesbian acts mentioned	−0.5	13.19	4.29
Explicit Mention Of:			
man as aggressor	0.4974	4.4	12.05
woman as aggressor	−0.7512	20.88	3.61
slang for "make love"	−0.5687	41.76	16.47
physical appearance	−0.6019	48.35	18.88
body type, parts, etc	−0.549	23.08	8.03

Note: these are variables with gamma values of +/−0.30 or greater.

types (significant other, "Mr[Ms] Right", taboo person, etc.); romantic/emotional content; sensual content (place, time described, etc.); sexual content (coitus, fellatio, cunnilingus, etc.); language (use of slang, "make love," etc.); and references to physical characteristics. Kappa, a statistic for assessing interrater reliability, yielded average interrater agreement of 96.52% agreement for the 33 coded variables (range = 82.8% to 100%). Values for kappa ranged from 0.51 to 1, indicating substantial to 'almost perfect' agreement (Table 4.1.2).

FINDINGS
Narrative and Sexual Elements

Narrative strategies differed for women and men. Everything from length of fantasies to descriptions of sensual and sexual elements to actual language employed varied according to gender of respondent. Take, for example, these mens' fantasies:

"Menage-a-trois."
"2 hot babes and myself going at it."

Table 4.1.2 Kappa Values for Interrater Reliability

Variable Name	Kappa	% of men mentioning	% of women mentioning
Partner Type:			
significant other	0.9104	95.7	51.99
famous person	0.7947	98.92	94.76
taboo person	1	100	86.08
multiple partners	0.9698	98.92	64.45
"mr(mrs) right"	0.8771	97.85	82.5
Fantasy Dimensions:			
Romance/romantic	0.7729	92.47	66.85
emotions/emotional	0.7617	93.55	72.92
place mentioned	0.93	96.77	53.9
time/moment specified	0.6782	83.87	49.88
time described	0.5131	82.8	64.67
sensual props?	0.8577	94.62	62.23
intercourse occurred	0.8656	93.55	51.99
fellatio occurred	1	100	93.76
masturbation occurred	1	100	93.76
lesbian acts mentioned	0.9275	98.92	85.17
Explicit Mention Or:			
man as aggressor	0.9173	98.92	86.99
woman as aggressor	0.7543	95.7	82.5
slang for "make love"	0.8028	93.55	67.28
physical appearance	0.9723	98.92	61.19
body type, parts, etc	0.9504	98.92	78.32

Note: these are variables with gamma values of +/–0.30 or greater. (See Table 1).

Kappa values are as follows:

0.41–0.60 moderate interrater agreement

0.61–0.80 substancial interrater agreement

0.81–1.00 almost perfect interrater agreement

"To have sex [crossed out, with "make love" substituted] with an older woman 10 or so years older."
"Have sex on the beach."

These are not *excerpts* from fantasies—they are the *entire* fantasies. Overall, we found that men's fantasies were shorter than women's, word for word, largely due to amount of emotional and sensual scenery women tended to describe (discussed later). This differs from Follingstad and Kimbrell's finding that men wrote more words and longer single fantasies than did women (1986).

Other language differences appeared when considering the explicitly sexual aspects of the fantasies. Both genders used the following terms for intercourse: *make love, have intercourse, have sex, do it, fuck, and*

make mad passionate love. However, there were more extensive gender differences. Some terms for intercourse in men's fantasies were *going at it, having her way with me, have, perform, inflict extreme pleasure on, knocking boots, satisfying them, penetration, and thrusting. Women's fantasies used terms such as get intimate, doing his dishes, jumping him, have me, be together, become one, impalement, sexual experience/situation, rolling and thrusting, it goes from there, you can guess the rest, pelvic thrust, inside me.*

The terms men used had more 'active' connotations than the terms women used. Women's terms were gentler, vaguer, and less precise than men's, exemplified by "you can guess the rest" versus "inflict extreme pleasure on." Notably, not one of the 249 women in the sample referred to male genitalia as anything other than

Table 4.1.3 Language Examples From Fantasies

Examples of Women's Passive Language	Examples of Women's Active Language	Examples of Men's Passive Language	Examples of Men's Active Language
being caressed	giving him pleasure	whatever the person's into	at my beck and call
turns me on	forced to eat me out	relate to me sexually	I watch them
knows where to touch me	tie up	get dominated	involve myself with them
man-handled	whip	he mounts and rides me	they fight for my penis
completely controlled	take photos of	taken control of	I perform anal sex
whatever happens, happens	watch	humiliated	going at it
be stranded	give oral sex	enslaved	I'm with two women
he enters me	tease	doing things to me	she falls down onto my penis
he creates the scenery	undress him	I'm a sex slave	I push her onto her back
he makes me feel things	I have multiple orgasms		I give her/him orgasms
he has me touch/lick/suck	I make love to him		my orgasm is the high point
he carries me	someone is watching		I satisfy her/him
he pulls me close	it's rough sex		I flip her over
he takes advantage of me			she's bent over the desk
he saves me from rape			I make love to
he wants me			inflict extreme pleasure on
I'm in danger			undress her
I pretend innocence			I press her against me
tied up			
he lays his body on mine			
we become one			
he shows me how to satisfy			
I experience/encounter			

"penis." However, both men and women reserved their most creative language for coitus. Frank and Anshen (1983) noted the profusion of sex-marked verbs, particularly for the stereotypic male role in coitus (conversely, there is a dearth of terms for the stereotypic female role). They concluded that, "Women are thus assigned passive roles in sex by our language" (1983, p. 68). Richter's 1987 analysis of English language sexual slang would support this. He notes terms for women's anatomy such as waste pipe, hole, slit, and teats. Terms for men's anatomy include tassel, prick, ladies' delight, bollocks, and rather 'active' words like pile-driver, hair-divider, and live rabbit.

Perhaps in correspondence with these differences in sexual language and slang, we found that men's descriptions of specifically sexual activities were direct, active and clear:

> "The women would wipe my cum all over themselves and lick it off one another."
> "She says, 'Put your cock in my ass'."
> "I'll be more interest[ed] if she started playing with those beautiful tits she has and starts fingering herself."
> "She falls down, slowly landing directly on my penis, moving in a motion I have never witnessed before. She makes me have orgasms I never had before."

In describing what *may* be sexual activities, women tended to be more vague:

> "We do not make love genitally, but whole bodily."
> "We begin to have intercourse."
> "One thing leads to another."

These differences in sexual explicitness hint at what we suggest is the underlying cultural sexual script. Women's fantasies subtly and overtly depicted the relatively standard foreplay-then-intercourse script, even when telling the reader to use the imagination to envision what happens next. Men's fantasies incorporated more description of sexual acts, particularly those that culminated in orgasm.

For these variables, qualitative analysis of differences in sexual slang and description of sexual conduct is crucial, because quantitative analysis cannot capture the extent of these differences. For example, 78% of men and 65% of women offered fantasies that implied or specified intercourse. About 12% of the men and 3% of the women described or implied fellatio. Half of the men and 56% of the women used the term "make love" in their fantasies. But simple frequencies do not show that men tended to specify, describe, and rhapsodize about intercourse, while women tended to imply and sidestep the event. We return to the sexual imagery and content of these fantasies after exploring the more emotional and sensual themes we observed.

Emotional and Romantic Elements

Our research revealed gender differences in the emotional content and tone of the sample's fantasies as well. Women often specified that the fantasy partner was a significant other, and typically used the words "boyfriend" or "husband" (47% of women), while only 15% of men referred to partners who were significant others. Moreover, 15% of the women specifically described opposite sex partners whom they called "Mr. Right," the "man of my dreams," or "wonderful in every way," while only 3% of men did so. Instead, men offered fantasies that involved a celebrity (6.5% vs. 1% of women), a taboo partner (teacher, employer) or multiple partners. Only 12% of men mentioned taboo partners (6% of women did so), but fully 40% of men's fantasies involved two or more partners. About 9% of the women's fantasies included multiple partners.

Typical women's fantasies instead included romantic and emotional ideas like these:

> "He would hold me close and cater to my every need. He would treat me like a princess."
> "I want this to be my honeymoon. I want this to be the first time that I make love."
> "Finally he comes right out and says really sensitively and emotionally how he needs me as more than a friend and we got into this huge fight and then he suddenly pins me against the wall, and starts kissing me and then stops and says he's sorry but he couldn't help it."

Women's fantasies were generally stories of love, affection, and romance. Men's fantasies involved less description of emotional or romantic themes and provided less emotional context. A few men's fantasies were, for this sample, gender-transgressive narratives, where the man described a loving, committed relationship with a significant other or "the woman of his dreams." Gender-transgressive fantasies for women in this sample described sexually active, ardent, assertive women, searching for multiple partners, who had multiple orgasms and multiple contexts for sexual expression.

Such differences conform to traditional gender stereotypes. Women learn to associate emotional commitment and affection with sexuality (Athanasiou, Shaver & Tavris, 1970; DeLamater & MacCorquodale, 1979; DeLamater, 1987; Lott, 1992; Simon & Gagnon, 1998). Women are often taught that sexuality should be intertwined with a "relational orientation," instead of being taught that sexuality can be viewed as a route to physical pleasure (a "recreational orientation"), as many men are (Gagnon & Simon, 1973; DeLamater, 1987). Thus, it is not surprising that women's fantasies maintain these conventions by incorporating sexual expression into committed, emotionally meaningful relationships. Men's fantasies display the learned ability to differentiate between sexual and emotional activities.

An area of quantitative difference in the fantasies in this sample involves specified or implied romantic and emotional content. Women provided more romantic fantasies with clear 'emotional' content—34.5% compared to 11% of the men. This squares with what women learn about sexuality via cultural sexual scripting. Some of the women's fantasies, such as, "He would hold me close and cater to my every need. He would treat me like a princess," (cited above) were essentially romantic, emotional *nonsexual* narratives. Thirty-one percent of the women's fantasies included romantic imagery, while only 7.5% of the men's did.

One possible measure of this sample's differences in emotional and affective content could be the amount of physical description of the fantasy partner(s). We observed that elaboration of the physical attributes of the fantasy partner seemed to be present in fantasies with less emotional and romantic imagery. About 48% of the men mentioned something about the appearance of the partner(s), and 23% of the men very specifically described physical attributes of the partner(s).

This may be due to fantasy partner choice. Since fewer men fantasized a specific, 'actual' partner (i.e.,

a significant other, spouse, lover), they may have felt more compelled to specify the distinct 'pieces and parts' of the fantasy partner(s). Cultural sexual scripts also teach some men how to attach sexual attraction to specific body parts or attributes—"I'm a leg/breast/butt man" is a common expression. However, we do not often hear heterosexual women saying. "I'm a butt/penis/chest woman."

To wit, men's fantasies included very clear depictions of physical characteristics, particularly when multiple partners were mentioned:

> "They must be thin with nice bubble asses and medium, upturned breasts (with nipples like pencil erasers)."
> "Elle McPherson type, gorgeous looking, hot woman, straight long hair, with lots of great hot looking clothes on."
> "These women are of course slim, trim and tan and obviously incredibly sexy."
> "The entire Swedish bikini team—big breasts, blond, unbelievably curvy asses."
> "One of the women would be blonde, the other dark haired, about 5'7" to 5'10", knock-out bodies."

Women did mention partner's physiques, but the language was more general:

> "I'm out on a date with a nicely built man. . . ."
> ". . . tall, built, and unbelievably gorgeous. . . ."
> ". . . really good looking."
> "Someone so gorgeous I have to have him."

Men described exactly what their fantasy partners looked like, and even mentioned celebrities who constituted visual 'blueprints' of their affinities, in case the reader was unclear about exactly how gorgeous or firm the fantasy partner ought to be. When women mentioned physical characteristics, generally they stated simply that the man was attractive and fit. Another way to explore these emotional differences is to look at the differences between sensual and sexual content.

Sensual Imagery

Sensual imagery refers to narrative elements that set a scene, evoke a mood, develop a story line, provide non-sexual detail, and, especially, provide descriptions of geographical and temporal settings and the use of props (like candles, clothing, food, etc.). Descriptions of fantasy location were more common among women (38% vs. 24% of men). Women also tended to situate their fantasies temporally (e.g., morning, afternoon) and then describe the moment. Fully 71.5% of women specified a time or moment for the fantasy, while only 45% of men did so. However, only 36.5% of women further described the temporal moment, along with 16.5% of men.

It should be noted that more often than expected, men did situate their fantasies, but rarely with the extensive description found in women's fantasies. About 64% of men specified some location, while about 74% of women did so. But this superficial numerical similarity does not fully show the gender differences in fantasy scene-setting. While many men mentioned that their fantasies occurred near water or on a beach, often this was all that they said. Most women not only mentioned the locale, but also things like the air and water temperature, the ocean surrounding the fantasized island, the number of other people in the area (if any), and various sensual props (dinner, a picnic, wine, etc.).

Women offered far more detailed descriptions of geographic location. For example, *men* offered these descriptions:

"If I had to pick a location, I guess I would choose a place a little out of the ordinary."
"My sexual fantasy involves being on an island with only sexually attractive and available females. . . ."
"I like to think of dogs barking and being in an industrial setting, during lovemaking that is. Fear and discomfort are integral parts of my fantasy."
"As far as the setting goes it makes no difference, only important factor is that we are both with her at the same time."

Women's fantasies were opposite in terms of length and clarity:

". . . A tropical island. I've always dreamed about making love in a crystal blue sea, with a waterfall in the background, then moving on shore to a white, sandy beach."
"It's eveningtime [sic], the sun is setting, I'm on a tropical island, a light breeze is blowing into my balcony doors and the curtains (white) are flutter-

ing lightly in the wind. The room is spacious and there is white everywhere, even the bed. There are flowers of all kinds and the light fragrance fills the room."
"The room would be filled with candles and soft music would fill the air, he would feed me strawberries, which we'd share, and in the morning we'd wake, bathe one another, and. . . ."
"We are out in the country. There is no one for miles around. There is an open yard in the back of the house surrounded by woods. All we can hear is the chirping of birds and the rustling of leaves. It is raining. Not a monsoon, not a drizzle, but a warm summer afternoon shower. There is a big, beautiful, white gazebo in the middle of the yard."

Regardless of whether women were fantasizing about the beach or some other locale, they described more specific elements of the setting than did men in this sample. Women tended to emphasize romantic and aesthetic elements. Some of the fantasies included very detailed settings, replete with colors, textures, and fabrics, with no mention of anything overtly sexual. It seems that women's fantasies displayed more elaborate "sensual imaginations" than did men's.

Sexual Imagery

The specifically sexual dimensions of the fantasies revealed that women may have developed sensual imaginations, but men displayed more developed "sexual imaginations." More men than women mentioned intercourse, giving/getting fellatio, masturbatory activities, lesbian activities, and "woman as aggressor"—the woman making the first move and/or orchestrating the encounter:

Variable	Men mentioned	Women mentioned
Intercourse	78%	65%
Fellatio	12%	3%
Masturbation	7.7%	3%
Lesbian activities	13%	4%
Woman as aggressor	21%	3.6%

Women described "man as aggressor" more often than "woman as aggressor"; 12% of women described male partners this way, while 3.7% described themselves as taking the lead (see above chart).

Men's descriptions of fantasized sexual activities tended to be explicit and clear, although not necessarily verbose. For example:

"The fantasy reaches a second high point during the longest and most powerful orgasm/ejaculation ever."

"Totally uninhibited sexual activity."

"Her voice will be sincere, yet playful. She will suggest that I take a good look at her breasts. In her attitude I would find no inhibitions whatsoever."

Women described sexual scenes such as:

"He tells me I mean more to him than anything else in the world and that he's never been happier in his entire life . . . I then look into his gorgeous eyes and say—'I do want this more than anything in the world—I love you'."

". . . Our secret, not even knowing each other's name. Like a mystery, and I'll never see him again."

"He'd get so excited that he wouldn't be able to control himself and he would grab me and make passionate love to me."

"Have my ideal man and myself together for the whole day. While we are together, we would play sports and then go home and take a shower together. Have no one else to bother us from the outside world and have it feel like eternity and never wanting to leave."

The primary difference in the moods and moments described by the respondents is that men envisioned sexual moments of wild abandon, no inhibitions, with sexually inventive, assertive women. Women rarely imagined themselves as sexual actors, aggressors or initiators, and certainly not as much as men imagined women as sexual actors.

The average man's fantasy in this sample, however, made sexual conduct clear and explicit, while providing the reader with some new slang for a vernacular collection. He tells us that he "got head" first, then she was turned onto her stomach while he entered her, and that after he came (explosively, of course), she climbed aboard him and "rode him like an angel on a bronco."

"To have sex with at least 3 women—one blond/blue eyes, brunette/brown eyes, and redhead/green eyes. All friends, 22 years old and bodies that stepped out of Penthouse. All 5′6″ or shorter. Have a totally wild, uninhibited time, knocking boots all night long then start again in the A.M. I'd do it in the shower, on the hood of my caddy, and on the kitchen table. And of course I'd satisfy all of them, repeatedly."

While a scene is set, at least formally, there is no mood created by the scene-setting as in the women's fantasies. Unlike women's fantasies, we don't know whether there were any lit candles, half-drunk glasses of bubbly, and soft, gentle breezes.

Just as men's descriptions of their sexual repertoire tended to be more elaborate, that repertoire also tended to be a bit more extensive. While neither women nor men tended to mention giving or receiving cunnilingus, men did mention receiving fellatio more than women mentioned giving it. In some cases, oral sex might have been subsumed in vague, reductive narratives such as "then we messed around for a while" or "we rub and kiss each other all over."

Qualitative analysis did show that explicit language, description, and developed sexual imaginations were present in a few women's fantasies. When women wrote fantasies that included their sexual agency, multiple partners, anonymous partners, and oral sex of both types—in short, the stereotypic elements of masculine fantasies—they did so in 'active', explicit language with sexual descriptiveness.

Similarities Between the Genders

We expected men to be much more likely to mention a stranger as the fantasy partner, but there was little difference between men's and women's responses (11% of men, 9% of women). There was also little difference in fantasies specifically mentioning a 'friend' as a partner (12% of men, 7.6% of women). However, more men did not specify exactly who the fantasy partner was or what the relationship was (if any) to that person. For example, some men mentioned that there were two blondes, but they were further undefined. They could have both been strangers to the fantasizer, they could have been friends—it was unclear and not implied.

As for other sexual activities, such as dominance and submission, few respondents went beyond the standard cultural script (e.g. kissing, intercourse). This could be due to lack of sexual experience, age cohort effects, and/or respondent bias. Participants may have been self-conscious about presumed researcher responses to fantasy content; inhibition may have prevented respondents from including avant-garde activities and scenarios about which they actually fantasized.

In the language of the fantasies, men and women did not differ in their use of the terms *make love/have sex/have intercourse*. But there may actually be a more subtle connection between fantasized partner and/or relationship status and word chosen. Individuals of either gender may use "make love" when describing conduct with a significant other, and "have sex" with a stranger or with multiple partners. Since more women than men specify significant others, women may thus be more likely to use "make love."

Neither sex mentioned "penis/vagina" very much or used slang for genitalia, although men described *intercourse* in more ways than did women. But researchers find that men are generally more likely to improvise with language, use slang, and speak more casually (Lakoff, 1990; Coward, 1985). It has been argued that men create language and therefore feel more entitled to expand it (Spender, 1985). Further, Sanders and Robinson (1979) found that, in conversation, women use more formal and clinical terminology for genitalia and sexual activities than do men.

LIMITATIONS

The generalizability of these findings is limited in several respects. First, we used a college-based convenience sample that was intrinsically self-selecting on many levels. The students in the classes we visited were studying intimate relationships, sexuality, and gender. There were disparities between the number of women enrolled and the number of men enrolled. Additionally, the men who enroll in these classes may differ from the women who enroll. The relatively small number of men (N = 91) included in this sample may also have some bearing on the results. In addition, there was no way to guarantee that all enrolled students would be in attendance on the day of fantasy collection. Every student who was present had the option of not participating; there is no way to know how many students elected not to write a fantasy but also did not return an answer to this effect.

Another kind of respondent bias may also be present. While comfortable with participating generally, some respondents may have felt uncomfortable writing fantasies that they considered avant garde, unusual, or "kinky," fearing negative researcher responses. Some respondents may have tried to anticipate what kinds of fantasies we wanted and may have thus tried to provide especially typical responses. Clearly, respondent and sample biases must be taken into account when interpreting the results.

These results are not fully generalizable to all men and women because of other independent variables that bear on the sample. Most of the respondents were between 18 and 22, a typical college student age range. An older or younger sample would be likely to provide different fantasies, connected perhaps to different life experiences and relationships. The research occurred in a college setting; respondents of a similar age range who are not in college might answer differently.

The sample may also be overly skewed away from white, middle-class respondents also. The campuses at which data were collected are highly diverse campuses; one actually has a majority of people of color on campus and a minority white student body (49%). However, there were no overt differences among the fantasies that lead us to suspect that "race" needed to be provided by respondents (along with "sex") as an independent variable. Nonetheless, if we *had* asked for other independent variables, non-gendered differences may have become more obvious. This is especially possible given that different racial and ethnic groups vary in religiosity and subcultural sexual scripts. The different experiences of minorities and non-minorities are visible in virtually every aspect of social and mental life, and sexuality intersects with race and ethnicity along with gender, class, and sexual orientation.

Beyond the limitations on generalizability imposed by the sample, there are other considerations posed by our methodology. An open-ended question enabled respondents to write almost nothing ("menage-a-trois," for example) or to compose long essays. Future research that asks respondents to specify certain elements (such as who? where? when?, etc.) of fantasies might yield responses with more comparability, although forced-choice response options can lead to other problems. Additionally, the coding scheme we devised was developed based on what we expected to find in the fantasies. Finally, regarding descriptive excerpts, the excerpted or actual fantasies included here were chosen to highlight typical gendered differences. Gender transgressive fantasies, and the few that seemed indistinguishable as to the author's sex were not included in this discussion.

THE SOCIOLOGY OF SEXUAL FANTASIES

Both women and men fantasize themselves as sexually irresistible objects of desire, and both fantasize themselves as the recipients of sexual activities. Women seem to use a more passive linguistic style than do men when describing penile-vaginal intercourse. Men seem to use more active language to describe sexual activities, even when fantasizing themselves as the recipients of these activities, even when tied up (from one fantasy with bondage: "I tell her to suck me and she does").

How can this be explained? How can men use the language of *activity* to describe something during which they seem to be powerless? In heterosexual encounters, men and women often interpret the same behaviors from different sides of the power equation. For example, men experience both fellatio and cunnilingus as expressions of their power—along the lines of, 'I can get her to suck me,' and 'When I go down on her I can make her come'—regardless of whether the man is 'actually' active or passive.

Symmetrically, women experience both fellatio and cunnilingus as expressions of their lack of power—"He forces my mouth onto his penis," and, "He goes down on me and I'm helpless" (from the fantasies in this sample)—regardless of whether the woman is 'actually' passive or active. Perhaps measures of activity and passivity may more accurately be cast as measures of interpersonal sexual power, in terms of who has more power in heterosexual interactions. These 'false symmetries' lead us to consider the ways in which a sociological discussion reveals important dimensions of sexual fantasy that have been overlooked by previous psychological researchers.

Although our findings corroborate earlier research findings, our interpretation is different. Psycho-

biological research on fantasies tends to locate fantasy in sex-linked, innate mental structures. Ellis and Symons, for example, claimed that evolutionary selection was responsible for the gender differences they observed. Thus, men's penchant for new, different, and unknown female partners was explained (the need to spread "seed") and women's penchant for emotional, committed male partners was explained (the need to find one male who would be responsible for the offspring of their union).

Instead, we suggest that gender differences in fantasies are rooted in deep *social* structures. Differential sexual scripting, with the goal of reinforcing socially constructed gender role identities, is the primary axis of disparity. With socialization into a binary gender system that also assumes heterosexuality, gender is enormously powerful in the construction of the sexual self. So we would expect to see gender differences trumping sexual orientation differences, although this idea has not been fully explored.

Since our social structures also have inequities built in, we would expect to see these inequities reproduced in even the most intimate realms of individuals—in sexual fantasies, the intrapsychic level of sexual scripting. These structural gender inequalities have consequences. By casting themselves as fantasy objects of desire, with less visible sexual agency, (heterosexual) women may ultimately be less able to exert sexual desires in social interactions. Meanwhile men, who cast themselves as sexual actors, filled with sexual agency, may ultimately enact a wider range of sexual behaviors without quandaries.

One possible consequence of how inequalities play themselves out in fantasies has an empirical element: in our sample, none of the men or women mentioned having safer sex. Respondents mentioned condoms (and contraception, for that matter) *only* to point out that their fantasies explicitly *did not* include latex, safety, or worries about disease/pregnancy. This superficial symmetry, however, only serves to mask the important difference. We could be concerned with these respondents' general inability to incorporate safer sex practices into their fantasies, but clearly women and men are differently affected by this inability.

Recall that when women fantasized about men, the men they fantasized about were loved, trusted, and intimate; most women fantasized about past or present significant others. When men fantasized about women, their relationships to the women were unclear, perhaps involving strangers, friends, or multiple partners. Here the potentially dangerous consequences of unsafe sexual practices are for more marked—especially for the female partners. Women's fantasized lack of sexual agency can thus translate into an inability to implement safer sex practices *and* insist on them. Men's abundant sociostructural sexual power can thus translate into an ability to avoid safer sex and to persuade partners to avoid it as well. In both cases, the women fantasizers and the anonymous women of men's fantasies are at risk.

We might also see arenas of difficulty between the sexes in the form of sexual harassment and date rape. With such visible incongruities between the ways in which heterosexual men and women *imagine* sexual encounters, it is possible that these disparities could be transformed into violent and aggressive sexual conflicts. Duncombe and Marsden (1996) describe "... the level of the basic discourses of sexual exchange [that] undermine women's ability and right to initiate or refuse sexual intercourse" (p. 224). We suggest that these basic exchanges and discourses are evident in the genders' fantasies. When inequitable power exchanges permeate the intrapsychic dimensions of sexual scripting, heterosex can be compromised in multiple ways.

The gray areas between fantasies and realities seem likely to be translated into problems for heterosexual women and men. If women translated their sexual fantasies into behaviors, then they would demand sensual intimate emotional connections with committed sexual partners. If men translated their fantasies into behaviors, then they would want highly sexual encounters with active and skilled women, without always requiring an emotional, relational context. Thus when women and men have sex with one another, each may experience a level of compromise from the ideal(ized) images expressed in fantasies. Duncombe and Marsden (1996) refer to these compromises collectively as 'sex work', expanding Arlie Hochschild's concept of emotion work (1983). In heterosexual 'sex work', partners interpret gendered sexual scripts in terms of necessary compromises, partic-

ularly regarding sexual needs and satisfaction. Duncombe and Marsden found, for example, that couples developed informal strategies to indicate sexual availability and prevent women from having "openly to show desire" (1996, p. 227).

This suggests that heterosexual men may believe that their sexuality would be "feminized" by demands for emotional displays of tender affection and cooperation in mood and scene setting. On the other, heterosexual women may feel that their sexuality would be "masculinized" by the anonymous and highly sexual interests of some men. During class discussion after data collection, one woman referred to men's more recreational fantasizing, saying. "It doesn't matter if it's me or someone else doing it to him right then. What seems more important is that it's being done right then by *someone*."

But Jayne Stake's research (1997) on how people integrate traditionally masculine and feminine characteristics suggests that successful "real-life" integrations are associated with well-being and enhanced self-esteem. When called on to be both expressive and instrumental, study subjects felt better in the work situations they described. Could sexuality be a similar "real-life" situation where the merging of traditionally gender-linked traits would benefit participants?

There are several areas of heterosexual men's and women's sexual fantasies that would benefit from a merging of interests. Women would profit by heeding the desires of their male partners, who long for ardent, aware, enthusiastic sexual mates. Men would profit from increasing their ability to be emotionally committed, passionate and sensual. Taken together, both men and women who seek each other as partners would reap the benefits of women's increased sexual agency and men's increased intimacy.

Gender differences within the most internalized aspect of sexuality—at the level of sexual fantasizing—suggest that the sociocultural structure of gender is pervasive. In heterosexual conduct, we see how fantasy and reality converge and diverge, with men looking for active, sexually experimental partners and women looking for emotional contexts and lush sexualized settings. In the "real-life" of sexuality, we see how partnered sex can involve compromises that range from the benign (e.g., choosing one position over another) to the horrible (e.g., nonconsensual force). The rich internal world of sexual fantasies needs fuller exploration so that we can better understand gender and sex.

REFERENCES

Athanasiou, R., Shaver, P., & Tavris, C. (1970). Sex. *Psychology Today,* (July) 39–52.

Barclay, A. M. (1973). Sexual Fantasies in Men and Women. *Medical Aspects of Human Sexuality, 7,* 205–216.

Barnes, N. M. (1998). Comparison of Sexual Fantasies. Unpublished doctoral dissertation. University of Missouri, Kansas City.

Bell, A., Weinberg, M., & Hammersmith, S (1981). *Sexual Preference: Statistical Appendix.* Bloomington, IN: Indiana University Press.

Chick, D., & Gold, S. R. (1987–1988). A Review of Innocences on Sexual Fantasy: Attitudes, Experience, Quilt and Gender. *Imagination, Cognition and Personality, 7,* 61–76.

Coward, R. (1985). *Female Desires: How They Are Sought: Bought and Packaged.* New York: Grove Press.

DeLamater, J. (1986). Sexual Desire and Social Norms: Sociological Perspectives on Human Sexuality. In: J. Geer & W. Donohue (Eds), *Theories and Paradigms of Human Sexuality.* New York: Plenum Publishing Co.

DeLamater, J. (1987). Gender Differences in Sexual Scenarios. In: K. Kelley (Ed.), *Females, Males, and Sexuality: Theories and Research.* Albany: State University of New York Press.

DeLamater, J., & MacCorquodale, P. (1979). *Premarital Sexuality: Attitudes, Relationships, Behavior.* Madison: University of Wisconsin Press.

Dubois, S. L. (1997). Gender Differences in the Emotional Tone of Written Sexual Fantasies. *Canadian Journal of Human Sexuality, 6,* 307–315.

Duncombe, J., & Marsden, D. (1996). Whose Orgasm is this Anyway? 'Sex Work' in Long-term Heterosexual Couple Relationships. In: J. Weeks & J. Holland (Eds), *Sexual Cultures: Communities, Values, and Intimacy.* Macmillan: New York.

Ellis, B. J., & Symons, D. (1990). Sex Differences in Sexual Fantasy: an Evolutionary Psychological Approach. *Journal of Sex Research, 27,* 527–555.

Follingstad, D. R., & Kimbrell, C. D. (1986). Sex Fantasies Revisited: an Expansion and Further Clarification of Variables Affecting Sex Fantasy Production. *Archives of Sexual Behavior, 15,* 475–486.

Frank, F., & Anshen, F. (1983). *Language and the Sexes.* Albany: State University of New York Press.

Freud, S. (1975). *Three Essays on the Theory of Sex.* New York: Basic Books.

Gold, S. R., & Clegg, C. L. (1990). Sexual Fantasies of College Students with Coercive Experiences and Coercive Attitudes. *Journal of Interpersonal Violence, 5,* 464–473.

Gold, S. R., & Gold, R. G. (1991). Gender Differences in First Sexual Fantasies. *Journal of Sex Education & Therapy, 17,* 207–216.

Goleman, D. (1983). Sexual Fantasies: What are their Hidden Meanings? *The New York Times,* February 28.

Iwawaki, S., & Wilson, G. D. (1983). Sex Fantasies in Japan. *Personality and Individual Differences, 4,* 543–545.

Hochschild, A. (1983). *The Managed Heart.* University of California Press: Berkeley.

Kaplan, H. S. (1974). *The New Sex Therapy: Active Treatment of Sexual Dysfunctions.* New York: Brunner and Mazel.

Kelley, K. (1984). Sexual Fantasy and Attitudes as Functions of Sex of Subject and Content of Erotica. *Imagination, Cognition, and Personality, 4,* 339–347.

Kinsey, A. C., Pomeroy, W. B., & Martin, C. E. (1948). *Sexual Behavior in the Human Male.* Philadelphia: W.B. Saunders.

Kinsey, A. C., Pomeroy, W. B., & Martin, C. E. (1953). *Sexual Behavior in the Human Female.* Philadelphia: W.B. Saunders.

Knafo, D., & Jaffe Y. (1984). Sexual Fantasizing in Males and Females. *Journal of Research in Personality, 18,* 451–462.

Lakoff, R. (1975). *Language and Woman's Place.* New York: Harper Colophon Books.

Leitenberg, H., & Henning, K. (1995). Sexual Fantasy. *Psychological Bulletin, 117,* 469–496.

Lewis, M. (1991). What Do Women Really Want? In: *GQ,* November.

Lott, B. (1992). *Women's Lives: Themes and Variations in Gender Learning* (2e). Pacific Grove, CA: Brooks/Cole Publishing.

Male Fantasies. In: *Time,* February 18, 1980.

Masters, W. H., & Masters, V. E. (1966). *Human Sexual Response.* Boston: Little, Brown.

Masters, W. H., & Masters, V. E. (1970). *Human Sexual Inadequacy.* Boston: Little, Brown.

May, R. (1980). *Sex and Fantasy: Patterns of Male and Female Development.* New York: W. W. Norton.

Mednick, R. A. (1977). Gender Specific Variances in Sexual Fantasy. *Journal of Personality Assessment, 41,* 248–254.

Plaud, J. J., & Bigwood, S. J. (1997). A Multivariate Analysis of the Sexual Fantasy Themes of College Men. *Journal of Sex and Marital Therapy, 23,* 221–230.

Richter, A. (1987). *The Language of Sexuality.* Jefferson, NC: McFarland and Co.

Rook, K. S., & Hammen, C. L. (1977). A Cognitive Perspective on the Experience of Sexual Arousal. *Journal of Social Issues, 33,* 7–29.

Simon, W., & Gagnon, J. (1998). Psychosexual Development. *Society, 35*, 60(8).

Spender, D. (1985). *Man Made Language*. London: Methuen.

Stake, J. (1997). Integrating Expressiveness and Instrumentality in Real-Life Settings: A New Perspective on the Benefits of Androgyny. *Sex Roles, 37*, 541–564.

Wilson, G. D. (1997). Gender Differences in Sexual Fantasy: An Evolutionary Analysis. *Personality and Individual Differences, 22*, 27–31.

Wilson, G. D., & Lang, R. J. (1981). Sex Differences in Sexual Fantasy. *Personality and Individual Differences, 2*, 343–346.

4.2 The Heterosexual Questionnaire

M. Rochlin

1. What do you think caused your heterosexuality?

2. When and how did you decide you were a heterosexual?

3. Is it possible that your heterosexuality is just a phase you may grow out of?

4. Is it possible that your heterosexuality stems from a neurotic fear of others of the same sex?

5. If you have never slept with a person of the same sex, is it possible that all you need is a good Gay lover?

6. Do your parents know that you are straight? Do your friends and/or roommate(s) know? How did they react?

7. Why do you insist on flaunting your heterosexuality? Can't you just be who you are and keep it quiet?

8. Why do heterosexuals place so much emphasis on sex?

9. Why do heterosexuals feel compelled to seduce others into their lifestyle?

10. A disproportionate majority of child molesters are heterosexual. Do you consider it safe to expose children to heterosexual teachers?

11. Just what do men and women *do* in bed together? How can they truly know how to please each other, being so anatomically different?

12. With all the societal support marriage receives, the divorce rate is spiraling. Why are there so few stable relationships among heterosexuals?

13. Statistics show that lesbians have the lowest incidence of sexually transmitted diseases. Is it really safe for a woman to maintain a heterosexual lifestyle and run the risk of disease and pregnancy?

14. How can you become a whole person if you limit yourself to compulsive, exclusive heterosexuality?

15. Considering the menace of overpopulation, how could the human race survive if everyone were heterosexual?

16. Could you trust a heterosexual therapist to be objective? Don't you feel s/he might be inclined to influence you in the direction of her/his own leanings?

17. There seem to be very few happy heterosexuals. Techniques have been developed that might enable you to change if you really want to. Have you considered trying aversion therapy?

18. Would you want your child to be heterosexual, knowing the problems that s/he would face?

From *Men's Lives*, 5th ed., edited by Michael S. Kimmel & Michael A. Messner, p. 407. From Changing Men, Spring 1982.
© 1982 by Changing Men.

4.3 Navigating Sex, Sexuality, and Christian Values

Lillie S. Ransom

Family Background

This is a story of a travel through time. It is written from the perspective of an African American bisexual woman, who grew up in a working class family in the Midwestern industrial city of Cleveland, Ohio. My parents, like many in their generation, migrated to the industrial urban area for better job prospects. Mom is from a small town in Georgia, and dad a small town in Missouri. Both of my parents grew up on farms, with hard working parents and close knit families. Each was the second from the youngest—southerners would call them "knee babies." Mom and dad are each serious Baptists too. In fact, they met at a Baptist church in Cleveland, Ohio. Being committed Baptists and died in the wool Christians, my parents are people who believe the Bible is the inerrant word of God, and the ultimate guide for living a successful life on earth. To them this Christian belief system guarantees salvation from sins, and a place in heaven with Christ Jesus. Growing up in their household, being a Christian also meant "loving your neighbor as yourself." One tangible example of how that worked is that I was expected to share my bicycle and toys freely with the other kids on our street whether they reciprocated or not. My parents did not look on me too favorably when I pointed out to them that my things seemed to get worn and torn up because of so much use

while my "friends" kept many of their toys looking new and squeaky clean because they saved them for themselves and special occasions. Being Christ-like meant being self-sacrificing. Another aspect of growing up Christian meant having an unimpeachable moral character. That translated into letting the store clerk know if s/he gave you too much change, never cursing or swearing or otherwise demonstrating anger, and not being in any circumstances that might call our characters into question. There is no way I can tell this story about navigating the intersections of race, class, gender, sexuality and concepts of morality without saying a bit more about each of my parents.

It happened that my mother's two oldest siblings were also her only two brothers. Mom was the middle of three girls who survived childhood. A sister born immediately before Mom died in a fire when my mother was too young to know or remember her. My mother worshipped the ground her brothers walked on. She talks about being really excited when they returned to rural Georgia from their exploits in the military or Cleveland. Her brothers brought loads of affection and gifts. Mom doesn't speak of her sisters with the same type of sweet nostalgia, she isn't as close to them. Her sisters, like she, are now in their late sixties. She has one cousin particularly close to her geographically and emotionally who is an octogenarian. These relatives describe my mother as a

From *Sexuality and Culture* 4(5): 65–79. Copyright © 2000 by Transaction Publishers. Reprinted by permission of Transaction Publishers.

"momma's girl." My mother was the daughter who stayed close to home and proudly hung out with her momma. She enjoyed caring for younger children, learning to cook, clean, and sew. Fond of Sunday School and participating in Easter and Christmas programs, mom imparted these latter interests to me. I loved practicing speeches with her and later delivering them in front of smiling, friendly audiences. I also enjoyed, and would like to take the liberty of saying, I was pretty good at giving presentations at school. Mom never questioned the limits the Baptist Church placed on her—or me—because we were female. She simply accepted them. Males with our oratory skills and proclivities would have been encouraged to become preachers. The fact that I am considered an excellent communicator is in great part due to the hours mom and I spent together talking, laughing, and practicing speeches. My mother also contributed to my love of learning by genuinely caring about my homework. One of my fondest memories is of mom developing multiplication charts and drills for me to supplement the teacher's efforts to teach us multiplication at school. Mom also tried to impart her interest in the piano and dance to me. However, she received little encouragement from my dad for these "extra" activities, and I was not inclined to practice very much. I love and appreciate art, music, and other cultural activities but I never developed exceptional abilities in these areas—much to my regret.

Mom was also smart as a whip but there was no talk of sending her to college, even though she was the salutatorian of her high school class. As a Negro woman graduating high school in the late forties her options were limited, even after moving to the Midwestern city of Cleveland. The kind of employment she was able to find was either as a domestic worker, cleaning homes (sometimes) coupled with being a nanny for the resident white children, or working in school cafeterias. Mom worked in these capacities from the time she arrived in Cleveland at age 18, until she married my dad and later gave birth to me one month after her 25th birthday. Before marrying dad, mom lived in a large second story unit of a duplex with her brothers and sisters, and one sister-in-law. The house was owned by their Uncle Ken, who had moved to Cleveland years before. Like many before

them and a large percentage of their contemporaries, she was still nurtured in an extended family even after she was an adult.

Mom continued to work off and on after she married, and always helped produce some income by baby-sitting and performing other home centered activities, but my primary image of her (and she of herself) is as a non-compensated homemaker. My parents had four other children after I was born, and my dad worked hard to earn enough money so that mom could stay home and personally supervise our growing up. He's very proud that he could earn enough to make ends meet, and have the luxury of not worrying whether his children were being properly cared for. This arrangement worked for them because it allowed my mom to do the things she loved most—caring for children, cooking, cleaning, sewing, and other domestic pursuits. She was also good at finding bargains and stretching dollars. Mom passed those money-managing skills on to me.

Dad was also a very good student. He was strong in math, and I'm convinced if he hadn't been born a Negro boy in segregated Missouri, he would have been encouraged to reach for greater heights. Dad moved from the small town of New Madrid, Missouri to Kansas City so he could go to high school. The next part is fuzzy, but I think he attended college and majored in Elementary Education before being drafted into the Korean War. Somewhere between high school and his stint for Uncle Sam, dad fathered his first child, my older sister, Carrie. After the war, dad moved to Cleveland and joined a moderate sized black Missionary Baptist Church. That's where he and mom met. My parents' stories agree on the notion that they did not have a long or whirlwind romance. To hear them tell it, they recognized common sense, attractiveness, and soundness in one another, and when they learned I was on the way, they decided to marry. My father worked as a painter, Fuller-Brush salesman, insurance salesman, parking lot attendant, and public housing manager during our formative years. He always managed to work and provide for us. Unfortunately, the jobs he held did not seem to utilize his college degree or confer the prestige and respect white men with college degrees in the 1950s, 1960s, and 1970s received.

Dad's hard earned income and mom's cleverness with money allowed them to purchase a modest duplex house when I was four years old; the house was in an inner city neighborhood rapidly changing from Jewish to Negro. They usually rented the upstairs portion of the duplex to relatives. We always had food, clothing, and shelter. My siblings and I benefited from being on the smaller side physically and inheriting hand-me-downs from family friends. Trips to the dentist and private doctors were unheard of, we visited public health facilities on an as needed basis. We did not have fancy furniture or the latest model cars. My parents did not hire plumbers, painters, etc., for home repairs. Neither parent was a natural "handyman" so things were often in disrepair or in a state of makeshift repair. I always felt embarrassed about that. My friends and relatives graduated to nicer, bigger homes and cars while our lifestyle never seemed to change. Many of them moved to the suburbs during the 1970s, while my parents chose to remain (and still do) in the deteriorating neighborhoods in the inner city of Cleveland.

Because my parents did not believe in spending to the limit, or spending what they did not have, those relatives and friends who had nicer material lifestyles often borrowed money from my parents for various things. That always baffled me, but I was influenced by that too and tend to be the friend most likely to have money to loan in whatever circles I find myself in. My parents are good Christian people, and they are responsible for instilling concepts of morality, ethical behavior, and social caring in me.

GENDER AWARENESS/SOCIALIZATION

One of my earliest memories of gender awareness is when my sister Vicki was born. I was three and a half years old when that happened. When someone told me, I assume it was dad but I honestly don't remember who it was, she was a girl and not a boy I cried. I was disappointed. I had gotten it into my head that I wanted a baby brother. I also assigned my first doll a male gender, and apparently I wanted everyone to be clear about his identity because I called him "Michael-boy." I can only speculate about these phenomena since I have no foolproof way of knowing what was

going on in my young mind. My best guess is that somehow I had internalized some messages about male children being "better" and more "desired." One of the ways this message probably got communicated was when I heard my dad repeatedly tell how he had already chosen a name for his first boy long before he met mom! It turns out he fathered four girls before his first son was born. But he was determined to have a son, and eventually sired two.

My parents' gender roles and power divisions were clear to me as a youngster. He got to make all the decisions and she quietly went along with them, even if she had other ideas. I observed this ritual and decided when I was little that I had to make sure I did not grow up and let a man boss me around like that. I also had no interest in the traditional feminine activities, e.g., cooking, sewing, etc., in which mom excelled. Vicki was pretty indifferent to these domestic activities too. Nikki, their third daughter, and our baby sister, seems to be the one who excels at these things. Dad often chided, "Nikki is the real woman around here." I have no idea how that affected Vicki, but when I would hear that, I would wonder to myself, "hmm, what does that say about me?" Even though my dad was never physically abusive and did not yell or curse at us, I was put off and felt putdown by his ravings about being the boss, and expecting the rest of us to blindly follow his mandates. I understand better now that this authoritarianism helped him cope better with the racist and limiting options he had in the larger world.

Their first son, my brother, Nicholas, was born when I was almost eight years old. When he was still a toddler my dad would call out to him, "you're the man around here, take care of your mother and sisters," as he left the house. That did not sit too well with me (and I learned years later, that it had not sat very well with my Mother either), especially since I was older and had worked hard to live up to my dad's admonitions to be good, responsible, and set an example for the younger children. Even though I was too young to articulate it, I knew if my brother actually believed what he was told, he would think he didn't have to listen to our mother. But that's another story. I loved Nick and doted on him, I treated him like my special doll baby for the first few years of his life. He still jokes to this day about how any one who wants to mistreat him has to deal with me first because I look out for him.

Chris, Mom and Dad's fifth and youngest child, was born two months before my 15th birthday, and we all adored him. I loved him and cared for him too, but this time I was always keenly aware that he could be mistaken for mine, and I did not want people thinking I was one of those teenage mothers. I had already accepted the values that "good girls" should be pure and non-sexual, and was afraid of the consequences if anyone suspected otherwise. I also realized that black girls had to work much harder to maintain respect and images of purity, so I did the work! It was only after Chris became a young adult that I realized something my mother used to say was true, "you two are more alike than any of my other children." We do have many of the same interests, tastes, and proclivities, and when I visit home, Chris and I have some good times together despite the years between us.

As may be quite obvious, my gender socialization was very much along traditional lines. I was always told, "little girls are sugar and spice and everything nice," and rewarded for behavior that conformed to this, and not for behavior expressing anger, disappointment, or "unnice" things. My Mom told all of her girls that if they didn't want to have to work after they had children, they should never let their husbands grow dependent on their incomes. In fact, if we could manage to not work outside the home, that would be better. Dad by example and word taught us that it was proper and natural for the man to be in charge, and that that is what God intended. In fact, Dad fondly reminds us that women are created for men, and that women cannot reach their full happiness and potential without being helpmates.

MILD IRONY

The same parents who wholeheartedly and enthusiastically believed my highest goals should focus on becoming a good wife and mother, and maybe a school teacher, interestingly enough made no distinction in their educational aspirations for their daughters and sons. They wanted all of us to attend college. This

is where their meager, non-changing standard of living came in handy. My parents were able to help each of us through undergraduate school, and all but one of us graduated with at least a bachelor's degree. The one who didn't complete his bachelor's also received parental and financial support but became distracted by other things.

There was much reinforcement for my parents' gender role beliefs in their families of origin, their church community, and even in the wider society when they married in the 1950s. But I grew up and started school in the 1960s, just when the outside world was beginning to challenge these socially constructed assumptions. I am unable to point to any one person or event that influenced me to question my parents' and the church's gender role constructions and their applicability for my life. Much of the questioning was probably prompted internally because I knew on some level I could not conform to these traditional roles and expectations. For many years those questions and doubts brewed beneath the surface. I kept playing the games I was taught to play but I always felt it was a losing proposition. More about that later.

SEX AND SEXUALITY
Childhood Years

The following sums up my early attitudes about sex. Sex: You won't do "it" until you're married. Do mom and dad do "it"? I don't know because I never see them kiss or touch affectionately. Later I figured out they must do it or have done it because that's how babies are made, but I surely didn't have any clues in their behavior toward one another.

For me, childhood sex play, an apparently common phenomenon, occurred more with girls than boys. In fact, I can only remember one incident where males were involved and I will elaborate on that shortly. Whenever I participated in sex play, while it was physically pleasant, there was a lingering sense of guilt, unworthiness, and feeling dirty. Once a female cousin and I got caught by my mom and aunt. We were disciplined with a good talking to. I can remember the tone of that conversation, it left me feeling bad and that I had really disappointed my mom, but for the life of me I cannot remember the actual content of the conversation. We did not get spankings, and that was a relief. Our parents did believe in corporal punishment though.

On the other hand, at some other point in my childhood, my mother and the same aunt whipped me, that same cousin, and her two brothers respectively for participating in a stripping game. A large part of the trauma of this discipline was hearing my cousins yelling and screaming upstairs while I was getting my whipping downstairs. (My cousins, aunt and uncle were living upstairs at the time.) This is the incident I alluded to earlier when I mentioned a childhood sexual incident involving males. My older male cousins gradually stripped a younger male cousin butt naked (one piece of clothing at a time) and would call us in to view him after each piece of clothing was removed. The older male cousins actually invited both their sisters, including the cousin already mentioned and her younger sister, me, and Vicki to view this activity. The two younger girls were not interested so they eventually went and told on us.

At any rate, I do not think there was any touching or fondling with this incident as there had been in the incident I described earlier, but the adult reaction was much stronger.

Those reactions and the constant church teaching about fornication and adultery convinced me that sex was sinful. During those years, I had no special guilt associated with sex play with girls rather than boys, it was more generalized about sexual activities and expressions.

It was during junior high school that I realized I could be strongly attracted to females, and had somewhere picked up enough information to be ashamed about it. The same girl friend that I had participated with in some of my earlier exploratory activities was now crazy about boys, and talking about them incessantly. She was now embarrassed about the silly past, and never wanted to talk about it, so I did not share with her that I had a serious crush on one of our female teachers. One by one, the older girls that I had connected with in sexual play had already moved on and transferred their affections to boys. I felt alone and confused, but who does a 14-year-old talk with about

a thing like that? I had no idea so I kept the stuff to myself.

Eventually I went to high school and started developing some interest in boys but two things seemed to confound the expression of that interest. One, my parents were very strict with me, their oldest daughter, so I was not allowed to date. (In fact, I often joke that if I had decided to wait for their permission to date, I would still be waiting!) And two, I was genuinely fond of books and learning and smart in school, so I got a reputation for being a bookworm rather than a social butterfly. I was an ordinary-looking girl, clean and neat, but not the type boys go crazy about. Back then I didn't think I was attractive at all, but hindsight and experience has made me realize I was never ugly, I just thought so. So, there was no way I had the natural nerve or parental encouragement to reach out to boys myself.

My developing interest in boys did not replace my attraction to women. The two attractions coexisted, and persist to this day. I had at least one more serious crush on a female teacher in high school, and could have been swept off my feet if she had been so inclined.

College Years

I started college at age 17, and almost immediately met a woman who intrigued me. Her name is Elaine, and you will hear a bit more about her in the Coming Out section. She was a Residence Hall Coordinator and one of the folks who welcomed me and my parents to Talcott Hall, a woman's dorm. Co-ed housing was common at my alma mater, and there was also an opportunity to live in an afrocentric residence hall, but my dad objected furiously to that, thinking it would pigeonhole me as someone unwilling to be broad-minded and integrate with the larger society. I think my parents were relieved when I chose a women's dormitory but I do not remember much discussion about it, I don't think I was seriously considering a co-ed dorm anyway.

Soon after my arrival on campus, I met three other people who became important parts of my college memories—Diane, the woman who became my best friend in college (she and I managed to become roommates in the middle of the fall semester), her life-long school buddy Greg, and the guy who became my second real but most long-term boyfriend, Lenny. All of these people played an integral part in my college years, but this is not the forum to elaborate on that. Greg was the first openly gay man I really got to know. He was smart, talented, and quite a comedian. Thinking of him even now brings a smile to my face. Greg spent time speculating about who was and was not gay. Diane and I started speculating too because it seemed an innocent enough game at the time. I later learned this wasn't the coolest thing in the world to do.

Coming Out?

This section turns out to be more about the first opportunity I had to come out, than my actual coming out. Elaine (the women I mentioned at the beginning of the College Years section) and I became really close friends during the second semester of my freshmen year. The following summer we wrote what I can now call, "love letters" to each other every week. I would not have called them that then. Diane remained my best friend but Elaine excited me emotionally in ways that Diane, other friends, and my boyfriend did not. During my sophomore year, Elaine confessed that she was in love with me and wanted to be sexually intimate with me. I was shocked, thrilled, and scared all at once. I told her how flattered I was, but began to quote scriptures about why and how that could never be. According to Elaine, she had been close to many of her woman friends before but never wanted sexual closeness, and she tried hard to understand why these feelings were different and needed to be expressed this time. Elaine never pressured me and was always respectful of my views, but unknown to me she was going through her own quiet hell, learning that she might be a lesbian.

Shortly after expressing her genuine feelings to me, we met someone who became Elaine's first female lover. I was devastated, love-lorn, and dejected, but my intellect and spiritual beliefs kept telling me I had no right to feel these things because two women cannot or at least should not be in love with one another. Elaine ended up in a counselor's office because of the stress of dealing with her self-discovery. Her counselor called me in because Elaine mentioned that I was the true object of her affection.

The counselor wanted to know how this revelation made me feel and if I needed to talk about things myself. How nice of her! I could not admit my mutual fondness and attraction beyond saying I really cared about Elaine and wanted her to be okay. I could not see that I needed counseling too, because I thought the answer was to keep praying to God that my inappropriate feelings would disappear. By the time all of this hit the fan, I had a fairly successful seven- or eight-month relationship with Lenny, and felt my romantic needs were being met through him. Besides, I wanted very much to do the right moral thing, and that by all accounts was to be heterosexual.

After Undergraduate School

I fell in love with another woman but only told her about it after she asked. She is straight as an arrow, has married twice in the years since my confession of unfailing love, and always prayed for my "healing" and deliverance from homosexual attractions. This woman convinced me to see my first counselor about this issue, and that counseling relationship lasted a mere two months. I did not have the terminology for it then, but I would now say the counselor was nearly homophobic, and could not deal with the issues I presented.

LOVE
Obeying God

This pattern of being attracted to one woman or another while dating men repeated itself many times in the years that followed. I would not reconcile my concepts of morality with heterosexual expression before marriage, bisexuality or lesbianism. I always admired Lenny's healthy and care free attitude about sex. To him, it was part of life's natural rhythms and functions and something to be shared with the special person in your life. The thought of feeling guilty about it was something he just could not get. Yet, in my opinion he was moral in his attitudes regarding sex. He was not promiscuous, forceful, or indiscriminate in his affections; for him sex was a special expression between two people who loved and cared for one another, and he was willing to share in contraception and to accept whatever consequences sexual activity might produce. To this day I believe he meant it when he said that, and would have tried to go the distance had I so desired. When we finally broke up after six rocky years, sometimes off, sometimes on, trying to make a go of it, it was because we could not see eye to eye on specific religious/spiritual expressions. The organized Church turned him off, and he was not sure what to think about this Jesus Christ person. I, on the other hand, was still fairly steeped in my religious upbringing and could not consider marrying someone who did not share my persuasion, at least in a general sense.

I tried to get my family's explicit support and perceptions about the scripture verse that convinced me we could not be together—this verse admonishes Christians not to be unevenly yoked with unbelievers (New Testament Bible, King James Version (KJV), II Corinthians 6:14). My parents were amazingly silent. To this day I do not know what they thought of my decision not to become engaged and later married to a man who did not accept the Christian faith. They really liked Lenny.

On the other hand, I know beyond a shadow of a doubt how they feel about homosexuality. To them it is quite simply an abomination! Though there was much more tacit family (and societal) acceptance for heterosexual activity outside of marriage, my inner voices kept saying if the scriptures mean what they said, I had to be sexual OR moral (since I was single), one or the other, but not both. My conscience could not fully accept the dichotomy about heterosexual activity being more okay than homosexual activity. So, for most of my adult life I abstained from sex to minimize the conflict.

Loving One Another

I later fell in love with and became sexually involved with a woman with whom I still associate. She comes from a similar religious and family background so we dealt with the sexual part of our relationship by constantly praying for forgiveness, and eventually developing the discipline to not be sexually involved with one another. "If the truth be told," as many black folks like to say, I did not feel as guilty as I expected I would. I was mostly bothered by seeing my partner so upset all the time. I had internalized esteeming others more highly than oneself [New Testament Bible, KJV, Philipians 2:3]; and because I love[d] her, I did not want to continue engaging in activities that seemed to wear her down. And though it was sometimes rough and rocky to be in love with someone and remain close, but not consummate the relationship, it seemed the kind of self-sacrificial love my faith called for.

At the urging of this former partner and yet another counselor, I participated in an ex-gay ministry. I asked God to change me, take away my sinful attractions to women, and make me and mold me as a loving heterosexual woman. I followed the program, became quite active, and even became a spokesperson of sorts. At the same time, I tried to conform my attitudes to accept a woman's rational "God-given" role in the universe and joined a conservative church that would reinforce these decisions. I was miserable. I became depressed, distraught, and entertained suicidal thoughts. Something was the matter. I started to think that God didn't love me. I mean, here I was trying to do everything I understood I should, and God was not blessing me with a good Christian man or healthy platonic Christian relationships for that matter.

Loving Myself

Later, I sought out counseling for the third time in my adult life. This time it became apparent that I had accomplished the "success" of long term abstinence and other sexuality issues by severing parts of myself. Gradually, I embraced my attraction for women, looked God in the eye, as it were, and said I have tried to conform to my understanding of your will. It doesn't seem to be working for me, here I am, with all my faults, gifts, and cares. I had academically and professionally reached the middle class, but still needed and wanted spiritual teaching and affirmation and a healthy relationship.

Through the years, without making conscious choices to reject my fundamental upbringing, I eventually became comfortable with women ministers, divorce for reasons other than literal adultery, and the belief that God is more interested in people's ability and willingness to love with integrity and care and doing unto others as we would have them do unto us, than in the biological sex of one's mate; these are examples of some of the inward changes I have undergone. All of the specific examples contradict literal interpretations of several Christian scriptures, and would therefore spell condemnation from the perspective of Christian sisters and brothers in congregations and traditions as fundamentalist as the one I grew up in—that would include my family of origin. I respect where they are, but I am thankful for where I am.

I know beyond a shadow of a doubt that God loves me, and that God asks only that I love God in return with all my heart, soul, and mind, and that I love others as myself. Now that I am on the path to loving and embracing all of me, I can love others more fully and freely and let this be the guiding concept of morality. For me, this is the essence of being Christian, or

Christ-like; it is not the attempt to rotely and blindly follow scriptural or pastoral mandates. Should I ever have a lifemate, it matters most if he or she conducts his or her life by this principle, not that it be a he rather than a she. I will no longer limit God or my life in that way. Or if I remain single, I embrace all the possibilities therein, and still commit to loving the people I encounter even when they are racist, sexist, homophobic or otherwise demeaning. Let me be clear though, loving them does not mean being passive and letting misdeeds go unchallenged. Loving is moral but it is hard work, it is constant work. So much in our capitalistic, competitive society goes against the principles of love. It is out of this Christian morality, this ethic of love, that I wrote this essay and attempt to live my life. And even though this public profession may make some who know me extremely uncomfortable (or proud), as well as expose me to harassment I might have otherwise escaped, so be it.

4.4 CASUAL SEX ON SPRING BREAK
Intentions and Behaviors of Canadian Students

Eleanor Maticka-Tyndale, Edward S. Herold, and Dawn Mewhinney

Although numerous studies have been conducted on the sexual behavior of young people, there is little research on sexual behavior occurring in specific contexts. One context that has been ignored by researchers is the North American spring break holiday, a one-week break in the school calendar in late February or early March. Approximately one million U.S. students participate in some form of spring break vacation (Josiam, Clements, & Hobson, 1995). Spring break vacations are also popular among Canadians, with thousands of students heading to popular vacation spots (S. Cox, Inter-Campus Programs, personal communication, September, 1995).

Mewhinney, Herold, and Maticka-Tyndale (1995), using focus groups and interviews with Canadian students who had traveled to Florida for spring break, found the key elements of a spring break vacation to include a group holiday with friends traveling and rooming together, a perpetual party atmosphere, high alcohol consumption, sexually suggestive contests and displays, and the perception that casual sex is common. Overall, there is the perception that sexual norms are far more permissive on spring break vacation than at home, providing an atmosphere of greater sexual freedom and the opportunity for engaging in new sexual experiences. Smeaton and Josiam (1996) reported similar findings from their survey of U.S. students on spring break vacation in Panama City Beach, Florida.

The behavior patterns found on spring break have also been found among nonstudent samples of holiday travelers. In their review of the tourism and vacation literature. Herold and van Kerkwijk (1992) identified the characteristics of vacations that were conducive to casual sex activity as a sense of freedom from at-home restrictions, a relaxation of inhibitions, a focus on having a good time, and high alcohol consumption.

We examined factors that might influence university students to engage in coitus with a new partner while on spring break. For the purpose of this paper, we refer to this behavior as *casual sex:* This was the term used by students in a preliminary study (Mewhinney et al., 1995) to refer to the type of sex engaged in while on spring break. The students portrayed spring break sexual partnerships as initiated rapidly, often within hours of meeting, and as temporary, not lasting beyond the spring break period. Given our focus on new, casual partnerships, we excluded from our analysis those young adults who were sexually active on spring break with a relationship partner from home or with someone whom they had known before spring break.

Triandis's theory of interpersonal behavior (TIB; 1977, 1980, 1994) was selected to guide data collection and analysis because it includes peer influences and situational characteristics in explaining behavior, both of which were identified in preliminary research (Mewhinney et al., 1995) as important influences on spring break sexual activity. The TIB belongs to the school of cognitive models that includes the theory of reasoned action (TRA; Ajzen & Fishbein, 1980) and the theory of planned behavior (TPB; Ajzen, 1985). These theories explain the influence of attitudes and norms on intentions, with these intentions, in turn, directly influencing behaviors. Triandis's model goes beyond the others by examining how factors other than intentions influence behavior, and by more fully specifying the factors that influence intentions. The TIB has proven useful in understanding complex behaviors, particularly those that may be influenced by the social and/or physical environment (e.g., in sexuality research, see Boyd & Wandersman, 1991; Godin, et al., 1996).

Using the framework of the TIB, we predicted that whether a young adult on spring break in Daytona Beach would engage in casual sex would be influenced by an expectation or intention to engage in coitus with a new partner on spring break, prior experience with casual sex, and an environment conducive to new coital partnerships. The first factor, intention, has received considerable attention in the social psychological literature (e.g., Fishbein & Jaccard, 1973; Jorgensen & Sonstegard, 1984; White, Terry, & Hogg, 1994). Although factors that might intervene in the intention-behavior link have been discussed (e.g., Randall & Wolff, 1994), only Triandis has explicitly focused on variables such as prior experience and situational conditions that may facilitate, impede, or replace intentions as determinants of behavior.

Previous research supports the inclusion of these additional variables in explanations of sexual behavior. For example, researchers have found that for individuals with a greater number of past coital partners, erotic cues (e.g., arousal and situational cues) have a stronger influence on whether coitus occurs than does the quality of a relationship (Christopher & Cate, 1984; D'Augelli & D'Augelli, 1977). The TIB would make a similar prediction, although prior experience is conceptualized somewhat differently. In the TIB, prior experiences that closely approximate the current sexual situation, such as having coitus with someone within hours of meeting him or her, can replace intentions and independently influence a behavior. The influence of prior experience is strongest when the new event closely parallels the prior experiences (for this study, if the prior experience of casual sex occurred while on a previous spring break vacation in Daytona Beach) and when there are multiple instances of that prior experience.

Situational conditions work with intentions and prior experience to facilitate the likelihood of particular behaviors by providing opportunity and cues that contribute to an individual's erotic expectations (see also D'Augelli & D'Augelli, 1977; Rook & Hammen, 1977). In the TIB, situational conditions that are conducive to actions are specific to the action and situation of interest. Thus, for this study, we must consider conditions associated with being on vacation (Herold & van Kerkwijk, 1992).

Triandis suggests that intentions and prior experiences are the dominant influences on behavior, with situational conditions acting as mediators that facilitate or impede behaviors. Thus, if the situation prohibits or impedes casual sex, prior behavior and/or intentions will not result in the predicted behaviors. If conditions conducive to casual sex are present, then its realization will depend on prior experience with casual sex and/or intentions.

The TIB also provides an explanation of how intentions are formed. As in other cognitive models (e.g., TRA and TPB), personal attitudes and social norms are presented as influencing the formation of intentions or plans. However, the TIB more fully specifies the personal and social dimensions. Personal attitudes include affective and evaluative components. The affective component of attitudes toward casual sex involves the feelings that one anticipates as part of casual sex (e.g., pleasure, elation, fear, disgust). The evaluative component of attitudes is the cognitive evaluation of the probable consequences of casual sex (e.g., desirable, undesirable, good, bad). These two forms of attitudes are specified separately because each has a distinct influence on the formation of intentions. For example, a young adult may anticipate feelings of pleasure and excitement at the thought of casual sex on spring break but may judge the potential results of engaging in casual sex to be undesirable.

Social norms emanating from an individual's reference group are the second component influencing the formation of intentions. Here the TIB's predictions are similar to those of reference group theory (Christopher & Cate, 1984; Winslow, Franzini, & Hwang, 1992). As with personal attitudes, Triandis specifies several dimensions of reference group influence: (a) agreements or promises that are formed between friends (pacts either to engage or not to engage in casual sex); (b) the perceived norms and expectations of one's immediate reference group (subjective social norms); (c) beliefs about what is appropriate for a member in one's position or status

(role beliefs); and (d) the internalized personal standards or moral codes (personal normative beliefs). The first two dimensions represent the social group as the point of reference. The second two dimensions represent the individual's transformation of social norms into self-expectations and standards and take the self as the point of reference. As with affective and evaluative components of attitudes, each of these may exert different pressures on the individual. For example, there may be pressure to fulfill the pacts or agreements made with friends or to act in accordance with the norms and expectations set by the reference group. There may also be pressure to act in a way that is considered appropriate to one's age, gender, or relationship status, or that is in accord with one's personal standards or moral code.

The conceptualization of the components of the theory of interpersonal behavior, the relationships among them, and the inclusion of new components have evolved over time (Triandis, 1977, 1980, 1994). Figure 4.4.1 presents the full structural model for the

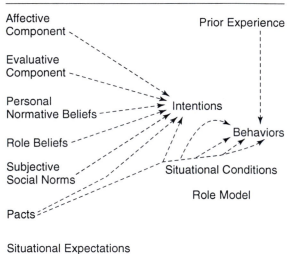

Paths not in original model

Figure 4.4.1

theory of interpersonal behavior as used in this study. In accordance with Triandis's suggestion that additional factors may be tested for their potential contribution to the explanatory power of the model, we have added situational expectations to the prediction of intentions and two measures of peer influence to the prediction of behavior.

Situational expectations are the expectational predecessors of situational conditions. These are conceptualized as the individual's expectations about whether spring break experiences will be conducive to casual sex. It is similar to the control belief concept in the TPB (Ajzen, 1991), a variable that is indicative of the degree to which a behavior is under the control of an individual. We suggest that when there are situational expectations conducive to casual sex, the individual expects that casual sex will occur. Triandis models participation in activities (situational conditions) as directly influencing the behavior. The addition of the expectation of participation as an influence on intentions permits us to examine more precisely the impact of the spring break environment, both as anticipated and as experienced, on casual sex.

We also added two peer influences to the explanation of casual sex activity: pacts and role modeling. These fit within Triandis's conceptualization of social norms and relate to our specific interest in the spring break environment. In preliminary research (Mewhinney et al., 1995), we found that a spring break vacation was a group activity. By including characteristics of peer influence that are part of the spring break experience, we are able to examine the direct effect of these aspects of the environment on engaging in casual sex.

We completed this study in two parts. First, in the prebreak study, we examined expectations and intentions before a spring break trip and tested the portion of the TIB that explains the formation of intentions. Second, in the Daytona study, we examined experiences on the trip and tested the portion of the TIB that explains behavior. The methodology, results and discussion specific to each study are presented separately. The discussion following these presentations addresses portions of the results that bridge both studies.

STUDY 1: PREBREAK STUDY
Methods
Recruitment of Participants
In February, 1996, students from four universities in southern Ontario who were planning a one-week spring break vacation in Daytona Beach, Florida were recruited before their trip through travel agents, advertisements in campus papers, posters on campus, class announcements, and campus information booths. Self-administered questionnaires were given or mailed to students following telephone or face-to-face contact with a research assistant. In addition, questionnaires were distributed and collected by research assistants at the beginning of chartered bus rides to Daytona Beach. In this prebreak sample, 151 surveys were completed.

Questionnaire Development
Triandis's (1977, 1980) theory includes a measurement model that operationalizes each concept in a manner that is specific to the time, context, and behavior of interest. Triandis provides the structure and form of measurement for each concept (e.g., personal attitudes are measured using semantic differential scales, social norms are measured using Likert scales), but the specific items and indicators must be established based on preliminary elicitation research. Elicitation research was conducted following Triandis's guidelines (Ajzen & Fishbein, 1980; Triandis, 1977, 1980). Students who had traveled to Florida for spring break before 1996 participated in semistructured, open-ended group and individual interviews. Concepts were operationalized based on content analysis of the interviews.

A draft of the prebreak questionnaire was tested and refined in a two-week test-retest procedure with a sample of 10 men and 10 women who anticipated going on a spring break vacation. Items that did not meet criteria set for test-retest reliability (kappa coefficient of at least 0.70) or that were more weakly correlated with other items measuring the same construct (evaluated using Cronbach's alpha) were eliminated from the final questionnaire. The specificity of items used in the scalar measures of constructs was tested using confirmatory factor analysis to ensure that items loaded only on their designated constructs. Construct validity was assessed by examining correlation matrices to verify that scalar measures correlated with criterion factors of gender, age, and prior coital experience in a manner consistent with prior research in the field.

The prebreak surveys included questions about sexual history, spring break plans and expectations, and the constructs used to predict intentions to engage in sexual activity. The final prebreak questionnaire could be completed in an average of 20 minutes.

Measurement of Constructs

Seven-point semantic differential scales consisting of adjective pairs used by students in the elicitation research to describe the experience and consequences of casual sex on spring break measured affective and evaluative attitude components. Participants were asked to rate their feelings about and evaluation of the consequences of "having sex with someone you meet on spring break." To ensure that this was a measure of attitudes toward coitus and not toward condom use, we asked participants to make this assessment without consideration of whether condoms were used. The adjective pairs measuring feelings when thinking about casual sex (affective component) were fun-loving/serious, exciting/dull, pleasant/unpleasant, adventuresome/ordinary. The adjective pairs measuring cognitive evaluations of the potential consequences of casual sex were good/bad, smart/stupid, responsible/irresponsible. Mean scores of the pairs for each attitude were used to measure the affective attitude and cognitive evaluations toward casual sex on spring break. Cronbach's alpha for the affective and cognitive measures was 0.76 and 0.82, respectively.

The four dimensions of social norms—personal norms, subjective social norms, role beliefs, and pacts—were measured. The strength of personal norms supporting casual sex was measured by the mean score of responses to three questions, each with a 7-point bipolar response: (1) "When on Spring Break . . . you feel you *should* have sex with someone you meet there if you want to"; (2) " . . . you would

feel guilty if you have sex with someone you meet there" (reverse-coded); (3) " . . . it would be against your values to have sex with someone you meet there" (reverse-coded). Cronbach's alpha for this measure was 0.83.

Subjective social norms, or the perception of how much one's reference group approves or disapproves of his or her casual sex activity, was measured using the mean score of 7-point bipolar responses to three questions. Respondents indicated how likely or unlikely it was that each of three groups of referent others (male friends, female friends, and friends who went with them to Daytona Beach) would think that they *should* have sex if they met someone who was appealing. Cronbach's alpha for subjective social norms was 0.85.

Role beliefs, or the strength of beliefs about whether casual sex is appropriate for someone given his or her status or position, was measured using the mean score of 7-point bipolar (*strongly agree* (1) to *strongly disagree* (7)) responses to three questions. Respondents were asked whether having sex with someone met on spring break was "OK for someone of my gender . . . of my age . . . of my relationship status." Cronbach's alpha for role beliefs was 0.79.

To measure pacts, we asked participants whether they had made promises, agreements, or pacts with the friends who would accompany them to Daytona either to engage or not to engage in casual sex. The presence and nature of these pacts or agreements was effect coded as −1 for an agreement not to have sex, 0 for no pact or agreement, and 1 for an agreement to have sex.

Because situational expectations closely parallel Ajzen's (1991) control belief, Ajzen's method for operationalizing control beliefs was used to assess situational expectations. During the elicitation phase, students identified specific situations or experiences that had occurred in Daytona Beach that they thought were conducive to or impeded engaging in coitus with a new partner while in Daytona. Ten experiences were identified and used in measuring the influence of anticipated situations on engaging in casual sex: partying, being in a break-loose mood, drinking alcohol, getting drunk, watching contests such as "hot body" and "wet t-shirt," dancing dirty, trying to "pick someone up," someone trying to "pick up" the respondent, the appearance that everyone was having sex, and someone wanting to have sex with the respondent. Participants used a 4-point scale ranging from *never* (1) to *frequently* (4), to rate the frequency with which they expected to be involved in each of the experiences. The perceived degree of influence of each experience on whether they engaged in casual sex was scored on a 7-point bipolar scale (*strongly agree* (1) to *strongly disagree* (7)) in response to the question "How likely is it that you would have sex with someone you meet on Spring Break if. . . ." The score for each experience or situation was constructed from the product of the frequency rating and the degree-of-influence rating. Cronbach's alpha for the total situational expectation score consisting of the mean of the 10 items' scores was 0.96.

To measure the criterion variable, we asked participants how often they expected or intended to engage in casual sex on spring break (defined as sexual intercourse with someone they had met on spring break). Answers ranged from *never* (1) to *frequently* (4).

Data Analysis

In the TIB, personal and status characteristics, such as gender, are external to the model: Their influence on intentions and behaviors is mediated through their influence on attitudes, norms, and experiences. Research on sexuality, however, has documented interactions between gender and attitudes, norms, experiences, and behaviors, suggesting that gender may also influence intentions and behaviors from within the model. These interactions include the way peer influences affect attitudes and behaviors (e.g., Christopher & Cate, 1984), the way attitudes and behaviors are linked (e.g., Oliver & Hyde, 1993), the way prior experiences influence future behaviors (Christopher & Roosa, 1991), and the characteristics of relationships that are necessary for coital interaction (e.g., Christopher & Roosa, 1991). These findings necessitate a consideration of potential gender interactions when designing an analysis plan. In this study, men's and women's covariance matrices for all variables used in the multivariate procedures were tested for significant differences using LISREL VI (Joreskog & Sorbom, 1986). This procedure permitted us to

identify the number and location of interactions. With the exception of the covariance of subjective social norms and intentions, there were no significant differences between the covariance matrices for men and women. The interaction of gender with subjective social norms was accommodated in this analysis by using gender-specific terms for men's and women's subjective social norms. Because there was only one interaction between gender and an independent variable, the remainder of the data for men and women were aggregated.

During exploratory research, students argued that the interpretation of spring break activities was influenced by one's peer group. If friends endorsed casual sex, for example, then a student expected and interpreted the activities on spring break as conducive to casual sex. If friends did not endorse casual sex, the same activities would not necessarily be seen as leading to or facilitating casual sex. The possible mediator role of peers with respect to situational expectations was tested using four regression analyses. In each, intention was regressed on situational expectations along with one measure of social norms and the interaction between expectations and social norms. The interaction between situational expectations and pacts was the only significant interaction. Therefore, it was included in the final analysis.

Including several dimensions of complex constructs such as personal attitudes and social norms in an analysis allows us to identify the contribution and relative strength of each dimension in explaining the dependent variable. However, because dimensions are expected to be closely related to one another, they present the possibility of multicollinearity. The presence of multivariate collinearity was tested using measures of tolerance and variance inflation, comparisons of the eigenvalues of the variables uncentered cross-products matrix, and examination of the proportion of variance of each independent variable associated with each eigenvalue (Smith & Sasaki, 1979). These supported the conclusion that each predictor variable represented a sufficiently independent portion of variance in intentions to conduct multivariate analyses. Because the inclusion of interaction and gender-specific terms in the proposed analysis further heightened the possibility of multicollinearity, all independent variables measured at the interval level were centered around their mean values as suggested by Smith and Sasaki (1979) and Aiken and West (1991). The measure for agreements with friends (pact) retained its original unweighted effect coding.

The model for intentions was tested using hierarchical ordinary least squares regressions. The predictor variables in the original TIB were entered as a block in the first regression followed by the addition of situational expectations and the interaction between pacts and situational expectations.

Results

Profile of the Sample

Participants were 66 males and 85 females aged 18–31 (77% were ages 21–23). All participants were White and identified themselves as heterosexual and single. Thirty-five percent of men and 38% of women reported they were in a long-term relationship.

Spring Break Expectations

As seen in Table 4.4.1, this was the first spring break trip and the first trip to Daytona Beach for most students. Consistent with descriptions in the elicitation research, spring break in Daytona is a social event, with 82% of men and 88% of women accompanied by friends. However, this is not necessarily a vacation for couples: Forty-eight percent of the men and 68% of the women who were in relationships reported that their partners would not accompany them to Daytona.

Almost all who traveled to Daytona Beach had prior coital experience. The median number of prior coital partners was six for men and three for women. Fewer women than men intended to engage in casual sex on spring break. Women were less likely than men to form pacts or agreements with friends about casual sex: but when they did, women made agreements with friends *not* to engage in sex while in Daytona (15%), whereas men formed agreements to have sex (46%). In the elicitation interviews, students described agreements among women to "pull your friend out of a situation" if it appeared she might become sexually

involved: men described competitive pacts to see who could "get laid" the most. The gender pattern seen in Table 4.4.1 is replicated in the mean scores on the scalar measures of attitudes, norms, and expectations related to casual sex. Men's scores were higher than women's on each measure, indicating that men's attitudes and beliefs were more supportive of casual sex on spring break than were women's.

Intentions to Engage in Casual Sex

The Pearson product moment correlations between all variables used in the analysis ranged from .14 to .71.

Table 4.4.1 Percentage of Men and Women With Different Sexual and Spring Break Experiences and Intention

Variable	Males	Females
Prior Sexual Experience		
Previous coital experience	95%	92%
Ever coitus within 24 hrs. of meeting partner	65%[++]	34%
Spring Break Experience		
1st spring break trip	73%[++]	48%
1st Daytona Beach trip	73%	87%
Plan to Go With Friends	82%	88%
Plan to Go with Relationship Partner[a]	18%	12%
Pacts or Agreements Formed With Friends:		
Not to engage in casual sex	8%	15%
To engage in casual sex	46%[+++]	1%
Coital Intentions for Spring Break		
Intend coitus with relationship partner	18%	9%
Intend coitus with acquaintance[b]	62%[+++]	25%
Intend coitus with someone met on spring break[c]	76%[+++]	19%
Do not intend to engage in coitus	8%[+++]	61%

Note. Sample comprised of 66 males and 85 females.

[a]48% of men and 68% of women are in a relationship and report their partners will *not* accompany them. [b]Someone the participant knew before coming on spring break but with whom the participant had not engaged in coitus. [c]Casual sex.

[++]Difference between percentages significant at $p < .01$ (chi-square test). [+++]Difference between percentages significant at $p < .001$ (Chi-square test).

Those between intentions and predictor variables were positive and ranged from .18 (attitudes with intentions) to .71 (situational expectations with intentions). Table 4.4.2 reports the results of the ordinary least squares regression of intention to engage in casual sex on centered predictors. Both the TIB (Model 1) and the enhanced TIB (Model 2) explained sizable portions of the variance in intentions ($R^2 = .70$ and .74 respectively). The enhanced TIB explained a significantly larger portion of the variance than the original TIB, $F(2,134) = 12.51$, $p < .001$. The strongest influence on men's intentions was their perceptions of the degree of endorsement they would receive from their friends for participation in casual sex while on spring break. Women, however, were not influenced by the perceived endorsement of others. For both men and women, all indicators except personal standards and role beliefs had a significant influence on the formation of intentions. Thus, it was the social norms using the peer group as the point of reference rather than those using the self that influenced intentions. The results of the interaction between pacts and situational expectations coincided with the comments students made during the elicitation phase. The positive effect of situational expectations was enhanced when there was a pact to engage in coitus with a new partner while on spring break. However, when there was a pact *not* to engage in coitus with a new partner, the association disappeared—the pact counteracted the anticipated environmental influence.

STUDY 2: DAYTONA STUDY
Methods
Recruitment

One male and one female graduate student who had experience and training in research methods and who were in the age range of students on the spring break trip collected the data for the Daytona study during the 1996 spring break season. Three methods of recruitment were used: on-site at Daytona Beach, on buses returning home, and through the mail. On-site recruitment procedures were similar to those followed by Smeaton and Josiam (1996) in their study of spring break in Panama City Beach, Florida, and by Eiser and Ford (1995) in their study

Table 4.4.2 Ordinary Least Squares Regression Coefficients for Intentions to Engage in Casual Sex on Centered Predictors

Variable	Model 1: TIB			Model 2: Enhanced TIB		
	B	*S.E.*	β	*B*	*Σ.E.*	β
Affective Component	0.12**	0.04	0.15	0.12**	0.04	0.15
Evaluative Component	0.18***	0.04	0.27	0.16***	0.04	0.25
Personal Standard	0.05	0.04	0.10	0.01	0.03	0.03
Role Belief	0.04	0.03	0.08	0.03	0.04	0.06
Subjective Social Norm: Women	0.05	0.04	0.06	0.02	0.04	0.02
Subjective Social Norm: Men	0.38***	0.05	0.45	0.27***	0.05	0.32
Pact[a]	0.39***	0.11	0.20	0.26**	0.11	0.14
Situational Expectation				0.13**	0.05	0.20
Pact x Situational Expectation[b]				0.21***	0.06	0.20
Constant	1.55	0.06		1.49	0.06	
R^2		.70			.74	

Notes. N = 151. All independent variables except *Pact* are centered around their mean.
[a]Effect coded -1 = pact not to engage in coitus; 0 = no pact; 1 = pact to engage in coitus. [b]Interaction between pacts and situational expectations.
**$p < .05$. *** $p < .001$.

of a British beach resort. Participants were recruited on beaches and pool decks between 11 a.m. and 4 p.m. from Wednesday to Saturday of each of the two weeks when Canadian students were in Daytona. This timing ensured that participants had been in Daytona for at least 2 days before completing the questionnaire and that they were likely to be sober, as the heaviest alcohol consumption began in the late afternoon. Students were approached by the research assistants who explained the survey procedures and ethical guidelines and verified that potential participants were from Canada (all were from eastern Ontario). Those who agreed to participate were provided with a pencil and the questionnaire on a clipboard. Up to five questionnaire were distributed at one time. Research assistants ensured that each participant completed the questionnaire privately and out of the range of vision of others. Of the 494 students approached in this manner, 484 completed questionnaires, for a response rate of 98%. This closely matches Smeaton and Josiam's (1996) response rate of 99%.

In the second recruitment strategy, questionnaires were distributed to students for completion at the beginning of the return bus trip home. Research assistants explained the purpose and procedures of the study, and one person on the bus was delegated to collect and return completed surveys in a pre-addressed envelope. It was not possible to calculate a valid response rate: A number of students declined to complete a survey because they had already done so, but 119 questionnaires were completed in this manner.

In the final recruitment strategy, questionnaires were mailed to the 151 students who had completed prebreak surveys (all had agreed to receive a postbreak survey) within one week of returning home. These students were provided with an addressed, stamped return envelope and a separate stamped, addressed postcard. All who did not return a postcard received up to three phone reminders. Seventy-eight participants returned these questionnaires, for a response rate of 52%.

Participants' birthdates and university student numbers were used to match questionnaires and to eliminate duplicates. Three duplicates were found.

In each case, the questionnaire completed after the longest time in Daytona was retained.

Comparison of Surveys from Different Recruitment Strategies

Responses on questionnaires using the three recruitment strategies were compared on 60 items, controlling for gender and duration of time in Daytona. Of the 60 comparisons, 3 were significant at $p < .05$. This number of significant comparisons would be expected by chance at this level of significance. Based on these results, the three sampling strategies were judged to produce similar results, and data were combined for the Daytona analyses.

Questionnaire Development and Measurement of Constructs

The Daytona survey contained questions on sexual and spring break history and activities and experiences while in Daytona Beach. It could be completed in 10 minutes. Questions for this survey were developed using the same procedures described for the prebreak survey. Where questions addressed the same concepts in both surveys, wording was modified to accommodate the different time frame. Several constructs were unique to the Daytona survey: the spring break experience, prior casual sex experience, role modeling, and engaging in casual sex.

First, the degree of participation in spring break experiences conducive to casual sex was measured using mean scores of participants' ratings (on a 4-point scale ranging from *never* to *frequently*) of how often they participated in each of the ten experiences listed in the prebreak questionnaire as situational expectations. Cronbach's alpha was 0.82.

In the TIB, prior experience is measured as the number of times an individual has already engaged in the behavior of interest. Because few students had ever been to Daytona Beach for spring break vacation before this trip, the use of experiences specific to this environment was judged unfeasible. As an alternate indicator of similar prior experience, we examined whether an individual had ever engaged in coitus with someone they had known for less than 24 hours. This was scored dichotomously (0 = no, 1 = yes).

Participant reports of the proportion of friends who had participated in coitus while on spring break (0 = none; 1 = few; 2 = about half; 3 = most) were used as a measure of perceived role modeling of coital activity.

To measure the criterion variable we asked participants whether they engaged in coitus while on spring break and what their relationship was to the partner. For purposes of this analysis, a *casual sex* variable was created that was coded 0 if the respondent had not engaged in coitus while on spring break ($N = 499$) and 1 if the respondent had engaged in coitus with someone they met while on spring break ($N = 94$).

Data Analysis

The tests for equivalence of men's and women's covariance matrices and the collinearity diagnostics conducted for the prebreak analysis were replicated for the Daytona sample. Although men's and women's covariance matrices were not significantly different for the original TIB constructs, they were significantly different when the two peer influence variables were added. Consequently, separate regression analyses were conducted for each gender. No multicollinearity was identified, and there were no interaction terms in these regression models. Therefore, variables were not centered.

The models for coitus with someone who was met on spring break were tested separately for men and women using hierarchical logistic regressions with forced entry of blocks of variables. The predictor variables in Triandis's original model were included in the first model. Two variables were added in the second: proportion of friends who had engaged in coitus on spring break and the form of agreement or pact struck with friends about casual sex on spring break.

Results

Sample Profile

Participants were 306 males and 375 females from six universities in Ontario, Canada. They ranged in age from 18 to 30 years with 69% clustering between ages 21 and 23. All participants were White and identified themselves as heterosexual and single. Twenty-eight percent of men and 35% of women reported that they were in a long-term relationship.

Spring Break Experiences

Table 4.4.3 reports responses to questions about sexual history and spring break intentions and experience. The gender differences identified in the prebreak sample were replicated here. Consistent with these differences, men reported participating in significantly more spring break activities conducive to casual sex ($M = 2.96$, $SD = 0.58$) than did women ($M = 2.79$, $SD = 0.57$; $p < .05$), and a significantly larger percentage of men's friends engaged in coitus on spring break ($M = 0.22$, $SD = 0.24$) than did women's friends ($M = 0.12$, $SD = 0.21$; $p < .001$). However, there were no significant differences in the coital activity that men and

Table 4.4.3 Percentage of Men and Women Reporting Sexual and Spring Break Experience and Intentions

Variable	Males	Females
Prior Sexual Experience		
Previous coital experience	91%	87%
Ever coitus within 24 hrs of meeting partner	61%[+++]	34%
Pacts or Agreements Formed With Friends		
Not to engage in casual sex	5%[+++]	21%
To engage in casual sex	30%[+++]	5%
Intend to Engage in Casual Sex	55%[+++]	11%
Coital Activity on Spring Break		
Coitus with relationship partner	7%	8%
Coitus with acquaintance[a]	6%	4%
Coitus with someone met on spring break[b]	15%	13%
No coital activity	72%	77%

Note. Sample comprises 306 males and 375 females.

[a]Someone the participant knew before coming on spring break but with whom the participant had not engaged in coitus. [b]Casual sex.

[+++]Difference between percentages significant at $p < .001$ (Chi-square test).

women reported on spring break. Seventy-four percent of students did not engage in coitus during the spring break trip. Those whose relationship partners accompanied them restricted coital activity to these partners. Most others engaged in casual sex.

Fewer men engaged in coital activity with new partners than intended to (55% of the men in this sample intended to engage in coital activity, but only 15% did). For women, however, there was almost no difference in the percentages who intended and who engaged in coitus with a new partner. For those who engaged in coitus with a new partner, there was no significant gender difference in the number of partners. During spring break, 68% had one partner, 13% had two partners, and 19% had more than two partners.

Explaining Participation in Casual Sex

When considered separately (Table 4.4.4), intentions to engage in casual sex, prior casual sex experience, participation in spring break activities, the proportion of friends who engaged in coitus while on spring break, and the formation of pacts about casual sex with friends were significantly different for those who engaged and did not engage in casual sex while on spring break. Having a relationship partner at home did not necessarily impede engaging in casual sex on spring break.

Table 4.4.5 reports hierarchical logistic regressions of the dichotomous measure of participation in casual sex first on the variables in the TIB, and then with the addition of two measures of peer influence. Regressions were conducted separately for women and men. In the first regression, using variables from the TIB, results were similar for men and women. Intentions and spring break experience significantly differentiated between those who engaged and did not engage in casual sex, with spring break experiences the stronger of the two predictors. The absence of a significant effect for prior casual sex experience could be related to the measurement of this construct. Because of the novelty of the Daytona Beach experience for the majority of students, prior experience was measured using any casual sex experience rather than the more specific measure of casual sex on spring break recommended by Triandis.

Results of the second regression were different for men and women. For men, the addition of two measures of peer influence did not improve the predictive power of the model, as seen in the absence of a significant increase in the improvement in chi-square or in the percentage of cases that were correctly classified. Intentions and prior casual sex experience remained the significant predictors of engaging in casual sex. For women, however, there was a significant improvement in the predictive power of the model. The

Table 4.4.4 Percentages and Mean Scores on Selected Predictor Variables, by Casual Sex Activity

	Coital Activity on Spring Break	
Variable	No Coital Activity	Casual Sex
Women		
Intend to engage in casual sex	8%+++	31%
Prior casual sex experience	23%+++	55%
Spring break activities	2.75***	3.28
Proportion of friends engaged in coitus	0.07***	0.38
Pacts formed with friends		
No casual sex	24%+++	8%
Casual sex	2%+++	19%
Currently in a relationship[a]	31%	26%
Men		
Intend to engage in casual sex	50%+++	88%
Prior casual sex experience	51%+	71%
Spring break activities	2.93***	3.41
Proportion of friends engaged in coitus	0.19***	0.38
Pacts formed with friends		
No casual sex	2%++	7%
Casual sex	27%++	48%
Currently in a relationship[a]	26%	18%

Notes. This table excludes data for students who engaged in coitus with someone they knew. Sample comprises 268 women and 205 men who did not engage in coital activity, and 48 women and 46 men who engaged in casual sex.

[a]None of these relationship partners were in Daytona Beach.

***$p < .001$ it-test). +$p < .05$ (Chi-square test). ++$p < .01$ (Chi-square test). +++$p < .001$ (Chi-square test).

Table 4.4.5 Hierarchical Logistic Regression Coefficients for Casual Sex[a] on Predictors From Two Models, Women and Men Regressed Separately

Variable	Model 1: TIB			Model 2: Enhanced TIB		
	Odds (Antilog)	Log Odds	Partial Correlation	Odds (Antilog)	Log Odds	Partial Correlation
Women						
Prior experience[b]	1.85	0.62	0.03	1.40	0.34	0.00
Intentions[c]	2.94	1.08*	0.11	2.41	0.88	0.00
Spring break experience	5.57	1.72***	0.25	2.81	1.03	0.09
Role model[d]				3.59	1.28***	0.28
Pact[e]				11.92	2.48**	0.16
Constant		−7.30			−5.79	
Men						
Prior experience[b]	0.74	−0.30	0.00	0.806	−0.23	0.00
Intentions[c]	3.68	1.30**	0.14	4.83	1.58**	0.15
Spring break experience	6.14	1.82***	0.24	12.27	2.51***	0.28
Role model[d]				1.22	0.20	0.00
Pact[e]				0.51	−0.67	0.00
Constant		−8.04			−10.49	

Notes. $N = 306$ women: $N = 251$ men. All coefficients are maximum-likelihood estimates. Models 1 and 2 both correctly classified 80% of the cases. For women. 1 over baseline. Chi-square improvement was 38.236 ($df = 3$; $p < .01$); and for 2 over 1, Chi-square improvement was 35.747 ($df = 2$; $p < .01$). For men, 1 over baseline. Chi-square improvement was 33.300 ($df = 3$; $p < .01$), and for 2 over 1, Chi-square improvement was 5.441 ($df = 2$; $p = .06$).

[a]0 = no coital activity: 1 = coitus with a partner met on spring break. [b]0 = no prior casual sex experience; 1 = prior casual sex experience. [c]0 = no intentions to engage in casual sex on spring break: 1 = intend to engage in casual sex on spring break. [d]Measured as proportion of friends who engaged in coitus on spring break. [e]1 = pact to engage in casual sex: 0 = no pact: −.1 = pact not to engage in casual sex.
*$p < .05$. ** $p < .01$. *** $p < .001$.

two peer influences, perceived role modeling and pacts, were the significant factors in classifying students correctly. Although the frequency of participation in spring break experiences conducive to forming new coital partnerships had the strongest effect in Model 1, it was just below statistical significance ($p = .06$) in Model 2. In Model 2, the proportion of friends engaging in sex had the strongest effect on whether women engaged in casual sex.

DISCUSSION

In their review of research on premarital sexual decision-making Christopher and Roosa (1991) noted that the contexts and settings in which coital partnerships

are formed have received little research attention. The research reported in this paper focused on the North American spring break vacation and its influence on a young adult to engage in casual sex. It built on the review of characteristics of vacations that contribute to engaging in sex by Herold and van Kerkwijk (1992), and on the research on "vacation sex" conducted by Eiser and Ford (1995) and Smeaton and Josiam (1996). In this study, 21% of men and 17% of women reported engaging in coitus with a new partner, 15% and 13%, respectively, with someone they met on spring break.

Three factors stand out about these percentages. First, there is greater similarity in the percentages of men and women who engaged in casual sex than would be expected considering the degree of dissimilarity between men and women on all other variables examined in this research. On variables used to predict either the formation of intentions or engaging in casual sex, men's scores clustered in the direction of acceptance, endorsement, and expectation of situations conducive to casual sex; women's clustered in the opposite direction. This finding is consistent with previous research (for reviews, see Christopher & Roosa, 1991; Oliver & Hyde, 1993). Despite this clustering, casual sex did not occur for most men. This suggests that women's attitudes, norms, expectations, and intentions, which were less supportive of engaging in casual sex, determined whether coitus occurred, consistent with the traditional image of women as "gatekeepers" (Herold, 1984).

The second factor of interest is that the percentages reporting coital activity with a new partner were similar to the British beach resort vacationers in Eiser and Ford's (1995) study (22% for men and 20% for women). However, the percentages for women in our study and in the British study were considerably higher than that reported by Smeaton and Josiam (1996) in their Panama City Beach spring break study where only 4% of women reported sex with a new partner. In our study and the British study, data were collected by male and female research assistants who were close in age to the vacationers, whereas Smeaton and Josiam's data were collected by two male professors. Our procedure may have produced greater comfort and honesty among the female participants, resulting in greater consistency in women's and men's reports.

The third factor to note is that the percentage of men and women reporting casual sex on spring break was considerably lower than the percentage of students reporting prior casual sex. Thus, although spring break is a vacation conducive to new coital partnerships for some, most students on spring break did not participate in coitus.

Since Reiss' (1967) work on personal standards for sexual behavior, consideration of the relationship between standards and behavior has had a prominent place in sexuality research. In this research it was personal *attitudes* rather than personal *standards* (as differentiated by Triandis) that influenced casual sex,

with attitudes influencing intentions to engage in casual sex. Personal standards and role beliefs—that is, the variables that measured social norms as expressed in personal moral codes or standards—did *not* have a significant influence on intentions or expectations about casual sex. These results contrast with those of other studies using the Triandis model in which personal standards or role beliefs were found to have an effect that was stronger than that of attitudes (Boyd & Wandersman, 1991; Godin et al., 1996). This highlights a characteristic of the spring break environment and the behavior under consideration that was more fully described by students in the elicitation phase: Activities on spring break, including coitus, were described as exceptions to the everyday experience—as outside of usual expectations, standards, or norms. Students used phrases such as "what happens in Daytona, stays in Daytona," "nothing that happens there comes home," and "nothing counts." They portrayed an atmosphere in which the usual rules and moral codes did not apply. Students provided detailed descriptions of how some had behaved "totally out of character" or in ways that "they never would at home." These illustrations and the results of the statistical analysis support the picture of spring break as an environment in which personal codes are temporarily suspended.

Although personal codes did not influence spring break coital behaviors, perceptions of peer expectations and promises or pacts made with peers did. This also conformed to the image of spring break described in the elicitation phase of the research: Friends travel and "hang" together in Daytona Beach. In statistical analyses, peers had a significant influence on both the formation of intentions to engage in casual sex and in casual sex activity when in Daytona Beach. However, peer group influence took different forms for men and women. For men, peer influence operated through pacts formed with friends about casual sex and perceptions of friends' approval or disapproval of casual sex. In both cases this influence was on the formation of intentions to engage in casual sex. Peer influences did not have a direct effect on engaging in casual sex. For women, peer influence operated through the formation of pacts between friends about casual sex and through role modeling (i.e., the percentage of friends on spring break who participated in coitus). Pacts influenced intentions and, along with the percentage of friends who engaged in coitus on spring break, had a direct effect on engaging in casual sex in the Daytona sample. Thus, men's *intentions* were more strongly influenced by the effect of peers than were women's. However, peers had an additional direct influence on women's coital *activity* on spring break. A common finding in other studies is that peers have a stronger influence on men than on women (for a review, see Christopher and Roosa, 1991), though some have found that the influence is experienced equally by men and women (e.g., Winslow et al., 1992). However, in most research only one form of peer influence is tested. The effect of different forms of peer influence found in this study leads us to concur with Wilcox and Udry's (1986) suggestion that it is important to examine more fully the different types of peer influence in future work.

The activities and experiences that students considered conducive to casual sex paralleled those identified by Herold and van Kerkwijk (1992): a perpetual party atmosphere, high rates of alcohol consumption, sexual contests, dancing dirty, frequent attempts made to "pick up" a sexual partner, and being in a break-loose mood. Along with positive attitudes toward casual sex while on spring break and perceived peer support for casual sex, anticipation of this spring break experience led to the formation of intentions or expectations of engaging in casual sex. Once in Daytona Beach, participation in casual sex depended not only on prior intentions but also on the degree of participation in spring break activities. For women, however, peer influences in Daytona Beach were more important in determining casual sex activity than were intentions or participation in spring break activities. For men, the greater consistency in the importance of the spring break environment on both expectations of casual sex and casual sex activity suggests that they are more susceptible to influences from the external environment and potentially are more likely to interpret the environment as providing sexual cues.

There are limitations to the generalizability of the results of this research. First, because of the voluntary nature of the samples and the restriction to one research site it is difficult to know whether the results can be generalized to other vacations. The high response rate for recruitment at Daytona Beach, the consistency in results across the different sampling designs in the Daytona study, the similarity in the reports of prior sexual activity with reports obtained in Canadian studies using national probability samples (Maticka-Tyndale, 1997), and the similarities of our results to those of other studies of vacation sex in other locations (Eiser & Ford, 1995; Herold & van Kerkwijk, 1992; Smeaton & Josiam, 1996), support confidence in the findings. However, the generalizability of findings of a study of this nature must always be treated with caution until more research, ideally with improved sampling strategies, has been conducted.

A second limitation is the absence of a longitudinal design to test the full Triandis model. Initially, one of our goals was to obtain such a sample. However, because of the last-minute nature of spring break holidays and the intense academic schedule of midterm exams during the weeks just before spring break it was difficult to recruit a sufficient number of participants before spring break. Although the lack of a significant difference between the responses of students recruited in Daytona and those recruited before spring break gave us confidence that results in both studies were reflective of the same population, a full test of the Triandis model awaits a longitudinal sample.

Some researchers may feel that the absence of standardized measures of constructs introduced an additional limitation to the generalizability of our results. Triandis's theory stresses the importance of measurements specific to the time, place, event, and population, and provides a methodology for creating and testing such measures. We followed these recommendations for creating measures and testing their reliability and validity. However, Triandis's rejection of standardized scales for their lack of specificity to the topic of study may be viewed with skepticism by some researchers. Whether one sees the types of measures used in this study as enhancing or limiting the quality of the results depends on whether the measures are considered a strength or a weakness of the design.

These limitations point to two methodological directions for future work. The first is the exploration of more representative sampling designs either for studies of contexts such as vacations or for sampling diverse contexts and comparing them for their influence on different forms of sexual partnering. Second, an empirical comparison of Triandis's measurement model to the use of standardized scales could help resolve some of the questions raised about potential limitations of Triandis's approach.

The areas of gender difference and similarity also suggest areas for future inquiry. The gender differences in all but coital activity on spring break remind us that coitus occurs between partners. A full understanding of how sexual activity and partnerships occur requires future research at the level of the couple. In addition, further inquiry is necessary to understand the variations in peer influence on men and women.

The sexual activity on spring break was described by students as a temporary, rapidly progressing partnership. This raises questions about how different forms of sexual partnerships are formed, what meaning they hold, and how they fit within the overall sexual scripts of young adults. Further investigation of environments conducive to rapid and casual sexual encounters, the specific characteristics of these environments that encourage sexual partnering, and the differences between those who are influenced and those who resist the influence of the environment is another area of inquiry suggested by this research.

Finally, the TIB provided a powerful multivariate model that integrated personal, social, and situational factors in explaining sexual planning and activity. This suggests that this model could be helpful in more fully explaining sexual partnering in other contexts.

REFERENCES

Aiken, L. S., & West, S. G. (1991). *Multiple regression: Testing and interpreting interactions.* Newbury Park, CA: Sage Publications.

Ajzen, I. (1985). From intentions to actions: A theory of planned behavior. In J. Kuhl and J. Beckmann (Eds.), *Action-control: From cognition to behavior,* (pp. 11–39). Heidelberg, Germany: Springer.

Ajzen, I. (1991). The theory of planned behavior. *Organizational Behavior and Human Decision Processes, 50,* 179–211.

Ajzen, I., & Fishbein, M. (1980). *Understanding attitudes and predicting social behavior.* Englewood Cliffs, NJ: Prentice-Hall.

Boyd, B., & Wandersman, A. (1991). Predicting undergraduate condom use with the Fishbein and Ajzen and the Triandis attitude-behavior models: Implications for public health interventions. *Journal of Applied Social Psychology, 21,* 1810–1830.

Christopher, F. S., & Cate, R. M. (1984) Factors involved in premarital sexual decision-making. *The Journal of Sex Research, 25,* 255–266.

Christopher, F. S., & Roosa, M. W. (1991). Factors affecting sexual decisions in the premarital relationships of adolescents and young adults. In K. McKinney & S. Sprecher (Eds.), *Sexuality in close relationships.* (pp. 111–134). Hillsdale, NJ: Lawrence Erlbaum Associates.

D'Augelli, J. F., & D'Augelli, A. R. (1977). Moral reasoning and premarital sexual behavior: Toward reasoning about relationships. *Journal of Social Issues, 33,* 46–66.

Eiser, J. R., & Ford, N. (1995). Sexual relationships on holiday: A case of situational disinhibition? *Journal of Social and Personal Relationships, 12,* 323–339.

Fishbein, M., & Jaccard, J. (1973). Theoretical and methodological considerations in the prediction of family planning intentions and behavior. *Representative Research in Social Psychology, 4,* 37–51.

Godin, G., Maticka-Tyndale, E., Adrien, A., Manson-Singer, S., Willms, D., & Cappon, P. (1996). Cross-cultural testing of three social cognitive theories: An application to condom use. *Journal of Applied Social Psychology, 26,* 1556–1586.

Herold, E. S. (1984). *Sexual behavior of Canadian young people.* Toronto: Fitzhenry & Whiteside.

Herold, E. S., & van Kerkwijk. C. (1992). AIDS and sex tourism. *AIDS and Society, 4,* 1–8.

Joreskog, K. G., & Sorbom, D. (1986). *LISREL: Analysis of linear structural relationships by the method of maximum likelihood, Version VI.* Mooresville, IN: Scientific Software, Inc.

Jorgensen, S. R., & Sonstegard, J. (1984). Predicting adolescent sexual and contraceptive behavior: An application and test of the Fishbein model. *Journal of Marriage and the Family, 46,* 43–55.

Josiam, B., Clements, J. S., & Hobson, P. (1995). *Spring break student travel: A longitudinal study.* Unpublished manuscript.

Maticka-Tyndale, E. (1997). Reducing the incidence of sexually transmitted disease through behavioral and social change. *The Canadian Journal of Human Sexuality, 6,* 89–104.

Mewhinney, D. M., Herold, E. S., & Maticka-Tyndale, E. (1995). Sexual scripts and risk-taking of Canadian university students on spring break in Daytona Beach. Florida. *The Canadian Journal of Human Sexuality, 4,* 273–288.

Oliver, M. B., & Hyde, J. S. (1993). Gender differences in sexuality: A meta-analysis. *Psychological Bulletin, 114,* 29–51.

Randall, D. M., & Wolff, J. A. (1994). The time interval in the intention-behavior relationship: Meta-analysis. *British Journal of Social Psychology, 33,* 405–418.

Reiss, I. L. (1967). *The social context of premarital sexual permissiveness.* New York: Holt, Rinehart, & Winston.

Rook, K. S., & Hammen, C. I., (1977). A cognitive perspective on the experience of sexual arousal. *Journal of Social Issues, 33,* 7–29.

Smeaton, G., & Josiam, B. (1996). *Sex, drugs and alcohol on the beach: "Where the boys are in the age of AIDS."* Paper presented at the meeting of the Society for the Scientific Study of Sex. Houston, TX.

Smith, K. W., & Sasaki, M. S. (1979). Decreasing multicollinearity: A method for models with multiplicative functions. *Sociological Methods and Research, 8,* 35–56.

Triandis, H. C. (1977). Interpersonal behavior. Monterey, CA: Brooks/Cole.

Triandis, H. C. (1980). Values, attitudes, and interpersonal behavior. In H. Howe & M. Page (Eds.). *Nebraska Symposium on Motivation 1979* (pp. 195–295). Lincoln. NE: University of Nebraska Press.

Triandis, H. C. (1994). *Culture and social behavior.* New York: McGraw-Hill Inc.

White, K. M., Terry, D. J., & Hogg, M. A. (1994). Safer sex behavior: The role of attitudes, norms, and control factors. *Journal of Applied Social Psychology, 24,* 2164–2192.

Wilcox, S., & Dury, W. (1986). Autism and accuracy in adolescent perceptions of friends' sexual attitudes and behaviors. *Journal of Applied Social Psychology, 16,* 361–374.

Winslow, R. W., Franzini, L. R., & Hwang, J. (1992). Perceived peer norms, casual sex and AIDS risk prevention. *Journal of Applied Social Psychology, 22,* 1809–1827.

4.5 INFLUENCES OF CULTURE ON ASIAN AMERICANS' SEXUALITY

Sumie Okazaki

While sharing their Asian ancestry and vestiges of Asian cultural heritage to varying degrees, Asian Americans comprise an ethnic minority group that defies simple characterizations. Consisting of approximately 4% of the total U.S. population, Asian Americans trace their roots to one or more of 28 Asian countries of origin or ethnic groups. The largest proportions of Asian Americans in 1990 were Chinese (24%) and Filipino (20%), followed by Japanese, Korean, and Asian Indian at approximately 11% to 12% each and Vietnamese at 9% (U.S. Bureau of the Census, 1993). However, the continuing influx of new immigrants from Southeast Asia and South Asia as well as from China and Korea provide a backdrop for diversity among Americans of Asian ancestry on important dimensions such as national origin, language, nativity, generational status, religion, acculturation to the mainstream American values and customs, and so on. The majority (66%) of Asian Americans in 1990 were born in foreign countries (U.S. Bureau of the Census, 1993).

The present review concerning the impact of Asian and Asian American cultures on sexuality will first examine aspects of various Asian cultural traditions and values that influence sexual attitudes and behavior among Asian Americans, then examine the available scientific literature in several major areas (but excluding materials related to HIV, other STDs, and safe sex practices). Some topics, namely sexual dysfunction and treatment, are not covered because no data exist. Most studies that are reviewed here do not specifically test the link between aspects of Asian or Asian American culture and sexual variables but instead use Asian American ethnicity as a proxy for culture.

From *Journal of Sex Research* 39(1): 34–41. Copyright © 2001 by The Society for the Scientific Study of Sexuality. Reprinted by permission of The Society for the Scientific Study of Sexuality.

CULTURAL ROOTS

Sexuality is linked to procreation in most Asian cultures. Gupta (1994) argues that sexuality was not a taboo subject in ancient Hindu culture granted that it was discussed within the context of marriage. Rather, sexuality was openly discussed in religious and fictional texts (e.g., the Kama Sutra) and depicted in paintings and sculptures, some with explicit erotic details. Japanese and Chinese erotica also date back to ancient times. On the other hand, sex is a taboo subject in contemporary Chinese culture, where sex education in schools is minimal and parents as well as health professionals are reluctant to discuss sexuality and sexual information (Chan, 1986). Traditional Cambodian society believed that a lack of knowledge regarding sexuality would prevent premarital sexual activity that would tarnish the family honor; consequently, discussions of information regarding sexual intercourse and sexuality were kept to a minimum (Kulig, 1994). Filipino culture, with the strong influence of Catholicism, tends to have a strong moral undercurrent that scorns premarital sex, use of contraceptives, and abortion (Tiongson, 1997).

Regardless of each Asian culture's degree of openness surrounding sexual discourse, expressions of sexuality outside of marriage are considered highly inappropriate in most Asian cultures. Most Asian cultures are highly collectivistic and patriarchal; thus, sexuality that is allowed open expression (particularly among women) would repr sent a threat to the highly interdependent social order as well as to the integrity of the family. Many Asian cultural traditions place emphasis on propriety and the observance of strict moral and social conduct, thus modesty and restrained sexuality are valued (Abraham, 1999). The sexually conservative beliefs and behavior that many Americans of Asian ancestry may exhibit may, in turn, be misinterpreted by the larger American society as asexual (Tsui, 1985).

SEXUAL KNOWLEDGE, ATTITUDES, AND NORMS

Available data regarding the sexual knowledge, attitudes, and norms among Asian Americans reflect relative conservatism. In a 1993 study in British Colum-

bia comparing 346 Asian Canadian and 356 non-Asian Canadian[1] university students enrolled in introductory psychology courses, Meston, Trapnell, and Gorzalka (1998) found that Asian Canadians held more conservative sexual attitudes and demonstrated less sexual knowledge than non-Asian Canadians. Among Asian Canadians, the more acculturated they were to the Canadian culture the more permissive their sexual attitudes. In a survey of 574 girls in sixth through eighth grades at public junior high schools in southern California, East (1998) compared the girls' sexual, marital, and birth expectations across four ethnic groups (White, Black, Hispanic, and Southeast Asians). Southeast Asian American (Vietnamese, Cambodian, Laotian; $n = 70$) girls reported the oldest "best" age for first intercourse ($M = 21.7$) and first birth ($M = 24.4$) and the oldest "desired" age for first birth ($M = 26.4$) of the four ethnic group girls. Southeast Asian American girls indicated the least desire to have children, the least likelihood of having children out of wedlock, and the least intention of having sexual intercourse in the near future. In a survey of 452 unmarried young adults (ages 18 to 25) attending 2-year community colleges, Feldman, Turner, and Araujo (1999) also found that Asian Americans ($n = 104$) held significantly later normative and personal sexual timetables for initiating all types of sexual behavior relative to other ethnic groups. In another survey with 474 college students in the Southwest (17 of whom were Asian American) regarding sex education, Asian Americans' reported age at which they understood what sexual intercourse was ($M = 15.1$) and the age at which they plan to begin their future children's sex education ($M = 14.1$) were older than those of any other ethnic group (Harman & Johnson, 1995).

There are some data suggesting that Asian Americans' sexually conservative attitude may erode with higher degrees of exposure to the American culture. Abramson and Imai-Marquez (1982) administered a measure of sex guilt to three different generations of Japanese American men and women and matched groups of White Americans in the metropolitan Los Angeles area. The researchers found that each subsequent younger generation of Japanese Americans and White Americans reported less guilty thoughts and feelings concerning sexual matters, although Japanese Americans still reported more sex guilt than White Americans within each age cohort group. However, in a different study of 18 Japanese American, 22 Mexican American, 20 African American, and 27 White American parents in Los Angeles regarding their attitudes toward sex education, the attitudes of Japanese American parents were found not to differ from those of other ethnic group parents once father's education and mother's religiosity were controlled for (Abramson, Moriuchi, Waite, & Perry, 1983). Notably, all of the Japanese American parents were born in the U.S.

SEXUAL BEHAVIOR

Most studies of sexual activity among Asian Americans have been conducted with adolescents and college students. The most comprehensive survey of American adults' sexual behavior, the National Health and Social Life Survey conducted in 1992, did not oversample Asian American individuals (Laumann, Gagnon, Michael, & Michaels, 1994). Consequently, only 2% of the total sample was Asian American, making it difficult to sufficiently characterize the sexual behavior of Asian American (particularly female) adults in the general population.

Adolescents

In a survey of 2,026 high school students in Los Angeles County, Asian American adolescents ($n = 186$) were more likely to be virgins (73%) than African American (28%), Latino (43%), and White Americans (50%) (Schuster, Bell, & Kanouse, 1996). Further analyses of the same data revealed that Asian American adolescents were less likely to have initiated a vaginal intercourse at an early age and were less likely to report having participated in other heterosexual genital sexual activities during the prior year than their non-Asian counterparts as well (Schuster, Bell, Nakajima, & Kanouse, 1998). The researchers found that Asian American nonvirgins also reported the lowest number of lifetime partners for vaginal intercourse, even though the reported frequency of sexual activity did not differ from those of other ethnic group adolescents. Asian American adolescents in homes where English is the primary language spoken were

more likely than other Asian Americans to be nonvirgins and to have engaged in heterosexual genital sexual activities. Asian American adolescents were also more likely than non-Asian Americans to think that their parents and friends would disapprove if they had vaginal intercourse and that people their own age should not have vaginal intercourse.

Another study of an ethnically diverse sample of 877 Los Angeles County youths (Upchurch, Levy-Storms, Sucoff, & Aneshensel, 1998) found that Asian American males had the highest median age of first sex (18.1) and that Asian American females (as well as Hispanic females) had rates of first sex that was about half that of White females. Finally, an analysis of the national Youth Risk Behavior Survey data (total $N = 52,985$) collected by the Centers for Disease Control and Prevention (Grunbaum, Lowry, Kann, & Pateman, 2000) also found that Asian American high school students were significantly less likely than Black, Hispanic, or White students to have had sexual intercourse or to have had four or more sex partners. Only 28% of Asian American students reported lifetime experience of sexual intercourse compared to 77% of Black, 55% of Hispanic, and 48% of White students. However, among those who were currently sexually active, Asian American students were found to be as likely as other groups to have used alcohol or drugs during last sexual intercourse or to have used a condom at last intercourse. It should be noted that there is variability among Asian ethnic groups with respect to sexual behavior. Horan and DiClemente (1993) reported that among 11th and 12th grade students in San Francisco, only 13% of Chinese American students were sexually active but 32% of Filipino students were sexually active.

College Students

The patterns found with Asian American adolescents also extend to college students. In a 1982 survey of 114 Chinese American college students in northern California (60% of whom were U.S.-born), Huang and Uba (1992) found that the majority (over 60%) approved of premarital sexual intercourse when partners are in love or engaged to be married; however, only 37% of the men and 46% of the women surveyed had ever engaged in coitus. In this sample, Chinese American women were generally more sexually experienced than men, with more women having engaged in kissing, necking, and petting, although men ($M = 18.5$) and women ($M = 18.8$) did not differ in age of first vaginal intercourse experience. There was a positive correlation between the level of acculturation to the U.S. and engagement in premarital sexual intercourse, and those Chinese Americans dating only White Americans consistently had more sexual experience than those dating only Chinese Americans. Huang and Uba concluded that Chinese American college students were not avoiding premarital sex because they do not find it permissible. Rather, the authors speculated that Chinese Americans' sexual behavior and gender differences may reflect internalized racism (e.g., less positive body images), more conservative standards for engaging in premarital sexual relations, and racialized stereotypes of Asian American men as asexual and undesirable sexual partners.

In a 1987–1988 survey of 153 Asian American college students in Southern California (half of who were born in the U.S.), Cochran, Mays, and Leung (1991) found that 44% of the men and 50% of the women had engaged in heterosexual sexual intercourse at least once. The rate of Asian Americans who were sexually active (47%) was significantly lower than their age cohorts in other ethnic groups. Among those who were sexually active, the rates of engagement in oral sex was high (86% for women, 75% for men). In an analyses of their 1993 data on 346 Asian and 356 non-Asian Canadian college students, Meston, Trapnell, and Gorzalka (1996) found significant and substantive ethnic differences in all measures of interpersonal sexual behavior (i.e., light and heavy petting, oral sex, intercourse) and intrapersonal sexual behavior (i.e., frequency of fantasies, masturbation incidence and frequency, and ideal frequency of intercourse), and all sociosexual restrictiveness measures (e.g., lifetime number of partners, number of partners in the past year, predicted number of partners, lifetime number of one-night stands). Overall, 35% of Asian Canadian college students in this survey reported having experienced intercourse. This study did not find any differences among Asian Canadians in their sexual behavior according to their length of residency in Canada.

A survey of 148 White American and 202 Asian American college students in Southern California (McLaughlin, Chen, Greenberger, & Biermeir, 1997) also found that Asian American men (over 55%) and women (60%) were significantly more likely than White American men (25%) and women (<30%) to be virgins. Among those who were sexually experienced, Asian American men ($M = 2.3$) and women ($M = 2.2$) reported fewer lifetime sexual partners than White American men ($M = 5.5$) and women ($M = 3.5$). Within the Asian American sample, women from least acculturated families were more likely to be virgins (77%) than those from moderately or highly acculturated families (52% and 53%, respectively). This pattern did not hold for Asian American men. Of note, Asian Americans and White Americans endorsed casual sex to a similar degree even though the groups differed significantly in the number of partners. McLaughlin et al. interpreted this attitude-behavior inconsistency among Asian American college students as possibly reflecting the larger and more effective role that their parents play in controlling the adolescents' behavior.

In sum, the available data indicate that Asian Americans tend to be more sexually conservative than non-Asian Americans of the same age group, particularly with regard to the older age of initiation of sexual activity. One exception is a study by Sue (1982), who reported in a survey of 36 Asian American college students enrolled in a human sexuality course that rates of premarital sexual behavior did not differ from those of non-Asian students. However, Sue's anomalous data are likely the result of the selective nature of Asian American students who voluntarily enrolled in a human sexuality course.

SEXUAL AND REPRODUCTIVE HEALTH

Almost all studies examining sexual and reproductive health among Asian Americans have been conducted with women. The studies of participation in breast and cervical cancer screening among the Asian American population paint a fragmented picture. Some studies have shown moderate rates of cancer screening among Asian American women. For example, 57% of 189 Chinese American women in Michigan, aged 50 or older, had had mammograms in the past 2 years (Yu, Seetoo, Tsai, & Sun, 1998), and over 70% of the Chinese American women sampled in San Francisco had had a mammogram, Pap test, clinical breast examination (CBE), and breast self examination (BSE) (Lee, 1998).

However, the majority of the studies have found extremely low rates of screening in Asian Americans compared to the non-Asian American population. In a study conducted in the Puget Sound area, Asian American women were found to be less likely than other ethnic group women to enroll in breast cancer screening programs even when out-of-pocket expenses for the screening tests were paid by managed care (Tu, Taplin, Barlow, & Boyko, 1999). In a study of women 18 to 74 years old in the San Francisco Bay Area, Chinese American and Vietnamese American women had the lowest rates of first time utilization and recent utilization of breast and cervical cancer screening among all the ethnic groups (Hiatt et al., 1996). Specifically, 33% of Chinese American women had never obtained a pap test and 30% had never performed BSE, whereas 58% of Vietnamese American women had never had a Pap test and 66% had never performed BSE. An interview study of 332 Chinese American women (ages 40–69) recruited through a two-stage probability sampling method in the Chinatown area of Chicago (Yu, Kim, Chen, & Brintnall, 2001) also found a low level of knowledge of cancer screening tests and low use rates. Only 52% and 54% of the Chinese American women surveyed had ever heard of the CBE and Pap smear test, respectively, for cancer screening purposes, and much lower percentages had actually undergone screenings (35% for CBE, 12% for mammogram, 26% for BSE, and 36% for Pap test). Levels of education, English fluency, and source of health care (Eastern vs. Western medicine) were significant predictors of reproductive health behavior in this population.

The pattern of low use of screening also extends to younger age groups. Only 14.9% of 174 Chinese American students at a midwestern university practiced BSE (Lu, 1995). In a 1996 reproductive and sexual health survey of 674 Asian American women (age 18–35; the majority foreign-born) in California, 67% of the women reported having had at least one sexual partner in their lifetime, yet half of the women (50%) had not received any reproductive or sexual health services within the past year and 25% had never received such services in their lifetime (National Asian Women's Health Organization, 1997). More than one third of the respondents reported that they had never discussed pregnancy, sexually transmitted diseases, birth control, or sexuality in their households. A survey of high school students in Los Angeles County also found that Asian American adolescents reported lower levels of communication with physicians about sexual activity and risk prevention than other ethnic groups (Schuster, Bell, Peterson, & Kanouse, 1996).

In a rare study that specifically examined the role of Asian cultural variables, Tang, Solomon, Yeh, and Worden (1999) studied BSE and cervical cancer screening behavior in 156 Asian American and 50 White American female college students. In this sample, 48% of Asian American and 68% of White American women reported having had sexual intercourse with a male partner. The ethnic differences extended to screening behavior, as only 27% of Asian American women reported performing BSE at least once in their lifetime in contrast to 47% of White American women. Similarly, only 32% of Asian American but 70% of White American women reported having had at least one Pap test in their lifetime. Asian American women were found to have more cultural barriers to screening (more communication barrier with mother surrounding sexual and gynecological issues, less openness around sexuality and more modesty, less prevention orientation in health care, and less utilization of Western medicine). Even after controlling for differences between the two ethnic groups (e.g., mother's education, year in college, family history of breast or cervical cancer, knowing someone with breast cancer, being sexually active, etc.), Asian Americans were still less likely than White Americans to have had BSE and pap test. However, Asian American women who were more acculturated were more likely to participate in these screening behaviors.

Consistent with Tang et al.'s (1999) results, similar cultural reasons for the low utilization of reproductive health services were elucidated through a qualitative analysis of interview data with 9 Asian

American health care practitioners and educators who worked with Asian American women and focus group data with 6 second-generation Asian American women (National Asian Women's Health Organization, 1995). This study found that Asian American women's sense of risk regarding reproductive and sexual health appeared to be downplayed, as the women tended to view gynecological services as important and legitimate only when they concerned reproductive functions or when the pain or symptoms of infection became unbearable or interfered with daily functioning. In the interviews, health advocates and practitioners agreed that recent immigrants in particular may perceive gynecological exams such as Pap tests as invasive and inappropriate prior to marriage, and that the perception that gynecological care is only acceptable after marriage likely prevents many Asian American women from accessing appropriate care. Additionally, Mo (1992) argued that the idea of a visit to a medical doctor for a checkup without receiving some form of intervention (namely medication) does not fit immigrant Chinese patients' expectations. Mo explained that a Cantonese term, *ham suup,* which is a colloquial term for sexuality that is most often used in a derogatory manner, is used to describe anyone who is sexually inappropriate. Talking about or touching one's body and being knowledgeable about the body are considered as *ham suup,* thus discouraging traditional and immigrant Chinese women from gaining knowledge regarding sexuality and sexual health. In sum, there appears to be a pervasive tendency for Asian American girls and women to be more reluctant than White American girls and women to seek care for their sexual and reproductive health.

As a possible consequence of their relatively low use of screening, Asian American women tend to be diagnosed with more advanced stages of cervical cancer (Frisch & Goodman, 2000) and breast cancer (Jenkins & Kagawa-Singer, 1994) than White American women, thereby increasing the disease burden at diagnosis (Hedeen, White, & Taylor, 1999). Cervical cancer rates among Vietnamese American women was the highest of all ethnic groups in the U.S., with the incidence of 43 per 100,000, a rate that is almost five times that of White American women (Miller et

al., 1996). These statistics indicate that there are high health costs associated with Asian American women's reluctance to become knowledgeable about, and to engage in, sexual and reproductive health practices.

One study regarding the sexual and reproductive health issues of Asian American men does exist. A telephone survey of 802 English speaking Asian American men between the ages of 18 and 65 was conducted in Los Angeles, San Francisco, and New York (National Asian Women's Health Organization, 1999). Over half of the respondents (54%) were single and the majority (75%) was foreign-born. Although 87% of the surveyed Asian American men had at least one sexual partner in the past year, the vast majority of the respondents (89%) had never received sexual or reproductive health care services.

SEXUAL ABUSE AND AGGRESSION

The scope of sexual abuse in the Asian American community is unknown, as most state and national agencies that collect such data fail to segregate the data for Asian American victims. Where data are available, the reported incidence among Asian Americans appears relatively low compared to other ethnic groups, possibly due to their lack of access or reluctance to use mental health services and public agencies (Kenny & McEachern, 2000). However, many service providers assert that the actual incidence is much higher than reported (Okamura, Heras, & Wong-Kerberg, 1995). High rates of history of sexual victimization among Cambodian American refugees women and children, which they suffered during the Khmer Rouge reign of terror or at refugee camps, have been extensively documented (e.g., Mollica, Wyshak, & Lavelle, 1987; Rozée & Van Boemel, 1989; Scully, Kuoch, & Miller, 1995). In a study of abuse history among 102 Vietnamese Amerasian refugee young adults in the Philippine Refugee Processing Center who were awaiting placement in the United States, 12% of men and 9% of women reported having been sexually abused (McKelvey & Webb, 1995).

Those who work with Asian American communities speak of the Asian American victims' extreme reluctance to disclose or report sexual abuse or assault

(Okamura et al., 1995; Tsuneyoshi, 1996). For example, most Southeast Asian refugees surveyed by Wong (1987) stated that they would respond to sexual abuse in their own family by keeping it a family secret. Further, sexual abuse within the context of marriage may be fatalistically tolerated among some Asian American communities. As a result, immigrant Asian American women may be at a higher risk of marital sexual abuse than U.S.-born Asian American women because they may have been socialized to believe that they had fewer sexual rights than their husband (Lum, 1998). An analysis of interviews with 25 South Asian immigrant women who were abused by their spouses found that 60% of the women reported being forced to have sex with their husbands against their will, and sexual abuse took many forms such as marital rape and violence and the husbands' control of women's reproductive choices (e.g., forcing the wife to get an abortion, refusal to allow the use of contraceptives, etc.) (Abraham, 1999). Similarly, an interview study with 150 immigrant Korean American women in Chicago revealed that 60% of the women reported being battered, and 37% of those who were physically abused also reported being forced to have sex by their partners (Song, 1996).

Given the cultural tendency to hide sexual abuse from others, it is difficult to ascertain the accuracy of sexual abuse reports.[2] A review of 158 Asian American cases referred for child maltreatment to a San Diego social service agency serving Asian American immigrants and refugees found that sexual abuse constituted only 5% of the total cases, with most sexual abuse victims being Filipino and female (Ima & Hohm, 1991). Another retrospective chart review study of a child abuse clinic in San Francisco generated 69 substantiated cases of sexual abuse between 1986 and 1988 in which the victims were Asian Americans (Rao, DiClemente, & Ponton, 1992). A comparison of this sample of Asian American child sexual abuse victims with randomly selected samples of other ethnic group counterparts found that Asian American victims tended to be older ($M = 11.5$ years) and more likely to be living with both parents than other ethnic group victims. Notably, Asian American victims were much less likely to display inappropriate

sexual behaviors or express anger and hostility but most likely to express suicidal ideation or attempt suicide. Although Asian American mothers were as likely as White Americans and Hispanic Americans to be the primary caretakers to the child victims, they were much less likely than the other groups to have brought the abuse to the attention of authorities and most likely to disbelieve the report of the abuse. Asian American victims were also the least likely to disclose sexual abuse to their mothers; 61% either never spontaneously disclosed the abuse or disclosed the abuse to someone other than their mothers. Asian American victims were also the most likely group to be abused by a male relative (including the father).

Meston and her colleagues (Meston, Heiman, & Trapnell, 1999; Meston, Heiman, Trapnell, & Carlin, 1999) conducted a survey of 466 Asian Canadian and 566 non-Asian Canadian undergraduates regarding abuse experience before age 18 and their current sexuality. The researchers found that 25% of Asian Canadian women and 11% of Asian Canadian men had at least one experience with sexual abuse (defined here as being involved in some sexual activity against their wishes). In contrast, 40% of non-Asian Canadian women and 11% of non-Asian Canadian men reported at least one experience with sexual abuse. However, associations between early abuse and adult sexual behavior did not differ significantly between Asian and non-Asian Canadians, and reports of sexual abuse were not significantly correlated with socially desirable responding in either group. In another survey of 243 college women (38 of whom were Asian American), rates of reported childhood sexual abuse and being a victim of rape among Asian American college women (21% and 11%, respectively) were lower than those of their White American and African American counterparts (Urquiza & Goodlin-Jones, 1994). The researchers also found that for White and African Americans, women with a history of childhood sexual abuse were three times as likely to be raped as an adult than women without a history of childhood sexual abuse. However, this pattern did not hold for Asian American women.

Hall and Barongan (1997) noted that there appeared to be a lower prevalence of sexual aggression in Asian American communities. A national survey of sexual aggression found that fewer Asian American men perpetrate rape and fewer Asian American women are victims of rape than other ethnic groups (Koss, Gidycz, & Wisniewski, 1987). In their review of risk and protective factors for sexual aggression among Asian Americans, Hall, Windover, and Maramba (1998) argued that the patriarchal aspects of Asian culture, in which women hold subordinate status to men, may create a risk for, and a tolerance of, sexual aggression by Asian American men. On the other hand, Asian cultural emphases on self-control and interpersonal harmony may serve as protective factors for sexual aggressive behavior among Asian Americans. To test culture-specific models of sexual aggression, Hall, Sue, Narang, and Lilly (2000) examined intra- and inter-personal determinants of Asian American and White American men's sexual aggression. In this sample of college students, 33% of Asian American and 38% of White American men reported that they had perpetrated some form of sexual aggression. Whereas a path model for White American men suggested that only an intrapersonal variable (misogynous beliefs) predicted sexual aggression, both interpersonal (concern about social standing) and intrapersonal (misogynous beliefs, alcohol use) variables were predictive of Asian American sexual aggression.

Other studies point to a possible role of Asian cultural factors in the attitudes toward sexual violence. For example, a study of 302 Asian American and White American college students (Mori, Bernat, Glenn, Selle, & Zarate, 1995) found that Asian Americans were more likely to endorse negative attitudes toward rape victims and greater belief in rape myths than their White counterparts. Moreover, less acculturated Asian Americans held more negative attitudes toward rape victims than more acculturated Asian Americans. A telephone survey about domestic violence attitudes with 262 Chinese Americans in Los Angeles County (Yick, 2000) found that although 89% of the respondents agreed that sexual aggression constituted domestic violence, the respondents' gender role beliefs (traditional or egalitarian) emerged as a significant factor that shapes their definitions of abuse. In summary, certain facets of traditional Asian cultures (e.g., traditional gender roles, concerns about

loss of face) appear to be implicated in Asian Americans' attitudes toward, reporting of, and perpetration of sexual abuse and aggression.

SEXUAL ORIENTATION

Little empirical research exists concerning sexual orientation and sexual identity among Asian Americans apart from the HIV-risk studies, although a body of scholarly work (largely in the humanities) regarding Asian American gay, lesbian, and bisexual identities and sexual orientation exists (e.g., Leong, 1994, 1996). One study of 13 Japanese American gay men revealed that only half of their respondents were open with their families regarding their gay identity (Wooden, Kawasaki, & Mayeda, 1983). In a survey of 19 women and 16 men (ages 21–36) who identified as both Asian American and lesbian or gay, Chan (1989) found that they tended to be more involved in social and political activities in the lesbian-gay community than in the Asian American community. More than half of the respondents (57%) reported being more comfortable in the lesbian/gay community than in the Asian American community and identified more strongly with the gay or lesbian aspects of their identity, although a minority of the respondents reported a synthesized ethnic and sexual identities. Although the majority (77%) had come out to a family member (e.g., sibling), only 26% had disclosed their gay identity to their parents because of fear of rejection.

Finally, in a study investigating whether cultural backgrounds moderate the relationship between sexual orientation and gender-related personality traits, Lippa and Tan (2001) found that participants from more gender-polarized cultural backgrounds (Hispanics and Asian Americans) showed larger homosexual-heterosexual differences in gender-related traits than White Americans for both men and women. That is, Hispanic and Asian American gay men assumed more feminine roles and Hispanic and Asian American lesbians assumed more masculine roles with respect to occupational and hobby preferences as well as self-ascribed masculinity and femininity. Hispanic and Asian American gays and lesbians were also found to fear social disapproval of their homosexuality more than their White counterparts. Taken together, the findings from the few existing studies on sexual orientation among Asian Americans suggest possible influences of cultural and community factors in their sexual identity, disclosure of homosexuality, and gender-related traits.

CONCLUSION

Although there are significant gaps in the social science literature concerning Asian Americans' sexuality and sexual behavior, the existing data converge on notable differences between Asian Americans and other ethnic groups on major aspects such as sexual timetables and behaviors and attitudes surrounding sexuality, reproductive health, and sexual abuse. Many characteristics of the Asian Americans' sexual attitudes and behavior have significant implications for public health and clinical work. The next generation of empirical work must begin to test specific hypotheses regarding the Asian cultural characteristics as well as the impact of minority status on sexuality of Asian Americans.

NOTES

1. In this and all other studies conducted by Meston et al. (1996, 1997, 1999), individuals born in South Asia (India and Pakistan) were classified as non-Asians rather than Asians. (South Asians are considered in this review as Asians, following the convention in Asian American scholarship and the U.S. Census classification.) However, because South Asian Canadians typically constituted less than 3% of Meston et al.'s (1996, 1997, 1999) non-Asian samples, the results of their ethnic comparisons are likely to be reliable. The Asian Canadian group in their studies consisted primarily (70%) of ethnic Chinese.

2. For a more in-depth discussion of cultural factors that may influence in the reporting and treatment of child sexual abuse in Asian American communities. see Futa, Hsu, and Hansen (2001).

REFERENCES

Abraham, M. (1999). Sexual abuse in South Asian immigrant marriages. *Violence Against Women, 5,* 591–618.

Abramson, P. R., & Imai-Marquez, J. (1982). The Japanese-American: A cross-cultural, cross-sectional study of sex guilt. *Journal of Research in Personality, 16,* 227–237.

Abramson, P. R., Moriuchi, K. D., Waite, M. S., & Perry, L. B. (1983). Parental attitudes about sexual education: Cross-cul-

tural differences and covariate controls. *Archives of Sexual Behavior, 12,* 381–397.

Chan, C. S. (1989). Issues of identity development among Asian-American lesbians and gay men. *Source Journal of Counseling & Development, 68,* 16–20.

Chan, D. W. (1986). Sex misinformation and misconceptions among Chinese medical students in Hong Kong. *Archives of Sexual Behavior, 19,* 73–93.

Cochran, S. D., Mays, V. M., & Leung, L. (1991). Sexual practices of heterosexual Asian-American young adults: Implications for risk of HIV infection. *Archives of Sexual Behavior, 20,* 381–391.

East, P. L. (1998). Racial and ethnic differences in girls' sexual, marital, and birth expectations. *Journal of Marriage & the Family, 60,* 150–162.

Feldman, S. S., Turner, R. A., & Araujo, K. (1999). Interpersonal context as an influence on sexual timetables of youths: Gender and ethnic effects. *Journal of Research on Adolescence, 9,* 25–52.

Frisch, M., & Goodman, M. T. (2000). Human papillomavirus-associated carcinomas in Hawaii and the mainland U.S. *Cancer, 88,* 1464–1469.

Futa, K. T., Hsu, E., & Hansen, D. J. (2001). Child sexual abuse in Asian American families: An examination of cultural factors that influence prevalence, identification, and treatment. *Clinical Psychology: Science & Practice, 8,* 189–209.

Grunbaum, J. A., Lowry, R., Kann, L., & Pateman, B. (2000). Prevalence of health risk behaviors among Asian American/Pacific Islander high school students. *Journal of Adolescent Health, 27,* 322–330.

Gupta, M. (1994). Sexuality in the Indian subcontinent. *Sexual & Marital Therapy, 9,* 57–69.

Hall, G. C. N., & Barongan, C. (1997). Prevention of sexual aggression: Sociocultural risk and protective factors. *American Psychologist, 52,* 5–14.

Hall, G. C. N., Sue, S., Narang, D. S., & Lilly, R. S. (2000). Culture-specific models of men's sexual aggression: Intra- and interpersonal determinants. *Cultural Diversity & Ethnic Minority Psychology, 6,* 252–267.

Hall, G. C. N., Windover, A. K., & Maramba, G. G. (1998). Sexual aggression among Asian Americans: Risk and protective factors. *Cultural Diversity & Ethnic Minority Psychology, 4,* 305–318.

Harman, M. J., & Johnson, J. A. (1995). Cross-cultural sex education: Aspects of age, source, and sex equity. *TCA Journal, 23*(2), 1–11.

Hedeen, A. N., White, E., & Taylor, V. (1999). Ethnicity and birthplace in relation to tumor size and stage in Asian American women with breast cancer. *American Journal of Public Health, 89,* 1248–1252.

Hiatt, R. A., Pasick, R. J., Perez-Stable, E. J., McPhee, S. J., Engelsatd, L., Lee, M., Sabogal, F., D'Onofrio, C. N., &

Stewart, S. (1996). Pathways to early cancer detection in the multiethnic population of the Francisco Bay Area. *Health Education Quarterly, 23(Suppl.),* S10–S.

Horan, P. F., & DiClemente, R. J. (1993). HIV knowledge, communication and risk behavior among White, Chinese-, and Filipino-American adolescents in a high-prevalence AIDS epicenter: A comparative analysis *Ethnicity & Disease, 3,* 97–105.

Huang, K., & Uba, L. (1992). Premarital sexual behavior among Chinese college students in the United States. *Archives of Sexual Behavior,* 227–240.

Ima, K., & Hohm, C. F. (1991). Child maltreatment among Asian and Pacific Islander refugees and immigrants: The San Diego case. *Journal of Interpersonal Violence, 6,* 267–285.

Jenkins, C. N. H., & Kagawa-Singer, M. (1994). Cancer. In N. W. S. Zan D. T. Takeuchi, & K. N. J. Young (Eds.), *Confronting critical heal issues of Asian and Pacific Islander Americans,* (pp. 105–147) Thousand Oaks, CA: Sage.

Kenny, M. C., & McEachern, A. G. (2000). Racial, ethnic, and cultural factors of childhood sexual abuse: A selected review of the literature *Clinical Psychology Review, 20,* 905–922.

Koss, M. P., Gidycz, C. A., & Wisniewski, N. (1987). The scope of rape. Incidence and prevalence of sexual aggression and victimization in a national sample of higher education students. *Journal of Consulting & Clinical Psychology, 55,* 162–170.

Kulig, J. C. (1994). Sexuality beliefs among Cambodians: Implications for health care professionals. *Health Care for Women International, 15,* 69–76.

Laumann, E. O., Gagnon, J. H., Michael, R. T., & Michaels, S. (1994). *The social organization of sexuality: Sexual practices in the United States.* Chicago: The University of Chicago Press.

Lee, M. (1998). Breast and cervical cancer early detection in Chinese American women. *Asian American & Pacific Islander Journal of Health, 6,* 351–357.

Leong, R. (Ed.) (1994). Dimensions of desire [Special issue]. *Amerasia Journal, 20*(1).

Leong, R. (Ed.) (1996). *Asian American sexualities: Dimensions of the gay and lesbian experience.* New York: Routledge.

Lippa, R. A., & Tan, F. D. (2001). Does culture moderate the relationship between sexual orientation and gender-related personality traits? *Cross-Cultural Research, 35,* 65–87.

Lu, Z. J. (1995). Variables associated with breast self-examination among Chinese women. *Cancer Nursing, 18,* 29–34.

Lum, J. L. (1998). Family violence. In L. C. Lee & N. W. S. Zane (Eds.), *Handbook of Asian American psychology* (pp. 505–525). Thousand Oaks, CA: Sage.

McKelvey, R. S., & Webb, J. A. (1995). A pilot study of abuse among Vietnamese Amerasians. *Child Abuse & Neglect, 19,* 545–553.

McLaughlin, C. S., Chen, C., Greenberger, E., & Biermeier, C. (1997). Family, peer, and individual correlates of sexual experience among Caucasian and Asian American late adolescents. *Journal of Research on Adolescence, 7,* 33–53.

Meston, C. M., Heiman, J. R., & Trapnell, P. D. (1999). The relation between early abuse and adult sexuality. *The Journal of Sex Research, 36,* 385–395.

Meston, C. M., Heiman, J. R., Trapnell, P. D., & Carlin, A. S. (1999). Ethnicity, desirable responding, and self-reports of abuse: A comparison of European- and Asian-ancestry undergraduates. *Journal of Consulting & Clinical Psychology, 67,* 139–144.

Meston, C. M., Trapnell, P. D., & Gorzalka, B. B. (1996). Ethnic and gender differences in sexuality: Variations in sexual behavior between Asian and non-Asian university students. *Archives of Sexual Behavior, 25,* 33–72.

Meston, C. M., Trapnell, P. D., & Gorzalka, B. B. (1998). Ethnic, gender, and length-of-residency influences on sexual knowledge and attitudes. *The Journal of Sex Research, 35,* 176–188.

Miller, B. A., Kolonel, L. N., Bernstein, L., Young, J. L., Swanson, G. M., West, D., Key, C. R., Liffy, J. M., Glover, C. S., Alexander, G. A., et al. (Eds.). (1996). *Racial/ethnic patterns of cancer in the United States, 1988–1992, NIH Publication No. 96 4104.* Bethesda, MD: National Cancer Institute.

Mo, B. (1992). Modesty, sexuality, and breast health in Chinese-American women. *Western Journal of Medicine, 157,* 260–264.

Mollica, R., Wyshak, G., & Lavelle, J. (1987). The psychological impact of war trauma and torture on Southeast Asian refugees. *American Journal of Psychiatry, 144,* 1567–1571.

Mori, L., Bernat, J. A., Glenn, P. A., Selle, L. L., & Zarate, M. G. (1995). Attitudes toward rape: Gender and ethnic differences across Asian and Caucasian college students. *Sex Roles, 32,* 457–467.

National Asian Women's Health Organization. (1995). Perceptions of risk: An assessment of the factors influencing use of reproductive and sexual health services by Asian American women. San Francisco: Author.

National Asian Women's Health Organization. (1997). Expanding options: A reproductive and sexual health survey of Asian American women. San Francisco: Author.

National Asian Women's Health Organization. (1999). The Asian American Men's health survey. Sharing responsibility. San Francisco: Author.

Okamura, A., Heras, P., & Wong-Kerberg, L. (1995). Asian, Pacific Island, and Filipino Americans and sexual child abuse. In L. A. Fontes (Ed.), Sexual abuse in nine North

American cultures: Treatment and prevention (pp 67–93). Thousand Oaks, CA: Sage.

Rao, K., DiClemente, R. J., & Ponton, L. E. (1992). Child sexual abuse of Asians compared with other populations. *Journal of the American Academy of ChiM & Adolescent Psychiatry, 31*, 880–886.

Rozee, P. D., & Van Boemel, G. (1989). The psychological effects of war trauma and abuse on older Cambodian refugee women. *Women & Therapy, 8(4)*, 23–50.

Schuster, M. A., Bell, R. M., & Kanouse, D. E. (1996). The sexual practices of adolescent virgins: Genital sexual activities of high school students who have never had vaginal intercourse. *American Journal of Public Health, 86*, 1570–1576.

Schuster, M. A., Bell, R. M., Nakajima, G. A., & Kanouse, D. E. (1998). The sexual practices of Asian and Pacific Islander high school students. *Journal of Adolescent Health, 23*, 221–231.

Schuster, M. A., Bell, R. M., Petersen, L. P. & Kanouse, D. E. (1996). Communication between adolescents and physicians about sexual behavior and risk prevention. *Archives of Pediatric and Adolescent Medicine, 150*, 906–913.

Scully, M., Kuoch, T., & Miller, R. A. (1995). Cambodians and sexual child abuse. In L. A. Fontes (Ed.), *Sexual abuse in nine North American cultures: Treatment and prevention* (pp 97–127). Thousand Oaks, CA: Sage.

Song, Y. I. (1996). Battered women in Korean immigrant families. New York: Garland.

Sue, D. (1982). Sexual experience and attitudes of Asian American students. *Psychological Report, 51*, 401–402.

Tang, T. S., Solomon, L. J., Yeh, C. J., & Worden, J. K. (1999). The role of cultural variables in breast self-examination and cervical cancer screening behavior in young Asian women living in the United States. *Journal of Behavioral Medicine, 22*, 419–436.

Tiongson, A. T., Jr. (1997). Throwing the baby out with the bathwater: Situating young Filipino mothers and fathers beyond the dominant discourse on adolescent pregnancy. In M. P. P. Root (Ed.), *Filipino Americans: Transformation and identity* (pp. 257–271). Thousand Oaks, CA: Sage Publications.

Tsui, A. M. (1985). Psychotherapeutic considerations in sexual counseling of Asian immigrants. *Psychotherapy, 22*, 357–362.

Tsuneyoshi, S. (1996). Rape trauma syndrome: Case illustration of Elizabeth, an 18-year-old Asian American. In F. H. McClure & E. Teyber (Eds.), *Child and adolescent therapy: A multicultural relational approach* (pp. 287–320). New York: Harcourt Brace College Publishers.

Tu, S., Taplin, S. H., Barlow, W. E., & Boyko, E. J. (1999). Breast cancer screening by Asian-American women in a managed care environment. *American Journal of Preventive Medicine, 17*, 55–61.

Upchurch, D. M., Levy-Storms, L., Sucoff, C. A., & Aneshensel, C. S. (1998). Gender and ethnic differences in the timing of first sexual intercourse. *Family Planning Perspectives, 30*, 121–127.

Urquiza, A. J., & Goodlin-Jones, B. L. (1994). Child sexual abuse and adult revictimization with women of color. *Violence & Victims, 9*, 223–232.

U.S. Bureau of the Census. (1993). We the Americans: Asians. Washington, DC: U.S. Government Printing Office. Wong, D. (1987). Preventing child sexual assault among Southeast Asian refugee families. *Child Today, 16*, 18–22.

Wooden, W. S., Kawasaki, H., & Mayeda, R. (1983). Lifestyles and identity maintenance among gay Japanese-American males. *Alternative Lifestyles, 5*, 236–243.

Yick, A. G. (2000). Domestic violence beliefs and attitudes in the Chinese American community. *Journal of Social Service Research, 27*, 29–51.

Yu, E. S. H., Kim, K. K., Chen, E. H., & Brintnall, R. A. (2001). Breast and cervical cancer screening among Chinese American women. *Cancer Practice, 9*, 81–91.

Yu, M. Y., Seetoo, A. D., Tsai, C. K., & Sun, C. (1998). Sociodemographic predictors of Papanicolaou smear test and mammography use among women of Chinese descent in Southeastern Michigan. *Womens Health Issues, 8*, 372–381.

CHAPTER FIVE

SAME-SEX SEXUALITIES

One of the most frequently asked questions by students enrolled in classes on human sexuality is "why are some people gay?" A more appropriate question might be "why are most people heterosexual and some people homosexual in every culture of which there is a record?" Same-sex sexual behavior is found in every culture and in most animal species as well. But just because homosexuality is ubiquitous doesn't mean it is treated the same way. Some cultures are quietly tolerant; others noisily intolerant. Some cultures prescribe definite roles and behaviors for homosexuals; others want to pretend they don't exist at all.

Homosexual and heterosexual identities and behaviors are constructed in the same cultural arena and from the same basic cultural materials: proliferating images, sexual shame, gender inequality, and sexual inequality. Instead of asking why "so many" people seem to be gay these days, one might just as easily ask another question: Given the dramatic discrimination, hatred (homophobia), and violence that gays and lesbians face, isn't it a miracle that anyone at all would be gay?

The essays in this section explore the varieties of same-sex sexualities. Most of the selections explore the gendered nature of same-sex behavior; that is, the ways in which homosexual identity and behavior conform to gender norms. For example, in a classic article, Adrienne Rich casts lesbianism as a form of feminist resistance to both sexism and what she calls "compulsory heterosexuality," the cultural demand that everyone be straight—or else.

Steven Seidman and his colleagues, Laura Brown and Bianca Murphy explore the differences in gay and lesbian sexual, romantic, and political behavior, using gender as a way to understand sexuality.

Paula Rust, Patricia Gagné and her colleagues, and E. J. Graff all complicate the picture dramatically by exploring bisexuality and transgenderism as sexualities. These are both based on gender, but transcend gender, putting gender into play as yet another variable in the construction of sexualities.

5.1 LESBIAN IDENTITIES
Concepts and Issues

Laura S. Brown

The concept of a lesbian *identity,* a sense of oneself as lesbian, which gives meaning to behavior across dimensions of time and place, as distinct from simply being an unidentified participant in certain kinds of sexual behavior between two women, is a relatively new one. Until the work of such late nineteenth- and early twentieth-century sexologists as Ellis (1922) and Hirschfield (1936) came to the intellectual foreground, lesbian relationships, when they were identifiable to the outside world, tended to be perceived as perverse relationships between women who were essentially heterosexual. This view prevailed largely because there was no framework for understanding the concept that a person might be fundamentally homosexual. We know little about how such women perceived themselves, aside from knowing that many of them identified themselves as loving and bonded to one another. More commonly, close affectional ties between women were not seen by the larger culture as possessing a sexual cast; as Faderman (1982) and other historians of lesbian heritage have noted, intimate and romantic (although not necessarily sexual) relationships between women have been normative in many cultures over time without a lesbian identity attaching to the behavior. Following the arrival of psychoanalytic concepts on the Western intellectual scene, such relationships were construed as containing an inevitable sexual component.

In addition, the notion of lesbian identity is culture bound as well as time bound. Outside of Western, Eurocentric cultures, definitions of sexuality differ widely from those currently subscribed to by European and North American behavioral scientists and in popular culture. Although women behave as lesbians cross-culturally—that is, having sexual and affectionate relationships with one another—"lesbian identity" as such may be absent in contexts which do not define persons as having particular sexual orientations or which are not directly influenced by Western cultural concepts of sexuality (Weinrich & Williams, 1991; Williams, 1986).

The definition of lesbian identity that I work with in this chapter is one I have found useful in organizing my thinking on this matter. I define lesbian identity as primarily a self-ascribed definition held by a woman over time and across situations as having primary sexual, affectional, and relational ties to other women. This identity may or may not be congruent with overt behavior at any point during the lifespan, and the variables making up this definition may come and go from the foreground of a woman's definition as life circumstances change. A lesbian identity may also be ascribed to a woman by others, even if she does not accept this definition, and the development of such a woman's sexual identity must also be considered in any discussions of lesbian identity development. One of the issues to be examined in this chapter is the question of how to define and describe the process of sexual identity development for women to whom lesbian identity is ascribed by others, who behave in ways that both dominant and lesbian cultures would describe as lesbian, and who intentionally define themselves as nonlesbian. Because such women fall within what Rich (1980) has described as a "lesbian continuum," the development of their identity falls within my discussion even though they may reject the terminology of the self-defined lesbian.

This very broad, flexible, and somewhat ambiguous definition defines the contours of the concepts under discussion in this chapter. They include these three questions: Who decides what makes a woman a lesbian? By what paths do women arrive at a definition of themselves as lesbian? And, related to the second, are there paths by which a woman who has so identified herself then departs from that definition? In those cultural contexts where there is no separate lesbian social identity or role, what are the processes of sexual identity development; how do cultural differences in understanding the nature of attraction and intimate pair-bonding in humans transform the meaning of being or behaving in a lesbian fashion?

WHO ARE THE LESBIANS?

The arguments over who and what makes a lesbian can be found throughout both modern and postmodern literature, psychology, and philosophy, not to mention in the pages of popular magazines published for this sexual minority. It is useful to review these questions here to demonstrate the complexities inherent in defining the parameters of empirical study of lesbian identity development. The singer Holly Near personifies some of the issues in the current debate; a woman who has been sexually and romantically involved with women, who currently, as well as prior to her brief period of same-sex relationships, is sexually and romantically involved with men, and who yet proudly describes herself as a lesbian in writing and in performance. Is she, or isn't she? Then there is another public figure, Patricia Ireland, the president, as of this writing, of the National Organization for Women. She has recently revealed that she lives with a female companion, although she also maintains her marriage to a man. Is she bisexual? lesbian? Or, as she stated, does it matter what her behavior is named? She has chosen to have an ambiguous public sexual identity. And what of the women in a Boston marriage; that is, two women who live together as a couple, are tied by bonds of affection and emotional intimacy, but who have never or rarely been sexual with one another (Rothblum & Brehony, 1993). This pair will probably be perceived as lesbian by others, although they may or may not identify themselves as such.

Some women describe themselves as having known of their attraction to their own gender from a very young, even prepubescent age. Others may feel heterosexually attracted in adolescence, then gradually find their interest becoming more directed to other women as they grow older. Still other women may be securely ensconced in heterosexual adult relationships, even marriage, then find themselves strongly drawn to another woman or women. This may occur as late as the sixth or seventh decade of life, judging by some first-person accounts (Adleman, 1986). A woman who is strongly politically feminist may make a conscious choice, regardless of feeling, to relate sexually and emotionally to other women because of strong belief in the importance of women bonding with one another or in protest against the dominance hierarchies in which most heterosexual relationships are embedded. In this case her socially defined sexual orientation and lesbian identity exist to some degree detached from her actual experiences of arousal and sexual attraction. Some of these women identify themselves as lesbians; some, including those who have had life-long exclusive sexual and affectional attraction to women, do not, or do so only with difficulty. Who among these women is the "real" lesbian, whose identity development we are attempting to comprehend?

This question of who are "genuine" lesbians betrays several interesting underlying concerns both from the dominant culture and from the perspective of lesbians. The dominant culture has wished to know who lesbians were at times because special, negative treatment is reserved for lesbians that is not considered appropriate for women who merely "appear" to be lesbian but are not. In addition, women who are lesbian, but who actively deny or hide their status, are treated similarly to women who are not lesbian, "forgiven," as it were, their sexual orientation as long is it is hidden from public view; intentional and public commitment to a lesbian identity carries meaning within a dominant cultural context above and beyond an individual woman's self-perceptions.

Well-defined boundaries around the concept of lesbian are important in dominant North American culture for purposes of discrimination, for the same reasons it is important in this culture to know whether a person has any African ancestry so that she or he may be classified as "African-American." The need for a strict definition of lesbian reflects the tendency toward dichotomous thinking that typifies much white, Euro-centric cultural philosophies, a dichotomy which for the most part assumes separate and mutually exclusive categories of sexual orientation. At the same time, the dominant culture has tried to define certain women as "not lesbian" because the value accorded a particular woman was at odds with the devaluation of lesbians. The extended public debate over the nature of Eleanor Roosevelt's relationship with the journalist Lorena Hickok, which judging by their letters was at least emotionally intimate, sensuous, and passionate, is an example of this phenomenon. Various biographers, depending on their degree of discomfort with lesbian-ism, have argued for or against the notion that Roo-sevelt, seen as a paragon of public virtue, might have had a lesbian relationship or identity (Cook, 1992).

For lesbians ourselves, the question has different meanings that have to do with safety, affiliation, and the possibilities of sexual and intimate relations, as well as the importance of having roles and lesbian women models of superlative function available in both historical and contemporary context. As lesbian author and theorist Julia Penelope has pointed out (1992), the question of who is a lesbian can become extremely important for women who wish to define a space as "lesbian-only." It may also enter, for individ-ual women, into questions of to whom one will dis-close one's own lesbian identity, or with whom one will contemplate the possibility of an intimate sexual relationship. It is not uncommon for women newly coming into a lesbian identity after a history of het-erosexual experience to find themselves rebuffed by other women for not being "sufficiently" lesbian, somehow tainted in their "purity" by having related to men. How then, is lesbian to be defined by lesbians, and which lesbians possess the authority to define? Is one lesbian's definition of herself adequate to the needs of another lesbian's quest to create boundaries defining to whom and in what circumstances she will reveal herself most intimately?

One recent controversy in white U.S. lesbian cul-tural feminist circles, which reveals the dimensions of the definitional question, centers on whether a male-to-female transsexual who is now partnered with a woman can be considered a lesbian for purpose of inclusion in such lesbian-only spaces, and whether the woman in a relationship with this newly created female person is herself in a lesbian relationship (Let-ters, *Lesbian Connection,* Spring 1992). Arguments strongly for and against each position have appeared (Raymond, 1982), with nothing resembling consensus emerging in the public discourse (although consensus is not really to be expected). The question raised in these debates of whether a person must be born and raised female to be socially constructed and accepted as a woman, and thus lesbian, highlights all aspects of the discourse over the parameters of lesbian identity.

As Golden (1987) has pointed out, these defini-tional debates also raise questions regarding the degree to which a lesbian identity (as differentiated from an erotic orientation to which no particular identity may be attached) is fixed, invariant, and stable, in contrast to flexible and changeable over time. This is not a triv-ial concern for either the student of lesbianism or les-bians ourselves. For theorists and researchers of les-bian identity development, the tendency to see sexual identity in one or another manner leads to models which are descriptive and predictive of those out-comes. A model which encompasses the ambiguous definition described by Golden and others may in turn lead to more ambiguous outcomes, although perhaps more interesting questions regarding the overall con-struction, both socially and phenomenologically, of women's sexual identity development in general. For lesbians, the fixedness of a lesbian identity speaks more strongly to issues of trust and predictability. If a woman has always and only related sexually and affec-tionally to other women, she may be perceived as "safer" to invest in for relationships than a woman who has past experiences of heterosexual relationships. Golden suggests that as this definitional question is played out, in some lesbian communities whether a woman has ever been sexual with men is more impor-tant than whether she has been sexual with women. In this analysis, a formerly celibate woman has no appar-ent loyalties to heterosexual relationships, while a women who has behaved heterosexually may be per-ceived as at risk for returning to men.

A model such as Golden has proposed implies that a lesbian identity may, at some point, be a possible outcome for any woman's sexual identity develop-ment, whereas biological models such as those currently popular among some students of gay male identity restrict lesbian identity to those women who diverge biologically from a heterosexual "norm," or those with an erotic orientation entirely consistent with their sexual identity. Questions of fixed versus fluid also inform debates over whether conversion therapies aimed at "reorienting" women to heterosexuality are ethical or efficacious (Haldeman, 1991), as well as public policy questions regarding civil rights protections for sexual minority persons.

A history of lesbian relationships does not appear to be a necessary predictor of ongoing lesbianism, however, as the first-person accounts of several women who now identify themselves as bisexual illustrate quite clearly (Wiese, 1992). Such narratives illustrate the degree to which sexual orientation and sexual identity are not always congruent. These women describe their distress at discovering in midlife that they wish to take up an intimate relationship with a man, perhaps for the first time in their lives. Not only is the individual identity of such a woman challenged; her identity within a social context and community will also undergo transformation. The transformation to bisexuality in later adulthood from a prior life history of lesbian identity raises questions about the fixed nature of sexual orientation and identity. The "bisexual lesbian" perceives herself as having a lesbian identity, independent of her sexual orientation or her current sexual behavior. Ironically, the woman who describes herself in this manner may have a stronger attachment to a lesbian identity in the public context than might a woman who has always related sexually and affectionally only with women, but for reasons of culture or homophobia has an asexual or heterosexual public identity. While the frequency with which such transitions occur is currently unknown, given the very closeted nature of many women in this position, evidence exists that lesbian identity development is a process with not only several different initial stages, but variations in later stages as well.

Motherhood and the possibility of motherhood in the past decade and a half through donor insemination have also raised questions in some lesbian cultures about what constitutes a "genuine" lesbian self-definition. Some separatist lesbians (Penelope, 1992; Ruston, Jo, & Strega, 1986) have argued that lesbian

motherhood, which requires contact with sperm, constitutes an oxymoron in which lesbian "energy" is diverted from its proper place among lesbians to a task which is paradigmatic of women's enslavement in patriarchal cultures. For these authors, contact with sperm, however divorced from sexual experience, renders a woman no longer lesbian. In addition, for many lesbians in age cohorts preceding the baby boom generation, motherhood was thought to be excluded by lesbian identity, except for those women who had borne children out of prior heterosexual connections. Lesbian mothers, in addition, have written about their sense of being "invisible" to other lesbians in their parental role; in effect, these women describe feeling stripped of their lesbian identity by the more visible identity of motherhood, which is strongly tied to heterosexuality in the dominant discourse.

This discourse reflects the struggle over who is to control the definition of lesbian identity, and what other features of women's identity in general are included in or excluded from the boundaries of lesbian identity. Dominant cultural definitions tend to contain direct or indirect inferences of deficit and deviance, while lesbian cultural definitions tend to use lesbian experience as normative and orthogonal to questions of abnormality. Psychology as a discipline has wavered from one stance to another, depending on the politics and identities of the psychologists writing about lesbian issues. However, even within these categories disagreement exists over a number of factors which leave definitions uncertain. Within each setting, distinguished simplistically here for purposes of outlining the conceptual problems, the discourse is not unitary.

In understanding the concept of lesbian identity development, in developing research or theory, one is first faced with this complex definitional question. Which answer a scholar chooses reflects a willingness to align primarily with certain explanatory models, which in turn define the parameters of ensuing theory or research. For example, if one adopts a model of lesbian definition that rests solely on overtly expressed sexual behavior, then questions of how and when arousal to same-sex stimuli and sexual contact in same-sex contexts first occurred will be important because they represent data about important defining variables. If one adopts the writer Adrienne Rich's model of a "lesbian continuum" (1980), in which overt sexual expression is simply one of several forms of lesbian relating to be examined, then questions of affection, bonding, and valuing of women as aspects of lesbian identity development become paramount. If one uses a political model of lesbians as resisters to culturally imposed norms of femininity, this might lead to attempts to study and understand gender nonconformity. Attention to multicultural issues raises questions regarding the degree to which the external dominant context informs the process of identifying oneself as lesbian, and the degree to which cultural perceptions regarding gender role nonconformity enter into consideration for individuals defining themselves as not-heterosexual. Because our current state of knowledge does not lend stronger support to one or another definition, scholars of lesbian identity development will continue to need to clarify what paradigm of lesbianism they are adopting and embedding in their work. In addition, the ethical scholar needs to attend to whether, how, and to what degree the model adopted attributes deviance or pathology to lesbians. The definitional questions are foundational to our understanding and critiques of models currently advanced for describing the development of lesbian identity.

To organize a discussion of the diverse models of how lesbian identity develops, I define a lesbian as a woman whose primary sexual and affectional attractions are to other women and who has a sexual minority identity, that is, recognizes through the use of language or symbolic expressions that her sexual orientation places her apart from a sexual mainstream, even though she may not use the term "lesbian" per se. (For example, she may call herself "gay," purposely eschewing the term lesbian, reflecting class and cultural origins where the latter term is more stigmatized than the former. Or she may call herself "queer," a more inclusive term arising from postmodern constructions of sexual identity popular in some groups of younger women, in which gender politics has lost the significance it held in an earlier generation of lesbian-feminists.) This definition does not speak to questions of gender-role stereotypy and leaves open the question of how the term "woman" is socially constructed. Overt sexual expression of lesbian identity is not

required, only that any such expression if it occurs be primarily invested in women. In addition, women who have related to men, and some who continue to relate to men sexually and affectionally, are not necessarily excluded from this definition, depending on the position in which such heterosexual behavior in placed. What is core to this definitional model is that the lesbian sees her relationships and connections to women as *primary,* whether acted upon or not, and identifies herself as outside the sexual mainstream.

MODELS OF IDENTITY DEVELOPMENT

Following on the diversity of paradigms arising from definitional questions is the variability of models of identity development themselves. I categorize lesbian identity development into biological models, traditional psychodynamic models, feminist psychodynamic models, and cognitively mediated "stage" models. Each model reflects different definitional assumptions and inferences regarding the nature of lesbianism, and each is problematic in its own way. Many such models have been derived from paradigms of gay male identity development, or are subsumed under such paradigms, reflecting what this writer believes to be an erroneous and sexist assumption regarding the isomorphism of homosexuality in women and men, as well as the historical neglect of lesbians in the research and theoretical literatures. One important factor informing my own critique of models of lesbian identity is whether and to what degree they make the experiences of lesbians as women, with distinct forms of socialization experiences, primary in their understanding of the development of erotic and affectional same-gender connections for women. Lesbians and gay men often have only sexual minority status in common. As the following review of the literature notes, women's experience of our sexual selves, an important component of lesbian identity, appears to be sufficiently different from the parallel process in men as to render suspect any model that purports to explain both gay men and lesbians equally well.

In addition, some of these models explored here arise within a context of more general models of women's psychosexual development. It is my bias that lesbian identity is an aspect of female identity which cannot be completely understood apart from a general understanding of women's development within a particular cultural context. This placement of lesbian identity development within a framework of women's development conceives of lesbianism as a common and normal, if minority, outcome of the development of sexual and affectional relating and overall self-development in women. In fact, my own tendency is to wonder, given some recently proposed models of women's identity development, why more women are not lesbian, since such models tend to highlight women's attachments and affectional connections to other women as central to the development of identity and self. I believe this question to be important, and address it at length in discussions of feminist models of lesbian identity.

In evaluating the various paradigms for lesbian identity development, it is useful to ask whether and to what degree such models posit a set of necessary and sufficient conditions for the development of a lesbian self. I believe that the utility of any model which fails to do so will be truncated, and the model will be unable to stand alone as a paradigm for understanding lesbian identity development. In addition, any model that will be useful to current scholars and clinicians must encompass the range of lesbian phenomenological experiences, accounting for the variability of realities exposed in the rich autobiographical literature by lesbians. The inherent assumptive frameworks of a variety of models of "coming out"—that is, coming to identify oneself as lesbian or gay—are that something unspecified is a precursor to the awareness of same-sex affection and attraction. Thus, an ideal model will be able to describe that precursor state. While the ethical implications of pursuing such a line of questioning are challenging, since risk is inherent in the exploration of questions of the origins of lesbian identity, the ethics of neglecting to ask such important questions about the nature of sexual orientation override concerns about how findings will be used.

BIOLOGICAL MODELS

Biological models have been proposed since Ellis to explain the presence of homosexuality in both women

and men. Early models arise from a construction of homosexuality as a disease, deficit, or error. These paradigms include, most famously, Hirschfield's description of homosexuals as a "third sex," as well as many folk stereotypes of lesbians as "mannish" women. As a result of this underlying assumptive stance, such models tend to contain several prominent and consistent metamessages. First, there is usually an assumption of pathology: too much or too little or a particular hormone, pre- or-postnatally, "wrong" sizes of genital organs, malfunction of reproductive capacity. This image of the lesbian as a biological "invert" or "third sex" was especially popular in the late nineteenth and early twentieth centuries. These views were often used to support calls for tolerance and understanding of behavior that, since biologically fixed, could not be changed. Second, there is a message of inevitability and fixedness of sexual orientation. That is, such models either state or infer that a woman's lesbianism is innately present for her to discover, and will be present in such a woman regardless of external experience.

Difficulties with such models are both empirical and conceptual. Despite many attempts to uncover meaningful, nonoverlapping biological differences between lesbian and heterosexual women, the weight of the evidence does not support this position (Kirsch & Weinrich, 1991). Lesbians tend to demonstrate the same within-group variability on such factors as level of sex hormones, size of clitoris, and reproductive capacity as do heterosexual women. There also appears to be no evidence of difference in size or development of central nervous system structures of the sort recently reported to differentiate gay and heterosexual men. The only current piece of empirical research suggesting some biological component to lesbianism is a recent study that found greatly increased numbers of lesbian or bisexual sisters of a group of lesbians compared to a matched sample of heterosexual women (Bailey & Benishay, 1993). The concept of the biological "invert" first promulgated by Ellis and Hirschfield and popularized by Hall's lesbian classic *The Well of Loneliness,* in which lesbians and gay men represent a biological third sex, betrays the confusion between gender role and anatomical sex that permeates biological models in which lesbians are masculinized, "butch" women only.

Conceptually, such models are problematic because of their assumption of a fixed, nonchanging sexual self for lesbians and, by implication, for all women. Arguably, such a model may be important in understanding gay men, who subjectively report a more unchanging experience of sexual identity; but lesbian sexuality, like other aspects of female sexuality, does not appear to be well-described by any model assuming fixed sexual orientation. If, as proposed earlier, lesbian identity development is placed within a context of the overall development of female sexual identity, the biological models appear to be even less useful. In addition, such biological models do not account well, if at all, for the nonsexual, affectional aspects of lesbian identity. They are reductionistic, paring lesbianism down to *only* sexual acts and arousal, rather than placing lesbianism in the broader frame of affiliation, affection, and sense of community which are the subjective experiences of many lesbians.

Such models are seductive, however, because of their potential value in the political arena. Lesbian and gay rights activists have argued that if homosexuality is fixed and primarily biologically determined, then lesbians and gays should not be discriminated against. Such an argument plays into a dominant paradigm, but this position should be adopted only with extreme caution by both scholars and activists, since it implies that the dominant culture may freely punish those who have any choice in their deviance from a dominant norm and accord fair treatment only to those who are "victims," so to speak, of their biology. The degree to which biological models fail to reflect lesbian phenomenology in many cases makes them problematic and suspect.

TRADITIONAL PSYCHODYNAMIC MODELS

As is the case for biological models, traditional psychodynamic formulations of lesbian identity development carry the message of psychopathology. These models address questions of etiology as linked to the genesis of lesbian identity. Despite his focus on female sexuality, Freud himself addressed the question of lesbian identity only briefly, in one of his famous "Three Essays" on sexuality in which he hypothesized it mir-

rored in some ways the development of male homosexuality, representing a perverse as distinguished from neurotic adaptation to internal conflict. In addition he published one case study of a lesbian patient (Freud, 1920). The proposed mechanisms leading to lesbian identity were unclear. Freud suggested that homosexuality in women represented a failure to resolve issues at the oedipal stage of development, leading to an identification with the father and a desire to possess the mother sexually, while simultaneously rejecting the mother because of her deficient lack of penis. Freud's followers have embellished considerably upon this formulation, increasing the degree of pathology ascribed to lesbianism, and describing it as an important aspect of failure to accept normal femininity (Deutsch, 1933; Jones, 1927; Socarides, 1968). One school of psychodynamic thought on lesbianism proposes that such an identity develops out of a wish to return to and merge with the mother (Eisenbud, 1981).

Attempting to provide empirical support for the notion that pathological processes are at the foundation of lesbian identity, Kaye et al. (1967) queried the psychoanalytic therapists of a small number of lesbian patients and purported to find a disturbance of gender role arrangements in the families of these women. More recent psychoanalytic thinking on lesbianism (Siegel, 1988) has placed it within the framework of characterological personality disturbance; interestingly, none of the women described in the dozen or so case studies in Siegel's volume were self-defined as lesbian; most had strong heterosexual self-definitions and patterns of sexual behavior interspersed with some same-sex fantasy or incidental same-sex contact.

Traditional psychodynamic formulations appear extremely problematic on the surface because of their pathologizing bent and the tendency to infer patterns of identity development from the case histories of women in distress. These models are also quite monocultural, assuming Eurocentric paradigms of family structure and process, which severely limits their usefulness in describing identity development for lesbians from non-Western cultures or non-nuclear family structures. Largely because of these limitations, such classic psychoanalytic formulations have understandably been avoided by most modern scholars of lesbian identity (Golden, 1987; Kitzinger, 1987).

However, these models contain a paradigm of sexual identity development as fluid and changeable over time and in response to certain types of interpersonal and social/contextual experiences. As a consequence, such psychodynamic models potentially provide useful conceptual and heuristic steppingstones, once their normative assumptions have been critiqued and stripped away. If we abandon (as I suggest) the heterosexist notion of one normal stream of sexual identity development, in which outcomes other than heterosexual identity and behavior are constructed as deviant and pathological, and instead adopt a paradigm of multiple, diversely normal streams of sexual identity development with many possible successful outcomes, then the questions traditional psychodynamic models raise are very intriguing; they ask us to consider how the complex experiences of girls within their familial and social contexts can lead to identification with a certain sense of self and attention to certain aspects of erotic and affectional arousal.

Politically, such questions are dangerous. Because these identity development models also contain assumptions about the origins of lesbianism within potentially fluid, modifiable interactive experience, there is always a risk that dominant cultural institutions might attempt to use such information to prevent the emergence of lesbianism. This is not a paranoid concern, since there is ample evidence of such attempts based on folk "wisdom" about the origins of lesbian identity (e.g., the campaigns of Anita Bryant, framed as a "saving of children" from homosexuals, or recent ballot measures in Colorado and Oregon aimed at stopping homosexuality by declaring it illegal and perverse). Consequently, many students of lesbian identity development have been understandably wary about the use of such a conceptual framework, preferring to ignore causal questions and simply assume that the required (if unspecified) seeds upon which to construct a lesbian identity are present in personality.

FEMINIST PSYCHODYNAMIC MODELS

Feminist psychodynamic models of the development of sexual self in women avoid some, if not all, of the problematic normative assumptions of traditional psychodynamic formulations and biological models. These models tend to address lesbian identity development within a broader framework of women's sexual identity processes, thus framing a lesbian outcome as one of several normative possibilities for women (Galenson, 1986; Golden, 1987). Although, as Palladino and Stephenson (1990) have noted, these models are flawed by their monocultural nature, with assumptions about family structure, child-rearing patterns, and gender role norms that almost exclusively reflect white, northern European paradigms, they tend to be more encompassing of women's phenomenology than are other models of lesbian identity development. Feminist psychodynamic models use the object relations formulations popularized by Nancy Chodorow (1979), which posit that the core of female personality development rests in the mother-infant daughter relationship. This pairing enables the daughter to develop a sense of self through interaction and projective identification. One prominent feminist model of female personality development, the self-in-relation paradigm (Jordan, Kaplan, Miller, Stiver, & Surrey, 1992; Surrey, 1985), expands upon the possibilities Chodorow proposed to posit that women's adult development, which includes the development of a sexual self, occurs in a relational matrix characterized by increasing competence in relationality and for which the sense of self is constructed as self-in-relation to others. Empathy and the capacity for mutuality in relations are defined as successful outcomes of this developmental process.

Curiously, few of these theorists (aside from Carla Golden, cited earlier) have commented directly on the development of lesbian identity. In fact, much of the theoretical literature in the feminist psychodynamic field can be described as heterosexist, since it assumes heterosexualit of women implicitly even while explicitly endorsing a diverse-outcome norm for women's sexual development. As Palladino and Stephenson (1990) note, the feminist psychodynamicists fail to explicate how a girl whose passionate relational attachments are to a woman (the mother) is transformed into a woman whose relational self is directed to men, while similarly failing to address what might occur in the developmental process of those girls who, to some degree, continue to direct their passion, arousal, and relationality toward women throughout the lifespan. They note how Eichenbaum and Orbach (1987), another prominent pair of feminist psychodynamic theorists, describe their own erotic charge for one another without ever examining the erotic implications of their friendship, thus falsely separating questions of lesbian identity development from those of women's overall relational process. These problems and critiques aside, feminist psychodynamic formulations are potentially powerful paradigms for the study of lesbian identity development.

Golden's (1987) work exemplifies how feminist psychodynamic formulations can be extrapolated to understand certain patterns of lesbian identity development in some groups of women. In her examples, feminist psychodynamic formulations provide important elements for understanding lesbian identity as a normal aspect of female sexuality. In addition, Golden's work reflects other useful assumptions of the feminist psychodynamic literature. These elements include a foundation in women's embodied experiences rather than a view of women as "other," an (at least theoretical) embrace of a normative stance in which lesbianism is one of many equally valued outcomes of female adult development, and a broader, less genitally focused model of passionate relating than is found in male-dominant paradigms. Such conceptual threads could be woven together so as to allow a more complex and rich response than would otherwise be possible to some of the definitional questions addressed earlier in this chapter.

Such models, with their emphasis on the quality of relationships, place lesbian identity within the broader question about how women come to love and bond with other women, and ask the more subversive question as to why some women *fail* to develop primary sexual and affectional bonds to women, rather than seeing the development of such bonds as representing a separate, relatively infrequently taken, and possibly deviant developmental pathway. However, it is incumbent upon researcher or theoretician using these paradigms to address the very real limits of phenomenology, to borrow a phrase from Lerman (1992) in response to questions of cultural diversity as they affect the development of sexual self in women. Because the phenomenologically based models proposed by feminist psychodynamicists have been so seductive to white women, their reduced applicability and usefulness for women of color in North America and women in non-Euro-American cultures is often not noticed. As Espin (1987) has noted, one cannot simply "add women of color and stir" to make an intrapsychic model generalizable beyond its culture of origin, even when that model is feminist.

"STAGE" MODELS

The period since 1970 has seen a flurry of proposed models to explicate the "coming out" process in lesbians and gay men (for a complete review see Gonsiorek & Rudolph, 1991). These models derive from Atkinson, Morten, and Sue's (1979) model of minority identity development, and attempt to identify stages by which the individual lesbian learns, within the social context, to identify to self and others as lesbian. Stages usually consist of such elements as noticing same-gender attractions, working through ambivalent feelings about these attractions, ascribing meaning and names to those feelings, and then attaching the feelings to a minority group identity.

In stage models, identity development is construed as a process of learning to name one's sexual self, and then place oneself within various social contexts at increasing degrees of social distance from the person. Many of the models developed to date have taken the experience of gay men as their norm, extrapolating this to assumptions about lesbians. Each of these models proposes that becoming lesbian requires a process of identifying oneself as such, giving meaning to that self-identification, and then communicating that identity to other lesbians, gay men, and members of the general community. The sine qua non of identity development is hypothesized as the ability to be more open about one's sexual orientation in more settings.

Like traditional psychodynamic formulations, these stage models lack explanations for the roots of lesbian feelings. Same-sex attraction is simply assumed to exist. This can be read as either a taking for granted the normative nature of such feelings (i.e., they are simply there, like the color of one's hair) or a strategy for avoiding politically dangerous etiological considerations. Depending on the other intellectual traditions influencing the individual who is generating these paradigms, one can detect assumptions regarding the possible biological and/or psychological roots of sexual identity development. For example, Malyon's (1982) model of identity development in gay men demonstrates clearly the author's grounding in psychodynamic theory, whereas DeMonteflores and Schultz's (1978) proposal reflects a social constructivist perspective. All of the models reviewed by Gonsiorek and Rudolph also have a hint of the biological in their explanatory fictions.

Such models are also limited by the inherent assumption that the process of sexual identity development have one outcome. That is, such models do not account for the fluidity and changing nature of sexual identities, or for nonlinear processes of coming to terms intellectually with one's felt and embodied experiences. Such models explain the woman who comes to a lesbian identity later in her adult life by defining the period of heterosexual behavior and/or identity as one of denial or repression of awareness of same-sex attraction. These models reflect their genesis in a period when the notion of bisexuality did not receive serious consideration, however, and fail to make sense of the woman who identifies initially as lesbian, based on her behaviors and the meanings ascribed to them in the social discourse, then relates heterosexually either again or for the first time, and finally arrives at a bisexual or heterosexual identity. The models manifest the influence of the dichotomous model of sexual orientation, in which one is either lesbian or heterosexual for life, but not both at various points in the life cycle.

The strength of the stage models is their power to explain and describe how the development of sexual self in lesbians is one of constant interaction and interchange between internal reality and external cultural context. They demonstrate how social discourse influences the process of naming oneself lesbian as well as the meaning ascribed to that name. They offer the scholar or researcher frames within which to raise questions about what might happen in lesbian identity development in a lesbian-defined, lesbian-affirmative social context rather than the heterosexist and antiles-

bian social discourse which informs the developmental process of almost every lesbian.

Empirical research derived from these models has also underscored the importance of examining lesbian identity development separate from that of gay men; a number of researchers note that the awareness of same-sex attraction for women begins as a primarily affectional rather than sexual phenomenon (Gramick, 1984; Schippers, 1990; Sears, 1989). While such an awareness is essential for taking the next step of naming such feelings as lesbian, our knowledge that these feelings are not narrowly sexually defined in women can lead to further questions regarding what happens to those women who feel affection for a member of their own gender but do not name themselves lesbian. This might fruitfully enlarge the discourse regarding the definitions of lesbianism, and will probably point the way toward situating questions of lesbian identity development within the broader framework of the development of female sexuality.

CONCLUSION

As I have noted elsewhere (Brown, 1989), the psychological study of lesbian and gay issues has been severely hampered by our tendency, until recently, to engage in such study from the models and constructs of dominant, heterosexist paradigms in which assumptions about the non-normative, if not deviant, nature of lesbianism and the dichotomous nature of sexual orientation were embedded. These problems are reflected in the conceptual issues discussed in this chapter. That is, our definitional questions and theoretical models have arisen to one degree or another from outside lived lesbian experience. This limits them in various ways.

A problem common to all extant models is that they have been overly Eurocentric; no well-developed models of lesbian identity development speak to the meaning of same-sex relationships for women in cultures where no clearly demarcated lesbian identity exists. Similarly, only partial explorations are available in the behavioral science literature of how race, culture, and class interact with the process of lesbian identity development in the North American and

European cultural matrices from which most of the current models spring, although several authors have begun to address this question regarding African-American (Greene, 1986, 1994), Latina (Espin, 1987), and Asian-American (Chan, 1989) lesbian groups. The autobiographical literature is repleat with such material from personal and phenomenological perspectives, offering rich conceptual possibilities for the psychological theoretician and researcher.

A related problem of extant models is the failure of any one model to account for the diversity of lesbian definitions and experiences in the development of lesbian identity. Partly because the discussion of this topic in a nonpathologizing manner is relatively recent, the thinking reflected in many paradigms has been overly simplistic, attempting to narrow the scope of discussion prematurely to impose some order on the creative chaos of the material at hand. What is needed in the future is models that use a biopsychosocial framework to understand the interaction of humans with both physical and emotional environmental contexts. Such models must eschew the concept of sexual orientations as dichotomous and mutually exclusive and embrace a paradigm of human sexuality as a collection of complex and fluid phenomena.

In this chapter I have chosen not to address questions of gender role as they relate to lesbian identity. This is partially to narrow the focus of my discussion. It also reflects my difficulties with what I believe to be a conflation of gender role and sexual orientation in many definitions of lesbian identity, and my view that much of this confusion represents certain limited points in temporal and cultural discourses on female sexuality. The discussion of such matters as butch and femme roles in certain North American lesbian communities, while fascinating aspects of the public invention of lesbian erotic selves, falls beyond the scope of the present chapter. However, future studies of lesbian identity development will need to inquire about the relationship of these phenomena in the more general framework of human development. That is, where and when are the seeds of erotic and affectional orientation sown as children gain a sense of themselves as members of a gender, then move toward gen-

dered schemata of their own and others' behavior? One cannot, after all, have a gender orientation until gender becomes an important emotional category of analysis.

We also need to ask ourselves how we can apply a lesbian voice and vision to our understanding of lesbian identity development. That is, how can we assume a lesbian stance to be central rather than marginal; and what questions and frameworks can we expect to arise from such a different view of lesbian realities? As Kitzinger (1987) has noted, the social constructions of lesbianism by the general public and by theoreticians and researchers have tended to distort our views of lesbian realities and to depoliticize the discussion by ignoring the subversive nature of lesbian existence in heterosexist and misogynist dominant cultures.

This transformational dilemma continues to be a demanding task for theoreticians and researchers because our professional socialization in heterosexist dominant cultures is a powerful limiting factor on our imaginations. Models derived from qualitative studies of lesbian communities and lesbian families have promise, because they will begin to offer us the experiences of women for who being lesbian has always been a viable and valuable possibility rather than a hidden, feared, or stigmatized one. As we approach the second decade of lesbian liberation, the social cradle for the age cohort of these women, the possible models for understanding lesbian identity will be changed by the differences between these women's realities and those of their foresisters. As it is difficult to separate our understanding of gendered phenomena from those that are simply the result of power and dominance hierarchies (Unger, 1989), so it is extremely difficult to differentiate theoretically or empirically those aspects of lesbian identity development that are primarily or solely about the management of stigma or marginality from those that are simply about being lesbian.

Concretely, all of these suggestions may require scholars of lesbian identity development to reinvent our methodologies in light of the currently available data. The questions that have informed research on lesbian issues until the present have largely reflected earlier knowledge bases. Our knowledge, much of which is experiential, has expanded exponentially in the past two decades. Ironically, our best hopes for better understanding lesbian identity may lie in the development of a lesbian-informed study of women's overall sexual development, including the development of heterosexuality in women. Those models, arising from feminist psychodynamic formulations, seem to best describe embodied lesbian experience and assume the primacy of women's passionate relationships to other women. It may be possible to better understand how lesbians hold on to and eroticize these attachments if we comprehend how such passions are lost or distorted for women who are not lesbian. In other words, we may be asking the wrong questions. We may need to ask not only why are some women lesbians and how do they come to that identity, but also why do some women lose their lesbianism as they develop?

Scholarship in this field is arriving at a new level of maturity after two decades of increasingly public and affirmative discourse by lesbians and our allies regarding the processes by which we come to name and know ourselves as lesbian. The challenge for the future is to move beyond the limitations imposed by dominant cultural norms and to develop definitions and paradigms based in the diversity and variability of embodied lesbian experiences across time and culture.

REFERENCES

Adleman, J. (1986). Falling and rising in love. In M. Adelman (Ed.), *Long time passing: Lives of older lesbians* (pp. 35–50). Boston: Alyson Publications.

Atkinson, D. R., Morten, G, & Sue, D. W. (1979). *Counseling American minorities*. Dubuque, IA: Brown.

Bailey, J. M., & Berishay, D. S. (1993). Familial aggregation of female sexual orientation. *American Journal of Psychiatry, 150,* 272–277.

Brown, L. S. (1989). New voices, new visions: Toward a lesbian/gay paradigm for psychology. *Psychology of Women Quarterly, 13,* 445–458.

Chan, C. S. (1989). Issues of identity development among Asian-American lesbians and gay men. *Journal of Counseling and Development, 68,* 16–20.

Chodorow, N. (1979). *The reproduction of mothering*. Berkeley, CA: University of California Press.

Cook, B. W. (1992). *Eleanor Roosevelt, Volume One, 1884–1933.* New York: Viking.

DeMonteflores, C., & Schultz, S. (1978). Coming out: Similarities and differences for lesbians and gay men. *Journal of Social Issues, 34,* 59–72.

Deutsch, H. (1933). Female sexuality (homosexuality in women). *International Journal of Psychoanalysis, 14,* 34–56.

Eichenbaum, L., & Orbach, S. (1987). *Between women: Love, envy and competition in women's friendships*. New York: Viking.

Eisenbud, R. J. (1981). Early and late determinants of lesbian choice. *Psychoanalytic Review, 69,* 85–109.

Ellis, H. (1922). *Studies in the psychology of sex: Vol. 2* (3rd ed.) Philadelphia: F. A. Davis.

Espin, O. M. (1987). Issues of identity in the psychology of Latina lesbians. In Boston Lesbian Psychologies Collective (Eds.), *Lesbian psychologies: Explorations and challenges* (pp. 35–55). Urbana, IL: University of Illinois Press.

Faderman, L. (1982). *Surpassing the love of men: Romantic friendship and love between women from the Renaissance to the present.* New York: William Morrow.

Freud, S. (1953). Three essays on the theory of sexuality. In *Standard Edition, 7* (pp. 125–243). London: Hogarth Press.

Freud, S. (1920). Psychogenesis of a case of homosexuality in a woman. In *Standard Edition, 18.* (pp. 143–175). London: Hogarth Press.

Galenson, E. (1986). Early pathways to female sexuality in advantaged and disadvantaged girls. In T. Bernay & D. W. Cantor (Eds.), *The psychology of today's woman: New psychoanalytic visions* (pp. 37–50). Hillsdale, NJ: The Analytic Press.

Golden, C. (1987). Diversity and variability in women's sexual identities. In Boston Lesbian Psychologies Collective (Eds.), *Lesbian psychologies: Explorations and challenges* (pp. 18–34). Urbana, IL: University of Illinois Press.

Gonsiorek, J., & Rudolph, J. (1991). Homosexual identity: Coming out and other developmental events. In J. Gonsiorek & J. Weinrich (Eds.), *Homosexuality: Research implications for public policy* (pp. 161–176). Newbury Park, CA: Sage.

Gramick, J. (1984). Developing a lesbian identity. In T. Darty & S. Potter (Eds.), *Women-identified women* (pp. 31–44). Palo Alto, CA: Mayfield.

Greene, B. (1986). When the therapist is white and the patient is Black: Considerations for psychotherapy in the feminist heterosexual and lesbian communities. *Women and Therapy, 5,* 41–66.

Greene, B. (1994). Mental health concerns of lesbians of color. In L. Comas-Diaz & B. Greene (Eds.), *Women of color and mental health*. New York: Guilford.

Haldeman, D. (1991). Sexual orientation conversion therapy for gay men and lesbians: A scientific examination. In J. Gonsiorek & J. Weinrich (Eds.), *Homosexuality: Research implications for public policy* (pp. 149–160). Newbury Park, CA: Sage.

Hirschfield, M. (1936). The homosexual as an intersex. In V. Robinson (Ed.), *Encyclopaedia sexualis.* New York: Dingwall-Rock.

Jones, E. (1927). Early development of female homosexuality. *International Journal of Psychoanalysis, 8,* 459–472.

Jordan, J., Kaplan, A. G., Miller, J. B., Stiver, I., & Surrey, J. (1992). *Women's growth in connection: Writings from the Stone Center.* New York: Guilford.

Kaye, H. S., et al. (1967). Homosexuality in women. *Archives of General Psychiatry, 17,* 626–634.

Kirsch, J. A. W., & Weinrich, J. (1991). Homosexuality, nature, and biology: Is homosexuality natural? Does it matter? In J. Gonsiorek & J. Weinrich (Eds.), *Homosexuality: Research implications for public policy* (pp. 13–31). Newbury Park, CA: Sage.

Kitzinger, C. (1987). *The social construction of lesbianism.* London: Sage.

Lerman, H. (1992). The limits of phenomenology: A feminist critique of the humanistic personality theories. In L. S. Brown & M. Ballou (Eds.), *Personality and psychopathology: Feminist reappraisals* (pp. 8–19). New York: Guilford.

Letters Column (1992, Spring). *Lesbian Connection.* Lansing, MI: Elsie Publishing.

Malyon, A. (1982). Biphasic aspects of homosexual identity formation. *Psychotherapy: Theory, Research, and Practice, 19,* 335–340.

Palladino, D., & Stephenson, Y. (1990). Perceptions of the sexual self: Their impact on relationships between lesbian and heterosexual women. In L. S. Brown & M. P. P. Root (Eds.), *Diversity and complexity in feminist therapy* (pp. 231–254). New York: Haworth.

Penelope, J. (1992). *Call me lesbian: Lesbian lives, lesbian theory.* Freedom, CA: The Crossing Press.

Raymond, J. (1982). *The transsexual empire: The making of a she-male.* Boston: Beacon.

Rich, A. (1980). Compulsory heterosexuality and lesbian existence. *Signs: Journal of Women in Culture and Society, 5,* 631–660.

Rothblum, E. D. & Brehony, K. A. (Eds.) (1993). *Boston marriages: Romantic, but asexual relationships among contemporary lesbians.* Amherst: University of Massachusetts Press.

Ruston, Jo, B., & Strega, L. (1986). Heterosexism causes lesbophobia causes butch-phobia: Part II of the big sellout: Lesbian femininity. *Lesbian Ethics, 2,* 22–41.

Sears, J. T. (1989). The impact of gender and race on growing up lesbian and gay in the South. *National Women's Studies Association Journal, 1,* 422–457.

Schippers, J. (1990, August). "Gay affirmative counseling and psychotherapy in the Netherlands." Paper presented at the Convention of the American Psychological Association, Boston MA.

Siegel, E. V. (1988). *Female homosexuality: Choice without volition.* Hillsdale, NJ: The Analytic Press.

Socarides, C. W. (1968). *The overt homosexual.* New York: Grune and Stratton.

Surrey, J. (1985). The "self-in-relation": A theory of women's development. *Work in progress.* Wellesley, MA: Stone Center Working Papers Series.

Unger, R. K. (1989). Explorations in feminist ideology: Surprising consistencies and unexamined conflicts. In R. K. Unger (Ed.), *Representations: Social constructions of gender* (pp. 203–211). Amityville, NY: Baywood Publishing.

Weinrich, J., & Williams, W. (1991). Strange customs, familiar lives: Homosexualities in other cultures. In J. Gonsiorek & J. Weinrich (Eds.), *Homosexuality: Research implications for public policy* (pp. 44–59). Newbury Park, CA: Sage.

Wiese, R. B. (Ed.) (1992). *Closer to home: Bisexuality and feminism.* Seattle: Seal Press.

Williams, W. L. (1986). *The spirit and the flesh: Sexual diversity in American Indian culture.* Boston: Beacon.

5.2 BEYOND THE CLOSET?

The Changing Social Meaning of Homosexuality in the United States

Steven Seidman, Chet Meeks, and Francie Traschen

INTRODUCTION

In late 20th-century America, the closet has become a central category for grasping the history and social dynamics of gay life. This concept is intended to capture social patterns of secrecy and sexual self-management that structure the lives of 'gay individuals' in societies organized around a norm of heterosexuality.[1] The concept of the closet is linked, perhaps inseparable from, the notion of 'coming out'. The latter category gives expression to the dramatic quality of privately and publicly coming to terms with a contested social identity. The categories of the closet and coming out have then been foundational to accounts of modern homosexuality.

Moreover, as many social thinkers have argued, concepts and narratives are to be assessed not only by their empirical and conceptual adequacy, but by their social effects—for example, the ways they shape identities, group life, and political movements (Bravman, 1997). In this regard, the narrative of coming out of the closet constructs gay individuals as suffering a common fate in a society organized around normative heterosexuality. Gay individuals are said to share an experience of secrecy and social isolation, the ordeal of refashioning a stigmatized identity, and negotiating social inclusion. This narrative shapes a common identity and politicizes it by making homosexuals into unjust social victims.

Despite the analytically and politically productive aspects of the narrative of the closet, we have reservations. Politically speaking, to the extent that this narrative has been linked to identity politics, it shares the strengths and weaknesses of the latter. Rallying around a shared 'minority' identity has contributed to gay political empowerment. Yet, there are considerable costs attached to identity politics—for example, the repression of differences among lesbians and gay men, a narrow focus on legitimating same sex preference, the isolation of the gay movement from other movements, and as queer perspectives argue, normalizing a gay identity leaves intact the organization of sexuality around a hetero/homosexual binary. Furthermore, by making the closet into the key focus of gay oppression, coming out and affirming a gay identity is often viewed as the supreme political act—as if mere gay visibility undermines heterosexism. The latter is, however, institutional and cultural, not simply a matter of individual prejudice. Finally, the narrative of coming out of the closet creates divisions between individuals who are 'in' and 'out' of the closet. The former are stigmatized as living false, unhappy lives and are pressured to be public without considering that the calculus of benefits and costs vary considerably depending on how individuals are socially positioned.

The focus of this article though is less the politics than the sociology of the closet. We argue two main points. First, we defend the analytical value of a concept of the closet but aim to be clear about its historical and sociological meaning. Specifically, we are in broad agreement with the revisionism of Chauncey (1994) who holds that the concept of the closet has unique sociohistorical preconditions—most importantly, the foregrounding of sexual identity and a systematic mobilization of social agencies (e.g. the state, medical—scientific institutions, the criminal justice system) aimed at enforcing a norm of heterosexuality. However, we believe that historians such as Chauncey have not questioned a one-sided sociological view that emphasizes the repressive character of the closet. We argue that central to this concept is a double life and strategies of everyday sexual self-management. While such practices aim to avoid the risks of unintended exposure, they also create a 'protected' space that permits individuals to fashion a gay self and facilitates the making of gay social worlds (e.g. gay bars or informal networks). In short, we propose to view the closet as a strategy of accommodation and resistance which both reproduces and contests aspects of a society organized around normative heterosexuality.

Our second argument focuses on emergent social patterns that indicate the declining social significance of the closet in contemporary America. Our research suggests that many individuals who identify as lesbian, gay, or bisexual have 'normalized' (subjectively accepted) and 'routinized' (socially integrated) their homosexuality. Consequently, a double life involving patterns of concealment and sexual self-management is less defining of their lives.

Although our research suggests that many Americans have today fashioned lives 'beyond the closet', we are not intending to narrate a one-dimensional story of the progressive social inclusion and equality of gay individuals. First, normalization and routinization have been incomplete. Our respondents continue to manage their homosexuality in part because of shame, guilt or fear. In this regard, our point is not that sexual self-management practices are obsolete. Rather, we contend that such practices are more situation-specific then patterning of a whole way of life, as is suggested by the concept of the closet. Second, we distinguish between 'interpersonal' and 'institutional' routinization. The former indicates informal ways individuals integrate homosexuality into their conventional social lives, e.g. disclosing to family members or coworkers. Institutional routinization refers to incorporating policies and practices into organizations that do not subordinate nonheterosexuals. We are not convinced that progress at the interpersonal level has been paralleled at the institutional level. However, the focus of this article is interpersonal routinization.

In 1996–97 we interviewed 25 individuals who identified as lesbian, gay, or bisexual. As other social researchers have argued (e.g. Esterberg, 1997; Whisman, 1996), a representative sample of homosexually identified individuals is not possible. We sought a sample population that was diverse in terms of gender, race, and class.

Our aim was to interview individuals who have not organized their lives around a gay subculture. We assumed that 'subculturally' identified individuals would have normalized and routinized their homosexuality. Instead, we sought individuals who would be less subculturally identified and therefore more likely to be 'closeted'. Although most of our respondents reported a feeling of belonging to a gay community, the extent to which they participated in this community varied considerably. None were political activists or organized their lives in relation to a gay subculture.[2]

We have divided this article into three parts. In the first section, we critically examine the way the concept of the closet has been used in folk and expert discourses. We defend a view of the closet which narrows its historical and sociological scope of application. Specifically, we view 'closet practices' as a response to repressive strategies aimed at maintaining a norm of heterosexuality by excluding homosexuality from public life. This strategy (roughly inaugurated in the 1940s but intensified in the 1950s and 1960s) created the conditions of the closet—a concept of homosexuality as a distinct sexual identity and a double life. The latter involved intensive and extensive strategies of sexual self-management that created a protected space that allowed individuals to fashion gay selves and to navigate between a straight and gay world. In the second section, we present a series of case studies to make plausible our claim of a trend towards the normalization and the (interpersonal) routinization of homosexuality. We point to social patterns that, though organized by a norm of heterosexuality, are not adequately described by the concept of the closet. In the third section, we consider the implications of these trends for viewing homosexuality as a source of identity, community, and politics. We argue that one effect of normalizing and routinizing trends is the 'decentering' of gay identities and communities—that is, homosexuality shifts from being narrated as a core to a partial, more voluntary aspect of identity and basis of community. We conjecture that these social shifts are a source of the 'queer' currents in gay culture. In other words, it is the successes, as much as the failures of identity politics, that has contributed to the rise of a queer political culture that is critical of a movement aimed exclusively at normalizing homo-sexuality.

I. RETHINKING THE SOCIOLOGY OF THE CLOSET

Since the Stonewall riots in 1969 the closet has become a core concept for understanding gay life in the US. Our preliminary research indicates that it was initially in the political literature that the closet made its public debut. The major gay liberationist anthology was tellingly entitled, *Out of the Closets* (Jay and Young, 1972). In her 'Introduction', Karla Jay states that this collection was published 'in the hope that one day all gay people will be out of the closet' (p. lxii). In Laud Humphreys's sociology of gay liberationism (1972), he states that the rallying cry of this movement was 'Out of the closet, into the streets!' (p. 3). As gay liberationism gave way to a civil rights, pride-based politics in the mid-1970s, and as institutionally elaborated subcultures were created in the 1980s (D'Emilio, 1983; Levine, 1979; Wolf, 1979), the act of coming out, as publicly ritualized in National Coming Out Day and pride marches, became a sacred personal and political event (Herdt, 1992; Herrell, 1992). The renewal of gay radicalism in the early 1990s, in the form of the politics of outing, underscores the continued significance of the politics of the closet (Gross, 1993). Today, political strategies focused on dismantling the closet remain central—whether the site is the classroom (Harbeck, 1992), the industrial-media complex (Signorile, 1993), corporate America (Woods, 1993), the civil service bureaucracy (DeCrescenzo, 1997), or the military forces (Cammermeyer, 1994).

If a political investment underpins a discourse of the closet, this narrative figure was gradually absorbed into the gay mainstream. Between the mid-1980s and the late 1990s, the framing of gay life in terms of the closet and coming out became pervasive. For example, a flourishing industry of self-help literature advises lesbians and gay men, but also their family, friends, and employers, on managing daily life beyond the closet, dealing with the shame and residual homophobia of the closet, and so on (Buxton, 1994; Johnson, 1997; Kaufman and Raphael, 1996). Thus, in Mary Borhek's *Coming Out to Parents* (1993), parents are advised on how to ease their children's exodus from the closet. They are instructed that disclosure by a daughter or son creates closet dynamics for them. For example, the mother must decide who to 'come out' to as a parent of a gay child (Hom, 1996).

Shifting from 'low brow' to 'high brow' literary culture, much of what has been canonized as 'classic' gay literature has a coming out story as its dramatic center (e.g. Rita Mae Brown's *Rubyfruit Jungle* or Edmund White's *A Boys Own Story*). Consider the memoir as a literary genre that blends folk and literary culture. From Merle Miller's *On Being Different* (1971), *The Original Coming Out Stories* (Penelope and Wolfe, 1989), to the testimonies of people of color (Beam, 1986; Ramos, 1987), the struggle around the closet is the core dramatic motif (see McRuer, 1996; Plummer, 1995; Zimmerman, 1984). For example, Miller's memoir is structured around a shift from a life of passing, which included marriage, to a finale when, unable to countenance his own shame and others' bigotry, he 'comes out of the closet' (p. 47). Some 20 years later, Paul Monette (1992) narrates his life story as a 'narrow escape from the coffin world of the closet' to the 'giddy circle of freedom' that accompanied the public affirmation of his homosexuality.

The concept of the closet has been central in the social scientific literature. In one of the earliest studies in the sociology of homosexuality, Humphreys (1970) analyzes participants in 'tearoom trade'. The tearoom is a public space where the quest for sexual pleasure is linked to heightened risks of exposure and danger. Humphreys views tearoom participants as exhibiting a 'closeted' type of social adaptation. In response to a stigmatized desire, these individuals fashion a double life. Passing in their public life, homosexual expression is confined to furtive sexual encounters involving intense self-management to avoid unwanted exposure. In recent social science, which is often focused on coming out, the closet is typically non-thematized but foundational. For example, Herdt (1992) criticizes views of 'coming out as a uniform, ahistorical, stage-driven process'. Coming out is approached as an initiation rite marking a transition to an adult gay identity. The dynamics of this rite of passage are complicated by gender or generational difference. The idea of coming out assumes of course an initial condition involving the secretive management of homosexuality, i.e. the closet. However, whereas coming out is analyzed with attention to sociological and historical complexities, the closet is the taken-for-granted, ahistorical ground of gay life (Jenness, 1992; Rust, 1993).[3] Although queer perspectives are critical of much of gay culture, the concept of the closet remains foundational. As Sedgwick says, 'the gay closet is not a feature only of the lives of gay people. But for many gay people it is still the fundamental feature of social life' (1990: 68).

One theme that runs through this literature is the claim that the closet always accompanies homosexuality in a normatively heterosexual society. In an early sociological study, Edward Delph wrote: 'An alternative to the "closet" developed after the Stonewall riot gave birth to the gay liberation movement: coming out of their own closets by disclosing secret identities . . . If the closet is a result of the fear of stigmatization, it is the major way in which one's social and sexual life is integrated. It has served faithfully for decades and probably centuries as the way to make "sense" out of conflicting demands or expectations of homosexual desires in a heterosexually defined social world' (Delph, 1978: 158–60). Theorizing in a very different milieu, Diana Fuss echoes this view. 'Paradoxically, the "ghosting" of homosexuality coincides with its "birth." For the historical moment of the first appearance of the homosexual as a "species" rather than a "temporary aberration" also marks the moment of the homosexual's disappearance—into the closet' (1991: 4).

Recently, Chauncey (1994) has criticized perspectives that apply the concept of the closet to all patterns of homosexual concealment without attention to unique sociohistorical conditions. He argues that the primary cultural division in the early decades of this century in New York City was around gender. The dominant currents of this culture distinguished between 'normal' masculine men (who could—and did—have sex with men) and 'fairies' or effeminate men (who were thought to be woman-like and to desire sex with 'normal' men). Moreover, fairies created a gay world that was public and integrated into at least some (working-class) neighborhoods. Chauncey argues that the homosexual closet is a product of the repression of this working-class gay world. He maintains, moreover, that the notion of a closet assumes that the hetero/homosexual binary, as a framework defining sexual identity by sexual object choice, marginalized the normal/fairy binary—an event that he dates from the 1930s.[4]

We think that Chauncey's argument is persuasive but needs to be amended. He acknowledges that secrecy and self-management were integral to the public gay life created by fairies. Although they were tolerated in some working-class neighborhoods, fairies were also the targets of citizen and state harassment. Chauncey argues that the concealment practices of fairies should not be described by the concept of the closet. He prefers the concept of 'double life' because the secretive practices of fairies were not part of a comprehensive pattern of deception and passing, but were strategies to avoid public censure in order to enjoy a public gay life. However, this distinction between the double life (which made possible a positive gay life) and the closet (which repressed a gay life) involves a reductionistic sociological view of the latter as a state of repression.

It is hardly surprising that Chauncey understands the closet as exclusively repressive. This view is pervasive. Consider two contemporary literary and political documents.

In *Becoming a Man* (1992), Monette reverses the conventional coming-of-age narrative. Instead of a story of childhood and adolescence as formative of an adult self, he relates a tale of youth that involved the loss of self to the suffocating logic of the closet. 'Until I was 25, I was the only man I knew who had no story at all. I'd long since accepted the fact that nothing had ever happened to me and nothing ever would. That's how the closet feels, once you've made your nest in it and learned to call it home'. For Monette, the struggle for self-possession is told as a struggle against the closet which he describes variously as an 'internal exile', an 'imprisonment', and as 'the gutting of all our passions till we are a bunch of eunuchs'.

If Monette makes the escape from the closet into the chief act of self-possession, Signorile (1995) makes destroying the closet into the supreme political act. The closet is said to preserve the power of heterosexism by fashioning a 'cowering, sad, self-loathing homosexual' (p. 365). It reproduces homosexual oppression by creating a dominated self. 'The closeted, as captives, suffer such profound psychological trauma that they develop a relationship to their closets similar to that of hostages to their captors . . .' (p. xviii). To the extent that the closet is viewed as the cornerstone of gay oppression, Signorile defends 'outing' as a libratory political act.

We question whether the concept of the closet is coherent if it refers exclusively to a condition of repression. This view assumes an original, already formed homosexual self who is constrained 'in' the closet. This assumption is inconsistent with social constructionist ideas which view gay selves as socially formed and never fully consolidated (Butler, 1991; Phelan, 1993). From this perspective, the closet would be viewed as not only repressive but productive in a double sense.

First, practices of concealment not only protect the individual from the risks of exposure but create a 'protected' psychic space to imaginatively construct a gay self. As Foucault (1980) might say, the self-management practices imposed by normative heterosexuality to suppress homosexuality ironically incite a heightened self-consciousness about such desires. In other words, the prohibition against homosexuality makes it into a preoccupation to the point where the individual may consolidate an identity around this desire.

For example, despite Monette's explicit claim that concealment is only repressive, his autobiographical sketch relates a tale of the formative role of the closet in the making of a gay self. It was in the closet that he began to cultivate his homosexual desires. 'I couldn't tell my claque of girls how riveted I'd been on the Prom King's grinding hips—his football hands stroking Connie's bare back up and down' (p. 45). Similarly, Paul speaks of struggling to suppress an impulse to stare at the other boys during high school gym. The language he uses to describe this experience suggests only repression. Yet, Paul relates that these boys became part of his fantasy life. 'Jerking off every night in the dark thinking about them, summoning them in their nakedness . . . I was able to picture in stupefying detail a hundred different naked bodies . . .' (pp. 70–71). It was in the public silence of the closet that

these fantasies were elaborated—shaping Paul's gay self and ultimately driving him 'out' of the closet: 'I had no choice but to keep on looking for the thing I'd never seen: two men in love and laughing. For that was the image in my head . . . [which] I'd fashioned out of bits of dreams . . . The vision of the laughing men dogged me and wouldn't be shaken . . . till I sometimes thought I'd lost my mind—but I also think it kept me alive' (p. 178). Thus, while Monette self-consciously tells a story of how heterosexism produced a dominated self, he also narrates a tale of the making of a resisting gay self. The chief drama of his story is that of an inauthentic, unfree self who rebels against the closet in order to recover his true self. If we take the closet as a metaphor only of containment and denial, we cannot explain how a dominated self manages resistance and liberation.

A second sense of the productivity of the closet relates to the making of community. While some individuals conceal in order to avoid any public exposure, others pass as a strategy to make possible a public gay life. This socially productive aspect of the closet was recognized in a study of lesbian identity and community formation. Barbara Ponse (1978) observes that:

> the secrecy around gay life provides a protective milieu for trying on the lesbian identity in a favorable ambience. Once a lesbian identity has been acknowledged and accepted, the lesbian subculture created by the binding and separating powers of secrecy supports and strengthens commitment to that identity, through associations with validating others.

Similarly, Mariana Romo-Carmona underscores the ironic role of the closet in contributing to the making of a Latina lesbian community. While emphasizing the oppression that accompanies practices of silence and secrecy (e.g. misrecognition, invisibility, disenfranchisement), Romo-Carmona remarks that such practices unintentionally create a heightened feeling of difference and solidarity:

> How many daughters, mothers, sisters, Godmothers and grandmothers, aunts, cousins and best friends have lived and died unknown? Each woman's forced silence was a denial of her existence, as if she never loved another woman. . . . Saliendo del closet is ultimately helping to create . . . a Latina lesbian community. (Ramos, 1987: xxiii; cf. Trujillo, 1991).

Defining the closet as exclusively repressive assumes moreover that 'closeted' individuals reproduce it by internalizing polluted self-images (e.g. Signorile, 1993; Vaid, 1996). The combination of social and self-hatred is said to inevitably result in personal despair and pathology. Indeed, we have heard many stories of excess with drugs and alcohol, sad tales of depression and loneliness that were linked to a closeted life. For example, Adam, a 40-year-old professional, drank his way through adolescence and early adulthood, through a marriage and a family, in order to manage a life of profound duplicity and shame:

> I was living a lie. I was in a marriage to someone I couldn't stand. I was miserable all the time. I was uncomfortable with myself, but I didn't have the balls to come out of the closet. . . . In the six months before I came out and got sober, I tried to commit suicide twice. I was just an extremely unhappy individual.

Without minimizing the oppressive aspects of homosexual concealment and self-management, we found that such patterns do not have a uniform psychological and social meaning. For example, some respondents fashioned satisfying lives, despite living with considerable ambivalence.

Phil described himself as 'very closeted'. He was aware of his desires for men as a youth, but their relation to his self-identity was unclear. Growing up in a small town in the 1940s and 1950s, he was barely exposed to ideas about homosexuality. It was not until Phil was in his 30s and 40s (1960s–1970s) that he realized same-sex feelings are often interpreted as indicating a homosexual identity. However, he did not at the time nor does he now define himself as gay, despite acknowledging that his primary desires are for men. He identifies as bisexual as a way to make sense of the fact that his feelings for his deceased wife were real. He does not describe his marriage as a lie or a strategy to pass. 'I married because that's what I wanted to do. I wanted that kind of a life'. Phil's decision to continue to conceal is in part motivated by shame and fear of social disapproval; he also described it as a positive choice to live a publicly heterosexual life. Phil embraces a heterosexual identity in part because of the image he wants those he loves to have of him, in order

to maintain the kind of intimacy he now shares with family and friends, and because it is a social life that he has enjoyed, despite some anguish in having to marginalize his homosexuality.

Jim (born 1967) was aware of his homosexual feelings as a youth though unsure of their meaning. He grew up in a small town and had little exposure to ideas about homosexuality. As late as the 1980s, Jim reports that the only images that made a lasting impression were those heard in church and his family. Homosexuality was said to be immoral and unnatural. Jim says that through adolescence he was unsure of the importance of homosexual feelings in his life. Jim had a girlfriend through high school whom he eventually married. He told his wife about his feelings for men, but he was committed to making the marriage work. After his wife died in an accident Jim choose to publicly identify as gay. Yet, he never reinterpreted his heterosexual past as inauthentic. 'I did love my wife; there was a commitment there, and we were best friends. She knew everything about me, there were no secrets, nothing hidden there'.

Some respondents were very clear about the meaning of homosexual feelings in their lives. For example, some individuals interpreted their homosexuality as indicating a discredited identity. Their decision to conceal was driven by shame, guilt, and fear. Some married or rigidly conformed to gender stereotypes in order to conceal; others turned to alcohol or drugs.

There is no escaping ambivalent feelings towards homosexuality in a society that makes heterosexuality normative. Yet, some individuals do not interpret homosexual feelings as revealing their true selves. They understand homosexuality as marginal in their psychic economies. They minimize their homosexuality without feeling self-loathing or estrangement. We should not assume that all individuals experience homosexuality as an identity and therefore experience its marginalization as a betrayal of a true self. Moreover, even individuals who interpret their homosexuality as integral to their selves may choose to marginalize it without necessarily surrendering to self-loathing. The presumption that the presence of homosexual feelings marks the individual as a homosexual fails to consider that many individuals experience both homosexual and heterosexual feelings in psychically integral ways. At some point, Phil and Jim made a decision to live heterosexually not simply to avoid social disapproval but because of deeply felt psychological longings for heterosexual intimacy and integration into a conventional social world. Our interviews suggest that not all individuals who identify as gay always distinguish clearly between homosexual and heterosexual feelings, experience them as mutually exclusive, understand them as markers of identity, and describe the suppression of homosexual feelings as necessarily betraying their true selves (Davis, 1992; Esterberg, 1997; Markowe, 1996).

To bring this discussion to a close, we believe that the concept of the closet is analytically useful if its specific sociohistorical scope is clarified. We find plausible Chauncey's claim that the era of the closet began in the 1930s and 1940s. We conjecture that by the 1950s and 1960s the norm of heterosexuality operated by maintaining a symbolic and social separation between a 'pure' heterosexuality and a 'polluted' homosexuality. Enforcing this social division involved the exclusion of homosexuality from public life. A series of repressive strategies—from censorship to civic disenfranchisement and violence—were deployed. A heterosexist order maintained by a logic of repression created the social practices that have come to be called the closet. Central was a double life—a private life where homosexuality could be acknowledged and expressed in a quasi-public gay world (bars, cruising areas, informal gatherings) and a public life of 'passing' as heterosexual (Escoffier, 1997). We have argued, moreover, that practices of concealment were not only suppressive and reproductive of domination, but were productive of gay selves and quasi-public worlds.

II. Case Studies in the (Incomplete) Normalization and Routinization of Homosexuality

The concept of the closet is compelling to the extent that the core areas of an individual's life—work, family, and intimate ties—are structured by practices of managing homosexuality in order to avoid unwanted exposure. The closet refers to a division between a private life where homosexuality can be expressed and a public life where one passes as heterosexual. To the extent that homosexuality continues to be polluted and subject to criminal sanction and civic disenfranchisement, there will be individuals for whom the management of their homosexuality is so intensive and extensive that such practices shape a whole way of life.

In this section, we argue that many Americans have normalized and routinized their homosexuality to a degree that the concept of the closet is less descriptive of their lives. Our thesis is that the behavior of these individuals in the core areas of their lives is not systematically shaped by the need to conceal and manage their homosexuality. The choice for these Americans is no longer between denial or a double life, but how to live a public life that integrates homosexuality while still making decisions about disclosure.

Normalization refers to a subjective condition in which homosexuality is described as natural or normal. Homosexuality is said to make the individual neither inherently inferior nor superior to those who identify as heterosexual. Normalizing homosexuality means that while individuals may still feel some shame or guilt, they describe such feelings as the residues of living in a normatively heterosexual society rather than as judgments about the inherently inferior status of homosexuality. Normalization makes interpersonal routinization possible. This concept refers to individual efforts to integrate homosexuality into the conventional social world. Key indicators of interpersonal routinization would be whether individuals disclose information about their homosexuality to family, close friends, and coworkers, or whether individuals date, form relationships, and make their intimacies public.

We approach normalization and routinization in terms of a continuum. Individuals normalize and routinize their homosexuality to varying degrees over the course of a lifetime. We assume that in a society organized around the norm of heterosexuality, normalization and routinization will be incomplete. This may reflect incomplete normalization (e.g. sustained feelings of shame and guilt around homosexuality), incomplete interpersonal routinization (e.g. intolerance by heterosexuals), or incomplete institutional routinization (institutional practices that subordinate nonheterosexuals).

We describe the lives of some individuals who have normalized and routinized their homosexuality to a considerable extent. Their lives are less plausibly understood by the concept of the closet. Homosexuality does not dictate their lives, e.g. it does not pressure individuals to marry, uncouple sex from one's emotional and social life, or conceal this identity from family or friends. For these individuals, disclosure decisions are less prompted by shame, guilt or fear than by decisions about drawing boundaries between personal information that is private and public. Despite lives that are 'beyond the closet', normalization and routinization are incomplete. Subjective ambivalence and interpersonal and institutional resistance to routinization underscore the continued power of normative heterosexuality in the US.

We present several abbreviated case studies. Aspects of the lives of individuals are sketched with the intent of illustrating a series of positions on a continuum—with one pole indicating a life in the 'closet' and the other indicating lives 'beyond the closet'.

Phil came of age as an adult in the 1950s. He was raised in a working-class, Catholic family in a small rural town. Phil relates the story of his homosexuality in terms of a conventionalized narrative of the closet. Aware of homosexual feelings as a youth, Phil initially denied them and later separated them from the rest of his life. He did what was expected of him— he married and raised a family. His masculine self-presentation and his marital status reduced the risk of exposure. His few homosexual experiences were anonymous or with men who shared his fear of exposure. Nevertheless, Phil was 'always concerned that somehow it would be found out'. Accordingly, he engaged in intensive daily self-management. He did not associate with gay people, avoided staring at men, was silent in the face of homophobic comments, avoided arguments about homosexuality, maintained a public interest in women, and so on. Even now, widowed for several years, Phil reports that few people know of his homosexuality.

Phil's account of his decision to remain 'closeted' is likewise conventionalized. He reported that his fam-ily of origin would not have tolerated his homosexuality. His father would have been devastated. His mother would have been very disappointed and it would have strained their intimacy. Similarly, Phil is unsure whether he would have been fired from his job, but his coworkers would certainly have disapproved and made work tense. Once married and having raised a family, the price of integrating his homosexuality into his life became too high. Even now, a widower, economically secure, and his children grown, Phil insists he will never come out. Although his children would probably accept him, Phil wants them to view him in a socially approved way—as heterosexual. The threat of disturbing the rich intimacy of his family stops Phil from living a life which, in his own words, expresses who he is. '[Homosexuality is] very important for my sense of self, but I can't act on it like I wished I could. I can't come out. I have to keep it a secret'.

If Phil illustrates the closeted end of the continuum, Clara exemplifies a life that is conducted largely beyond the closet. Clara describes herself as an 18-years-old black lesbian. Clara comes from a large working-class family. Her father and mother were separated when she was a child. She has lived mostly with her mother in a Maryland suburb, but spends some time with her father in Harlem. Clara is a college freshman.

Clara's 'coming out' process was remarkably painless. She disclosed her lesbian preference to her mother—and then to her whole family—at the age of 14. Today she is open about her homosexuality to everyone in her family, which she describes as close. The extent to which Clara has normalized and routinized her homosexuality is indicated by the scope of disclosure to her family. 'I talk about everything with my mother and my sisters and one brother. They know my lover and everything like that. They know just about everything [about my lesbian life]'. Her comments on disclosing to her father, who, as a Jamaican, is described as less understanding, illustrates the extent of Clara's normalizing of her homosexuality: 'He had the biggest problem with it but it didn't matter to me, cause I just told him to be telling him. I wasn't telling him for approval'.

Clara's description of her social life points to a similar degree of normalization and routinization. She is open with friends, classmates, and teachers. For example, living in a college dorm Clara had to deal quickly with issues of disclosure. She reports the following incident. Invited by dorm mates to a fraternity party, Clara declined. ' "I'm not going", and they were like, "why?" I'm like, "I don't do dick". They were like, "What do you mean?" I was like, "I'm a lesbian" '. The normalization of homosexuality exhibited in Clara's behavior with family and classmates was stated directly in comments to the effect that her homosexuality was 'normal' or her 'norm'.

Clara describes a life in which her homosexuality has been interpersonally routinized. People who matter to Clara have been accepting. Her dorm mates were surprised at how open she was but they have accepted her. For example:

when we sit in the dorm room sometimes and we're having conversations about an ex-boyfriend, if I find them talking about something that maybe was similar to something that went on with me I [would say], 'oh you know, my ex-girlfriend one time so and so' and they'd be like, 'really, they do the same thing like that?'

Similarly, Clara reports the following incident with her dentist: He [the dentist] knows [about me being a lesbian] because when I went to get my teeth checked . . . my girlfriend came with me. It wasn't like I sat down and told him, but he asked who she was and I was like, 'oh, that's my girlfriend'. The dentist was very accepting. 'Every now and then he'll ask about her, [ask] how she's doing, [and] what she's doing and all of that'.

Clara's relatively smooth integration of homosexuality into her life was exceptional. It was more common for our respondents to narrate a shift from a double life to a life beyond the closet.

Bill is a white, 40-year-old, middle-level state worker who comes from a working-class family in a small town close to his present residence in Albany, New York. Bill was aware of his homosexual feelings as a child. These became more vivid between the ages of 10–12 when heterosexual dating began in his peer group. Despite being attracted to men, Bill dated only women in order to conceal his homosexuality. Homosexuals were described by family and peers as 'fag-

gots'. Bill feared being disowned by family, ridiculed by friends, and condemned by his church. By adolescence Bill had, in his own words, 'stepped into the closet'. Subsequently, Bill married, joined the marines, and started drinking to manage a closeted life.

His marriage ended in the mid-1980s. Perhaps triggered by a decision to get sober and his abiding loneliness, Bill decided to integrate his homosexuality into his life. He disclosed initially in the gay world of bars and fashioned a gay friendship circle. This social network allowed him to disclose to his mother and eventually to his entire family, friends, coworkers, ex-wife, son, and his hometown: Bill was interviewed by a local newspaper on being gay and Christian.

Bill's relation to his son illustrates the normalizing of his homosexuality. Bill has joint custody of Larry. When his son was 10 years old, Bill tried to explain that he was gay. Larry didn't respond. From time to time Bill would reintroduce this topic but Larry remained inattentive. Bill decided to be relaxed about it:

I would be completely myself in front of him, and that included conversations with gay friends, or talking about gay people or places. . . . I was in a relation and I let him see us hold hands and hug and kiss goodbye. . . . I was just trying to show him that we're a normal gay couple. I kind of hate that word normal but . . . you know, that it was natural for us.

Bill has, to a significant degree, routinized his homosexuality. For example, Bill has disclosed to his supervisor and his two regular coworkers. 'I don't try to hide it in my conversations. I think that most everybody knows'. Asked if he talks about the gay aspects of his life (e.g. friends, lovers, social events) with his coworkers in a way that would be similar if he were heterosexual, Bill replied, 'Yeah, with two of them, definitely, [because] they're closer friends than the other one'. Asked if there was anything important relating to the gay aspects of his life that he conceals with them, he replied 'Not at all'.

Rachel was born in 1964. She is now completing her PhD thesis. Rachel was married for 8 years. She did not become aware of any lesbian feelings until she got involved with a woman in the early 1990s. This surprised and excited her but it was several years before she would identify as a lesbian. Rachel prefers to identify as a lesbian rather than a bisexual, because she believes that while she chose, out of real needs and feelings to marry, she has subsequently chosen to be with a woman as a life partner.

Rachel initially disclosed to her friends who were very accepting. Disclosure to her family was difficult. She describes her father, with whom she is close, as bigoted. Moreover, her parents pressured her to stay married. Nevertheless, as her marriage ended, and her involvement with Phyllis became serious, Rachel revealed her homosexuality to her family. Although her parents are ambivalent, Rachel insists on integrating the lesbian aspects of her life into her family relations:

> They don't like to talk about that kind of stuff [i.e. lesbian life] but they know about Phyllis. I nudge them every once and awhile when they forget to say something or when they forget to include her . . . I'm much more sensitive, much more quick to jump on them about it [or] to say something to them.

Phyllis is included in all family events.

Rachel describes a life in which her homosexuality is routinized. She lives with Phyllis in a New England suburb. They bought a home together and both are listed on the mortgage. Their daily lives are conducted publicly as a couple. 'When we have contractors to the house, when we go buy furniture . . . , we make no effort to pretend as if, these are going in my room, or her room. We make every decision as a couple and talk as if we are a couple'. In this regard, Rachel says her doctor and dentist know that she is a lesbian. Neighbors also know about her and Phyllis. The disclosure logic here is revealing of Rachel's effort to routinize this practice. 'What I don't think is important is that I put my hand out and say "hello, my name is Rachel and I'm a lesbian". I think that's awkward but . . . people know that we live in that house together, and make joint decisions, and our names are on the mailbox. [Also], people when they ask me how I'm doing, [also] say things like, "gee I haven't seen Phyllis around and how is she doing?" So I don't hide it but on the other hand I don't make anybody uncomfortable'.

Rachel says that today her homosexuality does not influence her choice of friends (except that they be accepting of her homosexuality), where she lives, the kind of work she does, or the ways she interacts with family, coworkers, neighbors, and service providers. Rachel does not view her life in terms of a division between a straight and gay world.

Albert was born in 1972. He is a middle-class African-American. Albert described a strong sense of feeling different throughout growing up. He attended an all-white primary and secondary school. Although Albert grew up in Albany, a capital city, he recalls only negative images of homosexuality through high school (1987–91). Albert managed daily life so as to avoid any risk of exposure.

Albert attempted suicide when he was 18 years old. This promoted a disclosure process. His family was supportive. 'My mother loves me for who I am'. Albert has boyfriends over to their home, and they are considered 'family' by his parents. He admits that there is much about his gay life that is not talked about but this reflects a family culture that excludes personal matters from public discussion. Moreover, while his homosexuality 'feels ordinary, it's a little awkward for my mother. She's like, "I don't have to like it but I accept that's who you are" '. Normalizing his homosexuality entailed integrating it into his daily life. Albert disclosed to his high school friends: 'It was really good because they were just encountering friends of theirs that they met at school [college] who had come out to them and so it was really very good. They were sorry about what I'd gone through but there was no negative reactions'. Albert says that, so far, 'I haven't found any [friend] that hasn't been accepting'.

As Albert's suicide attempt indicates, coming to terms with his homosexuality was agonizing. Today, though, 'I finally have accepted it for myself, it's who I am and I don't really care what the other person thinks'. When asked if there was still anxiety about disclosing, he said, 'its just something that's normal [for me]'. Albert is trying to normalize the practice of disclosure. 'If someone ask[s] me . . . if I have a girlfriend I say no I have a boyfriend . . . I'm not gonna just come out and tell someone because I don't feel like I have to tell somebody'.

Except for two (older) respondents, all of our interviewees have, to a considerable degree, normalized and routinized their homosexuality. Today, concealment and coming out are not their primary concerns. Instead, their (gay) concerns revolve around dating, developing gay friends, gaining legal rights and accompanying social benefits, and social recognition of their relationships. For example, Albert says: 'I'm not really focused on coming out of the closet. I've done that already. I guess now I'm dealing with being a gay man who is HIV positive'.

To the extent that homosexuality is normalized and interpersonally routinized, we would expect that decisions about disclosure would be prompted less by shame, guilt, or fear. We found that some concealment decisions involved judgments about how to draw boundaries between information about the self that is private—but not necessarily because it is discrediting—and information that is public.

For example, since Mike's marriage ended in 1991 he has lived a publicly gay life. Mike works in a large State agency. He has a picture of his partner (Andy) on his desk. He reports that he talks as openly about his life with Andy as his coworkers talk about their heterosexual partners. For example, 'we went to a union ceremony two weeks ago and I brought in all the pictures and showed them to my secretary and the people I'm closest to'.

Mike must still make decisions about disclosure. For example, with new clients and coworkers, disclosure 'depends on the way the conversation runs. If someone asks me if I'm married . . . I say that I'm with a man'. Mike treats homosexuality as part of a class of 'intimate information' that is not routinely shared. He makes disclosure decisions by considering the degree of intimacy established or desired. With most coworkers he does not disclose because 'I probably would never have an opportunity to share anything personal with them'. Mike's comments on his disclosure practices in relation to his son are similarly revealing of a logic that is not driven by shame or fear. Mike is open to his son (16 years old) who stays with him on weekends. However, when his son invites friends to his home, 'Andy and I don't kiss in front of them and we don't sleep in the same bed'. Mike's decision to conceal is motivated by respect for his son who has not fully normalized his father's homosexuality. 'I think it's sensitivity to my son's relationships with his friends and understanding that it's not easy for everybody to be out, including possibly my son with his friends, being out about me'.

Consider the disclosure decisions of Jeff (born 1965). He talks easily about the gay aspects of his life with family, coworkers, and friends, including fraternity brothers. However, Jeff has not disclosed to all his coworkers. 'If they don't know it's not because I'm hiding it from them'. Jeff says his homosexuality is often irrelevant to his professional life (research scientist). 'It just doesn't come up. . . . There is no personal stuff from either side'. With regard to his family, Jeff insists that he is as open to them as he would be if he were heterosexual. He brings dates to meet his parents, and his boyfriend has joined his family for holiday gatherings. Yet, Jeff acknowledges that some information linked to his gay life is withheld. For example, Jeff has not told his uncles and aunts that he is gay. 'You know if I tell them it will rifle through my family in a second. I couldn't care less [but] I don't know if [my parents are] ready for all our relatives to find out I'm gay'. Jeff's decision to accommodate his parents needs is for him, but perhaps not for his parents, a concealment decision that reflects neither shame or fear.

Marcia is a 20-year-old college student who is very public about her lesbian identity. However, she does not disclose to everyone, and varies how much she reveals. Two considerations guide her disclosure decisions. First, Marcia considers the timing of disclosure in order to avoid stereotypical reactions. 'If I tell a person that I'm queer immediately then they don't really know who I am'. Thus, while she has disclosed to most of her coworkers, a new employee does not yet know. 'I get the feeling from him that I need to wait a little. . . . He needs to know me, because he seems like the type of person who's going to judge me on my sexuality'. Second, Marcia considers the level of intimacy that is socially appropriate or personally desired. Thus, with one coworker 'I can talk about anything to her [because we're intimate]', but with others 'I don't like to bring my personal life to work. . . . It's none of their business'.

As individuals try to make their homosexuality into a routine part of their daily lives, decisions to conceal pivot around considerations other than, or in addition to, fear, shame, or guilt. Individuals withhold information about their homosexuality because it is defined as personal, because disclosure would involuntarily 'out' others (e.g. parents or friends), or because they wish to minimize a stereotypical reaction. Today, many individuals disclose not only to gain approval or contest social disapproval, but in order to achieve and sustain intimacy, to avoid misrecognition, to get respect for themselves and their partners, and to integrate their homosexuality into their everyday lives. These are not concealment and disclosure decisions that reflect the social logic of the closet.

In social contexts organized by normative heterosexuality, normalization and routinization will be incomplete. Despite his emphatic rhetoric of self-acceptance, Mike admitted continued ambivalence. Asked to clarify why he has not spoken with his son about what it feels like to conceal when his son has friends in the house, Mike said that 'part of it might be that little bit of self-homophobia that I still carry'. Or, consider Ralph (born 1958), who owns a hairdressing business. Ralph deliberately conceals with middle-aged, working-class male customers because of a 'fear of rejection'. Similarly, although he is open with his parents, Ralph has not disclosed to his larger kin network because 'I fear rejection'. Rejection means that family and clients will 'say that I'm not as good as anyone else'. Ralph is in part vulnerable to self-devaluation because of his own ambivalence towards homosexuality.

Subjective ambivalence is connected to incomplete interpersonal routinization. Thus, perhaps Mike did not press his son because he feared reproducing his estrangement with his parents. Mike's parents have not accepted his being gay. Although they live just a few miles apart, they never call him at home and refuse to meet Andy. Forced to choose between integration into his family of origin and maintaining an integrated, affirmative sense of self and family of choice, Mike has 'separated from [his parents]'. Similarly, despite normalizing a bisexual identity, Andrea, a college student still financially dependent upon her parents, cannot integrate this identity into her family. Asked how they would react to her disclosure, she commented: 'I would be kicked out; I wouldn't even be able to get my stuff from my house. I would not be able to speak to them. My parents are really just like that'.

Pressures to self-manage in order to avoid unwanted exposure also underscores a reality of incomplete institutional routinization. Thus, Clara anticipates heightened public self-monitoring as she pursues a career:

> I'm not going to be so loose about it because you do have to watch who you say something to and that's not . . . like going back in the closet. I just feel like it's protecting your job, your career, not everybody has to know and when they find out that could cause a problem.

As a doctoral student, Rachel has not experienced workplace discrimination. However, because her partner is a physician who fears loss of patients and collegial support, Rachel and Phyllis engage in intensive sexual self-management. 'When we're in more professional situations, and what she [Phyllis] terms as threatening situations, our behavior changes, and it feels like a double life' (on the heterosexist organization of the workplace, see Badgett and King, 1997; Friskopp and Silverstein, 1995; Schneider, 1984; Woods, 1993). As these two examples suggest, subjective normalization and interpersonal routinization have not necessarily been paralleled by institutional routinization.

A shift in the social logic of normative heterosexuality in American society is occurring. There has been a considerable relaxing of social repression at the personal and interpersonal levels. Many individuals have fashioned affirmative gay identities; the symbolic and social boundaries between straights and gays have lessened considerably. Many individuals live beyond the closet. It is equally clear, however, that the US remains a nation organized by the institution of heterosexuality. If it operates less through repression, and if it is less directed at regulating individuals at the interpersonal level, it remains embedded at the institutional level as manifested in law, social policy, civic disenfranchisement, institutional practices and public culture.

III. THE SOCIOLOGY AND POLITICS OF HOMOSEXUALITY IN A PERIOD OF THE DECLINING SIGNIFICANCE OF THE CLOSET

The era of the closet has not passed. Representations continue to typify the homosexual as polluted and civic and social disenfranchisement and violence structure gay life in the US. As a set of practices responding to the repressive logic of normative heterosexuality, the closet continues to organize the lives of many Americans.

Nevertheless, we have argued that dynamics of normalization and routinization point to the marginalization of the closet in contemporary US. This dynamic has not been analyzed, in part because of the politically mobilizing force of a discourse of the closet. By underscoring lives trapped in the repressive space of the closet, a reality of unjust homosexual oppression is emphasized. We have not denied the continued power of the social conditions producing a politics of the closet. Rather, we have sought to document normalizing and routinizing processes suggesting that accordingly social analysts need to rethink practices of sexual self-management in a way that does not collapse them into a uniform, homogenizing language of the closet.

In this concluding section, we sketch some of the implications of normalization and routinization for issues of identity, community, and politics.

In the course of our interviews, an apparent contradiction surfaced between assertions of the centrality of a gay identity and reported social practices. For example, Mike stated that 'being gay is who I am and I don't want anyone to assume otherwise'. Yet, Mike hardly participates in gay culture, and his closest friends are heterosexual. He describes a life that revolves around his partner, children, Alcoholics Anonymous, work, and sports. Mike at times invoked a rhetoric of a primary gay identity but his life suggested otherwise. In fact, at one point in the interview he offered an identity description that was more consistent with his practice. 'Being out . . . doesn't change who I am as a person or as a boss or as a father. Being gay is just another part of me'.

We contend that since normalization and routinization involve integrating homosexuality into one's life, this will involve a desire to be publicly recognized as gay. If homosexuality is experienced as an acceptable, integral aspect of oneself, and especially one that is not signaled by the surface of the body and conventional behaviors—and one that individuals normalize in relation to a history of shame and secrecy—we would expect individuals to be deliber-

ate about asserting a public gay identity. At the same time, normalization and routinization prompt individuals to 'decenter' or marginalize homosexuality as a basis of personal identity.

Our research suggests that normalization and routinization are paralleled by a shift in the way individuals frame homosexuality in relation to identity. The conditions producing the closet often make homosexuality into a way of life and therefore into a primary (even if discredited) identity. If the 'first phase' of normalizing gay identities has typically involved affirming this identity as primary, a 'second phase' may occasion decentering homosexuality as a basis of identity. For at least some individuals who have normalized their homosexuality, it is described as a 'thread' rather than a core aspect of identity. For example, Jeff says that his homosexuality influences aspects of his life without overdetermining his self-definition. 'It's not a separate part of me. Its an overall theme [in my life] . . . I guess being gay has a little bit of influence in how I behave at work and a little bit of influence in the way I go shopping, and a little bit of influence in who I'm seeing'. Marcia echoes this 'decentering' theme. 'I wouldn't say that when I think of myself the first thing I think of is a lesbian. Or, I wouldn't say that I think that when people first meet me that's what they need to know. . . . Being a lesbian [is] just like being a woman, or being a redhead. These are things that are part of me'.

If the conditions of the closet often compel individuals to make their homosexuality into a primary self-identity, normalization gives individuals the latitude to define its relation to identity, and many individuals seem to be choosing to decenter it.

Despite these decentering trends, our respondents expressed an emphatic sense of belonging to a gay community, even though they participate minimally, if at all, in group activities. We conjecture that this collective identification stems in part from the continued nonnormative status of homosexuality. Normalization and routinization have, however, decentering collective effects. To the extent that homosexuality becomes a normalized thread of identity, we would expect a weakening identification of the gay 'community' with urban subcultures, as they have typically demanded a 'maximum' gay self-identification. In the context of normalizing and routinizing trends, the 'gay ghetto' (New York's West Village or San Francisco's Castro) becomes just one form of community, rather than the emblem of the gay community. We anticipate heightened contestation over the question of what the gay community signifies, which collective form represents this gay community, and who speaks for gay people.

Our research points to diverse patterns of group identification and integration. At one extreme are individuals who conceal or disassociate their homosexuality in a systematic (i.e. 'closeted') way. They report an abstract identification with a gay community, and exhibit a highly segmented collective involvement. Thus, David, 63 years old and reportedly happily married, expressed a collective identification by self-defining as gay even though his participation in this culture is limited to furtive sexual encounters. At the other extreme are individuals who have normalized and routinized their homosexuality to a considerable degree. They exhibit at least two clear patterns. First, individuals who have chosen to make their homosexuality into a primary identity evidence high levels of community integration. Gordon, an African-American in his mid-30s, found the Black community to be unfriendly towards gay individuals. He substituted a gay identity for the primary Black identity he learned while growing up. His primary group ties are with gay people. Second, individuals who define homosexuality as an aspect of identity exhibit degrees of collective identification from weak to strong but consistently weak social integration. Despite an emphatic normalizing of a gay identity, Rachel and Jeff publicly signal this identity almost exclusively symbolically—for example, by wearing a 'freedom ring' or attaching a rainbow sticker to their cars. For these individuals, homosexuality resembles white European ethnicity in contemporary America. Their link to a gay community is optional, partial, and symbolic. As with white ethnics, there will be an individualizing and symbolic marking of collective identification without extensive social obligations and integration.

We conclude by commenting on some political implications of normalizing and routinizing trends. Gay politics since Stonewall have been predominantly a version of identity politics. The gay movement has sought to legitimate homosexuality. In effect, sexual orientation has been collapsed into gender preference and gay politics into efforts to normalize a gay identity. The closet has served as a marker of the lack of homosexual legitimacy, while coming out has symbolized progress. We recognize that lesbian and gay politics in the post-Stonewall period has been far more varied. For example, gay liberationism was as much about challenging gender roles and capitalism as about legimating a homosexual identity. Lesbian feminism made the critique of male domination and the institution of the family pivotal to its politics (see Adam, 1987). Yet, it has been the politics of normalization and social integration that has dominated mainstream gay politics from the mid-1970s through the 1990s.

Political efforts to normalize a gay identity have had considerable success, despite continued institutional heterosexism, interpersonal intolerance, and subjective ambivalence. Hence, although we are critical of a unidimensional narrative of progress, our research underscores trends towards normalization and social inclusion. An immediate social impetus of these trends has been identity-based political mobilization—from efforts at civic and political legislation to antiviolence and cultural political strategies.

Paradoxically, these very trends have encouraged the decentering of gay identity politics. Specifically, while normalizing gay identities may consolidate a triumphant identity politic, it also encourages political strategies that marginalize such a politic. On the one hand, as gay identities are legitimated, movements organized around other discredited sexual practices such as bisexuality or S/M mobilize as independent sources of sexual identity, community, and politics. On the other hand, normalizing trends encourage a post-identity sexual politics. A gay politics focused exclusively on legitimating a gay identity leaves uncontested norms and practices regulating the ways homosexual and nonhomosexual bodies, pleasures, and intimate practices, including families, are organized.

The rise of queer politics in the 1990s represents a post-identity sexual politic (Seidman, 1997). It does not focus on legitimating identities but on challenging the regulatory power of norms of sexual health and normality. Embedded in medical, legal, criminal, familial, psychiatric, and state institutional practices are social norms that control behavior by pathologizing conduct—including consensual adult practices—that deviate from conventional or normalized gender, sexual, and intimate norms, e.g. S/M, phone sex, multiple-partner sex, or nonmarital, noncohabiting forms of 'family'. Queer political perspectives criticize sexual identity movements to the extent that they freeze identities thereby producing marginalizing and excluding effects, support a narrow range of ways of organizing bodies, pleasures, gendered selves, and intimacies, and do not question medical norms (normality and health) that invest sexual desires with moral significance and therefore legitimate extensive state and social institutional intervention. Queer politics do not signal the end of gay identity politics. Instead, we imagine an ongoing tension between sexual identity politics and forms of post-identity politics.

ACKNOWLEDGMENTS

We have benefitted greatly from the comments of Jeff Alexander, Margaret Cerullo, Steven Epstein, Josh Gamson, Linda Nicholson, and Arlene Stein.

NOTES

1. 'Homosexual' or 'gay' refers to a behavior or an acquired social identity. We do not assume that homosexuality per se makes individuals into a distinct personality or social type.

2. The interview was divided into three parts. The first obtained demographic information; the second part focused on concealment decisions at work, with friends and family, and in daily life; and the third part addressed disclosure practices and reactions.

Interviews were transcribed and analyzed. We looked for statements from respondents which were indicative of 'normalization' and 'interpersonal routinization'. An example of the former would be: 'I have now accepted my sexuality and if friends or family cannot accept it that's their problem'. Interpersonal routinization would be indicated by statements such as, 'everyone knows about my sexuality at work because I talk openly about it and even bring my partner to work social functions'. We also looked for responses which would highlight the incompleteness of these patterns. The statements included in this article are indicative of what we found throughout the interviews.

Of the 25 respondents, 13 were men, 12 were women; 19 were white, 6 were either Black or Hispanic; 9 could be classi-

fied as working or lower middle class, 16 as middle class; 6 respondents were aged 25 years or less, 11 were below 40, and 8 were older than 40.

3. The struggle against the closet is often said to create a shared experience of oppression and desire for freedom associated with coming out. The closet is therefore assumed to be a social fact whose meaning is uniform. However, there are reasons to suspect that social differences complicate this view. For example, some African-Americans emphasize unique racial aspects to the social patterns of homosexuality (Beam, 1986; Hemphill, 1991). The combination of the racism of a white-dominated gay community and the lack of institutionally elaborated black gay public cultures, along with the reserved public support of black elites, creates distinctive patterns of secrecy, disclosure, and identity formation. Similarly, Latina lesbians describe being situated between the racial worlds of black and white, the worlds of America and their nation of origin or identification, between their heterosexual families, which are solidaristic but homophobic, and lesbian communities that are racist, as shaping a unique social context for experiencing homosexuality (Ramos, 1987).

4. Whereas Chauncey argues that a public gay (fairy) culture declined to be replaced by a 'closeted' middle-class homosexual culture in the 1950s, the work of Kennedy and Davis (1993) maintains that working-class (butch) lesbians often live outside the closet.

REFERENCES

Adam, Barry (1987) *The Rise of a Gay and Lesbian Movement.* Boston, MA: Twayne.

Altman, Dennis (1971) *Homosexual Oppression and Liberation.* New York: Avon Books.

Badgett, M. V. and King, Mary (1997) 'Lesbian and Gay Occupational Strategies', in Amy Gluckman and Betsy Reed (eds) *Homo Economics,* pp. 73–86. New York: Routledge.

Beam, Joseph, ed. (1986) *In the Life.* Boston, MA: Alyson.

Borhek, Mary (1993) *Coming Out to Parents.* Cleveland, OH: Pilgrim Press.

Bravman, Scott (1997) *Queer Fictions of the Past.* Cambridge: Cambridge University Press.

Butler, Judith (1991) 'Imitation and Gender Insubordination', in Diana Fuss (ed.) *Inside/Out,* pp. 13–31. New York: Routledge.

Buxton, Amity (1994) *The Other Side of the Closet.* New York: John Wiley and Sons.

Cain, Roy (1991) 'Disclosure and Secrecy Among Gay Men in the United States and Canada: A Shift in Views', in John Fout and Maura Shaw Tantillo (eds) *American Sexual Politics,* pp. 289–309. Chicago, IL: University of Chicago Press.

Cammermayer, M. (1994) *Serving in Silence.* New York: Penguin.

Chauncey, George (1994) *Gay New York*. New York: Basic Books.

Davies, Peter (1992) 'The Role of Disclosure in Coming Out Among Gay Men', in Ken Plummer (ed.) *Modern Homosexualities*, pp. 75–83. London: Routledge.

DeCrescenzo, Teresa, ed. (1997) *The Social Service Closet*. Binghamton, NY: Haworth Press.

Delph, Edward (1978) *The Silent Community*. Beverly Hills, CA: Sage.

D'Emilio, John (1983) *Sexual Politics, Sexual Communities*. Chicago, IL: University of Chicago Press.

Escoffier, Jeff (1997) 'The Political Economy of the Closet: Notes Toward an Economic History of Gay and Lesbian Life Before Stonewall', in Amy Gluckman and Betsy Reed (eds) *Homo Economics*, pp. 123–34. New York: Routledge.

Esterberg, Kristin (1997) *Lesbian & Bisexual Identities*. Philadelphia, PA: Temple University Press.

Foucault, Michel (1980) *The History of Sexuality*, Vol. 1. New York: Pantheon.

Friskopp, Annette and Silverstein, Sharon (1995) *Straight Jobs, Gay Lives*. New York: Simon & Schuster.

Fuss, Diana (1991) 'Introduction', in *Inside/Out*, pp. 2–10. New York: Routledge.

Gross, Larry (1993) *Contested Closets*. Minneapolis: University of Minnesota Press.

Harbeck, Karen, ed. (1992) *Coming Out of the Classroom Closet*. New York: Haworth Press.

Herdt, Gilbert (1992) 'Coming Out as a Rite of Passage', in Gilbert Herdt (ed.) *Gay Culture in America*, pp. 124–50. Boston, MA: Beacon Press.

Hemphill, Essex (1991) 'Looking for Langston: An Interview with Isaac Julien', in Essex Hemphill and Joseph Beam (eds) *Brother to Brother*, pp. 174–83. Boston, MA: Alyson.

Herrell, Richard (1992) 'The Symbolic Strategies of Chicago's Gay and Lesbian Pride Day Parade', in Gilbert Herdt *Gay Culture in America*, pp. 225–52. Boston, MA: Beacon Press.

Hom, Alice (1996) 'Stories from the Homefront: Perspectives of Asian-American Parents with Lesbian Daughters and Gay Sons', in Russell Leong (ed.) *Asian American Sexualities*, pp. 37–50. New York: Routledge.

Humphreys, Laud (1970) *Tearoom Trade*. Chicago, IL: Aldine.

Humphreys, Laud (1972) *Out of the Closets*. Englewood Cliffs, NJ: Prentice Hall.

Jay, Karla and Young, Allen, eds (1972) 'Introduction', in *Out of the Closets and Into the Streets*. New York: Douglas.

Jenness, 0306Valerie (1992) 'Coming Out Lesbian Identities and the Categorization Problem', in Ken Plummer (ed.) *Modern Homosexualities*, pp. 65–74. New York: Routledge.

Johnson, Bret (1997) *Coming Out Every Day*. Oakland, CA: New Harrington Press.

Kaufman, Gershen and Raphael, Lev (1996) *Coming Out of Shame*. New York: Doubleday.

Kennedy, Elizabeth and Davis, Madeline (1993) *Boots of Leather, Slippers of Gold*. New York: Routledge.

Levine, Martin (1979) 'Gay Ghetto', in Martin Levine (ed.) *Gay Men*, pp. 182–204. New York: Harper and Row.

McRuer, Robert (1996) 'Boys Own Stories and New Spellings of My Name: Coming Out and Other Myths of Queer Positionality', in Carol Siegal and Ann Kibbey (eds) *Eroticism and Containment*, pp. 260–84. New York: Routledge.

Markowe, Laura (1996) *Redefining the Self*. London: Polity.

Miller, Merle (1971) *On Being Different*. New York: Random House.

Monette, Paul (1992) *Becoming a Man*. New York: Harper-Collins.

Penelope, Julia and Wolfe, Susan, eds (1989) *The Original Coming Out Stories*, 2nd edn. Freedom, CA: The Crossing Press.

Phelan, Shane (1993) '(Be)Coming Out: Lesbian Identity and Politics', *Signs* 18 (Summer): 765–90.

Plummer, Ken (1995) *Telling Sexual Stories*. London: Routledge.

Ponse, Barbara (1978) *Identities in the Lesbian World*. Westport, CT: Greenwood Press.

Ramos, Juanita, ed. (1987) *Companeras*. New York: Routledge.

Rust, Paula (1993) ' "Coming Out" in the Age of Social Constructionism: Sexual Identity Formation among Lesbian and Bisexual Women', *Gender and Society* 7 (March): 50–77.

Schneider, Beth (1984) 'Peril and Promise: Lesbians' Workplace Participation', in Trudy Darty and Sandee Potter (eds) *Women-Identified Women*, pp. 21–30. Palo Alto, CA: Mayfield.

Sedgwick, Eve (1990) *The Epistemology of the Closet*. Berkeley: University of California Press.

Seidman, Steven (1997) *Difference Troubles*. Cambridge: Cambridge University Press.

Signorile, Michelangelo (1993) *Queer in America*. New York: Random House.

Trujillo, Carla, ed. (1991) *Chicana Lesbians*. Third Women Press.

Vaid, Urvashi (1996) *Virtual Equality*. New York: Doubleday.

Whisman, Vera (1996) *Queer by Choice*. New York: Routledge.

Wolf, Deborah (1979) *The Lesbian Community*. Berkeley: University of California Press.

Woods, James with Lucas, Jay (1993) *The Corporate Closet*. New York: The Free Press.

Zimmerman, Bonnie (1984) 'The Politics of Transliteration: Lesbian Personal Narratives', *Signs* 9 (Summer): 663–82.

5.3 GAY AND LESBIAN RELATIONSHIPS

Letitia Anne Peplau, Rosemary C. Veniegas, and Susan Miller Campbell[1]

LOVE AND COMMITMENT

> The engraved invitation read, "After 20 years of love and life together, Emalee and Sarah would like to renew the vows they made to one another. You are invited to share in the joy of the 20th anniversary of their commitment ceremony. A reception and dinner at their home will follow the ceremony."

Love and companionship are important ingredients for a happy life. A national survey of Americans found that most people, regardless of sexual identity, consider love to be extremely important for their overall happiness (Freedman, 1978). Ample research documents that intimate relationships are a key factor in psychological health and happiness. In a recent review, Myers (1992) concluded, "Whether young or old, male or female, rich or poor, people in stable, loving relationships do enjoy greater well-being" (p. 156).

Many gay men and lesbians desire an enduring love relationship (Bell & Weinberg, 1978) and are successful in achieving this goal. Empirical surveys about intimate relationships report that 40% to 60% of gay men and 45% to 80% of lesbians are currently in a romantic relationship (Peplau & Cochran, 1990). These figures may underestimate the true proportions because most studies survey relatively young individuals, who may be less likely to have settled into a committed relationship. Studies that include older adults report that many lesbians and gay men establish lifelong partnerships (Blumstein & Schwartz, 1983; McWhirter & Mattison, 1984). For example, a study of lesbians over the age of 60 found relationships lasting 30 years and longer (Kehoe, 1989).

Love and Satisfaction

Many people believe that gay and lesbian relationships are unhappy. For example, one study found that heterosexual college students expected gay and lesbian relationships to be less satisfying and more prone to discord than heterosexual relationships, and they believed gay and lesbian couples to be "less in love" than heterosexual partners (Testa, Kinder, & Ironson, 1987). However, available research provides no evidence that same-sex couples are typically troubled or less successful than heterosexual couples.

Several studies have compared gay, lesbian, and heterosexual couples in order to investigate differences in the partners' love for each other and their satisfaction with the relationship. These studies often matched same-sex and heterosexual couples on age, income, and other background characteristics that might otherwise bias the results. In an illustrative study, Peplau and Cochran (1980) selected matched samples of 50 lesbians, 50 gay men, 50 heterosexual women, and 50 heterosexual men who were currently in a romantic/sexual relationship. Among this sample of young adults, about 60% said they were in love with their partner, and most of the rest said they were "uncertain" about whether they were in love. On Rubin's standardized Love and Liking Scales, the lesbians and gay men generally reported very positive feelings for their partners and rated their current relationships as highly satisfying and close. No significant differences were found among lesbians, gay men, and heterosexuals on any measure of relationship quality. Other studies using standardized measures of satisfaction, love, and adjustment have found the same pattern—no significant differences among couples based on sexual orientation. Gay men and lesbians report as much satisfaction with their relationships as do heterosexuals (Cardell, Finn, & Marecek, 1981; Dailey, 1979; Duffy & Rusbult, 1986; Kurdek & Schmitt, 1986a, 1986b, 1987; Peplau & Cochran, 1980; Peplau, Padesky, & Hamilton, 1982).

Thus, contrary to prevailing stereotypes, research indicates that most gay and lesbian couples are happy.

These findings do not imply that all gay men and lesbians have problem-free relationships. As reported later in this chapter, there are sources of conflict in same-sex relationships, just as there are in heterosexual relationships. Rather, the point is that lesbians and gay men are no more likely than heterosexuals to have dysfunctional relationships.

In the last decade, researchers have begun to identify factors that enhance satisfaction in same-sex relationships. Social exchange theory predicts that satisfaction is high when a person perceives that a relationship provides many rewards, such as a partner's intelligence, interesting personality, sense of humor, or sex appeal. Satisfaction is also high when a relationship entails relatively few costs, for instance, when conflict is low and a partner has few irritating behaviors. Several studies have found that perceived rewards and costs are significant predictors of happiness in lesbians' and gay men's relationships (Kurdek, 1991a; Kurdek & Schmitt, 1986a). For example, Duffy and Rusbult (1986) compared the relationships of lesbians, gay men, and heterosexuals. In all three groups, greater satisfaction was significantly associated with the experience of relatively more personal rewards and fewer personal costs. In a study of lesbian relationships, Peplau et al. (1982) found support for another exchange theory prediction, that satisfaction is higher when partners are equally involved in or committed to a relationship.

Other correlates of satisfaction in gay and lesbian relationships have been investigated as well. For example, partners' values about relationships can make a difference. Individuals vary in the degree to which they value "dyadic attachment" (Peplau, Cochran, Rook, & Padesky, 1978). A person is high in attachment to the extent that he or she emphasizes the importance of shared activities, spending time together, long-term commitment, and sexual exclusivity in a relationship. Lesbians and gay men who strongly value togetherness and security in a relationship report significantly higher satisfaction, closeness, and love for their partner than do individuals who score lower on attachment values (Eldridge & Gilbert, 1990; Peplau et al., 1978; Peplau & Cochran, 1981).

Individuals can also differ in the degree to which they value personal autonomy, defined as wanting to have separate friends and activities apart from their primary relationship. Although some studies have found that lesbians and gay men who place strong emphasis on autonomy report significantly lower love and satisfaction than individuals who score lower on autonomy values (Eldridge & Gilbert, 1990; Kurdek, 1989), other studies have not (Peplau et al., 1978; Peplau & Cochran, 1981).

There may also be links between the balance of power in a relationship and partners' satisfaction. Several studies of lesbians and gay men have found that satisfaction is higher when partners believe they share relatively equally in power and decision-making (Eldridge & Gilbert, 1990; Harry, 1984; Kurdek, 1989; Kurdek & Schmitt, 1986a; Peplau et al., 1982.) Finally, a recent study suggests that happy and unhappy couples may differ in their approach to problem-solving (Kurdek, 1991a). In both lesbian and gay relationships, satisfied partners were more likely than unhappy partners to use positive problem-solving approaches, such as focusing on the specific problem at hand. Partners in happy couples were less likely than other couples to use such negative approaches as launching a personal attack, growing defensive, or withdrawing from the interaction.

Commitment

It is estimated that roughly one in every two recent heterosexual marriages will end in divorce (Martin & Bumpass, 1989). These figures are a forceful reminder that romantic relationships do not necessarily last "until death do us part" or even for a very long time. How do lesbians and gay men fare in their efforts to maintain enduring intimate relationships? Those interested in heterosexual relationships can use official marriage records and census reports to chart the length of relationships, but comparable data are not available for gay men and lesbians.

One of the few large-scale studies of lesbian, gay, and heterosexual couples (Blumstein & Schwartz, 1983) assessed the stability of relationships over an 18-month period. For couples who had already been together for at least 10 years, the breakup rate was quite low: Only 6% of lesbian couples, 4% of gay couples, and 4% of married couples separated during the 18-month period. Among couples together for 2 years or less, some differences in the breakup rates were found: 22% for lesbian couples, 16% for gay couples, 17% for heterosexual cohabiting couples, and 4% for married couples. It is noteworthy that the largest difference among these short-term couples was not between heterosexual and same-sex couples, but rather between legally married couples and unmarried couples, regardless of sexual orientation.

Relationship researchers have identified several factors that affect the longevity of intimate relationships and that help to explain the greater duration of legally married couples (e.g., Levinger, 1979). A first factor concerns positive attraction forces that make one want to stay with a partner, such as love and satisfaction with the relationship. As we noted earlier, research shows that same-sex and male-female couples typically report comparable levels of happiness in their relationships.

Second, the duration of a relationship is also affected by barriers that make it difficult for a person to leave a relationship. Barriers include anything that increases the psychological, emotional, or financial costs of ending a relationship. Heterosexual marriage can create many barriers to separation, such as the cost of divorce, investments in joint property, concerns about children, and one partner's financial dependence on the other. These obstacles may encourage married couples to work toward improving a deteriorating relationship, rather than ending it. In contrast, gay and lesbian couples are less likely to experience comparable barriers to the ending of a relationship—they cannot marry legally, they are less likely to co-own property, their relatives may prefer that they end their relationship, they are less likely to have children in common, and so on.

Kurdek and Schmitt (1986a) systematically compared the attractions and barriers experienced by partners in gay, lesbian, and heterosexual cohabiting couples and in married couples. They found no differences across the four groups in attractions; all groups reported comparable feelings of love and satisfaction. However, barriers, assessed by statements such as "many things would prevent me from leaving my partner even if I were unhappy," differed. Married couples

reported significantly more barriers than either gay men or lesbians, and cohabiting heterosexual couples reported the fewest barriers of all. Similarly, in their study of lesbian, gay, and heterosexual couples, Blumstein and Schwartz (1983) found that couples who pooled some or all of their financial assets together were less likely to break up. Not surprisingly, married heterosexuals were the couples most likely to have joint finances. In a recent longitudinal study of cohabiting lesbian and gay couples followed over a four-year period, Kurdek (1992) also found that couples who pooled their finances were less likely to break up.

A third factor affecting the longevity of a relationship is the availability of alternatives to the present relationship. To the extent that people want to be involved in an intimate relationship, having fewer potential partners available may encourage partners to work out their problems. In contrast, a person who believes that many attractive partners are readily available or who would be just as happy single may be quicker to end a relationship. Only two studies have compared the perception of available alternatives among gay, lesbian, and heterosexual couples, and they differ in their findings. One study found that lesbians and married couples reported significantly fewer alternatives than did gay men and heterosexual cohabitants (Kurdek & Schmitt, 1986a). In contrast, a second study found no significant differences among lesbians, gay men, and heterosexuals—all of whom reported having moderately poor alternatives (Duffy & Rusbult, 1986).

In summary, research finds that gay and lesbian couples can and do have committed, enduring relationships. On average, heterosexual and same-sex couples report similar high levels of attraction toward their partner and satisfaction with their relationship. Couples differ, however, in the obstacles that make it difficult to end a relationship. Here, the legal and social context of marriage creates barriers to breaking up that do not typically exist for same-sex partners or for cohabiting heterosexuals. The relative lack of barriers may make it less likely that lesbians and gay men will be trapped in hopelessly miserable and deteriorating relationships. However, weaker barriers may also allow partners to end relationships that might have improved if given more time and effort. As lesbians and gay men gain greater recognition as "domestic partners," the barriers for gay and lesbian relationships may become more similar to those of heterosexuals. Currently, for example, several large companies have extended health benefits to same-sex domestic partners and increasing numbers of lesbian couples are raising children jointly (see Patterson, this volume). The impact of such trends on the stability of same-sex relationships is an important topic for further investigation.

POWER AND THE DIVISION OF LABOR

Jim is deeply in love with Tom, and the two have been together for almost a year. When Jim suggested that they move in together, Tom gave excuses. Jim wonders just how much Tom cares for him and tries hard to make their relationship work. When they disagree about something, Jim usually gives in and lets Tom have his way, rather than risking an argument.

Power

Who has more say in a relationship? Does one partner dominate the other? Researchers have studied the balance of power, that is, the general way in which power is distributed in a relationship. Today, many Americans endorse power equality as an ideal for love relationships, and this emphasis on egalitarianism is especially strong among young adults. For example, Peplau and Cochran (1980) compared the relationship values of matched samples of young lesbians, gay men, and heterosexuals. All groups rated "having an egalitarian (equal power) relationship" as quite important. When asked what the ideal balance of power should be in their current relationship, 92% of gay men and 97% of lesbians said it should be "exactly equal." Not everyone, however, was successful in attaining this egalitarian ideal. Only 59% of lesbians, 38% of gay men, 48% of heterosexual women, and 40% of heterosexual men reported that their current relationship was "exactly equal." The percentage of people who describe their relationship as equal in power has varied across studies. For instance, equal power was reported by 59% of the 140 lesbians studied by Reilly and Lynch (1990) and by 60% of the 243 gay men studied by Harry and DeVall (1978).

Several factors can tip the balance of power away from equality. Social exchange theory predicts that greater power accrues to the partner who has relatively greater personal resources, such as education, money, or social standing. Several studies have provided empirical support for this hypothesis. In two separate studies of gay men, Harry found that unequal decision-making was associated with partner differences in age and income; men who were older and wealthier tended to have more power than their partner (Harry, 1984; Harry & DeVall, 1978). Similarly, in their large-scale study of couples, Blumstein and Schwartz (1983) concluded that "in gay male couples, income is an extremely important force in determining which partner will be dominant" (p. 59). For lesbians, research findings on personal resources and power are less clear-cut. A study of 77 young adult lesbians in Los Angeles found that differences in income and education were significantly related to power (Caldwell & Peplau, 1984). Another study reported that perceptions of which partner had "more say" were unrelated to education or age but were associated with large differences between the income of the two women (Reilly & Lynch, 1990). In contrast, Blumstein and Schwartz (1983) concluded, "Lesbians do not use income to establish dominance in their relationship. They use it to avoid having one woman dependent on the other" (p. 60). Further research on the balance of power among lesbian couples is needed to clarify these inconsistent results.

A second prediction from social exchange theory is that when one person in a relationship is relatively more dependent or involved than the other, the dependent person will be at a power disadvantage. This has been called the "principle of least interest" because the less interested person tends to have more power. Studies of heterosexuals have clearly demonstrated that lopsided dependencies are linked to imbalances of power (e.g., Peplau & Campbell, 1989). To date, only one study has tested this hypothesis with same-sex couples. Among the young lesbians studied by Caldwell and Peplau (1984), there was a strong association between unequal involvement and unequal power, with the less involved person having more power.

Another approach to understanding power in relationships focuses on the specific tactics that partners use to influence each other. For example, Falbo and Peplau (1980) asked lesbians, gay men, and heterosexuals to describe how they influence their romantic partner to do what they want. These open-ended descriptions were reliably categorized into several influence strategies. The results led to two major conclusions. First, gender affected power tactics, but only among heterosexuals. Whereas heterosexual women were more likely to withdraw or express negative emotions, heterosexual men were more likely to use bargaining or reasoning. But this sex difference did not emerge in comparisons of lesbians and gay men influencing their same-sex partner. Second, regardless of gender or sexual orientation, individuals who perceived themselves as relatively more powerful in the relationship tended to use persuasion and bargaining. In contrast, partners low in power tended to use withdrawal and emotion.

Another study comparing the intimate relationships of lesbians, gay men, and heterosexuals also found that an individual's use of influence tactics depended on his or her relative power in the relationship (Howard, Blumstein, & Schwartz, 1986). Regardless of sexual orientation, a partner with relatively less power tended to use "weak" strategies such as supplication and manipulation. Those in positions of strength were more likely to use autocratic and bullying tactics, both "strong" strategies. Further, individuals with male partners (i.e., heterosexual women and gay men) were more likely to use supplication and manipulation. Similarly, Kollock, Blumstein, and Schwartz (1985) found that signs of conversational dominance, such as interrupting a partner in the middle of a sentence, were linked to the balance of power. Although interruption has sometimes been viewed as a male behavior, it was actually used more often by the dominant person in the relationship, regardless of that person's gender or sexual orientation. Taken together, the results suggest that although some influence strategies have been stereotyped as masculine or feminine, they may more correctly be viewed as a reflection of power rather than gender.

Division of Labor

All couples face decisions about who will do what in their life together. For a dating couple these decisions range from who will do the driving to who will take the lead in initiating sexual intimacy. When a couple decides to live together, new questions arise about responsibilities for housework, finances, and entertaining guests. Traditional sex roles have provided ready-made answers to these questions for heterosexuals—the man is the leader and breadwinner and the woman is the follower and homemaker. Heterosexuals who reject traditional roles may find that it takes considerable effort to forge new patterns of relating.

How do gay and lesbian couples organize their lives together? Tripp noted, "When people who are not familiar with homosexual relationships try to picture one, they almost invariably resort to a heterosexual frame of reference, raising questions about which partner is 'the man' and which 'the woman'" (1975, p. 152). Historical accounts of gay life in the United States before the advent of gay rights organizations and the modern feminist movement suggest that masculine-feminine roles were fairly common (see Jacobson & Grossman, this volume). For example, Wolf (1980) described lesbian experiences in the 1950s in these terms:

> The old gay world divided up into "butch" and "femme." . . . Butches were tough, presented themselves as being as masculine as possible . . . and they assumed the traditional male role of taking care of their partners, even fighting over them if necessary. . . . Femmes, by contrast, were protected, ladylike. . . . They cooked, cleaned house, and took care of their "butch." (p. 40)

Today, most lesbians and gay men actively reject traditional husband-wife or masculine-feminine roles as a model for enduring relationships (Blumstein & Schwartz, 1983; Harry, 1983, 1984; McWhirter & Mattison, 1984; Peplau & Gordon, 1983).

Most lesbians and gay men are in dual-worker relationships, so that neither partner is the exclusive breadwinner and each partner has some measure of economic independence. The most common division of labor involves flexibility, with partners sharing domestic activities or dividing tasks according to personal preferences. For example, in Bell and Weinberg's (1978) study nearly 60% of lesbians and gay men said that housework was shared equally. Asked if one partner consistently does all the "feminine tasks" or all the "masculine tasks," about 90% of lesbians and gay men said "no." Indeed, some gay men and lesbians report that one of the things they appreciate about same-sex relationships is being able to avoid traditional roles: "Role playing seems to me by nature to involve dominance and control," one gay man explained, "both of which make me feel uncomfortable" (Jay & Young, 1977, p. 369). A lesbian explained that she and her partner joke about butch-femme roles. "She will say, 'Well, I guess I'm the femme today,' but we really aren't into role playing at all. . . . If we see couples into butch-femme relationships, we go, 'Oh, yick!'" (Blumstein & Schwartz, 1983, p. 451).

Several researchers have suggested that today many lesbians and gay men base their relationships on a friendship model (Harry, 1983, Peplau, 1991). In best friendships, partners are often of relatively similar age and share common interests, skills, and resources. Unlike traditional marriages, best friendships are usually similar in status and power.

Additional research about the division of labor in same-sex relationships is needed. One particularly valuable direction for inquiry is the examination of the ways in which same-sex couples juggle the various responsibilities they have to their partner, job, children, aging parents, and community activities (e.g. Shachar & Gilbert, 1983). When both spouses in a heterosexual marriage have full-time jobs, women shoulder the majority of housework and child care, creating a substantial imbalance in workload (Crosby, 1991). Perhaps an understanding of the more egalitarian division of labor in same-sex relationships will provide clues about how all couples can arrive at a more equitable sharing of responsibilities.

PROBLEMS AND CONFLICT

Joan and Kate have lived together for six years. Joan's career as an attorney frequently takes her out of town and Kate's work as a librarian at a local college is also very demanding. Increasingly Joan and Kate have little time to spend with each other. They often argue out of frustration and fear that their relationship is headed for a breakup. Both women are unwilling to compromise their careers but do not want to lose the relationship.

Disagreements and conflicts occur in all intimate relationships. A study of heterosexual newlyweds identified 85 different types of conflicts (Gottman, 1979). Among lesbian and gay couples, the range of possible conflicts is probably equally large. Because most of the available information about problems in lesbian and gay relationships comes from reports by therapists about their clients, the full range of problems encountered in same-sex partnerships may not be represented. Issues described in the literature include differences in background or values, concerns about finances or work, sexual problems, jealously or possessiveness, and problems with family members (Berger, 1990; Berzon, 1988; Browning, Reynolds, & Dworkin, 1991; George & Behrendt, 1988). In short, many problems in same-sex relationships are similar to those in heterosexual relationships. There are, however, problems specific to same-sex couples. We consider two problems that arise from gender socialization and from homophobia.

Merger and Competition

Some authors have speculated that the gender socialization of men and women may create unique problems for same-sex couples that are not encountered by heterosexuals. For example, it has been suggested that lesbians are at special risk of becoming overly involved and identified with each other, in part because our society teaches women to value intimacy and emotional closeness. Evidence for this point comes from clinicians who work with lesbian couples in therapy and have described a problem called "merger," "fusion," or "enmeshment" (Falco, 1991; Krestan & Bepko, 1980; Roth, 1984; Smalley, 1987). *Merger* has been defined as "the difficulty of maintaining separate identities within the relationship, and a tendency for merging in thoughts, actions, or feelings" (Browning et al., 1991, p. 185). In therapy, merger is inferred when partners seem to be too emotionally close, or when partners appear confused about their individual feelings, opinions, or personal identity. Burch (1986) provided the following illustration of a merger problem:

Judith and Maria both complained that they did not follow their own desires because that would disturb the other. Maria said, "She makes me feel guilty when I go out with my friends without her, so I can't do it." Judith said, "I can't tell Maria when I'm unhappy because she takes it so personally." (p. 60)

Burch noted that merger can occur in all types of relationships but suggested that lesbians have a greater tendency toward enmeshment because of their psychological development as women and because the larger society does not recognize or value lesbian relationships. These clinical reports illustrate that merger can be a problem for some lesbian couples. However, in the absence of systematic research comparing the frequency of merger problems among lesbians and among heterosexual couples, the claim that this problem is more common among lesbians remains untested.

It has been suggested that gay couples are vulnerable to unique problems that result from men's traditional socialization. For instance, Hawkins (1992) linked male socialization for achievement, competitiveness, sex, and aggression to problems commonly reported by therapists who work with gay couples, including conflicts over finances or jobs, anger and violence, jealousy, and sexual difficulties. Hawkins also commented on gay men's communication skills, asserting that male socialization "leaves men ill-equipped to deal with relationships. . . . When two men then try to build a relationship, the problem is compounded because both are lacking in the interpersonal skills needed" (p. 82). Other clinicians have also emphasized that gay couples have problems because of adherence to stereotypic male roles (e. g., George & Behrendt, 1987; Shannon & Woods, 1991).

Although these speculations and clinical observations about problems in gay couples are intuitively plausible, counterevidence is also available. For instance, in interviews with 156 gay couples not in therapy, McWhirter and Mattison (1982) found no pervasive lack of verbal expressiveness. "In fact gay men have a tendency to over-communicate with each other. At times they process their feelings and behaviors 'to death,' causing relationship fatigue and distress" (p. 88). Systematic research is needed to test the accuracy, prevalence, and generalizability of clinical beliefs about gender-linked problems in gay and lesbian couples.

Coming Out and Being Out

Bill and Roger have lived together for a year. Bill is active in a local gay political organization and regularly asks Roger to attend organization events with him. Roger refuses because he fears that his boss or family might find out that he is gay. When Roger's parents visit, he asks Bill to spend the week with friends. The couple had a major fight about Roger's decision not to come out to his family, and Bill stomped out of the apartment without packing any of his things.

Society's negative attitudes toward homosexuality create problems for gay and lesbian couples. A common dilemma for lesbians and gay men concerns whether to reveal their sexual orientation to friends, family, coworkers, and others in their social network. Decisions about whether to "come out" or "be out" about their relationship can be a source of conflict for gay and lesbian couples.

Reports by therapists have identified ways in which disclosure about one's sexual orientation can affect relationships. In some couples, partners disagree about how much they want to reveal about themselves and their relationship. For example, Roger prefers to keep his relationship hidden, fearing harassment at work or rejection by his parents. Bill prefers a more open approach. Disagreements of this sort can be particularly stressful; the less open partner may feel pressured into more disclosure than is comfortable, and the more open partner may interpret the other's fear of disclosure as a lack of commitment to the relationship (Murphy, 1992; Shannon & Woods, 1991). As an illustration, Decker (1984) explained that if one member of a couple wants to give a party for coworkers at home and expects the other to pretend that he or she is "just a roommate," confusion, anger, and depression may result.

Even when partners agree about the extent to which they will be open, problems can arise because of negative reactions from family, friends, or coworkers. Murphy (1989) found that the anticipation of negative reactions from parents created stress in lesbian relationships. Writing about a woman whose father disapproves of her lesbianism, Murphy (1989) reported, "She and her lover felt so much conflict about seeing her father that they would fight with each other 'over any stupid thing' before visiting him" (p. 48). Many therapists believe that resolving issues about "outness" is central to a successful same-sex relationship (e.g., George & Behrendt, 1988; Murphy, 1992; Shannon & Woods, 1991).

Belonging to an ethnic-minority group can make coming out even more difficult (see Manalansan, this volume). Two small studies have suggested that gay and lesbian Asian Americans may experience considerable stress concerning coming out (Chan, 1989; Wooden, Kawasaki, & Mayeda, 1983). On the one hand, Asian American place great importance on family and community relationships and so being cut off from these ties is a serious threat. On the other hand, Asian American culture is extremely negative about homosexuality, and individuals who identify openly as gay or lesbian risk bringing shame not only on themselves but also on their family and community. As one Asian American explained, "I wish I could tell my parents—they are the only ones who do not know about my gay identity, but I am sure they would reject me. There is no frame of reference to understand homosexuality in Asian American culture" (Chan, 1989, p. 19). Thus, the common fears of lesbians and gay men that coming out may lead to rejection and stigmatization may be heightened for Asian Americans and members of other ethnic groups that emphasize strong family ties and have strong antigay attitudes.

Violence and Partner Abuse

"The fighting began with intense arguments that were devastating. . . . When she was angry it was like being stabbed in the chest. She was the source of that pain; she was also the only source of comfort, understanding and affirmation of love. . . . One day we had an argument, and she hit me. We were on my motorcycle, I was driving, and all I could think was what an insane thing it was—to hit my arm and risk our lives." (Lisa, 1986, p. 38)

In some relationships conflicts escalate into psychological abuse and physical violence. Estimates of battering and prolonged physical abuse in heterosexual relationships range from 25% to 33% (Herbert,

Silver, & Ellard, 1991; Koss, 1990). Adequate information about the frequency of abuse in gay and lesbian relationships is not currently available. Understandably, some lesbians and gay men have been reluctant to discuss violence in same-sex couples for fear of contributing to negative attitudes toward homosexuality. In a book about violence in lesbian relationships, Hart (1986) explained, "We recognized how threatening the reality of lesbian battering was to our dream of lesbian utopia—a nonviolent, fairly androgynous . . . community struggling for social justice" (p. 13). Nonetheless, there is growing evidence that violence is a problem for some lesbian and gay couples (e.g., Kanuha, 1990; Lobel, 1986; Morrow & Hawxhurst, 1989; Renzetti, 1992; Waterman, Dawson, & Bologna, 1989).

As in heterosexual relationships, abuse in same-sex couples can take many forms, including verbal abuse (e.g., demeaning the partner in front of others), negative actions (e.g., destroying partners' property), sexual coercion, and physical violence. Many of the same factors that contribute to heterosexual partner abuse appear to affect violence in gay and lesbian couples. For example, the misuse of alcohol or drugs is a common precursor to violence. Jealously, dependency, and dominance may also contribute to abuse (Renzetti, 1992; Schilit, Lie, & Montagne, 1990). Individuals who stay in an abusive relationship often report that they are socially isolated and have no one to turn to for help. In addition, homophobia may create unique problems for lesbians and gay men who face violence in a relationship. For example, Renzetti (1982) reported that many of the abused lesbians she studied did not turn to their family for help. In some cases, the family did not know that the woman had a lesbian partner. In other cases, the family knew that a woman was lesbian but the woman nonetheless chose not to seek help from relatives because she feared that knowledge of the battering would reinforce their negative, homophobic attitudes.

More research is needed to clarify the magnitude of the problem of abuse in gay and lesbian couples and to understand the factors that contribute to this violence. To date, most published studies of violence in same-sex relationships have investigated lesbian relationships. Even less is known about abuse in gay relationships. Also needed are better community services to help lesbians and gay men who are victims of abuse. Currently, social service agencies lack adequate information and resources to address gay and lesbian battering (Hammond, 1988). Indeed, existing shelters for battered women are often hesitant to extend services to lesbians (Lobel, 1986; Renzetti, 1992). Although public discussion of battering in same-sex couples is relatively new, it is already apparent that violence is a significant problem.

WHEN RELATIONSHIPS END

> Jennifer and Michelle lived together for two years. Their relationship was always stormy, but both women tried to work out their problems. Finally deciding that the relationship would never get any better, Jennifer moved out last weekend. Jennifer feels guilty about ending the relationship but is relieved that their stressful fights are over. Michelle was very surprised by Jennifer's decision and feels deeply hurt and depressed.

Couples who have dated casually may break up after a few months. More enduring relationships may end as partners grow apart or discover incompatibilities. Sadly, relationships of any length can end tragically when a partner dies. During the current AIDS epidemic, bereavement has become an all too familiar experience for many gay couples. In this section, we examine research about the experience of breaking up and bereavement in gay and lesbian couples.

Breaking Up

Relationships end for diverse reasons, many of which have been considered in our discussion of the problems and conflicts experienced in gay and lesbian relationships. Two studies have specifically addressed the reasons lesbian and gay partners give for a breakup. In one study, 50 lesbians rated the extent to which each of 17 possible factors had contributed to the ending of a past relationship (Peplau et al., 1983). Among this sample of young lesbians (median age 26), who may not have been ready for a permanent commitment, issues of independence were the most important factor cited. One half of the women rated their desire to be independent as a major factor, and nearly one third

indicated that their partner's desire to be independent was a major factor. A second theme concerned differences between the partners in interests (36%), attitudes about sex (24%), background (17%), intelligence (10%), and/or political views (7%). These findings highlight the potential importance of similarity for relationship satisfaction among lesbians, a point amply documented among heterosexuals (Brehm, 1992). Perhaps surprising in light of society's hostility toward homosexuality, issues about being lesbian were not commonly cited as reasons for a breakup. Less than 20% of women cited as a major factor their feelings about being a lesbian, 14% cited "societal attitudes toward lesbian relationships," and only 2% cited pressure from their parents.

In a longitudinal study of cohabiting couples, Kurdek (1991b) investigated factors contributing to the breakup of lesbian and gay relationships. Although only 12 gay men and 14 lesbians were included in this breakup sample, the results offer preliminary evidence about the reasons for dissolution. In open-ended descriptions of reasons for the breakup, the most common themes were nonresponsiveness (e.g., "There was no communication between us and little support"), partner problems (e.g., "He had a big drug and alcohol problem"), and sexual issues (e.g., "She had an affair"). Participants also rated the importance of 11 specific issues that might have contributed to their separation. Highest ratings were given for the partner's frequent absence, sexual incompatibility, mental cruelty, and lack of love. Kurdek noted that these diverse explanations for separation are similar to those reported in studies of heterosexuals.

A final source of information about factors leading to breakups is a large-scale study of lesbian and gay couples conducted by Blumstein and Schwartz (1983). They followed a sample of 493 gay and 335 lesbian couples for an 18-month period and compared those who ended their relationship to those who stayed together. Money mattered: Couples who argued about money, fought about their level of income, and did not pool their finances were more likely to break up than other couples. The partners' commitment to their jobs was also a factor. Couples who said that work intruded into their relationship were more likely to break up, and partners who were more ambitious and spent more time at work were more likely to leave the relationship. In contrast, couples who spent a lot of time together were more likely to survive the test of time. Sexual satisfaction also contributed to the longevity of a relationship.

The ending of an important relationship is usually an emotion-laden experience. In the Kurdek study (1991b), participants rated their emotions following separation. The most common negative emotional reactions were loneliness, confusion, anger, guilt, and helplessness. Common positive emotions included personal growth, relief from conflict, increased happiness, and independence. Research with heterosexual dating couples found similar emotional reactions (Hill, Rubin, & Peplau, 1976). This study also showed that the kind of emotional reactions experienced depend on the part that each person played in the breakup: Individuals who had initiated the breakup were more likely to feel guilty, free, and happy, whereas partners who wanted to continue the relationship but were left behind felt lonelier and more depressed.

The severity of emotional reactions to a breakup depends on many factors. Kurdek (1991b) found that lesbians and gay men who placed great emphasis on attachment to a partner had more difficult emotional reactions than did individuals who gave less emphasis to attachment (see also Peplau & Cochran, 1981). In addition, individuals had a more difficult emotional adjustment when their relationship had been of longer duration, when the couple had pooled their finances, and when they had felt greater love for their partner.

The Death of a Partner

One of the most stressful events in life is the death of a spouse (Holmes & Rahe, 1967). Much is known about the psychological reactions of heterosexuals to bereavement and about the sources of social support usually available to a grieving spouse. When a heterosexual partner dies, a period of public grieving is commonly allowed. In addition to the support of friends and family, widows and widowers can turn to religious institutions and to self-help groups for the widowed. There is no reason to believe that the emotional anguish of bereavement is different for lesbians and gay men who lose a beloved partner. After the death

of her partner of 15 years, one older lesbian reacted the following way:

> I became a hermit. For at least a year I wept when I looked at anyone—this I hid—but I still became depressed. For several years I frequently visited the mausoleum and talked to her (No one else around). My work is my savior. (Kehoe, 1989, p. 49)

Although the personal pain of loss may be similar for people regardless of their sexual orientation, the social circumstances of bereavement often differ considerably.

Same-sex partners who have been closeted about their relationship may receive little social support. They may be unable to talk about the nature of their loss or the meaning that it has for them. According to mental health professionals, their grief may never be adequately expressed and so the period of mourning may be prolonged (McDonald & Steinhorn, 1990). Even when lesbian and gay partners have been open about their relationship, a surviving partner may encounter difficulties. For example, they may not be granted bereavement leave from work. Without legal documents such as wills or joint insurance policies, widowed partners may not have rights to their joint property (see Rubenstein, this volume). Even when partners take legal precautions, problems can still arise. An older woman who had been named the beneficiary of her lover's part in the house and business they owned together explained:

> Her will is being contested by her family and the property we had in joint ownership is in litigation. Even the burial plans were overruled by them, and they finally made the medical decision to remove her life support systems. (Kehoe, 1989, p. 49)

A gay man described the problems created by the family of his lover:

> Not two months after he died they were accusing me of stealing from him and demanding a complete accounting for the money spent during the time he was sick. . . . Right after the funeral, . . . they wanted to get into the apartment . . . as if it was his house, not mine. . . . I really wonder, do straight people go through this, or is there more respect? (Shelby, 1992, p. 146)

Currently, information on the bereavement process for lesbians and gay men remains sparse. Clinicians are only beginning to develop therapeutic approaches to help lesbians and gay men who have lost their partners (Saunders, 1990; Siegal & Hoefer, 1981).

Losing a Partner to AIDS

Gary's partner Miguel recently died from AIDS. Gary had cared for Miguel through the night sweats, delusions, and pain. As he watched over Miguel every night, Gary asked himself why he had not gotten the virus. He felt guilty for being the healthy one and sometimes wished that he also had AIDS.

Because the AIDS epidemic struck first in the United States in gay communities, many gay men have lost a loved partner to this disease. The difficulties of bereavement are heightened when AIDS is the cause of death, both because victims tend to die at an untimely young age and because of the social stigma of AIDS (Stulberg & Smith, 1988). Before the AIDS crisis, it would have been unusual for a young adult to confront the death of many friends to disease. But in many gay communities, attendance at funerals has become a familiar part of life. A study of 745 gay men in New York City found that nearly one third had suffered the loss of a lover or close friend to AIDS. Some had experienced multiple losses. The more people an individual knew who had died of AIDS, the greater the person's risk of experiencing serious psychological distress, including anxiety, depression, sleep problems, and increased use of recreational drugs and sedatives (Martin, 1988).

An additional problem experienced by some surviving partners and friends has been termed "survivor guilt" (Wayment, Silver, & Kemeny, 1994). Men who have engaged in risky sexual behavior but do not test positive for HIV may believe that they "should" be HIV positive and have been spared by chance. As one man explained:

As a surviving partner, one whose number of living friends has dwindled steadily from 1983 to 'mostly deceased by 1989,' I'm here to tell you that the stress and anxiety are real. It's very difficult to figure out why some of us are left and others are not, especially when we all did the same things. (p. 21)

Experts acknowledge that professional services to assist people whose partners have died from AIDS are inadequate (Kubler-Ross, 1987).

COUPLES COUNSELING

Lesbians and gay men seek counseling for many of the same relationship problems as do heterosexuals. Yet their experiences in therapy can be quite different because gay men and lesbians often confront antihomosexual bias from therapists. Only recently have clinicians begun to acknowledge this problem and to create gay and lesbian affirmative approaches to therapy. Another recent trend has been the development of couples counseling for same-sex partners.

Bias in Psychotherapy

Karen began seeing a psychotherapist because she was having problems in her relationship with Amy. The therapist, believing that homosexuality reflects psychological immaturity, encouraged Karen to break up with Amy. The therapist told Karen that her affair with Amy was just a "phase" she would outgrow and advised Karen to start dating men.

The process of psychotherapy is inevitably influenced by the values and biases of the therapist (Murray & Abramson, 1983). A large-scale survey of members of the American Psychological Association identified many ways in which therapists sometimes provide biased and inadequate care to lesbian and gay clients (Garnets, Hancock, Cochran, Goodchilds, & Peplau, 1991). For instance, therapists may view a client's homosexuality as a sign of psychological disorder, trivialize or demean gay and lesbian lifestyles, or be poorly informed about lesbian and gay identity development and the societal context of antihomosexual prejudice. When relationship problems are the reason for entering therapy, lesbians and gay men may encounter additional types of bias (DeCrescenzo 1983/1984; Falco, 1991; Ussher, 1991). A therapist may underestimate the importance of intimate relationships for gay men and lesbians or regard same-sex partnerships as unhealthy or transient. A therapist may be insensitive to the nature and diversity of lesbian and gay relationships, perhaps relying on inaccurate stereotypes about masculine and feminine roles in same-sex couples (Eldridge, 1987). In addition, a therapist may fail to consider couples counseling when it might be more appropriate than individual psychotherapy. Therapists who are themselves gay or lesbian are not necessarily invulnerable to these biases (Anthony, 1981/1982; Stein, 1988).

Affirmative Therapies for Lesbian and Gay Couples

> Peter started seeing a therapist because of increasing conflicts with his lover, Sean. They argued a lot about money, housework, and sexual values. The therapist suggested that Sean and Peter consider couples counseling so they could work together to solve their problems.

Some therapists believe that it is not enough to provide unbiased therapy for lesbians and gay men. Rather, clinicians should go further by developing approaches to therapy that affirm the value and legitimacy of gay and lesbian lifestyles. Gay and lesbian affirmative psychotherapies place importance on the development of a positive gay or lesbian identity in the context of loving and healthy relationships with same-sex others (DeCrescenzo, 1983/1984; Malyon, 1981/1982). Affirmative therapists are especially sensitive to the psychological consequences of societal prejudice and homophobia, including the possibility that lesbians and gay men may have internalized negative attitudes and beliefs about homosexuality (Gonsiorek, 1988).

Within the framework of affirmative psychotherapy, clinicians are now creating therapeutic approaches specifically for lesbian and gay couples. For some relationship problems, a couples approach may be preferable to seeing one or both partners individually. In a discussion of therapy with gay couples, Shannon and Woods (1991) noted that all couples in healthy relationships, regardless of sexual orientation, share such characteristics as commitment, respect for each other, the expression of feelings, and the ability to resolve conflicts. Based on their knowledge of gay men's experiences, Shannon and Woods highlighted additional issues that are often important for gay cou-

ples. These include each partner being able to accept and value his homosexuality and giving up rigid male stereotypic roles that can detract from a successful same-sex relationship. In a discussion of affirmative therapy for lesbians, Browning and colleagues (1991) noted the potential value of feminist therapy in helping lesbian clients understand the influences of both sexism and homophobia in their lives. Currently, therapists are developing treatment models for specific relationship issues that can affect gay and lesbian couples, including sexual problems (Hall, 1988; Reece, 1988), alcohol abuse (Glaus, 1988/1989; Kus, 1990), and physical abuse (Hammond, 1988; Morrow & Hawxhurst, 1989).

Affirmative therapies emphasize the role of therapists as advocates for social change as well as service providers (Brown, 1989; Browning et al., 1991; Shannon & Woods, 1991). Although many gay affirmative therapists are themselves gay men or lesbians, an affirmative approach can be used by therapists regardless of their sexual orientation. The key is drawing on knowledge about the personal and relationship experiences of lesbians and gay men, being sensitive to the diversity of lesbians and gay men, and developing expertise in effective treatment approaches (Fassinger, 1991).

CONCLUSION

We have reviewed a growing body of scientific research on gay and lesbian relationships. Although many gaps remain in our knowledge, much has been learned about same-sex couples in the past 20 years. Public interest in same-sex couples appears to be increasing, perhaps spurred by the recent efforts of lesbians and gay men to secure legal rights in such arenas as health benefits for domestic partners, child custody, marriage rights, and service in the armed forces.

Research has demonstrated that most lesbians and gay men desire intimate relationships and are successful in creating them. Many same-sex couples want an equal-power relationship, although not all couples attain this ideal. Many times, differences between partners in personal resources and psychological dependency on the relationship set the stage for power inequalities. However, same-sex couples do not typically adopt "husband" and "wife" roles in their relationships. Instead, most lesbian and gay couples have a flexible division of labor, sharing housework and other chores. Contrary to stereotypical beliefs, same-sex partnerships are no more vulnerable to conflicts and dissatisfactions than their heterosexual counterparts. The loss of a close relationship through breakup or death is always a painful emotional experience. Because of the AIDS epidemic, many gay men have confronted the untimely loss of friends and lovers. In recent years, therapists have developed new gay affirmative approaches to helping lesbian and gay couples cope effectively with problems that occur in their relationships.

Many similarities have emerged in the relationship experiences of lesbians, gay men, and heterosexuals, suggesting that there is much commonality in the issues affecting all contemporary couples. That which most clearly distinguishes same-sex from heterosexual couples is the social context of their lives. Whereas heterosexuals enjoy many social and institutional supports for their relationships, gay and lesbian couples are the object of prejudice and discrimination. Drawing on their clinical observations, therapists have begun to analyze the impact of social rejection on the adjustment of gay and lesbian couples. However, additional research is needed to understand more fully how traditional social institutions and hostile attitudes affect all facets of gay and lesbian relationships.

Scholars are increasingly emphasizing the rich diversity that exists among gay and lesbian couples. Gender differences between the relationships of lesbians and gay men have received the most attention (e.g., Peplau, 1991). Additional studies are needed, however, to understand the varieties of same-sex partnerships and how such factors as culture and ethnicity influence lesbian and gay couples. Virtually all studies discussed in this chapter examined the relationships of White, educated, middle-class people. The few studies that considered ethnic-minority lesbians or gay men typically focused on issues such as identity development or AIDS (e.g., Chan, 1989; Espin, 1987; Loiacano, 1989; Wooden et al., 1983), not on

relationships. Additional research on ethnic-minority couples will help to clarify issues that are especially prominent among ethnic-minority lesbians and gay men. These issues include how relationships are shaped by racial or ethnic identity, how conflicting loyalties to families and to love relationships are balanced, how couples react to potential homophobia in their ethnic communities and to racism or other prejudice in gay and lesbian communities, and how different forms of spirituality affect couples' lives.

NOTE

1. We are grateful for the advice of Linda Garnets, Ph.D., and for the assistance of Talia Barag.

REFERENCES

Anthony, B. D. (1981/1982). Lesbian client-lesbian therapist: Opportunities and challenges in working together. *Journal of Homosexuality, 7,* 45–57.

Bell, A. P., & Weinberg, M. A. (1978). *Homosexualities: A study of diversity among men and women.* New York: Simon & Schuster.

Berger, R. M. (1990). Men together: Understanding the gay couple. *Journal of Homosexuality, 19,* 31–49.

Berzon, B. (1988). *Permanent partners: Building gay and lesbian relationships that last.* New York: Dutton.

Blumstein, P., & Schwartz, P. (1983). *American couples: Money, work, sex.* New York: Morrow.

Brehm, S. S. (1992). *Intimate relationships,* (2nd ed.). New York: McGraw-Hill.

Brown, L. S. (1989). Toward a lesbian/gay paradigm in psychology. *Psychology of Women Quarterly, 13,* 445–458.

Browning, C., Reynolds, A. L., & Dworkin, S. H. (1991). Affirmative psychotherapy for lesbian women. *Counseling Psychologist, 19,* 177–196.

Burch, L. (1986). Psychotherapy and the dynamics of merger in lesbian couples. In T. S. Stein & C. J. Cohen (Eds.), *Contemporary perspectives on psychotherapy with lesbians and gay men* (pp. 57–71). New York: Plenum.

Caldwell, M. A., & Peplau, L. A. (1984). The balance of power in lesbian relationships. *Sex Roles, 10,* 587–599.

Cardell, M., Finn, S., & Marecek, J. (1981). Sex-role identity, sex-role behavior, and satisfaction in heterosexual, lesbian, and gay male couples. *Psychology of Women Quarterly, 5,* 488–494.

Chan, C. S. (1989). Issues of identity development among Asian-American lesbians and gay men. *Journal of Counseling and Development, 68,* 16–20.

Crosby, F. (1991). *Juggling*. New York: Free Press.

Dailey, D. M. (1979). Adjustment of heterosexual and homosexual couples in pairing relationships: An exploratory study. *Journal of Sex Research, 15,* 143–157.

DeCrescenzo, T. A. (1983/1984). Homophobia: A study of the attitudes of mental health professionals toward homosexuality. *Journal of Social Work and Human Sexuality, 2,* 115–135.

Decker, B. (1984). Counseling gay and lesbian couples. *Journal of Social Work and Human Sexuality, 2,* 39–53.

Duffy, S. M., & Rusbult, C. E. (1986). Satisfaction and commitment in homosexual and heterosexual relationships. *Journal of Homosexuality, 12,* 1–24.

Eldridge, N. S. (1987). Gender issues in counseling same-sex couples. *Professional Psychology: Research and Practice, 18,* 567–572.

Eldridge, N. S., & Gilbert, L. A. (1990). Correlates of relationship satisfaction in lesbian couples. *Psychology of Women Quarterly, 14,* 43–62.

Espin, O. (1987). Issues of identity in the psychology of Latina lesbians. In Boston Lesbians Psychologies Collective (Ed.), *Lesbian psychologies* (pp. 35–51). Urbana, IL: University of Illinois Press.

Falbo, T., & Peplau, L. A. (1980). Power strategies in intimate relationships. *Journal of Personality and Social Psychology, 38,* 618–628.

Falco, K. L. (1991). *Psychotherapy with lesbian clients*. New York: Brunner/Mazel.

Fassinger, R. E. (1991). The hidden minority: Issues and challenges in working with lesbian women and gay men. *Counseling Psychologist, 19,* 157–176.

Freedman, J. (1978). *Happy people*. New York: Harcourt Brace Jovanovich.

Garnets, L., Hancock, K. A., Cochran, S. D., Goodchilds, J., & Peplau, L. A. (1991). Issues in psychotherapy with lesbians and gay men. *American Psychologist, 46,* 964–972.

George, K. D., & Behrendt, A. E. (1988). Therapy for male couples experiencing relationship problems and sexual problems. In E. Coleman (Ed.), *Psychotherapy with homosexual men and women: Integrated identity approaches for clinical practice* (pp. 77–88). New York: Haworth Press.

Glaus, K. H. (1988/1989). Alcoholism, chemical dependency and the lesbian client. *Women and Therapy, 8,* 131–144.

Gonsiorek, J. C. (1988). Current and future directions in gay/lesbian affirmative mental health practice. In M. Shernoff & W. A. Scott (Eds.), *The source book on lesbian and gay healthcare* (2nd ed.) (pp. 107–113). Washington, DC: National Gay and Lesbian Health Foundation.

Gottman, J. M. (1979). *Marital interaction: Experimental investigations*. New York: Academic Press.

Hall, M. (1988). Sex therapy with lesbian couples: A four stage approach. In E. Coleman (Ed.), *Psychotherapy with homosexual men and women: Integrated identity approaches for clinical practice* (pp. 137–156). New York: Haworth Press.

Hammond, N. (1988). Lesbian victims of relationship violence. *Women and Therapy, 8,* 89–105.

Harry, J. (1983). Gay male and lesbian relationships. In E. Macklin & R. Rubin (Eds.), *Contemporary families and alternate lifestyles: Handbook on research and theory* (pp. 216–234). Beverly Hills, CA: Sage.

Harry, J. (1984). *Gay couples*. New York: Praeger.

Harry, J., & DeVall, W. B. (1978). *The social organization of gay males*. New York: Praeger.

Hart, B. (1986). Preface. In K. Lobel (Ed.), *Naming the violence: Speaking out about lesbian battering* (pp. 9–16). Seattle, WA: Seal Press.

Hawkins, R. L. (1992). Therapy with male couples. In S. Dworkin & F. Guiterrez (Eds.), *Counseling gay men and lesbians* (pp. 81–94). Alexandria, VA: American Association for Counseling and Development.

Herbert, T. B., Silver, R. C., & Ellard, J. H. (1991). Coping with an abusive relationship: How and why do women stay? *Journal of Marriage and the Family, 53,* 311–325.

Herek, G. M. (1994). Assessing heterosexuals' attitudes toward lesbians and gay men: A review of empirical research with the ATLG Scale. In B. Greene & G. M. Herek (Eds.), *Lesbian and gay psychology: Theory, research, and clinical applications* (pp. 206–228). Thousand Oaks, CA: Sage.

Hill, C. T., Rubin, Z., & Peplau, L. A. (1976). Breakups before marriage: The end of 103 affairs. *Journal of Social Issues, 32,* 147–168.

Holmes, T. H., & Rahe, R. H. (1967). The social readjustment rating scale. *Journal of Psychosomatic Research, 11,* 213–218.

Howard, J. A., Blumstein, P., & Schwartz, P. (1986). Sex, power, and influence tactics in intimate relationships. *Journal of Personality and Social Psychology, 51,* 102–109.

Jay, K., & Young, A. (1977). *The gay report: Lesbians and gay men speak out about sexual experiences and lifestyles*. New York: Summit Books.

Kanuha, V. (1990). Compounding the triple jeopardy: Battering in lesbian of color relationships. *Women and Therapy, 9,* 169–184.

Kehoe, M. (1989). *Lesbians over 60 speak for themselves*. New York: Haworth Press.

Kollock, P., Blumstein, P., & Schwartz, P. (1985). Sex and power in interaction: Conversational privileges and duties. *American Sociological Review, 50,* 34–46.

Koss, M. P. (1990). The women's mental health research agenda: Violence against women. *American Psychologist, 45,* 374–380.

Krestan, J., & Bepko, C. (1980). The problem of fusion in the lesbian relationship. *Family Process, 19,* 277–289.

Kubler-Ross, E. (1987). *AIDS: The ultimate challenge.* New York: Macmillan.

Kurdek, L. A. (1989). Relationship quality in gay and lesbian cohabiting couples: A 1-year follow-up study. *Journal of Social and Personal Relationships, 6,* 39–59.

Kurdek, L. A. (1991a). Correlates of relationship satisfaction in cohabiting gay and lesbian couples: Integration of contextual, investment, and problem-solving models. *Journal of Personality and Social Psychology, 61,* 910–922.

Kurdek, L. A. (1991b). The dissolution of gay and lesbian couples. *Journal of Social and Personal Relationships, 8,* 265–278.

Kurdek, L. A. (1992). Relationship stability and relationship satisfaction in cohabiting gay and lesbian couples: A prospective longitudinal test of the contextual and interdependence models. *Journal of Social and Personal Relationships, 9,* 125–142.

Kurdek, L. A., & Schmitt, J. P. (1986a). Relationship quality of partners in heterosexual married, heterosexual cohabiting, and gay and lesbian relationships. *Journal of Personality and Social Psychology, 51,* 711–720.

Kurdek, L. A., & Schmitt, J. P. (1986b). Relationships of gay men in closed or open relationships. *Journal of Homosexuality, 12,* 85–99.

Kurdek, L. A., & Schmitt, J. P. (1987). Partner homogamy in married, heterosexual cohabiting, gay, and lesbian couples. *Journal of Sex Research, 23,* 212–232.

Kus, R. J. (1990). Alcoholism in the gay and lesbian communities. In R. J. Kus (Ed.), *Keys to caring: Assisting your gay and lesbian clients* (pp. 66–81). Boston: Alyson.

Levinger, G. (1979). A social psychological perspective on marital dissolution. In G. Levinger & O. C. Moles (Eds.), *Divorce and separation* (pp. 37–63). New York: Basic Books.

Lisa. (1986). In K. Lobel (Ed.), *Naming the violence: Speaking out about lesbian battering* (pp. 37–40). Seattle, WA: Seal Press.

Lobel, K. (Ed.). (1986). *Naming the violence: Speaking out about lesbian battering.* Seattle, WA: Seal Press.

Loiacano, D. K. (1989). Gay identity issues among Black Americans: Racism, homophobia, and the need for validation. *Journal of Counseling and Development, 68,* 21–25.

Malyon, A. (1981/1982). Psychotherapeutic implications of internalized homophobia in gay men. *Journal of Homosexuality, 7,* 59–69.

Martin, J. L. (1988). Psychological consequences of AIDS-related bereavement among gay men. *Journal of Consulting and Clinical Psychology, 56,* 856–862.

Martin, T. C., & Bumpass, L. L. (1989). Recent trends in marital disruption. *Demography, 6,* 37.

McDonald, H. B., & Steinhorn, A. I. (1990). *Homosexuality: A practical guide to counseling lesbians, gay men and their families.* New York: Continuum.

McWhirter, D. P., & Mattison, A. M. (1982). Psychotherapy for gay male couples. *Journal of Homosexuality, 7,* 79–91.

McWhirter, D. P., & Mattison, A. M. (1984). *The male couple.* Englewood Cliffs, NJ: Prentice-Hall.

Morrow, S. L., & Hawxhurst, D. M. (1989). Lesbian partner abuse: Implications for therapists. *Journal of Counseling and Development, 68,* 58–62.

Murphy, B. C. (1989). Lesbian couples and their parents: The effects of perceived parental attitudes on the couple. *Journal of Counseling and Development, 68,* 46–51.

Murphy, B. C. (1992). Counseling lesbian couples: Sexism, heterosexism and homophobia. In S. Dworkin & F. Guiterrez (Eds.), *Counseling gay men and lesbians* (pp. 63–79). Alexandria, VA: American Association for Counseling and Development.

Murray, J., & Abramson, P. R. (1983). *Bias in psychotherapy.* New York: Praeger.

Myers, D. G. (1992). *The pursuit of happiness.* New York: Avon.

Peplau, L. A. (1991). Lesbian and gay relationships. In J. C. Gonsiorek & J. D. Weinrich (Eds.), *Homosexuality: Research findings for public policy* (pp. 177–196). Newbury Park, CA: Sage.

Peplau, L. A., & Campbell, S. M. (1989). The balance of power in dating and marriage. In J. Freeman (Ed.), *Women: A feminist perspective* (4th ed.) (pp. 121–137). Mountain View, CA: Mayfield.

Peplau, L. A., & Cochran, S. D. (1980, September). *Sex differences in values concerning love relationships.* Paper presented at the annual meeting of the American Psychological Association, Montreal, Canada.

Peplau, L. A., & Cochran, S. D. (1981). Value orientations in the intimate relationships of gay men. *Journal of Homosexuality, 6,* 1–19.

Peplau, L. A., & Cochran, S. D. (1990). A relationship perspective on homosexuality. In D. P. McWhirter, S. A. Sanders, & J. M. Reinisch (Eds.), *Homosexuality/heterosexuality: Concepts of sexual orientation* (pp. 321–349). New York: Oxford University Press.

Peplau, L. A., Cochran, S., Rook, K., & Padesky, C. (1978). Women in love: Attachment and autonomy in lesbian relationships. *Journal of Social Issues, 34,* 7–27.

Peplau, L. A., & Gordon, S. L. (1983). The intimate relationships of lesbians and gay men. In E. R. Allgeier & N. B. McCormick (Eds.), *Gender roles and sexual behavior: The changing boundaries* (pp. 226–244). Palo Alto, CA: Mayfield.

Peplau, L. A., Padesky, C., & Hamilton, M. (1982). Satisfaction in lesbian relationships. *Journal of Homosexuality, 8,* 23–35.

Reece, R. (1988). Causes and treatments of sexual desire discrepancies in male couples. In E. Coleman (Ed.), *Psychotherapy with homosexual men and women: Integrated identity approaches for clinical practice* (pp. 157–172). New York: Haworth Press.

Reilly, M. E., & Lynch, J. M. (1990). Power-sharing in lesbian partnerships. *Journal of Homosexuality, 19,* 1–30.

Renzetti, C. M. (1992). *Violent betrayal: Partner abuse in lesbian relationships.* Newbury Park, CA: Sage.

Roth, S. (1984). Psychotherapy with lesbian couples: The interrelationships of individual issues, female socialization, and the social context. In E. S. Hetrick & T. S. Stein (Eds.), *Innovations in psychotherapy with homosexuals* (pp. 89–114). Washington, DC: American Psychiatric Association.

Saunders, J. M. (1990). Gay and lesbian widowhood. In R. J. Kus (Ed.), *Keys to caring: Assisting your gay and lesbian clients* (pp. 224–243). Boston: Alyson.

Schilit, R., Lie, G., & Montagne, M. (1990). Substance abuse as a correlate of violence in intimate lesbian relationships. *Journal of Homosexuality, 19,* 51–65.

Shachar, S. A., & Gilbert, L. A. (1983). Working lesbians: Role conflicts and coping strategies. *Psychology of Women Quarterly, 7,* 244–256.

Shannon, J. W., & Woods, W. J. (1991). Affirmative psychotherapy for gay men. *Counseling Psychologist, 19,* 197–215.

Shelby, R. D. (1992). *If a partner has AIDS: Guide to clinical intervention for relationships in crisis.* New York: Haworth Press.

Siegal, R. L., & Hoefer, D. D. (1981). Bereavement counseling for gay individuals. *American Journal of Psychotherapy, 35,* 517–525.

Smalley, S. (1987). Dependency issues in lesbian relationships. *Journal of Homosexuality, 14,* 125–135.

Stein, T. S. (1988). Theoretical considerations in psychotherapy with gay men and lesbians. *Journal of Homosexuality, 15,* 75–95.

Stulberg, I., & Smith, M. (1988). Psychosocial impact of the AIDS epidemic on the lives of gay men. *Social Work, 33,* 277–281.

Testa, R. J., Kinder, B. N., & Ironson, G. (1987). Heterosexual bias in the perception of loving relationships of gay males and lesbians. *Journal of Sex Research, 23,* 163–172.

Tripp, C. A. (1975). *The homosexual matrix.* New York: Signet.

Turque, B. (1992, September 14). Gays under fire. *Newsweek,* pp. 35–40.

Ussher, J. M. (1991). Family and couples therapy with gay and lesbian clients: Acknowledging the forgotten minority. *Journal of Family Therapy, 13,* 131–148.

Waterman, C. K., Dawson, L. J., & Bologna, M. J. (1989). Sexual coercion among gay male and lesbian relationships. *Journal of Sex Research, 26,* 118–124.

Wayment, H. A., Silver, R. C., & Kemeny, M. E. (1994). *Spared at random: Survivor reactions in the gay community.* Unpublished manuscript, Department of Psychology, University of California, Los Angeles.

Wolf, D. G. (1980). *The lesbian community.* Berkeley: University of California Press.

Wooden, W. S., Kawasaki, H., & Mayeda, R. (1983). Lifestyles and identity maintenance among gay Japanese-American males. *Alternative Lifestyles, 5,* 236–243.

5.4 TWO MANY AND NOT ENOUGH
The Meanings of Bisexual Identities

Paula C. Rust

THE MEANING OF BISEXUAL IDENTITY

The question "What does your sexual identity mean to you?" was designed to elicit discussions of the aspects of their self-concepts that respondents feel are called into play when they use a particular identity, not their definitions of the sexual orientation categories to which these identities refer. Further instructions invited respondents who had indicated that they have more than one sexual identity to explain each of their sexual identities, and many respondents did discuss more than one of their identities. The following discussion focuses only on those respondents living in the United States who have bisexual identities and on the explanations they gave of the meanings of these bisexual identities. The reader should keep in mind that many of these respondents also identify as lesbian, gay, heterosexual, queer, or have a variety of other identities, and that the explanations they gave of those identities call on other aspects of their self-concepts that are not mentioned below. Therefore, in most cases, the portrait painted of individual respondents is incomplete. To help complete the picture, I include a brief discussion of respondents' use of bisexual identities in conjunction with other identities.

Feelings of Sexual Attraction and Capacities

When asked to discuss the meaning of their bisexual identities, the vast majority of respondents said that their bisexuality is their potential to be sexually, emotionally, and/or romantically attracted to members of both sexes or genders. Most respondents said, simply, that they are attracted to both men and women. Many specified that their attraction is sexual, several said the attraction is sexual and emotional, and some described their attractions as erotic, romantic, physical, psychological, spiritual, social, affectional, or mental. A few respondents pointed out that they are not attracted to all men and all women, but only to some members of each gender. A few specified that their attractions toward women and men are equal in strength and one said he is not really very attracted to either gender at all—but most apparently see their bisexuality as a reflection of the fact that they are attracted to both genders to some degree and did not consider the relative strength of their attractions to women and men important enough to mention. For example, Respondent #346 explained that "I call myself [bisexual] because I am emotionally, sexually, psychologically, and spiritually attracted to women as well as to men."

Although most respondents used the word *attraction,* some said they are bisexual because they have sexual or romantic *feelings* toward, fall in love with, are "interested in," or "lean toward" both men and women, or because they have the *potential, capacity, or ability* to have such feelings. Respondent #518 wrote "I consider myself 'Bi' or 'Bisexual' because I am *able* to have romantic, emotional, and sexual feelings for people of both genders" (emphasis added). In practice, the distinction between the experience of *having* feelings and the *capacity* to feel might be trivial; most respondents who identify as bisexual in acknowledgement of their capacity to have feelings for both men and women probably recognized this capacity as a result of having had feelings for both, and those who identify as bisexual because they have had feelings for both women and men ipso facto have—or at least, had—the capacity for feelings for both women and men. Despite the close relationship between the capacity to have feelings and the experience of having had feelings, however, these two criteria do reflect different concepts of bisexuality. Bisexuality as a capacity to have feelings for both women and men is a more abstract concept than bisexuality defined in terms of having feelings for both women and men. The former refers to a state of being, whereas the latter approaches a behavioral definition of bisexuality because having feelings is an experience.

Sexual attraction to, or romantic feelings toward, another person does not necessarily imply that one would enjoy having sex with that person, that one desires to have sex with that person, or that one is open to the possibility of having sex or a romantic involvement with that person. Individuals can feel sexually attracted to people with whom they would never consent to have sex, and they can fantasize romances with people they would not even want to meet. Many respondents explained that their bisexual identity is based, not only on a sexual attraction for both women and men or on their capacity for feelings toward both women and men, but also on a desire or willingness to have sex with both women and men, on the belief or knowledge (often based on previous experience) that they enjoy sex with both women and men, or on their willingness to become romantically involved with either a woman or a man. These respondents are clearly saying that their bisexual identity reflects more than sexual attraction to or feelings for both genders; it reflects desire or willingness to act on those attractions or feelings. For example, "I experience sexual and sensual desire, + choose to act on these desires (when they are mutual) for/with both men and women."

Other respondents went yet another step further, explaining that their bisexual identities reflect not only a willingness to act on their attractions or feelings for both women and men, but also a capacity for and willingness to have *relationships* with either women or men. For example,

I have always found both women and men attractive and had erotic fantasies about both women and men. However, this is not the primary component of my sexual identity. I call myself bisexual because I can build and sustain intimate relationships with both women and men, and I feel I could choose either a woman or a man as a lifetime monogamous partner.

For some bisexual individuals, their openness to having relationships with either women or men is, at the moment, theoretical because they are currently involved in a monogamous relationship. Respondent

#231 calls herself bisexual because "I have been, and am, attracted to both men and women. I have had, and am open to having (were I not monogamously committed) relationships with both men and women." For such individuals, this theoretical openness to having a relationship with either a man or a woman was manifest in their choice of their current partner, and would presumably become manifest again if their current relationship were to end. As Respondent #61 explained, "[my bisexual identity] signifies the pool of people from whom I picked my lover *and* who I might find attractive on the street."

Past and Present Sexual Behavior and Romantic Relationships

For most bisexual-identified individuals, bisexual identity does not depend on actually having had sexual contact with both women and men. Actual past or present behavior was much less frequently mentioned than feelings of sexual attraction or willingness to have sex or relationships with both women and men as a source of meaning for bisexual identity. Among respondents who did mention their behavior, most also mentioned their feelings of attraction toward both women and men and many also mentioned their ability to enjoy or willingness to have sexual contact or relationships with both women and men, indicating that they did not base their bisexual identities solely on their past or present behavior. Respondent #119 described his attractions and his sexual behavior history,

I am sexually/emotionally attracted to both sexes— my sexual history involves relationships with both sexes in a serial fashion: for the past 4 years I've had a 7 month relationship with a man, a 4 month relationship with a woman, a year relationship with a man & now a 1 1/2 year relationship with a woman.

and Respondent #8 bases her identity on her potential future sexual behavior as well as her past sexual behavior: "by identifying as bisexual, I acknowledge that I'm potentially capable of emotional and/or sexual intimacy with either men or women. It also describes my recent sexual behavior."

Identifying as bisexual as a reflection of one's previous and/or expected future sexual relationships with both women and men requires a longitudinal view of one's sexual life. By this definition, one is not bisexual because of the experiences one is having at any given moment, but because of the sum of one's experiences over the course of one's lifetime. As Respondent #435 put it, "[My] primary attraction at this time is to men [but] looking at my life holistically, I have had satisfying, loving, intimate, sexual relationships with women." Some respondents are, however, currently having sexual relations with both women and men and draw the meaning of their bisexual identity at least partially from their concurrent same- and other-gender involvements. For example, Respondent #696 reported that "I am bisexual because I have a girl-friend, with whom I have sex often and am very attracted to, but am still attracted to men, with whom I also have sexual relations" and Respondent #227 has, "at present, . . . one female lover and two male lovers in a quadradic relationship (two of my lovers are also bisexual, while the third is exclusively gay)."

Although a few respondents who mentioned their past or present sexual behavior as a source of meaning for their bisexual identities made the point that they have had—or are having—"equal" amounts of sexual experience with women and men, many described histories involving substantially more contact with one gender than with the other. Some respondents whose bisexual identities are behavior-based have had several lovers of one or both genders, whereas others have had only one or a few. These individuals obviously do not feel that their sexual behavior must be equally divided between women and men to be described as "bisexual." For example, one woman reported that "over 99% of my sexual interactions have been heterosexual. But I fantasize about women a great deal and enjoyed the one-on-one encounter I had."

Only twenty-four respondents mentioned past or present sexual behavior as the sole source of meaning for their bisexual identity. Some of these respondents called themselves "technical bisexuals." Respondent #591 wrote that "I have had meaningful valuable sexual relationships with men [and women] which makes me technically bisexual." The adjective "technical" has clinical, ego-dystonic implications, usually implying that although one's behavior might be bisexual, other—perhaps more personally meaningful—aspects of one's sexuality are not bisexual. For example, some bisexual-identified women would prefer to be lesbians

for political reasons but acknowledge that they are attracted to or have had sexual relationships with men and therefore reluctantly describe themselves as "technically bisexual." Respondent #27 has had relationships with both men and women but is left cold by her own bisexual self-description because it does not reflect her true desire, which is to be in a relationship with a woman: "In terms of my actual sexual & emotional relationships, I would have to be considered, technically, BIsexual; I've been involved with about equal numbers of men & women. In terms of importance of those relationships, of my ideals, I'd like to be with a woman" (emphasis on "bi" in original).

"I Have" or "I Haven't," But "That Doesn't Matter"

Several respondents mentioned both their feelings of attraction or willingness to become involved with either women or men and their sexual behavior—or lack thereof—when discussing the meanings of their bisexual identities, and then commented that their bisexual identities are based solely on their feelings and potentials and not on their behavior. These individuals do not feel that their bisexual identities are in any way contingent on their behavior; their bisexual identities are or would be no less valid or meaningful if they lacked sexual experience with both genders and they deny or resist pressure to demonstrate their bisexuality by acting on their attractions for both genders. For example, "Bisexual is most accurate for me since 1991 . . . The fact that I have not had any significant relationships with either men or women recently is less a factor for identifying than for my reparative therapy work." Some respondents commented that basing their sexual identities on their behavior would deny part of themselves. Respondent #342 is currently active with a same-gender partner and explained that the term bisexual is "closest to home for me. I would be lying if I said I was gay, because I'm attracted sensually & sexually to both men and women. Even tho' I'm in a primary relationship w/ a gay man, to *not* label as Bi means that I'd lose an integral part of who I am."

Some bisexual-identified respondents find that the reasons for the differences between their feelings or potentials and their actual behavior are social, such as pressure toward certain kinds of sexual behavior or social structures that make certain kinds of sexual behavior more available or likely. For example, the cultural presumption of heterosexuality facilitates heterosexual contact. One woman explained that because she has been socialized toward heterosexual relating she has difficulty developing potentially sexual relations with members of her own gender. She likes "the idea of being sexual with both men & women. I am attracted to both, but don't always act on that attraction. I more easily & naturally relate to men because of social conditioning—I'd like that to change." The cultural presumption of heterosexuality is also reflected in and promoted by social institutions such as legally sanctioned marriage. Some respondents had married other-gender partners in accordance with social expectations despite their same-gender or bisexual feelings, and then found that the expression of their same-gender feelings became even more difficult because of the expectation of marital monogamy. For example,

> I have been married to a woman for 13 years, almost monogamously. I have a 9-year old daughter. I first became aware of my gay tendencies at age 5. I basically believe in family monogamy, but I have also spent most of my marriage fantasizing exclusively about men. At this point in my life (age 40) I am considering other options besides a monogamous, married relationship.

Individuals' opportunities for sexual relationships are also limited by social structures that constrain the types of people they are likely to meet. Those who have engaged in predominantly other-gender sexual activity in the past are likely to interact mostly with heterosexuals and might find it difficult to break into social circles containing potential same-gender partners, whereas those who have engaged in predominantly same-gender sexual activity or who have identified as lesbian or gay might find that their opportunities for other-gender sexual contact are not only limited, but discouraged, by friends. Those who seek partners who identify as bisexual might find it difficult to find partners of either gender if they live in an area that lacks a visible bisexual population. Respondent #190, a bisexual woman, has had difficulty finding other bisexual women with whom she

can relate; she is "equally attracted to men and women, but since it is hard to find compatible bi women, most of my sexual experience has been with men. I consider myself bi because of my feelings rather than actions."

Although social structures generally exert consistent pressures that tend to make the same types of potential partners available to a particular person time after time, Respondent #316 believes that age-related demographic structures have changed her opportunities as she grew older. As a younger woman, she married a man in a heterosexual relationship but, now that she is nearly 70 years old, she thinks that:

> Although [I have had] no actual sexual experience with women as yet, I have concluded, following death of my husband 2 years ago, my sexual needs are more likely to be met at my age by intimate relationship to a woman, in mutually shared relationship. I do not rule out chance of meeting and development of intimate relationship to man but age statistics are less likely for that.

"I Haven't, and Maybe It Does Matter"

Not everyone with a bisexual identity and lack of either same-gender or other-gender experience is certain that a bisexual identity can be based on attractions or potentials alone. Two women respondents are not sure of their bisexual identities because they lack sexual experience with both genders. Both expressed uncertainty about the validity of their identities, one because she has not yet had an experience with another woman, and the other because she has not yet had a longterm relationship with a woman. For example,

> I hesitate to call myself [bisexual] because I have only thought about having relationships w/ women. I feel closer to women than to men, and I find women sensual, yet I tend to seek out heterosexual relationships. Perhaps because they're more socially acceptable . . . or maybe because that's just what I prefer?

Because she has not yet had an experience with a woman, this woman is not sure that she really feels attracted to women; in other words, she needs to have a sexual experience to be sure she is properly interpreting her feelings. Although she might eventually identify herself as bisexual based on her feelings and not on her sexual experiences, for her a sexual experience will be necessary evidence of those feelings. Similarly, one man said that he is "probably bisexual" and "intend[s] to find out how I feel after having a physical relationship with a woman." Although this man does not consider having had sexual relationships with both women and men a criterion for bisexual identity, he finds that he needs to have a sexual relationship with a woman in order to find out if he meets the criterion he does find important—whether or not he enjoys a relationship with a woman.

Asymmetry and Flexibility

Some individuals base their bisexual identities on asymmetrical combinations of experiences and feelings with women and men. Some feel more strongly attracted to one gender but actually enjoy sex more with the other gender, finding that their actual sexual experiences fail to live up to their fantasies with either one gender or the other. Respondent #606 explained that "I call myself bisexual because the best sexual fantasies I have are gay, but the best sex I've had is straight. My sex with men has never been as good. I feel great in gay bars + dance clubs, however. I'm married + have been monogamous for 1 year." Other respondents are more emotionally attracted to one gender but more sexually attracted to the other gender, or prefer different types of relationships with the different genders. Both women and men tend to be more emotionally attracted to women and more sexually attracted to men, or find it is easier to have casual sex with men. One man wrote, "I seem to get into emotional relationships with women but enjoy quick sex with men" and a woman wrote, "I feel a greater physical attraction to men, but a greater spiritual/emotional attraction to women." A few respondents reported the reverse, however; one man wrote that "I desire to have sex w/ males and females, but seek emotional relationships w/ men," and a woman wrote "I am sexually attracted to both men and women. My more profound romantic feelings have occurred only with men."

Like bisexual-identified respondents who are more strongly attracted to one gender than the other or who have substantially more sexual experience with one gender than the other, respondents who identify themselves as bisexual based on asymmetrical feelings and experiences reject popular conceptions of bisexuality as involving equal attractions or equal amounts of sexual experience with women and men. As Respondent #10 put it, "[My] attractions/experiences are not balanced 50–50, but then again most of us know that's mostly a stereotype." In fact, one man argued that the difference between his feelings toward women and men is an integral part of his bisexual identity. He identifies as bisexual "because I am attracted to and aroused by both men and women. And because my sexual response to men is very different from my sexual response to women."

Because the term "bisexual" can cover such a wide range of feelings and experiences in any proportion, with both women and men, some respondents find bisexual or bi identity to be a "flexible" identity that provides greater freedom of being or expression. As Respondent #137 explained, "the Bi identity gives me more freedom to be me." The flexibility of bisexual identity allows individuals to maintain consistent sexual identities even as their sexual feelings and experiences change over time. Several respondents described their sexualities as "fluid" or explained that bisexual identity is the only identity that can encompass the range over which their feelings and experiences vary with time. For example, "over the long term range of my life, 'bisexual' describes the complete composite of my sexual/romantic relationships in the most inclusive way possible. I don't need to redefine myself internally when my external relationship changes."

Several respondents specifically contrasted bisexual identity with monosexual identities, arguing that monosexual identities are restrictive because they limit one's possibilities to only one gender or because they are accompanied by social and sexual scripts that constrain self-expression not only in terms of the genders of one's partners but also in terms of the sexual and non-sexual aspects of one's relationships with those partners. For Respondent #429, "being bisexual means being open to different possibilities. I reject hetero or homosexuality because they limit my options" and Respondent #37 "attempted the lesbian label and found it stifling/rigid." Respondent #573 wrote, "I call myself 'Bi' because I feel it best expresses the multi-gender interest I enjoy. It frees me from the rigid heterosexual role" and Respondent

#151 is bisexual because "too many 'scripts' exist for straight people, making it harder to have authentic experiences with those of the opposite sex."

Some individuals dislike labels in general, but hesitatingly call themselves "bisexual" because it is the broadest, least defining, and therefore the least offensive. Respondent #379 uses bisexual identity "because anything else would drive me insane. I hate labels but it is one of the few I am totally comfortable with, partly because it is so difficult to define and make assumptions about."

Political Meanings of Bisexual Identity

For many individuals, bisexual identity describes not only their sexual feelings or behaviors but also their politics. Three political meanings emerge from respondents' comments. First, many respondents see bisexual identity as related in some way to gender politics. Second, some respondents use bisexual identity to combat bisexual invisibility in an effort to reshape the landscape of sexual politics. Third, bisexual identity is used by some individuals as an expression of political solidarity, either with bisexuals in particular or with all non-heterosexual people in general.

Different individuals see bisexual identity as related to gender politics in different ways. Most commonly, bisexuality is seen as a challenge to the central importance of gender in defining sexual orientation. Heterosexuality and homosexuality are defined in relation to gender; heterosexuality is sexuality as experienced between other-gendered individuals and homosexuality is sexuality as experienced between same-gendered individuals. Although bisexual identity is a rejection of the gender restrictions characterizing heterosexuality and homosexuality, the concept of sexuality as gender-based is incorporated into many bisexuals' self-conceptions as evidenced by respondents' comments that they call themselves bisexual because they are "sexually attracted to *both men and women*" or have had "sex with *both men and women*." But some bisexual-identified individuals object to the reification of gender implicit in this conception of bisexuality, asserting that their own sexuality is not a combination of sexuality-toward-men and sexuality-toward-women but a sexuality in which others' genders are irrelevant or incidental.

Many respondents who question the role of gender in conceptualizing bisexuality distinguish between *sex* and *gender* and clearly state that their attractions to others are independent of one or both of these characteristics. Respondent #658 said that both are irrelevant; "who I am sexually attracted to has nothing to do with their sex/gender," whereas Respondent #418 focuses specifically on the irrelevance of sex:

> I find myself attracted to either men or women. The outside appendages are rather immaterial, as it is the inner being I am attracted to. On the rare occasions I find a *body* attractive before I know who lives in it, it really doesn't matter if it is a male body or a female body. And, during lovemaking, I thoroughly enjoy being with *either* sex—or both!

Some respondents recognize gender, and even sex, as concepts with more than two possibilities, explaining that the lack of importance of gender means that they can be attracted not to *both* genders or sexes, but to *any* gender or sex. Respondent #495 recalled that "the best definition I've ever heard is someone who is attracted to people & gender/sex is not an issue or factor in that attraction. To make things simpler, someone who can/would be/is attracted to people of both sexes & *any* gender. And since this is true for me, I call myself bisexual" (emphasis added), and Respondent #619 is attracted to "Females, males, pre-op males in some cases and some masculine female bodies. . . . beauty in body and spirit is attractive regardless of gender and dress."

Many respondents who reject the reification of gender in the conceptualization of sexuality stop short of declaring gender completely irrelevant to their own sexuality. These respondents find that other characteristics are more important than gender in affecting their attractions to and experiences with others, but that gender also has some influence on their sexual feelings or expression. Some explain that, because gender is a socially important characteristic, it tends to be correlated with other characteristics such as personality traits, sexual appetite, and sexual availability. Therefore, even if gender per se is not the basis for their attractions to others or for their choices of sexual partners, gender is likely to play a role in their attractions and in the quality of their sexual experiences. Quotes from two respondents illustrate some of the ways in which gender might play a role in sexuality even among individuals who question gendered conceptions of sexuality:

I don't have genderless attractions, as some other people do. My attractions towards men & women feel different, and I'm still trying to figure out/identify *how*. I think I'm attracted to some qualities that are more common and stronger in women (for whatever reasons—cultural conditioning or whatever), and some that may be more common in (some) men than (some) women (lack of interest in clothes, hair, shopping, etc.). Still, there are many exceptions to gender generalizations, so I can't categorically eliminate either sex. Sexism is a problem w/ men, though (sexism both from them & the rest of the world).

I identify myself as bisexual. To me, this means that of the people that I find myself attracted to or interested in developing an intimate or sexual relationship with, some are male and some are female. I would like to say simply that "I don't discriminate on the basis of gender," but having grown up in a sexist culture, and having been bombarded with roles and stereotypes all my life, I don't think that's possible. To me, being bisexual means that I don't walk through life with strange blinders on, refusing to acknowledge feelings I might have for another person, because of her or his gender.

The question of the role of gender in sexuality is particularly problematic for individuals whose own genders do not fall neatly into either the "woman" or the "man" category. If one is both a woman and a man oneself, then any interaction with another individual—even an individual with a fixed, traditional gender—is neither clearly same-gender nor clearly other-gender. Seven bisexual respondents in the current study identify themselves as bisexual not only because they are attracted to both women and men, but because they are, themselves, either both women and men, neither women and men, both passive and active in sex, or both genitally male and female—the latter occurring in one respondents' fantasies only. "Bisexual" is the only term readily available that can incorporate these respondents' senses of their own genders. For example, "My sexual identity reflects both my attraction to women + men, and that I feel

largely feminine + masculine with respect to my behavior, dress, "personality patterns", etc. though my prime sense of self is feminine and female. All this is so loaded by culture, it's very hard to sort out, + mostly I don't bother. I just am."

Another common way in which respondents see bisexual identity as related to gender politics is to see one's bisexuality—whether gender-based, nongender-based, or gender-influenced—as a challenge to traditional gender simply by virtue of one's refusal to limit one's self sexually to one gender or the other. As Respondent #269 put it, "I do not exclude a person from consideration as a possible love interest on the basis of sex/gender." In this view, bisexuality is a form of gender non-discrimination, and hence a challenge to traditional gender hierarchies if not necessarily a challenge to qualitative gender differences. Even if their sexual feelings for or experiences with women and men are different from each other, i.e., gendered, the fact that they do not restrict their feelings or partner choices to one gender is a form of gender equity for these individuals. Most see their non-discriminatory stance as a rejection of mainstream patriarchal and heterosexist discrimination. Respondent #280 identifies as bisexual

Becuz i have strong feeling for/attractions to men occasionally but am learning to recognize how compulsory heterosexuality, heterosexism & homophobia shape those feelings, while at the same time i'm learning to recognize &/or acknowledge my feelings for/attractions to womyn as feelings to be celebrated & nurtured. "Bisexual" best describes the continuum of feelings that i have for both men and womyn.

In contrast, one woman sees her non-discriminatory stance as a rejection of the [lesbian] cultural feminist preference for women to the exclusion of men; Respondent #279 has, "in the past, attempted to restrict my dating to women, for a variety of political or personal reasons, but have found myself unable, and in the long run, unwilling, to restrict my attractions on the basis of gender alone."

Finally, some respondents see their bisexuality as a way of challenging dichotomous thinking itself, including not only dichotomous gender, but also the straight/gay distinction that is based on dichotomous gender distinctions. Respondent #209 feels that bisexual is "the most convenient term to begin getting away from dichotomous thinking (gay/straight) to a Kinsey continuum or Klein continuum of human behavior, thinking and feeling," and Respondent #404 feels that bisexuality challenges the distinction between sexual and non-sexual human interactions:

> Bisexual (to me) challenge traditional notions of intimacy and other "set" boundaries . . . attractions aren't limited to sexual ones; [there are] also emotional, social, etc. [attractions] . . . Also, I feel as though the label "bi" challenges the either/or polarization that our culture (USA) teaches.

The second political meaning of bisexual identity, that is, the goal of promoting bisexual visibility and asserting the validity of bisexuality as a form of sexuality, incorporates the desire to challenge dichotomous distinctions; valid and visible bisexuality challenges dominant constructions of sexuality as composed of a heterosexual-homosexual dichotomy. Several respondents explain that they call themselves bisexual to promote bisexual visibility, fight biphobia, or create a cultural space for bisexuality. Respondent #13 wrote that "for years I described myself as 'sexual' but took on 'bisexual' as a political response to invisibility." Respondent #77 feels that it is particularly important for her to be visible as a bisexual when she is among gay men and lesbians, whereas visibility as a lesbian will do when she is among heterosexuals. She explained that "It is important to me that gay & lesbian folk see me as bisexual, but I feel less strongly about that around straights, especially most straight men, whom I like to avoid. I let them assume when I say queer I mean lesbian."

Third, some respondents identify as bisexual as an expression of political solidarity with other bisexuals, or with non-heterosexual people in general, toward the common goal of eradicating heterosexism. As Respondent #456 put it,

> We can talk about my identity on 2 levels. First, we can consider my inherent nature, which is bisexual with a greater tendency towards same sex attraction. However, ironically, in practice, I have been exclusively heterosexual and monogamous for over three years. I choose, however, to identify myself as bi to

express my political solidarity with all queer people. Many of my friends are gay and obviously they would be offended if I denied my same sex attraction.

Social Meanings of Bisexual Identity

One source of social meaning for any sexual identity is the ability of the identity to connect an individual to a community. Eight respondents mentioned that the identity "bisexual" represents their membership in a bisexual community and, for a few, also in a larger queer community. One man is "almost exclusively with women" but identifies as bi for a few reasons, including "culturally, my roots are in the bi/gay community. The people are cooler!" One woman feels "a sense of pride and belonging to community" when she calls herself bisexual, and another woman is "capable of being romantically/sexually attracted to both men and women" but finds that the term bisexual "doesn't always fit [because] sometimes I feel a lot more 'straight,' and sometimes I feel asexual. However, I almost always feel like going to dinner on Tuesday nights with fun people, so I keep the label!"

Sometimes bisexual identity draws its meaning from a relationship not with a whole community, but from a relationship with a single other bisexual individual. Respondent #527 finds that her bisexual identity has an added depth of meaning because her husband is also bisexual. Now that she and her husband have decided to "explore how we can [express our bisexuality] in a way that is safe for our relationship . . . I no longer identify as bisexual living a heterosexual lifestyle, but [as] a bisexual who wants to be out . . . and who does not want to be pegged as 'het.'" In other words, her bisexuality holds a different meaning for her now that it is no longer hidden within an apparent heterosexual relationship.

Another social source of meaning for bisexual identity lies in the understandings that other people have of the term "bisexual." Some respondents describe themselves as bisexual not because the term reflects their own self-understandings completely or accurately, but because it is the term that is most intelligible, acceptable, or believable to others, or because it conveys a particular aspect of their sexuality that they want to convey clearly even at the expense of misrepresenting other aspects of their sexuality. A few quotes illustrate some of the reasons individuals use bisexual identities that do not accurately or completely convey their self-conceptions:

> I am not happy with, or sure of, the label "bisexual." I use it by default, since other labels are confusing to some audiences. "Bisexual" seems to be the most believable, based on my history of being attracted to and having sexual/romantic relationships with both men and women. I would rather call myself a "lesbian," but no one would buy it if I continued to love men 'romantically.'

> I use the term "bisexual" mostly with other people where I want to make my attraction to women and men perfectly clear and it's the easiest word to make this clear. However, I don't like the way it is so specific about bi/two sex attractions.

> Until recently I felt I was hetero-identified bisexual. All of my intimate & long term relationships were with women, but sometimes my fantasies included men. Then I started using pan-sexual. To me that term has the benefit of not referring to even the concept of gender, it's all inclusive, rather than definitive. However sometimes I ran across people that assumed it to mean having sex with people other than consensual adults, i.e.: children, animals, objects. So for easy clarification I adopted the "Bisexual" moniker.

Some individuals would prefer not to label themselves at all, but call themselves bisexual in capitulation to social pressures to adopt a sexual identity or to ease social interaction with others who expect them to have a sexual identity. Respondent #186 reported that, when filling out the questionnaire for this study, he almost chose the response option "I prefer not to label myself," explaining that "I avoid using the label [bisexual] except with likeminded people. But I use it, because, as with most labels, it saves time and is approximately correct. It means I'm open to sensuality and sexuality with men and with women."

Miscellaneous Meanings for Bisexual Identity

When asked to discuss the meaning of their bisexual identities, a few respondents took the question as an opportunity to discuss what their bisexual identities did not mean, for example, that contrary to stereotypes bisexuality does not imply simultaneous same- and other-gender sexual activity, and that monogamy is consistent with bisexuality.

One respondent stated that his bisexual identity was not honest; he indicated that he calls himself bisexual because he is avoiding a homosexual identity, writing "I call myself bisexual, because I am currently married. And it is easier to accept personally than "homosexual" even though that is what I really am (I think)." In contrast, several respondents said that they identify as bisexual because it is the most honest identity. These individuals have the feelings or behaviors that they themselves consider bisexual, but recognize that many people with the same feelings or behaviors do not call themselves bisexual. Therefore, their own bisexual identities are based, not only on their bisexual feelings or behaviors, but on their willingness to be open, not closeted, about their bisexuality. For these individuals, bisexual identity represents honesty with themselves and with others.

For the Record: A Quantitative Accounting of the Meanings of Bisexual Identities

In summary, most individuals who describe themselves as bisexual explain that their bisexual identity means that they are sexually, emotionally, and/or romantically attracted to both women and men, but many also mention their sexual experiences or connections to a bisexual community or politics. Quantitative interpretations of qualitative data are imprecise because complex qualitative relationships are lost in the act of quantifying. However, information about the numbers of respondents who mentioned each aspect of the meaning of bisexual identity can provide a useful assessment of the meaning of bisexual identity at an aggregate, or social, level.

Out of 407 respondents who discussed the meanings of their bisexual identities, 324 wrote answers that are clear, informative, and classifiable enough for quantitative purposes. Of these, 234 (72%) mentioned feelings and capacities only and made no mention of their sexual behavior unless to discount it as a source of meaning for their bisexual identities. Among these 234 respondents, 163 explicitly mentioned feelings of attraction, and an additional twenty-four mentioned other feelings including love or unspecified emotions. Of these 187 respondents, most described themselves as being attracted to or having feelings for both women and men, but twenty-nine said that their feelings were independent of gender such that their attractions were toward people, rather than toward "women and men." Twenty-three of the 187 respondents, plus an additional thirty-one respondents, said that their bisexual identities reflect not only feelings of attraction—either stated or assumed—but also their enjoyment of or their desire or willingness to have sex with either women or men. Twenty-one of the 187 respondents, plus an additional sixteen respondents, went even farther and said that their bisexual identities reflect not only their stated or assumed attractions to women and men and their willingness to have sex with either women or men, but their capacity for or willingness to have relationships with either women or men.

Only twenty-four (7%) of the 324 respondents mentioned their past or present sexual behavior only, with no mention of their feelings or capacities as a source of meaning for their bisexual identities. Half of these mentioned the sexual act only and half described sexual relationships or sexual acts in the context of emotional or romantic relationships. Five of these twenty-four respondents, plus four additional respondents, mentioned having experienced attractions toward both women and men, thus describing attractions as an experience rather than as a state of being or capacity. Two respondents mentioned having had emotional relationships without explicitly mentioning having had sexual contact with either women or men.

Sixty bisexual-identified respondents, nineteen percent of the 324 whose discussions of the meanings of their bisexual identities were classifiable, mentioned both their feelings or capacities and their behaviors as sources of meaning for their bisexual identities. Forty (67%) of these respondents explained that their bisexual identities represent both their feelings of attraction toward both men and women and the fact that they have had sex, often in the context of emotional or romantic relationships, with both women and men. Eight of these forty respondents also said that their bisexual identities reflect their openness to having relationships with either women or men. The other twenty respondents did not explicitly mention feelings of attraction to both women and men as an

aspect of their bisexual identity, but they did mention either their ability to enjoy or willingness to have sex with either women or men or their willingness to have relationships with either women or men in addition to the fact that they had already had sex with and/or loved both women and men.

Many individuals whose bisexual identities reflect their attractions toward or past, present, or potential sexual experiences with both women and men also ascribe social or political meanings to their bisexual identities. For many, their bisexuality is a political challenge to traditional gender. In addition to the twenty-nine respondents mentioned above who describe their feelings of sexual attraction as being independent of gender, another thirteen respondents did not go so far as to declare gender irrelevant but did discuss the role of gender in their attractions, frequently questioning the reification of gender in the cultural construction of sexuality. Nine respondents described their bisexuality as a form of gender nondiscrimination and thereby a challenge to traditional gender hierarchies—either the masculinism of mainstream culture or the feminism of lesbian culture. Seven respondents discussed bisexuality as a challenge to dichotomous thinking, including dichotomous gender and sexual categories. Promoting bisexual visibility is another political goal that motivates some individuals' use of bisexual identity; seven respondents mentioned this.

Regarding social meanings of bisexual identity, eight respondents said that their bisexual identities connect them to a bisexual community or to other bisexual individuals. Seventeen said that they use the term "bisexual" because of the way it is understood by others or because it is, at least, a term that others recognize although for many of these individuals it does not quite reflect the way they see themselves.

THE USE OF MULTIPLE SEXUAL IDENTITIES TO DESCRIBE COMPLEX SEXUAL SELVES

For most respondents who identify as bisexual, the bisexual identity does not suffice to fully describe their conceptions of themselves. Many use additional monosexual, alternative, or compound identities to complete the picture. Although a full exploration of the use of multiple sexual identities among individuals who are attracted to or have had sexual contact with both women and men must await a detailed exploration of not only bisexual but also non-bisexual identities by these individuals, a brief discussion is necessary here to place bisexual identity in context as one of many identities used by these individuals as they seek to identify themselves in a monosexist world.

Individuals use multiple sexual identities for many reasons. First, some individuals use different identities in different contexts, either because different terms have different meanings in different contexts or because their purposes for using a sexual identity are different in different contexts. For example, some respondents are content to use lesbian or gay identities in heterosexual contexts to increase the visibility of minority sexualities in general or because they do not feel heterosexuals would appreciate the difference between lesbianism or gayness and bisexuality, but assert their bisexuality in lesbian or gay contexts where they feel a more immediate need to challenge biphobia. Other individuals prefer alternative identity terms like "queer" or "pansensual" over "bisexual," but they identify as "bisexual" in mainstream contexts where their preferred terms are considered pejorative or would be unfamiliar to others, reserving their use of alternative terms to bisexual, lesbian, gay, or queer cultural contexts where they are understood.

Second, some respondents use multiple sexual identities because they do not feel any one identity term describes them accurately. So, they use several identity terms in an effort to piece together the appropriate aspects of each term to create an identity that more accurately reflects their self-conceptions. For example, many individuals call themselves both bisexual and either lesbian, gay, or heterosexual because they have attractions toward or have had sexual experiences with both women and men but feel much more strongly attracted toward, enjoy sex more with, form stronger emotional bonds with, or plan in the future to have relationships only with members of their own gender and therefore don't believe they fit neatly into either the "bisexual" or the "lesbian/gay"

category. Often, these individuals use compound identities such as "bisexual lesbian" or "heterosexual-identified bisexual," linking two terms into a single identity to show that these terms must be used jointly to achieve a more accurate identity. Such individuals are analogous to individuals of biracial descent who find that neither of the available racial identities—for example, "White," and "African American"—accurately describes themselves.

Third, some respondents use multiple sexual identities to describe multiple aspects of themselves. For these respondents, each identity might, in fact, accurately describe particular aspects of themselves but fail to reflect other aspects. For example, many individuals use one identity to describe their sexual feelings or behaviors and another to describe their social affiliations or their political position vis-à-vis sexual and gender politics and liberation movements. A "bisexual queer," for example, is often a person who is attracted to both women and men and who ascribes to queer political philosophies regarding the breakdown of cultural categories. A "polyfidelitous bisexual" is a bisexual who practices sexual fidelity within a group of three or more people, as opposed to a polyfidelitous heterosexual or a monogamous bisexual. Individuals who use multiple sexual identities to describe different aspects of themselves are analogous to a deaf African-American woman who finds that both the available identities—"African American" and "deaf"—are accurate, although neither is complete because each describes only one aspect of herself.

DISCUSSION

Summary

For individuals who do not fit neatly into culturally sanctioned monosexual categories, the task of developing a sexual identity is challenging. Each individual must somehow construct a self-description that balances her or his need to accurately describe her or his own sexual sense of self with the need to effectively convey an intelligible self to others. To the extent that one's own sexual sense of self differs from culturally available concepts of lesbianism, gayness, and heterosexuality one will have difficulty finding terms for self-description that are both accurate and effective in social interaction. Some individuals strike the balance in favor of easing social interaction, using monosexual identities because they are commonly understood although they might not be entirely accurate. Other individuals reject the pressure to identify altogether, refusing to adopt any sexual identity at all despite the social difficulties this produces. However, most individuals who were aware enough of their departure from conventional monosexual categories to respond to this survey struggled to find a compromise between these two extremes. The results are creative and varied. Many individuals use bisexual identities, but for most a bisexual identity alone is not enough. In addition to their bisexual identities, some individuals use other terms to convey different aspects of their sexual selves or because different identities have different meanings in different contexts. Some individuals combine bisexual identity with monosexual identity to create a single compound identity. Some individuals create their own identities, or draw upon alternative identities that are gaining currency within queer culture. Each individual develops her or his own solution.

For most individuals who call themselves bisexual, bisexual identity reflects feelings of attraction, sexual and otherwise, toward women and men or toward other people regardless of their gender. Among bisexual-identified individuals, there is very widespread agreement that bisexuality is a capacity or state of being that might or might not be expressed through behavior, and that behavior alone cannot be used as an indication of bisexuality. In particular, one can be bisexual regardless of whether one has ever had sexual contact with members of either or both genders and one can be bisexual while involved in a monogamous relationship with one other person. For many individuals, their bisexuality inheres in their mere ability to be attracted to either women or men, whereas others perceive their bisexuality as their willingness to act on their sexual attractions for women and for men, or on their openness to having romantic relationships with either women or with men. Only a small proportion of bisexual-identified respondents mentioned whether they actually had acted on these desires or had had such relationships, and many of those who did mention their sexual behavior proceeded to emphatically state that it

is their willingness to engage in such activity or to have such relationships, and not the activity or relationships themselves, that makes them bisexual. Their behavior might be relevant insofar as it is evidence of their feelings, but behavior itself is not a criterion upon which most bisexual-identified individuals base their bisexual identities. Most bisexual-identified individuals draw their sense of who they really are sexually from their internal feelings; the extent to which their behavior might not match their feelings is often explained as a result of social factors that constrain the expression of sexuality.

A few respondents did cite only their past or present sexual behavior when discussing the meanings of their bisexual identities. Some of these respondents referred to their bisexuality as "technical," implying or explicitly stating that their behavior-based bisexual identity fails to acknowledge other important but non-behavioral aspects of their sexualities.

Whether basing their bisexual identities on their feelings and capacities or on their behaviors, many bisexual-identified respondents reject popular conceptions of bisexuality as consisting of equal degrees of sexual attraction toward women and men or of equal amounts of sexual experience with women and men. Most respondents did not mention the relative proportions of their feelings toward or experiences with women versus men, saying only that they "are attracted" to both women and men or that they had had sexual contacts with members of both genders. However, many respondents clearly stated that they are more strongly attracted to one gender than the other or that they have had more sexual contacts with members of one gender than the other. Although it is apparent that all of these bisexual-identified respondents consider their unequal experiences to be consistent with a bisexual identity, several respondents saw fit to make explicit the point that bisexuality can encompass any proportion of attractions or experiences with women and men.

The Concept of "Potential" in Conceptions of Bisexuality

Because most individuals use bisexual identity to refer to their feelings or capacities rather than their actual behavior, the meaning of bisexual identity invokes the concept of "potential." Everyday discourse usually demands recognition of one level of potential; that which might happen is "potential," whereas that which has already happened is "actualized." Amid the various meanings of respondents' bisexual identities, however, at least one additional layer of potential can be recognized. For example, those individuals who said that their bisexual identities reflect their openness to having sex or relationships with either women or men invoke one level of potential, that is, the possibility that one will actually have sex or a relationship with either a woman or a man in the future. But some respondents indicated that this potential itself is, at the moment, theoretical because they are currently involved in committed monogamous relationships and would not become involved with anyone else unless their current relationship were to end. They are, therefore, *not* currently open to having relationships with either men or women because they are not currently open to having a relationship with anyone other than their current partner. They are only *potentially* open to *potential* relationships, that is, their potential itself is potential.

The concept of potential is related to the distinction between feelings, capacities, and behaviors. At first glance, the feeling-capacity-behavior distinction appears to be clear-cut. A feeling is an internal emotional state, a capacity is an ability, and a behavior involves action; for example, attraction is a feeling, the ability to feel attracted is a capacity, and a sex act is a behavior. But the concept of potential creates relationships between feelings, capacities, and behaviors that blur the distinction between them. For example, for individuals whose bisexual identities mean "I am attracted to women and men," is their bisexual identity reflecting a feeling, a capacity, or a behavior? Was the individual feeling sexually attracted toward a woman and a man at the moment s/he wrote the sentence? Or, is the individual referring to a state of being capable of sexual attraction to both women and men? Or, was the individual referring to a previous experience of feeling attraction toward women and men? The statement could mean any of these things, and probably means all three for most bisexual-identified individuals because they are all related to each other by the concept of potential. If one is capable of attrac-

tion to women and men, then one might say one has the potential for actually feeling attracted to women and to men. One is probably also inferring one's ability to feel attraction and one's potential for future feeling experiences from a past experience of feeling attracted. So, a capacity might be a potential feeling or an inference based on a previous feeling, and a current potential is a future feeling or behavior. Nevertheless, one thing is abundantly clear from current findings: despite the fact that many individuals might have inferred their capacity to be attracted to both women and men or their willingness to have sexual contact or relationships with either women or men from their previous experiences or behaviors, it is their perception that they remain *capable* of feelings for and/or sexual contacts with both women and men—not the fact that they have had such feelings and experiences—that is central to their conceptions of themselves as bisexuals.

Can a Sense of Self Co-Exist with the Breakdown of Essentialist Identity Categories?

The meaning of bisexual identity is different from the definition of bisexuality. Respondents were asked to discuss the *meanings* of their bisexual identities; whether the aspects of themselves that they mentioned in response to this question are, in fact, criteria that they use to *define* bisexuality is an entirely different issue. The difference between the meaning of bisexual identity and the definition of bisexuality is most clearly evident in the answers of respondents who mentioned that they are attracted to both women and men and that they have had sexual contact with both women and men, and then protested that only the attractions and not the behaviors are necessary to their self-conception as bisexual. Their sexual behavior is part of the *meaning* of their bisexual identity; that is, when they describe themselves as bisexual to someone else or to themselves, this behavior is one aspect of themselves that might come to mind and be reflected in this identity—after all, it came to mind when they were asked to discuss their bisexual identity in the IBICIP questionnaire. However, their sexual behavior is not part of their *definition* of bisexuality; that is, had they not had these experiences they would nevertheless feel justified in calling themselves bisexual. We cannot conclude, therefore, that the aspects of self mentioned by any individual are in any sense "criteria" for their own bisexuality, much less that that individual would apply these "criteria" to any other person. A woman whose own bisexual identity reflects her willingness to choose either a woman or a man as a life partner would not necessarily define bisexuality as the willingness to have either a woman or a man as a life partner; she might well consider another woman who is attracted to both women and men, but unwilling to act on her attractions to men, to be bisexual also.

The distinction between the meaning of bisexual identity and the definition of bisexuality underlies one of the discussions taking place periodically in bisexual newsletters and electronic discussion groups. On one hand, in the context of a culture in which sexuality is essentialized and sexual politics are ethnicized, there is cultural pressure to define a bisexual population whose interests would be championed by a bisexual liberation movement. To the extent that this happens, bisexuals can take their place as another player in sexual identity politics. But becoming a player in ethnic-style sexual identity politics means defining the boundary that separates those who belong to the population from those who don't, that is, defining bisexuality. This, in turn, would merely reconstruct the sexual landscape and perpetuate sexual oppression in a slightly altered form; the bisexual category, like the lesbian, gay and heterosexual categories, would become part of the oppressive structure awaiting the next generation of sex rebels. Many bisexual activists wish to avoid following this path, eschewing identity politics in favor of a more queer approach that involves breaking down sexual categories instead of using them as bases for identities. Toward this end, there is resistance to any discussion that appears to lay the groundwork for an ethnic-style bisexual identity, such as discussion of the definition of bisexuality. At the same time, as seen in the current study, individuals are engaged in a struggle to develop a sexual sense of self. Discussing one's sense of self, and the possible meanings of the terms one might use to describe it, is an important part of the process of developing a sexual sense of self, if not a sexual identity. But, because the concept of the meaning of bisexual identity is difficult to distinguish from the concept of a definition of bisexuality, such discussions are often either riddled with apologies or cut short in an effort to thwart the development—or even the appearance of the development—of a definition of bisexuality. The irony is that the most effective deterrent to the development of new, oppressive sexual categories is this very discussion, because it is only through this type of discussion that the individual differences that belie cultural categories can be made visible.

REFERENCES

Ault, Amber. 1996. Ambiguous identity in an unambiguous sex/gender structure: The case of bisexual women. *The Sociological Quarterly*, 37(3): 449–463.

Katz, Jonathan. 1990. The invention of heterosexuality. *Socialist Review*, 20: 7–34.

Katz, Jonathan Ned. 1995. *The Invention of Heterosexuality*. New York: Dutton.

5.5 COMING OUT AND CROSSING OVER
Identity Formation and Proclamation in a Transgender Community

Patricia Gagné, Richard Tewksbury, and Deanna McGaughey

Coming out is a term generally used to refer to the processes whereby gay men, lesbians, or bisexuals inform others of their sexual identity. Despite this popularized notion, the social scientific literature has shown coming out to be a broader and more complex process whereby people recognize and accept their sexual preference, adopt a sexual identity, inform others of their sexual orientation, and become involved in relationships with others of similar sexual identity (Cass 1979, 1984; Coleman 1981–82; Isay 1990; Troiden and Goode 1980; Weinberg 1978). Research on the discovery of sexual preference, the development of sexual identity, and public disclosure has focused primarily on lesbians and gay men, with an emergent literature concerning bisexuals (Garber 1995; Weinberg, Williams, and Pryor 1994; however, see Mason-Schrock 1996). While this work is an important component in our understanding of the dynamic nature of the formation, acceptance, and public disclosure of sexual preference and identity, it has, by its nature, been restricted from examining the complex interplay of sex, gender, and sexuality.[1]

In Western societies, gender identity has been largely dictated by external genitalia, the initial signifier of "sex," and other reproductive anatomy (see Laqueur 1990). With the rise of technology, reduced infant mortality, greater life expectancy, contraception, infant feeding formula, and the feminist movement, the immutable relationship between sex and gender has been questioned (see Huber 1989; Huber and Spitze 1983). Nonetheless, the expression of alternative forms of gender has been largely limited to the expansion of existing norms and roles—a liberal form of social change. Ironically, those hoping to freely express alternative gender identities have largely reacted against the binary system and thus

have been restricted by it. Gender becomes something one must "confess" through social signifiers that may only be interpreted within the existing social order (see Foucault [1978] 1990). Falling in "between" the gender binary will often result in assumptions of homosexuality, as in the case of the feminine man or the masculine woman. Expressions of gender that fall "outside" the dominant gender system make social presentations of gender undecipherable. Frequently, those who fall outside or between the gender binary are encouraged to conform to the dominant system. Those who cannot or will not conform may be counseled to alter their bodies or encouraged to perfect a new gender presentation so that they may "pass" as the "other sex" (Raymond 1994). Those who start out challenging the dominant gender system by enacting gender in ways that are comfortable for themselves but disturbing to others often end up by redefining their identities in ways that conform to hegemonic belief systems and institutional demands.

Much of the social scientific focus on transgendered individuals has derived from an interest in understanding "deviation" from the "normal" and "natural" two-sex system (see Herdt 1994). While extremely diversified, this literature is organized around psychiatric and psychological concerns (Blanchard 1988; Brown 1990; Docter 1988; Persinger and Stettner 1991; Person and Ovesey 1984), anthropological examinations of transgenderism (Blackwood 1984; Bullough and Bullough 1993; Callender and Kochems 1983, 1985; Whitehead 1981), and defining and describing various categories of transgenderists and their cultural manifestations (Chauncey 1994; Newton 1979; Talamini 1982). With the exception of Weinberg, Williams, and Pryor's (1994) research on transsexual bisexuals and treatises written by trans-

From *Gender & Society* 11(4): 478–508. Copyright © 1997 by Sage Publications, Inc. Reprinted by permission of Sage Publications, Inc.

gendered individuals (Bornstein 1994; Morris 1974; Rothblatt 1995), the literature on transgenderism has focused primarily on issues of sex and gender. Within this literature, there has been little examination of sexuality (but see Herdt 1994) and a virtual absence of research on the coming-out experiences of transgendered individuals.

Traditionally, coming-out processes for gay men and lesbians have been seen as a sequence of psychological and social progressions. The stages of coming out have been conceptualized as (a) self-definition as lesbian or gay, (b) tolerance and acceptance of self-defined identity, (c) regular association with other gay men or lesbians, (d) sexual experimentation, and (e) exploration of gay subcultures (Troiden 1988). Obviously, not all out bisexuals, lesbians, or gay men progress through these stages in similar order or speed. Lesbians, bisexuals, and gay men may slowly pronounce new identities, with fluctuating periods of openness or being closeted (de Monteflores and Schultz 1978). Not every gay or lesbian coming-out process leads to a similar outcome. For some, the effects of externally imposed stigma (perhaps reinforced by internalized homophobia) lead individuals to be "out" but to capitulate to stigmas and avoid gay/lesbian activities or to seek to pass as heterosexual (Troiden 1988). For lesbians, gay men, and bisexuals, being known and labeled is not necessarily the goal of coming out. Even for the most political and those who manage stigmas best, disclosure is not universal (Bell and Weinberg 1978; Troiden 1988). Gay men and lesbians can and frequently do enjoy selecting and controlling to whom their identities are known.

In this article, we examine the coming-out experiences of a nonrandom sample of individuals who were members of the transgender community at the time we solicited volunteers for our project. Transgenderism refers to "the lives and experiences of diverse groups of people who live outside normative sex/gender relations" (Namaste 1994, 228). Persons who enact alternative gender presentations or who have internalized alternative gender identities are referred to as "transgenderists" (Tewksbury and Gagné 1996). When looking at the experiences of transgenderists, identity management concerns are at least as complex as those of bisexuals, gay men, and lesbians, if not more so.

While there are some similarities between the coming-out processes of transgenderists and gay men, lesbians, and bisexuals, there are also salient differences. First, since around the end of the nineteenth century, homosexuality has been defined as an identity (D'Emilio 1983; Foucault [1978] 1990). As that identity and the communities and institutions built around it have become more visible, lesbians and gay men, and more recently bisexuals, have had opportunities to find similar others. Thus, feelings of "difference" are more easily identified, labeled, and accepted than they were before homosexuality defined "who" the person was. While gay men, lesbians, and bisexuals have challenged the medical definition of homosexuality as a mental illness, they have for the most part, adhered to the notion that sexuality is an important component in defining who the person is (Adam 1995; D'Emilio 1983). Challenges to this trend are only now emerging within queer communities and queer theory (Epstein 1994; Namaste 1994; Seidman 1994, 1996; Stein and Plummer 1994).

Although barriers to self-awareness and acceptance are declining, transgenderists continue to grapple with many of the issues that confronted sexual minorities in the United States prior to the 1970s. Most masculine-to-feminine transgenderists conform to traditional beliefs about sex and gender, whereas a minority attempt to step outside the gender binary by defining themselves in nongendered or multiply gendered ways (Raymond 1994). For example, within the transgender community, the declassification of transsexualism as a psychiatric diagnosis has been hotly debated, with those seeking to challenge medical definitions arguing that it should be removed from the *Diagnostic and Statistical Manual of Mental Disorders* (DSM-IV) and those still seeking access to hormones and sex reassignment surgery (SRS) arguing that being diagnosed transsexual is the only way they may become the women they truly are. In other words, they must "confess" their transsexualism in ways that adhere to medical models in order to proceed from one sex to the other. Similarly, most transsexuals adhere to beliefs that their desires to live as women were the result of biological "mistakes" that left them as feminine persons in male bodies (Pauly 1990; Stoller 1971). Rather than choosing to live as feminine males, they opt to cross over to full-time womanhood. Similarly, most cross-dressers look on their sartorial transitions as opportunities to express their feminine selves (Talamini 1981; Woodhouse 1989). They deem feminine behavior in masculine attire to be highly inappropriate. Among our sample, the exceptions to these trends tended to exist among individuals who, at one time, identified as transsexuals and/or cross-dressers and who, in the process of trying to understand who they were, began to question the legitimacy of gender as a defining characteristic of self. At the time we talked with them, these people were members of the transgender community who self-identified as either a radical transgenderist, ambigendered, or a third gender. They were looking for ways to defy categorization based on gender, rather than find a way to fit within the gender system.

While transgenderism is an issue of sex and gender, it does entail aspects of sexual *re*orientation. Thus, sexually active transgenderists must recognize, tolerate, and learn to accept an alternative gender identity; develop a repertoire of coping strategies to manage public presentations of gender; and, in some cases, manage the actual transformation of permanent identity and anatomy. Whether gender transformations are temporary or permanent, the sense that one really is the sex associated with the gender portrayed involves a reexamination of sexual identity. For example, some anatomically male transsexuals and cross-dressers, in the process of establishing a feminine self, engage in sexual activity with other anatomical male persons. While morphologically the experience may be defined by observers as *homosexual* or *same sexed,* the social women experiencing the interaction tend to define it as *heterosexual.* Such activity is highly valued as a way of exploring femininity. For transgenderists, the discovery of sexual identity, or a sense of who the individual is as a sexual person, frequently occurs within a sex/gender system that does not address sexual issues among those whose sex and gender do not fit within the binary system. Furthermore, those who do have SRS must sexually "come out" to themselves and others by reexamining their sexual preferences and orientations. As gender and/or sex changes, the subjective and social meanings of sexual interactions are also transformed. While gay

men, lesbians, and bisexuals must come out sexually, their experiences are not confounded by alterations in gender and genital makeup.

Research on the coming-out processes and experiences of transgenderists provides an opportunity to examine the management of the transformation of three aspects of socially normative expectations, rather than just one. Whereas lesbians, gay men, and bisexuals are able to carefully control information dissemination, transgenderists must manage both their actual and virtual social identities (Goffman 1963) on three dimensions. Lesbians, gay men, and bisexuals can selectively come out, whereas transgenderists, because of changes in gender or biological appearance, are often forced out of the closet, creating awkward or even dangerous situations. Transgenderists provide an opportunity to examine the private and public dimensions of achieving a new gender through interaction with others and the emergence and management of alternative sex, gender, and sexual identities.

METHOD

We completed 65 semistructured, in-depth, tape-recorded interviews with masculine-to-feminine individuals from several points along the transgender spectrum (see Tewksbury and Gagné 1996). *Transgenderism* is an umbrella term that encompasses a variety of identities—including transsexual, fetish, and nonfetishistic cross-dresser; drag queen; and other terms—as devised by individuals who live outside the dominant gender system. In this study, we have categorized individuals on the basis of the identity they proclaimed to us. All volunteers in our sample were members of the transgender communities through which we recruited volunteers for our study. The majority in our sample had refined their self-identifications in the process of coming out. Included in our sample are individuals who self-identify as pre- ($n = 27$), post- ($n = 10$), and nonoperative ($n = 4$) transsexual. Transsexuals are people who believe themselves to be female and who wish to, or do, live full-time as women. Preoperative transsexuals are those who desire to have, but have not yet had, SRS. Postoperative transsexuals are those who have had SRS. Nonoperative transsexuals are those who live full-time or nearly full-time as women but who do not wish to have SRS. Some have availed themselves of other medical and cosmetic procedures—including female hormones, breast implants, and electrolysis, whereas others alter their gender presentations without bodily alteration. During childhood (before age 10), about one-third ($n = 16$) felt a strong desire to become a girl or believed themselves to be female. The remainder began to recognize a desire to be female during adolescence ($n = 15$) or adulthood ($n = 10$). They self-identified as heterosexual, bisexual, lesbian, and asexual. Although our sample included many male individuals who had had sexual relationships or encounters with other male persons, no one in our sample self-identified as gay at the time of the interview or at any time during their lives. Also included in our sample are 2 fetishistic cross-dressers, one of whom began erotically motivated cross-dressing during adolescence and the other during adulthood. Such individuals—referred to in the psychiatric literature as transvestites—are male individuals who have a masculine gender identity, self-identify as heterosexual, and dress in women's clothing for erotic purposes. Our sample also includes 17 (nonfetishistic) cross-dressers.[2] Cross-dressers are men who usually self-identify as heterosexual, with a minority identifying as bisexual (Feinbloom 1977; Prince and Bentler 1972; Talamini 1982; Woodhouse 1989). Thirteen of the cross-dressers began cross-dressing in childhood, and 4 during adolescence. Cross-dressers are men who wear women's clothing to relax and permit the expression of their feminine selves. Seven of the cross-dressers in our sample began "dressing" in response to erotic motivations. By the time we interviewed them, the eroticism had dissipated. The remaining cross-dressers in our sample had always dressed for nonerotic reasons. All but 1 of the transsexuals in our study had, at one time, self-identified as a cross-dresser prior to developing a transsexual identity, with 15 reporting that their earliest experiences with cross-dressing were erotically motivated. Each continued cross-dressing even after the erotic component was gone and finally adopted a transsexual identity. In our sample, 4 cross-dressers were in the process of exploring the possibility they might be transsexual. We have categorized them according to the identities they presented to us at the time of the interview. Most cross-dressers in our sample held very traditional opinions about sex, gender, and sexuality. They were masculine, heterosexual men who, when they dressed as women, wished to be perceived as feminine, heterosexual female persons.

A small number of persons ($n = 5$) who cross-dressed and had no desire for SRS referred to themselves in more politically oriented terms. While there are subtle differences in politics, all five of these people have used transgenderism to challenge binary assumptions about sex, gender, and sexuality. Their intent is not to "pass" as women but to challenge the idea that gender is a "natural" expression of sex and sexuality. This group of five includes one "radical transgenderist"—an anatomical, heterosexual male person with a masculine gender identity, who uses cross-dressing as a means to express feminine aspects of self and to challenge traditional binary conceptualizations of sex, gender, and sexuality. It also includes one "ambigenderist," an individual who lives alternatively as a man and a woman, and who believes that categories of sexual orientation do not exist and that sexuality is a spectrum. Depending on how he or she feels, he or she frequently went out "in between"—as neither a man nor a woman (with long hair, makeup, high heels, tight pants, and a two-day growth of beard). In addition, this group includes three people who self-identified as a "third gender." These three individuals believed that all people have both masculine and feminine attributes. Their desire was to develop and be able to publicly present both aspects of self and to live as a combination of both genders. Like the ambigenderist, they resisted categorizing themselves according to sexual identity. In our discussions of the transgendered people in our sample, we have self-consciously adhered to the self-identifications used by our volunteers, with the exception of the final group of five. For purposes of clarity, we refer to this group as gender radicals. We have taken the liberty of doing this because all of them emphasized their desire to eliminate the existing system of gender, rather than just their own gender.

Our research was conducted over a one-year period, spanning 1994 and 1995. Early in the research process, we made a conscious decision to include all

masculine-to-feminine transgenderists who volunteered. Our reasons were twofold. First, within the literature on transgenderism, there has been a strong tendency to reify categories. While we have relied on the
literature for an understanding of ideal types of transgender expression, our early forays into the transgender community convinced us that such categorization
was often imposed on the community by outsiders,
including researchers and medical practitioners. We
have attempted to avoid doing this by relying on the
identities proclaimed to us. Second, although it is not
universally manifested among our sample, we have
found the transgender experience to be a process
whereby individuals experiment with various identities until they find one that "fits" or with which they
are comfortable. While some boys know from early
childhood that they are really girls, others come to that
realization more slowly, through a process of cross-
dressing (either fetishistically or non-fetishistically),
and perhaps on to transsexualism or gender radicalism. By including individuals from several points on
the transgender spectrum, we were able to gain a
richer understanding of the coming-out experience as
an ongoing process of gender exploration, rather than
one in which the goal is a rigid end product.

We solicited volunteers through 14 transgender
support groups, transgender online services, and by
responding to personal ads in a national transgender
publication. People in every region of the contiguous
48 states volunteered for interviews, making our
research national in scope. Participants resided in large
urban areas, small towns, suburbs, and rural areas. Our
sample includes 4 African Americans, 2 Asians, 1 Hispanic, and 58 Whites. Participants ranged in age from
24 to 68 years, with a mean age of 44. Occupationally,
they were diverse with jobs ranging from doctors, air-
line pilots, computer systems analysts, engineers, college professors, school teachers, enlisted members of
the military, police officers, welders, mechanics, food
service and clerical workers, and janitors. Although
our sample was occupationally diverse, the majority
was well educated and had long employment histories
in the skilled trades and professions. Most members of
our sample were either employed or voluntarily unemployed (i.e., retired or student) at the time we talked
with them. Nonetheless, one postoperative and eight

preoperative transsexuals were unemployed, and the
majority of those who lived full-time as the gender into
which they were not assigned at birth were vastly
underemployed.[3]

To provide the greatest reliability among interviews, all but one were conducted by the first author.
Where distance precluded a face-to-face meeting,
interviews were conducted over the telephone. They
were organized such that, after background information on age, education, occupational history, and family was gathered, respondents were encouraged to tell
their life stories as they pertained to their transgendered feelings and experiences. Respondents were
guided through several areas of inquiry, including
their earliest transgender experiences or feelings;
being discovered cross-dressed; acquiring girls' or
women's clothing, makeup, and wigs; learning about
and refining a feminine appearance or persona; participating in transgender support groups or on-line communities; finding therapists and surgeons and experiences with the medical community; identifying and
labeling emotions, feelings, behaviors, and identity;
telling others; transformations or stability in sexual
fantasy, behavior, and identity; and political and gender attitudes. Interviews ranged from 45 minutes to
eight hours in length, averaging about three hours.

Interviews were transcribed in full. An analytic-
inductive process was used in organizing and interpreting the descriptions and stories of the volunteers
in our sample (Miles and Huberman 1984). Data
analysis included three flows of activity: data reduction, which included the process of identifying emergent themes in the data; data display, the process of
organizing and clustering the information to be used
for deriving conclusions; and conclusion drawing and
verification, the process of deciding what experiences
mean, noting patterns and explanations, and verifying
our findings (Miles and Huberman 1984).

FINDINGS

Appearance is a central component in the establishment and maintenance of self and identity (Stone
1975). An alternative gender may be achieved only
through interaction, in which the recognition of others
has the potential to legitimate and reinforce the emer-

gent alternative identity. Therefore, in order to "be" themselves, whether on a temporary or permanent basis, transgenderists have a compelling need to present alternative expressions of gender. Many transgenderists choose to alter their external physical characteristics to conform to beliefs about "appropriate" appearance for the desired gender. Individual expressions of gender, as well as surgical, cosmetic, and medical procedures used to alter primary and secondary sex characteristics, are signifiers of identity. Such alternations help individuals explore and clarify who they are and may help them gain entrée to a community of others like themselves. Identity transformation is a social psychological process that develops with time, experiences, the management of emotions (Mason-Schrock 1996), conscious efforts, and interaction with others.

To examine the ways in which alternatively gendered identities are recognized, explored, evaluated, and declared (both privately and publicly), it is necessary to look at several developmental steps in the lives of transgendered persons. First, an identification of earliest memories of experiencing the "difference" or dissonant sex/gender sensations will be explored, followed by a look at how, when, and why transgenderists arrived at a self-definition as a transgendered person; and how, when, why, and to whom the processes of proclaiming this new identity to others was managed. Finally, we conclude with a discussion of where along the transgender spectrum individuals locate themselves and how they arrived at a salient and (relatively) stable identity.

Early Transgendered Experiences

Examination of the earliest recollections that transgendered individuals have of feeling that either their sex or gender was "wrong" or did not "fit" for them are useful in providing insight into the earliest manifestations that become alternative identities. Many recollections of childhood may, in fact, be reconstructed biographies. Nonetheless, these are materials from which individuals mold current identities and, therefore, are valid and significant.[4] This is the process in which the collective creation of biographical stories brings phenomenologically real "true selves" into being (Mason-Schrock 1996).

Gender constancy—a sense that a person's gender is a permanent aspect of self—is acquired between the ages of three and five years (Kohlberg 1966; Kohlberg and Ulian 1974). In our sample, 16 transsexuals recalled wanting to be girls or knowing that they really were girls during early childhood. For all but one of the remainder, feelings of being or wanting to be a woman emerged during adolescence or adulthood. Among cross-dressers, all reported knowing they were boys in early childhood and throughout adolescence, but four said they remembered wishing they could be girls during early childhood, and two reported knowing they were male but wishing they could become female during adolescence. Fetishistic cross-dressers and gender radicals did not report feeling they were or wanting to become women. Feminine behaviors and feelings of being or wanting to be girls created confusion for young children and adolescents, particularly when they received messages that they could not be or act that way.

For transsexuals and cross-dressers, one way of making sense of the incongruity between sex and gender was to explore whether a feminine boy might actually be able to become a girl. For example, one cross-dresser explained that at about the age of five, "I remember . . . asking my mother out in the backyard, 'Am I always going to be a boy? Could I change and be a girl someday?' " Such questions are undoubtedly common among young children. For most children, clothing and other expressions of gender are signifiers of maleness or femaleness. Cross-dressers explained that they were satisfied with explanations that they could not change their anatomy and become female but that they continued to want to temporarily "become" girls by wearing feminine clothing, makeup, and wigs. As adults, all but four cross-dressers (who were exploring the possibility they might be transsexual) reported knowing they were male and being happy with their sex and gender identity. Throughout their lives, they were able to conceal their transgenderism much more easily than were transsexuals, who felt compelled to act and be feminine at all times.

Among transsexuals, confusion over gender, desires to be female, or feelings of being female were commonly reported in childhood and over the life course. Many of the transsexuals in our sample thought they really were girls (in the dominant cultural sense) until they began to receive messages to the contrary. For example, one postoperative transsexual explained her earliest understanding of gender and the way in which it started to be corrected. She said,

> I was probably three or four years old. . . . I remember playing with paper dolls and Barbie dolls and stuff with my sisters and wearing their clothes. I didn't even know I wasn't a girl until [at school] I was told it was time to line up for a restroom break.

Differentiating themselves from girls did not come easily for these 16 transsexuals. Socializing messages might be gentle and subtle, as the ones above, or more laden with overt hostility and anger. For example, another preoperative transsexual explained,

> I can remember begging my mother to let me wear her clothes. . . . I kicked and screamed. . . . Another time she was ironing and I wanted my own ironing board and iron and be just like mommy. This time she got really angry and I guess I was becoming aware of the fact that I wasn't ever going to be a little girl, that it was socially unacceptable . . . because she said, "You want to be a little girl? Well, we'll put you in a little dress and tie your hair up i n ribbons." . . . She became aggressive about it and at that point I understood that it was socially unacceptable.

In early childhood, cross-dressing and cross-gender behavior appear to have been tolerated. However, as children advanced beyond the "toddler" stage, they were pressured by adults and other children to recognize and adhere to traditional conceptualizations of gender and conform to masculine stereotypes. Pressures to conform to the gender binary were often based on homophobic assumptions about gender "deviants." For example, a nonoperative transsexual said,

> Around the time I was 9 or 10 years old, there was one boy in the neighborhood . . . [who] was never allowed to spend the night at my house. . . . All he would tell me is, "My dad won't let me." One afternoon I approached his dad about it. . . . This man turned an incredible red-purple color and shaking and pointing a finger in my face [said], "Because

you're a fucking queer!" I didn't know what those words meant, but it was real clear from his body language that whatever those words were tied to was not OK.

The pressure to adhere to the masculine stereotype was strong, and many in our sample tried to conform. Cross-dressers hid their dressing, segmenting it off from the rest of their lives. Among transsexuals, such segmentation of the feminine aspect of self was more difficult. The majority felt more comfortable playing with girls, participating in "girls'" activities, and expressing and presenting themselves in more feminine ways. For those whose transgender feelings and behaviors began in early childhood, pressures to "fit" into the masculine stereotype and "act" like boys created confusion about identity, an internalized sense of deviance, and frequently strong self-loathing. For example, a preoperative transsexual said, "I didn't know it was transsexual. I just didn't feel like a male. Everyone was telling me I was and I felt I had to act that way . . . I felt it was something very, very wrong."

After an initial period of confusion about sex and gender, most children recognized that cross-dressing and feminine behavior were deviant and, therefore, they tried to repress it and keep it secret. This suggests that as children begin to understand the binary gender system, they become ashamed of feminine or transgendered feelings, learn to hide their behaviors, and become confused about who they are and how they fit into the world. Many in our sample talked about becoming addicted to alcohol or drugs later in life, in an effort to numb the emotional pain they experienced and to repress the "true self," which did not fit and, therefore, needed to be repressed. Throughout adolescence and adulthood, most went through periods of "purging," when they would stop engaging in transgendered behavior and throw out feminine clothing, makeup, and wigs. Despite the stigma attached to transgenderism, however, the need to "be themselves" was strong. Even as they tried to stop, and as their feminine attributes were criticized and sanctioned, they found it impossible to stop and learned to become more and more secretive. For example, a preoperative transsexual explained,

> I was being beat up, called sissy. . . . I didn't feel normal. I felt like, "Why are you doing this? This isn't

right. You're a boy." But I couldn't stop. The curiosity kept drawing me to it and I kept doing it. I felt guilty and I always thought after I . . . took the clothes off, "I'm not going to do this anymore. This is silly." A few days later . . . I was back doing it again.

Coming Out to One's Self

For many transgendered individuals, coming to terms with identity is driven by three factors: (1) events that inform them that to feel as they do is "wrong" (2) finding that there are names for their feelings, and (3) learning that there are others who have had similar experiences. The search for authenticity is a motivating factor in the desire to resolve identity (Gecas 1991). Because of the centrality of community in the formation and legitimation of identity (see Taylor and Whittier 1992), the efforts of transgenderists to find and express a "true self" are mitigated by their contacts with the transgendered world, just as they are affected by the dominant culture. To "confess" gender (or transgenderism), one must communicate in an established idiom or risk the desired authenticity. While new identities are emergent, they are created within the constraints of current understandings. Furthermore, because of dominant beliefs that incongruity between assumed sex and presented gender is indicative of homosexuality, and that such is deviant, as transgenderists mix or replace masculinity with femininity on either a temporary or permanent basis, they frequently wonder what this implies about their sexuality.

When individuals fail to adhere to the gender binary, they are often told they are wrong or bad, so they tend to initially think of themselves as sick or deviant. Until they find similar others who have rejected stigma, self-blame and the internalization of deviance are common. As the transgenderists in our sample became aware that there were others in the world like them, they experienced a sense of self-recognition, and most quickly aligned themselves with new potential identities. The refinement and adoption of relatively stable identities occurred within the possibilities offered by the transgender subculture, which has been heavily influenced by medical models of transgenderism.

For most individuals, the first display of feelings that are later labeled as transgendered come in the form of cross-dressing. Among adult transgenderists, cross-dressing is symbolically more important than "playing dress up." For fetishistic and nonfetishistic cross-dressers, it is an opportunity to express the feminine self; for gender radicals, it is a chance to blend the masculine and feminine aspects of self; and for transsexuals, it is a time to be one's self. Children learn at a very early age to attribute their own and others' sex and gender on the basis of clothing (Cahill 1989), and they find cross-dressing an accessible means of gender exploration. When others, especially valued and respected significant others, strongly oppose such actions, they effectively communicate a sense of deviance. All but two of our participants who engaged in transgender behaviors as children or adolescents told us that the message came through loud and clear: to cross-dress, or for that matter to do anything that was not "appropriately" masculine, was deviant and not to be discussed with others. Such messages worked to drive transgendered children into a secret world, where feelings about what was "natural" were held in private.

Most transsexuals and a minority of the cross-dressers in our sample reported being labeled "sissies" by parents, siblings, and school mates. The difference in experiences may be due to the fact that transsexuals reported an overwhelming urge to be feminine at all times, whereas cross-dressers could more easily segment the feminine self away from public scrutiny. Those labeled "sissy" or "girl-like" experienced extreme stigmatization, isolation, and at times abuse. Derogative comments from family members seemed to affect the self-esteem and self-concept more than insults from peers or other nonrelatives. One nonoperative transsexual married to a woman recounted how her parents and friends pressured her to be more masculine. She said,

> The kids in the neighborhood that I wanted to be friends with . . . were the girls. . . . I wanted my own doll and remember the boys in the neighborhood seemed to have a real problem with that. . . . In that same time period, my dad came into my bedroom one night and he took all the dolls out of my bed. He said I could keep the animals but the dolls had to go because, "You're a little boy and little boys don't sleep with dolls."

Even with such social sanctions, the feelings persisted. Among transsexuals and a minority of cross-dressers, to be doing what girls were doing felt comfortable and natural. For many, playing with boys was stressful, anxiety provoking, and often induced feelings of failure and low self-esteem. Consequently, many transgenderists found ways to separate themselves from those who reinforced the feeling of difference and deviance, staying to themselves as much as possible.

Just as children tried to conceal transgenderism or conform to the expectations of family and other socializing agents, adults were likely to engage in similar coping strategies until they began to accept themselves as transgenderists. Transsexuals tended to react to negative messages by being hypermasculine. As adults, many in our sample went into physically strenuous or high risk occupations where they could prove their masculinity. Some joined the military and others married, hoping to "cure" themselves of transgendered longings and behavior. For example, one preoperative transsexual, who got married at a time in her life when she identified as a cross-dresser, explained. "[Now] I'm okay. I'm one of the guys. I've scored. I'm a guy. I fit in with all the other guys. This will cure everything. Well, it didn't." She was cross-dressing within months of the wedding. Or, as an attempt to not be perceived as different during her life as a man, one preoperative transsexual explained, "[Working for a] moving company and the fact that I played windmill softball were both indicative of the many people in my situation where we overcompensate." Another said, "I would avoid doing anything that someone might see as being a remotely feminine kind of thing. I wouldn't even help my ex-[wife] plant a flower garden." Out of our entire sample, 18 had served in the military. Most said they hoped the experience would make men out of them. Although an extreme example of this sentiment, another preoperative transsexual explained,

> I knew there was something wrong with me and I wanted to do whatever I could to make a real man out of myself. So I joined the army. Voluntarily went to Vietnam. Voluntarily carried a machine gun in the jungle. I was a paratrooper. I was a Green Beret. I did everything I could do in a that three-year period to make a man out of myself. Cross-dressers were less likely to react in hypermasculine

ways, primarily because they kept their feminine side hidden.

Most transgenderists who recalled childhood, adolescence, and early adulthood as periods of confusion and turmoil found cross-dressing to be relaxing and comfortable and functioning as a woman to be natural. Their struggles with identity and relationships arose from society's sanctions.

Throughout childhood, adolescence, and early to mid adulthood most transgenderists in our study experienced shame and confusion for not being "right." They lived in a social region for which there was no idiom. Because they were sanctioned for feminine attributes and behavior, they learned that there was no place for feminine boys or men in society. Feeling more comfortable with girls, they began to understand gender and sex within the social options presented to them. The socially constructed aspects of reality were so strong that believing they were born with the wrong genitals seemed more plausible than violating the gender binary. Even in adulthood, transsexuals frequently made efforts to conceal their genitals, even from themselves, by tucking them between the legs or taping them up. While relatively uncommon in our sample (during adulthood, $n = 2$), when transsexuals were unaware of available medical options or were unable to afford SRS, they attempted self-castration. These efforts indicate the degree to which gender is signified by genitalia.

It was common in our sample for transgenderists to experience sexual attractions to other men, to have sexual fantasies about men, or both. At the same time, they experienced social sanctions and pressures to conform to dominant conceptualizations of gender. While they worried they might be gay, they began to experience and explore sexuality within the binary system and its ancillary compulsory heterosexuality (Rich 1989). As a 36-year-old bisexual cross-dresser explained, "You're getting all kinds of messages that men are men and women are women. Sissy boys and fags. The adolescent years are really, really hard on homosexuals and anything not mainstream sexually." Within our sample, adolescent male persons and adult men in the early stages of identity formation were frequently confused about the implications feminine behavior had on their sexuality. As men, they knew sex with male individuals was unacceptable; but as women, it was a source of validation. Most reacted by repressing attractions to men, at least until they began to go out in public as women, when sexual interactions with men were indicative of passage into social womanhood. Nonetheless, sexual interaction between social men was perceived by everyone in our sample as problematic. As a postoperative transsexual explained,

> There's been a few boys that I would have probably liked to have gotten it on with. The so-called labels back then of being homosexual, or gay, or something like that, kept me from doing it. . . . The fifties was when I grew up and you just didn't talk about things like that.

None of the people in our sample adopted a gay identity, even temporarily, although sexual experimentation with male persons was a common aspect of the coming-out experience. Because of an understanding that transgenderism, homosexuality, and femininity were wrong, all but two transgenderists made efforts to conceal, to purge, to deny, and to cure themselves in order to avoid acceptance of their transgenderism.

Most commonly, the triggering event for acceptance of an identity came when, either accidentally or intentionally, the individual encountered others who served as symbols for available identities. However, role models who challenged binary conceptualizations of gender were largely unavailable. Because "there is no place for a person who is neither a woman or a man" (Lorber 1994, 96), finding role models and formulating an identity outside the gender binary is virtually impossible. Thus, alternative identities were restricted to those available within the gender binary, usually found among those who had crossed *from* one gender *to* the only other one known to be legitimately available.

Symbolic others came from a variety of sources, including television, magazine articles, pornography, psychological or medical case reports, female impersonators and most recently, on-line computer services. However, most of these sources were not equally available to children and adolescents. Television appearances by pioneer transgenderists served to introduce many adolescents of the 1960s to Christine

Jorgensen and Jan Morris, and to Renee Richards in the 1970s. Learning of the availability of transsexualism and seeing such women on television and reading about them in newspapers and magazines provided opportunities to know that there were alternative identities available. One newly postoperative transsexual looked back on her late teens as generally unhappy and confusing but says that she made a major discovery about both herself and society when

> I was in high school and I started to hear about Renee Richards. I graduated high school in '72, so she was just coming out when I was just starting high school. At that time, I still thought that I was alone in the world. . . . When I started to hear about Renee Richards, then I said, Maybe there is somebody else, but this is the only other person that knows where I'm coming from.

Finding others who felt as they did helped to alleviate, but not remove, the sense of isolation experienced by transgendered individuals. Nonetheless, through such initial exposures, many individuals learned that there were alternatives to living in confusion and shame, if one was willing to transform (either temporarily or permanently) to the other gender. Simply learning that SRS was possible led some to reconfigure their identities and reassess their place in the world. One transsexual, who more than 20 years later is still awaiting SRS, recalled that when she was entering her teen years,

> I still didn't have those feelings of wanting to be a woman probably until about the age of 10 when the Christine Jorgensen thing broke. At that time, I knew it was possible for men to have sex changes. That's when I got my first feeling that I wanted to be a girl.

From this point onward, the way she perceived herself was different. Whereas she says that during childhood "I didn't feel like a girl, and I didn't feel like a boy. I just wanted to be myself," after learning about the possibility of SRS, she lived in a state of identity limbo. Finally, she says, "When [my feminine self] took her first injection [of hormones], she became a reality to me. She became a real person." While available role models and medical procedures may not dictate identity changes, they do provide alternatives that contribute to identity clarification. Feminine gender is culturally signified and, in Western society, dictated by anatomy (Laqueur 1990). Because such beliefs are internalized, many transgendered individuals feel compelled to physically alter their bodies.

Finding a symbol of sex and gender possibilities did not always occur in such a positive way. Although one might, for the first time, learn that alternatives to the gender binary exist, some transgenderists simultaneously learned that such people were "freaks" to be objectified. For instance, a Mormon preoperative transsexual, recounted how at about age 18, "[We would] pass around the pornography and look at it. It really didn't do anything for me until I actually saw a transgendered person in the magazine. . . . I really identified with that."

In a more positive fashion, a few years later in life, while searching out more information and identity reinforcement, this same person discovered a copy of a transgender organizational magazine, and recalled, "I felt like there were people like me. That was my niche and I more or less identified with that. I got more education through that magazine than anything else."

Finally, in today's information age, on-line computer services appear to be emerging as a primary location for finding both virtual and real mentors. It was common for transgenderists who deciphered and accepted their identities in the 1990s to have done so with the assistance of on-line bulletin boards and personal conversations with already-identifying transgenderists. Here, in the privacy of one's home or work area, contacts could be made that allowed both experimentation with identities and informational inquiries that did not jeopardize existing identities or social, occupational, and familial relationships. In addition, on-line services allowed individuals to access information beyond that concerning the strictly erotic aspects of cross-dressing. For some transgenderists, this was a critical factor, as tabloid media and sensationalist reports have created a common misperception of cross-dressing as primarily an erotic activity. A self-identified radical transgenderist credits his subscription to one on-line service with helping him understand that cross-dressing need not be sexually charged. He said, "It wasn't until I got a hold of [online service] that I got exposed to aspects other than the erotic aspects, which are all over the place."

Similarly, a preoperative transsexual who says she didn't understand most of her feelings found virtual role models in cyberspace when

> I was on [a service]. I was browsing through an adult area. There was a single topic on [it] called "Cross Dressing," and I bumped in the cross-dressing place there and read a biography. When I read that, I was shocked because I could have written that myself word for word. And then I read more biographies and each one of them was the same story I had. So what I had done was I found people that had similar histories as children that I did, and that validated me.

Not all persons who found virtual models defined them as helpful. For some, the occasion of encountering both real and reported transgenderists served only to raise more issues to be resolved. For example, one cross-dresser recalled finding fetishistic cross-dressers and transsexuals in cyberspace. He related, "Although there were similarities, there were also some grave differences, primarily in the fact that I felt more romantic interest. I didn't feel I was a heterosexual female trapped in a male body. I liked my male body." Still, finding others even tangentially similar provided a forum in which to discover options and explore alternative identities. Thus, while we "do" gender in interaction with others, it appears that the emergence of transgender identity and alternatives to the gender binary are dependent on others who will recognize one as an authentic social actor (West and Zimmerman 1987).

Coming Out to Others

Simply discovering (quasi-)similar others is not all that is needed for the transgendered individual to complete the coming-out process. Rather, finding a symbolic role model provides initial validation of a newly emergent identity and potential avenues to find further sources of external validation. The sources of validation that are most important for the stabilization of identity are the significant others in one's life and the community of similar others.

Accepting an identity for one's self was one thing; proclaiming and working to get others to accept it was quite different. Going public with a transgendered identity could be an intimidating experience, to say the least. Among our sample, cross-dressers, fetishistic cross-dressers, and gender radicals had greater control over the coming-out process than did transsexuals, primarily because the former, as a group, were more limited in their need and desire to publicly enact the feminine self. The two fetishistic cross-dressers in our sample had revealed their transgenderism to their sexual partners and to members of the support groups to which they belonged. In those groups, they were encouraged to come to meetings "dressed," despite the fact that neither had a desire to cross-dress except for sexual purposes. Most nonfetishistic cross-dressers in our sample had come out to their spouses before joining a support group. For a minority, finding a community of similar others gave individual cross-dressers the support they needed to explore their identity as transgendered individuals and to later inform spouses or other significant others. One cross-dresser said that his wife was relieved when he came out to her. He had been attending support group meetings and transgender conferences in another state, and she thought he was having an affair. Like cross-dressers, gender radicals could selectively come out or not reveal their transgendered identity to others. For them, support groups provided access to a community in which they could explore their gender identities.

Despite the differences among these categories, the years of mainstream socialization and messages about "proper" gender performance were influential on everyone in our sample. The degree to which transgenderists were intimidated about revealing their transgenderism may be heard in the words of a 10-month, postoperative transsexual, who said,

> For somebody who's been a freak, a hippie, and a marijuana dealer, . . . and a flamboyant dresser, and somebody who refuses to get a conventional job and all this, somebody who's not been afraid of public opinion, it's, I think, notable that the gender area of my life and the social expectations were the one area I was afraid of public opinion.

Intimidation was not limited to those desiring to go out publicly. One cross-dresser explained that his fear of coming out to his wife was so extreme that he thought the couple would have to separate so he could pursue his transgenderism. He said,

> I sat her down and we had a talk, and that's when I told her I couldn't live this way anymore and I was going to leave. [I told her] that I loved her and the kids, but I couldn't tell her why. . . . [After a few days] we talked this all out and I finally went ahead and told her. . . . She said, "You go in there and dress. I want to see what you look like." So then I dressed up for her the first time. I was nervous and scared to death. I was shaking from inside out. . . . We sat down and discussed the basic rules on how this was going to work. . . . That's been five years ago, and we're still together.

Intimidation came from two fronts: (1) fears about how one would be treated by others and (2) anxieties about how others would cope with what was certainly seen by many as "nontraditional" behavior. Fear of the responses one will receive is to be expected. With the close cultural association drawn between transgenderism and homosexuality (Altman 1982; Bullough and Bullough 1993; Talamini 1982), fears of violent and isolating homophobic reactions seem warranted.[5] In addition, as people involved in significant relationships with others, many expressed concerns about how the news that they were transgendered would affect those close to them. These concerns typically centered on one's family, both nuclear and extended.

According to the accounts of those who have proclaimed their transgender identities to significant others, the fears about negative reactions were largely exaggerated, but not altogether unwarranted. Less than one-fourth of all persons interviewed for this project reported that their first experience of coming out to someone else lead to a negative reaction. This was related to several factors. First, transgenderists had exaggerated fears about the reactions of most significant others. Second, most individuals were actually successful at controlling knowledge of their transgenderism. They consciously selected individuals to come out to who were, in fact, sympathetic to the alternative identity. Who would be accepting was ascertained through discussions of various potentially volatile issues. In that way, transgenderists learned if there was a need for caution or preparatory education of the recipient. Those who received negative reactions to their proclamations were least likely to have gathered information or to have laid the necessary groundwork. Instead, they simply announced the new identity. For example, a preoperative transsexual decided to tell an 18-year-old daughter, who did not even know that her father had been cross-dressing, when the daughter moved back home. She said,

> After a week or two there, it seemed inappropriate not to tell my daughter. The girl lives in the house. For crying out loud, she's 18 years old. So I told her and I didn't really build up to it or anything. . . . She was always in the bathroom, doing hair and makeup and stuff. I stopped in to chat. I suppose it was like a bomb or something like that. "By the way . . . I'm going to have a sex change." She turned into an ice cube.

Although the experience of telling one's first "other" was not necessarily a negative experience, fears remained, and careful, often painful, decisions were made regarding with whom to share an emergent identity. Interestingly, two factors stand out about these early disclosures. First, they were usually done only out of a sense of responsibility, when someone was perceived as "needing to know." Second, the individuals with whom this information was shared were almost always female, most often a significant other. This was true among all groups of transgenderists in our sample.

While some elected to share with their mothers, there was a characteristic tendency for most to report that it was extremely difficult to share their new identity with their parents. For some, this was more easily accomplished when the interaction with one's parents was not face-to-face or when the situation could be escaped quickly. Despite the urge to deliver the news and run, those who came out to others face-to-face, who had provided (or offered to provide) information about transgenderism, and gave others time and space to cope with the information were most likely to receive tolerant, accepting, or supportive reactions. Still, much of the reaction to being told was dependent on the values of the recipient of the news, as well as the relationship itself. For example, a two-year postoperative transsexual who had been living with her male partner prior to having surgery recalled telling her mother about her decision to have SRS. She said, "I told her, 'Mom, I'm transsexual and I'm going to have

SRS.' My mom's response was, 'Oh, thank God! I can deal with this.' She thought I was going to tell her [my partner] and I were HIV positive." While cross-dressers commonly came out only to spouses and other transgenderists, transsexuals typically enlisted the supportive family members they had told to help them inform other relatives. Because their transitions are permanent and public, coming out cannot be restricted. One transsexual explained, "From my mom, I told my two sisters. . . . [Then] I think it was my grandmother, then my father. And I just couldn't bring myself to tell my kids, and so my mom told them." Coming out to those one expected to be supportive, based on an established past, provided both difficulties and benefits. While it might be hard to risk the support, there was often a belief that (at least after an initial period of shock) the established foundation of the relationship would win out and the informed other would be supportive.

The arena where transgenderists (usually transsexuals) were least likely to receive positive reactions was at work. Although there were a few people who were permitted to transition on the job, it was more common for transsexuals to be fired, demoted, pressured to quit, and harassed by other workers. Some found employment in unskilled, low-wage jobs, such as janitors or in fast-food restaurants; others worked for temporary agencies. A few in our sample went back to college, transitioning as students. The loss of identity and the structure of one's daily routine that comes with a career was more difficult for transsexuals to cope with than the actual loss of income. After accepting a severance package in exchange for her silence about her job termination, one postoperative transsexual wrote to the first author, "I have spent my entire life becoming the best [job title] I could be. Today I sold myself for 50 pieces of silver." Frequently, the loss of professional identity and income came at the same time that relationships with old friends and family members were being risked and sometimes lost.

Early excursions into the public domain were commonly as frightening as coming out to significant others or on the job. While going out and passing in public may be thought to be different from coming out, it is important to recognize that for the majority of transgenderists, the goal is to be perceived and accepted as a woman, not a transgenderist. Telling others about their transgenderism is done primarily to lay the groundwork for greater expression, acceptance, and legitimation of a feminine identity, and this is accomplished in public and in private interactions. Although there was variation between going out in public or telling a significant other first, every person in our sample felt a need to expand their spheres of interaction with others. While control over access to information about the transgendered identity remained important, this became less salient as the need to interact with others publicly increased. Because of the fear of the danger inherent in negative public reactions, most transgenderists carefully planned and carried out their initial public excursions in limited-access locations.

When transgenderists began to go out in public, they did so because of a need to receive reactions from others to legitimate identity. While some have undoubtedly been driven back into the closet by their initial forays into public places, in our sample, such excursions served to increase commitment to the emergent identity. Selection of safe places for public ventures meant that transgenderists looked for locations where they could make quick and easy entrances and exits and where they are unlikely to encounter disapproving others. Transgenderists most commonly reported that their first ventures were to gay community events or locations, simply driving in their cars, or going to known meeting places for transgenderists. The most common site for first ventures was gay bars. Here, among other marginalized community members, individuals could try out their new identities. Despite a strong desire to avoid being perceived as homosexual, gay bars were defined as safe havens (Levine, Shaiova, and Mihailovic 1975). For example, a preoperative transsexual, who had been living as a woman full-time for seven months, related that "while I was working on coming out full-time, I needed a safe place to go while I practiced. The bar was it. I know the drag queens might not like that. It was still a safe place for me though." For others, the thought of venturing into such a public setting and actually interacting with others, even if they might be

expected to be understanding, was simply too intimidating. Instead, some felt a need to slowly transition into public outings. For these individuals, the easiest way to be out, but not relinquish too much control, was to drive through populated areas, often including the vicinity of gay community settings. In this way, especially since most did so after dark, they could be seen, but not so well as to seriously threaten their ability to pass. A radical transgenderist, who has an understanding and supportive female partner reported that "I think the first time out was just to drive around with my girlfriend. We were going to a local gay bar, but it wasn't open at the time. We just drove and got fast food."

Typically, successful ventures while driving provided the impetus and courage for transgenderists to move forward and present themselves face-to-face with others; however, these steps were taken slowly and carefully. Movement from the car was usually into either a gay bar or a gathering of other transgenderists. For example, a preoperative transsexual who is fully out only to one family member and acquaintances in the transgender community, explained her first time out in public as follows:

> About 10 years ago. . . . I was out very late one night, got in my car, drove downtown to the north side of the city which is known for its gays, lesbians, and an occasional transvestite. Walked to what I thought was a bar where transvestites hung out and sat down, had a couple of drinks, couple cigarettes. . . . I did things like get dressed and drove around. I'd go for a short walk around the block or something. I didn't think I was good enough yet to go out in daylight and try to pull it off as a woman.

In gay bars and neighborhoods, transgenderists were most likely to be interpreted as marginal members of the queer subculture. Such settings provide a place where one who is "neither woman nor man" (Lorber 1994, 96) is most likely to find a social place that does not disturb the social order.

While transgenderists are likely to be interpreted as marginal members of the gay or queer subculture, they can experiment with sex, gender, and sexual identity in such locales. Frequently, while out as women who are (relatively) obviously male, transgenderists will have their first experiences being treated "like ladies." Woodhouse (1989, 31) has described a category of male individuals who do not want to have sex with a man or with a woman but who still want sex; so, they have sex with men dressed as women. These so-called "punters" provide opportunities for transgenderists to perfect their feminine persona and, for those who wish to learn more about themselves, to explore their sexuality. The overwhelming motivation for flirting in the bar and having sexual relations with men was to be treated "like a lady" and to explore the gendered aspects of sexuality.[6] It is through such interactions that many transsexuals and some cross-dressers encounter the final rite of passage as authentic heterosexual women, whether or not they have undergone SRS.

For others, the impetus to appear in public for the first time surfaced when opportunities arose to meet other transgenderists in the context of a support group. Support groups were one location where the most important identity tests occurred, when the individual encountered other transgenderists. As they entered such groups, transgenderists commonly reported a feeling of total acceptance and freedom to be themselves, often for the first time in their lives. If these supposedly similar others were willing to accept the individual, and the individual felt safe in the group, this communicated that she or he truly was transgendered. The value of support groups, on-line services, organizations, and publications becomes most clear in this context.

Support groups can be very important in facilitating identity exploration and the arrival at a "final" identity, but they could also induce anxiety, confusion, and fright in individual transgenderists. While they may have already confronted their "difference" in their own minds and with others in their lives, to come face-to-face with "the real thing" could be intimidating. For those who were courageous enough to take such steps, support groups almost always functioned as they were intended: They provided support for a stigmatized identity. Nonetheless, such acceptance was provided within a narrow range of social options that were based on acceptance of a binary system of sex and gender. Transsexualism was commonly explained by biological theories, and those

who had completed the transition process gave advice on how to gain access to medical procedures to those in earlier stages. Among cross-dressers, "dressing" was encouraged as an acceptable way for men to express the feminine self. All transgenderists were encouraged to perfect their ability to pass during informal interactions and copious seminars on style, makeup, feminine body language, and the feminine voice and diction.

In addition to the facilitating function of support groups, many transgenderists reported that their public proclamations were in large part propelled by encouragement (or instructions) from a therapist. The overwhelming majority of our sample were or had been active in counseling/therapy. Many therapists, especially those who seemed to be well liked by their clients, encouraged coming out, appearing to others, and learning to pass as women. If one were to view transgenderism as "normal," it should be treated as such, particularly by the transgenderist; however, "normality" was defined as the desire to be and pass as a woman. Among our sample, only a small minority was willing to be publicly known as transgendered.

Resolution of Identity

After a lifetime of being stigmatized and feeling as if they did not fit, the transgenderists in our sample engaged in a long process of identity exploration. The majority in our sample explained that they had arrived at a "true" identity, with which they felt they could "be themselves." Only a minority of men who cross-dressed but were exploring transsexualism had not yet resolved their identities. In their efforts to resolve and establish an identity that was comfortable for themselves, the individuals in our sample shared diverse goals and visions for themselves and the community. Transsexuals sought to "completely" transform and live convincingly as their true (female) selves. Cross-dressers sought only to have opportunities to temporarily vary their public identity presentations, express their femininity, and be recognized and treated as women. Only the gender radicals in our sample wished to live and be recognized as transgendered. Significant differences appeared among specific transgender identities. Among most transsexuals and cross-dressers, there was an overwhelming desire to pass as women, for it was through such interactions that femininity and treatment as a woman were achieved. For a minority, as experience and confidence were gained, passing was a desirable, but no longer essential, aspect of going out in public. These people tended to recognize that physical stature, including height and musculature, made it difficult, if not impossible, for them to pass. Among gender radicals, concerns with presenting a convincing appearance as a woman were secondary, if at all important. For them, the goal was to challenge dominant conceptualizations of gender and create new possibilities.

Among transsexuals, because of the internalized identity as women, it was most common to find an aspiration to be seen and identified by others as real women. When discussing this feeling, transsexuals expressed a need to "pass" in their daily interactions. This desire was paramount for such individuals and taken as a symbolic testament of final arrival at their desired self and socially constructed identity. One divorced, preoperative transsexual summarized this sentiment well when she commented, "[Passing] to me is the most important aspect of the whole thing. If you can't do that, I don't see the point of living this way." Enduring the internal and social struggles encountered in the process of recognizing and accepting a new identity and introducing oneself to the outside world was valued only if there could be a non-stigmatizing, "normal" resolution to the process. Transsexuals did not wish to challenge the gender binary, although most perceived their transitions as very radical actions. Rather, their goal was to "become" the women they "truly are" and to pass from being their masculine selves into full womanhood. Often, after learning to pass and completing the transformation process, transsexuals dropped out of the transgender community and assumed their place as women in society.

Within the transgender community, a desire to pass and blend into society sometimes introduced tensions and additional levels of hierarchy and structure. Those who sought to pass, and believed they had the ability to do so, sometimes believed that varying statuses of achievement (passing ability) were important. Some passable transgenderists, therefore, viewed those who could not pass as liabilities. Being seen with a detectable transgenderist was believed to bring suspicion and possible detection to those who would otherwise pass. Once again, the above transsexual showed her aptitude for clear expression when she explained her withdrawal from a local support group because, "I didn't feel the group gave me anything. I was too far ahead of them. . . . We're still friends, but I won't walk down the street with them."

Although most transgenderists were concerned with passing as well as possible, there is an emergent group within the community that seeks a free expression of gender, outside of the binary system. For example, the ambigenderist in our sample explained that she had moved beyond such concerns, focusing on her own welfare and identity, not the perceptions of others.

> At one time, [passing] was important. I don't care anymore. A lot of times I'll go out in a dress . . . no makeup on. I'm not trying to pass and I know I'm not going to pass. I am who I am. . . . It is political, everything's political. A social statement about who I am and I'm going to express myself.

Similarly, a former self-identified transsexual, turned gender radical, had kept a masculine name and avoided feminine pronouns while living as a woman. This person expressed the belief that passing is something that many transgenderists experience and then move through, saying, "I think passing is more a fear that has to be overcome and when I overcame that fear to being nonchalant about it, I didn't care that I passed or not."

For both those who were and were not seeking to pass when in public, the most common, overwhelming desire was to simply be accepted. This was difficult unless they could find ways to fit within the binary and symbolically communicate identity within the idiomatic system of gender expression. To "blend in" to society as a woman was something most transgenderists, especially transsexuals, saw as an ultimate goal. The ultimate resolution was an identity that was not wrapped in the language of transgenderism. To be known as simply just another person was desirable.

Despite one's own aspirations for individual identity and ability to blend socially, there was a sense of community among the vast majority of transgenderists that facilitated a desire to work with others and to contribute to the developmental processes of other community members. Regardless of the variety of community members, the plurality of individuals expressed a keen ambition to contribute to the psychological, social, and physical development of other transgendered community members. Helping others transform appears to be an important final "step" in the transformation process. Nonetheless, there are variations within the community. For transsexuals, the desire to participate in, and contribute to, the transgendered community appears to be relatively temporary. Once a stable identity as "woman" has been established, many leave the community. For cross-dressers, the community provides an opportunity to go out in public. For those who wish to challenge cultural conceptualizations of gender, support groups serve as potential social movement organizations.

This attempt to contribute to the development of others in the community came in both implicit and explicit forms. For some, this could be accomplished simply by being visible to other community members. More often, such forms of encouragement and assistance were much more direct and overt. For example, a gender radical, who is an active member of a local support group, editor of a local transgender community newsletter, and who conducts research on the structure of the transgender community, merged the implicit and explicit. This person explained,

> I feel the best thing I can do to create change is just to thrive, to be myself, to present myself in a way that I am comfortable with. The hell with everything else. . . . We need to be more open. We need to be more proud of who we are as opposed to being more ashamed. I think our movement could be much stronger. . . . I want people to start questioning things even though they may look at me oddly. People always say that I am sick or insane. Maybe one person may start to look at things differently. If other people start seeing that, we can act normally in the open with people knowing about you and that they don't have to be frightened.

To help other individual transgenderists, it was necessary to work at social change. Without changing the cultural context, the social infrastructure, and the idiom in which transgenderists are perceived and alternative genders are achieved, it is highly unlikely that the experiences and identities of individual transgenderists can be "normalized," without placing them back within a binary system.

CONCLUSION

Gender is so pervasive that it is taken for granted and often completely over-looked, until the norms of gender presentation, interaction, or organization are inadvertently violated or deliberately challenged (Lorber 1994). Gender receives constant surveillance and is continually policed through social interactions that socialize new and existing members of society and sanction those who violate the rules (see Gagné and Tewksbury 1996). At the organizational level, individuals are categorized and assigned meaning and roles on the basis of gender. For example, one of the first questions asked on organizational applications is one's sex. This is based on the erroneous assumption that gender will be congruent with sex. In organizational settings, sleeping arrangements are often based on sex/gender (as in dormitory arrangements) and bathrooms and locker rooms are segregated by sex/gender (see Rothblatt 1995). Where individuals' gender does not "match" their sex, there is little organizational space in which they can exist. At the institutional level (in the military, economic, religious, legal, political, and medical realms), individuals' roles, rights, and responsibilities are determined by gender, under the assumption that gender is indicative of sex (or sexuality) and that labor must continue to be divided on that basis. For example, in the military, female persons have been restricted from combat duty and homosexuals have been restricted from military service because of the disruption they are believed to pose to the military system, which is firmly based on a binary system of sex, gender, and sexuality. Often thought of as part of the superstructure of society, gender is an inherent component of the infrastructure itself (Lorber 1994). Nonetheless, in everyday life, gender is achieved and reinforced through interactions, where its idiom is derived from, and either legitimated or stigmatized by, the very superstructure and infrastructure in which it exists (West and Fenstermaker 1995).

Individuals who attempt to challenge the binary conceptualization of sex and gender, by living androgynously between genders, are likely to be ridiculed and stigmatized (see Gagné and Tewksbury 1996). Those who attempt to live outside of the sex/gender binary, for example, by publicly confessing that they are male persons with (or who would like to have) breasts or vaginas, are also likely to be ostracized. Those who are willingly or unwittingly unconvincing in their gender presentations and interactions are subject to greater levels of emotional and physical abuse than are those who are able to pass. It is those who are publicly perceived as "not women/not men" who pose the greatest challenge to the binary system. Nonetheless, the goal of most is to be perceived as a woman and treated like a lady. Those who pass are perceived as women, and any challenge they might have posed to the gender system goes unnoticed.

To challenge the binary, individuals must overcome a number of interactional, organizational, and structural barriers. They must learn to live and find ways to cope with the discomfort and hostility that others express at not being able to categorize them within existing gender categories. They need to find ways to support themselves and interact with others in organizations that have social spaces for women and men only. And, they must find ways to establish themselves as legal and social actors within institutions that recognize only two sexes and two congruent genders. Given these pressures, it is understandable why most transgendered individuals come out quickly and cross over to the "other" gender category.

As we have shown, the recognition, exploration, establishment, and final resolution of an identity outside cultural understandings is a difficult, complex, and for some, impossible process. Despite the policing of gender that was experienced by the transgenderists in our sample, the need to express a "true self" was an overwhelming urge that could not be denied. Although many tried to hide their femininity through hypermasculine activity or self-isolation, and most tried to deny transgendered feelings and urges, all eventually found the urge to "be themselves" overwhelmingly undeniable. Among our sample, others' reactions to them playing with girls, engaging in "girls'" activities, cross-dressing, wearing makeup,

and other expressions of a feminine self caused confusion, anxiety, and a deep sense of shame. Only when they discovered that there were others like them were they able to begin to make sense of what they were experiencing and who they were. Entering into a community of supportive others allowed for an exploration and resolution of identity. Our data suggest that gender is not a natural and inevitable outgrowth of sex. Those who are not comfortable expressing gender that is congruent with genital configuration experience an overwhelming urge to express gender in alternative ways. Nonetheless, the vast majority stay within the gender binary as masculine men and feminine women. The tendency to stay within the binary gender system is so strong that as Hausman (1993) has asserted, gender determines sex, rather than the reverse. Given the limited range of identities available to them, it is interesting, but not surprising, that the overwhelming majority of transgendered individuals adhere to traditional conceptualizations of sex and gender.

NOTES

1. Where sex, gender, and sexuality have been most apparent in this literature has been in the research distinguishing differing patterns of self-definition and public pronouncements between lesbians and gay men. Among lesbians, there appears to be a pattern of self-definition in same-sex affectionate involvements (Cronin 1974), whereas among gay men self-definition is most likely in social/sexual contexts (Troiden 1988; Warren 1974).

2. In this article, unless otherwise stated, "cross-dresser" refers to a nonfetishistic cross-dresser.

3. We recognize that there is a transgender community within the impoverished class, but we were unable to solicit volunteers from that segment of the population through the routes we used.

4. This view, however, is disputed by others who believe that retrospective biography construction is actually a search for ways "to fashion this information into a story that leads inexorably to the identity" that is being constructed (Mason-Schrock 1996, 176–77).

5. A substantial minority of our sample talked about experiencing intimidation, harassment, and violence in public places. It was not uncommon for those learning to "pass" to be called "faggot" or other homophobic epithets. One very tall, muscular cross-dresser told us about having her wig pulled off and being physically assaulted, and one preoperative transsex-

ual had to move after receiving death threats from her neighbors.

6. Those who wished to determine whether they were gay reported having sex with men while not dressed as women. It appears that sexual interaction was a form of gender play and exploration of gender-based heterosexual identity.

REFERENCES

Adam, Barry. 1995. *The rise of a gay and lesbian movement.* Rev. ed. New York: Twayne.

Altman, Dennis. 1982. *The homosexualization of America.* Boston: Beacon.

Bell, Allen P., and Martin Weinberg. 1978. *Homosexualities: A study of diversity among men and women.* New York: Simon & Schuster.

Blackwood, Evelyn. 1984. Sexuality and gender in certain Native American tribes: The case of cross-gender females. *Signs: Journal of Women in Culture and Society* 10:27–42.

Blanchard, Roy. 1988. Nonhomosexual gender dysphoria. *The Journal of Sex Research* 24:188–93.

Bornstein, Kate. 1994. *Gender outlaw. On men, women, and the rest of us.* New York: Random House.

Brown, George. 1990. A review of clinical approaches to gender dysphoria. *Journal of Clinical Psychiatry* 51:57–64.

Bullough, Vern L., and Bonnie Bullough. 1993. *Cross dressing, sex, and gender.* Philadelphia: University of Pennsylvania Press.

Callender, Charles, and Lee M. Kochems. 1983. The North American berdache. *Current Anthropology* 24:443–70.

———. 1985. Men and not-men: Male gender-mixing statuses and homosexuality. *Journal of Homosexuality* 11:165–78.

Cass, Vivien C. 1979. Homosexual identity formation: A theoretical model. *Journal of Homosexuality* 4:219–35.

———. 1984. Homosexual identity formation: Testing a theoretical model. *Journal of Sex Research* 20:143–67.

Cahill, Spencer. 1989. Fashioning males and females: Appearance management and the social reproduction of gender. *Symbolic Interaction* 2:281–98.

Chauncey, George. 1994. *Gay New York: Gender, urban culture, and the making of the gay male world 1890–1940.* New York: Basic Books.

Coleman, Eli. 1981–82. Developmental stages of the coming out process. *Journal of Homosexuality* 7:31–43.

Cronin, Denise M. 1974. Coming out among lesbians. In *Sexual deviance and sexual deviants,* edited by Erich Goode and Richard Troiden. New York: William Morrow.

D'Emilio, John. 1983. *Sexual politics, sexual communities: The making of a homosexual minority in the United States, 1940–1970.* Chicago: University of Chicago Press.

de Monteflores, Carmen, and Stephen J. Schultz. 1978. Coming out: Similarities and differences for lesbians and gay men. *Journal of Social Issues* 34:59–72.

Docter, Richard F. 1988. *Transvestites and transsexuals: Toward a theory of cross-gender behavior.* New York: Plenum.

Epstein, Steven. 1994. A queer encounter: Sociology and the study of sexuality. *Sociological Theory* 12:188–202.

Feinbloom, Deborah H. 1977. *Transvestites and transsexuals.* New York: Delta Books.

Foucault, Michel. [1978] 1990. *The history of sexuality: An introduction.* Vol. 1, translated by Robert Hurley. Reprint, New York: Vintage.

Gagné, Patricia, and Richard Tewksbury. 1996. No "man's" land: Transgenderism and the stigma of the feminine man. In *Advances in gender research.* Vol. 1, edited by Marcia Texler Segal and Vasilikie Demos. Greenwich, CT: JAI.

Garber, Marjorie. 1995. *Vice versa: Bisexuality and the eroticism of everyday life.* New York: Simon & Schuster.

Gecas, Viktor. 1991. The self-consent as a basis for a theory of motivation. In *The self-society dynamic,* edited by J. A. Howard and P. L. Callero. Cambridge, England: Cambridge University Press.

Goffman, Erving. 1963. *Stigma: Notes on the management of a spoiled identity.* Englewood Cliffs, NJ: Prentice-Hall.

Hausman, B. L. 1993. Demanding subjectivity: Transsexualism, medicine and the technologies of gender. *Journal of the History of Sexuality* 3:270–302.

Herdt, Gilbert. 1994. Introduction: Third sexes and third genders. In *Third sex, third gender: Beyond sexual dimorphism in culture and history,* edited by Gilbert Herdt. New York: Zone Books.

Huber, Joan. 1989. A theory of gender stratification. In *Feminist frontiers II: Rethinking sex, gender, and society,* edited by Laurel Richardson and Verta Taylor. New York: Random House.

Huber, Joan, and Glenna Spitze. 1983. *Sex stratification: Children, housework, and jobs.* New York: Academic Press.

Isay, Richard A. 1990. Psychoanalytic theory and the therapy of gay men. In *Homosexuality/heterosexuality: Concepts of sexual orientation,* edited by D. P. McWhirter, S. A. Sanders, and J. M. Reinisch. New York: Oxford University Press.

Kohlberg, Lawrence. 1966. A cognitive-developmental analysis of children's sex-role concepts and attitudes. In *The development of sex differences,* edited by Eleanor E. Maccoby. Stanford, CA: Stanford University Press.

Kohlberg, Lawrence, and D. Z. Ulian. 1974. Stages in the development of psychosexual concepts and attitudes. In *Sex differences in behavior,* edited by R. C. Friedman, R. M. Richard, and R. L. Vande Wiele. New York: Wiley.

Laqueur, Thomas. 1990. *Making sex: Body and gender from the Greeks to Freud.* Cambridge, MA: Harvard University Press.

Levine, Edward M., Charles H. Shaiova, and Miodrag Mihailovic. 1975. Male to female: The role transformation of transsexuals. *Archives of Sexual Behavior* 5:173–85.

Lorber, Judith. 1994. *Paradoxes of gender.* New Haven, CT: Yale University Press.

Mason-Schrock, Doug. 1996. Transsexuals' narrative construction of the "true self." *Social Psychology Quarterly* 59: 176–92.

Miles, Matthew B., and A. Michael Huberman. 1984. *Qualitative data analysis: A sourcebook of new methods.* Beverly Hills, CA: Sage.

Morris, Jan. 1974. *Conundrum.* London: Faber & Faber.

Namaste, Ki. 1994. The politics of inside/out: Queer theory, poststructuralism, and a sociological approach to sexuality. *Sociological Theory* 12:220–31.

Newton, Esther. 1979. *Mother camp: Female impersonators in America.* 2d ed. Chicago: University of Chicago Press.

Pauly, Ira B. 1990. Gender identity disorders: Evaluation and treatment. *Journal of Sex Education & Therapy* 16:2–24.

Persinger, Michael, and Laurence Stettner. 1991. The relationship of transvestite behavior to self-rated personality characteristics. *Journal of Psychology and Human Sexuality* 4:83–96.

Person, E., and L. Ovesey. 1984. Homosexual cross-dressers. *Journal of the American Academy of Psychoanalysis* 12:167–86.

Prince, Virginia, and P. M. Bentler. 1972. Survey of 504 cases of transvestism. *Psychological Reports* 31:903–17.

Raymond, Janice G. 1994. *The transsexual empire: The making of the she-male.* New York: Teachers College Press.

Rich, Adrienne. 1989. Compulsory heterosexuality and lesbian existence. In *Feminist frontiers II: Rethinking sex, gender, and society,* edited by Laurel Richardson and Verta Taylor. New York: Random House.

Rothblatt, Martine. 1995. *The apartheid of sex: A manifesto on the freedom of gender.* New York: Crown.

Seidman, Steven. 1994. Symposium: Queer theory/sociology: A dialogue. *Sociological Theory* 12:166–77.

———, ed. 1996. *Queer theory/sociology.* Cambridge, MA: Blackwell.

Stein, Arlene, and Ken Plummer. 1994. "I can't even think straight": Queer theory and the missing sexual revolution in sociology. *Sociological Theory* 12:178–87.

Stoller, Robert J. 1971. The term "transvestism." *Archives of General Psychiatry* 24:230–37.

Stone, Gregory P. 1975. Appearance and the self. In *Life as theatre: A dramaturgical sourcebook,* edited by Dennis Brissett and Charles Edgley. Chicago: Aldine.

Talamini, John T. 1981. Transvestism: Expression of a second self. *Free Inquiry in Creative Sociology* 9:72–74.

———. 1982. *Boys will be girls: The hidden world of the heterosexual male transvestite.* Lanham, MD: University Press of America.

Taylor, Verta, and Nancy Whittier. 1992. Collective identity and social movement communities: Lesbian feminist mobilization. In *Frontiers in social movement theory,* edited by Aldon D. Morris and Carol McClurg Mueller. New Haven, CT: Yale University Press.

Tewksbury, Richard, and Patricia Gagné. 1996. Transgenderists: Products of non-normative intersections of sex, gender, and sexuality. *Journal of Men's Studies* 5:105–29.

Troiden, Richard. 1988. *Gay and lesbian identity.* Dix Hills, NY: General Hall.

Troiden, Richard, and Erich Goode. 1980. Variables related to the acquisition of a gay identity. *Journal of Homosexuality* 5:383–92.

Warren, Carol A. B. 1974. *Identity and community in the gay world.* New York: Wiley.

Weinberg, Martin S., Colin J. Williams, and Douglas W. Pryor. 1994. *Dual attraction: Understanding bisexuality.* New York: Oxford University Press.

Weinberg, Thomas S. 1978. On "doing" and "being" gay: Sexual behavior and homosexual male self-identity. *Journal of Homosexuality* 4:563–78.

West, Candace, and Sarah Fenstermaker. 1995. Doing difference. *Gender & Society* 9:8–37.

West, Candace, and Don H. Zimmerman. 1987. Doing gender. *Gender & Society* 1:125–51.

Whitehead, Harriet. 1981. The bow and the burden strap: A new look at institutionalized homosexuality in native North America. In *Sexual meanings: The cultural construction of gender and sexuality,* edited by Sherry B. Ortner and Harriet Whitehead. London: Cambridge University Press.

Woodhouse, Annie. 1989. *Fantastic women: Sex, gender and transvestism.* New Brunswick, NJ: Rutgers University Press.

5.6 THE M/F BOXES

E. J. Graff

A 15-year-old girl is incarcerated in a Chicago mental hospital in 1981 and kept there for three years because she won't wear a dress. A Winn-Dixie truck driver is fired from a job he held for twenty years when his boss learns that he wears women's clothes at home. A small-time hustler in Falls City, Nebraska, is raped and then murdered when he's discovered to be physically female. A woman bleeds to death after a Washington, DC, hit-and-run accident when, after finding male genitals under her clothes, paramedics stand by laughing.

M or F? For most of us that's a simple question, decided while we were in utero. Checking off that box—at the doctor's, on the census, on a driver's license—takes scarcely a thought. But there's an emerging movement of increasingly vocal people whose bodies or behavior unsettle that clear division. They're calling themselves "transgendered": It's a spongy neologism that, at its broadest, absorbs everyone from medically reassigned transsexuals to cross-dressing men to women so masculine that security guards are called to eject them from women's restrooms. Fellow travelers include intersexuals (once called hermaphrodites), whose bodies are both/and rather than either/or. The slash between M/F cuts painfully through these lives.

And so they've started to organize. Brought together by the Internet, inspired by the successes of the gay rights movement, and with national sympathy gained from the movie *Boys Don't Cry,* intersex and transgender activists are starting to get a hearing in organizations ranging from college campuses to city councils, from lesbian and gay rights groups to pediatric conferences. And, like the feminist and gay rights movements before them, the new sex-and-gender activists may force us to rethink, in life and in law, how we define and interpret the basics of sex.

A first clue to how zealously the M/F border is guarded—to how sex is literally constructed—comes at birth. One in 2,000 infants is born with genitalia ambiguous enough to make doctors hem and haw when parents ask that first question: boy or girl? Since the late 1950s/early 1960s, standard medical procedure has been to lie and obfuscate. Rather than explain that the child is "a mixture of male and female," writes Anne Fausto-Sterling, author of *Sexing the Body,* medical manuals advise physicians to reassign the child surgically to one sex or another, telling parents only that "the gonads were incompletely developed . . . and therefore required removal." A large clitoris may be cut down; a micropenis may be removed and a vagina built; a testis or testes are sliced out—sometimes over the parents' explicit objections.

Now some of those children have come of age and are telling their stories: severe depression, sexual numbness and a longtime despair at having been folded, spindled and mutilated. The leader of this nascent movement is Cheryl Chase, who in 1993 organized the Intersex Society of North America. ISNA opposes reassignment surgery on intersex infants and advocates raising intersex children as social males or females, educating them about their bodies and letting them choose at puberty whether they'd like surgical assistance or a shift in social sex. ISNA's cause was helped when Johns Hopkins sex researcher and PhD John Money, who wrote the intersex silence-and-reassignment protocol, was profoundly discredited. After a child he called "John" was accidentally castrated soon after birth, Money advised his parents to have him undergo surgery to construct a vagina, raise him as "Joan" and give him female hormones at puberty. Money reported this involuntary sex reassignment as fully successful. But in 1997, both a medical journal report and a *Rolling Stone* article revealed that the reassignment had been a disaster. Despite the insistence of parents, doctors, psychologists and teachers, "Joan" had always insisted that she was "just a boy with long hair in girl's clothes." In adolescence, John took back his manhood.

How did John "know" he was male—and by extension, how do any of us decide we're girls or boys? One theory is that, in utero, John had undergone the androgen bath that turns an undifferentiated fetus—which otherwise becomes female—male, giving him a male identity and masculine behavior. In the other rare cases where XY infants lose penises and are raised as girls, some insist on being boys—but others happily identify as (masculine, lesbian) women, which suggests that things aren't quite so simple. Scientists recognize that our brains and nervous systems are somewhat plastic, developing in response to environmental stimuli. Sexuality—all of it, from identity to presentation to sexual orientation—is no exception; it develops as a biological interaction between inborn capacities and outside influences. As a result, most of us have a narrow range in which we feel "natural" as we gender ourselves daily through clothes, stance, stride, tone. For most, that gendered behavior is consonant with biological sex: Girls present as female, if not feminine, and fall in love with boys; boys present as male or masculine and fall in love with girls. But those in whom gendered behavior is vice versa—feminine boys, highly masculine girls—get treated as unnatural, even though their gendering is just as biological as the rest of ours. What happens to these transgendered folks can be so brutal that the pediatric surgeons who cut off infant clitorises or penises look like merely the advance guard of the M/F border patrol.

Take, for instance, Daphne Scholinski, so masculine that at age 6, strangers chastised her when she tried to use women's restrooms. In her dry, pitiless memoir *The Last Time I Wore a Dress*, Scholinski tells the story of being committed to a mental hospital at 15 for some very real problems, including severe neglect, her father's violence and her own delinquency. The hospital ignored her shocking childhood and instead "treated" her masculinity. Scholinski got demerits if she didn't wear makeup. She was put on a boys' ward, where she was twice raped, to encourage her to be more feminine. Her confinement was so disturbing that she still gets posttraumatic stress flashbacks, including nightmares so terrifying that she wakes up and vomits. And so Scholinski is starting an organization dedicated to reforming the diagnosis of childhood GID, or gender identity disorder, under which she was treated.

Or consider the treatment of Darlene Jespersen and Peter Oiler. After working for Harrah's Reno casino for eighteen years, in the summer of 2000, Jespersen was fired from her bartending job when Harrah's launched a new policy requiring all its female employees to wear foundation, powder, eyeliner, lipstick and so on. "I tried it," says Jespersen in a plaintive voice, "but I felt so naked." The obverse happened to Peter Oiler, a weathered, middle-aged man with large aviator glasses, a pleasant drawl and a bit of an overbite. After twenty years of being rotated through progressively more responsible jobs in Winn-Dixie's shipping yards, in 1999 Oiler was driving a fifty-foot truck delivering grocery supplies throughout southeastern Louisiana—until Winn-Dixie learned that he called himself "transgendered." Oiler tried to explain that he simply wore women's clothes on the weekends: He wasn't going to become a woman; he didn't want to wear makeup and heels on company time. In January 2000 Oiler was fired.

Jespersen and Oiler are stunned. Jespersen is suing Harrah's. Says Oiler, "I was raised to believe that if you do an honest days' work, you'll get an honest day's pay." The ACLU Lesbian and Gay Rights Project has taken up his case, in part because of the sheer injustice—and in part to get courts to treat discrimination against people who violate sex stereotypes as illegal sex discrimination. If a woman can wear a dress, or if a man can refuse makeup, why not vice versa? In doing so, the ACLU, like the three national lesbian and gay legal organizations, would be building on the 1989 Supreme Court decision *Price Waterhouse v. Ann Hopkins*. Price Waterhouse had told Hopkins that she wasn't going to make partner because she was too masculine—and, in actual written memos, advised her to wear jewelry and makeup, to go to charm school, to be less aggressive. The Supreme Court declared such stereotyping to be sex discrimination.

Will judges see Peter Oiler's dismissal as illegal sex stereotyping? There have been some recent hints that they might. In Massachusetts, for instance, the US Court of Appeals for the First Circuit said Lucas Rosa could sue a bank that instructed feminine Rosa, who had shown up to apply for a loan wearing a dress, to go home and come back in men's clothes; a female, after all, would have been considered for the loan. Another Massachusetts judge said that a male student could come to school in a dress, since female students could. A Washington transsexual prisoner raped by a prison guard, and two New York municipal employees harassed for being gay, were allowed to sue when judges ruled they'd been attacked for violating stereotyped expectations of their sex.

Our society has learned to see why women would want masculine privileges like playing soccer and serving on the Supreme Court, but there's no matching force expanding the world for males. Boys and men still patrol each other's masculinity with a *Glengarry Glenn Ross* level of ridicule and violence that can seem, to women, nearly surreal. Those males who violate the M-box's limits on behavior are quite literally risking their lives.

Which means that, if you're a performing drag queen, a cross-dressing straight man like Peter Oiler, or a transsexual who still has some male ID, do not under any circumstances get stopped by a cop. In New York City, says Pauline Park, a co-founder of NYAGRA (New York Association for Gender Rights Advocacy), even if the police don't actually beat you, "you could be arrested and detained for days or weeks. They don't let people out until they plead guilty to prostitution. They put them in the men's cell, where they're often assaulted and sometimes raped, as a tactic to get people to plead guilty."

And don't turn to emergency medical personnel. In August 1995 Tyra Hunter's car crashed in Washington, DC. When firefighting paramedics cut away her dress and found male genitals, they laughed and mocked her. She bled to death in the hospital. In August 2000 a jury awarded Hunter's mother $1.75 million in a wrongful-death action. Hunter's experience, unfortunately, is not unusual. Once a month, someone transgendered is murdered, and those are just the documented cases. Transgender activists are beginning to mark November 28, the anniversary of another such death, as a Day of Remembrance, with

candlelight vigils and a determination to slow the steady drumbeat of murder.

"We're despised. We're pariahs in this society," says Miranda Stevens-Miller, chair of the transgender rights organization It's Time, Illinois, about transsexuals and otherwise transgendered people. Many transsexuals are fired once they begin to transition. Others lose custody and visitation rights, houses, leases. Many are shut out of office and other public restrooms for years—an indignity that cuts to the very core of being human, since every living body needs to pee. And so the most urgent transgender organizing is happening locally, in organizations such as TGNet Arizona, NYAGRA and It's Time, Oregon. They're teaching Trans 101 to local employers, doctors, city councils, lesbian and gay organizations, judges, families, landlords, friends. They're attempting to collect statistics on firings, beatings, murders, bathroom harassment, police abuse. Often these groups are driven by the energy and determination of one or two people who spend their own time and pennies writing and photocopying leaflets, giving workshops for corporate and college groups, and lobbying city councils and lesbian and gay organizations for inclusion in hate-crimes and antidiscrimination laws. Lately, they're having remarkable success at adding "gender identity and expression to the protected categories in local and state employment nondiscrimination and hate-crimes laws; they've won in locales ranging from Portland, Oregon, to DeKalb, Illinois, to the state of Rhode Island.

Nationally, trans groups are still in the skirmishing phase faced by any new movement, with the inevitable splits over strategy and personality. The group with the most name recognition, GenderPAC, angers some transgender activists by avoiding the "T" word in its advocacy, saying that it aims at gender freedom for everyone; it acts on behalf of such people as Darlene Jespersen and Peter Oiler, or boys called "faggot" for not being noticeably masculine. Currently the most significant transgender organizations nationally are IFGE (International Foundation for Gender Education), GEA (Gender Education and Advocacy) and the Working Group on Trans Equality, a loose network of grassroots trans activists aiming at a coordinated national presence. Perhaps the biggest success so far is that all the major lesbian and gay organizations and many smaller ones have added transgendered folks to their mission statements as folks who are equally, if differently, queer.

Or is it so different? All of us deviate from what's expected from our sex. While the relationship between transgender activists and lesbian and gay groups has at times been contentious, some lesbian and gay activists, notably Chai Feldblum, Georgetown law professor, are starting to urge that we all organize around our common deviance from sex stereotypes. The differences between homosexual, transgender and transsexual experiences are not that great: All are natural variations on the brain's gendered development that have cropped up throughout human history, from Tiresias to Radclyffe Hall, from Billy Tipton to Quentin Crisp. For the most part, the mainstream sees us on one sliding scale of queerness. And occasionally our struggles and goals intersect quite neatly. For instance, homos can't always tell whether we're harassed at work because someone figures out that we date others of the same sex, or simply because we're too butch or too fey.

And none of us can rely on having our marriages recognized by the institutions around us when we need them—because marriage is one of the last laws on the books that discriminate based on sex. Recently, Joe Gardiner asked a Kansas court to invalidate his dead father's marriage to transwoman (born male, medically and legally reassigned as female) J'Noel Gardiner, saying J'Noel was "really" a man—and therefore could not have legally married a man. The lower court agreed with the son that XY = man, which meant the son would inherit his father's fat estate. But the Kansas appeals judge remanded the case back down for a new trial. Sex, the appeals court declared, isn't decided simply by a chromosome test. Rather, sex is a complex constellation of characteristics that includes not only chromosomes but also "gonadal sex, internal morphologic sex, external morphologic sex, hormonal sex, phenotypic sex, assigned sex and gender of rearing, and sexual identity." The court approvingly quoted Johns Hopkins researcher and medical doctor William Reiner, who wrote, "The organ that appears to be critical to psychosexual development and adaptation is not the external genitalia, but the brain."

PART THREE

SEXUAL
BEHAVIORS

CHAPTER SIX

VARIATIONS AND ADAPTATIONS

Despite the fact that we almost never really seriously talk about what we do, what we like, what turns us on, and how we like to have sex, most of us stick to a fairly predictable routine of sexual behaviors (coitus, fellatio, and cunnilingus) and in a fairly predictable (and predictably small) number of positions. It's not that we're necessarily sexually boring, but rather that most of us find some things that are arousing and see no reason to wander from the tried and true.

But if the middle of a bell curve of sexual behaviors is where most of us find ourselves most of the time, there are plenty of people who venture away from that center and toward the outer reaches of a particular behavior, to places that most of us may wander inadvertently on occasion. Most of us stumble into those marginal behaviors and quickly return to the center; some of us, though, will set up camp there and organize our sexual interactions based on those preferences.

The articles in this section invite us to think of sexual variations as points on a continuum instead of as in an either/or dichotomy. It's not that some people like S/M and others don't; rather, most of us, at some point, have experienced a small amount of pain or the desire to inflict pain during a sexual encounter. Or we find ourselves being excited by the possibility of being seen having sex (exhibitionism), or by the possibility of seeing someone else having sex (voyeurism). Or we find that the sight of a black boot, a lacy garter belt, a thong, or a whip is sexually arousing.

Most of us don't freak out, we accept that it happened and return to home base. For some of us, though, the experience was a bit more thrilling, and we want to go back and try it again. And for a few of us, it becomes so exciting that we seek out others with whom we can do it again. A very people few reorganize their entire sexual identity around the reproduction of those scenes. They're deviants or connoisseurs, depending on your perspective.

Laurence Alison and colleagues examine the way power and violence are eroticized in the world of domination and submission and S/M. In a major development since Krafft-Ebing first explored sadism and masochism, we now understand these activities to be both cognitively and behaviorally linked, so we speak of sadomasochism, or S/M.

Clive Davis and colleagues and Celia Roberts and colleagues explore two sides of variations on female sexuality: the use of vibrators in masturbatory behavior and faking orgasm. Finally, Al Cooper and colleagues explore the ways in which cyberspace creates new sexual possibilities to play with behavior and identity and also results in new risks and dangers.

6.1 SADOMASOCHISTICALLY ORIENTED BEHAVIOR
Diversity in Practice and Meaning

Laurence Alison, Pekka Santtila, N. Kenneth Sandnabba, and Niklas Nordling

INTRODUCTION

The current conceptualization of sadomasochism relies on a label of convenience for a set of related sexual activities of particular subcultures (Haeberle, 1978; Katchadourian and Lunde 1972/1975). Facets include physical restriction and bondage (Baumeister, 1988) and humiliation (Baumeister, 1988; Moser and Levitt, 1987; Weinberg, 1987). Additionally, Weinberg et al. (1984), Lee (1979), and Kamel (1983) refer to a subset of behaviors commonly associated with the gay male 'leather' scene that, to observers, appears to be sadomasochistic in origin. These behaviors include enemas, catheters, anal fisting, and scatological practices, and are sometimes described by the subjects as displays of 'masculinity and toughness' (Weinberg et al., 1984, p. 387).

The evidence for these facets of pain, restriction, and humiliation and Weinberg et al.'s identification of hypermasculinity (Weinberg et al., 1984) as being related sets of actions remains speculative because there have, to date, been no correlative studies examining the notionally related facets of these groups of sexual behaviors. That is, are the behaviors associated with each of these suggested facets more empirically interrelated with one another than with behaviors of the other facets? Or, more specifically, are there subsets of, for example, physically restrictive acts (handcuffs, straitjackets, use of chains) or pain creating actions (skinbranding, caning, spanking) that are empirically related? This would provide empirical support for the existence of distinct themes within sadomasochistic sexual behavior.

The present study sought not to identify these sets of actions as defining of sadomasochism but rather to map out the empirical relationships between the individual acts performed by individuals engaged in the sadomasochistic subculture. The concern was to establish the extent to which individual actions bear an empirical relationship to one another. It is therefore important to bear in mind that while these sets of actions are commonly considered to be sadomasochistic and therefore take on the connotation of 'describing' sadomasochists, they are actually a set of descriptions about subsets of interactions that occur between individuals engaged in a variety of behaviors. For example, in Weinberg et al.'s exploration (Weinberg et al., 1984) of the 'leather' scene subjects engaged in dressing up in leather, using chains and anal fisting did not consider themselves sadomasochists.

Similarly, previous studies have not taken account of the potential preferences that may exist for individuals in engaging in one facet (i.e., the administration or receiving of pain) over another facet (i.e., humiliation). One possibility is that individuals would only engage in a limited set of behaviors and not in others suggesting that sadomasochism is in fact a label for a number of independent phenomena. Another possibility is that individuals emphasize a particular set of behaviors but also engage in other behaviors to a more limited extent. This would suggest that it makes sense to conceptualize sadomasochism as a distinct phenomenon. Also, there have been no investigations exploring whether a preference for one facet over another is related to the sex and the sexual orientation of the subjects, and whether there is a preference for the 'sadistic' or the 'masochistic' partner to engage in one facet more than any other.

Finally, the reasons for an individual developing a preference for a particular set of sadomasochistic sexual behaviors has not been thoroughly clarified. In fact, some recent studies (Nordling et al., 2000; Santtila et al., accepted) have shown evidence for associations between childhood experiences and aspects of sadomasochistic behavior whereas the importance of an ongoing process of adult socialization has been stressed by more sociologically oriented researchers. Weinberg et al. (1984) criticized traditional models for ignoring the sadomasochistic subculture. According to them, this subculture provides opportunities for persons to define and elaborate their sexual activities. Also, the finding that the sexual activity that occurs in a sadomasochistic scene is often, but not always, scripted and therefore collaborative (Weinberg, 1987), suggests that individual sexual repertoires are socially constructed. An attempt was made in the present study to explore whether the extent to which the subjects were integrated into the sadomasochistic scene (defined as the frequency of sadomasochistic sessions and involvement with pornographic material of a similar nature) would predict the flexibility of their sexual repertoires within each of the suggested sadomasochistic subthemes.

In summary, we were interested in establishing what evidence existed for identifying the facets of sadomasochism previously referred to by others (physical restriction, administration and receiving of pain and psychological and physical humiliation as well as hypermasculinity), the potential relationship that these domains may have with other factors in the individuals' lives as well as the extent to which the degree of involvement in the sadomasochistic subculture would predict the flexibility of the subjects' sexual repertoires. It was expected that female subjects would be more likely to engage in behaviors related to humiliation (Messman and Long, 1996) whereas gay male subjects would report more behaviors related to hypermasculinity (Weinberg et al., 1984).

METHOD

Subjects

One hundred and eighty-four subjects (22 women and 162 men) who were members of two sadomasochistically oriented clubs participated in this study (two subjects were discarded due to lack of responses on questions related to specific sexual behaviors). Ninety-five were recruited from Kinky Club, a club

for mainly heterosexual people with a variety of sexual preferences. Ninety-one subjects were recruited from the MSC-Finland association with mainly gay male members. Of the subjects, 43.0% reported being mainly heterosexual, 5.4% bisexual, and 51.6% mainly homosexual. Of all subjects, 27.0% identified themselves as mainly sadistic, 22.7% as both sadistic and masochistic, and 50.2% as mainly masochistic in their sadomasochistic behavior.

Subjects were highly educated (over a third had a university degree). They also had a higher income level than the population in general (Statistical Yearbook of Finland, 1993) with half having a monthly income of more than 2000 US dollars. This study group, as with others previously explored (Baumeister, 1988; Spengler, 1977; Weinberg, 1987) is suggestive of a group of subjects who are not psychologically disturbed or dysfunctional but are rather better educated and in a generally higher earning bracket than the general population. (For more details on the demographic and sexual characteristics of the males in the study group, see Sandnabba et al., 1999).

Materials

The Questionnaire

Information selected for this study was taken from a larger survey conducted by Sandnabba et al. (1999) in which the authors were investigating the social adaptation and variety of sexual behaviors of sadomasochists. The original questionnaire was designed as a descriptive analysis of the range of behaviors that sadomasochists indulged in and as a descriptive analysis of the study group. For the purposes of the present study the focus was upon the set of activities engaged in and the empirical relationships between them. Concentration was therefore upon elements of behavior within sadomasochistic encounters. This included items pertaining to the various practices of the subjects on a dichotomous basis, that is, had they indulged in a particular behavior at any point during the last 12 months. This list included a number of activities previously listed in studies on the behavior of individuals in the sadomasochistic scene. Additionally, questions (other than the demographic information already outlined) were asked regarding the number of sadomasochistic sessions during the preceding year and the extent to which the subjects had acquired sadomasochistic pornographic magazines during the same time period for the purpose of exploring any relationships between these variables and the sadomasochistic behaviors of the subjects.

Statistical Analysis: SSA

Based on the joint co-occurrence of behaviors, the 184 questionnaires were analyzed using Smallest Space Analysis (SSA). SSA is a nonmetric multidimensional scaling procedure that represents the associations between variables as the inverse of distances in a statistically derived geometric space—the greater the similarity between two variables the greater their proximity in the corresponding space (Guttman, 1968). SSA is based upon the assumption that the underlying structure of complex behavioral systems is most readily appreciated if the relationship between each and every other variable is examined (Canter and Heritage, 1990). The SSA-I program computes association coefficients between all variables and rank orders them, creating a triangular matrix consisting of association coefficients for each variable against every other variable. It is these rank ordered coefficients, rather than their absolute values that are used to form the spatial representation of variables. By using these rank ordered coefficients, SSA is able to represent the variables in the smallest possible dimensionality.

To find an optimal representation of the variables, SSA-I performs iterations that compare the rank order assigned to the *original* associations with the rank order of the distances between points in the plot (which the program calculates from a *derived* association matrix). With each iteration, adjustments are made to the geometric representation in an attempt to minimize the difference between the plot and the original association matrix. The closer the two sets of rank orders are, the better the fit. These iterations continue until the difference between these two matrices is at a minimum. The degree of fit between the geometric representation and the original input similarity data is indicated by Guttman's coefficient of alienation (Guttman, 1968). The coefficient of alienation ranges from 0 (*indicating a perfect fit*) to 1. A coefficient of

.20–.25 is considered a reasonably good degree of fit (Shye et al., 1994).

The resulting configuration of points in the SSA is based solely upon the relationships among variables. Therefore, these points can be examined directly without assuming underlying dimensions as in factor analysis (Canter and Heritage, 1990). Classifying variables through an examination of the regional structure in an SSA is part of an approach to research known as facet theory (Canter, 1985). The elements of 'facets' in this case refer to the overall classification of behaviors into 'types' (i.e., hypermasculinity, administration of pain, humiliation, and physical restriction). The spatial contiguity of the variables representing these facet elements provides a test of the major underlying differences among these variables as revealed through their co-occurrence in sadomasochistic behaviors, and is therefore a test as to whether the facet structure is empirically supported (Canter et al., 1998).

The postulation of facet elements goes beyond simply saying that behaviors belong in particular 'groups.' The principle of contiguity states that, " . . . variables which are more similar in their facet structure will also be more related empirically" (Foa, 1965, p. 264). Therefore, variables that share the same facet elements would be more highly correlated and thus should appear closer together in the multidimensional space. This idea can be extended as a general, regional hypothesis. Basically, items that have facet elements in common will be found in the same region of space. Likewise, variables that have very low intercorrelations will appear in different regions of the plot indicating dissimilarity.

For further elaboration of the technique, the range of applied fields within which it has been used, and its strengths and weaknesses see Canter (1983), Elizur and Sagie (1999), Guttman (1954), and Shye et al. (1994).

RESULTS

A two-dimensional solution was employed to represent the association matrix, where the coefficient of alienation was .27. This is a reasonably high coefficient indicating that the fit between the representation and the actual ranked associations was not particularly good. However, as Shye (1994, p. 125) states

> in the past it has been customary to attempt SSA solutions of increased dimensionality whenever the coefficient was considered high ... This procedure has, however, been found lacking both on technical and on theoretical grounds [since] the coefficient of alienation is sensitive to the number of items processed.

Although our results suggest that the geometric output is not a perfect representation of the variables, the two-dimensional arrangement of variables did approximate the conceptual system of sadomasochism as hypothesized in previous work (Baumeister, 1988; Messman and Long, 1996; Moser and Levitt, 1987; Weinberg et al., 1984). Moreover, employment of a three-dimensional representation did not significantly lower the coefficient of alienation, nor, more importantly did it change the first (two-dimensional configuration) projection of the points. Thus, whilst higher dimensional models may reveal other, more subtle nuances of this set of sexual activities, the two-dimensional model does reflect an interpretable, conceptually and empirically supported model. As Shye (1994, p. 126) states that, "If a regional contiguity pattern in a two-dimensional solution conforms well to a content facet formulated in advance and if evidence for this conformity is accumulated, the purpose of theory construction has been achieved."

Figure 6.1.1 therefore shows the projection of the two-dimensional space. Table 6.1.1 displays the behaviors (and frequency of occurrence) separated into the hypothesized polar regions along with their associated Cronbach's alpha coefficients. These ranged from .71 (*humiliation*) to .78 (*administration of pain*) and while not indicative of perfect scales of behavior are reasonably high given, in some of the regions, the relatively small number of items (i.e., only 5 items in *humiliation*). It is important, however, not to consider these as discrete regions, but rather as a polarizing spectrum of gradual change around the midpoint intersection of all the regions. Thus, cusp variables such as wrestling and bondage in the *physical restriction* region are associated relatively more with their adjacent *hypermasculine* region than with

mummification, which lies near the cusp of its contiguous set of related variables in the *humiliation* region. This visual map of the correlation matrix, therefore, reveals evidence of a circular ordering of the variables from *hypermasculine,* through to the *administration of pain,* to *humiliation, physical restriction* and back, full circle to *hypermasculine.* This also suggests that sadomasochism can be conceptualized as a set of interrelated behaviors where individuals give different emphases to particular themes rather than it being a label of convenience for a number of independent phenomena.

To establish whether there were relationships between the subjects' sex, sexual orientation, and sadomasochistic preference and any of the themes, summary variables reflecting the number of behaviors present in the separate regions of the plot were formed. Thereafter, any differences between the male and female subjects and between the predominantly and exclusively heterosexual male and predominantly and exclusively gay male subjects (bisexual subjects were discarded from this analysis) and also between the predominantly and exclusively sadistic male and predominantly and exclusively masochistic male (flexible subjects were discarded from this analysis) were explored using the Student's t-test. (Only male subjects were included in the two latter analyses due to the low number of female subjects in the study group). Female subjects engaged in significantly more of the behaviors in the humiliation region ($M = 3.14$, SD $= 1.70$) compared to male subjects ($M = 2.56$, SD $= 1.46$), $t(182) = 1.70$, $p < .05$, whereas the male subjects engaged in more of the behaviors in the hypermasculinity region ($M = 3.75$, SD $= 2.14$) compared to female subjects ($M = 2.50$, SD $= 1.90$), $t(182) = 2.62$, $p < .01$. The means and standard deviations for the other analyses are presented in Table 6.1.2. There were significant differences between the hetero- and gay male subjects in terms of their involvement in the *hypermasculinity* and *humiliation* regions. As expected, the gay male subjects were more likely to engage in a larger number of the behaviors of the *hypermasculinity* region ($t(151) = 2.57, p < .01$) compared to the heterosexual male subjects whereas the latter were more likely to engage in a larger number of

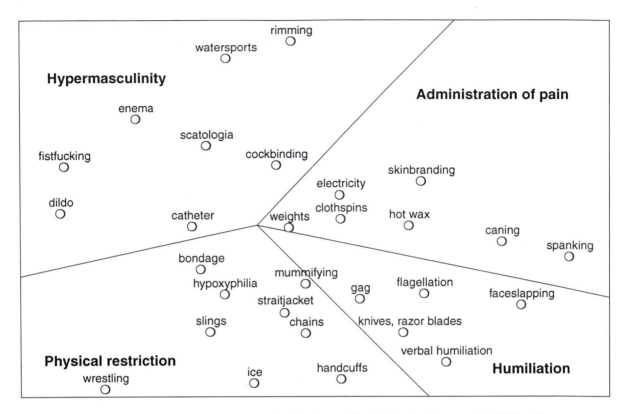

Fig. 6.1.1 A two-dimensional Smallest Space Analysis of sadomasochistic behaviors in a sample of 184 subjects.

Table 6.1.1 The Frequency of the Sexual Behaviors in the Different Regions of the SSA Space with Associated Cronbach's α Coefficients

Hypermasculinity (N = 8, α = .75)	%	Administration of pain (N = 7, α = .78)	%	Humiliation (N = 5, α = .72)	%	Physical restriction (N = 9, α = .75)	%
Rimming	77.5	Clothspins	67.6	Flagellation	81.8	Bondage	88.4
Dildo	70.2	Spanking	64.0	Verbal humiliation	70.1	Handcuffs	73.2
Cockbinding	68.3	Caning	50.7	Gag	53.0	Chains	70.8
Watersports	50.6	Weights	41.5	Faceslapping	37.2	Wrestle	45.1
Enema	42.7	Hot wax	34.8	Knives	10.9	Slings	39.0
Fistfucking	32.9	Electricity	16.4			Ice	31.7
Scatologia	18.2	Skinbranding	15.8			Straitjacket	17.0
Catheter	10.4					Hypoxyphilia	16.5
						Mummifying	13.4

Table 6.1.2 Number of Sexual Behaviors in the Different Regions of the SSA Space in Groups of Gay Male and Heterosexual Male Subjects and in Groups of Sadistic and Masochistic Subjects

Region	Heterosexual ($N = 64$)		Gay male ($N = 89$)		Sadistic ($N = 42$)		Masochistic ($N = 80$)	
	M	SD	M	SD	M	SD	M	SD
Hypermasculinity	3.17	2.17	4.03	1.95	3.40	2.07	4.05	2.04
Administration of pain	3.09	2.15	2.74	1.99	2.55	1.99	3.16	2.11
Humiliation	2.88	1.32	2.28	1.46	2.40	1.50	2.64	1.49
Physical restriction	3.91	2.24	3.97	2.11	3.81	2.27	4.02	2.32

Table 6.1.3 Correlations Between Measures of Involvement in Sadomasochistic Subculture and the Number of Behaviors Engaged in the Different Regions of the SSA Space

Number of behaviors engaged in the different regions	Number of sadomasochistic sessions	Use of sadomasochistic pornographic material
Hypermasculinity	.24***	.19**
Administration of pain	.23**	.24***
Humiliation	.18*	.21**
Physical restriction	.10	.19**

*$p < .05$; ** $p < .01$; *** $p < .001$.

humiliation behaviors ($t(151) = 2.59$, $p < .01$). In terms of the sadomasochistic preference, there were nonsignificant tendencies for the masochistic male subjects to have engaged in a larger number of behaviors in both the *hypermasculinity* ($t(120) = 1.65$, $p < .10$) and the *administration of pain* ($t(120) = 1.56$, $p < .12$) regions compared to the sadistic male subjects.

Next, Pearson's correlation coefficients were computed between the variables indicating the subjects' involvement in the sadomasochistic subculture (number of sadomasochistic sessions, use of sadomasochistic pornography) and the number of sexual behaviors within the different regions that the subjects had engaged in during the preceding year (see Table 6.1.3). As expected, positive and significant associa-

tions could be observed. However, the absolute values of the coefficients were not particularly impressive.

DISCUSSION

Our results are encouraging in supporting previous references to various facets of sadomasochistically oriented behavior. At a broad level, these appear to take on different functions for men and women on the one hand and gay men and heterosexual men on the other. The female subjects significantly preferred themes associated with humiliation whereas the male subjects were more likely to engage in themes related to hypermasculinity. In other words, at opposing poles lie the facets of hypermasculinity and humiliation and in adjacent regions lie the physical aspects of restriction and the administration of pain. Elements of humiliation are significantly preferred by the women and by the heterosexual males in the study group and were revealed in the correspondence between faceslapping, flagellation, the use of a gag, the use of knives and razors, and verbal humiliation. Thus, actions significantly preferred especially by the gay men involved rimming; watersports; cockbinding; fistfucking; scatologia; and the use of dildos, enemas, and catheters. We would suggest that adjacent facets (restriction and pain) to these two regions can take on rather different meanings for each group but are important components of the full picture of sadomasochistic behavior.

Our results confirmed that the following acts were associated with one another: subjecting individuals to (sadistic component) or receiving (masochistic component) electric shocks, skinbranding, caning, spanking, the use of hot wax, clothespins, and the use of weights. It is perhaps significant that the more extreme and intense of these experiences (skinbranding and electrocution) are located nearer the hypermasculine region, whereas spanking and caning appear next to the humiliation region. This may be suggestive of subtle variations in the context within which pain is administered and received and the meaning that it has for the different subjects and, potentially, for different sexes and for different sexual orientations. For example, as noted in Lee (1979), Kamel (1983), and Weinberg et al.'s examinations (Weinberg et al., 1984) of the gay 'leather' scene an emphasis is placed either upon the masculinity of the activities involved and/or the extent to which the bruises and welts received represent a 'sign of love and/or surrender' (Weinberg et al., 1984, p. 387). In contrast, the caning and spanking aspects of pain administration and reception may be more indicative of the associated facet of humiliation and the adoption of a set of activities associated with the 'illusion of violence' (Weinberg and Kamel, 1983). As Gebhard (1969) points out, individuals involved in the heterosexual sadomasochistic scene rarely highlight pain as a central facet. As Califia (1979, p. 21) points out, "The basic dynamic of S and M is a power dichotomy, not pain." Our results suggest that the administration and receiving of pain may take on rather different meanings depending upon the context within which it is received and, of course, depending upon the intensity of the sensation delivered/experienced. In other words, pain may, for some individuals, be rather more literal (hypermasculine) than be symbolic (humiliation).

Secondly, reference has been made to the physically restrictive acts associated with sadomasochistic practices. Bondage; mummification; hypoxyphilia; the use of straitjackets, chains, handcuffs, slings and ice, as well as wrestling with one's partner were all located in this region. Significantly, however, bondage, hypoxyphilia, and wrestling are adjacent to the hypermasculinity region whereas mummification, straitjackets, chains, and handcuffs are adjacent to the humiliation region. Once again, this emphasizes the potentially different psychological symbolism of different aspects of restriction for different parties.

The advantage of the multivariate scaling analysis presented here is that it represents the relationships between each and every variable and thus allows for refinements and more subtle developments of hypotheses regarding the nature of the domain under investigation. Thus, these findings are not definitive but rather generative of more refined hypotheses regarding associations of particular actions. Subsequent studies could follow up the extent to which different individuals draw upon facets of pain and restriction in order to heighten the intensity of their experiences. This contextualizing of these components clearly has significant psychological meaning for the acting out of the subjects of this particular group but of course, whether this is a generalizable finding to other sadomasochistic groups remains open to question. The particular structure here may be indicative of differences between the styles of the clubs examined rather than between the sexuality of the subjects. Subsequent work would need to clarify this issue and explore a range of homo- and heterosexual-oriented clubs to explore whether the differences established here are an artifact of the club rather than an association with an individual's sexual preferences. The subjects' involvement in the sadomasochistic subculture through sexual contacts and pornography was positively associated with greater variability in their sexual behavior. Although the design of the study does not warrant any causal conclusions, the results imply that sadomasochistic behavior is best understood as a product of adult socialization processes where real or imagined sexual contact leads the subjects to adopt new behaviors and sexual scripts. This finding accords well with social constructionistic explanations of sexual behavior (Weinberg, 1987; Weinberg et al., 1984).

In this study group, results suggest that for the gay male group the administration and reception of pain was a more intense and real perception and that the symbolic representation of pain was more important for the women and the heterosexual men. Similarly, the restrictive acts in this particular heterosexual group appear to have a more symbolically humiliating association than the more physically intense aspects of restriction located nearer to the hypermasculinity region preferred by the gay male subjects. The subtleties of the meanings of these actions, however, will remain speculative until further research is able to explore how individuals employ these facets within their own particular context. This may mean that the outcome of our study provides the basis for developing interviewing protocols or surveys that will help capture the meaning that restriction, pain, humiliation, and masculinization takes on for different subsets of the sadomasochistic population.

REFERENCES

Baumeister, R. F. (1988). Masochism as escape from self. *J. Sex Res.* 25: 28–59.

Califia, P. (1979, December 17). A secret side of lesbian sexuality. *Advocate:* 19–23.

Canter, D. V. (1983). The potential of facet theory for applied social psychology. *Quality and Quantity,* 17: 35–67.

Canter, D. V. (ed.). (1985). *Facet Theory: Approaches to Social Research,* Springer, New York.

Canter, D. V., and Heritage, R. (1990). A multivariate model of sexual offense behavior: Developments in 'offender profiling.' *J. Forensic Psychiat.* 1: 185–212.

Canter, D. V., Hughes, D., and Kirby, S. (1998). Pedophilia: Pathology, criminality or both? The development of a multivariate model of offense behavior in child sexual abuse. *J. Forensic Psychiat.* 9: 532–555.

Elizur, D., and Sagie, A. (1999). Facets of personal values: A structural analysis of life and work values. *Appl. Psychol: Int. Rev.* 48: 73–87.

Foa, U. G. (1965). New Developments in facet design and analysis. *Psychol. Rev.* 72: 262–274.

Gebhard, P. (1969). Fetishism and sadomasochism. In Masserman, J. H. (ed.), *Dynamics of Deviant Sexuality,* Grune and Stratton, New York, pp. 71–80.

Guttman, L. (1954). A new approach to factor analysis: The circle. In Lazarfeld, P. E. (ed.), *Mathematical Thinking in the Social Sciences,* Free Press, Glencoe, IL.

Guttman, L. (1968). A general nonmetric technique for finding the smallest co-ordinate space for a configuration of points. *Psychometrika* 33: 469–506.

Haeberle, E. (1978). *The Sex Atlas,* Seabury Press, New York.

Kamel, G. W. L. (1983). The leather career: On becoming a sadomasochist. In Weinberg, T. and Kamel, G. W. L. (eds.), *S and M: Studies in Sadomasochism,* Prometheus, Buffalo, NY, pp. 73–79.

Katchadourian, H., and Lunde, D. (1975). *Fundamentals of Human Sexuality,* 2nd Ed., Holt, Rinehart and Winston, New York.

Lee, J. A. (1979). The social organization of sexual risk. *Alternative Lifestyles* 2: 69–100.

Messman, T. L., and Long, P. S. (1996). Child sexual abuse and its relationship to revictimization in adult women: A review. *Clin. Psychol. Rev.* 16: 397–420.

Moser, C., and Levitt, E. (1987). An exploratory-descriptive study of a sadomasochistically oriented sample. *J. Sex Res.* 23: 322–337.

Nordling, N., Sandnabba, N. K., and Santtila, P. (2000). The prevalence and effects of self-reported childhood sexual abuse among sadomasochistically oriented males and females. *J. Child Sex. Abuse* 9, in press.

Sandnabba, N. K., Santtila, P., and Nordling, N. (1999). Sexual behavior and social adaptation among sadomasochistically-oriented males. *J. Sex Res.* 36: 273–282.

Santtila, P., Sandnabba, N. K., and Nordling, N. (in press). Retrospective perceptions of family interaction in childhood as correlates of current sexual adaptation among sadomasochistic males. *J. Psychol. Hum. Sex.,* in press.

Shye, S., Elizur, D., and Hoffman, M. (1994). *Introduction to Facet Theory: Content Design and Intrinsic Data Analysis in Behavioral Research,* Sage Publications, London.

Spengler, A. (1977). Manifest sadomasochism of males: Results of an empirical study. *Arch. Sex. Behav.* 6: 441–456.

Weinberg, M., Williams, C. J., and Moser, C. (1984). The social constituents of sadomasochism. *Soc. Probl.* 31: 379–389.

Weinberg, T. S. (1987). Sadomasochism in the United States: A review of recent sociological literature. *J. Sex Res.* 23: 50–69.

Weinberg, T. S., and Kamel, G. W. L. (1983). S & M: An introduction to the study of sadomasochism. In Weinberg, T., and Kamel, G. W. L. (eds.), *S and M: Studies in Sadomasochism,* Prometheus, Buffalo, NY, pp. 17–24.

6.2 FAKING IT
The Story of "Ohh!"

Celia Roberts, Susan Kippax, Catherine Waldby, and June Crawford

> I mean they say, well, women fake orgasm, I think it's pretty true.
>
> —*(female interviewee)*

In a recent issue of Australian *Cosmopolitan* magazine, women were advised to fake orgasm on occasions when they were feeling too tired or distracted to enjoy sex. "Faking it," they were assured, was the only polite response in that situation—after all, it would not be fair to offend the men who were working so hard to please them (*Cosmopolitan,* 1992, September). It is faking orgasm which this paper takes as its focus, for as *Cosmopolitan's* advice indicates, and as we will argue, faking orgasm is a compelling "showcase" site of heterosexual relations. The central aim of our analysis is to examine the ways in which heterosexual relations produce this phenomenon. The broader aim of this paper, which arises out of a larger project based at The National Centre for HIV Social Research, Macquarie University, is to demonstrate the centrality of an understanding of the complexities of heterosexual relations to the development of effective HIV/AIDS education campaigns aimed at heterosexual people.

Although *Cosmopolitan* tells women exactly when and why they should fake orgasm, explicit instructions are not given as to *how*. From our research it seemed that the American film "When Harry Met Sally" provides the most readily available representation of how to fake orgasm. Given the extravagant nature of Sally's performance—a full volume theatrical imitation of ecstasy—it is hardly surprising that most of the women we interviewed said that what they did was of a different genre. Statements like "I suppose I do moan and groan a bit more than I'd feel like it" and confessions of "untrue" affirmative answers to the question, "Did you come?" or "Was that good for you too?" were common. In almost every woman's interview these practices were mentioned as something they did, at least some of the time.

In stark contrast, very few of the men we talked to said that they had ever been in bed with a woman who was faking orgasm. Perhaps they too had an exaggerated expectation of theatricality. In general "the whole faking syndrome," as one man put it, was considered by our male interviewees to be a problem that other people encountered. One older man even went so far as to state categorically that "Nobody fakes orgasms any more . . . I think people have forgotten, people fortunately don't do that any more." Clearly, the refined performances which women are giving are extremely convincing.

The phenomenon of faking orgasm in its various forms is important for preventive education and research around HIV/AIDS and heterosexuality because it illustrates the peculiar complexities involved in sexual relations between women and men. It is a knowledge of these complexities which enables educational interventions to be effective—as we have argued previously, it does not make sense to structure an educational campaign around an imagined or ideal set of heterosexual relations which bear little relation to how most people experience their lives (Waldby, Kippax, Crawford, 1991). It is clear, for example, that heterosexual relations are not played out exclusively in conscious and articulated ways: Faking orgasm and men's and women's different responses to it indicate that sexual interactions are multilayered and to some extent unspoken, even unspeakable. Thus, as has been previously pointed out, the model of sexual negotiation and assertion advocated in governmental HIV/AIDS educational materials aimed at heterosexuals—one based

Reprinted from *Women's Studies International Forum* 18 (5/6), by Celia Roberts, Susan Kippax, Catherine Waldby, and June Crawford, "Faking It: The Story of 'Ohh!'," pp. 523–32, copyright © 1995, with permission from Elsevier Science.

on honest and open discussion between partners—is highly problematic (Waldby, Kippax, Crawford, 1991). Such a model assumes that sex is something which, at least after embarrassment has been overcome, can be freely spoken about. The complexities surrounding faking orgasm, as we will show, demonstrate the problematic nature of this model.

METHODOLOGY

The data for this paper comes from interviews with 73 heterosexual first year university students (mostly aged under 25 years, but some mature age students) and 19 focussed group discussions made up of 3–8 students of the same sex.[1] Both the interviews and groups were conducted by same-sex interviewers and group facilitators. Approximately two-thirds of our data came from women—a percentage which reflects the enrolment statistics in the course from which our subjects were recruited.

The individual interviews were semistructured and lasted between 45 minutes and 2 hours, while the group discussions were loosely structured and were of 2 hours duration. The interviews were very personal, with the interviewees talking about their own sexual and relationship histories and their feelings about initiating relationships, the differences between committed and casual relationships, talking and directing during sex, penetration, their own bodies, HIV and other STDs, contraception, and homosexuality. The group discussions on the other hand, although they often became personal, focussed more on the participants' social circles and perceptions of sexual and relationship issues within these circles and the wider society. The groups were asked to comment on statements made by the opposite sex which were taken from previous years' groups and interviews, and also to develop endings to half-finished "real life" stories. Both the groups and interviews were confidential so all names have been changed here.

The interviews and group discussions were transcribed and analysed. We looked for themes running through the data, for commonly used metaphors and/or similarities in statements of belief. This analysis was helped by the use of a qualitative data computer programme, *Kwalitan* (1990), which allowed us

to mark certain passages in the text as being relevant to a particular theme, and to recall all items so marked.

The underlying premise of our method is that the way people talk about and experience sexuality, as is explained in detail below, is culturally constructed. Thus in examining the ways in which a number of people talk about sex, we believe, we can identify commonalities which are important and meaningful and in so doing come to understand the experiences of individuals in a more comprehensive and useful way.

This paper uses contemporary feminist writing to provide the theoretical underpinnings of the arguments presented and builds also on previous work from the Heterosexuality and HIV/AIDS project (Kippax, Crawford, Waldby, & Benton, 1990; Waldby, Kippax, & Crawford, 1990, 1993a, 1993b; Waldby et al., 1991).

THE STORIES OF "OHH!"

The aim of this paper is not to provide the "truth" about faking orgasm but rather to discuss the ambivalences and slippages of meanings which circulate through and around it. What we wish to argue is that an understanding of the complexities and instabilities of heterosexual relations, which are demonstrated in the phenomenon of faking orgasm, is useful in attempting effective educational interventions. Our argument then is based on an examination of the narratives or stories which are woven into and constitute people's sexual experiences. In our data two important stories arise: a story of relationships and love, and another of technique and work.

The Love Bit

One of the most striking similarities across the women's interviews and group discussions was an almost exclusive focus on love and the importance of being in a monogamous relationship. Sex, although a "natural" progression once the women were in such relationships, seemed always to take second place. These statements from three women's groups indicate commonly held views:

KAREN   Sex is the wrong word I think. Like, you have
             sex with people that you don't really care about. You

know and like, it's sort of like, if you're gonna have sex with the person that you love (mm) it's like making love instead of having sex (right). It sounds so um like . . . so detached, like you're having sex with somebody (yeah) (mm) (yeah) I mean, it's obviously a way of showing, probably the ultimate way of showing someone that you care about them.

INTERVIEWER   So can you imagine the situation where you do love someone but you still feel like having sex with other people? Or do you consider that love has to be . . .

MICHELLE   But if you really loved someone then you wouldn't want to have sex with anyone else.

DIANA   I think that . . . [sex is] sort of, not natural but it comes with love, what you're doing . . . It comes with love, it's just, sort of an extension of your love for the person.

This focus by women on emotionality and relationships is not surprising. As our interviewees of both sexes confirmed, it is a well known "truth" in our culture that women are more "into" relationships than are men. That these women placed the stability of their relationships above their own sexual pleasure was not seen to be at all problematic by the vast majority of our interviewees.

Technique: Working in the Dark

In contrast to this story of love and relationships, the men we interviewed seemed to use a less emotional narrative: a story of technique and work. Wendy Hollway has argued that men usually construct their sexuality as being based on a strong "biological" drive (Hollway, 1984). As has been previously shown, this construction positions women as the passive recipient of men's desire—sex becomes something which men do to (or on) women, whose silence is interpreted as consent (Kippax et al., 1990). Although this "male sex drive" story was evident to some extent in our research, the men we interviewed were also very keen to discuss sexuality as an abstracted practice of knowledge and skill (Waldby et al., 1993a, pp. 250–251). This practice requires a thinking mind and a controlled body. The techniques it produces are also very static—once a man has learnt certain skills he does not need to change or develop them according to his situation. Thus again what is also required is a passive woman's body to

receive the technique and work—as is evident in the following quotes, women in this unemotional or "reasoned" approach to sexuality quickly lose their status as persons and their difference from one another.

INTERVIEWER   How capable are you, you know, of pleasing your partner?

PHIL   Ah. On a scale of one to ten?

INTERVIEWER   Why not!

PHIL   Oh, I think I'm doing a pretty good job, yeah.

INTERVIEWER   Do you ever feel anxious about your ability to please your partner?

TOM   Ah, sometimes I worry about it but nothing, I mean it's not a worry in my mind at all times. Especially if I'm with someone I knew, you know. If I slept with someone new for the first time you might be a bit worried about it then. And if they, if you see them again well you know that [giggles] it worked.

It became clear in our research that one particularly important aspect of the technique/work narrative is an emphasis on being able to give women an orgasm, a phenomenon which, at least in its present form, dates specifically from feminist-influenced sexology (Ehrenreich, Hess, Jacobs, 1986).[2] Whilst their own pleasure is "natural" and driven, men use their technique to bring women to orgasm.

STEVEN   I don't feel like I have to be, I don't place myself at the centre of the actual event so I feel like my partner is more central to the experience than me so I have to, I'm in a way there for her, to please her, so I have no problem with having an orgasm, so, I feel like it's my duty to make sure she has one as well. . . .

INTERVIEWER   Well, how important is orgasm? Female orgasm?

STEVEN   To me it's fairly central, yeah I think.

INTERVIEWER   Do you have any anxieties over your ability to er—

STEVEN   Yes, sometimes.

INTERVIEWER   Provide orgasm?

STEVEN   Yeah, sometimes, yeah. I think it's a constant thought when the act's actually taking place, it's something that you're thinking about most of the time. It's always in the back of your mind. You don't actually rate your performance but you're wondering, is she enjoying it or what else could you do, there's all thoughts going on at the same time.

Although many might at first be pleased that women's pleasure is being attended to, we suggest that what is happening here can be read as an elaboration on the male sex drive discourse. Giving women an orgasm is a demonstration of the man's sexual capacities and skill—again he seems to be "doing" sex on an undifferentiated woman's body. Women's pleasure, unlike men's, is not seen to be natural, but rather as dependent on men's work. Thus women's orgasm is not pleasure for pleasure's sake, but is used to prove the quality of men's technique.

SEXUALITY AND EMBODIMENT

So two stories emerge from our research: a women's story of love and relationships, and a men's story of technique and work. Where do these stories come from, and why do they seem to fit into sexually aligned groups?

In attempting to answer similar questions, feminist theorists have examined the underlying structures of our culture and the knowledges which inform them. They have found that much modern western thought is characterised by a privileging of a mode of thinking which utilises binarisms: a series of mutually dependent "opposite" pairs in which only one side of the pair has a positive definition, whilst the other side is defined as everything that the other is not (Grosz, 1987; Jay, 1991). Examples of these binarisms include: reason-emotion, mind-body, active-passive, public-private, culture-nature, presence-absence. In each of these, men are aligned with the first side, and women with the second. As we will argue, these splits fundamentally inform the ways our interviewees spoke about their sexual experiences.

But *how* do these binarisms actually come to affect individuals at the seemingly "personal" level of sexuality? In answering this, we have looked toward recent feminist writing which has taken the body as its subject—for, as these theories demonstrate, it is the body which seems to constitute the interface between culture and subjectivity.

This writing is based on a denaturalisation of the body—the body is no longer seen as a "purely" bio-

logical entity, but rather as socially and psychically constructed. In this way of thinking, individual bodies are situated in a particular cultural space and are lived, that is, they are experienced as having meanings and significances beyond anatomical or biological existence. Indeed, "biology must itself be amenable to psychical and cultural transformation, to processes of retracing or inscription" (Grosz, 1987, p. 7). Because human biology is always experienced within culture it is "always already cultural" (Grosz, 1987, p. 7). Bodies are sexed—that is they are either the bodies of men or women—and are in part brought into being by a "historically based culturally shared phantasy about male and female biologies" (Gatens, 1983, p. 152). In other words, these are bodies produced in and by a certain culture and which also produce themselves at an imaginary (or psychical) level, on both an individual and a cultural level (Gatens, 1983).

These bodily inscriptions also mark identities. As Gross (1986) explains in delineating the work of Luce Irigaray, the culturally inscribed body "internalised in the form of an image (an imaginary) forms the limits or boundaries of the subject's ego or sense of self" (p. 142). Thus, people's experiences of their bodies, feelings, and beliefs as their own are intrinsically connected to cultural inscriptions of their bodies. Thus, a woman experiences herself as a woman because she is inscribed with cultural stories of femininity (and of its dependent "opposite," masculinity). Thus, in our data, for example, it is not that women do not know about or believe in the masculine story of technique and work, or that men do not have any knowledge of or investment in the relationships narrative, but rather that when they are asked to speak about themselves they speak the stories associated with their own sex.

So, binarisms such as the mind-body split are inscribed onto the sexed bodies of individuals. This is evident also in the dominant account of masculine embodiment where the body is conceptualised as being the property of the person who is somehow separate or above his biology (Grosz, 1987, pp. 4–5). For this account to operate, there must be a body which is biologically given and which can be controlled by the mind. The mind must be able to transcend the body, but at the same time be able to use the body to achieve the mind's ends.

This traditional conceptualisation of the body seems to be reflected in our male interviewees' technique/work narrative. The emphasis on masculine technique and work shores up a notion of the body as controlled by the mind. As is evident in the following quote, women's orgasms are seen as being a result of masculine work and expenditure of effort. Sex is conceptualised as men using their bodies as tools to work on the bodies of women.

INTERVIEWER   How, how does it make you feel? [that his partner does not have orgasms.]

PETER   It makes me wonder what I'm doing [giggles] or what I'm meant to do. 'Cause I find myself spending four times as much time on her than me, she is on me. And mate I'm finding it, I'm, I'm orgasming, but she, she doesn't so.

INTERVIEWER   Mm.

PETER   That, I don't know if it's like that with all women or not, so.

INTERVIEWER   Mm.

PETER   Ah, but it doesn't seem to worry her. I mean I say, "I'll keep going" you know, and she says, "No, don't worry."

As with all binarisms, both sides are dependent on the existence of the other. Thus, when men's bodies are positioned as controlled by the mind, women's bodies are positioned as out of control, or needing control (or work). Women's positioning as the recipients of masculine technique reinforces the male-female binarism of active-passive: Women's bodies become reminders of men's activity and control. Thus, women's response to men's technique is also very important—for unlike men, women, who are already positioned on the body side of the binarism, are more able to fully immerse themselves in the body's pleasures. This immersion would be too risky for men, as according to the binarism, it entails a loss of mind. Thus, women's sexual pleasure—her loss of mind—reaffirms men's own control and stability (Waldby et al., 1991).

Women's position on the body side of the mind-body binarism is also linked to their alignment with emotionality. As Elizabeth Grosz (1987) argues, "patriarchal oppression justifies itself through the presumption that women, more than men, are tied to their fixed corporeality. They are thus considered *more* natural and biologically governed, and *less* cultural, to be more object, and less subject than men" (pp. 5–6). One result of this alignment with the body and with nature, Grosz goes on to explain, is that women are given a "pseudo-evolutionary function in the reproduction of the species" (p. 6). Because women are seen to be closer to nature than are men, they are seen to exist for the purposes of reproduction, and to be the people who are best suited for tasks such as child-rearing. Unsurprisingly, these tasks are also linked with emotionality, nurturing, and the maintaining of relationships.

FAKING IT

So how does this discussion help us to make sense of women faking orgasm? We have argued that what is demanded of women in the technique/work narrative is proof of the value of the man's work, of the soundness of his technique. Thus, women are expected to experience orgasm. But part of the "problem" with women's sexuality is that women's orgasm is not visible. Unlike men, women do not ejaculate visibly, and although in recent times it has been stated that women's capacity for orgasm is at least multiple, their partners still cannot see what is going on.[3] Thus, there is a demand for noisy and exaggerated display.

SALLY   He'd probably love it if I started to, not faking it but he'd probably like it if I was a bit more . . . vocal about it, what I was experiencing. 'Cause he sort of says I'm a silent achiever.

INTERVIEWER   Oh yeah? [laugh]

SALLY   But sometimes I think he's too much of, it's not that he makes a lot of noise either, but I mean . . . he vocalises a lot about how he feels and asks, you know, sort of asking questions all the time.

INTERVIEWER   So you don't actually like talking during sex?

SALLY   Ah, I like talking but . . . not during it, and the only thing I like saying during it is sort of . . . what you feel about that person. . . . Not about sex, the mechanics sort of it. I feel like he sort of gets into the mechanics a bit of it.

As is clear in Sally's case, the demand for display, for noise, is a demand for the affirmation of technique or "mechanics" as she puts it. The demand for noise also indicates that heterosexuality becomes an economy in which the woman's orgasm is exchanged for the man's work.[4]

This demand for noise as proof of orgasm not only indicates the limits of our male interviewees' understanding of feminine sexuality, but shows the importance of cultural constructions of sexuality in individual's experiences: cultural representations of women's orgasm as overwhelmingly pleasurable and, therefore, loud are common in women's popular magazines and pornography. Sally's initial equation of this affirmation with faking orgasm is also very telling. For indeed faking orgasm can only work because of this representation—it is far easier to make a bit of noise than, for example, to fake a vaginal spasm!

This "orgasm for work" economy of heterosexuality however, is not unproblematic. For as we outlined earlier, women's sexuality is seen as oppositional to men's "natural" sexuality, and their orgasms are thus "unnatural."[5] This also springs from women's alignment with the body: women's overimmersion in the body—their lack of mind—means that their bodies are perceived as being chaotic and out of control. Women's orgasms are thus seen as being difficult to achieve—bringing women to orgasm is seen by both men and women to require not only the correct state of mind (in fact a relinquishing of mind and a retreat into the body), but also a good deal of skilled masculine work.[6] Thus the value of men's technique is affirmed—if women *do* reach orgasm, their partner must be "good" at sex—but yet women's sexuality is in some way contained—the difficulties women experience "prove" that women are not as "naturally" sexual as men.

The economy of heterosexuality, as we have already suggested, can also only operate because women provide background networks of love and nurturing. In focussing on maintaining relationships, women make sure there is a space for the smooth functioning of this economy. When the economy is disrupted, for instance, when the woman does not reach orgasm despite the man's skilled work, there are disruptions also to the relationship.

TRACY   Like Jeff used to get really upset. Like he used to get so upset all the time . . . Cause he used to say, "Oh but why, why can't I make you come?" . . . he used to talk about it all the time and it used to sort of piss me off because like I thought, "Oh well there's something wrong with me". . . . And then I realised that it's not, it's just something I've just got to live with. I've just got to work at it. So he's, like we used to talk about it all the time 'cause he'd go, "Gonna happen one day" . . . and he was like "OK, this is what we're gonna do. [interviewer giggles] We're gonna try all these different ways [giggles] and we're gonna make you come," and it was like—and he'd be talking to me the whole way and he'd be going, "Oh, just imagine," he'd be going, "Imagine this, imagine that. Imagine your wildest fantasies," and I'd be going "Oh, shut up!" [both giggle] . . .

INTERVIEWER   Was it that important to you or was it . . .

TRACY   Yeah, it was, but it used to get me down so much.

INTERVIEWER   You'd rather sort of just . . .

TRACY   Yeah, I guess, oh you know, like . . . it's obviously a really good feeling, but you want it to happen all the time but it can't . . . So it still gets me down sometimes now, but I just can't let it get to me because I think, "Oh," but I mean, it's not everything.

Like Tracy, the women who had difficulties with orgasm reported experiencing a great deal of anxiety and spoke of numerous difficult encounters with their partners over the issue. When men "failed" to bring their lovers to this necessary "peak," this was dealt with by both partners in one of two ways. One response, as with Tracy's Jeff, was to assume that the "problem" was one of masculine technique, and thus the way to overcome it was with the man's ever renewed attempts, involving more and more complex skills. The other response was more pessimistic—here both partners assumed that the body of woman is simply faulty, that it is unrealistic to expect a woman to orgasm every time, and that it is better not to worry too much about it. This response springs from the previously mentioned cultural construction of women's bodies as intrinsically flawed and is also reinforced by the cultural discourses of sexuality which suggest that women enjoy "foreplay" much more than "real" sex (penetration)[7] anyway, and so will not mind if they do not reach orgasm.

Here we return to *Cosmopolitan*'s advice: if a woman cannot "achieve" orgasm she should fake one *to please her partner and to avoid relationship problems.* Hence, it is at the site of faking orgasm that the two narratives we have outlined—the technique/work narrative and the love/relationships narrative—intersect. Faking orgasm, as we stated in the beginning, is clearly involved with technique: the pretence techniques of the woman and the affirmation of masculine technical skills. However, it is also interwoven with the emphasis on relationships: The "reason" women give for faking is that it keeps the man happy and, thus, the relationship functioning.

INTERVIEWER   Do the guys you know sort of worry about giving a girl an orgasm, like they sort of (oh yeah), or do they just . . .

JANE   Oh yeah, did you get off, did you get off, did you get off.

MEGAN   Yeah.

JANE   'Cause otherwise it says something about them I think.

LIZ   Yeah it does.

JANE   And if I say "No," then that means like he wasn't good or . . .

MEGAN   Yeah, they feel inadequate.

JANE   So in a sense they're more worried about themselves. And so you think they're worried about you enjoying it but, I mean, (they're not) it's sort of, they're more worried about if they were good or not.

MEGAN   Yeah.

ALISON   That's why I think girls fake it, so that they can sort of like get it over with.

JANE   I fake it sometimes. Just . . . 'cause my boyfriend gets really worried . . . because . . . he wants to know that he's giving me pleasure too. And so sometimes I'll just fake it, if I'm not really in the mood . . .

ALISON   Yeah, I used to do that a lot.

JANE   I just, you know, just sort of fake it a little bit. I think everyone does sometime.

INTERVIEWER   So that he won't get upset?

ALISON   Yeah.

JANE   Not upset, but so he won't feel inadequate.

It is clear that as the site of intersection between the two narratives, faking orgasm generates anxieties and difficulties for both men and women. Women worry that it is unfair to their partners to fake, but, yet, are not willing to risk upsetting them by admitting the "truth" about their enjoyment. Men are concerned about their partners faking orgasm because of its connections with poor technique which they read as a questioning of their masculinity. The fact that faking orgasm is a well-known "syndrome" also creates further anxiety for men by touching upon the culturally prevalent fear that women's desire is in essence unknowable and insatiable. If women are faking orgasm, it might be that masculine technique is in itself lacking. Even worse, women could be experiencing some undetectable pleasure during sex which is not dependent on the man's skills.

Thus, we can see that faking orgasm is a site where cultural inscriptions of sexuality are played out—faking orgasm reaffirms women's position as the passive recipients of masculine technique. Paradoxically, however, (and this may also have something to do with both men and women's high anxiety levels surrounding faking orgasm) faking orgasm is simultaneously a disruption to the traditional alignment of women with the passive side of the binarisms—when women fake they are being active and are using their minds to perform (being) the body! This paradox shows the complexity of sexed subject positions: Women's position on the passive side of the binary is shown to require their activity.

FAKING ORGASM: WHAT DOES IT MEAN FOR HIV/AIDS EDUCATION?

In their problematisation of the dualism of a purely biological body and a controlling mind, the reconceptualisations of the body we discussed earlier provide us with a different way of thinking about subjectivity and desire. If the body and subjectivity are products of social inscription and conscious and unconscious workings over of these inscriptions, we can understand how the stories about sexuality we have been outlining in this paper come into play in individual people's lives. This does not mean that there are no possibilities for change—either on a individual or societal level—for this is precisely what these denaturalising theories allow. If subjects are exposed to different cultural inscriptions, or if their personal experiences allow for different interpretations of these inscriptions, they can begin to experience a different embodiment.

As we stated in the beginning, governmental HIV/AIDS educational materials aimed at heterosexuals tend to promote negotiation and assertion in sexual encounters. The underlying premises of these strategies are that men and women are on an equal footing in relationships, that they can talk together about sexuality, and that they will both negotiate to ensure that their own pleasure is obtained. In earlier work we have shown that the first of these assumptions is simply incorrect: Men and women are not on an equal footing in relationships, they do not have equal power to negotiate such things as condom use (Waldby et al., 1991).

The theories of the body we have outlined demonstrate the inaccuracy of the second two premises. If we accept the roles of social inscription and unconscious workings over of this inscription, then it is clear that there are many aspects of sexuality which are not available for discussion: People do not know where their ideas are coming from, or why they believe what they do. By definition, those things which are unconscious are unknowable to the subject. The stories which heterosexual people self-consciously use to make sense of their own behaviours are the ones which are culturally available and hence believed unproblematic. One of the most important of these is that heterosexuality is "natural" and "right"—thus for heterosexual couples there does not seem to be anything to discuss.

Our discussion of faking orgasm indicates that sexuality is not based on a rational decision making process, but, rather, is intensively written over with cultural inscriptions and unconscious desires. To understand faking orgasm we have shown that we need to understand that individuals' behaviour is produced within cultural stories such as those of technique and love, their different positions in the series of binarisms we have discussed, and culturally acceptable notions of what are appropriate feminine and masculine behaviour and attitudes. Sexual behaviour is not dictated by a mind which controls a body, but rather is part of, and springs from, the lived experience

of a culturally situated body. Sexuality is not an issue which individuals can openly and fully discuss. There are many more things at stake in a sexual encounter than pleasure or sexual satisfaction, or even safety from diseases such as HIV/AIDS.

So what then of HIV/AIDS education? We suggest that any serious attempt to encourage behaviour change amongst heterosexuals must take these sorts of issues into account. We must stop thinking of the body as a passive object of mental control. Instead, we believe, the (admittedly much harder) task of looking at such things as constructions of "proper" or "appropriate" masculinity and femininity, culturally shared unconscious fears and imaginary body maps (Gatens, 1983), and personal desires for intimacy and recognition must be undertaken. If these forces are not taken into account, education will be severely limited and will reinforce a status quo which not only makes the uptake of safe sex strategies very difficult, but which is oppressive to women. Educators would perhaps be best advised to encourage people to look at the narratives which they use to understand their sexuality and relationships, and to problematise ideas about what is "natural" and "normal," for only then can people begin to examine and understand their own attitudes and behaviours and, thus, undergo change.

NOTES

1. The percentage of mature age students was approximately 16% for the interviews, whilst the percentage was approximately 21% for the groups. The age range for the mature students was between 26 and 45 years.

2. In this historical episode we see what happens when a phallocentric culture takes on and, thus, changes a feminist demand.

3. In pornographic films the "come shot" or "money shot" (a picture of male ejaculation) stands in for both men and women's orgasm (Williams, 1989). Our women interviewees also suffered anxiety as to whether they actually had experienced orgasm, and some time was spent in at least one of the women's groups discussing whether what they had experienced actually was an orgasm.

4. Gilfoyle, Wilson, and Brown (1992) also see heterosexuality as a kind of economy, but for them orgasms are a gift men give to women in exchange for women's offering of their own passive bodies. The notion of heterosexuality as an exchange is also argued on a more general conceptual level by Luce Irigaray

(1985) and Carole Pateman (1989) who suggested that western culture is based on the exchange of women's bodies between men.

5. For a discussion of the historical development of this positioning of women's orgasm as "unnatural" see Laquer (1990) and Spongberg (1992). The positioning of men's orgasm as "natural" uncharacteristically positions men on the natural side of a culture-nature binarism. We would argue that this is an interesting and quite specific instance, as in fact the story of technique/work shows. During sex, men are seen to be driven by "nature," however, this is only in relation to their own orgasm. Their sexuality in every other respect is seen to require technique/work, which, as we argue in the text, repositions them on the culture side of the nature-culture binarism. Men's nature, as opposed to women's, is always seen in terms of possible or probable (mental) control. The men who are perceived to be unable to exercise control over their nature are usually considered criminals or deviants, or are excused by extenuating circumstances (such as provocative dress).

6. Both the men and the women we interviewed had numerous stories which they used to explain women's ability or inability to orgasm. These ranged from the psychologistic to the "scientific" and statistical, and from the practical and technical to the emotional. These complicated explanations, however, usually boiled down to the two basic "truths" outlined in the text: Women find it inherently "difficult" to orgasm (for either psychologistic or physiological reasons) and that it is men's technique which can, in some cases and where various conditions are "right," bring women to orgasm. Some women did feel a responsibility to help their partner in his endeavour by providing the information to help their partner "fine tune" his technique and to assist by getting themselves in the "right frame of mind," but the actual physical stimulation was seen to be the man's job.

7. Nearly all of our subjects defined "having sex" as vaginal penetration.

REFERENCES

Ehrenreich, Barbara, Hess, Elizabeth, & Jacobs, Gloria. (1986). *Remaking love: The feminization of sex*. New York: Anchor Books.

Gatens, Moira. (1983). A critique of the sex/gender distinction. In Judith Allen & Paul Patton (Eds.), *Beyond Marxism: Interventions after Marx* (pp. 143–160) Sydney, Australia: Interventions Publications.

Gilfoyle, Jackie, Wilson, Jonathon, & Brown. (1992). Sex, organs, and audiotape: A discourse analytic approach to talking about heterosexual sex and relationships. *Feminism and Psychology, 2*, 209–230.

Gross, Elizabeth. (1986). Philosophy, subjectivity and the body: Kristeva and Irigaray. In Carole Pateman & Elizabeth Gross (Eds)., *Feminist challenges: Social and political theory* (pp. 125–143). Sydney, Austalia: Allen and Unwin.

Grosz, Elizabeth. (1987). Notes toward a corporeal feminism. *Australian Feminist Studies, 5*, 1–16.

Hollway, Wendy. (1984). Gender difference and the production of subjectivity. In Julien Henriques, Wendy Hollway, Cathy Urwin, Couze Venn, & Valerie Walkerdine (Eds.), *Changing the subject: Psychology, social regulation and subjectivity* (pp. 227–263). London: Methuen.

Jay, Nancy. (1991). Gender and dichotomy. In Sneja Gunew (Ed.), *A reader in feminist knowledge* (pp. 89–106). Sydney, Australia: Routledge.

Kippax, Susan, Crawford, June, Waldby, Catherine & Benton, Pam. (1990). Women negotiating heterosex: Implications for AIDS prevention. *Women's Studies International Forum, 13*, 533–542.

Kwalitan [computer software]. (1990). Netherlands: University of Nijmegen.

Irigaray, Luce. (1985). *This sex which is not one*. New York: Cornell University Press.

Laquer, Thomas. (1990). *Making sex: Body and gender from the Greeks to Freud*. Cambridge, MA: Harvard University Press.

Pateman, Carole. (1989). *The sexual contract*. Cambridge, MA: Polity Press.

Singer Kaplan, Helen. (1992, September). 50 sex questions women ask most. *Cosmopolitan*, pp. 156–164.

Spongberg, Mary. (1992). *The sick rose: Constructing the body of the prostitute in nineteenth century medical discourse*. Unpublished doctoral dissertation, University of Sydney, Australia.

Waldby, Catherine, Kippax, Susan, & Crawford, June. (1990). Theory in the bedroom: A report from the Macquarie University AIDS and Heterosexuality Project. *Australian Journal of Social Issues, 25*, 177–185.

Waldby, Catherine, Kippax, Susan, & Crawford, June. (1991). Equality and eroticism: AIDS and the active/passive distinction. *Social Semiotics, 1*, 39–50.

Waldby, Catherine, Kippax, Susan, & Crawford, June. (1993a). Heterosexual men and "safe sex" practice: Research note. *The Sociology of Health and Illness, 15*, 246–256.

Waldby, Catherine, Kippax, Susan, & Crawford, June. (1993b). Cordon sanitaire: Clean and unclean women in the AIDS discourse of young men. In Peter Aggleton, Graham Hart, & Peter Davies (Eds.), *AIDS: The second decade* (pp. 29–39). Sussex: Falmer Press.

Williams, Linda. (1989). *Hard core: Power, pleasure and the "Frenzy of the Invisible."* Los Angeles, CA: University of California Press.

6.3 CHARACTERISTICS OF VIBRATOR USE AMONG WOMEN

Clive M. Davis, Joani Blank, Hung-Yu Lin, and Consuelo Bonillas

Although there are many historical accounts of women using sexual enhancement devices or "sex toys," such as dildos, ben wa balls, feathers, and other objects (e.g., Dengrove, 1977; Kinsey, Pomeroy, Martin, & Gebhard, 1953; Maines, 1989; Masters & Johnson, 1966; Tavris & Sadd, 1975), the electric vibrator is a relatively new addition to the array. Despite the fact that electromechanical vibrators have been in existence for more than 100 years and have undoubtedly been used for sexual stimulation during their entire history (Maines, 1989), only within the past 2 decades or so have they become more readily and widely available, and more commonly used. For example, Kinsey et al. found vibrator use to be rare 40–50 years ago. About 20 years ago, Hite (1976) reported that only 1% of her sample said they had ever used a vibrator.

Only a few years later, however, in a similar type of survey of self-selected women readers of Cosmopolitan magazine, Wolfe (1981) found that more than 25% of the sample reported at least occasional use of a vibrator in connection with masturbation. Although the sample was not representative of the larger U.S. population, it is clear that by the 1980s many women were using vibrators in their sexual activity. More than a decade later, however, we still know little about the characteristics of women who use vibrators as a part of their sexual activity and how they actually use them. To begin to address this lack of knowledge, we obtained descriptive accounts of vibrator usage, both alone and with a partner, from a convenience sample of more than 200 women.

Most of what little attention has been paid to vibrator use has been clinically focused, concerned primarily with vibrator use in the treatment of orgasmic dysfunction (e.g., Kaplan, 1974; LoPiccolo & Lobitz, 1972; Marquis, 1970; Riley & Riley, 1978; Williams & Orsmond, 1977; Zeiss, Rosen, & Zeiss,

1977). Even in that literature, controversy exists. Whereas some authors (e.g., Heiman, LoPiccolo, & LoPiccolo, 1976; Masters & Johnson, 1986) have encouraged women to use a vibrator to heighten their sexual arousal or to enhance orgasmic capacity, others (e.g., Kaplan, 1974) have been less enthusiastic, fearing that the woman might become too dependent on the vibrator. Kaplan argued that women may become unable to experience orgasm by other means if a vibrator is relied upon too extensively.

Researchers who have investigated women's masturbation in nonclinical samples have barely mentioned vibrator use (e.g., Clifford, 1978; Hite, 1976). Clifford, in her study of masturbation by college women, thoroughly examined many specific aspects of masturbatory behavior, but she did not pursue her finding that a "few" individuals reported masturbating using a vibrator. In the Cosmopolitan survey, Wolfe (1981) found that vibrators were used during solitary masturbation by 26% of all the respondents and by 37% of the women over 30. She expanded on vibrator use only by including a small number of the written descriptions provided by the respondents.

There is one exception. Levin and Levin (1975), reporting on the Redbook survey, found that 1 woman out of 5 in a sample of 100,000 had experimented with vibrators, phallic objects, oils, or feathers in conjunction with sexual intercourse. Furthermore, they found nonreligious women were more likely than religious women to employ vibrators to enhance sexual experience. Aside from a negative correlation with religiosity, no other variable (e.g., age, educational background, or income) was found to be reliably associated with vibrator use.

Thus, there is a paucity of information about the characteristics of women who use vibrators as a part of their sexual activity and the nature of their experience in using those vibrators. To explore these issues, we undertook this investigation. At the outset we should stress that the sample, although sizeable and diverse in many respects, is entirely self-selected and not representative of any known population. Thus, the data are best viewed as suggestive and should not be generalized beyond this sample.

METHOD

Respondents and Procedure

A questionnaire was sent to the 700 most recent purchasers of a vibrator from the mail-order division of a sexuality store in San Francisco. A cover letter explained the purpose of the research, solicited cooperation, and provided a discount coupon for future purchases from the store. Because we were interested in vibrator use among women and the questionnaire was written with women in mind, the cover letter invited men who received the letter and who had purchased a vibrator for a woman to give the questionnaire to that woman. Because purchasers often use initials, rather than first names, it was not possible to screen respondents in advance for their sex. The staff estimated that 25–33% of purchasers are men.

To preserve anonymity, questionnaires were returned to the first author without participant identification. This convenience sample was used because of the availability of the names and knowledge that this sample was geographically diverse. Of the 700 surveys sent out, 202 (29%) were returned. Based on interpretable postmarks, the diversity expectation was borne out in that questionnaires were returned from at least 38 states and 3 countries.

The descriptive characteristics of the sample are summarized in Table 6.3.1. It was an eclectic sample: Age ranged from 18–75; more than 60% were heterosexual, but one third were either lesbian or bisexual; about half were currently in a monogamous relationship, but 30% were not currently involved in any sexual relationship.

Questionnaire

The questionnaire was designed to allow women to describe, mostly in their own words, their experience with vibrator usage. Other data were collected to allow comparisons among women in background and usage experience. The questionnaire consisted of 31 items, 8 of which were open ended and will be identified specifically in the Results section. The questions were addressed to three broadly defined areas: (a) demographic background and relationship status (4 questions; see Table 6.3.1), (b) masturbatory and partnered sexual activity (11 questions, 9 of which are reported on Tables 6.3.2 and 6.3.3; 2 questions about preferred stimulation for nonorgasmic women alone and with a partner were not analyzed because only 2% of the sample was not orgasmic), and (c) vibrator usage in masturbatory and partnered sexual activity [16 questions, the data from 12 of which are reported in the text and Tables 6.3.4 and 6.3.5; 4 questions (3 open ended) dealt with types, brands, and the chang-

Table 6.3.1 Characteristics of the Sample ($N = 202$)

	%
Current age of respondents ($n = 194$)	
18–29	26
30–39	39
40–49	27
over 50 (highest = 75)	8
Sexual orientation ($n = 201$)	
Bisexual	21
Heterosexual	63
Lesbian	13
Other	3
Current relationship status ($n = 202$)	
Coupled, monogamous	49
Coupled, with a primary partner	13
No primary sexual partner	5
No sexual partner now	31
Other	2
Current sexual partner(s) ($n = 200$)	
Exclusively male	54
Exclusively female	12
Both female and male	6
No sexual partner now	28

Table 6.3.2 Aspects of the Sexual Behavior Histories of the Sample

Age of first masturbation (*n* = 198)	
Age	%
Never	1
4–9	17
10–12	18
13–15	20
16–19	15
20–25	18
26–35	9
36 and older	3

Frequency of pursuing sexual arousal and/or orgasm in past year		
	Alone (*n* = 199)	With a partner (*n* = 199)
Frequency	%	%
Never	6	15
< 2/month	13	12
2–3/month	24	19
1–3/week	38	39
> 3/week	20	15

Frequency of experiencing orgasm		
	Alone (*n* = 199)	With a partner (*n* = 177)
Frequency	%	%
Never	2	3
Rarely (1–15%)	3	10
Occasionally (16–50%)	3	12
Usually (51–85%)	16	27
Nearly always or always (>85%)	76	47

Degree of satisfaction with frequency/consistency of orgasm		
	Alone (*n* = 199)	With a partner (*n* = 198)
Rating	%	%
Not at all	10	22
Somewhat	8	10
Moderately	25	25
Very	58	43

ing of vibrators used; these data are not reported herein]. The content of the questions relevant to this report will be described further in the Results section.

Drafts of the questionnaire were reviewed by small convenience samples of women who were users of vibrators. Based on their suggestions, revisions of the wording of the survey were made at each stage of the development process until we concluded there was no need for further revision.

The coding of the open-ended items was straightforward in that in almost all cases it amounted to recording whether a specific element of content, such as a position, a sound, or a positive or negative reaction, was mentioned. During the early phase of coding, all coded open-ended items were reviewed by a second coder to ensure that all content was coded. After all coding was completed, a random sample of 50 questionnaires was selected for coding by both women coders. Agreement was 98%.

Table 6.3.3 Percentages of Respondents Reporting Various Types of Stimulation that Usually or Always Trigger Orgasm

Type of behavior	% Alone (*n* = 199)	% With Partner (*n* = 196)
Clitoral-manual	59	56
Clitoral-oral	NA[a]	61
Clitoral-vibrator	79	54
Vaginal-manual	15	26
Vaginal-nonvibrating dildo	12	10
Vaginal-oral	NA	22
Vaginal-intercourse	NA	44
Vaginal-vibrator	30	24
Vaginal-other	2	5
Anal-manual	6	12
Anal-dildo or anal plug	7	4
Anal-vibrator	5	3
Anal-intercourse	NA	10
Other	4	5

[a]Not applicable

Table 6.3.4 Descriptive Accounts of Behavior When Using a Vibrator Alone ($n = 158$)

	%		%
Body position ($n = 155$)		Breathing and sounds associated	
Sitting	5	with usage ($n = 196$)	
Lying down	77	Breathe heavily	24
Various positions	19	Breathe faster	23
		Moan/groan	26
Primary location of vibrator ($n = 115$)		Makes no sounds	23
Clitoris	58	Yell/scream	4
Labia	2	Uses words	8
Vagina	3	Miscellaneous other	13
Various genital sites	36		
		Time period of typical session ($n = 135$)	
Body/vibrator movement ($n = 132$)		<5 min	13
Primarily moves body	10	5–10 min	13
Primarily moves vibrator	43	11–15 min	16
Moves both about equally	39	15–20 min	14
Miscellaneous other	8	21–30 min	16
		>30 min	7
Vibrator movement styles ($n = 79$)		No typical time period/wide variability	22
Slow, gentle	8		
Slow, then fast	4	Number of orgasms using a vibrator ($n = 154$)	
Circular	23	One	57
Up/down; back/forth	36	Two	21
In and out	11	One or two	3
Vibrator on and off	3	Three	8
Combination	15	More than three	11
Vibrator movement or pressure		Intensity of orgasmic feelings with a vibrator	
changes as aroused ($n = 74$)		($n = 123$)	
Harder/more pressure	20	More intense	52
Softer/less pressure	15	Less intense	15
Faster movement	14	No difference	20
Slower movement	3	Other comments not related to intensity	13
Move vibrator	12		
Move body	4		
A combination of the things	16		
Turn off vibrator	7		
Miscellaneous other	9		

Table 6.3.5 Most Common Partner Behaviors While Respondent is Being Stimulated by a Vibrator ($n = 145$)

Activity	%[a]
Watches the user	69
Holds the vibrator	67
Holds/strokes user	66
Stimulates user's genitals[b]	62
Stimulates user's nipples	61
Talks to the user	52
Masturbates him/herself	33

[a]Percentages do not total 100 because multiple responses were accepted.

[b]Includes simultaneous coitus.

RESULTS

In addition to the demographic and relationship data shown in Table 6.3.1, nine questions dealt with the sexual behavior histories of the women. Because of the exploratory nature of the investigation and the fact that the ability to detect a relationship between two variables depends on adequate variability existing for both variables, we believe it is useful to begin by reporting these descriptive sexual background data. In so doing, a cautionary note about the number of statistical tests conducted in analyzing these data is in order. It was our goal, consistent with the exploratory nature of the investigation, to look for relationships between the background variables and the sexual behavior histories, and between each of those types of variables and vibrator-related behaviors. Thus, approximately 150 conceptually relevant statistical comparisons (cross-tabulations) were made. One effect of conducting so many tests was to increase the Type 1 error rate: the likelihood of finding a significant difference by chance alone. To compensate partially for that likelihood, only associations that met the $p < .01$ level are reported as statistically significant, whereas in exploratory work it is common to accept a significance level as high as .10. Furthermore, for those variables associated with vibrator usage, when a significant association is reported, the most relevant percentages are also reported, in either the text or a

table, thereby allowing readers to evaluate for themselves whether the absolute differences warrant further consideration. Finally, all significant findings should be taken as mere indications of the possibility of a meaningful relationship between the variables, a relationship that can only be confirmed by subsequent hypothesis-testing research.

To ensure adequate cell sizes for these statistical comparisons, collapsing across some of the more detailed categories shown in the descriptive tables (Tables 6.3.1 and 6.3.2) was necessary. Where this occurred, the broader categories are described.

In considering the reported results, the reader may ask about relationships not reported for the variables that are discussed repeatedly. In all cases, those relationships were nonsignificant. Occasionally, explicit mention of a nonsignificant result is made, however, because we felt the trend, or the size of an absolute difference within the larger matrix of results, might have an implication for future research.

Sexual Behavior History

Women were asked their age at first masturbation, defined as the first time they recalled "consciously engaging in sexual self-stimulation." These data are shown in Table 6.3.2. More than one third masturbated by age 12, and 71% had done so by age 19.

Also shown in Table 6.3.2 are the frequency of "pursuing sexual arousal and/or orgasm" alone and with a partner during the past year. Although a few women reported they had not pursued sexual arousal alone during that time, 58% indicated an average of at least once a week. Similarly, more than half (54%) had engaged in sexual activity with a partner at least once a week. The relationship between the two variables is of potential interest. Considering only those women who did engage in both behaviors, the overall association did not meet our criterion of significance, $\chi^2(9, N = 184) = 17.35, p > .01 < .05$. However, of those women who engaged in partnered sexual activity at least 4 times per week, 40% engaged in self-stimulation 4 or more times per week also, and of those women who engaged in masturbation at least 4 times per week, 32% also engaged in partnered activity at least 4 times per week. Although age of the women was not reliably associated with the frequency of pursuing sexual arousal alone either, $\chi^2(9, N = 179) = 16.09, p > .05 < .10$, only 25% of those women over 50 engaged in self-stimulation as often as once per week, compared to 50–70% for the other age groups.

The relationship between age of first masturbation and the frequency of sexual activity alone was similar to the age relationship. The 4–9 and 10–12 age groups were combined for this analysis. Although the Chi-square was not significant, $\chi^2(9, N = 184) = 14.77, p > .05 < .10$, more than 70% of those women who began masturbating before age 13 engaged in sexual self-stimulation at least once a week, whereas only 51% of those who began masturbating after 13 engaged in self-stimulation this frequently. Sexual orientation was not significantly associated with frequency of sexual activity alone, $\chi^2(6, N = 192) = 13.81, p > .01 < .05$, but more bisexual women (81%) engaged in autoerotic behavior at least once a week than either heterosexual women (50%) or homosexual women (57%).

The women were asked about how often they experienced orgasm, when they pursued an orgasm, both alone and with a partner. These data are also summarized in Table 6.3.2. As shown, women were much more likely to be *nearly always* or *always* [85%+] orgasmic alone than with a partner, $\chi^2(3, N = 166) = 38.96, p < .001$. Because there were so few women who did not experience orgasm alone, for this analysis, the categories were collapsed to two: nearly always or always orgasmic and all those in the other groups.

Next, the women were asked about their orgasmic sexual satisfaction, alone and with a partner. Again, the data are summarized in Table 6.3.2. More women were *very satisfied* with their autoerotic experience than with their partnered experience, although two thirds were at least *moderately satisfied* in the partnered situation. Among the women currently in a partnered relationship, however, 62% reported being *very satisfied* with the frequency/consistency, comparable to the figure for satisfaction alone. Younger women, compared to older women, were relatively more satisfied with their orgasmic experience alone, $\chi^2(9, N = 191) = 58.19, p < .001$. Mostly notably, only 25% of those over 50 indicated they were *very satisfied,* compared to 58–66% of the other age groups.

Those women who were orgasmic were invited to indicate the kind of stimulation that "usually or always

triggers orgasm." They were provided with a checklist of 13 items in which the primary site of stimulation (clitoris, vagina, or anus) was systematically paired with the type of stimulation (manual, oral, dildo [or anal plug], vibrator, and intercourse), as appropriate. These data are summarized in Table 6.3.3. Women experiencing orgasm alone found clitoral-vibrator and clitoral-manual stimulation to be most effective, nearly 80% indicating that clitoral stimulation with a vibrator usually or always triggered orgasm. Twenty-five percent fewer (54%) reported that clitoral-vibrator stimulation in the partnered context usually or always triggered orgasm. More than half of the women experiencing orgasm in partnered sexual activity also reported these two types of stimulation and oral-clitoral stimulation to lead to orgasm regularly. Of the 202 women, 145 indicated that they had used a vibrator with a partner. Recomputing the percentages for only those women resulted in 72% reporting clitoral-vibrator stimulation and 32% indicating vaginal-vibrator stimulation regularly triggered orgasm in the partnered situation also.

Each of the three (alone) or four (partnered) most commonly effective types of stimulation (see Table 6.3.3) was analyzed in relationship to age. More than 70% of the under-30 women, and 64% of those between 30 and 40 reported clitoral-manual stimulation to be effective for them, whereas only half of 40–49 age group and 25% of the over 50 group so indicated, $\chi^2(3, N = 194) = 13.84, p < .01$. Age also was linked to the effectiveness of oral-genital stimulation, $\chi^2(3, N = 194) = 12.64, p < .01$, with those women over 50 (25%) being much less likely to report experiencing orgasm through this technique than were the younger groups (56–71%).

Vibrator Use

Characteristics of Women Who Used a Vibrator

The women were asked how old they were when they first tried a vibrator. Of the 199 who reported an age, 17% were under 20, 47% were between 20 and 29, 27% were between 30 and 39, and 8% were 40 or over. The oldest age at which a woman indicated she began using a vibrator was 58. Age of first masturbation was positively associated with age of first vibrator usage,

$\chi^2(9, N = 194) = 32.37, p < .001$. Sexual orientation was also significantly associated with age of first vibrator use, $\chi^2(6, N = 192) = 24.15, p < .001$. More than one third (36%) of the lesbian women had tried a vibrator by age 20, compared to 15% of the bisexual and 11% of the heterosexual women. By age 30, 86% of the lesbian women had used a vibrator, whereas fewer than two thirds of the other two groups had done so.

Vibrator Use Techniques

Via an open-ended question, the respondents were asked to describe how they usually used a vibrator in their masturbatory activity. In so doing, they were asked to discuss (a) positioning of their body (e.g., standing, sitting, lying down), (b) how and where they hold the vibrator, (c) their breathing patterns and sounds they make, (d) their orgasmic experience with the vibrator use, and (e) how long they spend engaging in an episode of sexual activity when using a vibrator, as well as to describe any other aspect of the experience they wished. These major results are summarized in Table 6.3.4.

Most often, women reported using the vibrator while lying down, and the primary focus was on the clitoris, but it was also clear that many women used a variety of positions and stimulated the entire genital area to some degree. They either moved the vibrator around or moved both the vibrator and their body about equally. The most common movement was described as a "back and forth" or "up and down" movement, but a circular type of movement of the vibrator was common also. There appeared to be no dominant type of change in vibrator movement as the women become more aroused, as shown in Table 4. Many described their breathing as heavy or faster than normal, and it was common to vocalize moans or groans. A similar number indicated they make no audible sounds during stimulation with a vibrator.

Vibrator Use and Orgasm

As previously indicated (Table 6.3.2), 92% of the women reported that they were orgasmic more than half the time when they engaged in self-stimulation. Of these orgasmic women, 154 reported the number of orgasms they typically experienced during a single session of stimulation in which vibrator was used.

Most experienced one or two, but a few commonly experienced three or more.

Many women ($n = 123$) described the differences, if any, between the feelings they experienced when an orgasm was stimulated by vibrator use, compared to their feelings when a vibrator was not used. A majority reported orgasms were stronger with a vibrator (see Table 6.3.4). Ten women reported that they only experienced orgasm with the use of a vibrator.

Next, women were asked whether "during their most active period of vibrator use for masturbation, did you continue to masturbate without a vibrator?" Half did. Of these, 34% used another method up to 20% of the time, 13% did so between 21% and 40% of the time, 33% did so 40–60% of the time, and the remaining 20% did so more than 60% of the time. Thus, although many women who use a vibrator to masturbate always do so, many others continue to use other methods as well. In response to an open-ended question about what other techniques were used, explicitly mentioned by at least 10% of the sample were the use of their fingers for manual stimulation, the use of running water on the genitals, and placing some other object in the vagina.

Vibrator Use with a Partner

Seventy-two percent of the sample reported they had used a vibrator while engaging in sexual activity with a partner. Although it did not reach the established criterion of .01, 80% of lesbian women had done so, compared to 71% of the bisexual women and 73% of the heterosexual women, $\chi^2(2, N = 189) = 8.12, p < .02$. The initiative to use a vibrator was about equally often the respondent's idea (46%) and the partner's (42%). The remainder (12%) indicated the idea was mutual. Several ways of introducing the vibrator into the activity were reported as equally common in response to an open-ended question. These included just picking up the vibrator and using it without prior discussion of doing so, the respondents asking the partner about using it, and the partner asking the respondent about using it.

Next, the women were asked, via an open-ended item, about partner reactions. Although reactions to the introduction of the vibrator were mixed, the most common response of the partner was a positive one, with words such as "glad," "happy," and "enthusiastic" being frequently cited. Only about 10% indicated their partners were "unenthusiastic" or reacted negatively. Twelve percent of the women indicated, in answer to a separate open-ended question, why they had stopped using a vibrator with a partner, if they had stopped. The only two common reasons were that the partner was no longer available and that partner disliked using the vibrator.

The women were also asked about the specific techniques of using a vibrator with their partners. From a checklist provided (with an "other [please describe]" option), to a question concerning the "usual" behaviors of the partner while the respondent was being stimulated with the vibrator, the most common responses are summarized in Table 6.3.5. It is clear that many partners actively participated in the sexual interaction by either stimulating the woman with the vibrator or engaging in some other form of stimulating her at the same time as she is using the vibrator, such as holding and stroking her. It also was common for the partner simply to observe the woman, sometimes masturbating himself or herself at the same time. Twenty-eight percent of the women indicated that they sometimes hold the vibrator in a position where both partners can be stimulated genitally at the same time.

The women were asked if their partners were orgasmic with vibrator stimulation. Of the 140 (97% of the 145 who used a vibrator with a partner) women who responded to this item, 55% indicated their partners were not orgasmic with vibrator stimulation. This item was significantly linked to sexual orientation, $\chi^2(2, N = 138) = 15.22, p < .001$. Eighty-five percent of the lesbian respondents indicated their partners were orgasmic with vibrator stimulation, whereas only 37% and 39% of the bisexual and heterosexual women, respectively, indicated their partners were orgasmic with the vibrator. Of the 145 women responding, 21% indicated their partner did not like the vibrator being used on them, but 65% responded positively; 12% reported they did not know their partner's reaction.

DISCUSSION

Our primary goal in this exploratory study was to document what some women do and how some women

react when they use a vibrator for sexual stimulation. We interpret the results as revealing both considerable commonality in vibrator-use activity and experiences and considerable diversity as well. That is, in response to most questions, one or two responses usually dominated as the most common, but many women also provided other answers. For example, although a clear majority indicated that clitoral stimulation with a vibrator (manual and oral as well) was effective in regularly triggering orgasm, some women did not use this technique or find it effective. Although most women favored lying down while using a vibrator, others sat or used a variety of positions. Further, although it was most common for women to move the vibrator over their clitoris and/or genital area, some moved only their body and not the vibrator, and some did both. Some increased the vibrator pressure as arousal increases; others decreased it. By documenting these variations, we have established a foundation for asking about the correlates and causes of the diversity.

Our second goal was to identify some correlates among the variables investigated. The observed degree of variation in both sample characteristics and sexual behaviors permitted meaningful analyses of some relationships between potential predictor variables (background and sexual histories) and the vibrator-related behaviors. Although generalizations of the overall results beyond the sample cannot be made because of the unknown representativeness of the sample, internal comparisons, or correlations between variables within the database, can be made. These results can suggest hypotheses that need to be tested in subsequent research.

Nearly all women in this sample had masturbated; more than half were currently doing so at least once a week. About 85% also engaged in partnered sexual activity; again, more than half were doing so at least once a week. Overall, this is a sample of women who engaged in a relatively high frequency of sexual activity compared to society as a whole (see Janus & Janus, 1993; Laumann, Gagnon, Michael, & Michaels, 1994). Furthermore, it is clear that masturbation is not a substitute for the partnered sexual activity for most of these women. Indeed, among those who masturbated at least 4 times a week, nearly a third also engaged in partnered activity at least 4 times a week, and of those who engaged in partnered activity 4 or more times a week, 40% masturbated at least 4 times a week.

Most of these women were consistently orgasmic. Self-stimulation was more reliable in triggering orgasm than were partnered sexual activities. Most women were also at least moderately satisfied with the frequency or consistency of their orgasmic experience, both alone and with a partner. This is not a sample of women frustrated with their sexual experiences or using a vibrator to compensate for lack of sexual satisfaction by other means, either alone or with a partner.

These women *do* use vibrators to enhance their sexual experiences. Using a vibrator was usually more effective than other means in triggering orgasm and, for most, produced a more intense or stronger feeling. For some, the vibrator was used to assist them in experiencing more than one orgasm during a single session of sexual activity.

These data are suggestive with regard to the controversy about the potential of vibrator use having negative effects on sexual functioning and satisfaction without using a vibrator. They offer no support for such a concern in that the overwhelming majority of vibrator users in this sample continued to engage in other sexual activities since initiating vibrator use alone and/or introducing a vibrator into their partnered activities. These women reported that using the vibrator enhanced their sexual experiences, but the data do not suggest that they become dependent on it (Kaplan, 1974).

Younger women in the sample began masturbating at earlier ages, were more satisfied with their orgasmic experience alone, and engaged in more clitoral-manual stimulation and more oral-genital stimulation. These results suggest that some younger women are becoming more self-reliant and sexually assertive, but the lack of significant relationships between age and the majority of variables indicates that women of all ages in the sample had very active, diverse, and self-satisfying sexual experiences.

Nearly three quarters of the women had introduced vibrators into their partnered activity, and most who had done so continued to use a vibrator in this context at least occasionally. It is interesting to note

that 25% fewer women reported usually experiencing orgasm with clitoral-vibrator stimulation in the partnered context than they did when alone. Whether this is because partners using the vibrator were less likely to stimulate the woman's clitoris or did so in such as way as to be less likely to trigger orgasm, however, cannot be answered with these data.

Although nearly 10% more lesbian women had done so than had women in the other groups, sexual orientation was not associated with who introduced the vibrator into the relationship or reaction to it. Reactions were reported to be mostly positive in the vast majority of cases. Although several significant relationships between sexual orientation and other variables were found, no obvious pattern of differences emerged to suggest that any one of these groups was more or less active, responsive, or different from the others in any meaningful way.

Although the results of this exploratory investigation provide a foundation for further research concerning vibrator use by women, the limitations of this database should not be overlooked. The population from which the sample was derived was one of purchasers of vibrators from a store/mail-order company specializing in sexuality products. Further, only about 30% of those to whom the questionnaire was sent returned it. Although this is not a low rate of return for mailed questionnaires, particularly for a fairly lengthy questionnaire and when no follow-up procedures are used (Miller, 1991), it remains the case that this is a highly self-selected sample. Given the available information about selection bias in sexuality research (see Catania, Binson, van der Straten, & Stone, 1996, for a review), we speculate that this sample is somewhat more sexually active and more positive about their vibrator-related experiences than a more representative sample of users might be. Given that no empirical data on these questions exist, however, it remains an empirical matter to be determined by future researchers. Several other research questions are ripe for investigation.

An area not addressed that would be helpful in achieving a better understanding of the total picture is that of the reasons why some women who experiment with vibrators do not continue to use them, in contrast to this group of (mostly) regular users. A related issue is why women to whom vibrator use has been recommended choose not to try them. More information about the absolute and relative frequency of vibrator use would be valuable also. Finally, an investigation of men's attitude toward women's vibrator use and women's concerns about those attitudes would be worthwhile.

REFERENCES

Catania, J. A., Binson, D., van der Straten, A., & Stone, V. (1996). Methodological research on sexual behavior in the AIDS era. *Annual Review of Sex Research, 6,* 77–125.

Clifford, R. (1978). Development of masturbation in college women. *Archives of Sexual Behavior, 7,* 559–573.

Dengrove, E. (1977). The mechanotherapy of sexual disorders. In J. Fischer & H. L. Gochros (Eds.), *Handbook of behavior therapy with sexual problems* (pp. 84–92). New York: Pergamon.

Heiman, J., LoPiccolo, L., & LoPiccolo, J. (1976). *Becoming orgasmic: A sexual growth program for women.* Englewood Cliffs, NJ: Prentice Hall.

Hite, S. (1976). *The Hite report.* New York: Macmillan.

Janus, S. S., & Janus, C. L. (1993). *The Janus report on sexual behavior.* New York: Wiley.

Kaplan, H. (1974). *The new sex therapy.* New York: Brunner/Mazel.

Kinsey, A. C., Pomeroy, W. B., Martin, C. E., & Gebhard, P. H. (1953). *Sexual behavior in the human female.* Philadelphia: Saunders.

Laumann, E. O., Gagnon, J. H., Michael, R. T., & Michaels, S. (1994). *The social organization of sexuality.* Chicago: University of Chicago Press.

Levin, R. J., & Levin, A. (1975, September). Sexual pleasure: The surprising preferences of 100,000 women. *Redbook Magazine,* 51–58.

LoPiccolo, J., & Lobitz, W. (1972). The role of masturbation in the treatment of orgasmic dysfunction. *Archives of Sexual Behavior, 2,* 163–171.

Maines, R. (1989, June). Socially camouflaged technologies: The case of the electro-mechanical vibrator. *IEEE Technology and Society Magazine, 8*(2), 3–11.

Marquis, J. N. (1970). Orgasmic reconditioning: Changing sexual object choice through controlled masturbation fantasies. *Journal of Behavior Therapy and Experimental Psychiatry, 1,* 263–271.

Masters, W. H., & Johnson, V. (1966). *Human sexual response.* Boston: Little, Brown.

Masters, W. H., & Johnson, V. (1986). *Sex and human loving.* Boston: Little, Brown.

Miller, D. C. (1991). *Handbook of research design and social measurement* (5th ed.). Newbury Park, CA: Sage.

Riley, A. J., & Riley, E. J. (1978). A controlled study to evaluate directed masturbation in the management of primary orgasmic failure in women. *British Journal of Psychiatry, 133,* 404–409.

Tavris, C., & Sadd, S. (1975). *The Redbook report on female sexuality: 100,000 married women disclose the good news about sex.* New York: Delacorte.

Williams, W., & Orsmond, A. (1977). Rapid inpatient treatment of severe dysfunction. *Australian & New Zealand Journal of Psychiatry, 11,* 61–64.

Wolfe, L. (1981). *The Cosmo report.* New York: Arbor House.

Zeiss, A. M., Rosen, G. M., & Zeiss, R. A. (1977). Orgasm during intercourse: A treatment strategy for women. *Journal of Consulting and Clinical Psychology, 45,* 891–895.

6.4 SEXUALITY IN CYBERSPACE
Update for the 21st Century

Al Cooper, Irene P. McLoughlin, and Kevin M. Campbell

INTRODUCTION

An estimated 9–15 million people access the Internet each day at a rate that is growing by an estimated 25% every 3 months.[1–3] Work, school, and even social activities have become increasingly dependent upon, and centered around, computers. However, much of what is said about online relating is full of paradoxes. On the one hand, it seems to epitomize the alienation of the modern world, and on the other to lead to the development of supportive and sometimes intensely intimate, even deeply erotic, relationships.[4] Few can fathom how profound the changes will be as we increasingly spend more and more of our time connected to the information superhighway. Given its burgeoning growth and wide accessibility, the Internet or World Wide Web (WWW) is altering patterns of sexual behavior, sexual health and education, and social communication. At the same time, it is enhancing and complicating interpersonal relationships and is developing into an alternative place for a variety of commercial opportunities.

SEXUALITY AND RELATIONSHIPS ON THE INTERNET

Sexuality is one aspect of human social behavior that is being dramatically impacted by the Internet. In fact, sex is reported to be the most frequently searched topic on the Internet,[5] and the pursuit of sexual interests on the Internet, or "cybersex," is a remarkably common activity for users. A recent study reported that approximately nine million users (15% of the online population) accessed one of the top five "Adult" Websites[6] in a 1-month period. Cooper[1] suggested that there are three primary factors that "turbocharge" online sexual-

ity and make it such an attractive venue for sexual pursuits. He called these factors the "Triple-A-Engine." They include accessibility (i.e., millions of sites available 24/7), affordability (i.e., competition on the WWW keeps all prices low and there are a host of ways to get "free" sex), and anonymity (i.e., people perceive their communications to be anonymous).

The Internet has also become a fertile ground on which intimate relationships can be sown and grown. Computer mediated relating (CMR) contains several characteristics that are unique to the online medium that can enhance attempts to create positive interpersonal contacts and healthy romantic relationships. However, these same characteristics can also complicate or become an obstacle to interpersonal connection. Specifically, CMR reduces the role that physical attributes play in the development of attraction, and enhances other factors such as propinquity, rapport, similarity, and mutual self-disclosure, thus promoting erotic connections that stem from emotional intimacy rather than lustful attraction.

In a culture that emphasizes physical attractiveness, the Internet provides a different way of developing attraction. It is a world where what you write, not how you look or sound, is who you are. Online communication allows individuals more control over how they present themselves and what they tell others about themselves. This opens the possibility of people becoming acquainted before evaluating each other based upon physical appearance. Likewise, stereotypical assumptions about the personality of the individual based upon physical attributes, which are often inaccurate, may be postponed until more factual knowledge is known about that person. This provides a model of intimate yet separate relating and it allows adult (and teen) men and women more freedom to deviate from typically constraining gender roles that are often automatically invoked in face-to-face interactions.[4]

The Internet can also enhance erotic connection by focusing on emotional aspects of sexuality instead of the physical. This may also reduce limitations of gender roles; allow each partner to feel autonomous within the relationship; encourage open, intimate, and direct communication; and provide a safe environment for the inexperienced to practice flirtation and experimentation with different sex roles and personas. However, at the same time, Internet relationships can foster superficial erotic contacts and online relating that may then lead to destructive results such as people acting on or compulsively overindulging in an accelerated, eroticized pseudo-intimacy.[4]

Electric communication as a mode of relating may foster other unique benefits and characteristics including a greater sense of closeness and community, time to compose a response that accurately conveys the intention, and the ability to "go further" or take more of a risk than one otherwise might. It can create a feeling of greater spatial proximity and connection with others, regardless of their actual geographic dispersion. Virtual worlds with unique cultures can develop online and foster a sense of community.[7] The Internet can also be a convenient mode of communicating and relating because participants do not have to be concerned about how they look when online and can engage in conversations at any time of the day or night. Although it may seem that the ability to express oneself emotionally online is limited, emotion can be expressed with a variety of symbols or string of characters called "emoticons." These provide a way to clearly express an emotion, that might be missed or downplayed in an offline interaction.[8]

EFFECTS OF THE INTERNET ON FACE-TO-FACE (FTF) RELATIONSHIPS

It is already clear that the fascination people have with sexuality and sexual relationships is being prominently manifested on the Internet in a multitude of ways.[9] For those with great sexual relations, the Internet will provide another dimension for them to explore together, as well as a tool for them to create new ways to increase their intimacy. It is just as possible to send an erotic E-mail to a partner as to a stranger. Couples can be encouraged to use this particular communication medium to stretch and invigorate an ongoing relationship. Some may find the Internet facilitates their ability to initiate a sexual encounter with their lover, share a sensitive fantasy, or stay in contact during the day.[10] The Internet may also be helpful when one partner in a couple desires to engage in a particular sexual activity and the other partner is unable or unwilling to comply. Internet newsgroups exist that deal with virtually every legal (as well as many illegal) sexual variation. Online services and "virtual meeting places" provide users with the chance to be exposed to those activities, to learn why others find the experience enjoyable, and subsequently may be more open to the behavior themselves. Particularly around sexual issues and accompanying concerns of normalcy, finding others who share the same interest may facilitate self-acceptance.[11] In addition, the online world is a great place to experiment and to have a "virtual trial" of the behavior before deciding whether it is something to engage in real time.

However, for those whose emotional development is evolved enough to find a partner but not quite evolved enough to fully relate in an ongoing and intensive manner, the Internet may provide the perfect venue for these types of "quasi-relationships." This could prove helpful if these relationships are a transitional practice step toward the more difficult face-to-face (FTF) relationships. Or it could be deleterious if the person becomes "stuck" in cyber-space and finds that his or her motivation to further stretch themselves in FTF relations is reduced.

There are also increasing numbers of reports of Internet infidelity. These online relations may interfere with conflict resolution in FTF relationships or lead to triangulation. Partners struggling with conflict in their FTF relationships may seek comfort, understanding, and sexual intimacy in online relationships instead of working out the conflict in the FTF relationship. Other negative consequences of Internet infidelity include secrecy and shame that oftentimes accompanies the dishonesty of the infidelity and the draining of energy from the primary FTF relationship.

This prevents the type of open communication and feelings of distress between people that catalyze and often lead to discussions and working through of problems ultimately resulting in growth and improvement in the primary relationship.[12] Cybersex use can be a symptom of deeper problems with closeness, dependency, and abandonment and can cause difficulty in couple relationships. One partner may be heavily involved in cybersex use, leaving the other partner feeling shut out, ignored, and deprived of time alone with their partners.[13]

ONLINE SEXUAL COMPULSIVITY

As the use of adult websites for the purpose of sexual expression is becoming increasingly popular, the power of the Triple A engine may challenge the internal defenses and coping skills of individuals with a vulnerability to, or proclivity, for sexual compulsivity. There is little point in denying the obvious dark side to the seductive temptations offered by the Internet when it comes to sexual behavior online. Individuals may increasingly rely on the Internet for their social and sexual needs and wind-up spending greater amounts of time there, rather than investing energy in real-world relationships.

Leaders in the field assert that sexually compulsive behavior has reached epidemic proportions.[5,14] The National Association of Sexual Addiction Problems estimated that 6–8% of Americans are sex addicts, which is 16–21.5 million.[15] The exact numbers are difficult to estimate, as people with these issues are often fearful of the reactions of others, feel ashamed, and thus are more likely to hide the frequency and details of their behavior. The Internet further complicates this by facilitating anonymity and enabling sexual activities to be pursued in an even more isolated and hidden fashion.

The National Council on Sexual Addiction and Compulsivity[15] defined sexual addiction as "persistent and escalating patterns of sexual behavior acted out despite increasing negative consequences to self and others." Cooper[14] defined sexually compulsive behavior as "an irresistible urge to perform an irrational sexual act" (p. 1). Cooper identified five hallmarks of sex-

ual compulsion. Early indications are that these appear to be particularly prevalent in online users. They include the following, which must be present for a duration of at least 6 months: (1) denial; (2) unsuccessful repeated efforts to discontinue the activity; (3) excessive amounts of time dedicated to the activity; (4) the behavior having a negative impact on social, occupational, and recreational functioning; and (5) repetition of the behavior despite adverse consequences.

Young[16–18] warned about the dangers of excessive Internet use and found that there appears to be a correlation between time online and negative consequences. She reported that the "Internet addicts" in her sample used the Internet an average of 38 hours per week for nonacademic and nonprofessional purposes.[16] Greenfield[19] noticed a similar trend. His survey indicated that those with excessive usage patterns spent nearly double the amount of time on the computer as nonaddicts, and were far more likely to report negative repercussions. Finally, the Cooper, Scherer, Boies, and Gordon[6] study also found a strong correlation between time spent online for sexual pursuits and measures of sexual compulsivity and distress scores. They also noted that users who did not appear to have a problem with online sexual activities (46.6%) reported spending less than 1 hour a week doing so. On the other hand, the 8.5% of respondents who acknowledged spending at least 11 hours a week in online sexual pursuits reported the most distress and highest scores on a measure of sexual compulsivity.

Internet sexuality, like other forms of sexuality, is best viewed as falling along a continuum ranging from normal and life-enhancing forms of sexual expression and exploration, to problematic and pathological expressions.[6,13] Cooper, Putnam, Planchon, and Boies[20] identified three distinct profiles of individuals who go online for sexual pursuits using data from the first large-scale study of Internet sexuality.[20] They labeled these profiles: Recreational, Compulsive, and At-risk users.

Recreational or nonpathological users refers to those who simply aim to satisfy their curiosity about available online sexual material, to occasionally experiment or gratify a sexual urge, or to search for specific sexual information. A substantial number of people (46.6%) reported visiting Internet sexuality sites in a recreational way, less than 1 hour per week, with few reported negative consequences.

Compulsive users were described as individuals who exhibit sexually compulsive traits and experience negative consequences as a result. Compulsive users may have previously established patterns of unconventional sexual practices, such as: preoccupation with pornography, multiple affairs, sex with several or anonymous partners, phone sex, frequenting prostitutes, or any one of the more conventional paraphilias listed in the DSM-IV.[20] A large number of people with these proclivities are aware of the Internet and the abundant sexual opportunities that exist there. Thus, the Internet provides a new forum for them to act out their issues and often further exacerbate their problematic behaviors.

At-risk users included online users without a prior history of sexual compulsivity, but who experienced some problems in their lives from their online sexual pursuits since discovering the Internet. At-risk users may be the most interesting group in the study of online sexual behavior, as they may never have had difficulty with problematic sexual behavior if not for the seductive power of the Triple-A engine.

As a result of these new variations of sexual compulsivity, clinicians are now faced with the opportunity and challenge of treatment in this new area of practice. Cooper, Putnam et al.[20] recommend an individually tailored combination of group, individual, and systemic interventions, with medication used in more severe situations. In addition, they posit that the aforementioned treatment might be facilitated in certain cases through E-mail, interactive Internet mediated treatment modules, along with the use of online education and group social support. This approach provides patients with greater access to services and clinicians with new ways to impact their patients outside of the therapy session. Finally, there is little doubt that there needs to be many more opportunities for therapists to participate in comprehensive training in the assessment and treatment of the constellation of problems resulting from cybersex compulsivity.

ALTERNATIVE COMMUNITIES AND DISENFRANCHISED PEOPLE ON THE INTERNET

Meeting other people on the Internet also increases one's chances of connecting with like-minded others due to the computer's ability to rapidly sort along many dimensions simultaneously. People who have a hard time connecting with others in FTF interactions may have a better chance of meeting a compatible person online.[4] Online dating services can help minimize painful rejections. The decision to contact a particular person can be made only after both parties view the others personal profiles (these are created by various online dating services and include descriptive information about the person). Therefore, those with particular characteristics and interests might find likeminded others by searching or scanning these profiles to find commonalties. These areas of similarity can include important life issues such as health concerns, sexual abuse, disabilities, religious affiliation, etc. This type of confidential matching may be especially attractive to those in sexually disenfranchised communities including lesbian, gay, bisexual, or transgender communities, S/M, or fetish communities. The Internet can provide a safe means of affiliating and relating to these people when they live in areas where these communities are less common and/or visible, such as rural locations.

The Internet offers the opportunity for the formation of online or virtual communities in which isolated or disenfranchised individuals can communicate with each other around sexual topics of shared interest (e.g., gay, lesbian, and bisexual issues, transgender issues, and rape survivors[21,22]). The Internet has functioned as a way for gay, lesbian and bisexual minorities to become majorities in their own "virtual communities." These online communities are particularly beneficial to those concerned about prejudice and discrimination because they are available to anyone, no matter where they live and accessible from the safety of one's own home. This process of community formation was accelerated by the freedom provided by gay Usenet newsgroups. In a series of Internet studies, McKenna and Bargh[21] found that newsgroup participation during sexual identity formation lead to greater self-acceptance and disclosure of hidden sexual identity to family and friends. Lesbian women, gay men, and bisexuals use the Internet more often than their heterosexual counterparts for experimentation, networking, communication, and the expression of a variety of sexual behaviors. This is not surprising and indeed is even adaptive as the Triple-A engine provides dimensions that are particularly important to these populations (i.e., sense of safety and ready access to partners). However, this increased access is a two-edged sword and can both enhance and damage the lives of those who avail themselves of it. The Triple-A engine can pose a particular hazard for those users whose sexuality may have been suppressed and limited all their lives when they suddenly find an infinite supply of sexual opportunities. Individuals may enthusiastically embrace the opportunities provided by the Internet without considering the possible dangers associated with it. A recent study by Ross, Tikkanen, and Mansson[23] comparing gay men who used the Internet to gay men who did not provided helpful descriptive information about these populations. Those who used the Internet tended to be younger, to live in small towns, to have less sexual experience with other men, and were more likely to frequent bathhouses and video clubs. These findings support the idea that the Internet provides a medium for young individuals who are exploring their sexuality in geographically isolated places. Without Internet access, these individuals would have less opportunity to explore and become full members of these minority communities.[23]

In an interesting twist, Cooper, Delmonico, and Burg[24] consider women to be members of a "sexually disenfranchised population." And although the Internet offers women freedom from the constraints placed on their sexual expression by community standards and expectations regarding the "proper role" of sexuality in their life, this freedom again cuts both ways. As women more freely experiment and take sexual risks[24] in ever-greater numbers, more of them are at risk for contracting sexual diseases, as well as developing sexual compulsions.

The Internet can also provide connection and community to a variety of other groups that are traditionally ignored and have limited options for developing romantic relationships. Clearly elderly and individuals that are confined to their homes can correspond over the Internet, sometimes taking those relations offline, leading to fuller and more rewarding lives. Similarly those with chronic illnesses and/or disabilities can reach out to others for empathy, support, and either friendship, romantic exchanges, or frank sexual discussions, if they so choose.

A final example (though there could be countless others) includes those with social phobias and chronic shyness. These people might feel safer and more comfortable disclosing on the Internet by virtue of being in a familiar place, having time to think of their words and responses, and having a buffer protecting them from their fears of another's negative reaction.

COMMERCIAL ASPECTS OF SEXUALITY AND THE INTERNET

The Internet has become an ideal place for the exploration of sex through adult websites, the purchase of sexually related merchandise, and the exchange of sexual services in a society where sex and sexuality is often a source of shame and embarrassment. The prevalence of adult websites, sex sites, and erotica has been estimated to range from less than one-half of 1%[25] to 83%[26] of all Internet sites and functions. The Internet provides an essentially unlimited array of sexual material, which is frequently changed and upgraded. It may be actively selected by the individual in accord with his or her personality and preferences, accessed anonymously, and viewed privately.[27] Adult websites, both those that involve still photos, X-rated videos, and live sex shows are filled with every imaginable image and sexual act. The images are explicit and something can be found to meet anyone's particular sexual interests. Unfortunately, one can be assured that despite claims that all "models" are over the age of 18, many of the persons involved in the making of these images are in fact underage."[5] This is of particular concern with the new interest in "amateur" sites and pictures, which are even less regulated and predictable than the traditional commercial sites.[28]

Although erotica and sexually explicit material may not have an adverse effect on most viewers, for some it may reinforce preexisting inclinations, including objectifying, splitting off parts of one's sexuality, or antisocial or anti-woman inclinations.[27,29,30] At the same time, it should be recognized that the small amount of empirical data we have to date finds a lack of a relationship between exposure to online pornography and misogynist attitudes. This, of course, parallels more widespread findings about exposure to offline erotica.[27]

Another growth area for online sexuality appears to be as a place to purchase sexual products. Just as catalogue shopping continues to increase its share of the marketplace, the Internet is ideally suited for showcasing sexually related products and services because of the availability, anonymity, and affordability of the Internet (The Triple A). For example, one new type of business enterprise is known as the "condom store." The condom store is devoted to the sale of condoms and other sexually related products. The medium of the Net allows people to compare features and prices of a larger number of product lines (A for Affordability) at their convenience (A for Access). The medium of the net minimizes embarrassment by providing an alternative to furtively rushing through local drugstores and picking up whatever is quickest (A for Anonymity). "The implications for the advantageous promotion of expanded sexual products and services is obvious, with one important benefit being that facilitation of larger numbers of people having the opportunity to take adequate prophylactic measures against contraception and disease."[1]

In addition to products, the Internet has also become another medium for the sale of sexual services. Sex workers have found online chat rooms, bulletin boards, and listings on numerous search engines to be excellent venues to advertise their services. The Triple A also provides a unique context for this kind of commerce. Anonymity allows a certain amount of physical safety for both sex workers and potential sex customers to negotiate their transactions with greatly reduced concerns of intervention by law enforcement.

By and large, law enforcement agencies have chosen not to direct their energies into cyberspace (with the exception of child pornography and solicitation). However, when choosing to get involved, law enforcement agencies have used that same anonymity to their advantage by posing as potential escorts, customers, and oftentimes children (most commonly to intercede with issues of child exploitation).

The Internet also provides a medium to commit sex crimes as pedophiles use the Internet to deliver and receive child pornography, find children to molest, engage in "cyber-sex" with children, and communicate with other pedophiles.[31] In a 1999 study, Durkin and Bryant were able to conduct a sociological investigation of pedophiles at large by contacting them through an Internet newsgroup composed of pedophiles. Previously it was difficult, if not impossible, to study pedophiles outside of a clinical or correctional population because of the disease's hidden nature.[32]

For better or worse, the Triple A allows for a broader range of potential purveyors of an expanded range of sexual services. Men in rural areas or situations who might not have access to areas frequented by prostitutes may now find these services easily available through their modem, either by arranging FTF meetings online or confining their sexual activities to "virtual" meetings and sexual encounters. Likewise, potential escorts (e.g., students looking for extra cash to get through school or women struggling to make ends meet financially) might find the Internet to be a more sanitary and comfortable place to arrange an exchange of sex for money. Another type of online sex is the live sex shows (often called "live video streaming") that are readily available for a fee. While using this service, customers can either E-mail or call and talk to the model as they dance or engage in any number of sex acts. This clearly superior alternative to phone sex is an imminent threat to replace that billion-dollar component of the commercial sex industry.

Finally, another new type of business has developed to counter the pervasiveness of online sexuality. For those who want it, there are a host of ways to block access to Internet sex. From software, to hardware, to Internet Service providers who prefilter what they carry, and so on, as the availability and use of the Internet as medium for sexual pursuits increases so will the demand for technology-based means of controlling that access.[28]

VIRTUAL MORALITY IN THE WORKPLACE

The explosion of the Internet into the workplace has put temptations squarely in the face of millions of employees. With just a few keystrokes they may all too easily travel to areas that are implicitly and even explicitly forbidden and/or at odds with the companies' mores and mission. Organizations are being forced to deal with the mushrooming ethical questions such as workers frittering away a morning shopping online or secretly viewing sexually explicit websites. Every day, companies face unexpected twists in the world of virtual morality. This is a new spin on the old concern of employees making personal phone calls at work, but with greatly magnified possibilities. For one thing, the Web can be insidious in its power, seductively lulling users to click from screen to screen for hours at a time. Productivity can indeed suffer when workers find this sexual escape to be so readily available. Some will find it so gratifying that they will develop problems with sexual compulsivity. In addition, purveyors of sex rarely call on the phone and suggest out loud that we check out some "hot teen action." But they don't think twice about large-scale spamming of outrageously prurient advertisements.

In a recent *Wall Street Journal* (October, 1999) survey of a cross-section of workers at large companies nationwide on workplace ethics, 87% of respondents said it is unethical to visit pornographic sites at work. Thirty-four percent said personal E-mail on company computers is wrong. Cooper, Putnam et al.[20] found that the prevalence of cybersex activity at work was striking in their recent survey of 9,177 Internet users. Six out of 100 employees reported that their primary method of accessing online sexual material was via their work computers. In total, an amazing 20% of men and 12% of women are using their work computers for at least some portion of their online sexual activity. This corroborates data from other sources

reporting that adult content sites are the fourth most visited category while at work (Media Matrix, February, 1999) and that 70% of all adult content traffic occurs during the 9-to-5 workday.[33]

Caught off guard by the geometric growth of such issues, many companies have lost all hope of handling matters case by case. Some are using sophisticated software to monitor when and where workers are traveling on Internet. Others are having their legal teams take first stabs at setting boundaries. For example, some companies seem to accept the inevitable with a policy specifically allowing employees to use the Internet for personal reasons. Many start with the general premise that use has to be of "reasonable duration and frequency" and cannot cause "embarrassment to the company." In our litigious society it is questionable how long this type of ambiguous language will be sufficient and go unchallenged. Companies need to be cognizant that ultimately these relative terms (e.g., "reasonable" duration) will put the onus on them to define the precise parameters. Who will set these guidelines and what will they form as the foundation for their decisions. What training or expertise will these decision-makers have in sexual issues and their many meanings or potential outcomes. Many may ultimately retain independent experts in human sexuality as consultants to help inform these decisions and provide a basis in research and psychological theory.

Clearly the tensions between being an organization that trusts and fosters autonomy in its workforce will somehow need to be balanced against employees' participation in activities and using company equipment that are at odds with the preferred company image, mores, and social values. And, of course, there are a myriad of ways that this increased presence of sexual access and material will raise concerns about issues of sexual harassment and the development of a sexually charged and biased environment.

Again, larger organizations, while slow off the block, are now scrambling to take action. The American Management Association recently found 27% of large U.S. firms have begun checking employee E-mail, a huge jump from 15% in 1997. Some routinely do this to search for obscene language or images. Once again, this raises a host of questions in terms of who will make the decision on what deserves to be censored, and based on what criteria. Is investigating fertility treatments in your region ok? How about checking the latest edition of the MSNBC column "Sexploration" written by a nationally known sex therapist answering a question on premature ejaculation?[34] What if a wife sends an E-mail to her husband reminding him to be home early as this is their wedding anniversary . . . If she tells him her thoughts of what might happen during the night . . . If they engage in 20 minutes of "stoking of the fire" during the day via E-mail. Inevitably, the possibilities for disaster are endless when this type of private message is accidentally forwarded to the wrong address at work. A lonely and angry coworker could decide to forward it to the whole company's list-serv or to a coworker who declined a date, and we have all the ingredients for a sexual harassment suit. Once again, the answer lies in new types of sophisticated training (as well as access to immediate expert consultation) for managers, HR personnel, EAP counselors, and others who will be dealing with these situations on a daily basis. Overly broad policies will be found to be lacking, avoiding, and denying. The policies will be found negligent. Companies who can demonstrate some good faith efforts to seriously consider these issues will be both buffered and applauded.

The issue of workplace sexual addiction and compulsivity will also be greatly magnified by the availability of Internet sex all day long. In his landmark study of nearly 1,000 sexual addicts, Carnes[35] found that "by far the biggest losses recorded were in the workplace" (p. 87). The main loss was time. Most of the sex addicts studied by Carnes[35] were not being able to work up to their potential, and 80% reported a loss of productivity. In a more recent study, Lybarger[36] found that sexual harassment continues in spite of federally mandated training, reporting, and disciplinary action. According to Lybarger,[36] training and other prophylactic measures for dealing with sexual issues in the workplace in general are woefully inadequate. Those suffering from a range of sexually addictive tendencies may frequently be participants in harassment scenarios. In his survey, 86% of all sexual addicts (large numbers if one accepts estimates of people fitting this criteria that range from 4% to 6% of the population) act out

in the workplace.[37] Looking at early empirical findings on the prevalence of those who have problems with online sexuality, the figures may be between 8.5%[6] and 17%.[24]

Once again, the best way to navigate this legally and practically is through training and education at a number of levels. Twenty-eight percent of participants in a recent workplace study reported they would have taken advantage of training in the workplace if it had been offered, and 36% indicated that they believe training would have led to an earlier recovery.[36] Again, appropriate personnel need to have clear criteria for deciding whether the employees' online sexual activities constitute a problem for them and/or the company or not. Cooper, Putnam, Planchon, and Boies[20] provide four profiles of people who go online for sexual activities ranging from recreational to sexually compulsive. Further research to elucidate and define these types of people is needed. In addition, employers need to be sure to have trainings so that their personnel have a response that is appropriate to the situation when an employee is caught engaging in online sexual activities.

Another dimension of an organization's response to sexual surfing at work will, of course, have a heavy technological component. Advancing technology is rapidly extending the capability for electronic eavesdropping to every office that uses the Internet. There is a new set of Internet surveillance systems, with names like WEBsweeper, Disk Tracy, and SecureVIEW. Some can conduct desktop-to-laptop sweeps, monitoring Web use from the mail-room to the executive suite. Many companies are now blocking access to sex sites, hate sites, and gambling sites—but this is always incomplete as websites are just a small segment of online sexual activities. In addition, those who are motivated (and likely have the most serious problems) will find ways to circumvent software as fast as it is installed. In May 1999, Zona Research Inc., an Internet market researcher in Redwood City, CA, found that fully one-third of companies screen out any sites that are not on an approved list. In its survey of more than 300 companies, Zona also found that 20% of companies filter sites based on the user's job and another 13% of companies filter sites on the time of day.

But these forbidden sites are many times one step ahead of being detected. Adult, gambling, and other controversial sites are disguising or sanitizing their address names in order to continue operating under the radar of companies monitoring and blocking Internet content. For example, one site remained undetected to cybersmut police until it made headlines recently. Not to be confused with 1600 Pennysylvania Avenue, www.whitehouse.com offers X-rated content. As employees become more technically savvy, it is fairly easy to bypass these programs. For example, add a virus to the directory where it is located, run the Virus Scan, the scanner deletes the entire directory, but because it has a virus, the software doesn't allow it to be deleted. Without the virus, the directory will now allow a user to delete it without a password.

An interesting alternative to traditional blocking technologies doesn't block access, but keeps a detailed and unchangeable list of where the user has gone and what material has been downloaded. No doubt it has the effect of frightening employees into being guardians of their own morals. Not unlike employees knowing that their phonecalls could be traced, however, it also introduces an Orwellian abuse of technology and again raises hosts of practical questions such as who and how often will someone monitor these lists? What criteria will be cause for further investigation? Could an unethical "big brother" use this information for personal or nefarious purposes?

Despite these great technical advances in policing and blocking employee's cybersex use, little has been implemented in the area of corporate training to educate workers in general about healthy sexuality, healthy sexual boundaries, and the consequences of sexual boundary violations in the workplace. Ideally, the workplace should not be the forum for education in healthy sexuality, but apparently other places are doing an inadequate job. When sexuality enters the workplace, the employer has no choice but to fill this void. Employers are realizing that they may literally be paying the price of this neglect in the form of large sexual harassment lawsuits or productivity losses. The cost of ignoring it may finally be greater than the expense of addressing it. Now with the first of a wave of 88 million, Internet-generation, young adults entering the workforce, corporations need to reinvent

themselves. The next task at hand for our Nation's employers, with the collaboration of mental health professionals, is education, training, and public awareness about healthy sexuality and the consequences of its dysfunctional counterpart.

SEX INFORMATION SUPERHIGHWAY

There is an almost unlimited amount of information available to be accessed on the Internet, and a sizable chunk of it is related to sexuality. In fact, the topic most often searched on the Internet is sex.[1,5] From the Internet's earliest days, sites for sexually explicit material took root and flourished. The Internet brings together consumers who want to know and learn with providers who want to share, teach, preach, or titillate.[38]

The advantages of the Internet's power to communicate a staggering amount of information on sexuality education are abundant. An important development is the rapid increase in the number of specific websites that offer opportunities to educate people on sexual matters (sexual dysfunction, safe sex practices, information on reproduction, abstinence, sexually transmitted disease, etc.). Currently, a wide range of sites provides sexual education in the form of advice columns, discussion groups, and distribution lists of innovative information. Also, people can stand back and "lurk," actively explore and ask questions, or even "try on" any type of sexual interest or curiosity that they have, all from the comfort of their own living room.[10] It has been said that the lack of factual information is a major contributor to the enormous fear and anxiety many feel about sexuality.[39]

Online communication allows experts to more easily share information with those who are interested. The Triple-A Engine[1] makes the Internet particularly conducive to the dissemination of sexual information. Similarly the enormous number of people online allows sex educators to reach enough potential participants to deliver services on very narrow and specialized topics (e.g., sex and intimacy for a couple following prostate cancer surgery) to populations that might otherwise be neglected.

The Internet provides health educators a unique opportunity to bridge this gap and speak directly to millions of people about sexuality and sexual health in the privacy of their own homes. Consequently, various medical information sites are proliferating. Audiences that have never before received information about sexual health are now potential recipients of life-enhancing and life-saving information. Again, the public needs education on how to separate the wheat from the chaff, as anyone can put up a site and offer sexual advice, but not all of it will be worth taking.

A variety of professionals are delivering information using the Internet[40–43] along a wide range of services from simple short FAQS and advice columns, to offering classes and workshops, to helping people set up individually tailored skill enhancement. A number of directions have been suggested in Cooper's[1] review of these issues and selected examples follow. For instance, classes instructing parents how to talk with teens about safe sex could be offered via the Internet to a rural village in Mexico. Another possibility could be that the developer of a new medication for sexual problems could hold a virtual class from her laboratory in England and have the physician-enrollees scattered around the globe. Or lastly, the difficulty of filling a class on sexual enrichment for same-sex partners in a long-term relationship due to issues of proximity and embarrassment could be countered by offering the class online.

ONLINE CLINICAL INTERVENTIONS

Despite the growth of Telehealth and media attention regarding online psychotherapy, remarkably few licensed professionals are presently offering "virtual psychotherapy."[44] Concerns regarding the practice of online psychotherapy include variable quality of patient information, lack of credentialing and accountability of professionals, and consumer's inability to determine the training and qualifications of the practitioner. The absence of patient protection alternatives available to consumers has also been noted.[45,46] Furthermore, current technological limitations in accurately diagnosing and treating patients are making more cautious professionals wary, particularly as most Internet communications are confined to a very narrow band of information. Most computer assessments don't supply vital visual information about a patient's condition. For instance, they can be slumped in a chair,

crying and suicidal, or they could be smiling. They could have a neurological condition that makes their walking unsteady. Concealment of odors or other indicators of substance abuse or dependence is easier online. Professionals need to be very selective when considering Telehealth interventions as a substitute for in-person evaluation. However, as a screening modality and the essential first step in facilitating people to get help, the possibilities are only starting to be realized.

There are a number of ways that the Internet can serve as an adjunct to more traditional FTF therapy. These include (a) using interactive computer programs to learn new information and the behavioral techniques that comprise a central place in many sex therapists' armentariums; (b) having patients do home assignments via the internet or E-mail in conjunction with weekly FTF interactions with the therapist; and (c) because the net can serve as a place to practice and/or "try on" new social skills, behaviors, or roles all in the safety and relative anonymity of cyberspace, professionals can encourage people in couples therapy to first disclose difficult or awkward new communications over E-mail and then later discuss the content once it is "out on the table."

Resolution of ethical, legal, and regulatory issues is lagging behind current realities. Much is yet to be determined. Even those practitioners willing to venture into this new frontier are cautioned to be well prepared and provisioned prior to offering services on the Web and via behavioral telehealth technology. In addition to the suggested principles for the online provision of mental health services[47] and following the NBCC[48] Code of Ethics pertaining to the practice of professional counseling, WebCounselors shall:

1. Review pertinent legal and ethical codes for possible violations emanating from the practice of WebCounseling and supervision.
2. Inform WebClients of encryption methods being used to help insure the security of client/counselor/supervisor communications.
3. Inform clients if, how, and how long session data are being preserved.
4. In situations where it is difficult to verify the identity of the Web counselor or Web client,

take steps to address imposter concerns, such as using code words, numbers, or graphics.

5. When parent/guardian consent is required to provide WebCounseling to minors, verify the identity of the consenting person.

6. Follow appropriate procedures regarding the release of information for sharing WebClient information with other electronic sources.

7. Carefully consider the extent of self-disclosure presented to the Web client and provide rationale for the Web counselor's level of disclosure.

8. Provide links to websites of all appropriate certification bodies and licensure boards to facilitate consumer protection.

9. Contact the NBCC/CEE or the Web client's state or provincial licensing board to obtain the name of at least one counselor-on-call within the Web client's geographical region.

10. Discuss procedures for contacting the Web-Counselor when he or she is off-line with their Web clients.

11. Mention those problems believed to be inappropriate for Web counseling at their websites.

12. Explain the possibility of technology failure to clients.

13. Explain to clients how to cope with potential misunderstandings arising from the lack of visual cues from Web counselor or Web client.

SEX EDUCATION IN THE TWENTY-FIRST CENTURY

The Web is generating much excitement among educators of teens and young people. Many agree that there is a paucity of accurate, useful, and comprehensive sexual health information in the places teens are attracted to the most: television, popular music, movies, and within peer relationships—all arenas to which sexual health educators have little or no access. For teens, traditionally underserved and undereducated about sexual health matters, the Internet provides abundant opportunities in furthering adolescent sexuality education. Information can be continually updated and designed to specifically speak to their rapidly changing interests. According to Tapscott,[49] chat moderators, teachers, parents, and community workers who spend time with young adolescent Internet users, feel that this is a confident generation who think highly of themselves. Developmental psychologist Jean Piaget explained that the construction of the self occurs as the child acts on its environment—as the child takes actions to understand what he or she can do. This may explain why television is such an unproductive medium for self-esteem development—The child does not take actions but, rather, is acted upon. When contrasted with the interactive nature of the Internet it becomes possible to imagine a very different outcome. This may be particularly relevant for young women, fostering their empowerment, and feelings of mastery around their sexuality, countering other powerful messages that imply their sexuality to be an object, often one in which they do not feel fully in control.

Self-esteem also seems to be enhanced in chat groups online because young people can always have another chance—They can adopt another self. It is possible that through the Internet, young people, have a new tool and a new environment for the construction of their identities. This quest for identity, first explained by Erik Erikson as the most important personality achievement of adolescence, is said to be a critical step in becoming a productive, fulfilled, and happy adult. The implications of children having vast new avenues of exploration at their fingertips, taking action in games, E-mailing friends for advice, searching for sources of information, would imply that the active child, rather than the passive recipient, would have a greater sense of empowerment to make informed choices.

MIT sociologist Sherry Turkle, indicates that starting around age 10, online sexuality, from flirting to outright virtual sex, is a normal part of the social lives of kids who have computers. Often their online relationships are extensions of their in-person relationships, only with fewer of the social pressures and insecurities that accompany adolescent experiences at parties or one-on-one. It allows these young people the opportunity to explore more in-depth conversational and emotional aspects of their relationships rather than focusing on getting physical. This approach is of course very different than that seen in many places in society where the development of sexual curiosity and energy by young people is dealt with by avoidance, denial, or, suppression strategies, all doomed to failure.

A radical new approach that utilizes the Internet as a virtual "practice world" protected from many of the adverse consequences likely in the real world is worth considering. Supporting this idea is research[49] in which both girls and boys found online sexual experimentation a safer and less terrifying prospect than the face-to-face versions. Critics will point to the possibility (or inevitability) that even in moderated sites young people will find themselves on the receiving end of unwanted advances (just like in real life).[31] But as one 12-year-old girl who goes online pretending to be 18 indicates, "I feel safe because I can always just disconnect."[50] Giving young people a chance to build skills and practice dealing with difficult situations is a much more rational approach than "protecting" them from these and then hoping they will respond appropriately in a high-pressure real-time event.

The perception that cyberspace will result in uncontrolled and dangerous sexual behavior on the part of youth may be somewhat of an adult-centered projection. Most teenagers seem more interested in developing both the emotional and the physical side of real relationships, with the Internet as just one additional mode of communication and place to experiment. When a young person is found to be spending an inordinate amount of time on the computer in sexual, or other, activities it is often a symptom of larger problems. Again a more open, educative, and structured approach to online sexuality would minimize young people being seduced and deceived into moving the virtual relationship into the real world. An "eyes open" approach would teach young people the safety rules of online relationships (such as not giving out identifying information, addresses, etc) and involve adults in the process of translating those relations to face-to-face interactions when appropriate.

Whereas there are tremendous educational opportunities on the Internet, not all pursuits of sexual information on the Internet will foster growth and personal development. Some activities might reinforce negative societal stereotypes around sexuality and/or be developmentally inappropriate. However channeling the natural curiosity into more healthy and age appropriate outlets might well be the best available option. One example might be a chat room, the young person needs to sign up for (with parental consent and even intermittent structured involvement) facilitated by a trained and experienced sex educator. Because peers are a major source of sexuality information for teens and adolescents, training young people to facilitate these discussions is crucial to making the information seem attractive and relevant. The training of cadres of young people for highly coveted positions as dating, romance, and sexual survivor expert-facilitators would not only have a positive effect on the chat room participants, and the facilitators themselves, but also a much wider effect on others who they interacted with in their schools and communities. While access to information is critical to young people, developing communication, decision-making, and negotiating skills are equally important.[51]

As online communication rapidly gains importance in the lives of increasing numbers of Americans, there is a need for mental health professionals to be involved in these early stages of its development in order to minimize potential problems and adverse effects. In addition, there are tremendous educational opportunities to help shape, direct, and maximize the positive ways that sexuality in our society can be impacted. People are receiving more and varied information about sexuality than ever before. The Internet is already being used to address a host of sexual issues in our society. Disenfranchised minorities are meeting, forming virtual communities, and exploring sexuality and relationships online. Teens are taking their sexual questions from the locker room to their terminals. Lonely people are bringing their romantic hopes to online matchmaking services. Each group has unique questions, anxieties and fears. Psychologists and other mental health professionals can be instrumental in both disseminating information and ensuring that it is accurate, accessible, and specifically tailored to the intended sexual community, and ethically rendered. We can keep creating specially designed websites (with the capacity to address specific single-issues in great depth) that deal with anything from STDs to paraphillias. These might include detailed and comprehensive interactive behavioral treatment modules for common sexual problems (e.g., premature ejaculation) as well as frequently asked questions (FAQs). We can become expert moderators for scheduled interactive online chats. We can create online movies and animations that address the many sexual questions of the Internet populations. We can be a presence on the Internet as a critical adjunct and first line intervention for sexual concerns in the rapidly evolving Telehealth field, which promises to be increasingly important in the 21st century.

CONCLUSION

The digital media is increasingly a reflection of our world—a new culture of interaction and participation—the antithesis of the passivity of the broadcast culture. The Internet will provide a forum in which work, play, education, consumption, and socializing will merge. The implications of this evolution for our profession are just starting to be elucidated in forward-thinking articles and journals such as this. Clearly in the arenas of sexuality, sex education, and therapy, the Internet will afford unique and exciting approaches and alternatives. Internet access will allow for innovative new ways of treating a multitude of disorders via both direct and adjunct treatment options. Being aware of the technological advances and how they can be applied in novel therapeutic ways will allow us to be more proactive and a part of the evolving future, rather than simply defensive and reacting to changes that already have become realities. It will also provide another opportunity for us to explain to the general public who we are and the many types of interventions that we, as a profession, have to offer individuals and society. In doing so, we have the opportunity to not only enhance our own credibility, but also to expand the public's awareness, understanding, and application of the educational, developmental, and health concepts (including sexual health) that we most want to impart.

Clearly, if we are to have a say in shaping the future, we need to first understand the changes that are unfolding around us. For instance, understanding the nature of online relating will become increasingly important for all clinicians. As people spend more time online and look to the Internet to fulfill an ever-increasing amount of their various needs, the issues associated with online sexuality will become increasingly important and salient. We need to be involved in helping educate the public as to the ways that technology can enhance their lives and relations, as well as to warn them about, and be able to treat, the myriad of potential abuses and compulsions that may develop. Only those professionals with a grasp of the complexity of online interactions will be able to guide others to effectively use the power of the net without "being burned." Thus there needs to be an increase in the breadth and sophistication of professional trainings around these issues.

As technology continues to advance and as the eighty million strong Net Generation enter the adult world they bring with them profoundly different ideas of love and work, reward, responsibility, and morality. It is through the use of digital media that the Net Generation will develop and superimpose its culture on the rest of society. Already these young people are loving, learning, playing, communicating, working, and creating communities very different from their parents. They are the future, a force for social transformation.

As we have detailed throughout this article, the Internet is already having a profound influence on sexuality that will only increase as technology continues to develop. Therefore, if we (the leaders in the field of mental health) are going to continue to be relevant, we will need to defeat our own technophobias. We will have to embrace and make the Internet our own (at least in the sexual realm). We hope that this article will spark thought, debate, and ultimately involvement in this emerging area. As the world enters the 21st century we invite the reader to join us in shaping the future of sexuality!

NOTES

1. Cooper, A. (1999). Sexuality and the Internet: Surfing into the new millennium. *CyberPsychology & Behavior*, 1:181–187.

2. Fernandez, E. (1997). The new frontier: Net sex. *San Francisco Examiner*, p. 14.

3. Computerworld. (1998). Commerce by numbers—Internet population. Available: http://www.computerworld.com/home/Emmerce.nsf/All/pop

4. Cooper, A., & Sportolari, L. (1997). Romance in Cyberspace: Understanding online attraction. *Journal of Sex Education and Therapy, 22*:7–14.

5. Freeman-Longo, R. E., & Blanchard, G. T. (1998). *Sexual abuse in America: Epidemic of the 21st century.* Brandon, VT: Safer Society Press.

6. Cooper, A., Scherer, C., Boies, S. C., & Gordon, B. (1999). Sexuality on the Internet: From sexual exploration to pathological expression. *Professional Psychology: Research and Practice, 30*:154–164.

7. Walther, J. B. (1992). Interpersonal effects in computer-mediated interaction: A relational perspective. *Communication Research, 19*:52–90.

8. Lee, Y. (1995). Syllabus for social aspects of computer-mediated communication. Available: http://www.iworldnet/~yesunny/gendreps

9. Cooper, A. (1997). The Internet and sexuality: Into the new millennium. *Journal of Sex Education and Therapy, 22*:5–6.

10. Levine, D. (1998). *The joy of cybersex.* New York: Ballantine.

11. Newman, B. (1997). The use of online services to encourage exploration of ego-dystonic sexual interests. *Journal of Sex Education and Therapy, 22*:45–48.

12. Shaw, J. (1997). Treatment rationale for Internet infidelity. *Journal of Sex Education and Therapy, 22*:29–34.

13. Leiblum, S. R. Sex and the net: Clinical implications. *Journal of Sex Education and Therapy, 22*:21–28.

14. Cooper, A. (1998). Sexually compulsive behavior. *Contemporary Sexuality, 32*:1–3.

15. Amparano, J. (1998, September 25). Sex addicts get help. *The Arizona Republic,* p. A1.

16. Young, K. S. (1996). *Internet addiction: The emergence of a new clinical disorder.* Paper presented at the 104th Annual Convention of the American Psychological Association, Toronto, Canada.

17. Young, K. S. (1997). *Internet addiction: What makes computer-mediated communication habit forming?* Paper presented at the 105th annual convention of the American Psychological Association, Chicago.

18. Young, K. S., & Rogers, R. C. (1998). The relationship between depression and Internet addiction. *Cyber-Psychology & Behavior, 1*:25–28.

19. Greenfield, D. N. (1999). *Virtual addiction: Help for net-heads, cyberfreaks, and those who love them.* Oakland, CA: New Harbinger.

20. Cooper, A., Putnam, D. E., Planchon, L. A., & Boies, S. C. (1999). Online sexual compulsivity: Getting tangled in the net. *Sexual Addiction & Compulsivity: The Journal of Treatment and Prevention, 6*:79–104.

21. McKenna, K. Y. A., & Bargh, J. A. (1998). Coming out in the age of the Internet: Identity "de-marginalization" through virtual-group participation. *Journal of Personality and Social Psychology, 75*:681–694.

22. Cooper, A., Boies, S., Maheu, M., & Greenfield, D. (1999). Sexuality and the Internet: The next sexual revolution. In: Muscarella, F., & Szuchman, L., (eds.) *The psychological science of sexuality: A research based approach.* New York: Wiley Press, pp. 519–545.

23. Ross, M. W., Tikkanen, R., & Månsson, S. A. (2000). Differences between Internet samples and conventional samples of men who have sex with men: Implications for research and HIV interventions. *Social Science & Medicine,* in press.

24. Cooper, A., Delmonico, D. L., & Burg, R. (2000). Cybersex users, abusers, and compulsives: New findings and implications. *Sexual Addiction & Compulsivity: The Journal of Treatment and Prevention, 7*:51–67.

25. Langan, C. (1996). Cyberporn . . . a new legal bog. Available: http://www.public.asu.edu/~langel/index.html

26. Rimm, M. (1995). Marketing pornography on the information superhighway: A survey of 917,410 images, descriptions, short stories, and animations down-loaded 8.5 million times by consumers in over 2,000 cites in forty countries, provinces, and territories. *Georgetown Law Review* 83:1849–1934.

27. Barak, A., Fisher, W. A., Belfry, S., & Lashambe, D. R. (1999). Sex, guys, and cyberspace: Effects of Internet pornography and individual differences on men's attitudes toward women. *Journal of Psychology & Human Sexuality, 11*:63–91.

28. King, S. A. (1999). Internet gambling and pornography: Illustrative examples of the psychological consequences of communication anarchy. *CyberPsychology & Behavior, 2*:175–184.

29. Bogaert, A. F. (1993). *The sexual media: The role of individual differences.* Unpublished doctoral dissertation. The University of Western Ontario, London, Ontario, Canada.

30. Malamuth, N. M. (1981). Rape fantasies as a function of repeated exposure to sex stimuli. *Archives of Sexual Behavior, 10*:33–47.

31. Durkin, K. F. (1997). Misuse of the Internet by pedophiles: Implications for law enforcement and probation practice. *Federal Probation, 61*:14–18.

32. Durkin, K. F., & Bryant, C. D. (1999). Propagandizing pederasty: A thematic analysis of the on-line exculpatory accounts of unrepentant pedophiles. *Deviant Behavior, 20*:103–127.

33. Branwyn, G. (1999). How the porn sites do it. *The Industry Standard* 1999. Available at: http//www.thestandard.net.

34. Goldberg, A. (1998). *Monthly users report on MSNBC for April 1998.* Washington DC: Relevant Knowledge.

35. Carnes, P. J. (1991). *Don't call it love: Recovery from sexual addiction.* New York: Bantam Books.

36. Lybarger, J. S. (1997). Sexual addiction: A hidden factor in sexual harassment. *Sexuality and Compulsivity: Journal of Treatment and Prevention,* 4:77–90.

37. Carnes, P. J. (1999). Editorial: Cybersex, sexual health, and the transformation of culture. *Sexual Addiction & Compulsivity: The Journal of Treatment and Prevention,* 6:77–78.

38. Schnarch, D. (1997). Sex, intimacy and the Internet. *Journal of Sex Education and Therapy,* 22:15–20.

39. Williams, M. A. (1994). The Chicago study at a glance. *Contemporary Sexuality,* 28:2.

40. Frisse, M., Kelly, E., & Mercalfe, E. (1994). An Internet primer: Resources and responsibilities. *Acad Med* 69:20–24.

41. Maheu, M. (1997). Will online services for consumer self-help improve behavioral healthcare? *Behavioral Healthcare Tomorrow Journal,* 6:6.

42. Rusovick, R. M., & Warner, D. J. (1998). The globalization of international informatics through Internet mediated distributed medical intelligence. *New Medicine,* 2:155–161.

43. Sleek, S. (1977). Providing therapy from a distance. *APA Monitor,* 38:1.

44. Maheu, M., & Gordon, B. (1999). *Survey of mental health practitioners on the Internet.* Manuscript in preparation.

45. Murry, B. (1998). Data smog. Newest culprit in brain drain. APA Monitor, 29. Available at: http://www.apa.org/monitor/mar98/smog.html

46. Health on the Net Foundation. Code of Conduct for Medical and Health Web Sites. (1998). Available at: http://www.hon.ch/HONcode/Conduct.html.

47. International Society for Mental Health Online. Available at: http://www.ismho.org/suggestions.html.

48. National Board for Certified Counselors, Inc. (1999). Available at: http://www.nbc.org/ethics/westandards.htm.

49. Tapscott, D. (1998). *Growing up digital: The rise of the net generation.* New York: McGraw-Hill.

50. Turkle, S. (1995). *Life on the screen: Identity in the age of the Internet.* New York: Simon and Schuster.

51. Kirby, D., Barth, R.P., Leland, N., & Fetro, J.V. (1991). Reducing the risk: Impact of a new curriculum on sexual risk-taking. *Family Planning Perspectives,* 23: 253–263.

— CHAPTER SEVEN —

SEX AS A GLOBAL COMMODITY

Part of the proliferation of sex in our lives—in the media, our conversations, our thoughts and fantasies—has to do with the way our economies are organized. Not only is the advertising slogan "sex sells" accurate, but it is also true that sex, itself, is for sale. In a consumer society, everything is turned into a commodity and desire is mobilized to entice us to consume. Even our bodies have become commodities to be bought and sold in the sexual marketplace. And just as the marketplace is globalized, so, too, is the sexual marketplace. Sex is bought and sold on a world scale, by telephone or computer modem and in real life as sex tourists travel to exotic locales to find sex for sale.

Martin A. Monto asks a basic question: why do men buy women's bodies in prostitution? What are they exactly looking for? What do they get? Julia Davidson and Jacqueline Sanchez Taylor explore the fascinating new form of sex tourism, which finds wealthier businessmen from the economic north seeking out the sexual services of women in the economic south in a strange political economy of sexual commodification.

Katherine Frank looks at these experiences from the other side. Frank, an anthropologist, critically reflects on her "field work" experiences as an exotic dancer in a heterosexual strip club, while Joanna Brewis and Stephen Linstead address identity and sex work.

7.1 THE PRODUCTION OF IDENTITY AND THE NEGOTIATION OF INTIMACY IN A 'GENTLEMAN'S CLUB'

Katherine Frank

THE COMMODIFICATION OF INTIMACY

At first it might seem as if a commercialized relationship could not possibly be intimate as we *commonly* understand the term. Arlie Hochschild's groundbreaking work on emotional labor, however, is useful in examining the effects on the laborer who is asked to provide a particular 'feeling' along with a service. In this way, one's labor can affect one's deepest sense of self. In *The Managed Heart,* Hochschild (1983) distinguishes between the emotion work that we do privately (such as trying to enjoy a party) and that which we do as part of a job (such as summoning up a sympathetic smile for an irate customer). When human feeling becomes commercialized and organized within the workplace, a certain transmutation must take place, according to Hochschild. As social beings, we learn to manage our feelings in many different situations—by 'trying to remain calm' when angry, for example, or by 'letting ourselves feel sad'. What Hochschild means by the 'transmutation of an emotional system', however, is that 'what it is that we do privately, often unconsciously, to feelings that nowadays often fall under the sway of large organizations, social engineering, and the profit motive' (1983: 19). *Seeming* to love their job, for flight attendants and other workers who perform emotional labor, has

become *part of that job,* and actually trying to love the job—trying to make that smile *real*—makes the work easier. For employees who are subject to the tipping system, like dancers, censure for failing to achieve the correct presentation of self will come not only from the management but directly from the customers as well. Ronai, for example, has noted that striptease dancers must 'act right', or control their emotional displays, in order to do their job well, and that this usually means stifling negative emotions for their customers (1992: 110).

Emotional labor differs from physical labor, according to Hochschild, by the fact that it requires one to coordinate mind and feeling, to draw on a deep source of self, in order to produce a particular state of mind in others. There is a similarity to physical labor, however, in that there remains the possibility that the worker can become alienated from the aspect of self used to perform the work. When a man's arm is used like a piece of machinery to produce an object, that arm is being used as an instrument from which he might become alienated. In the same way, when one's 'self' is used to produce a service, an individual may become estranged from that self—feeling a tension between the 'real' and the 'on-stage' selves. This is partly a defense, a means of avoiding stress and burnout, but it can also cause problems, especially in the sense that the more a worker's true self is offered up for sale, 'the more that self risks seeming false to the individual worker, and the more difficult it becomes for him or her to know which territory of self to claim' (1983: 196). While Hochschild acknowledges that 'the negative effects of emotional labor may be more severe for some workers than others', the job-related stress that emotional labor can engender is quite generally seen by researchers as having potential 'negative social-psychological consequences' (Wharton, 1993: 209). The study of emotion management, then, blurs the line between public and private, between 'real' and manufactured intimacy in general. As Ronai writes about her customers in the strip club: 'They are always inside me. . . . They are in me because I have feelings about them' (1992: 119).

Sandra Lee Bartky distinguishes between emotional involvement in commercial caregiving from that which occurs in intimate relationships, writing:

> [T]he flight attendant, like the good wife, must feed egos and heal wounds. . . . But the one relationship is casual and brief, the other more enduring and profound. Intimate relationships require more complex sensitivities and engage more aspects of the self. (1990: 105)

This distinction might seem adequate for the flight attendant who is providing a particular service along with her emotional support or for the dancer who is simply engaging with a particular man for a brief table dance. However, the service provided by the dancer to her regulars is an ongoing performance of a relationship, coupled with a visual access to her body that is often deemed appropriate for only the most private situations. Recently, some researchers have noted that workers' relationships with regular customers in the service industry can be as emotionally involving and fulfilling (or disturbing) as other close relationships (Tolich, 1993). The performance given by the dancer to her regulars, whether through bodily display or conversation, is thus both intimate (given that it is more involving than the relationships that she has with other men in the club) and illusory (given the fact that she may have an outside partner or many regulars). Moreover, as these relationships may be long-term, they may engage more and more aspects of both parties' selves over time.

The customer is often not unaware when the pleasantries of an interaction have been purchased. Relationships with regulars in the strip club are thus always threatened by a fundamental, possibly explosive, contradiction rooted in common ideologies surrounding intimacy and companionship. Intimacy is supposed to be 'real', love and friendship are not supposed to be bought with money. True relationships are not supposed to be based on lies or performances. The idea that there are some things that should not be sold is quite powerful ideologically—as many feminist theorists have pointed out, the figure of the female prostitute who would sell her sexual services to men needs to be debased so that 'the appropriation of women's services without compensatory benefit can be sold to women in the name of their own autonomy, dignity' (Singer, 1993; 49). Our cultural imaginary insists that there be outrage at the woman who accepts an 'indecent proposal', who throws away a chance at real love for money. Corresponding to this is the notion that there are still some things that just cannot be bought as well—money can buy you a lot of things, but it cannot buy love, friendship or happiness.

For the customers, then, an emphasis on developing a 'real' relationship may also help mitigate the psychological dissonance caused by the commodification of interpersonal interaction. Presents thus come to take on an importance in relationships with regulars, and gifts were constantly being given to dancers by these men—clothes, vacations, flowers, and even cars. These things mediated and *personalized* the relationships, simply because they were not in the form of money. Many of the regulars (purposefully?) bought the dancers useless gifts that could not be exchanged, and frequently a dancer would complain in the locker room, saying that she wished he had just given her the money instead. Gifts, then, could serve as 'the props of a love affair', symbols of a romantic love. Because there is no way to actually determine 'the sincerity of a gesture within an intimate relationship', intrinsically symbolic gifts, like flowers, could also be emotionally empty gestures (Nelson and Robinson, 1994: 146). As symbols, however, their very ambiguity can function as a means of legitimation. Darien's regular could send her a dozen red roses on Friday in anticipation of their 'date' at the same time as he remained married to his wife. Inside the club, the roses functioned as a multi-dimensional symbol—of passion, of possession, of an 'other'-worldly fantasy—to stabilize the interaction.

The payment of money thus has the potential to unsettle an interaction because its symbolic value is one that is ideologically incommensurable with romantic love or true friendship. Herein lies an important contradiction—if a dancer's performance is believable enough, the relationship between the dancer and her regular seems genuine; an exchange of money during the interaction, then, undermines that authenticity. It is the exchange of money, however, which always facilitated the interaction in the first place. Regulars were invaluable in that they were nearly always prepared to pay—it was an accepted (and, certainly at some level, a *desired*) aspect of the relationship. Nevertheless, it could still be disruptive and with some customers, a system of payment could be negotiated such that it did not intrude too much on the conversation. I had regulars who paid me up front, for example, so that neither of us would then need to think about the monetary aspect of the interaction again. This made it easier for me to concentrate on the situation at hand, and meant that when our time was up the man could leave without being reminded of the fact that he had purchased my time.

On the other hand, the payment of money could also serve to stabilize an interaction and serve to redress any possible power imbalances brought out by the interaction. First of all, it could offer an easy escape if the intimacy became too intense. After all, a man simply had to leave the club (or stop paying) to be free of his obligations. Secondly, to be able to pay highly for an intangible service is, to some extent, a mark of wealth and esteem and in some cases payment reflected a particular desirable class status. After all, men who wanted to be listened to, who wanted to avail themselves of the dancer's time and attention, needed to pay highly for that privilege. The $100 an hour fee (plus tip) was too steep for many men. On a slow night, less affluent men might be able to sit with a woman between her sets; on a weekend night, however, it could be painfully obvious which men had money and which men did not (and this information was also shared amongst the women in the dressing room). Further, as regulars needed to resist the stigma which is associated with someone who *needs* to pay for companionship on a recurrent basis, the large sums of money that they gave to the dancers over time could somehow prove that the money was irrelevant to them. If money is unimportant or irrelevant, the payment of money does not then disrupt the illusion of authentic intimacy that binds the relationship.

FANTASY-REALITY AND THE DUAL PRODUCTION OF IDENTITY

Relationships in the strip club between dancers and their regulars take place within a larger gendered and heterosexualized network of power relations. Further, these relationships are based on 'an exchange of sexual self-identities', and as such, involve a complex entanglement of fantasy and reality that can complicate our understandings of intimate relationships in general. They must be interpreted, then, within a framework which allows fantasy and reality to be conceptualized as irrevocably intertwined. For this framework, I am drawing on Zizek's Lacanian conception of fantasy as that which 'gives consistency to what we call reality' (Zizek, 1989: 44). Intimate relationships in a strip club seem to evolve as a result of a mutual manufacturing of fantasy and identity. In a strip club, a man will most likely be denied sexual access to the women. A fantasy of sexual possibility, identity, and interpersonal intimacy is cultivated, however, and the combination of these elements may make it an attractive atmosphere for some customers. The illusory nature of the interaction between a dancer and her regular is never seamless. Indeed, the suspension of the 'real' seems to underlie the very existence of a strip club. My regulars gave me many reasons behind their presence in the club which implied that the *illusion* of intimacy provided by the interaction was more desirable than an outside relationship—in the club, they were granted safety from the struggle to attract 'real' women, from the necessity to form 'real' commitments and from the demands of those 'real' women on their time and emotions. Further, behaviors that were unacceptable in the 'real' world, such as an obvious appraisal of women's bodies, were allowed in the club, even encouraged by the women themselves (Want to buy a table dance?).

This notion of the 'real' needs to be problematized, however. Clearly, one of the verbalized goals of a customer who *frequents* a strip club is escape from the 'real' world. This may mean several different things, however. There are, of course, regulars in the club who do have commitments with women outside the club, women who are making demands on their time and emotions and for whom the club provides an 'escape from'. There were many other men, however, who were actively seeking an 'escape to', searching for an intimacy that was clearly not available to them in that outside world—men who were recently divorced, who had few social skills, who had physical handicaps. Repeatedly, I listened to men who claimed that they 'didn't know how to talk to women', 'had difficulty meeting people', or just 'didn't have the time to develop a relationship'. These men, then, paid the dancers to listen to their work stories, laugh at their jokes, and eat dinner with them. In my experience in the strip club, 'realness' was thus more highly valued, or at least more realistically expected, than what was actually 'real'.

Denzin writes: 'Desire stands at the center of any intimate relationship, for what is desired is self-realized through the intimacy offered by the other' (1990: 92). There is thus a fetishization that underlies the provision of sexual services. In *Nightwork*, Anne Allison writes that in paying money for a sexual service:

> men are not only buying a commodity but putting themselves into the commodity too. That is, there is a fetishization of subject (man) as much as of object (woman), and the customer is not only purchasing one thing or an *other* but is also paying to become one other as well. He seeks to be relieved of his everyday persona—the one to which various expectations are attached—and given a new script in which he plays a different role. (1994: 22)

Thus, while the man might know that it is a fantasy persona, its 'realness' makes it all the more desirable. Here we can see the multiple commodification of bodies, identities, and intimacy at work, and there are several 'imaginary' relationships involved in the transaction. The dancer, as an employee of the club in which she works, is produced as a particular commodity, a body that can be viewed upon demand. The special lighting, the costumes, and the make-up all combine to make her very body imaginary, something that would not be exactly reproducible outside of the club or in a different venue. Through the physical presence of the dancer, the customer is visible as a heterosexual 'man' who desires women. This is a specular *image;* the other dancers and customers are witnesses to the transaction (this witnessing is a crucial element—if a man was not looking for a public encounter he most likely would not have chosen a strip club). Further, while the dancer herself is also manufacturing or presenting a particular identity, a public *image,* in her interaction with the customer, she is simultaneously involved in the production of a particular *male* subjectivity, that of 'being a male who can pay a female to service him' (Allison, 1994: 204). The man's private *image,* his self-representation, is thus also involved.

As any individual in the club can be provided with such a service, however, as long as he can afford it, a 'genuine' interaction, no matter how brief, becomes a mark of distinction. Insofar as all interactions in the club are mediated by money, these interactions are thus also always open to the suspicion of being false. In her interactions with a regular, then, a dancer is also trying to produce for him the subjectivity of a man who is worth being listened to *regardless* of the money that he pays her. This subjectivity may already be experienced by the man as a 'real' one, however, in which case it becomes the 'realness' of the dancer's identity and the (phantasmatic?) intimacy that they mutually manufacture which sutures the relationship. Peggy Phelan, using psychoanalytic theory to discuss performance, writes:

> As a representation of the real the image is always, partially, phantasmatic. In doubting the authenticity of the image, one questions as well the veracity of she who makes and describes it. To doubt the subject seized by the eye is to doubt the subjectivity of the seeing 'I'. (1993: 1)

Self-identity, according to Phelan, fails to secure belief because our own origins are both real and imagined. Identity needs to be 'continually reproduced and reassured', because we prefer to see ourselves as 'more or less securely situated', our beliefs as secure and coherent (1993: 5).

In a discussion of 'realness' in performance,[1] Judith Butler writes that 'realness' is a standard used to judge any given performance, 'yet what determines the effect of realness is the ability to compel belief, to produce the naturalized effect'. The performance that works, then, is that which effects realness such that 'what appears and what it means coincide' (1993: 129). All the while, however, this 'passing' is the effect of a realness based on the performance of a recognizably impossible ideal. The club in which I did my fieldwork was marketing an image of class, specializing in providing the customer with a particular (not found in *every* club) yet interchangeable type of dancer (any dancer will do—they are all 'beautiful', they are all composed, they will all take off their dresses). In such a situation, the only differences between the women becomes their own images which are created within the club and how they appeal to different men in distinct and 'private' interaction.

The dancers in the club, then, as mentioned earlier, were selling their 'selves', their identities. Certain elements of these selves were continually created and recreated in order to generate and sustain different male desires—a dancer might act like a serious, hardworking student with a much older man, for example, while performing quite differently for a bachelor party. Nevertheless, each dancer also used a variety of strategies to solidify the 'realness' of her own working identity. This realness was not important so much for its details or its truth value, but more for its ability to 'compel belief' in the entire interaction, and in the man's fantasized identities. Nearly every dancer used a fake name, and this was expected by the customers. Stage names, however, were carefully chosen to be 'revealing', to fit the woman's image—Chloe sounded elegant, Kim sounded like the girl-next-door. The management would not allow names that were obviously fake—Serrana and Peaches, for example, were told that they needed to choose new stage names when they came to work at the club. Men often attempted to find out a dancer's 'real name', though, and this becomes part of the performance. Finding out things about a dancer, to a certain extent, made her more real. As it was not the 'truth' that was significant so much as the discovery, I found that when I danced under my real name and shared this with my customers they seemed disappointed. Therefore, I continued to use my real name as my stage name and made

up a fake-real name to give them when they asked for it. This seemed to please them—they believed they found out something about me as a person and something about me that possibly few other people in the room knew. My disclosure, then, worked to 'compel belief' in the interaction.

Certainly, there are very real reasons why dancers do not like to provide their customers with much information. Many dancers attract stalkers, prank-callers, or obsessive individuals, and for this reason they were usually advised by the management not to use their own name and to fabricate a life-story. Even in the dressing rooms, real names were reserved only for dancers who were close friends. The danger of providing customers with too much personal information was openly acknowledged, and in fact provided an alibi when a dancer became caught in a lie. 'Well I had to lie about where I lived when I first met you', I found myself explaining when I accidentally mixed up stories, 'because I've had men try to follow me home before. But, of course, I know that you're different now'. In fact, this type of gradual disclosure itself fostered a kind of intimacy and trust. Over time, a dancer might quite willingly share more and more of her actual history with her regulars. One man laughed as he told me about his experiences with a dancer who called herself Andie. 'First she told me it was her real name, then her middle name. Then she told me that her middle name was Julie and that everyone calls her that at home in Alabama. Later, though, she admitted that Julie was the name she used when she worked in Texas and that her real name was Jackie'. Nevertheless, the rest of her story was consistent enough that he did not question her home state as Alabama or the truth of her experience working as a dancer in Houston. He returned to see her often and spent thousands of dollars on her inside the club. As the name is usually the first disclosure in a relationship, a lie is expected. Later disclosures, however, had to be more carefully presented as 'truths'.

If a customer did not believe that a dancer was genuine in her attentions, he would not become a regular. Developing a network of regulars, then, depends upon a certain consistency in one's stories and identity, both for practical reasons (How old am I tonight? What is my name?) and for the consistent production of authenticity. One way in which I learned to present an 'authentic' performance of identity in interaction with my regulars was through the control of information about my life and my 'self'. As a commodity—a thing, a body—one's image is relatively stable, as height, weight, and bone structure are not easily changed. Having red hair and freckles, always wearing white, and dancing very reservedly made my body and my appearance a certain kind of commodity that would only appeal to particular men. The services that I provided to individual men, however, were different in each interaction—sometimes I merely listened to their stories and sometimes I talked. When I talked, I talked about different parts of my 'history', mixing truth and story—sometimes I talked about the college I went to (a lie); sometimes I talked about not being able to find a man I liked enough to date (a lie); sometimes I talked about my interests in rock-climbing or hiking (the truth); about my family or my dog (the truth).

There is a concatenation, then, of lies, truths, and partial truths which underlie relationships between dancers and their regulars, and thus the interactions become more complicated as time passes. Just as a dancer's identity needs to 'compel belief', so must the relationship itself. One of the complications lies in the fact that despite appearing as a 'real' woman (who might really desire a man like him) a dancer must also remain a fantasy to her customers. While most of the dancers were involved in relationships with men or women outside of the club, these facts were rarely disclosed to the regulars. Further, men expressed disinterest in dancers who complained too much about financial problems, kids, or difficulties at work. Dancers admitted that if the relationships ever did lead to contact outside the club they were almost guaranteed to lose the man as a regular *customer*. Personally, I found it beneficial to speak very carefully of my life outside the club. While men would often ask many questions about me, I found that even telling them too much about my friends or activities would tend to upset the balance of our interaction. If I had such a good social life, was I maybe lying about being single? (Which could lead to: But all these women say that they are single. Are they all lying about everything?). If I simply said that my social life was

severely curtailed because I worked all of the time, however, it left intact the possibility of the mutual construction of an ongoing fantasy relationship. Maybe we could go to dinner together, go dancing or horseback riding someday. The creation of *possibility*, then, was essential at the outset. When it became obvious that the possibility of an outside relationship would never be realized, as it did in some cases, the man might terminate the relationship by simply not returning.

There were other men who seemed to recognize, however, consciously or unconsciously, that it was really the possibility that was important. These men would not ask me to see them outside of the club often, and when they did ask it was often *already impossible* for me to say yes—a pilot continually asked me to go on fantastic but infeasible last-minute vacations, for example, while another man would take me off the list for hours to discuss the possibility of 'living together'. He did not want to hear my practical excuses about returning to North Carolina in a few months; rather, I found that he was thrilled by my fictitious excuse that I did not believe in living together before marriage.

In the ongoing relationships developed with regulars, the dancers become distinct from the other women in the club and the men become distinct from the other customers—if only in the immediacy of the interaction. 'You're different from all of the other girls here', one of my regulars would tell me. Did he tell this to other dancers on nights that I was not working? To dancers at other clubs? But he knew that I liked red wine, the name of my dog, and where my parents lived. He would tell me that he 'needed me' and would pay for hours of my time. I found myself jealous when I came to work unexpectedly one night and found that he had taken another dancer off-the-list. Was this mutual emotion 'simulated'? Was it part of the transmutation that Hochschild is referring to in her concept of emotional labor? Where does real intimacy begin and end after all?

POWER AND GENDER

In *Gigolos and Madames Bountiful,* Nelson and Robinson (1994) argue that while these relationships between wealthy women and their 'kept' men are quite complicated, it is the heterosexual 'intimacy script' which exists in our society that lends a basic framework to the interactions. Nelson and Robinson support the idea that when intimacy is commodified, however, or explicitly facilitated with money, the power differentials in the transaction become too great for 'true' intimacy. The relationship between the gigolo and the woman, they argue, is thus an illusion, a masquerade. Real 'intimacy', then, should accompany real, desirable, legitimate relationships, and other types of arrangements are socially devalued. Indeed, the authors noted that women who supported gigolos were often seen by their friends as having been 'duped' or fooled. As Pat Califia writes:

> One of the dominant myths of our culture is that everybody longs to participate in romantic heterosexual love; that it is romance which gives life meaning and purpose; and that sex is better when you do it with somebody you love. We are also taught to assume that romance and money are mutually exclusive, even though the heroes of romance novels and neogothics are almost always as wealthy as they are handsome. (1994: 243)

The idea of 'true' intimacy as something which is ultimately desirable and which cannot be found in commodified relationships, then, is held by many individuals at a deep, unreflective level.

As this heterosexual intimacy script is always dependent upon gender roles which exist within a power matrix, how is 'true' intimacy ever achieved? For years, women have been configured as the caretakers of heterosexual 'relationships', as caregivers to men, as the guardians of intimacy. In the field of personal intimate relationships, women take primary responsibility for the management of emotion, adjusting their behavior and emotional display to provide emotional support to their male companions (Bartky, 1990; Duncombe and Marsden, 1993; Hochschild, 1983). It is recognized in the literature that men and women approach intimate relationships differently, whether this is seen as an outcome of some essential psychology or socialization into particular gender roles (Bartky, 1990; Brooks, 1995; Perlman and Fehr, 1987). Men and women bring different resources, desires, and emotional knowledges to intimate rela-

tionships, with women often expected to provide more nurturing interactions, convincing men of the value of their projects and identities. There are various positions taken in the literature on the exact nature of this transaction—some conservative theorists argue that while the emotional contributions of men and women to intimacy certainly differ, a balance is achieved in that he provides economic support while she provides emotional support through her nurturance; on the other hand, some feminist theorists write that this bargain is inherently unequal because economic dependence is disempowering in itself (Bartky, 1990: 102). When women offer comfort and assurance, or feed a man's self-esteem, without receiving such support in return, such provision 'can be understood as a conferral of status, a paying of homage by the female to the male' (Bartky, 1990: 109). This private provision of emotional sustenance by women to men, in turn, actually works to shore up the dominant social order. This inequality may be masked, however, as women learn to identify with such nurturing behavior.

Of course, these comments can be said to rest on stereotypes of masculine and feminine behavior. Indeed, Craib has criticized Duncombe and Marsden (1993) for mistaking a 'well established stereotype for reality' when they discuss differences in the emotional life of men and women. He argues that men and women do not behave in such stereotypical ways, citing colleagues and patients 'who could be stereotypically masculine and could also talk with sensitivity and insight about their own feelings, engage in comforting and supporting others and take part in all the routine emotional interchanges' in group psychotherapy settings (Craib, 1995: 155). Nonetheless, stereotyped behavior can indeed create problems in intimate personal relationships (Duncombe and Marsden, 1996: 155), and an analysis of such behavior has led to many a popular self-help guide. As Williams and Bendelow suggest, these emotional stereotypes:

> still exert a powerful and pervasive impact on our lives, particularly through the media and marketing, and amongst certain segments of the sociocultural order who remain firmly wedded to traditional beliefs and values about 'masculine' and 'feminine' roles and duties. Indeed, it is clear that, despite a general growth in social reflexivity in late moder-

nity, not all men are 'in touch' with their emotions. In this respect, there are still marked, albeit less clear-cut, gender differences in emotionality. (1996b: 149)

A lot of the work that a dancer does for her customers is that which women have *traditionally* been expected to do in relationships outside of the club— listening to his stories, boosting his ego, entertaining him with light conversation, and looking attractive for him. Many men who frequent strip clubs *are* 'firmly wedded to traditional beliefs and values about masculine and feminine roles and duties', and even if they are not, the interactions in the club often suggest these beliefs. The women's bodies, in all of their 'difference', are clearly visible. Further, the women are all willing to please, whether by taking off their clothes or conversing on topics that the man chooses.

In the gentleman's club, almost any man who can afford it can receive this kind of attention from nearly any woman he chooses, and as long as the financial compensation is immediate and generous enough, the women are as happy to sit with unattractive men as they are with men that they find attractive. In the case of a marriage or a long-term partnership, this bargain—the provision of emotional support for economic benefit—might be implicit; in the relationship between a dancer and a regular this bargain is normative and explicit—one of the things that dancers often note that they appreciate about the work. In the strip club there is a slippage between public and private that takes place. What is supposed to be private— nudity, sexual desire, intimacy—suddenly becomes publicly and financially negotiated. The idea that a relationship between a dancer and her regular is indeed authentically intimate *in some way* can serve to legitimate a relationship that might be belittled in other social arenas, but which nonetheless provides some deep satisfactions and feelings of power and autonomy.

Interpretations of power and autonomy, however, are linked to our self-representations, our personal mythologies. Many couples in satisfying intimate relationships, after all, would most likely say that the power differentials within their own relationship do not mirror those of society. Regardless of the truth or falsity of this statement, power imbalances may once

again be recorded in terms of personal choice or autonomy. Intimate relationships bring together the personal and the cultural, self and other, the image and the imaginary. 'Memory, sight, love', Phelan writes. 'All require a witness, imaginary or real' (1993: 5). The fantasy that underlies self-identity may mean that the notion of an individual maximizing his or her costs and benefits in an intimate relationship is too simple a construction. Many people, however, myself included, believe that there is indeed *something more* involved in 'real', 'true' intimacy, whether or not it can be proven, defined, or observed. Yet, the phantasmatic and the real can be intricately intertwined; that is, 'images are (already) reality, and the real is (also) imaginary' (Allison, 1996: xvii).

In this way, relationships in the strip club may also be satisfying a man's desire for self-realization by providing him with an interaction that compels belief in his imagined self. '[L]ove', Peggy Phelan writes, (like the 'real' self), 'is always an interrogation—a series of questions about the self and the other'. It is 'a question, occasionally an imperative, hardly ever an assurance', it is, in effect, a 'doubt' (1993: 121). The commodified intimate relationship can both assuage 'doubt' and redouble it.

CONCLUSION

In relationships between dancers and their regulars in the strip club, there is a multiple commodification of bodies, identities, and intimacy. To deny the fact that these relationships are intimate brings us to the idea that somehow it is only that which is free of any economic constraints or commodification that is genuine, and the tendency to categorize one type of relationship (uncommodified) as more 'real' than another (commodified) is a product of deeply entrenched cultural ideology. Granted, these relationships are often *different,* to value one over another, however, may lead us to miss the many diverse ways that people arrange to fill their economic, emotional, and sexual needs.

As I mentioned earlier, the men who frequent strip clubs do so for many diverse and complicated reasons. While some profess 'love' for a particular dancer, others are just there for an experience which is different or exciting. Whether they are escaping 'to' a world in which masculinity, companionship, and the spectacle of female bodies can be purchased, or escaping 'from' a world where their other responsibilities and relationships are becoming burdensome, these men are perfectly willing to pay for the fantasy exchanges. Certainly, as dancers, we *performed* during these exchanges. Sometimes, for example, I stifled my political views with a particular regular; not wanting to lose his business, I pretended to agree with whatever he said, pretended to enjoy his company. Sometimes the dancers laughed in the dressing room at the shallowness of their own performances—how does Keith really think Sarah would date him? How can Tom say he loves me when he doesn't even know my real name? The men, though, performed as well. Most claimed to be single or divorced, but how would we have known? One man insisted that I was his 'favorite' dancer, and that I was different from all of the other dancers in the club. I knew, though, that on nights I was not working he took Tiffany off the list for hours.

While we were always performing, however, we were not always *pretending*. After all, I cannot say that the intimacy I developed with my regulars in the strip club was really false, for sometimes our mutual performances were also authentic. There was positive affect involved; I sometimes held their hands or kissed them on the cheek; I listened with interest (sometimes) to their stories; I missed them when I returned to North Carolina for school. I became familiar with their idiosyncrasies in conversation and the multiple ways that they reacted to my talk and my body. Would I have listened if they hadn't been paying me? Maybe. Maybe not.

In this paper I have attempted to illuminate the fantasy-reality which structures interpersonal intimate relationships. There is a joke about the 'Lacanian' valentine which reads: 'Love is giving something you don't have to someone who doesn't exist'. I do not want to claim that inter-subjectivity and intimacy are not ever possible, however. What is important here, perhaps, is the realization that rational, utilitarian notions of relationships—such as 'counterfeit intimacy', or the 'pure relationship'—are too simplistic. Even these relationships—while seemingly based on rational calculation of an individual's wants and needs—contain a

remarkable element of fantasy. Further, they call into question the very possibility of intimacy *outside of* fantasy. Not just 'sexual' fantasy, but a fantasy of self-identity. As such, the hope for a conscious ability to calculate the costs and benefits of personal relationships in market terms may be quite complicated.

NOTE

1. Here I am using Butler's reading of 'realness' in order to discuss performance, and not using these strip club performances to discuss her theory of performativity.

REFERENCES

Acitelli, Linda K. and Duck, Steve (1987) 'Postscript: Intimacy as the Proverbial Elephant', in D. Perlman and S. Duck (eds) *Intimate Relationships: Development, Dynamics, and Deterioration*. Newbury Park, CA: Sage.

Allison, Anne (1994) *Nightwork: Sexuality, Pleasure, and Corporate Masculinity in a Tokyo Hostess Club*. Chicago, IL: University of Chicago Press.

Allison, Anne (1996) *Permitted and Prohibited Desires: Mothers, Comics, and Censorship in Japan*. Boulder, CO: Westview Press.

Bartky, Sandra L. (1990) *Femininity and Domination: Studies in the Phenomenology of Oppression*. New York: Routledge.

Bell, Shannon (1994) *Reading, Writing, and Rewriting the Prostitute Body*. Bloomington: Indiana University Press.

Bell, Shannon (1995) *Whore Carnival*. New York: Autonomedia.

Bildstein, Jay (1996) *The King of Clubs*. New York: Barricade Books.

Boles, Jacqueline and Garbin, Albeno P. (1974) 'The Strip Club and Customer-Stripper Patterns of Interaction', *Sociology and Social Research* 58: 136–44.

Bourdieu, Pierre (1984) *Distinction: A Social Critique of the Judgement of Taste*. C'mbridge, MA: Harvard University Press.

Brooks, Gary R. (1995) *The Centerfold Syndrome: How Men Can Overcome Objectification and Achieve Intimacy with Women*. San Francisco, CA: Jossey-Bass.

Butler, Judith (1993) *Bodies That Matter: On the Discursive Limits of Sex*. New York: Routledge.

Califia, Pat (1994) *Public Sex: The Culture of Radical Sex*. San Francisco, CA: Cleis Press.

Coontz, Stephanie (1992) *The Way We Never Were: American Families and the Nostalgia Trap*. New York: Basic Books.

Craib, Ian (1995) 'Some Comments on the Sociology of Emotions', *Sociology* 29(1): 151–8.

Delacoste, Frederique and Alexander, Priscilla, eds. (1987) *Sex Work: Writings by Women in the Sex Industry.* San Francisco, CA: Cleis Press.

Denzin, Norman (1990) 'On Understanding Emotion: The Interpretive-Cultural Agenda', in T. Kemper (ed.) *Research Agendas in the Sociology of Emotions,* pp. 85–116. New York: State University of New York Press.

Duncombe, Jean and Marsden, Dennis (1993) 'Love and Intimacy: The Gender Division of Emotion and "Emotion Work". A Neglected Aspect of Sociological Discussion of Heterosexual Relationships', *Sociology* 27(2): 221–41.

Duncombe, Jean and Marsden, Dennis (1996) 'Extending the Social: A Response to Ian Craib', *Sociology* 30(1): 155–8.

Enck, Graves E. and Preston, James D. (1988) 'Counterfeit Intimacy: A Dramaturgical Analysis of an Erotic Performance', *Deviant Behavior* 9: 369–81.

Giddens, Anthony (1992) *The Transformation of Intimacy: Sexuality, Love, and Eroticism in Modern Societies.* Stanford, CA: Stanford University Press.

Harvey, David (1990) *The Condition of Postmodernity.* Oxford: Blackwell.

Hochschild, Arlie R. (1983) *The Managed Heart: Commercialization of Human Feeling.* Berkeley: University of California Press.

Keen, Sam (1991) *Fire in the Belly: On Being a Man.* New York: Bantam Books.

Lasch, Christopher (1977) *Haven in a Heartless World: The Family Besieged.* New York: Basic Books.

Mattson, Heidi (1995) *Ivy League Stripper.* New York: Arcade Publishing.

Morgan, Peggy (1987) 'Living on the Edge', in F. Delacoste and P. Alexander (eds) *Sex Work: Writings by Women in the Sex Industry,* pp. 21–8. San Francisco: Cleis Press.

Murawaki, L. Katherine and D'Unger, Amy (1995) 'Objectification and Consciousness: Women's Views of Self and Power in the Adult Entertainment Industry', unpublished manuscript, Duke University.

Nelson, Adie and Robinson, Barrie W. (1994) *Gigolos and Madames Bountiful: Illusions of Gender, Power, and Intimacy.* Toronto: University of Toronto Press.

Perlman, Daniel and Fehr, Beverly (1987) 'The Development of Intimate Relationships', in Daniel Perlman and Steve Duck (eds) *Intimate Relationships: Development, Dynamics, and Deterioration.* Newbury Park, CA: Sage.

Phelan, Peggy (1993) *Unmarked: The Politics of Performance.* New York: Routledge.

Pheterson, Gail (1989) *A Vindication of the Rights of Whores.* Seattle: Seal Press.

Prewitt, Terry J. (1989) 'Like a Virgin: The Semiotics of Illusion in Erotic Performance', *American Journal of Semiotics* 6(4): 137–52.

Prus, Robert (1996) *Symbolic Interaction and Ethnographic Research: Intersubjectivity and the Study of Human Lived Experience.* New York: State University of New York Press.

Ronai, Carol R. (1992) 'The Reflexive Self Through Narrative', in C. Ellis and M. Flaherty *Investigating Subjectivity: Research on Lived Experience,* pp. 102–25. Newbury Park, CA: Sage.

Salutin, Marilyn (1973) 'Stripper Morality', in George P. Csicery, *The Sex Industry.* New York: Signet.

Singer, Linda (1993) *Erotic Welfare.* New York: Routledge.

Tolich, Martin B. (1993) 'Alienating and Liberating Emotions at Work: Supermarket Clerks' Performance of Customer Service', *Journal of Contemporary Ethnography* 22(3):361–81.

Wharton, Amy S. (1993) 'The Affective Consequences of Service Work: Managing Emotions on the Job', *Work and Occupations* 20(2):205–32.

Williams, Simon J. and Bendelow, Gillian A. (1996a) 'The "Emotional" Body', *Body and Society* 2(3): 125–39.

Williams, Simon J. and Bendelow, Gillian A. (1996b) 'Emotions and "Sociological Imperialism": A Rejoinder to Craib', *Sociology* 30(1): 145–53.

Zizek, Slavoj (1989) *The Sublime Object of Ideology.* London: Verso.

7.2 Prostitution and Fellatio

Martin A. Monto

Like prostitution policy, research on prostitution has focused primarily on prostitutes rather than on their clients (Carmen & Moody, 1985). Some argue that the neglect of clients, virtually all of whom are male, reflects a double standard in which women are held responsible for male deviance (Davis, 1993). Others argue that the lack of attention to male clients is due to the assumption that seeking prostitutes is natural behavior in men, hardly worthy of explanation (Prasad, 1999). A more common explanation for the lack of research on male clients is that they are inaccessible. Clients usually seek to keep their activities hidden, and the justice system may assist them to spare embarrassment to them and their families (Faugier & Cranfield, 1995; Special Committee on Prostitution and Pornography, 1985).

Recently, efforts to curtail prostitution have begun to focus on clients. Since 1995, weekend educational programs for arrested clients have developed in San Francisco, Las Vegas, and Portland, Oregon. These "johns schools" provide unprecedented access to this formerly hidden population. San Francisco's First Offenders Prostitution Program (FOPP), the largest and longest-running program of this kind, sees as many as 80 men per month (Monto, 2000). For a description of a similar but now defunct program in Portland, Oregon, see Monto (1998).

The little existing research on clients points to multiple explanations for seeking prostitutes. Indeed, Monto (2000), in a study of arrested clients, argued that most of the popular explanations as to why men seek out prostitutes are supported by existing data. Clients may seek sex with prostitutes because they are attracted to the illicit or risky nature of the encounter (Holzman & Pines, 1982; McKeganey & Bernard, 1996; Monto, 2000), because they want to have greater control over their sexual experiences (Monto, 2000), because they have difficulty becoming involved in

conventional relationships (Jordan, 1997; Monto, 2000), because they want to avoid the responsibilities or emotional attachments of a conventional relationship (McKeganey & Bernard, 1996; Monto, 2000), or because they are interested in companionship, intimacy, or love (Holzman & Pines, 1982; Monto, 2000). Additionally, research supports the idea that one of the main reasons clients pursue encounters with prostitutes is that they are interested in sexual practices to which they do not have access, either because they have no regular partners or because their partners are unable or unwilling to accommodate their desires (Jordan 1997; McKeganey & Bernard, 1996; Monto, 2000; Sullivan and Simon, 1998).

If some men seek prostitutes because they desire sexual practices that are not regularly available to them in their conventional relationships, then what are these desired practices? Findings from the nationally representative National Health and Social Life Survey (NHSLS) suggest a substantial discrepancy between men's and women's interest in fellatio. While 45% of men found receiving fellatio *very appealing,* only 17% of women found performing fellatio *very appealing.* In contrast, the proportion of men who found performing cunnilingus *very appealing* (34%) was slightly higher than the proportion of women who found receiving it *very appealing* (29%). While results showed that there were other practices, such as anal sex and group sex, that men found more appealing than women, fellatio was distinctive in that such a large proportion of men found it appealing and the discrepancy between men's and women's attitudes toward it was substantial (Laumann, Gagnon, Michael & Michaels, 1994).

Despite the appeal of fellatio to men, only 28% reported that they experienced it during their most recent sexual encounter (Laumann et al., 1994). While this discrepancy in the appeal and experience of fella-

---

From *Journal of Sex Research* 38(2): 140–45. Copyright © 2001 by The Society for the Scientific Study of Sexuality. Reprinted by permission of The Society for the Scientific Study of Sexuality.

tio seems to suggest that a significant minority of men in the U.S. may not have their perceived sexual needs met in conventional relationships, one cannot assume that men who find fellatio *very appealing* necessarily desire it during the majority of their sexual encounters. Additionally, even if some men experience less fellatio than they would prefer, most do not respond to the deficit by seeking prostitutes. In fact, only a small proportion of men completing the NHSLS reported ever having visited a prostitute (16%), and less than 1% reported having visited a prostitute during the previous year (Michael, Gagnon, Laumann, & Kolata, 1994).

Utilizing a large sample of men arrested for trying to hire prostitutes, the present study evaluates the importance of fellatio in prostitution encounters. I hypothesize that respondents will be more likely to select fellatio than any other practice when asked which sexual practices they (a) have ever experienced with a prostitute, (b) usually experience with a prostitute, (c) experienced during their most recent sexual encounter with a prostitute, and (d) find most appealing. I also hypothesize that respondents will generally report that their sexual interests are different than those of their regular partner, and that they want a different kind of sex than their regular partner wants.

METHOD

Participants

Participants were all men arrested for trying to hire prostitutes in three Western cities. Most of the data reported in the present study come from questionnaires administered to 1281 men participating in programs in San Francisco, California (N = 950); Las Vegas, Nevada (N = 254); and Portland, Oregon (N = 77). An additional set of questions concerning the degree to which respondents found various sexual practices appealing was asked of 55 men participating in the Portland program, and one question concerning respondents' practices during their most recent prostitution encounter was asked of 424 men participating in the San Francisco and Las Vegas programs.

Demographic characteristics of the participants included in the primary sample are presented in Table 7.2.1. Chi-squared tests revealed no statistically significant differences between the samples from these

Table 7.2.1 Clients' Background Characteristics

Characteristic	Percentage
Ethnicity (N = 1252)	
White	60%
Hispanic, Chicano, or Latino	17%
Asian	13%
Black	5%
Other or combination	5%
Level of education (N = 1270)	
Did not graduate from high school	9%
High school graduate	18%
Some college training	37%
Received bachelor's degree	25%
Received graduate degree	11%
Marital status (N = 1267)	
Married	42%
Never married	35%
Divorced	15%
Separated	6%
Widowed	2%
Work status (N = 1242)	
Working full time	81%
Working part time	6%
Retired	2%
Student	2%
Other	9%
Age (N = 1204)	
18–21	4%
22–25	9%
26–35	33%
36–45	31%
46–55	17%
56–65	4%
66 or older	2%
Sexual orientation (N = 1281)	
Strictly heterosexual	94%
Experience with both	5%
Strictly homosexual	1%
Number of sexual partners past year (N = 1261)	
None	9%
1	38%
2	16%
3 or 4	17%
5 to 10	13%
11 or more	7%

three cities on all but two variables, ethnicity and education. Mirroring the differences between these communities, the Portland sample was less ethnically diverse than the other two samples, and the San Francisco sample included a higher proportion of Asians. Additionally, the Las Vegas sample had a higher proportion of individuals who had not completed high school, and the San Francisco sample had a higher proportion of individuals with graduate degrees. Because most of the background characteristics were similarly distributed in all three cities, the samples were combined for reporting here.

Overall, 59% of the men who completed surveys reported that they had sexual relations with a prostitute at least once over the last 12 months. Twenty-one percent reported one episode, while 28% reported having had sexual relations with a prostitute more than one time but less than once per month. Eight percent reported having had sexual relations with a prostitute one to three times per month, and 2% reported having had sexual relations with a prostitute once or more per week. Another 21% reported that they had not had sexual relations with a prostitute during the past year. And 20% claimed never to have had sexual relations with a prostitute, indicating that their only experience had been propositioning the police decoy, which led to their arrest.

Procedures

Anonymous questionnaires were administered while men were gathered together immediately prior to their participation in intervention programs designed to discourage reoffense. Because attendance at these programs eliminates the arrest records of those who participate, nearly all men who are arrested for trying to hire prostitutes in these jurisdictions choose to attend. Participants were informed of their right not to participate through an attached letter. A signed consent form was not used because pretests revealed that respondents felt threatened by leaving a signature. All procedures were approved by the Institutional Review Board at the author's host institution, which operates in full compliance with the standards established by the National Institute of Health.

About 80% of men gathered for these programs completed questionnaires. Though refusals probably account for the largest proportion of the remaining 20%, language problems, late arrivals, and misunderstandings also accounted for a substantial proportion.

Measures

Measures were selected from among 87 items developed to provide basic information about the arrested clients of street prostitutes. The original intent of the questionnaire was not primarily to explore sexual behavior but to address motivations, to characterize attitudes, and to generally provide an overview of this heretofore inaccessible population. Items were selected to explore popular and scholarly assumptions about the clients of prostitutes and to provide information that might be of use to those who provide intervention programs for these men. These issues are explored in other articles (Monto, 1999a, 1999b, 2000). An opportunity to conduct qualitative interviews was not available.

Most of the measures reported here rely on single questions developed specifically for this study. The exact wording of the questions and the response frequencies are presented in Table 7.2.2. The four questions concerning the degree to which respondents found various sexual practices appealing were borrowed from the National Health and Social Life Survey (Laumann et al., 1994). The wording of these questions is also presented in Table 7.2.2.

RESULTS

The sexual interest and behavior items that are the focus of this study are presented in Table 7.2.2. Among the small sample of respondents (N = 55) answering questions about the degree to which they found various sexual practices appealing, 66% rated the idea of receiving oral sex as *very appealing*. This percentage is substantially higher than the 45% endorsing this response among men participating in the nationally representative National Health and Social Life Survey (Laumann et al., 1994). While this comparison would seem to support the central proposition of this study, that some men seek prostitutes because they desire fellatio, one should note that an even greater proportion of the client sample (76%) found vaginal sex very appealing. The hypothesis that

Table 7.2.2 Clients' Sexual Interests and Behaviors with Prostitutes

Item	N	Sample	Location
How would you rate each of these activities?			
Vaginal intercourse		54	Portland
Very appealing	76%		
Somewhat appealing	17%		
Not very appealing	2%		
Not at all appealing	5%		
A partner performing oral sex on you		55	Portland
Very appealing	65%		
Somewhat appealing	22%		
Not very appealing	6%		
Not at all appealing	7%		
Performing oral sex on a partner		55	Portland
Very appealing	58%		
Somewhat appealing	31%		
Not very appealing	2%		
Not at all appealing	9%		
Having anal intercourse with a partner		55	Portland
Very appealing	18%		
Somewhat appealing	15%		
Not very appealing	20%		
Not at all appealing	47%		
What kind of sexual activities have you ever engaged in with a prostitute?		995	Portland, Las Vegas, and San Francisco
Blow job	81%		
Vaginal sex	55%		
Half and half (oral and vaginal sex)	36%		
Hand job	35%		
Anal sex	10%		
Performing oral sex on her	9%		
What sexual activities did you engage in during your most recent encounter with a prostitute?		424	Las Vegas and San Francisco
Blow job	68%		
Vaginal sex	43%		
Hand job	14%		
Anal sex	4%		
Performed oral sex on her	6%		
What kind of sexual activity do you engage in most often with a prostitute?		926	Portland, Las Vegas, and San Francisco
Blow job	51%		
Vaginal sex	12%		
Half and half (oral and vaginal sex)	10%		
Hand job	6%		
Anal sex	1%		
Performing oral sex on her	0%		
Selected 2 or more responses	18%		
Other	2%		

(continued)

Table 7.2.2 Clients' Sexual Interests and Behaviors with Prostitutes (continued)

Item	N	Sample	Location
I would rather have sex with a prostitute than have a conventional relationship with a woman		1197	Portland, Las Vegas, and San Francisco
Agree strongly	5%		
Agree somewhat	13%		
Disagree strongly	18%		
Disagree somewhat	64%		
I want a different kind of sex than my regular partner.		1191	Portland, Las Vegas, and San Francisco
Agree strongly	12%		
Agree somewhat	29%		
Disagree somewhat	21%		
Disagree strongly	38%		
Now, thinking about the sexual relationship with your wife or partner . . . How similar are your sexual interests?		831	Portland, Las Vegas, and San Francisco
Very similar	36%		
Somewhat similar	39%		
Somewhat different	17%		
Very different	8%		

respondents would rate fellatio as more appealing than other sexual practices is not supported.

Results are consistent with the hypotheses that respondents would be more likely to select fellatio than any other sexual practice when asked about which practices they had ever experienced with a prostitute, usually experienced with a prostitute, and experienced during their most recent encounter with a prostitute. When 995 respondents from all three cities were asked whether they had ever participated in various sexual practices with a prostitute, 81% reported that they had received oral sex, or a "blow job." The second most frequently reported practice was vaginal sex at 55%. Many of the clients (36%) reported participating in "half and half," which includes both oral and vaginal sex. Being manually masturbated, or receiving a "hand job," was reported by 35% of respondents.

Of 926 men asked to identify the practice in which they participated most often when with a prostitute, 51% selected blow job, followed by 12% who selected vaginal sex, 10% who selected half and half (which includes oral sex), and 6% who selected hand job. Eighteen percent misunderstood instructions and selected two or more responses, and of those, fellatio was the most frequently chosen.

Among a separate sample of 424 respondents from Las Vegas and San Francisco who were asked about their most recent encounter with a prostitute, 68% reported that the encounter included oral sex, while 43% reported that it included vaginal sex, 14% reported being manually masturbated, and 4% reported anal sex.

The results do not support the hypotheses regarding two other attitudinal items. When 1191 arrested men from all three cities were asked to respond to the statement "I want a different kind of sex than my regular partner," 41% agreed somewhat or strongly. The responses of those 41% are consistent with the central proposition of this article. Of the remaining 59%, some may have disagreed because they were among the 20% of the sample who were not married and/or had no regular sexual partner. The remaining men, about 39% of the total sample, did not indicate that they wanted a different kind of sex than their regular partner wanted. Additionally, among 831 men from all three cities who reported having a wife or regular sexual partner, 36% reported that their sexual interests were *very similar* to those of their wife or regular sexual partner, while 39% answered *somewhat similar*. Twenty-five percent reported that their sexual interests were *somewhat different* or *very different* than those of their wife or regular sexual partner. While the desire for fellatio may be a major reason some men consort with prostitutes, it would be incorrect to assume that the majority of clients with partners find their sexual interests unreciprocated.

DISCUSSION

These simple descriptive findings indicate that men arrested for trying to hire street prostitutes were more likely to select fellatio than any other sexual practice when asked which practices they had ever experienced with a prostitute, experienced most frequently with a prostitute, and experienced during their most recent sexual encounter with a prostitute. Additionally, respondents were more likely than men in general to find fellatio highly appealing. All of these findings point to the importance of fellatio in the prostitution encounter. This contrasts sharply with nonpaid sexual practice in which vaginal sex is overwhelmingly preferred and practiced (Laumann et al., 1994). These findings tend to support the proposition that the desire for fellatio may be one reason some men seek prostitutes.

However, other findings leave room for alternative explanations. Despite the appeal of fellatio, vaginal sex was still described as *very appealing* by more of the respondents. Additionally, only a minority of respondents agreed that they wanted a different kind of sex than their regular partner wanted, and only 25% of respondents with partners rated their sexual interests as somewhat or very different than the desires of their partner. In other words, the predominance of fellatio during prostitution encounters cannot be fully explained by its appeal to potential clients or by its lack of availability in conventional relationships.

There are other possible explanations for the frequency of fellatio during prostitution encounters. Clients may believe that there is a lower risk of AIDS

from fellatio than from other practices. They may believe that there is less need to wear a condom during fellatio than during vaginal or anal intercourse. They may perceive vaginal sex to be more intimate than oral sex, and hence pursue fellatio when with prostitutes. Alternatively, the prevalence of fellatio during prostitution encounters may reflect the preferences of prostitutes themselves, who may prefer fellatio to less easily accomplished sexual practices.

The results of this study are limited in that the respondents participating were not a representative sample of prostitution clients. Virtually all were arrested while trying to hire street prostitutes rather than while patronizing escort services or indoor establishments. It may be that sexual practices differ in these settings. In a recent study by Lever and Dolnick (2000), street prostitutes were more likely to report performing oral sex (57%) during their most recent encounter with a client than were "call girls" (45%). One of the reasons for higher rates of fellatio in street prostitution encounters may be that such encounters often occur in vehicles, where fellatio may be more easily accomplished that vaginal sex. Additionally, since it is relatively easy to avoid arrest while trying to hire prostitutes, less experienced clients may be overrepresented among the participants in this study. The motivations and sexual practices of less experienced clients could differ from those with greater experience. Nevertheless, the data gathered and the results presented represent an opportunity to move beyond idiosyncratic impressions and anecdotal accounts, and to evaluate current understandings of the prostitution client in light of a large body of data collected from a previously inaccessible population.

It is clear that the desire for fellatio alone is not sufficient to cause men to seek out prostitutes. Though data from the National Health and Social Life Survey indicate that a substantial minority of men in the U.S. desire fellatio and suggest the possibility that some may not receive it as often as they would prefer, the overwhelming majority of men in the U.S. do not visit prostitutes. In fact, fewer than 1% of men participating in the NHSLS reported having engaged in sex with a prostitute over the previous year (Michael et al., 1994). Clearly, there must be additional predictors that discriminate between men who seek to fulfill their sexual desires through prostitution and men who do not. These could include many of the explanations described in the beginning of this paper, such as an attraction to risky sex, shyness, the desire to be in control, the desire to avoid emotional attachments, or an interest in companionship. One promising predictor is the degree to which individuals conceive of sex as a commodity rather than as a mutually fulfilling aspect of an intimate relationship. Monto (1999b) found a strong correlation between this construct and the frequency with which clients visited prostitutes.

Overall, the findings presented here reaffirm the importance of fellatio in the prostitution encounter. While there are multiple explanations for the prevalence of fellatio in prostitution encounters, findings suggest that some clients seek prostitutes because they are interested in fellatio, a sexual practice to which they may not have regular access through socially approved means. Clearly, this explanation does not apply to all clients, many of whom seek other sexual practices with prostitutes or who have partners who share their sexual interests. Additionally, results should not be misconstrued to suggest that women who choose not to perform fellatio lead their partners to seek prostitutes. Fellatio may be appealing for some men partly because it is unavailable. If given greater access to fellatio, some clients might simply move on to other practices that remain unavailable through conventional relationships.

REFERENCES

Carmen, A., & Moody, H. (1985). *Working women: The subterranean world of street prostitution.* New York: Harper and Row.

Davis, N. (1993). *Prostitution: An international handbook on trends, problems, and policies.* London: Greenwood Press.

Faugier, J., & Cranfield, S. (1995). Reaching the male clients of female prostitutes: The challenge for HIV prevention. *AIDS Care, 7,* S21–S37.

Holzman, H. R., & Pines, S. (1982). Buying sex: The phenomenology of being a john. *Deviant Behavior, 4,* 89–116.

Jordan, J. (1997). User buys: Why men buy sex. *Australian and New Zealand Journal of Criminology, 30,* 55–71.

Laumann, E. O., Gagnon, J. H., Michael, R. T., & Michaels, S. (1994). *The social organization of sexuality: Sexual practices in the United States.* Chicago: University of Chicago Press.

Lever, J., & Dolnick, D. (2000). Clients and call girls. In R. Weitzer (Ed.), *Sex for sale: Prostitution, pornography, and the sex industry* (pp. 85–100). New York: Routledge.

McKeganey, N., & Barnard, M. (1996). *Sex work on the streets: Prostitutes and their clients.* Philadelphia: Open University Press.

Michael, R. T., Gagnon, J. H., Laumann, E. O., & Kolata, G. (1994). *Sex in America: A definitive survey.* Boston: Little Brown.

Monto, M. A. (1998). Redefining prostitution by focusing on the johns: The unique approach of the Sexual Exploitation Education Project. *Violence Against Women, 4,* 503–517.

Monto, M. A. (1999a, April). *Meaningful differences: A comparison of the male clients of female street prostitutes with a national sample of men.* Paper presented at the meeting of the Pacific Sociological Association. Portland, OR.

Monto, M. A. (1999b, August). *Prostitution and human commodification.* Paper presented at the meeting of the American Sociological Association, Chicago, IL.

Monto, M. A. (2000). Why men seek out prostitutes. In R. Weitzer (Ed.), *Sex for sale: Prostitution, pornography and the sex industry* (pp. 67–83). New York: Routledge.

Prasad, M. (1999). The morality of market exchange: Love, money, and contractual justice. *Sociological Perspectives, 42,* 181–214.

Special Committee on Prostitution and Pornography. (1985). *Pornography and prostitution in Canada.* Ottawa, Canada: Canadian Government Publishing Centre.

Sullivan, E., & Simon, W. (1998). The client: A social, psychological, and behavioral look at the unseen patron of prostitution. In J. E. Elias, V. L. Bullough, V. Elias, & G. Brewer (Eds.), *Prostitution: On whores, hustlers, and johns,* (pp. 134–154). Amherst, NY: Prometheus.

7.3 'THE WORST THING IS THE SCREWING' (1)
Consumption and the Management of Identity in Sex Work

Joanna Brewis and Stephen Linstead

INTRODUCTION

In this paper, and a second linked paper (forthcoming in Volume 7 Number 3 of this journal), it is argued that the development of late modernity has been characterized by a reversal of the classic assumption that identity was defined by what the individual did or made, by their involvement in production. Identity is now more frequently distinguished by how we consume and what is consumed, as the consumption process itself becomes a process of symbolic production and reproduction—the consumption of signs as much as commodities. How and what we consume have become key identity markers and the boundaries between work and leisure have become blurred by more ambiguous considerations of lifestyle (Giddens 1991; 1992; Hawkes 1996, pp. 113–23). Those sites where work and leisure, production and consumption, naturally intersect are therefore of particular interest to the theorist of contemporary self-identity.

The sex industry is one such site. However, this is an occupation where the consumption that takes place is of the body, or its parts. Such occupations, where the person(ality) of the worker is an important part of the service on offer, often threaten to 'consume' them in the process—experienced as a loss of self-identity (Höpfl and Linstead 1993, p. 86; Roach 1985, p. 138). This may require the prostitute to engage in the emotional labour necessary to maintain a sense of self-identity which is distinct from that involved in the business arrangement. Prostitutes, due to the intensity and intimacy of their physical involvement in their work, do not necessarily find the distancing process easy, and a variety of styles and methods are employed by working girls (and boys) to sustain the mask, or series of masks, which make earning a living through the sale of sex possible. Consequently, our interest in prostitution, and its link to consumption and self-identity, derive here from the fact that the prostitutes themselves are the commodity that is consumed, and the implications that this has for their identity, as opposed to issues around the consumption undertaken by the client and how their identity may be constructed or consolidated through this process.[1]

In our discussion we draw on a review of qualitative research in the UK (Scotland and England) as well as on similar research, and accounts of sex work published by prostitutes, in Melbourne and Victoria, Sydney and New South Wales, South and Western Australia, and one of the authors' own research in New South Wales. Data concerning sex work in other geographical locations are also reviewed in passing. However, although qualitative studies of sex workers have been conducted in several localities to date, none of these have been comparative in their objectives and none have attempted to take an overview of several studies in areas which may be considered to have broad similarities, from which a rich picture of the occupation in a region may emerge. For this paper, studies from two 'advanced', English-speaking Western societies with similar legislative and enforcement frameworks were reviewed, making the assumption that any variation in context is therefore likely to be minimized, and any emergent differences the result of the stratification of a mature industry operating in a segmented and politicized (if not entirely 'free') market under conditions of late modernity.[2] The points made, therefore, are not intended to be applied to prostitution globally, even in the most highly abstract sense—at least not without very careful consideration.

From *Gender, Work & Organization* 7(2): 84–97. Copyright © 2000 by Blackwell Publishing Ltd. Reprinted by permission of Blackwell Publishing Ltd.

We have concentrated on adult female prostitution for the same reason, and regard the analysis of male, transgender or child prostitution as separate studies in their own right (although where appropriate we do note significant observations from such studies where they emerged in the literature reviewed).[3] We do not regard the situations of a 30-year-old entrepreneurial dominatrix from Leicester, a 21-year-old gay male student working as an escort in Melbourne and a 14-year-old Nepali girl sold into a Bombay brothel as being commensurable, nor would we advocate similar responses to their problems.[4] This paper is therefore a review of qualitative studies of Western female prostitution in two late modern, capitalist societies which attempts to discern patterns, similarities and contradictions in the processes by which these women manage their self-identity, rather than being a definitive statement of the issues of identity management affecting *all* prostitutes.

Our project of the exploration of the process of the negotiation and construction of prostitutes' identity within and around the commercial sexual transaction falls into two parts—the present paper which concentrates on the interactional features of identity construction, and a second paper which concentrates on the contextual and structural features which shape this construction. What we conclude is that the process is complex and subject to considerable local variation, despite the overall similarities of the situations covered in our literature review—as one might expect with any industry which is simultaneously truly global and local. What the sexual act means is always socially and culturally determined, affected by place and history, as Michel Foucault (1979; 1986; 1990) reminds us, and these variations are discernible in the micro-practices observable in the present-day sex industry, even when the distance involved may only be a matter of a few blocks. Moreover, the work itself, by its very nature, places pressure on the relationship between personal and professional identities. The ways in which these pressures are handled sheds light on the complexity of sex work and, by extension of this perspective from the margins, allows us an alternative purchase on the reflexive project of the self in modernity (Giddens 1991; 1992).

SEX AS WORK

The *meaning* of the sex act itself is what is at stake in interactions between prostitutes and clients, and the categorization of different types of sexual encounter—relational, professional or recreational—is often important for the prostitute to maintain the proper distance from the emotional demands of the client encounter and to enable the maintenance of self-identity beneath the public, professional mask. However, although what we discuss in this paper primarily falls into the category of work or professional sex, we shall see that the boundaries between categories are permeable, requiring constant attention, and that the mask is always in danger of slipping.

The detailed origins of the ideologies behind sex work are discussed in our second paper, but it is important to note here that the idea of the commodification of the body as an object for consumption—where the legitimate leisure activity of the client is serviced by the legitimate business activity of the prostitute—has been fully embraced by certain sectors of the sex industry itself. This has produced the 'sex worker' argument wherein prostitutes represent themselves (and are represented by certain commentators) as service workers who happen to be selling their sexuality rather than their social skills or other dimensions of their labour power, such as their physical strength. A prostitute interviewed by O'Neill, for example, comments: 'I'm a working girl . . . I work with my body' (Mary, cited in O'Neill 1996, p. 20). O'Connell Davidson (1994, p. 1; 1995; 1996, pp. 180–1) suggests that this discursive representation of the prostitute is under-pinned by the understanding that those who sell sex for money, and are not obviously coerced into such work—that is, the kind of sex worker discussed in this paper—are labouring in the same way as other workers under capitalism (i.e. they are free to sell their labour to the highest bidder in a mutual exchange). It is emphasized by advocates of the sex worker perspective that all prostitutes seek this freedom within their labour process, even those who seem to work in the most dangerous and unpredictable of situations. For example, McRae reports how Leila, a young female prostitute working on the street in

London's Notting Hill, observes potential clients through their car windows, and rejects them if they make her feel uncomfortable, even though this often makes the clients angry (McRae 1992, p. 242; see also discussion of making the sex contract in McKeganey and Barnard 1996, pp. 31–5). Similarly, Mary states that she is careful both to 'suss' her clients out, to try and get inside their heads, but also to keep a distance between her and the client so that, if they turn out to be dangerous, she has a chance to get away. She says that: 'I always have my head clear to work . . . I've got to be alert' (Mary, cited in O'Neill 1996, p. 20—also see McKeganey and Barnard 1996, pp. 43–7). This implies the risks of working when one is drunk or under the influence of drugs, when important boundaries may break down. Here then the line between *sex as leisure activity* (as required by clients) and *sex as work* (as performed by the prostitute) is easy to draw, but important to maintain.[5]

The prevailing context of prostitution in late modernity, then, is that of a consumer service industry, and we can now turn to examine the various techniques which prostitutes may (and equally may not) rely on to construct and manage their personal and professional identities, to fulfil the demands of their jobs at least cost to themselves in terms of emotional labour. One requirement for the emotional management of one's self is the maintenance of an appropriate degree of psychological distance from the encounter, or at least from certain aspects of it. One means of achieving this distance and bolstering the work persona for some prostitutes is the use of drugs.

STAYING COMPOS MENTIS: DRUG USE AND SELF-MANAGEMENT

Drug use appears to play a paradoxical role in prostitution. Soft drugs, from caffeine and nicotine through alcohol to pills such as valium and 'organic' drugs like marijuana, are widely used—sometimes to keep the workers awake during long days and nights, often with nothing to do, sometimes to relax them and dull the sensation of the potential unpleasantness of the job. Sometimes this also helps them to play the role/s

required, to become the product that clients demand and to distance their everyday selves from the work. La Toya, a Sydney transsexual working as a prostitute talks about how her use of soft drugs enables her to keep her work personality separated from her 'real' self:

> I take speed, pills—for the personality change but it keeps you warm as well. Especially on cold nights. It keeps your mouth going. If I was straight I could not do it . . . When I'm down at work I'm not me, Lisa, any more, I'm La Toya and that's where the drugs come in. You have to put on the attitude that you're that other person. Keep away from reality. When I'm down at work I'm in a totally different world. At first it was hard, splitting the two apart. (cited in Cockington and Marlin 1995, pp. 94–5)

There is widespread evidence in the literature of soft drug use by prostitutes as a means of coping with the pressures of the job. In contrast, the use of hard drugs seems to be incidental to these pressures—at least in any causal sense—as most injecting prostitutes take to sex work as a means of funding an already established habit, either their own or that of their partners. Nevertheless, all McKeganey and Barnard's (1996) injectors did claim that they took a dose before their night's work and that it helped them to cope with the work. These prostitutes suggested that they need to take a 'hit' to numb their awareness of the work they are doing:

> If I've no had a hit, you jus' want it over an' done with. If you've had a hit, you can stand and work nae bother, it doesnae bother you, you know what I mean. But ye see if you're straight, ye start to think about it, then things start flooding back intae your mind and you're sayin' 'I don't want to dae this', you know what I mean. (cited in McKeganey and Barnard 1996, p. 91)

However, Webb and Elms (1994, p. 283) report that their drug-dependent respondents indicated that, although drug use made the work more bearable, it could compromise their ability to negotiate safe sex with clients. Drug usage is more common among street prostitutes because parlours (brothels) usually ban hard drugs; many parlours will not even tolerate marijuana or pills, or in some cases alcohol, especially in the higher class establishments. Inga (cited in Cockington and Marlin 1995, p. 172), who admits to having used valium, ecstasy and marijuana in the past, now remains drug-free and clear-headed at all times; primarily because she says that she found that 'the straighter I was, the more money I made'. Now working in an upmarket parlour in Melbourne, there is the expectation that she will make conversation with clients, which requires her to concentrate, and places greater demands on the worker for the maintenance of the professional mask.

Furthermore, working to finance a habit tends to breed a vicious circle—the more money that is available, the more that gets spent on drugs. Consumption here becomes addictive, but the users report that they are able to break the habit and reduce their consumption again when they feel it is getting too much, so the addiction may be as much to the consumption as to the substance, depending on their drug of choice. Of course, some users do not make it back from the street, and drug-related murders of prostitutes, usually ones involved in dealing in some way, are not uncommon in all the locations covered by the research reviewed here.

Street prostitutes, whether involved with drugs or not, also live in the shadow of violence and rape to a greater extent than others. Escorts are also at risk, and even parlour workers have been threatened and attacked. Across the states of Australia, legislation varies such that in Perth and usually in Western Australia more generally only controlled brothels are tolerated, whereas in Queensland a recent law change means that only prostitutes who work independently are allowed to operate, which led to a spate of violent attacks on lone sex workers on escort assignments in Brisbane and on the Gold Coast (Perkins 1994, p. 149). This situation is not helped by the penalties which the law imposes on perpetrators, as the rape of a prostitute has frequently been treated with less severity than the theft of a product in Australia. In 1991, the Supreme Court of Victoria upheld a ruling by Judge Jones in the Victorian County Court that a prostitute, as a result of her work, would be less psychologically damaged by sexual assault than a 'chaste' woman, and used this to justify the imposition of a light sentence for the rape of a prostitute

(Scutt 1994). The consequent need to be constantly aware of personal safety issues leads some women to be vehemently anti-drugs:

> Because if you're putting it across to the punters that you're a timorous wee thing, they're gonna treat you like a mug, they will and I think that's the trouble. I don't get much hassle because they can see that I'm straight. I'm compos mentis all the time and that and very matter of fact about it, you know, I don't mess about. (cited in McKeganey and Barnard 1996, p. 33)

Thus the use of drugs by prostitutes is complex—whereas many may turn to soft drugs in particular as a way of tolerating the rigours of selling sex for money, they also recognize that this is not without its attendant difficulties. In particular, it may be the case that drug use renders the individual worker less able to take care of herself in an environment where there is very little legislative protection of prostitutes. Having judgement unimpaired by substance abuse is critical for the assessment and selection of clients and also, in B&D (bondage and domination) sessions in particular, for the assessment of where and when client 'breaking point' is likely to occur, in terms of flagellation etc. becoming too intense (see, for example, Martine's account, cited in Perkins 1994, p. 171). However, this increased effectiveness in terms of (a) being able to judge how far it is advisable to 'go' with clients and/or (b) being better able to sequentially manage encounters is mitigated against by the advantages drug use gives in overcoming long periods of inactivity during the day or through the night. In this sense, managing time as a prostitute can be compared to managing time in other occupations where boredom is a problem and psychological survival is a paramount concern (Brewis and Linstead 1998; Burawoy 1979; Collinson 1988; Roy 1960; Willis 1977).

FILLING THE EMPTINESS OF THE DAY

The demands of the sexual encounter may in fact comprise only a small proportion of the prostitute's working day. Where the encounter may be unpredictable, potentially frightening and risky, extensive 'downtime' waiting for clients between encounters may prove extremely tedious, and requires other strategies for its management. O'Connell Davidson points out that Desiree (the self-employed prostitute upon whom her research is based):

> has days when only one or two men turn up . . . A great deal of her time is spent sitting or pacing around in a state of restless boredom. She can chat to the receptionist, drink cups of coffee, endlessly reapply her make up, but she must keep herself psychically prepared for work and cannot settle to anything else, as a punter might knock on the door at any moment. (O'Connell Davidson 1993, p. 3)

Desiree's boredom is created in the main by the regularity with which the punters fail to turn up for scheduled appointments—and is made all the more difficult to cope with, as O'Connell Davidson suggests, by unpredictability. Desiree is never sure whether her clients will appear (unless they are regulars, whom she tries to cultivate). She therefore must remain on guard for their arrival. She frequently makes appointments with more than one punter for the same time of day, assuming that none or only one will arrive. Hence her boredom is not precisely equivalent to the boredom experienced by the unskilled manual worker. Desiree can never totally switch off and daydream; her occupation falls into the stressful category of boring, yet demanding of full attention always (Brewis and Linstead 1998).

Time spent with clients may also hang heavily, especially if the client is one that the prostitute is frightened of (Brewis and Linstead 1998). We can see this in the case of dominatrix prostitute Mandy Kavanagh and Alistair, one of her regular clients:

> time never flew when Mandy was with Alistair. Instead, the minutes between three and four dragged, as if they made up a day rather than an hour . . . [also] the hours preceding and following his every visit left their own trail of slime down her day. She had learnt the long way that this slippery feel of dirt did not become easier to bear with repetition. (McRae 1992, pp. 13–14)

Many of the women who held the lowest opinion of the clients in McKeganey and Barnard's (1996) research were, in fact, the ones who were working to finance a drug habit, and presumably felt they had little choice regarding what they did and for whom they worked. This view is not homogeneous, and the researchers also report that there was a full range of views of the clients held by their population of workers. But, given that prostitution may by turns be boring, terrifying, unpredictable, disgusting and risky in potentially equal measure, how do those who labour as prostitutes make it through the working day psychologically speaking *without* resorting to the use of drugs? In the next section we consider some of their strategies for psychological survival.

MAINTAINING THE MASK: TEMPORAL BOUNDARIES

One of the most important techniques in framing the sexual encounter is the ability to generate categories in order to define it. Browne and Minichiello (1995), in a study of male sex workers in Melbourne, identify several categories which parallel reported accounts from females in the industry, yet are expressed more systematically. Their approach is interactionist, starting with the assumption that each individual, whether client or prostitute: 'brings their own unique life experiences, values and beliefs, needs and expectations, images of [him]self and the other, past sexual experiences, and knowledge of sexual skills and safe sex strategies to the encounter' (Browne and Minichiello 1995, p. 602). Each is challenged and may be changed in the interaction with the other in the dyad—thus self-identity is always potentially at risk and needs to be enacted (see also Chapkis 1997, pp. 211–12). The meaning of the sex act is especially important here; male prostitutes differentiate between *relational sex,* which is reserved for partners and 'being in love' (which female sex workers also display); *work sex,* which is purely physical and uninvolved, and may involve making the client feel wanted (also a category for female sex workers); and *recreational sex,* where the worker, not working, needs to be wanted for themselves, although this is relatively impersonal. Female sex workers do not appear to report this last category as frequently as males, which may be a result of different lifestyles, many of these women being single parents, whereas many male prostitutes only work part-time, having other employment commitments.

How, then, do prostitutes manage to engage in 'work sex' on a daily basis? O'Neill's (1996, p. 23) respondents indicate the particular importance of controlling time in the client encounter. These women claim that the average time spent with a client is seven minutes—and it is interesting that they are mainly street, or ex-street, prostitutes. In these accounts of sex work, so that sex bought on the street can perhaps be seen as a straightforward commercial transaction which is to be completed as quickly as possible—the literal 'turning' of a 'trick'. A prostitute such as Desiree's higher priced services, on the other hand, must be delivered with more care. Here the street prostitute is perhaps better off than the women who work from their own home or from a parlour/brothel (Brewis and Linstead 1998).

O'Neill also repeats a story told to her by Mary which further suggests that sex workers may want to end a client session quickly:

> one time I remember doing a double with Sam and I was mouthing 'fucking hurry up' . . . she was in hysterics . . . and then I went into my 'YES . . . YESS . . . YESSS' and when he came I shouted 'EUREKA' . . . she nearly pissed herself with laughter. (Mary, cited in O'Neill 1996, p. 23)

This story echoes similar anecdotes told by Desiree about using techniques to get clients to orgasm quickly (such as using her pelvic floor muscles to literally 'milk' a man)—here Mary theatrically fakes her own orgasm to encourage the client's. Her success, however, also reveals the fragile control that the worker has over the length of an encounter—that she reduced Sam to laughter by her act implies how easy it is for the prostitute to, as Goffman (1971) puts it, make a mess of role in making it obvious to the client how disinterested they are in the sex. In a similar vein, Inga (cited in Cockington and Marlin 1995, p. 179) tells her story of how hard she has to work to keep up the façade. She suggests that she has to be surreptitious in looking at her watch during an encounter to see how long she has been with a client: '[b]ecause it's high class it would be the wrong thing to do. You know when your time's up. Then you get buzzed and you check your watch [openly]' (see also Brewis and Linstead 1998).

Another device which enables prostitutes to erect a psychological barrier between themselves and the client is the condom, and the generally non-negotiable nature of safe sex. In one of the authors' own research, in Port Kembla, Sydney and Wollongong, only one worker, a more mature parlour worker, claimed to offer unprotected sex to selected clients at her discretion; one street worker offered unprotected oral sex, again at her discretion, but not penetration. All other workers were fastidious, especially the parlour workers, and one younger street worker insisted that she always used two condoms. In contrast, there is widely reported evidence that drug users may offer unprotected sex and that many clients still demand it. However, the incidence of HIV positive prostitutes in Australia and the UK (and, incidentally, in the US) seems generally to be related to the sharing of needles by injectors rather than unsafe sexual activity, although the relationship is complex and variable, both within localities and globally.[6] Nonetheless, not one case of HIV seropositivity has been demonstrated to be the result of commercial sex in Australia, and the numbers of the population of sex workers who are HIV positive is relatively small (Harcourt 1994, pp. 205–13; Sharp 1994, pp. 228–35).

Both male and female prostitutes also have a series of strategies for establishing the psychological context of the encounter, involving self-programming; running through preparatory routines through which the role-playing becomes automatic; and sussing out the client which involves both attracting them, and figuring out what they want and are likely to need (Browne and Minichiello 1995, pp. 612–13; Goodley 1994, pp. 127–8; McKeganey and Barnard 1996, p. 34). This also entails a reading of body language to anticipate potential problems, a skill which extends into the encounter. The workers also have a range of internal dialogues which operate either to keep them detached or aroused as the need may arise, to take their minds off unpleasant things, and to help them to leave the work behind when necessary.

PUBLIC AND PRIVATE SPACE

The techniques described above, which help the prostitute to retain control over their labour process, are focused on maintaining the boundaries between 'private' and 'public' space, between work and non-work. This, it would appear, is due to what O'Connell Davidson (1994; 1996) calls the 'liminal' status of the prostitute—the fact that they are selling something which has not been *fully* commodified and which is usually associated with the non-commercial private sphere, governed as it is by values of intimacy, love and affect. This liminality arguably means that the *place* where prostitution happens, whether actual geographical location, part of the body or symbolic location (in terms of its positioning in the prostitute's psyche), is also crucial to the prostitute's sense of self, to their self-esteem. One might even suggest that the successful management of place marks female prostitutes out to themselves (and perhaps to others) as not being stereotypical fallen women.

This stereotype, as O'Neill (1996, pp. 4–5) makes clear, has existed from the earliest years of written language. She describes the Epic of Gilgamesh, a Babylonian poem dating from 1700 BC, as telling of a 'harlot' who 'made her breast bare, uncovered her nakedness and welcomed his eagerness' (Kishtainy, cited in O'Neill 1996, p. 5). The 'harlot', in so doing, enticed away a man who was living among animals to a new and civilized existence in the city. This image of the prostitute as enjoying her work, revelling in her lusts and desires, became particularly powerful with the advent of Christianity. For example, as O'Neill (1996, p. 6, citing Mazo Karras's work) points out, even though medieval commentators reluctantly accepted that prostitutes were necessary to satisfy men's sexual drives, they did not extend this rather strained tolerance to the prostitute herself.[7] Lust here was identified as entirely a woman's sin, and the prostitute as the worst exemplar of lust. The contemporary female prostitute, then, may be rejecting this enduring image of herself as morally destitute, as a sex-crazed harlot striving to satisfy her lusts by selling herself for money, by drawing a line between her private and working life, and in particular between her private sex life and the sex that she has for money. Part of this process is to locate these different kinds of sex in different geographical, bodily and symbolic contexts.

For example, Desiree, as reported by O'Connell Davidson (1994; 1995; 1996; O'Connell Davidson and Layder 1994), has decorated the house from which she works entirely in pink and grey. The working areas are also described as extremely neat and tidy, to the point of seeming sterile and impersonal—O'Connell Davidson says they have the feel of a 'fashionable private dentist's surgery' (O'Connell Davidson 1996, p. 183). O'Connell Davidson has also stated at conferences that Desiree uses separate linen and towels for her customers than she does in her actual living quarters. All of the above attempts to manage geographical place seem to underline her desire to clearly demarcate her life into work and non-work. Furthermore, not only does Desiree seek to maintain a professional image in the way she decorates her work environment, she also follows strict guidelines as to what she is willing to actually do for clients. She will not, as we may expect, perform acts which she believes are potentially damaging to her health, such as anal penetration, or vaginal penetration without a condom, but, further: 'she will not agree to practices which she personally finds too repulsive (like giving enemas), too intimate (like kissing) or too hostile (like ejaculating in her face)' (O'Connell Davidson 1995, p. 6). Hence Desiree has developed a code as to which areas of her body she is prepared to allow her clients access, and which are off limits, so as to protect her sense of herself as a professional prostitute, as selling sex *for money alone* in her working life. Kissing, for example, is rejected because it is too similar to the kind of behaviour in which one would engage with a non-commercial sexual partner; it smacks too much of genuine desire and love for the other person (also see McKeganey and Barnard 1996; O'Neill 1996; Salvadori 1997).[8] Other activities indicated by prostitutes which fall into this category of management of the body as place include using condoms with clients but not with partners, faking penetrative sex ('trick sex' between the well lubricated upper thighs) or faking oral sex using the hand.

Furthermore, the irrelevance of Desiree's personal feelings about clients—her not selecting/rejecting clients on the basis of any attraction to or repulsion from them (O'Connell Davidson 1994, p. 16; 1996, pp. 191–2)—while first ensuring that she is able to make a good living from prostitution, also ensures that she is not 'merely indulging a personal taste for anonymous sexual encounters involving the exchange of cash' (O'Connell Davidson 1996, p. 193). Her acceptance of any kind of client, as long as they will play by her rules, can therefore be seen also to function as part of her attempt to keep work and non-work distinct. This management of the symbolic location of commercial sex as reported by other workers may also include treating clients very differently from non-commercial sexual partners (for example, using a pseudonym with and never disclosing personal information to clients). Some respondents report stealing from difficult clients, or taking their money and then refusing to service them on the grounds, for example, of having begun to menstruate.

For these women, then, their 'real' selves are located outside of work, removed from encounters with clients (O'Neill 1996, p. 23)—and it is their distancing practices which allow them to maintain this self-image as working in prostitution only for the economic rewards which it offers (to which O'Connell Davidson (1995, p. 7) refers as the 'dull economic compulsion' of prostitution). Interestingly, the function of the distancing practices described above is reminiscent of that of the humour employed by the male manual workers studied by Collinson (1988), which consisted of constant references to their own sexual capacities or to their role as family bread-winner and head of household. This humour, Collinson argues, points to a need on the part of these men to prove themselves to be something more than shopfloor employees working for low wages in a tightly controlled and alienating work environment. The use of humour as a method of identity management is also evident among prostitutes—for example, Sam and Mary telling O'Neill that they wind their clients up to 'get one over on them' (O'Neill 1996, p. 22). Here these women use humour seemingly to emphasize to punters that they are not simply pieces of sexual meat; that their intelligence and sarcasm are very much part of who they are.

THE SOCIAL AND POLITICIZED BODY

In the same vein, prostitutes may also emphasize the multi-faceted nature of their lives in, it might be

argued, an effort to compartmentalize their work—to lock it into a specific and tightly bounded place in their identities. For example, O'Neill (1996, p. 22) reports that Sam and Mary:

> talked about the many different roles they play, mothers, their lives in the black community; visiting their own families, working class employed and extended families; and going out with clients 'dressed up to the nines' and then doing 'feminism' by supporting other women working as prostitutes.

O'Neill also recounts the activities of feminist prostitutes at the First European Whores Congress, in 1991 (see Leigh 1994), as well as an interesting anecdote from Moira, who argues: 'Who better to educate the clients but the prostitute?' (cited in O'Neill 1996, p. 21). Here Moira tells O'Neill of a client who wanted to have oral sex without a condom—she refused and told him that the other girls in her area would do the same. In the end the client returned to her—some two hours later—and agreed to her terms. Moira says that she made sure that 'everybody' heard her when she insisted that he use a condom—implying that her work is not just about satisfying the pent-up sexual desires of lonely or frustrated men, but is also a matter of social responsibility. She therefore lends herself legitimacy by characterizing her work as potentially educational, at least in part. The self-description of Kinky Miss Whiplash (Sara Dale, the woman who sold sex from former Chancellor Norman Lamont's London home) as a 'sex therapist' might also be seen as evidence of this attitude on the part of prostitutes. She (cited in McRae 1992, p. 110) states emphatically that, although being labelled as a prostitute by the media is hurtful, she still believes that her work is 'healing'.

Further to this issue of prostitution happening in a symbolic place in the individual prostitute's psyche, prostitutes may also demand that they are granted the same rights as others both in performing the work that they do and in other walks of life.[9] One could argue that, in doing this, they are rejecting society's attempts to label their selling of sexual services as their 'master status' (Becker 1973)—refusing to accept that prostitution must by definition assume the most significant place in their lives. Thus prostitutes may claim that they should enjoy the same degree of, for example, police protection as the rest of the working population. As Sara, cited by Webb and Elms (1994, p. 275), says:

> Whether you're a worker or not, whether it's an older worker or a new one, you have the right to go to the police, just like any other male or female in this world whether you are a prostitute or not. It's not fair the way a lot of girls get treated like dirt. They get pushed over. They are not there to be used and abused. They are there to do a job.

In a similar vein, Leigh refers angrily to the perception that a prostitute cannot really be raped—that, by commercially offering their bodies for others to use, they disbar themselves from any claim that they have been forced to have sex against their will. This follows an account of her work at a massage parlour, which resulted in her being raped at knifepoint by two men who had forced their way inside the premises. As she argues, her rape was traumatic because she feared she was going to be killed or seriously hurt—not because she didn't get paid for sex in this particular instance (Leigh 1994, pp. 247–9).

THE CLIENT BODY: TYPOLOGIES

It seems, then, that prostitutes may rely on a variety of distancing techniques, including the management of time and place, to secure their sense of themselves as only offering sex to punters *for money.* However, different logics with regard to the need to maintain strict boundaries between self and the commercial sex act may be applied with different types of client; again, these appear very similar for prostitutes of both sexes. Browne and Minichiello (1995) report that the service provided depends on the categorization by the worker of the client into type, for example, *marrieds,* looking for something their wives can't give them, and tending to expect discretion and very little beyond the act of sex itself; or *easy trade,* who are clean, gentlemanly, come quickly or only want non-penetrative sex, pay and go. *Undesirables* are those the workers would prefer not to service, including violent, dirty or obese types, and those who try to break the safe sex rules of the encounter. Distancing, therefore, is arguably more necessary with undesirables than it is with marrieds or easy trade clients.

These categories of punter also, for both male and female sex workers, include *romantics:*

> It's worse when you get a client who actually falls in love with you, which is really hard. The Golden Rule of the sex industry is don't fall in love with a client . . . it's just too hard emotionally . . . They always want you to get out of the industry and it just makes it too hard. (cited in Browne and Minichiello, 1995, p. 609)
>
> Oh I hate that, really that is ma hate, when they try and get all lovey dovey. I mean any guy that tries to get lovey dovey with a prostitute is off his head . . . I mean I've had one guy in a big fight . . . I stopped having him because it was just a nightmare, he was going 'I love you, I love making love to you . . . 'you don't fall in love with prostitutes and this guy was, I mean, I broke this guy's heart. (cited in McKeganey and Barnard 1996, pp. 89–90)

Sugar daddies may also turn out to be more trouble than they are worth, being so much older than the workers that they have little in common with them, and often proving unreliable financially. *Heaven trade* (clients whom the worker finds irresistibly attractive) may also prove difficult, as prostitutes here may be tempted to cross the barrier between work and personal life, or even allow unsafe sex. One way they guard against this temptation is to remember that:

> It's never going to happen because the clients see you as a worker. That is all you are to them. They don't want to make a boy [/girl] friend out of a worker. (cited in Browne and Minichiello 1995, p. 611)

As the above suggests, it is therefore problematic to claim that every prostitute will necessarily seek to establish a strict boundary between work and non-work with every client—encounters are influenced not least by the category in which the prostitute places individual punters. However, even when the desire to differentiate is clear, the dividing line between work sex and relational sex is always permeable.

WORK VERSUS LEISURE IN PROSTITUTION

As we have argued, maintaining the mask that preserves self-identity is not necessarily an easy matter for sex workers. O'Neill's Jane states quite explicitly that a prostitute's life becomes part of her work, rather than the other way around, because of the demands of 'being used' by others for money. Mary, also cited by O'Neill (1996, p. 19), suggests a similar problem in separating work from non-work. She implies that a prostitute is never strictly speaking off duty, because everything is subsumed by the need to make money; and she also suggests that a prostitute may end up working even if they are officially 'resting' because of this:

> You give everything of your life into prostitution...that is all that is around you all the time ... on [the] street the car stops 'are you doing business?' you tell them the price ... with a durex and you get in and go ...

The constant demands of working as a prostitute are also evident in Jane's comment that it is difficult for her and other women to tell others what they do for a living—and that, as a result, prostitution results in a 'closed circuit' (O'Neill 1996, p. 21) where one's co-workers (i.e. prostitutes) also become the friends with whom one socializes. One's world therefore becomes tightly circumscribed by one's occupation. There are echoes of this in O'Connell Davidson's (1994, p. 17) account of how Desiree: 'has very little contact with her family, who do not know what she does for a living, no social life outside her business and requires constant emotional support and reassurance from her receptionists'. Inga (cited in Cockington and Marlin 1995, p. 172) adds that prostitutes are her only friends, and that she actually tends to avoid socializing more widely because of questions about what she does for a living.

The way in which prostitution can spill over into one's non-work life is, to some extent, reflected in the blurring of work and non-work lines in another socially undesirable occupation—that of the slaughterman (Ackroyd and Crowdy 1990). Here, however, the work conducted in the abattoir becomes very important to these men in defining their overall social identity—they make little or no effort to disguise or compartmentalize what they do for a living, indeed their display of pride in the stigmatized elements of the occupation is an important part of their collective

identity work. This tactic is adopted by prostitutes as well—for example, by activists like Annie Sprinkle, or Carol Leigh, who is emphatic that she is proud to be a prostitute—but one could suggest that the bourgeois consciousness finds it easier to publicly accept the necessity of killing animals for sustenance than it does the open hiring of women's bodies for pleasure.

It is also true that the spillover of work into personal life is perhaps most evident in the prostitute's own sex life. The section which follows outlines the specific difficulties which may be encountered by an individual who sells sex for money in their intimate relationships, but also, and importantly, acknowledges evidence that suggests that some prostitutes actually derive pleasure from the work that they do.

HAVING FUN AND MANAGING FEELINGS

Perhaps the most evocative evidence of the distance that many prostitutes attempt to put between themselves and the work that they do is that female prostitutes in particular may engage in sex only with other women in their personal lives. Thus sex with men does not intrude into their identities as sexual beings—it belongs to their working identities only. A recent interview with four very young prostitutes (ranging from the age of 16 to their early 20s), working in the North of England, revealed that two of the women had become sexually involved with each other as a direct result of their work (source unknown). The group had all entered the sex industry because of a lack of real alternatives for supporting themselves financially—they reported disadvantaged home lives and educational underachievement, to say nothing of the depressed labour market in their locale. Thus, while the girls had all become prostitutes of their own volition, it is questionable as to how far this was a *free choice*—as suggested by Chapkis's (1997—see note 2) analysis of 'consensual' prostitution. Probably as a consequence of the circumstances of their entry into prostitution, the girls found their work disgusting and degrading, and harboured feelings of contempt for their male clients. This contempt had spilled over into the private lives of two of these girls so that they found it impossible to derive real pleasure from sleeping with men even on a non-commercial basis. It appeared therefore that they had sought 'sexual solace' in becoming lesbians, even though both had heterosexual 'pasts'.

As suggested above in the discussion of the maintenance of the divide between personal and professional space, this distancing of 'real desires' from 'work' can be very difficult—the emotional labour required to work as a prostitute may mean that one's sexual activities even outside of the commercial realm are distinguished by a certain 'coldness':

> You need to learn to separate and that it isn't just your body being used . . . you come home from work and your man wants to be kept happy and you've been at work all day pretending and you can't be bothered and sometimes you have to pretend with your man. (Jane, cited in O'Neill 1996, p. 20)

Jackie, interviewed by McRae, says that she actually never feels like sex with her partner Tyrone when she comes home after work: 'there's no chance of a sex-life then—I'm fucked, forty times over . . . I miss it sometimes, you know, fucking for love, fucking 'cos it's what *I want* . . .' (Jackie, cited in McRae 1992, p. 146—emphasis in the original). Inga similarly reports that her work places pressure on her relationship with her partner Steve. She says that he is jealous of her male clients, even though for her sex with them is 'just a job', and that it is often difficult for her to have sex with Steve because her prostitution means that she transfers her feelings of hatred for her male clients to him, and/or that she, like Jackie, frequently is so tired that all she wants from him is a 'cuddle' (cited in Cockington and Marlin 1995, p. 186). Sheena claims that she copes with the difference between punters and intimates by 'switching off' the 'wee switch I've got in ma head' (cited in McKeganey and Barnard 1996, p. 84). Others manage rituals of separation before they leave for work and, after returning, change clothes, bathe or shower, sit quietly and shed their assumed identity; yet even so they have difficulty coping with what they have done. For some even drugs are no help:

> It doesnae matter how much you take or what you take, you've still got to wake up in the morning and go 'I done that, I went out and done that'. Nothing's

going to stop you waking up next day and knowing what you done last night. (cited in McKeganey and Barnard 1996, p. 92)

Nevertheless the importance of the symbolic location of affective and erotic feelings in prostitution is complicated by evidence that some prostitutes enjoy their work and derive sexual pleasure from it. McKeganey and Barnard (1996, p. 86) were told of the content of a discussion between two of the girls on the subject:

> she says to me, 'Do you ever enjoy it when you go wi' a punter?' I says 'No!' And I went 'I hate them,' and she went 'Oh I do.' I says, 'How do you?' an' she says 'Like do you ever come when you're wi' a punter?' 'cos she does all the time.

Greta is another example: 'she practised prostitution which was not so much "post-Big Bang modernism" than [*sic*] "pre-Crash revelry", the Wall Street Crash of 1929 . . . For Greta, pleasure and prostitution were not mutually exclusive entities' (McRae 1992, pp. 254–5). Greta, by McRae's account, likes to insist that her clients have a drink and chat before sex and reacts in disgust to his stories of other prostitutes specializing in sadism-masochism, because she cannot see where the pleasure might lie in such activities.[10] Her management of place and time demonstrates how different Greta is from, say, Desiree, who places a great deal of emphasis on a quick turnaround of clients in a sterile and business-like environment.[11] It is a quirk of Greta's that McRae himself notes. However, what is perhaps particularly interesting about Greta is that she is a post-operative transsexual who sets much store by her surgically acquired femininity. Brewis, Hampton and Linstead (1997) suggest that the transsexual is frequently driven by a sensed biological imperative to physically become the other sex. Their activities often therefore reinforce the discursive rigidity of the gender divide—by surgical alteration of their bodies, they seek to become another sex and thereby another gender. A confirmed and stable gender identity, then, is crucial to the psychological health of many transsexuals—one could therefore argue that Greta enjoys her work for the pleasure it affords *because* this fits her image of what a woman should be like.

Nonetheless, as suggested in the McKeganey and Barnard research cited above, there is also evidence from non-transsexual prostitutes that real desire and real love might be present within the prostitute-client encounter, not least two members of the profession interviewed by one of the authors here (see also Brewis and Linstead 1998). Katrina said that she worked as a prostitute because she enjoyed it and that most of the clients were really very nice. She enjoyed the sex, having orgasms, dressing up, 'developing new talents', and the conversation. Taylor liked all her regulars; indeed, she had dated one and was falling in love with him. Further, high class Melbourne brothel worker Kelly said, in response to a question, from interviewer Tottie Goldsmith on the Australian Channel 10 TV programme *Sex/Life* as to whether she ever gets bored at work:

> Ohhh . . . [laughs] . . . I'd be lying if I said yes . . . honestly . . . I sort of like . . . in my bookings . . . I sort of like to put my whole effort into it . . . but there is days when you think to yourself . . . oh God, do I really have to do this? . . .
>
> . . . *Do you ever orgasm when you're having sex with clients?*
>
> Oh yes . . . [emphatically]
>
> *How many a day?*
>
> It can depend on the clientele that come in . . . if you get someone that you really get into it with you can actually really [nods head emphatically] enjoy it.

CONCLUSION

This paper has sought to contribute to the existing research on prostitution by offering an overview of qualitative research into and accounts of female prostitution in the UK and Australia, two contexts selected for their relative cultural commensurability. This comparative review of the data, an approach which has not been undertaken in previous work, has enabled discussion of the management of identity by prostitutes in the locations mentioned, given that the consumption of their bodies in the process of commercial sex can be seen to place pressure on their sense of themselves both professionally and personally. The discussion has established, through this comparison of data from different locations, that while there is a degree of similarity between the tactics and approaches employed by prostitutes in terms of maintaining the professional mask and distancing their work from their personal

lives, there are also significant differences depending on individual circumstances and, moreover, a need for caution given that prostitutes do not necessarily, in every encounter, want or need to maintain these strict divides. Moreover, it is clear from our review of the literature that the boundary between work sex and relational sex is not easy to maintain, even for those workers who labour in this regard.

The management of identity in prostitution, then, while frequently pointing to a seeming need on the part of the prostitute to maintain boundaries between their commercial and non-commercial sexual activities, cannot be said to be uniform—it has like all social constructions, to be accomplished and is done so through a variety of means. Control and enjoyment are two contrasting aspects of this everyday accomplishment, and the patterns and tensions which emerge between them vary according to time, place, mood and the interactants. Prostitutes, on the one hand, may need to try to fill their day with some kind of meaningful activity between business encounters, yet when they are within the encounter itself they may also need to empty it of significance and meaning. Similarly, on re-entering their normal everyday lives, sex workers often report needing to almost ritually shed the events of the working day/night, to empty themselves of the personae they assumed to get them through their shift. The varying ways in which prostitutes understand the work that they do, and in which they seek to represent this to themselves and to others, point to the variety of different discourses of prostitution, sex and sexuality through which participants in the sex industry define themselves and their clients. There has already been an indication in this paper that there are many discourses of prostitution, sex and sexuality in existence in late modernity. In our second paper, this issue will be expanded because it is, as suggested above, through the more or less powerful operations of these various discourses that individual prostitutes strive to make sense of the work that they do, and re-construct the selves who do it.

NOTES

1. We discuss the issue of the construction/consolidation of the client's identity through their consumption of the prostitute('s services) in another paper (see Brewis and Linstead 1998).

2. The extent to which 'free choice' is a useful concept in the discussion of prostitution is discussed by Chapkis (1997, pp. 51–3). Chapkis distinguishes between 'forced' prostitution (e.g trafficking, child prostitution) and 'consensual' prostitution but argues, nevertheless, that the lack of sound, realistic alternatives from which to choose often means that not all consensual prostitution is necessarily 'free' (she gives the example of migratory prostitution from Eastern Europe). Globally, women's choices are limited by their generally disadvantaged position 'within hierarchical structures of sex, race and class' and such inequality, coupled with 'extreme differences of wealth within and among nations, creates tremendous pressure on women to engage in any available form of employment, including sex work' (Chapkis 1997, p. 52). Whether and what choices exist for the prostitute therefore depend on a relation between self and context which may be complex and contradictory.

3. Much of the literature on prostitution tends to deploy the term automatically to denote female prostitution. While we are aware that male prostitution both exhibits similarities to and some very significant differences from female prostitution, there is not the space here to fully do justice to this gender dimension. Additionally, we set out in this paper to draw upon and synthesize themes emerging from available contemporary studies of prostitution in the UK and Australia, of which data on male prostitution form only a small part.

4. Race is another significant dimension of prostitution, and of the economic and identity choices available to prostitutes, which does not reduce to geographical location. Issues of trafficking, sex tourism, bartered brides and similar exploitation certainly involve race as a dimension, but in Western society simply being a member of a non-white ethnic group—even one which is culturally well established—changes the prostitute's situation. See Chapkis's (1997, pp. 207–9) interview with Gloria Lockett. However, space does not permit discussion of racialized differences between prostitutes in the locations which our data cover.

5. There are, however, many other discursive representations of the prostitute-client relationship, which place less emphasis on prostitution as a consumer industry and more on it as a political activity, as a strategy for survival, as an exemplar of patriarchal society and so on. So, while a prostitute who defines herself as a sex worker will define herself as labouring during the client encounter, and may impose strict demarcations between her work and her free time, it is possible that a prostitute who, say, defines herself as a political activist will not see herself as labouring in such a precise way. Thus the boundaries between work and leisure may be more or less blurred depending on the particular discursive representations through which prostitutes define themselves and their activities. A degree of such blurring is evident in the following passage, written by Carol Leigh (aka Scarlot Harlot), a prostitute who takes a highly politicized view of her work, describing herself as a 'rebel' and a 'famous slut':

> I'm not saying I loved the tricks or the work. It can be fun, especially if you like things like skydiving or hang gliding. But

what I liked was getting this insider's view, this secret story to tell. The silence of prostitutes became over-bearingly loud. (Leigh 1994, p. 246)

6. On the one hand, in the Centers for Disease Control and Prevention HIV/AIDS Surveillance Report, a mere 123 of 202,665 adult and adolescent males diagnosed with AIDS since 1981 suggested that the only risk factor to which they had been exposed was sex with a female prostitute. On the other, in Latin America, India and sub-Saharan Africa (with 20 million cases of HIV sero-positivity according to the World Health Organization), as many as 80% of prostitutes may be infected (Centers for Disease Control and Prevention 1994, pp. 7, 11, 17).

7. It is interesting here to note the durability of what Holloway (1989) refers to as the male sexual drive discourse.

8. This is not necessarily the practice nor the rationale adopted by other prostitutes—since AIDS, the caution has been to avoid kissing as research has been inconclusive as to whether saliva can spread HIV. While the intimacy argument certainly has some credibility in the prohibition of kissing, the safe sex argument is much more widespread. To some extent the intimacy argument has been mythologized, but it is unclear whether this is by the researchers or some of the prostitutes themselves. However, it is clear that other prostitutes as well as Desiree manage the physical terrain of their bodies as part of this 'labour of demarcation'.

9. Another part of this 'likening' strategy may be to point out that prostitutes do exactly what other women do, except that a prostitute at least charges, explicitly and upfront. Leigh (1994, p. 243) suggests that women who have sex with men to avoid being accused of frigidity, or to keep a relationship going, for example, are 'cheaper' than prostitutes. McIntosh (1994, p. 6) also points out that all heterosexual sex could be understood to be dangerous and exploitative to some degree, and therefore that prostitutes can be seen as more honest because at least they demand money for their sexual services.

10. Compare this to Mandy Kavanagh, who freely admits to deriving pleasure in her work only from beating or torturing her S/M client Alistair, because she loathes him so much and feels him to be utterly beyond redemption (McRae 1992, p. 15).

11. Greta's home, where she entertains clients, is described as 'a domain where it appeared that it was 1927 forevermore . . . with gramophones, Bix Beiderbecke records, cut-glass bowls, feather-boas, silk curtains and photographs of Lilian Gish, Louise Brooks, Scott and Zelda Fitzgerald, Noel Coward, Josephine Baker, Anna Akhmatova and the definitive Garbos' (McRae 1992, p. 255).

REFERENCES

Ackroyd, S. and Crowdy, P.A. (1990) Can culture be managed? Working with raw material: the case of the English slaughtermen. *Personnel Review*, 19,5, 3–13.

Becker, H. (1973) *Outsiders: Studies in the Sociology of Deviance*. New York: Free Press.

Brewis, J., Hampton, M.P. and Linstead, S. (1997) Unpacking Priscilla: subjectivity and identity in the organization of gendered appearance. *Human Relations,* 50,10, 1275–304.

Brewis, J. and Linstead, S. (in press) Time after time: the temporal organization of red-collar work. *Time and Society,* 7,2, 223–48.

Browne, J. and Minichiello, V. (1995) The social meanings behind male sex work: implications for sexual interactions. *British Journal of Sociology,* 46,4, 598–622.

Burawoy, M. (1979) *Manufacturing Consent: Changes in the Labour Process under Monopoly Capitalism.* Chicago: University of Chicago Press.

Centers for Disease Control and Prevention (1994) HIV/AIDS *Surveillance Report.* Vol. 5, No. 4, Atlanta: US Department of Health and Human Services.

Chapkis, W. (ed.) (1997) *Live Sex Acts: Women Performing Erotic Labour.* New York: Routledge.

Cockington, J. and Marlin, L. (1995) *Sex Inc: True Tales from the Australian Sex Industry.* Sydney: Ironbark Pan Macmillan.

Collinson, D.L. (1988) 'Engineering humour': masculinity, joking and conflict in shopfloor relations. *Organization Studies,* 9,2, 181–99.

Foucault, M. (1979) *The History of Sexuality, Volume 1: An Introduction.* London: Allen Lane.

Foucault, M. (1986) *The History of Sexuality, Volume 2: The Use of Pleasure.* Harmondsworth: Viking/Penguin.

Foucault, M. (1990) *The History of Sexuality, Volume 3: The Care of the Self.* Harmondsworth: Penguin.

Giddens, A. (1991) *Modernity and Self-Identity: Self and Society in the Late Modern Age.* Cambridge: Polity Press.

Giddens, A. (1992) *The Transformation of Intimacy: Sexuality, Love and Eroticism in Modern Societies.* Cambridge: Polity Press.

Goffman, E. (1971) *The Presentation of Self in Everyday Life.* Harmondsworth: Penguin.

Goodley, S. (1994) A male sex worker's view. In Perkins, R., Prestage, G., Sharp, R. and Lovejoy, F. (eds) *Sex Work and Sex Workers in Australia.* Sydney: UNSW Press, 126–31.

Harcourt, C. (1994) Prostitution and public health in the era of AIDS. In Perkins, R., Prestage, G., Sharp, G. and Lovejoy, F. (eds) *Sex Work and Sex Workers in Australia.* Sydney: UNSW Press, 203–4.

Hawkes, G. (1996) *A Sociology of Sex and Sexuality.* London: Open University Press.

Hollway, W. (1989) *Subjectivity and Method in Psychology: Gender, Meaning and Science.* London: Sage.

Höpfl, H.J. and Linstead, S.A. (1993) Passion and performance: suffering and the carrying of organizational roles. In Fineman, S. (ed.) *Emotion in Organizations.* London: Sage, 76–93.

Leigh, C. [Scarlot Harlot] (1994) Thanks Ma. In Sappington, R.

and Stallings, T. (eds) *Uncontrollable Bodies: Testimonies of Identity and Culture.* Seattle: Bay Press, 243–61.

McIntosh, M. (1994) *The Feminist Debate on Prostitution.* Paper presented to the British Sociological Association Annual Conference, Preston, March.

McKeganey, N. and Barnard, M. (1996) *Sex Work on the Streets: Prostitutes and Their Clients.* Buckingham: Open University Press.

McRae, D. (1992) *Nothing Personal: The Business of Sex.* Edinburgh: Mainstream.

O'Connell Davidson, J. (1994) *On Power, Prostitution and Pilchards: The Self-Employed Prostitute and Her Clients.* Paper presented to the 12th Annual Labour Process Conference, Birmingham, March.

O'Connell Davidson, J. (1995) The anatomy of 'free choice' prostitution. *Gender, Work and Organization,* 2,1, 1–10.

O'Connell Davidson, J. (1996) Prostitution and the contours of control. In Weeks, J. and Holland, J. (eds) *Sexual Cultures: Communities, Values and Intimacy.* British Sociological Association Explorations in Sociology, 48, London: Macmillan, 180–98.

O'Connell Davidson, J. and Layder, D. (1994) *Methods, Sex and Madness.* London: Routledge.

O'Neill, M. (1996) *The Aestheticization of the Whore in Contemporary Society: Desire, The Body, Self and Society.* Paper presented to the Body and Organization Workshop, Keele, September.

Perkins, R. (1994) Female prostitution. In Perkins, R., Prestage, G., Sharp, R. and Lovejoy, F. (eds) *Sex Work and Sex Workers in Australia.* Sydney: UNSW Press, 143–73.

Roach, J.R. (1985) *The Player's Passion: Studies in the Science of Acting.* Newark: University of Delaware Press.

Roy, D.F. (1960) Banana time: job satisfaction and informal interaction. *Human Organization,* 18, 158–68.

Salvadori, H. (1997) UK report: my life in a London brothel. *Marie Claire,* October, 116–22.

Scutt, J. (1994) Judicial vision—rape, prostitution and the chaste woman. *Women's Studies International Forum,* 17, 345–56.

Sharp, R. (1994) Female sex work and injecting drug use: what more do we need to know? In Perkins, R., Prestage, G., Sharp, R. and Lovejoy, F. (eds) *Sex Work and Sex Workers in Australia.* Sydney: UNSW Press, 225–36.

Thompson, P. and McHugh, D. (1995) *Work Organizations: A Critical Introduction.* Basingstoke: Macmillan Business.

Webb, L. and Elms, J. (1994) Social workers and sex workers. In Perkins, R., Prestage, G., Sharp, R. and Lovejoy, F. (eds) *Sex Work and Sex Workers in Australia.* Sydney: UNSW Press, 271–8.

Willis, P. (1977) *Learning to Labour: How Working Class Kids Get Working Class Jobs.* Farnborough, Sussex: Saxon House.

7.4 FANTASY ISLANDS
Exploring the Demand for Sex Tourism

Julia O'Connell Davidson and Jacqueline Sanchez Taylor

In a useful review of prostitution cross-culturally and historically, Laurie Shrage observes that "one thing that stands out but stands unexplained is that a large percentage of sex customers seek (or sought) sex workers whose racial, national, or class identities are (or were) different from their own" (1994:142). She goes on to suggest that the demand for African, Asian, and Latin American prostitutes by white Western men may "be explained in part by culturally produced racial fantasies regarding the sexuality of these women" and that these fantasies may be related to "socially formed perceptions regarding the sexual and moral purity of white women" (1994:48–50). Kempadoo also draws attention to the "over-representation of women of different nationalities and ethnicities, and the hierarchies of race and color within the [international sex] trade" and observes, "That sex industries today depend upon the eroticization of the ethnic and cultural Other suggests we are witnessing a contemporary form of exoticism which sustains post-colonial and post-cold war relations of power and dominance" (1995:75–6).

This chapter represents an attempt to build on such insights. Drawing on our research with both male and female Western heterosexual sex tourists in the Caribbean,[1] it argues that their sexual taste for "Others" reflects not so much a wish to engage in any specific sexual practice as a desire for an extraordinarily high degree of control over the management of self and others as sexual, racialized and engendered beings. This desire, and the Western sex tourist's power to satiate it, can only be explained through reference to power relations and popular discourses that are simultaneously gendered, racialized and economic.

WHITE WESTERN MEN'S SEX TOURISM

Empirical research on sex tourism to Southeast Asia has fairly consistently produced a portrait of Western male heterosexual sex tourists as men whose desire for the Other is the flip side of dissatisfaction with white Western women, including white Western prostitute women. Lee, for example, explores the demand for sex tourism as a quest for racially fantasized male power, arguing that this is at least in part a backlash against the women's movement in the West: "With an increasingly active global feminist movement, male-controlled sexuality (or female passivity) appears to be an increasingly scarce resource. The travel advertisements are quite explicit about what is for sale: docility and submission" (1991:90; see also Jeffreys 1997). Western sex tourists' fantasies of "docile" and "willing" Asian women are accompanied, as Kruhse-Mount Burton notes, by "a desexualization of white women . . . who are deemed to be spoiled, grasping and, above all, unwilling or inferior sexual partners" (1995:196). These characteristics are also attributed to white prostitute women. The sex tourists interviewed by Seabrook compared Thai prostitutes "very favorably with the more mechanistic and functional behavior of most Western sex workers" (1996:3). Kruhse-Mount Burton states that where many Australian participants in sex holidays criticized prostitutes in Australia "for being emotionally and sexually cold and for making little effort to please, or to disguise the commercial nature of the interaction," they stressed "the warmth, affection, femininity, youth and beauty of Asian prostitutes, combined with an aptitude for disguising the mercenary aspect of the arrangement" (1995:193–4).

Our own interview work suggests that Western male heterosexual sex tourists to the Caribbean typically share these attitudes and beliefs—a finding that is unsurprising given that many have also been prostitute users in Southeast Asia, either as tourists or as members of the armed forces. They often believe that Western women enjoy excessive powers in relation to men. The following extract from an interview with an American sex tourist and an American expatriate in the Dominican Republic in 1998 illustrates just how bitter such men can be about Western women's (perceived) encroachment on men's territory and traditional authority:

EXPATRIATE   I pay $1,100 child support a month [to his American ex-wife] . . . 17 percent of your gross income for one child she gets, 25 percent for two, 33 percent for three. I've no idea what happens to men who have four kids. . . . Women's lib in America in the United States has killed marriage in America for any man who has brains. . . . I wouldn't even marry a rich woman. . . . [In the Dominican Republic] they're raised different. Women's lib hasn't hit here. . . .

SEX TOURIST   In the States, [women] hire folks with cameras. . . . They go to bed with cameras. If they wake up with a bruise, they take a picture of it. Call it abuse. Possible abuse.

EXPATRIATE   In the United States, if you grab your wife like that, and you yell at her, put a little black blue mark, just a little one, she'll . . .

SEX TOURIST   When you've got a goddamn female announcing the NBA basketball game. . . . These females go into the men's locker rooms, but the males cannot go into the ladies' locker rooms. Most of these girls are dykes anyways.

Our interview work with sex tourists who are or have been domestic prostitute users also lends support to the view that their sex tourism is a means of accessing the gendered power that they feel they lack in the West:

> They're not like prostitutes. . . . They stay with you all day. . . . They rub in the sun tan oil, bring us the towel, she even washes your feet. What English tart

would do that? . . . The problem is getting rid of them. Once you've bought them, they stick to you. They even fight with each other over you. It's wicked (English sex tourist in the Dominican Republic).

> [Prostitution in Europe and North America is] all businesslike. It's by the hour, like a taxi service, like they've got the meter running. . . . There's no feeling. If I wanted to fuck a rubber doll, I could buy one and inflate it. . . . A prostitute in Europe will never kiss you. In Canada, it's ridiculous. You know, if you go with a prostitute and you don't pay her, you know what? They call it rape. You can be in court on a rape charge (Canadian sex tourist in Cuba).

There is a sense in which Western men's sex tourism can be said "to constitute . . . a collective behavior oriented toward the restoration of the 'generalized belief' of what it is to be male" (Kruhse-Mount Burton 1995:201). These are people who, by and large, equate true masculinity with unbridled sexuality over women more generally. Men like this experience the fact that some (though certainly not all) Western women are in a position to take legal action against men who physically abuse them as an infringement of rightful male authority. The fact that many (though again certainly not all) Western prostitutes are in a position to impose their own boundaries on the degree of physical intimacy implied by the prostitution contract (for example by refusing to kiss clients on the mouth or to engage in unprotected penetrative and/or oral sex) and are also in a position to turn down clients' requests to spend the night or a few days with them is likewise experienced as a threat to, or denial of, traditional male identity.

Though we recognize that sex tourism provides Western men with opportunities "to reaffirm, if only temporarily, the idealized version of masculine identity and mode of being," and that in this sense sex tourism provides men with opportunities to manage and control both themselves and others as engendered beings, we want to argue that there is more to the demand for sex tourism than this (Kruhse-Mount Burton 1995:202). In the remainder of this chapter we therefore interrogate sex tourists' attitudes toward prostitute use, sexuality, gender, and "race" more closely, and further complicate matters by considering white Western women's and black Western men and women's sex tourism to the Caribbean.

WESTERN SEXUALITY AND PROSTITUTE USE

Hartsock observes that there is "a surprising degree of consensus that hostility and domination, as opposed to intimacy and physical pleasure" are central to the social and historical construction of sexuality in the West (1985:157). Writers in the psychoanalytic tradition suggest that the kind of hostility that is threaded through Western sexual expression reflects an infantile rage and wish for revenge against the separateness of those upon whom we depend. It is, as Stoller puts it, "a state in which one wishes to harm an object," and the harm wished upon objects of sexual desire expresses a craving to strip them of their autonomy, control and separateness—that is, to dehumanize them, since a dehumanized sexual object does not have the power to reject, humiliate or control (1986:4).

The "love object" can be divested of autonomy and objectified in any number of ways, but clearly the prostitute woman, who is in most cultures imagined and socially constructed as an "unnatural" sexual and social Other (a status which is often enshrined in law), provides a conveniently ready-dehumanized sexual object for the client. The commercial nature of the prostitute-client exchange further promises to strip all mutuality and dependency from sexual relations. Because all obligations are discharged through the simple act of payment, there can be no real intimacy and so no terrifying specter of rejection or engulfment by another human being. In theory, then, prostitute use offers a very neat vehicle for the expression of sexual hostility and the attainment of control over self and others as sexual beings. Yet for many prostitute users, there is a fly in the ointment:

> Prostitute women may be socially constructed as Others and *fantasized* as nothing more than objectified sexuality, but in reality, of course, they are human beings. It is only if the prostitute is imagined as stripped of everything bar her sexuality that she can be *completely* controlled by the client's money/powers. But if she were dehumanized to this

extent, she would cease to exist as a person. . . . Most clients appear to pursue a contradiction, namely to control as an object that which cannot be objectified (O'Connell Davidson 1998:161).

This contradiction is at the root of the complaints clients sometimes voice about Western prostitutes (Graaf et al. 1992, Plumridge et al. 1997). It is not always enough to buy access to touch and sexually use objectified body parts. Many clients want the prostitute to be a "lover" who makes no claims, a "whore" who has sex for pleasure not money, in short, a person (subject) who can be treated as an object. This reflects, perhaps, deeper inconsistencies in the discourses which surround prostitution and sexuality. The prostitute woman is viewed as acting in a way wholly inconsistent with her gender identity. Her perceived sexual agency degenders her (a woman who takes an impersonal, active, and instrumental approach to sex is not a "real" woman) and dishonors her (she trades in something which is constitutive of her personhood and cannot honorably be sold). The prostitute-using man, by contrast, behaves "in a fashion consistent with the attributes associated with his gender (he is active and sexually predatory, impersonal, and instrumental), and his sexual transgression is thus a minor infraction, since it does not compromise his gender identity" (O'Connell Davidson 1998:127). A paradox thus emerges:

> The more that men's prostitute use is justified and socially sanctioned through reference to the fiction of biologically determined gender roles and sexuality, the greater the contradiction implicit in prostitution. In order to satisfy their "natural" urges, men must make use of "unnatural" women (O'Connell Davidson 1998:128).

All of this helps to explain the fact that, even though their sexual interests may be powerfully shaped by a cultural emphasis on hostility and domination, prostitute use holds absolutely no appeal for many Western men.[2] Fantasies of unbridled sexual access to willingly objectified women are not necessarily fantasies of access to prostitute women. Meanwhile, those who do use prostitutes in the West imagine and manage their own prostitute use in a variety of different ways (see O'Connell Davidson 1998). At one extreme are men who are actually quite satisfied with brief and anonymous sexual use of women and teenagers whom they imagine as utterly debased and objectified "dirty whores." (For them, the idea of using a prostitute is erotic in and of itself.) At the other extreme are those who regularly visit the same prostitute woman and construct a fiction of romance or friendship around their use of her, a fiction which helps them to imagine themselves as seen, chosen, and desired, even as they pay for sex as a commodity. Between these two poles are men who indulge in a range of (often very inventive) practices and fantasies designed to create the illusion of balance between sexual hostility and sexual mutuality that they personally find sexually exciting. How does this relate to the demand for sex tourism?

Let us begin by noting that not all Western male sex tourists subjectively perceive their own sexual practices abroad as a form of prostitute use. This reflects the fact that even within any one country affected by sex tourism, prostitution is not a homogeneous phenomenon in terms of its social organization. In some countries, sex tourism has involved the maintenance and development of existing large scale, highly commoditized sex industries serving foreign military personnel (Truong 1990, Sturdevant and Stoltzfus 1992, Hall 1994). But it has also emerged in locations where no such sex industry existed, for instance, the Gambia, Cuba, and Brazil (Morris-Jara 1996, Sanchez Taylor 1997, Perio and Thierry 1996). Moreover, even in countries like Thailand and the Philippines, where tourist-related prostitution has been grafted onto an existing, formally organized brothel sector serving military demand, tourist development has *also* been associated with the emergence of an informal prostitution sector (in which prostitutes solicit in hotels, discos, bars, beaches, parks, or streets, often entering into fairly protracted and diffuse transactions with clients).

This in itself gives prostitution in sex tourist resorts a rather different character to that of prostitution in red-light districts in affluent, Western countries. The sense of difference is enhanced by the fact that, in many places, informally arranged prostitution spills over into apparently noncommercial encounters within which tourists who do not self-identify as prostitute users can draw local/migrant persons who do not self-identify as prostitutes into profoundly unequal and exploitative sexual relationships. It also means that sex tourism presents a diverse array of opportunities for sexual gratification, not all of which involve straightforward cash for sex exchanges in brothels or go-go clubs or on the streets, and so provides the sex tourist with a veritable "pic'n'mix" of ways in which to manage himself as a sexual and engendered being. He can indulge in overt forms of sexual hostility (such as selecting a numbered brothel prostitute from those on display in a bar or brothel for "short time" or buying a cheap, speedy sexual service from one of many street prostitutes), or he can indulge in fantasies of mutuality, picking up a woman/teenager in an ordinary tourist disco, wining and dining and generally simulating romance with her for a day or two and completely denying the commercial basis of the sexual interaction. Or, and many sex tourists do exactly this, he can combine both approaches.

Now it could be argued that, given the fact that Western men are socialized into a view of male sexuality as a powerful, biologically based need for sexual "outlets," the existence of multiple, cheap, and varied sexual opportunities is, in itself, enough to attract large numbers of men to a given holiday resort. However, it is important to recognize the numerous other forms of highly sexualized tourism that could satisfy a wish to indulge in various sexual fantasies and also a desire for control over the self as a sexual and engendered being. Sex tourists could, for example, choose to take part in organized holidays designed to facilitate sexual and romantic encounters between tourists (such as Club 18–30 and other singles holidays), or they could choose to take all-inclusive holidays to resorts such as Hedonism or destinations renowned for promiscuous tourist-tourist sex, such as Ibiza or Cap d'Azur. These latter offer just as many opportunities for anonymous and impersonal sex in a party atmosphere as well as for intense but ultimately brief and noncommitted sexual romances. What they do not offer is the control that comes from paying for sex or the opportunity to indulge in racialized-sexual fantasies, which helps to explain why sex tourists reject them in favor of sexual experience in what they term "Third World" countries. This brings us to questions about the relationship between the construction of "Otherness" and sex tourism.

"OTHERNESS" AND WESTERN MEN'S SEX TOURISM

For obvious reasons, sex tourists spend their time in resorts and *barrios* where tourist-related prostitution is widespread. Thus they constantly encounter what appear to them as hedonistic scenes—local "girls" and young men dancing "sensuously," draping themselves over and being fondled by Western tourists, drinking and joking with each other, and so on. Instead of seeing the relationship between these scenes and their own presence in the resort, sex tourists tend to interpret all this as empirical vindication of Western assumptions of "non-Western peoples living in idyllic pleasure, splendid innocence or Paradise-like conditions—as purely sensual, natural, simple and uncorrupted beings" (Kempadoo 1995:76). Western sex tourists (and this is true of black as well as white informants) say that sex is more "natural" in Third World countries, that prostitution is not really prostitution but a "way of life," that "They" are "at it" all of the time.

This explains how men who are not and would not dream of becoming prostitute users back home can happily practice sex tourism (the "girls" are not really like prostitutes and so they themselves are not really like clients, the prostitution contract is not like the Western prostitution contract and so does not really count as prostitution). It also explains the paranoid obsession with being cheated exhibited by some sex tourists, who comment on their belief that women in certain sex tourist resorts or particular brothels or bars are "getting too commercial" and advise each other how to avoid being "duped" and "exploited" by a "real professional," where to find "brand new girls," and so on (see O'Connell Davidson 1995, Bishop and Robinson 1998).

It also points to the complex interrelations between discourses of gender, "race" and sexuality. To begin with, the supposed naturalness of prostitution in the Third World actually reassures the Western male sex tourist of his racial or cultural superiority. Thus we find that sex tourists continue a traditional Western discourse of travel which rests on the imagined opposition between the "civilized" West and the "barbarous" Other (Grewal 1996:136, Kempadoo 1996:76; see also Brace and O'Connell Davidson 1996). In "civilized" countries, only "bad" women become prostitutes (they refuse the constraints civilization places upon "good" women in favor of earning "easy money"), but in the Third World (a corrupt and lawless place where people exist in a state of nature), "nice girls" may be driven to prostitution in order to survive ("they have to do it because they've all got kids" or "they're doing it for their families"). In the West, "nice girls" are protected and supported by their menfolk, but in the Third World, "uncivilized" Other men allow (or even demand that) their womenfolk enter prostitution. In interviews, Western male sex tourists contrast their own generosity, humanity, and chivalry against the "failings" of local men, who are imagined as feckless, faithless, wife-beaters, and pimps. Even as prostitute users, Other men are fantasized as inferior moral beings who cheat and mistreat the "girls."

In this we see that sex tourism is not only about sustaining a male identity. For white men it is also about sustaining a *white* identity. Thus, sex tourism can also be understood as a collective behavior oriented toward the restoration of a generalized belief about what it is to be white: to be truly white is to be served, revered, and envied by Others. For the black American male sex tourists we have interviewed, sex tourism appears to affirm a sense of Western-ness and so of inclusion in a privileged world. Take, for example, the following three statements from a forty-five-year-old black American sex tourist. He is a New York bus driver and ex-vice cop, a paid-up member of an American-owned sex tourist club, Travel & the Single Male, and he has used prostitutes in Thailand, Brazil, Costa Rica, and the Dominican Republic:

> There's two sides to the countries that I go to. There's the tourist side and then there's the real people, and I make a habit of going to the real people, I see how the real people live, and when I see something like that . . . I tend to look at the little bit I've got at home and I appreciate it. . . .
>
> I've always been proud to be an American. . . . I always tip in U.S. dollars when I arrive. I always keep dollars and pesos, because people tend to think differently about pesos and dollars. . . .

They always say at hotels they don't want you to bring the girls in; believe me, that's crap, because you know what I do? Reach in my pocket and I go anywhere I want.

Meanwhile, sexualized-racisms help the sex tourist to attain a sense of control over himself and Others as engendered and racialized sexual beings. Here it is important to recognize the subtle (or not so subtle) variations of racism employed by white Western men. The sex tourists we have interviewed in the Caribbean are not a homogeneous group in terms of their "race" politics, and this reflects differences of national identity, age, socio-economic background, and racialized identity. One clearly identifiable subgroup comprised of white North American men aged forty and above, who, though perhaps not actually affiliated with the Klan, espouse a white supremacist world view and consider black people their biological, social and cultural inferiors. They use the word "nigger" and consider any challenge to their "right" to use this term as "political correctness." As one sex tourist complained, in the States "You can't use the N word, nigger. Always when I was raised up, the only thing was the F word, you can't use the F word. Now you can't say cunt, you can't say nigger."

For men like this, black women are imagined as the embodiment of all that is low and debased, they are "inherently degraded, and thus the appropriate partners for degrading sex" (Shrage 1994:158). As unambiguous whores by virtue of their racialized identity, they may be briefly and anonymously used, but they are not sought out for longer term or quasi-romantic commercial sexual relationships. Thus, the sex tourist quoted above told us that when he and his cronies (all regular sex tourists to the Dominican Republic) see another American sex tourist "hanging round" with a local girl or woman who has the phenotypical characteristics they associate with Africanness, they call out to him, "How many bananas did it take to get her down out of the tree?" and generally deride him for transgressing a racialized sexual boundary which should not, in their view, be openly crossed.

The Dominican females that men like this want sexual access to are light skinned and straight haired (this is also true in Cuba and in the Latin American countries where we have undertaken fieldwork). They are not classified as "niggers" by these white racists, but instead as "LBFMs" or "Little Brown Fucking Machines," a catch-all category encompassing any female Other not deemed to be either white or "African." The militaristic and imperialist associations of this term (coined by American GIs stationed in Southeast Asia) simultaneously make it all the more offensive and hostile and all the more appealing to this type of sex tourist, many of whom have served in the armed forces (a disturbing number of whom have also been or currently are police officers in the United States) and the rest of whom are "wanna-be vets"— men who never made it to Vietnam to live out their racialized-sexualized fantasies of masculine glory.

Shrage and Kruhse-Mount Burton's comments on the relationship between fantasies of hypersexual Others and myths about white women's sexual purity are also relevant to understanding this kind of sex tourist's world-view. An extract from an article posted on an Internet site written by and for sex tourists entitled "Why No White Women?" is revealing:

Q   Is it because white women demand more (in terms of performance) from their men during Sex? and white men cannot deliver?

A   In my case, it's just that my dick is not long enough to reach them up on the pedestal they like to stand on.

If whiteness is imagined as dominance, and woman is imagined as subordination, then "white woman" becomes something of a contradiction. As Young notes. "For white men, white women are both self and other: they have a floating status. They can reinforce a sense of self through common racial identity or threaten and disturb that sense through their sexual Otherness" (1996:52). White supremacists *have to* place white women on a pedestal (iconize them as racially, morally and sexually pure), since whiteness and civilization are synonymous and "civilization" is constructed as the rejection of base animalism. But keeping them on their pedestal requires men to constantly deny what they imagine to be their own needs and nature and thus white women become the object of profound resentment.

Not all Western male sex tourists to the Caribbean buy into this kind of overt, denigrating racism. In fact, many of them are far more strongly influenced by what might be termed "exoticizing" racisms. Younger white Europeans and North Americans, for example, have been exposed to such racisms through the Western film, music, and fashion industries, which retain the old-school racist emphasis on blackness as physicality but repackage and commoditize this "animalism" so that black men and women become the ultimate icons of sporting prowess, "untamed" rebelliousness, "raw" musical talent, sexual power and so on (see hooks 1992, 1994; Young 1996). As a consequence, many young (and some not so young) white Westerners view blackness as a marker of something both "cool" and "hot."

In their own countries, however, their encounters with real live black people are not only few and far between, but also generally something of a disappointment to them. As one British sex tourist to Cuba told us, black people in Britain are "very stand-offish. . . . They stick to their own, and it's a shame, because it makes divisions." What a delight it is for men like this to holiday in the Caribbean, then, where poverty combined with the exigencies of tourist development ensure that they are constantly faced by smiling, welcoming black folk. The small black boy who wants to shine their shoes; the old black woman who cleans their hotel room; the cool, young, dreadlocked black man on the beach who is working as a promoter for some restaurant or bar; the fit, young black woman soliciting in the tourist disco—all want to "befriend" the white tourist. Finally, interviews with black American male sex tourists suggest that they too sexualize and exoticize the women they sexually exploit in the Third World ("Latin women are hot," "Latin girls love sex").

Both the sexualized racism that underpins the category LBFM and the exoticizing sexualized racism espoused by other sex tourists help to construct the Other prostitute as the embodiment of a contradiction, that is, as a "whore" who does it for pleasure as much as for money, an object with a subjectivity completely attuned to their own, in short, the embodiment of a masturbatory fantasy. Time and again Western sex tourists have assured us that the local girls really are "hot for it," that Third World prostitutes enjoy their work and that their highest ambition is to be the object of a Western man's desire. Their belief that Third World prostitutes are genuinely economically desperate rather than making a free choice to prostitute for "easy money" is clearly inconsistent with their belief that Third World prostitutes are actually acting on the basis of mutual sexual desire, but it is a contradiction that appears to resolve (at least temporarily) an anxiety they have about the relationship between sex, gender, sexuality, and "race."

The vast majority of the sex tourists we have interviewed believe that gender attributes, including sexual behavior, are determined by biological sex. They say that it is natural for women to be passive and sexually receptive as well as to be homemakers, child rearers, dependent upon and subservient toward men, which is why white Western women (prostitute and nonprostitute alike) often appear to them as unsexed. Thus the sex tourist quoted at the beginning of this chapter could only explain women's presence on traditional male terrain by imagining them as sexually "unnatural" ("Most of these girls are dykes anyways"). White women's relative economic, social and political power as well as their very whiteness makes it hard for Western male sex tourists to eroticize them as nothing more than sexual beings. Racism/ethnocentrism can collapse such tensions. If black or Latin women are naturally physical, wild, hot and sexually powerful, there need be no anxiety about enjoying them as pure sex. Equally, racism settles the anxieties some men have about the almost "manly" sexual power and agency attributed to white prostitutes. A Little Brown Fucking Machine is not unsexed by prostituting, she is "just doing what comes naturally." Since the Other woman is a "natural" prostitute, her prostitution does not make her any the less a "natural woman." All these points are also relevant to understanding the phenomenon of female sex tourism.

"OTHERNESS" AND FEMALE SEX TOURISM

Western women's sexual behavior abroad (both historically and contemporaneously) is often viewed in a rather different light compared to that of their male counterparts, and it is without doubt true that Western women who travel to Third World destinations in search of sex differ from many of the Western male sex tourists discussed above in terms of their attitudes toward prostitution and sexuality. Few of them are prostitute users back home, and few of them would choose to visit brothels while abroad or to pay street prostitutes for a quick "hand job" or any other sexual service (although it should be noted that some women do behave in these ways). But one of the author's (Sanchez Taylor) ongoing interview and survey research with female sex tourists in Jamaica and the Dominican Republic suggests that there are also similarities between the sexual behavior of Western women and men in sex tourist resorts.

The Caribbean has long been a destination that offers tourist women opportunities for sexual experience, and large numbers of women from the United States, Canada, Britain, and Germany as well as smaller numbers of women from other European countries and from Japan (i.e., the same countries that send male sex tourists) engage in sexual relationships with local men while on holiday there (Karch and Dann 1981, Pruitt and La Font 1995, Chevannes 1993). Preliminary analysis of data from Sanchez Taylor's survey of a sample of 104 single Western female tourists in Negril, Sosúa, and Boca Chica shows that almost 40 percent had entered into some form of sexual relationship with a local man.[3] The survey data further suggest that these were not chance encounters but rather that the sexually active female tourists visit the islands in order to pursue one or more sexual relationships. Only 9 percent of sexually active women were on their first trip; the rest had made numerous trips to the islands, and over 20 percent of female sex tourists reported having had two or more different local sexual partners in the course of a two- to three-week stay. Furthermore, female sex tourists, as much as male sex tourists, view their sexual experiences as integral to their holiday— "When in Jamaica you have to experience everything that's on offer," one black American woman explained, while a white woman working as a tour representative for a U.S. package operator said: "I tell my single women: come down here to love them, fuck them, and leave them, and you'll have a great time here. Don't look to get married. Don't call them."

Like male sex tourists, these women differ in terms of their age, nationality, social class, and racialized identity, including among their ranks young "spice girl" teenagers and students as well as grandmothers in their sixties, working class as well as middle class professionals, or self-employed women. They also differ in terms of the type of sexual encounters they pursue and the way in which they interpret these encounters. Some are eager to find a man as soon as they get off the plane and enter into multiple, brief, and instrumental relationships; others want to be romanced and sweet-talked by one or perhaps two men during their holiday. Around 40 percent described their relationships with local men as "purely physical" and 40 percent described them as "holiday romances." Twenty percent said that they had found "true love." Almost all the sexually active women surveyed stated that they had "helped their partner(s) out financially" by buying them meals, drinks, gifts, or by giving cash, and yet none of them perceived these relationships as commercial sexual transactions. Asked whether they had ever been approached by a gigolo/prostitute during their stay in Jamaica, 90 percent of them replied in the negative. The data collected in the Dominican Republic revealed similar patterns of denial.

The informal nature of the sexual transactions in these resorts blurs the boundaries of what constitutes prostitution for Western women just as it does for Western men, allowing them to believe that the meals, cash, and gifts they provide for their sexual partners do not represent a form of payment for services rendered but rather an expression of their own munificence. It is only when women repeatedly enter into a series of extremely brief sexual encounters that they begin to acknowledge that, as one put it, "It's all about money." Even this does not lead them to view themselves as prostitute users, however, and again it is notions of difference and Otherness that play a key role in protecting the sex tourist from the knowledge that they are paying for the sexual attentions they receive. As Others, local men are viewed as beings possessed of a powerful and indiscriminate sexuality that they cannot control, and this explains their eagerness for sex with tourist women, regardless of their age, size, or physical appearance. Again, the Other is not *selling* sex, just "doing what comes naturally."

As yet, the number of black female sex tourists in Sanchez Taylor's survey and interview sample is too small to base any generalizations upon,[4] but so far, their attitudes are remarkably consistent with those voiced by the central character in Terry Macmillan's 1996 novel *How Stella Got Her Groove Back,* in which a black American woman finds "love and romance" with a Jamaican boy almost half her age and with certainly less than half her economic means.[5] Stella views her own behavior in a quite different light from that of white male sex tourists—she disparages an older white male tourist as "a dirty old man who probably has to pay for all the pussy he gets" (1996:83). It is also interesting to note the ways in which Macmillan "Otherizes" local men: the Jamaican boy smells "primitive"; he is "exotic and goes with the Island"; he is "Mr Expresso in shorts" (1996:142, 154). Like white female sex tourists interviewed in the course of research, Macmillan further explains the young Jamaican man's disinterest in Jamaican women and so his sexual interest in an older American woman by Otherizing local women through the use of derogatory stereotypes. Thus, Jamaican women are assumed to be rapacious, materialistic, and sexually instrumental—they only want a man who owns a big car and house and money—and so Jamaican men long for women who do not demand these things (i.e., American women who already possess them).

Like their male counterparts, Western female sex tourists employ fantasies of Otherness not just to legitimate obtaining sexual access to the kind of young, fit, handsome bodies that would otherwise be denied to them and to obtain affirmation of their own sexual desirability (because the fact is that some female sex tourists are themselves young and fit looking and would be easily able to secure sexual access to equally appealing male bodies at home) but also to obtain a sense of power and control over themselves and others as engendered, sexual beings and to affirm their own privilege as Westerners. Thus they continually stress their belief that people in the Caribbean "are different from Westerners." Sexual life is one of the primary arenas in which this supposed difference is manifest. More than half of the female sex tourists surveyed in Jamaica stated that Jamaicans are more relaxed about teenage sex, casual sex, and prostitution than Westerners. In response to open-ended questions, they observed that "Jamaican men are more up front about sex," that "Jamaicans are uninhibited about sex," that "Jamaicans are naturally promiscuous," and that "sex is more natural to Jamaicans." In interviews, female sex tourists also reproduced the notion of an opposition between the "civilized" West and the "primitive" Third World. One Scots grandmother in her early forties described the Dominican Republic as follows: "It's just like Britain before its industrial phase, it's just behind Britain, just exactly the same. Kids used to get beat up to go up chimneys, here they get beaten up to go polish shoes. There's no difference."

Western female sex tourists' racisms, like those of male sex tourists, are also many-layered and nuanced by differences in terms of nationality, age, and racialized identity. There are older white American female sex tourists whose beliefs about "race" and attitudes toward interracial sex are based upon an ideology that is overtly white supremacist. The black male represents for them the essence of an animalistic sexuality that both fascinates and repels. While in their own country they would not want to openly enter a sexual relationship with a black man, in a holiday resort like Negril, they can transgress the racialized and gendered codes that normally govern their sexual behavior, while maintaining their honor and reputation back home. As one Jamaican gigolo commented:

> While they are here they feel free. Free to do what they never do at home. No one looking at them. Get a Black guy who are unavailable at home. No one judge them. Get the man to make they feel good then they go home clean and pure.

This observation, and all the sexual hostility it implies, is born out by the following extract from an interview with a forty-five-year-old white American woman from Chicago, a regular sex tourist to Negril:

> [Jamaican men] are all liars and cheats. . . . [American women come to Negril because] they get what they don't get back home. A girl who no one looks twice at back home, she gets hit on all the time here, all these guys are paying her attention, telling her she's beautiful, and they really want her. . . . They're obsessed with their dicks. That's all they think of, just pussy and money and nothing else. . . . In Chicago, this could never happen. It's like a secret, like a fantasy and then you go home.

When asked whether she would ever take a black boyfriend home and introduce him to her friends and family, she was emphatic that she would not—"No, no, never. It's not like that. This is something else, you know, it's time out. Like a fantasy." This is more than simply a fantasy about having multiple anonymous sexual encounters without getting caught and disgraced. It is also a highly racialized fantasy about power and vengeance. Women like the sex tourist quoted above are looking for black men with good bodies, firm and muscle-clad sex machines that they can control, and this element of control should not be overlooked. It is also important to female sex tourists who reject white supremacist ideologies, and there are many of these, including white liberals and young white women who value Blackness as a "cool" commodity in the same way that many young white men do, and black American and black British female sex tourists.

These latter groups do not wish to indulge in the overtly hostile racialized sexual fantasy described by the woman quoted above, but they do want to live out other fantasies, whether they be "educating and helping the noble savage," or being the focus of "cool" black men's adoring gaze, or being the central character of a Terry Macmillan novel.[6] No matter what specific fantasy they pursue, female sex tourists use their economic power to initiate and terminate sexual relations with local men at whim, and within those relationships, they use their economic and racialized power to control these men in ways in which they could never command a Western man. These are unaccustomed powers, and even the female sex tourists who buy into exoticizing rather than hostile and denigrating racisms appear to enjoy them as such.

For white women, these powers are very clearly linked to their own whiteness as well as to their status and economic power as tourist women. Thus they contrast their own experience against that of local women (remarking on the fact that they are respected and protected and not treated like local women) *and* against their experience back home (commenting on how safe they feel in the Caribbean walking alone at night and entering bars and discos by themselves, observing that local men are far more attentive and chivalrous than Western men). Take, for example, the comments of "Judy," a white American expatriate in the Dominican Republic, a woman in her late fifties and rather overweight:

> When you go to a disco, [white] men eye up a woman for her body, whatever. Dominicans don't care because they love women, they love women. It's not that they're indifferent or anything. They are very romantic, they will never be rude with you, while a white man will say something rude to you, while Dominican men are not like that at all. A white man will say to me, like, "slut" to me and I have been with a lot of Dominican men and they would never say anything like that to you. They are more respectful. Light cigarettes, open doors, they are more gentlemen. Where white men don't do that. So if you have been a neglected woman in civilization, when you come down here, of course, when you come down here they are going to wipe you off your feet.

The Dominican Republic presents women like Judy with a stage upon which to simultaneously affirm their femininity through their ability to command men and exact revenge on white men by engaging sexually with the competition, i.e., the black male. For the first time she is in a position to call the shots. Where back home white female sex tourists' racialized privilege is often obscured by their lack of gender power and economic disadvantage in relation to white men, in sex tourist resorts it is recognized as a source of personal power and power over others. Meanwhile, their beliefs about gender and sexuality prevent them from seeing themselves as sexually exploitative. Popular discourses about gender present women as naturally sexually passive and receptive, and men as naturally indiscriminate and sexually voracious. According to this essentialist model of gender and sexuality, women can never sexually exploit men in the same way that men exploit women because penetrative heterosexual intercourse requires the woman to submit to the male—she is "used" by him. No matter how great the asymmetry between female tourist and local male in terms of their age or economic, social, and racialized power, it is still assumed that the male derives benefits from sex above and beyond the purely pecuniary and so is not being exploited in the same way that a prostitute woman is exploited by a male client.

This is especially the case when the man so used is socially constructed as a racialized, ethnic or cultural Other and assumed to have an uncontrollable desire to have sex with as many women as he possibly can.

CONCLUSION

The demand for sex tourism is inextricably linked to discourses that naturalize and celebrate inequalities structured along lines of class, gender, and race/Otherness; in other words, discourses that reflect and help to reproduce a profoundly hierarchical model of human sociality. Although sex tourists are a heterogeneous group in terms of their background characteristics and specific sexual interests, they share a common willingness to embrace this hierarchical model and a common pleasure in the fact that their Third World tourism allows them either to affirm their dominant position within a hierarchy of gendered, racialized, and economic power or to adjust their own position upward in that hierarchy. In the Third World, neo-colonial relations of power equip Western sex tourists with an extremely high level of control over themselves and others as sexual beings and, as a result, with the power to realize the fantasy of their choosing. They can experience sexual intimacy without risking rejection; they can evade the social meanings that attach to their own age and body type; they can transgress social rules governing sexual life without consequence for their own social standing; they can reduce other human beings to nothing more than the living embodiments of masturbatory fantasies.

In short, sex tourists can experience in real life a world very similar to that offered in fantasy to pornography users: "Sexuality and sexual activity are portrayed in pornography as profoundly distanced from the activities of daily life. The action in pornography takes place in what Griffin has termed 'pornotopia,' a world outside real time and space" (Hartsock 1983: 175). To sex tourists, the resorts they visit are fantasy islands, variously peopled by Little Brown Fucking Machines, "cool" black women who love to party, "primitive smelling" black studs who only think of "pussy and money," respectful Latin gentlemen who love women. All the sex tourist has to do to attain access to this fantasy world is to reach into his or her pocket, for it is there that the sex tourist, like other individuals in capitalist societies, carries "his social power as also his connection with society" (Marx 1973:94). That the Western sex tourist's pocket can contain sufficient power to transform others into Others, mere players on a pornographic stage, is a testament to the enormity of the imbalance of economic, social, and political power between rich and poor nations. That so many Westerners *wish* to use their power in this way is a measure of the bleakness of the prevailing model of human nature and the human sociality that their societies offer them.

NOTES

1. In 1995, we were commissioned by ECPAT (End Child Prostitution in Asian Tourism) to undertake research on the identity, attitudes, and motivations of clients of child prostitutes. This involved ethnographic fieldwork in tourist areas in South Africa, India, Costa Rica, Venezuela, Cuba, and the Dominican Republic. We are currently working on an Economic and Social Research Council—funded project (Award no. R 000 23 7625), which builds on this research through a focus on prostitution and the informal tourist economy in Jamaica and the Dominican Republic. Taking these projects together, we have interviewed some 250 sex tourists and sexpatriates and over 150 people involved in tourist-related prostitution (women, children and men working as prostitutes, pimps, procurers, brothel keepers, etc.).

2. The fact that not all men are prostitute users is something that is often forgotten in radical feminist analyses of prostitution which, as Hart has noted, encourage us to view "either all men as prostitutes' clients or prostitutes' clients as somehow standing for/being symbolic of men in general" (1994:53).

3. Because the survey aims to support exploration and theory development in a previously underresearched field, purposive (nonprobability) sampling methods were employed (Arber 1993:72). Sanchez Taylor obtained a sample by approaching all single female tourists in selected locations (a particular stretch of beach, or a given bar or restaurant) and asking them to complete questionnaires.

4. Four out of eighteen single black British and American female tourists surveyed had entered into sexual relationships with local men. Sanchez Taylor also interviewed four more black female sex tourists.

5. In Negril, gigolos often refer to black American female sex tourists as "Stellas," after this fictional character

6. Macmillan hints at the transgressive elements of a black Western female sex tourist's excitement—Stella's desire for the "primitive"-smelling younger man makes her feel "kind of slutty," but she likes the feeling.

CHAPTER EIGHT

PORNOGRAPHY

One of the most politically controversial issues in the study of sexualities is sexual representation, also known as pornography. Nearly all men confess to having some exposure to pornography; indeed, for many men the first naked women they see are in pornographic magazines. And pornography has been the site of significant political protest, from the right wing (which considers pornography to be as degrading to human dignity as birth control information, homosexuality, and abortion) to radical feminist campaigns (which see pornography as a vicious expression of misogyny, on a par with rape, spouse abuse, and genital mutilation).

While the right wing's efforts rehearsed America's discomfort with all things sexual, the radical feminist critique of pornography transformed the political debate, arguing that when men looked at pornographic images of naked women, they were actually participating in a culture-wide hatred and contempt for women. Pornographic images are about the subordination of women; pornography "makes sexism sexy," in the words of one activist. One pornographic director and actor commented on his "craft" as follows:

> My whole reason for being in the [pornography] Industry is to satisfy the desire of the men in the world who basically don't much care for women and want to see the men in my Industry getting even with the women they couldn't have when they were growing up. . . . So when we come on a woman's face or somewhat brutalize her sexually, we're getting even for their lost dreams. I believe this. I've heard audiences cheer me when I do something foul on screen. When I've strangled a person or sodomized a person or brutalized a person, the audience is cheering my action, and then when I've fulfilled my warped desire, the audience applauds.

The claims of antipornography feminists—that pornography causes rape, or that it numbs us to the real effect of real violence in women's lives—have been difficult to demonstrate empirically. Few studies have shown such an empirical relationship, though several have documented modest changes in men's attitudes immediately after exposure to violent pornography. Yet, whether or not there is *any* empirical evidence that pornography alone causes rape or violence, there remains the shocking difference between us: on any given day in the United States, men masturbate to images of women enduring sexual torture, genital mutilation, rape, and violence. Surely, this points to a dramatic difference between women's and men's sexualities—one can hardly imagine many women masturbating to reenactments of Lorena Bobbitt's ministrations to her husband. Violence is rarely sexualized for women; that such images can be such a routine and casual turn-on for many men should at least give us pause.

The articles in this section explore the political and psychology of pornography. Sharon Abbott asks why any woman would be motivated to think about the pornography industry as a career choice. Gail Dines and Robert Jensen offer a coherent radical feminist critique of pornography and its impact on men. The selections by Martin Barron and Michael Kimmel and by William Fisher and Azy Barak examine the new, and often unsettling, explosion of Internet pornography: Barron and Kimmel by comparing the levels of violence in Internet chat rooms, and Fisher and Barak on the possibilities and perils of cybersex.

8.1 SEXUAL VIOLENCE IN THREE PORNOGRAPHIC MEDIA
Towards a Sociological Explanation

Martin Barron and Michael S. Kimmel

With almost three decades of social science research on sexual violence in pornography, many of its characteristics are now well understood. We know that pornography contains images of both violence and sexual violence (Palys, 1986; Scott & Cuvelier, 1993; Smith, 1976). We have some idea of the negative effect of sexually violent pornography, especially on men's attitudes towards women (Allen, D'alessio, & Brezgel, 1995; Brannigan & Goldenberg, 1987; Fisher & Grenier, 1994; Linz, 1989; Malamuth & Check, 1985; Mayerson & Taylor, 1987).

Unfortunately, however, the vast majority of previous research on sexual violence in pornography has approached pornography as an undifferentiated mass with regards to sexual violence. This study seeks to determine if this assumption is justified. Does pornography differ across media? In what ways, and to what degree? How can these differences be explained? These are the primary questions of concern to this paper. We begin our inquiry by reviewing past efforts to understand the content of pornography, and then present some tentative hypotheses concerning the levels of sexual violence across media. Through an empirical investigation of three contemporaneous pornographic media—magazines, videos, and Internet newsgroups (the Usenet)—we discuss differences in violent content, and speculate about some of the possible explanations for these differences.

THE CONTENT OF PORNOGRAPHY

Most social and behavioral science research on pornography has studied either the effects of pornographic images on viewers, or examined the content of the pornography itself. (As our empirical analysis focuses only on the changing content of pornography, we have confined our review of the literature to that branch of the research.) Although Smith (1976) found remarkable homogeneity in his sample of "adult-only" paperbacks, Malamuth and Spinner (1980) found increasing violence in their study of *Playboy* and *Penthouse* over a 5-year period, from approximately 1.5% of all pictorials for both magazines in 1973 to 6% in *Penthouse* and 4% in *Playboy* in 1977.

The debate surrounding these studies generated important additional research. Scott and Cuvelier (1987a, 1987b) disaggregated the two magazines and examined them over a longer time span, to eliminate the possibility that the original studies had conflated them and examined an anomalous period. They found a curvilinear relationship between year and sexual violence, from virtually no violence in its earliest years, with increases until the late 1970s (the endpoint for the study by Malamuth & Spinner, 1980), when the violent content began to subside. It appears that *Playboy* responded to the proliferation of more violent magazines and the introduction of videotapes by returning to its traditional, more economically affluent and upscale consumerist readership.

Criticized for methodological synecdoche—letting *Playboy* stand for all pornographic magazines, especially at a time of proliferation—Scott and Cuvelier (1993) examined sexual violence in *Hustler* from its inception (July 1974) through July 1987. While they found a higher level of violent content (1.6% of all pictorials) in *Hustler* than in *Playboy* (.038%) overall, they found no changes in the magazine over time, and argued that their work "refutes the alleged increase in sexually violent portrayals" (Scott & Cuvelier, 1993, p. 367).

Other researchers used more synchronic approaches. Winick (1985), for example, examined 430 pornographic magazines found in an adult bookstore in New York City's Times Square. After classifying these magazines into 22 categories, Winick found that 4.9% of the magazines examined were dedicated to bondage and discipline, while violent content accounted for only 1.2% of his sample. However, lack of reliability of the sample (Winick only went into one store) and coding validity (all coding was done on the premises) make his findings less useful to other researchers.

The rapid development of video technology revolutionized the pornography industry. The rental of pornographic movies rose from 75 million in 1985 to 490 million in 1992 (Schlosser, 1997). Research followed suit. Comparing sexual aggression in "Triple-X" videos and in more mainstream "adult" videos, Palys (1986) found virtually no differences—6.6% of the scenes from adult videos and 6.4% of the scenes from Triple-X videos contained sexual aggression— but enormous differences between pornographic videos and pornographic magazines (where 1% was more typical). Virtually every study of pornographic videos has found similar levels of sexual violence, substantially higher than in magazines (see, for example, Brosius, Weaver, & Staab, 1993; Duncan, 1991; Yang & Linz, 1990).

Little research has been done on pornography and the Usenet (Internet newsgroups), although it has become a very controversial topic. One study (Rimm, 1995) was both methodologically and ethically suspect—supplemental data were collected from an adult bulletin board (which requires a credit card and age verification to use) and surreptitiously from students using the Usenet (DeLoughry, 1995; Elmer-Dewitt, 1995). Other, less typical forms of pornography—from pornographic cartoons (Matacin & Burger, 1987) to dial-a-porn recordings (Glascock & Larose, 1993)—have also been examined. These studies tend to underscore the fact that all pornographic media contain violence, and that each displays violence differently.

Only one study has attempted to compare pornographic media. Dietz and Sears (1988) examined books, magazines, and films in adult bookstores in four cities. They found that 12% of the magazines, 20% of the books, and 7.7% of the films portrayed some violent theme. While this study proposed the reverse in the amount of violence in magazines and videos, Dietz and Sears only examined the covers and display boxes of the pornography being investigated, thereby making it impossible to understand the actual content of the material (see Linz & Donnerstein, 1988).

Studies of the content of pornography have thus been suggestive at best, but beset by both substantive and methodological problems that make reliability questionable and comparability impossible. Only the research on the effects of pornography on men's attitudes and behaviors have yielded any reliable, albeit often contradictory, results. We still know little about the differences in the actual content of pornography among various pornographic media. This study is an attempt to remedy this serious lacuna in our understanding of the content of pornography. We provide a careful methodological procedure to compare different pornographic media to ascertain the differing levels of violence.

The introduction of these different pornographic media at different historical moments (with magazines being introduced first, followed by videos, and then the Usenet) offers several intriguing possibilities that might affect the differing amounts of violence we might find within them. Violent content might remain constant across all three media. Levels of violence might increase in a linear way, moving from low (magazines) to intermediate (videos) to higher (Usenet). Or it might decrease in a linear way. Finally, the relationship might be curvilinear, with either a peak or trough in the middle. Given that previous research found a significant increase in level of violence between magazines and videos, we hypothesized that a constant level, decrease, or curvilinear (trough) model was unlikely. The plausible relationships in which we were interested were that the level of violence would continue to increase from videos to the Usenet, or that it would decline from videos to the Usenet. At the same time, we wanted to retest the relationship between magazines and videos.

METHODOLOGY

Our sample of magazines and videos was drawn from a suburban New York township. The population of this suburb is predominantly white and middle class. We collected 50 cases from each of the three pornographic media. The unique nature of each media, however, necessitated slightly different sampling schemes for each medium. Videos and magazines were chosen through a multilevel cluster sampling design. For both media, pornography was operationalized as being any sexually explicit material to which access was limited, either by signs or physical structure, to adults. At each of five stores, 10 videos were randomly selected to comprise the video sample. (See Appendix A for list of films.) Because the majority of stores selling pornographic magazines did not sell 10 different magazines, 5 magazines were selected from five different stores, and two stories were randomly taken from within each magazine to comprise our magazine sample. (See Appendix B for a list of magazines.)

Our Usenet sample was confined to stories taken from the newsgroup alt.sex.stories. It is important to remember that the Usenet portion of the Internet is only one portion of what is considered the Internet, and only one way to access pornography via the Internet. We decided to concentrate on this portion for several reasons. First, it provides a convenient data pool. While the World Wide Web has certainly caught the public's eye more than newsgroups, there is virtually no way to construct a list of all pornographic web sites from which to sample. Further, while some pornographic web sites contain stories, the majority primarily contain pictures, and thus do not provide the narratives elements important to this study. We used alt.sex.stories precisely for its narrative content. Finally, while many web sites with pornographic material have begun to charge for access, the Usenet remains free to all with access to the Internet.

The sampling population for this study was made up of all sexual stories of at least 250 words posted to the newsgroup during one month in 1997 (approximately 28% of the postings for this month fit this description). From this population, a random sample of 50 cases was drawn.[1]

Coding Scheme

The unit of analysis within each story (textual or visual) was the scene. We used Palys' (1986) definition as "a thematically uninterrupted sequence of activity in a given physical context" (p. 25). Each scene was examined for sexual and/or violent content. Coders were provided a list of specific violent acts (see Table 8.1.1) and recorded whether each scene contained each particular act and, if the scene did contain that act, the sex of both the person performing the violent act and the victim. Coders only measured the presence of the behavior. They were not instructed to measure the number of times it occurred within a scene or the intensity of that occurrence.

Table 8.1.1 is divided into 4 violence strata (indicated by the spacing between categories). These divisions were made during data analysis by placing the individual violent acts in a roughly hierarchical order and making logical divisions among them.

In addition to examining specific violent acts, coders were instructed to identify the sex of the participants; whether each was in a dominant, submissive, or ambiguous power position; and whether each appeared to be a consensual, coerced, or nonconsensual participant.

Two points are important to note here. First, no attempt was made to measure the level of intensity contained in any particular violent act. Thus specific instances of the same violent act may vary in intensity.

Table 8.1.1 Violence Categories

Violence category
Verbal aggression
Pushing, shoving
Being rough in an otherwise "normal" activity
Pulling hair/biting
Pinching
Open hand punch (e.g. slap, spank)
Threaten with weapon
Choking
Closed fist punch or kick
Confine, bondage
Use weapon on victim
Torture, mutilation
Attempted, actual murder

While this is true for all forms of violence examined, it is especially noteworthy for those forms of violence that are more "culturally ritualized," such as verbal aggression, slapping/spanking, and confine/bondage, all of which oscillate between what might be considered light and heavy violence.

Five coders were employed to code the 150 cases. Four were undergraduate volunteers, and the fifth was one of the authors. Two of the coders were male and three were female. All were white and had some social science background, and all completed an extensive training seminar prior to participating.

Reliability

Ten percent of our sample was coded by two different coders in order ascertain intercoder reliability. Cohen's Kappa Coefficient was computed for each of these cases and their recode. This measure of association provides the percent agreement between coders rescaled to correct for chance. The average Kappa Coefficient for the 15 recoded cases was .8302.

RESULTS

The amount of sexual violence found in our sample is shown in Table 8.1.2. The first row aggregates the individual types of violence to give a summary of the percentage of scenes containing any violence, while each subsequent row summarizes the percentage of scenes containing particular forms of sexual violence.[2]

According to our findings, the Usenet is most likely to contain violence by a wide, and statistically significant (χ^2 = 10.34, df = 1, p < .0025), margin. Videos contain the second highest proportion of violent scenes, followed closely by magazines. However, while the videos in this sample contained a higher percentage of violence than magazines, these differences were not statistically significant at the .05 level. Although the difference between media in the percentage of cases containing *any violence* is statistically significant, more than half of the differences in individual violence items were not statistically significant. The majority of statistically significant differences occur in the most violent stratum, with one sta-

Table 8.1.2 Percentage of Scenes Containing Sexual Violence by Media

Type of violence	Magazine[a]	Video[b]	Usenet[c]	χ^2
Any violence	24.8	26.9	42.1	12.83**
Verbal aggression	7.6	12.6	15.0	3.11
Rough in otherwise normal activity	2.9	4.1	10.0	8.48*
Pushing, shoving	7.6	3.8	3.6	3.06
Pinch	1.0	3.8	2.1	2.79
Pull hair/biting	4.8	8.0	3.6	3.83
Threaten with weapon	0.0	0.8	9.3	31.72**
Open hand punch (i.e., slap, spank)	4.8	9.3	8.6	2.23
Choke	0.0	0.8	0.7	.86
Punch/kick	1.9	0.8	2.1	1.70
Confine, bondage	5.7	2.7	25.7	69.59**
Weapon	1.0	1.6	15.7	48.17**
Torture, mutilation	1.0	0.3	8.6	32.01**
Attempted/actual murder	0.0	0.0	1.4	6.72*

[a]n = 105. [b]n = 364. [c]n = 140.
*p < .05. **p < .001.

tistically significant form of violence occurring in each of the other three strata.

Table 8.1.3 illustrates the percentage of scenes containing violence in particular strata by medium. The row variables (*low, medium, high,* and *extreme*) are derived from dichotomous variables representing the presence (or absence) of violence from that stratum. Thus, any scene containing any verbal aggression, being rough in an otherwise normal activity, or pushing/shoving would be coded as containing violence in the low stratum.

Note that for both magazines and videos, violence decreases in a monotonic fashion. As violence becomes more intense, or extreme, fewer scenes contain it. For both media, approximately 15% of scenes contained low intensity violence. Both have fewer scenes with medium intensity violence (roughly 13%), fewer still with high intensity violence (roughly 5%), and very few scenes with extreme violence (2%). Differences between magazines and videos were not significant at $\alpha = .05$. The Usenet, however, does not follow such a linear pattern. Most of the violence in Usenet newsgroup pornography falls into the low and high categories, while the medium and extreme categories contain slightly less violence. For all strata, a higher percentage of scenes from the Usenet contain violence (the differences between the Usenet and the other two media combined are statistically significant at the $\alpha = .05$ level for all strata except medium).

When we examined the level of violence from more to less recent technology, we also found that the Usenet contains more coercive and less consensual

sex in the scenes depicted. Over one fourth (26.4%) of scenes from the Usenet contain coercive or nonconsensual sex, followed by videos and magazines (4.9% and 4.8% respectively). While we can again note the Usenet-video-magazine pattern, the difference between magazine and video is not significant ($\chi^2 = .006$, df = 1, p = .939).

When we examined the question of power in sexual relationships, we again find that the Usenet differs dramatically from the other media. While the majority of scenes in magazines and videos contained neither dominant nor submissive participants (i.e., portrayed egalitarian sexual relations, with 69.5% and 80.8% respectively), only 49.3% of Usenet scenes did. The difference between magazine and video here is significant (egalitarian sex, $\chi^2 = 6.055$, df = 1, p = .014).

When these power positions are disaggregated by gender an interesting pattern emerges. Table 8.1.4 shows power positions broken down by gender. Percentages are for all scenes containing that type of power position; thus, of all magazine scenes containing a participant in a dominant power position, 9.7% of those scenes have a male in the dominant power position. (The percentage of males and females in a given power position in a given medium do not add to 100%, because some scenes contain two people of opposite sexes maintaining the same power position.)

Two things are worth noting here. First, while videos and the Usenet follow the expected gender role patterns (woman are more often submissive, men are more often dominant), in the magazines dominant power positions are virtually always held by women.

Table 8.1.3 Sexual Violence in Scenes by Strata

	Magazine[a]	Video[b]	Usenet[c]	χ^2
Low	14.3%	16.5%	23.6%	4.51
Medium	9.5	15.4	17.1	3.03
High	6.7	4.4	26.4	56.72*
Extreme	1.9	1.9	17.1	48.76*

[a]n = 105. [b]n = 364. [c]n = 140.
*p < .001.

Table 8.1.4 Percentage of Scenes Containing Nonegalitarian Sex by Sex of Participant and Media

	Magazine[a]		Video[b]		Usenet[c]	
	Male	Female	Male	Female	Male	Female
Dominant	9.7	93.5	74.2	33.3	68.6	41.4
Submissive	74.2	35.5	26.5	77.9	16.2	85.3

[a]n = 31 (dominant), n = 31 (submissive). [b]n = 70 (dominant), n = 68 (submissive). [c]n = 66 (dominant), n = 68 (submissive).

At the same time, men are twice as likely to be in the submissive position as women. Second, across all media both sexes are shown relatively frequently in both dominant and submissive roles (with, perhaps, the exception of dominant men in magazines). This suggests a greater level of fluidity of dominance and submission than some theories, which hold that these images always accurately mirror gender stereotypes, might have predicted.

We then turned to an examination of the victims and perpetrators of violence. Where violence occurs it is disproportionately caused by men in Usenet scenes. Men make up a smaller percentage of aggressors in video scenes, and an even smaller percentage in magazines. In magazines, 38.5% of sexually violent scenes had male perpetrators and 65.4% had female perpetrators. However, in videos 60.2% of the sexually violent scenes had male perpetrators and 49% of the scenes had female perpetrators. In the Usenet sample 62.7% of the scenes had male perpetrators and only 42.4% of the scenes had female perpetrators. (Again, since a scene can contain perpetrators of both sexes, the percents do not sum to 100.) It is worth noting that magazines not only have a greater gender difference in the perpetrator of violence than the other two media, but they also display women inflicting violence more often then men.

The opposite gender relationship is expressed when we examine the victims of the violence. In magazines, 50% of the sexually violent scenes had male victims, and 61.5% had female victims. Percentages may not add up to 100% because the same scene may have had more than one victim of the violence. In the videos, 32.7% of the scenes depicted male victims, compared with 79.6% of the scenes depicting female victims. And on the Usenet, 23.7% of the scenes depicted male victims and 84.7% of the scenes had female victims. As we can see, the victims of violence in pornography are far more frequently female: Over 61 percentage points separate males and females at the extreme (Usenet), and 11.5 percentage points (magazines) is as close as the sexes come to parity. Magazines, which showed the greatest gender difference in terms of perpetrators of violence, are the most egalitarian in terms of the victims of violence.

Finally, we turn to the issue of consensual sex together with violence. To what extent were victims of violence consensual participants? What we found here was surprising. The vast majority of violence in magazines and videos occurs in the context of a consensual relationship. In magazines, 88.5% of the violence was depicted as consensual, compared with 3.8% as coercive and 7.7% as nonconsensual. In the videos, 91.8% of the violence was depicted as consensual, 5.1% as coercive, and 3.1% as nonconsensual. On the Usenet, however, 42.4% was depicted as consensual, while 10.2% was coercive and 47.5% was depicted as nonconsensual. Thus, less than half of the Usenet scenes that contained violence were consensual, statistically different from both magazines and videos ($\chi^2 = 51.38$, df = 2, p < .001).

DISCUSSION

Our results clearly demonstrate differing levels of violence among the three pornographic media. What types of theoretical arguments would explain these differences? Although we cannot conclusively point to any single theoretical trend, we outline some of the possible interpretations of the different levels, and offer some evaluation of those explanations.

Several differences among the different media must be factored into the explanation. Magazines, videos, and the Usenet represent three different historical "moments" in the history of erotic representation, from the 1950s and 1960s (the rise of mass-market magazines), to the 1970s and 1980s (the dramatic explosion of videotapes), to the current era, in which the Usenet (and the Internet in general) has emerged as one of the most versatile and accessible venues for pornography. This historical progression also illustrates the increasing "democratization" of pornographic media. As new technologies (video, telephone, computer, etc.) have been adapted to pornography, the cost of production has dropped and control of production has diffused. Successful pornographic magazines require massive production and distribution requirements, making them the province of media elites. For example, while Hugh Hefner began *Playboy* with a initial investment of only $600 in 1953 (Leerhsen, 1986), a magazine start-up today can require as much as $20 million—the amount needed by John F. Kennedy Jr. to inaugurate *George* (Handy, 1995).

Adult videos, which became the preferred pornographic medium during the mid-1980s, are far less expensive to produce than magazines. A typical adult feature can cost as little as $3,000 (Schlosser, 1997). The relatively inexpensive production price of videos, compared to magazines, has allowed for an enormous upsurge in both the number of producers creating pornographic videos and the number of features made each year.

The Usenet offers the greatest access to the largest number of users at the least expense: One need only have a computer, a telephone line, and access to the Internet to enter its pornographic world. Usenet pornography production is also unique in that there is complete individual ownership of the means of production. Magazine production requires large printing presses as well as numerous specialized employees (typesetters, graphic artists, etc.). Video production requires cameras, lighting, sound systems, duplication equipment, and people to run them. Usenet pornography production requires nothing more than a computer, a telephone line, and an imagination.

In addition, pornographic magazines are dependent upon advertising, which may require the magazine to mute the violent content to express a more mainstream association with erotica and high-end consumerism. Videos and the Usenet are less dependent upon advertising, and may actually eschew it altogether. This independence, coupled with the lower costs of production and distribution, means that many of the participants in the Usenet world are as much creators of pornography as they are consumers of it. We believe that this blurring of the lines between consumer and creator contains some threads of explanation that may be worth exploring.

Democratization has led to an increase in violent scenes from magazines to videos to the Usenet, with the largest increase in violence in the move between videos and the Usenet. Perhaps this is the illustration of nothing more than simple psychological notions of addiction working themselves out on an aggregate scale. We might expect, for example, that just as individual consumers of pornography tend to tire of a certain level of explicitness and need more, so, too, would the market, acting as an individual. Thus, the more pornography is consumed at one level, the less arousing this material becomes, as the consumer becomes used to—satiated with—the material. This satiation leads the consumer to seek out newer, more explicit, and more violent forms of sexual material that will again arouse him/her (Russell, 1993; Zillmann & Bryant, 1984). Thus we might expect that as new pornographic technologies emerge, one will find them increasingly violent, because they must satisfy both the demand previously satisfied and an increased demand for even more.

Such an explanation, however, can take us only so far in terms of the historical sequence of pornographic form. Our second finding concerned the differing *content* of the victim and victimizer among the three media, and this difference could not be explained by a simple addiction model. We found that the Usenet shows men in dominant positions, as victimizer and not victim, in far greater proportion than do magazines and videos, which is also suggestive that democratization of pornography has increased both the violence and the amount of misogyny—women as victims—contained in the images. Such a finding confirms some of the arguments offered by radical feminist critics of pornography: that pornography illustrates a universal misogyny and that its function in male supremacist society is to eroticize male supremacy, to "... keep sexism looking sexy." (Stoltenberg, 1989, p. 129; see also MacKinnon, 1987).

Unfortunately, radical feminist critics often tend to treat pornography as an undifferentiated whole, a monolith, rather than as a set of diverse and often competing genres. Their critique is not

> ... presented against the background of any attempt to analyze pornography into different forms, some catering for more peculiar perversions and some not, some concerned with women, some wholly directed towards homosexual men. Pornography is treated as simply an individual phenomenon... (Simpson, 1983, p. 71)

How, then, can we explain not only the increasing violence in the progression of pornographic media but also the qualitative difference in the depiction of victims and victimizers between the Usenet, on the one hand, and magazines and videos on the other? We believe that several specific elements of the Usenet tailor it for a particular type of pornographic representation. As we noted above, it is more democratic, with greater mass access and far less dependence on commercial advertisers. It is as close as one can get to men's[3] direct expressions of their own fantasies, unconstrained by the demands of the marketplace or the high costs of producing and distributing those fantasies to others.

More than this, though, these Internet newsgroups are the closest things to the all-male locker room that exist in the pornographic world: A world, in a sense, entirely without women, a world in which men control absolutely all facets of the scene and in which women do not insert themselves as corporeal beings, even in the highly stylized forms offered by magazines or videos. Any adequate explanation of the increased violence and the shifting relationships of victims and victimizers, then, must take into account the distinctly, purely, and uncorruptedly *homosocial* element in the Internet newsgroup.

Surely, this homosocial element has been noted before. After all, most pornography is produced *by* men and *for* men; it is in this sense *about* masculinity (see, for example, Kimmel, 1990; Kimmel & Linders, 1997). If, as Kimmel argued, pornography is "gendered speech," it provides a communicative system among and between men.

This homosocial element—men communicating with other men using a particularly gendered speech—has been largely absent from most empirical discussions of pornography and its impact, in part because of the surface level "reading" that pornography is about men's relationships with women. Yet with the Usenet, the relationship between producer and consumer is so blurred as to become nonexistent. And perhaps what is different between the Usenet and the other pornographic media is that the apparent collusion between producer and consumer is broken. Magazine and video producers enter into at least a tacit alliance with consumers. This is necessitated by the pornography producer's desire for profits, and the pornography consumer's desire for arousal. No such alliance exists

between the producers and consumers of Usenet pornography (at least not those who have continued to produce pornography free of charge). Perhaps what the Usenet offers is *homosocial competition*—a relationship among men in which the sexual victimization of women is a currency among men, used as a way to facilitate upward mobility in a masculine hierarchy.

Bird (1996) argues that homosociality is vital to the maintenance of hegemonic masculinity, acting to institutionally and interpersonally segregate men and women, and also acting to suppress nonhegemonic masculinities. Three characteristics of hegemonic masculinity are crucial to Bird's conceptualization, and may suggest some of the elements of an adequate explanation of our findings:

> (a) *emotional detachment,* a meaning constructed through relationships within families whereby young men detach themselves from mothers and develop gender identities in relation to that which they are not (Chodorow, 1978); (b) *competitiveness,* a meaning constructed and maintained through relationships with other men whereby simple individuality becomes competitive individuality (Gilligan, 1982); and (c) *sexual objectification of women,* a meaning constructed and maintained through relationship with other men whereby male individuality is conceptualized not only as *different* from female but as *better* than female (Johnson, 1988). (Bird, 1996, p. 121)

Perhaps the pornography found on Internet newsgroups is so much more violent than magazine and video pornography precisely because of the homosocial competition that exists between individual producers and between producers and consumers. Internet pornography, particularly the newsgroup stories used in this study, is written by men about their fantasies, and is intended for other men to read without marketplace considerations. The producers of this pornography are freed from formal market constraints and, therefore, participate in an informal masculinist marketplace, competing with other men in an effort to prove who can "do the most . . . ," "last the longest," "have the biggest . . . ," and so on.

Violence against women is thus a currency among men as they jockey for position in the eyes of other men. This is, of course, facilitated by the sexual objectification of women discussed by Bird (1996). The Usenet contains producers and consumers who are no less a social group because their interactions take place in virtual space. They have their own norms, values, symbols, and modes of interaction. We suggest here that this social group is particularly conducive to the hegemonic masculinity that promotes homosocial competition among pornography producers.

Neither magazine nor video pornography suggests such a relationship between producer and consumer. Indeed, constrained by the formal marketplace, magazines and videos promote homosocial collusion between producer and consumer. It is in the best interest of pornography producers from these media to provide their consumers with the most arousing material possible. The lines between consumers and producers is clear and well defined, thus facilitating their apparent collusion. By contrast, the boundaries between produce and consumer on the Usenet are blurred; consumers are producers and vice versa.

This collusion between producer and consumer helps explain the minor variations between videos and magazines. As we have noted, in most aspects videos and magazines are not significantly different. The homosocial competition model predicts this, since producers of these pornographic forms are trying to maximize their profits by providing the most arousing material to the largest proportion of consumers. This should be possible since hegemonic masculinity (and feminist theory) both suggest that men will tend to find the same material arousing. Marketplace adjustments in the amount of violent material contained in pornography would, therefore, eventually stabilize at relatively equal levels.

Of course, hegemonic masculinity is not absolute. Variations on the dominant masculine identity do exist. Hence, certain segments of pornography consumers would not be served by the homogenous pornography produced according to the demands of a hegemonic definition. Instead, microlevel variations would appear in some forms of pornography in attempt to tap these consumers. However, these microvariations are just that—small scale. Variations from the hegemonic ideal still conform to its general ideology. Hence, women in magazines can be shown

as causing violence, but they still are shown as suffering violence more often than men.

CONCLUSION

This article has provided the first systematic and methodologically coherent comparison among three contemporary pornographic media. We found not only increasing levels of violence as we moved from one medium to the next, but also a dramatic shift from magazines and videos on the one hand and the Usenet on the other when we examined both level of violence and the gender of victim and victimizer. While we offered no definitive explanation of these results, we suggested that explanations that stressed simple democratization, psychological addiction, or misogyny were inadequate to fully explain our results. We have therefore offered a sketch of a model that might explain the differences among these media by virtue of homosocial competition. This places the changing levels of violence within a context of men's relations with each other, and in their constant and ceaseless efforts to prove their masculinity in the eyes of other men. The changes in violent content among media, then, has more to do with the definition of hegemonic masculinity than it does with technological proliferation and democratization, or with the psychological propensity to require greater and greater thrills before satiation. Contrary to radical feminist theory, though, these changes in pornography may say more about men's relationships with other men than they do about men's relationships with women. One potentially fruitful avenue of further research would be an examination of commercial Internet pornography sites. Presumably, these sites operate under market constraints similar to those experienced by magazines and videos and, therefore, would experience the same collusion between producer and consumer leading to similar rates of violence. Only further research will be able to demonstrate the continued utility of this homosocial competition explanation of the changing violent content of pornography over different media and over time.

NOTES

1. While the pornographic videos and magazines we sampled may be nationally distributed, we sampled only those

available in this one area. However, the Usenet, by design, allows users in many different countries to access the same material, with only language restriction. Thus the generalizability of these findings for the Usenet may be far greater than the findings for the other media. On the other hand, little research has addressed the geographic variations in pornographic content, and there is some evidence that suggests a great variation (Dietz & Sears, 1988). Care should therefore be taken in generalizing these results to other geographic locales.

2. Thirty-six scenes (5.6% of all scenes) contained violence but not sex. Since the majority of the theoretical literature on the harm of violence in pornography has focused on sexual violence not violence per se, these scenes are not included in our subsequent analysis. Also included is the row's chi-square score. Chi-square tests the null hypothesis that there is no association between the presence of a particular form of violence and media. Thus, a significant chi-square indicates that there is an association between media and presence of violence.

3. Unfortunately, it is virtually impossible to know what proportion of Usenet pornography is produced or consumed by women. We believe that the vast majority of producers and consumers are male. However we have no hard evidence to support this and, if incorrect, our explanation for differences in violent content would be weakened significantly.

REFERENCES

Allen, M., D'alessio, D., & Brezgel, K. (1995). A meta-analysis summarizing the effects of pornography II. *Human Communication Research, 22,* 258–283.

Bird, S. R. (1996). Welcome to the men's club: Homosociality and the maintenance of hegemonic masculinity. *Gender and Society, 10,* 120–132.

Brannigan, A., & Goldenberg, S. (1987). The study of aggressive pornography: The vicissitudes of relevance. *Critical Studies in Mass Communication, 4,* 262–283

Brosius, H.-B., Weaver, J. B., and Staab, J. F. (1993). Exploring the social and sexual "reality" of contemporary pornography. *The Journal of Sex Research, 30,* 161–170.

Chodorow, N. (1978). *The reproduction of mothering.* Berkeley, CA: University of California Press.

DeLoughry, T. J. (1995, July 21). Researcher who studied online pornography gets invitation from Congress, criticism from scholars. *Chronicle of Higher Education,* A19.

Dietz, P. E., & Sears, A. E. (1988). Pornography and obscenity sold in 'adult bookstores': A survey of 5132 books, magazines, and films in four American cities. *Journal of Law Reform, 21,* 7–46.

Duncan, D. F. (1991). Violence and degradation as themes in "adult" videos. *Psychological Reports, 69,* 239–240.

Elmer-Dewitt, P. (1995, July 24). Fire storm on the computer nets. *Time, 146,* 57.

Fisher, W. A., & Grenier, G. (1994). Violent pornography, anti-woman thoughts, and antiwoman acts: In search of reliable effects. *The Journal of Sex Research, 31,* 23–38.

Gilligan, C. (1982). *In a different voice: Psychological theory and women's development.* Cambridge, MA: Harvard University Press.

Glascock, J., & LaRose, R. (1993). Dial-a-porn recordings: The role of the female participant in male sexual fantasies. *Journal of Broadcasting & Electronic Media, 37,* 313–324.

Handy, B. (1995, September 18). "Ich bin ein magazine editor." *Time, 146,* 127.

Johnson, M. (1988). *Strong mothers, weak wives.* Berkeley, CA: University of California Press.

Kimmel, M. (Ed). (1990). *Men confront pornography.* New York: Crown.

Kimmel, M., & Linders, A. (1997). Does censorship make a difference?: An aggregate empirical analysis of pornography and rape. *Journal of Psychology and Human Sexuality, 8,* 1–20.

Leerhsen, C. (1986, August 4). Aging playboy. *Newsweek, 108,* 50–56.

Linz, D. (1989). Exposure to sexually explicit materials and attitudes toward rape: A comparison of study results. *The Journal of Sex Research, 26,* 50–84.

Linz, D., & Donnerstein, E. (1988). Methodological issues in the content analysis of pornography. *Journal of Law Reform, 21,* 47–53.

MacKinnon, C. A. (1987). *Feminism unmodified: Discourses on life and law.* Cambridge, MA: Harvard University Press.

Malamuth, N. M., & Check, J. V. P. (1985). The effects of aggressive pornography on beliefs in rape myths: Individual differences. *Journal of Research in Personality, 19,* 299–320.

Malamuth, N. M., & Spinner, B. (1980). A longitudinal content analysis of sexual violence in the best-selling erotic magazines. *The Journal of Sex Research, 16,* 226–237.

Matacin, M. L., & Burger, J. M. (1987). A content analysis of sexual themes in Playboy cartoons. *Sex Roles, 17,* 179–207.

Mayerson, S. E., & Taylor, D. A. (1987). The effects of rape myth pornography on women's attitudes and the mediating role of sex role stereotyping. *Sex Roles, 1987,* 321–338.

Palys, T. S. (1986). Testing the common wisdom: The social content of video pornography. *Canadian Psychology, 27,* 22–35.

Rimm, M. (1995). Marketing pornography on the information superhighway: A survey of 917,410 images, descriptions, short stories, and animations downloaded 8.5 million times by consumers in over 2000 cities in forty countries, provinces, and territories. *Georgetown Law Review, 83,* 1849–1934.

Russell, D. (1993). *Against pornography: The evidence of harm.* Berkeley, CA: Russell Publications.

Schlosser, E. (1997, February 10). The business of pornography. *U.S. News & World Report, 122,* 43–52.

Scott, J. E., & Cuvelier, S. J. (1987a). Violence in Playboy magazine: A longitudinal analysis. *Archives of Sexual Behavior, 16,* 279–288.

Scott, J. E., & Cuvelier, S. J. (1987b). Sexual violence in Playboy magazine: A longitudinal analysis. *The Journal of Sex Research, 23,* 534–539.

Scott, J. E., & Cuvelier, S. J. (1993). Violence and sexual violence in pornography: Is it really increasing? *Archives of Sexual Behavior, 22,* 357–370.

Simpson, A. W. B. (1983). *Pornography and politics: A look back to the Williams Committee.* London: Waterloo.

Smith, D. D. (1976). The social content of pornography. *Journal of Communication, 26,* 16–24.

Stoltenberg, J. (1989). *Pornography and freedom.* Portland, OR: Breitenbush Books.

Winick, C. (1985). A content analysis of sexually explicit magazines sold in an adult bookstore. *The Journal of Sex Research, 21,* 206–210.

Yang, N., & Linz, D. (1990). Movie ratings and the content of adult videos: The sex-violence ratio. *Journal of Communication, 40,* 28–42.

Zillmann, D., & Bryant, J. (1984). Effects of massive exposure to pornography. In N. Malamuth (Ed.), *Pornography and sexual aggression,* (pp. 15–138). New York: Academic Press.

APPENDIX A
Videos in the Sample

The following videos comprise the sample reviewed by this study:

All Little Women	Damp Spot	Snakedance
Amateur A Cuppers	Danish Hard Core 104	Spunk Suckers
Anal Mystique	Dirty Dozen #67	Strap on Sally #9
Anal Persuasion	Ebony Experience	Super Diamond Double XX #6
Anal Playground	Eros Extreme	Super Tramp
Analtown USA #3	Filthy Fuckers #60	Superstar Sex Challenge #1
Asses Galore	Girls Who Love it Ass Backwards	The Big One
Bad Attitude	Hidden Obsession	Tits a Wonderful Life
Bad Girls #2	Impact	Totally Naked
Bad Girls #5	Jizz and Tonic	UFO Tracker
Because I can	Junkyard Dogs	Up and Cummers #32
Bisexual Anal	Kink-o-Rama	Upbeat Love
Buttfucker #3	Pleasure Zone #22	Wall to Wall #33
Butt Banged Bicycle Babes	Plum and Dumber	White Chicks #13
Casting Call #18	Private Profits	Wicked Women
Cum in my Holes	Sex Freaks	Zane's World
Cumming Clean	Sex Spa	

APPENDIX B
Magazines in the Sample

The following magazines were comprise the sample reviewed by this study:

40 +	Girls[a]	Original Porn Stars[a]
Adult Cinema Review	Girls of Penthouse	Panther[a]
Asian Beauties	Graham Cracker[a]	Penthouse
Big Busts	Hot Buns	Penthouse Letters
Celebrity Skin[a]	Hot Stuff	Playboy[a]

Club Confidential	Just Eighteen	Playboy Playmates[a]
College Girls[a]	Kinky Babes[a]	Playgirl
Confidential Letters	Leg Action	Portfolio[a]
Dirty	Leg Sex	Rage[a]
D-Cup	Live Nude Girls	Ravers
Dolly[b]	Lovers in Heat[a]	Score
Family Fun	Nugget	Turn-ons
Gallery		

[a]contained no stories [b]text not in English

8.2 INTERNET PORNOGRAPHY
A Social Psychological Perspective on Internet Sexuality

William A. Fisher and Azy Barak

Spectacular growth in availability of sexually explicit material on the Internet has created an unprecedented opportunity for individuals to have anonymous, cost-free, and unfettered access to an essentially unlimited range of sexually explicit texts, still and moving images, and audio materials (Cheney, 2000; Elmer-Dewitt, 1995; Freeman-Longo, 2000; Harmon & Boeringer, 1996; Mehta & Plaza, 1998; Rimm, 1995; Wysocki, 1998). In a fashion never before imagined, men and women—and boys and girls—can acquire sexually explicit content on the Internet, effortlessly and privately, as a direct expression of their sexual and personal characteristics and inclinations. Sexually explicit materials so obtained, in turn, may act to alter, not at all or more or less profoundly, the sexual and personal dispositions that incline individuals to seek out Internet sexuality in the first place.

Growth in access to Internet sexually explicit material challenges sexual science to conceptualize antecedents and consequences of experience with such content. One view, based upon relevant theory and research (e.g., Bogaert, 1993, 2001; Eysenck, 1978; Malamuth, 1989a, 1989b; Malamuth, Addison, & Koss, 2001; Mosher, 1980, 1988; Rimm, 1995; Snyder

& Ickes, 1985), suggests that antisocial personality characteristics will encourage some individuals to seek out antisocial sexually explicit materials from among those available on the Internet. The "goodness of fit" of antisocial personality characteristics with antisocial sexual content will, it is speculated, promote a tremendous depth of involvement in antisocial sexual stimuli. Individuals may lose awareness of the constraints of reality regarding enactment of antisocial sexual behavior, and uniquely strong negative effects of antisocial sexual content on the Internet may be seen among those predisposed to access such material.

A related view, also based upon relevant theory and research (e.g., Barak & Fisher, 1997; Barak, Fisher, Belfry, & Lashambe, 1999; Bogaert, 1993, 2001; Fisher & Barak, 1991; Malamuth et al., 2001; Mosher, 1980, 1988; Snyder & Ickes, 1985), suggests that normal range individuals will ordinarily choose sexually explicit Internet materials which are not anti-social in nature. The "poorness of fit" of normal range personality characteristics with antisocial sexual content will, in fact, provoke avoidance of antisocial sexual stimuli, termination of contact with such stimuli if encountered, and rejection of the antisocial sexual messages of such stimuli. According to this analysis, most individuals have a lifetime learning history and set of expectancies about acceptable and unacceptable sexual behavior that is sufficient to deter them from accessing or acting on antisocial sexual content on the Internet.

The current discussion attempts to provide a conceptual and empirical context for considering antecedents and consequences of experience with Internet sexually explicit materials. At present, research concerning experience with Internet sexuality is at an early stage of development, and focused discussion of these issues may prove particularly valuable as sexual science moves toward more intensive study of this area. We begin this paper with a summary of some of what has been learned from existing research concerning sexually explicit materials, in contexts other than the Internet, and consider lessons from this work that may inform the study of Internet sexuality. A social psychological theory, the Sexual Behavior Sequence (Byrne, 1977), is then applied as an heuristic guide in an initial effort to conceptualize a number of antecedents and consequences of experience with Internet sexuality. Our discussion closes with consideration of an agenda for future research concerning Internet sexually explicit materials. What follows, then, is *a* social psychological perspective—and certainly not *the* social psychological perspective—on aspects of Internet sexuality.

WHAT DO WE KNOW ABOUT SEXUALLY EXPLICIT MATERIALS OUTSIDE THE CONTEXT OF THE INTERNET? LESSONS FOR THE STUDY OF INTERNET SEXUALITY

What Do We Know About Defining Sexually Explicit Materials?

Conceptual and operational definition of terms is prerequisite to meaningful scientific discussion and research concerning sexually explicit materials, on or off the Internet. A three-part conceptualization of *erotica, degrading pornography,* and *violent pornography* has been suggested to guide theory and research in this area (Check & Guloien, 1989; Donnerstein &

Berkowitz, 1981; Fisher & Barak, 1989; Zillmann & Bryant, 1989).

Definitions of erotica, degrading pornography, and violent pornography are based on the manifest content of sexually explicit materials. It is assumed that the content of sexually explicit material will be a distinguishing characteristic of such material and critical determinant of antecedents and consequences of experience with it (Fisher & Barak, 1991). Content-based definitions of *erotica* generally hold that such material involves sexually explicit, nondegrading, and noviolent portrayal of consensual sexual activity (Check & Guloien, 1989; Donnerstein & Berkowitz, 1981; Fisher & Barak, 1989). Content-based definitions of *degrading pornography* hold that such material is sexually explicit and degrades, debases, and dehumanizes people, generally women, in a fashion that endorses such degradation (Check & Guloien, 1989; Zillmann & Bryant, 1989). Content-based definitions of *violent pornography* assert that such material is sexually explicit and depicts and endorses the utility and normativeness of sexual violence, usually directed by men against women (Check & Guloien, 1989; Donnerstein & Berkowitz, 1981; Fisher & Barak, 1989).

Definitions of erotica, degrading pornography, and violent pornography can be problematic. A primary concern is that achieving agreement about whether sexually explicit materials—on or off the Internet—fall into the broad categories of erotica, degrading pornography, or violent pornography, remains an unrealized objective. Although researchers such as Barron and Kimmell (2000) and Cowan and Dunn (1994) have studied the reliability of judgments of degradation and violence in small fragments of sexually explicit materials (e.g., 5-minute clips from full-length videos, and individual scenes in magazines, videos, and stories), our ability to reliably categorize complex and intact sexually explicit offerings, in the units in which they are experienced and interpreted by users, remains to be established. Moreover, whether or not sexually explicit materials that are categorized as erotica or as degrading pornography or violent pornography are actually spontaneously perceived and interpreted as such by consumers of sexually explicit material remains an entirely unanswered empirical question. Is it the case that what the researcher designates as violent pornography is spontaneously perceived and interpreted by the average male as an endorsement of the utility and normativeness of violence against women? Is it the case that what the researcher designates as erotica is spontaneously perceived and interpreted by the average female as a nondegrading sexual portrayal?

What lessons can be taken from efforts to define sexually explicit materials and applied to inform research on Internet sexuality? We would suggest that concerns regarding reliability and validity of definitions of sexually explicit materials can and should be addressed empirically, in order to facilitate meaningful study of Internet sexuality. Research concerning categorization of sexually explicit materials, in the complex and intact forms in which they are experienced, can address reliability concerns in an ecologically valid fashion. Research concerning the crucial question of whether or not categorizations of erotica, degrading pornography, and violent pornography reflect spontaneous perceptions and interpretations of consumers of such material can address critical validity issues that have been raised. Until reliability and validity concerns about the definition of sexually explicit materials have been addressed, it will be difficult to map the content of Internet sexuality, to conceptualize or study effects of Internet sexually explicit materials, or to craft educational interventions or sociolegal policies concerning Internet sexuality.

What Do We Know About the Prevalence of Sexually Explicit Materials?

Research interest in sexually explicit materials is historically associated with concern that such materials are enormously prevalent and are saturating society at an accelerating rate with each passing year (Fisher & Barak, 1991). During the 1980s, a time of intense research interest in sexually explicit materials, a report in the *Psychology of Women Quarterly* informed readers that X-rated materials in the U.S. represented ". . . an estimated $8 billion industry of misogyny per year" (Cowan, Lee, Levy, & Snyder, 1988, pp. 309–310) and the U.S. Attorney General's Commission reported that violent pornography was ". . . the most prevalent form" of sexually explicit material (U.S. Attorney

General's Commission, 1986, p. 323). At the same time, a best-selling human sexuality textbook speculated that $1 billion per year of the U.S. sexually explicit media industry involved sales of child pornography (Hyde, 1986) and the important antipornography documentary film, *Not a Love Story,* informed its viewers that the sexually explicit media are controlled by organized crime (Sherr-Klein, 1981).

Systematic studies of the prevalence of sexually explicit materials appear at first glance to to verify views about the saturation of western society with violent pornography (see Barron & Kimmel, 2000; Cowan et al., 1988; Dietz & Evans, 1982; Malamuth & Spinner, 1980, Smith, 1976). A closer look at research findings in this area, however, provides a cautionary tale of conflicting and inconsistent results. We find, for example, that Malamuth and Spinner (1980) report a steady increase in sexual violence in *Playboy* and *Penthouse* across the 1970s, from about 1% to 5% of all text and pictures. Scott and Cuvelier (1987; see also Scott & Cuvelier, 1993), however, studied some of the same magazines over some of the same years and found that, over all of the 30 years of *Playboy's* publication, sexually violent pictures (.16 per issue) or cartoons (.58 per issue) were extraordinarily rare, and were actually decreasing in frequency of occurrence over time. In the realm of sexually explicit videos, Cowan et al. (1988) reported that fully 51% of X-rated videos sampled portrayed the rape of a woman, whereas Palys (1986) and Garcia and Milano (1991) found vastly less sexual violence in such videos, and Palys (1986) determined that levels of sexual violence in X-rated videos had been declining across the decade under study. Other researchers (Barron & Kimmel, 2000) report very high levels of sexual violence overall in sexually explicit magazines, videos, and Internet sex story postings, but at the same time note that the perpetrators of sexual violence in these media are usually or often women (65%, 49%, and 42% of perpetrators of sexual violence were women in magazines, videos, and Internet postings, respectively).

Initial reports of the prevalence of sexually explicit material on the Internet are eerily reminiscent of initial reports of the prevalence of print and video pornography. For example, Rimm's (1995) *George-*

town Law Review paper, "A Survey of 917,410 Images, Descriptions, Short Stories, and Animations Downloaded 8.5 Million Times by Consumers in Over 2000 Cities . . ." (since heavily criticized for methodological flaws; see Hoffman & Novak, 1995) provoked a *Time* magazine cover story concerning the saturation of the Internet with pornography (Elmer-Dewitt, 1995). The *Time* magazine cover story was quickly followed by passage of the U.S. Communications Decency Act of 1996, designed to suppress the flood of Internet pornography, but the Communications Decency Act itself was quickly declared unconstitutional. Current reports indicate variously that the online pornography industry will gross $366 million by 2001 (Spenger, 1999) or that it *already* grosses in excess of $1 billion ("Blue Money," 1999), and reports indicate that a spectacular 69% of all e-commerce involves the purchase of sexual materials ("Blue Money," 1999). Other sources report that 15% of all Internet users accessed one of the top five "Adult" websites in a recent month (Cooper, Scherer, Boies, & Gordon, 1999), that sex is the most frequently searched topic on the Internet (Freeman-Longo & Blanchard, 1998), and that all of the top eight word searches on the Internet involve pornography (Sparrow & Griffiths, 1997). In another example, Canada's national newspaper of record recently printed a two-part series entitled "The Triple-X Crisis. Is Pornography Out of Control?" (Cheney, 2000). This report informs readers that 3.8 million Canadians visited an Internet sex site in October of 2000 and reports that the average user visits Internet sex sites on 4 days per month. We note in passing that taking these statistics seriously requires us to believe that approximately 25% of all Canadian males, aged birth to death, visited an Internet sexuality site last month, and did so on an average of 4 different days.

In addition to inconsistencies and prima facia questionable claims in research on the prevalence of sexually explicit materials, on and off the Internet, we note the nearly complete absence of research on the central and obvious issue of consumer preference for different types of sexual content. In an effort to address the critical question of what sort of sexually explicit material, if any, men might choose to see in a free-choice situation, Bogaert (1993; see also Bogaert,

2001) conducted a very simple and very informative study. Undergraduate males who were already participating in a study were given the opportunity to sign up, for experimental credit, for additional research that would involve viewing their choice of 14 videos. Subjects were permitted to choose to see videos depicting common sexual acts, novel sexual acts, sexually insatiable females, sexual violence, or child pornography. Results showed that undergraduate men's modal choice—51% of all men—was to decline to see *any* sexually explicit video, either because they did not need further experimental credit or because they were simply not interested. The second most frequent choice (15% of all men) was to see erotic depictions that were nonviolent and involved female sexual insatiability. The next most frequent choices were to view a control film, *Saturday Night Live* (8%), a video that portrayed sexual novelty including sexual activity with animals (8%), or a video depicting common sexual acts (7%). Men's least common choices, in this free-choice setting, were to see sexually violent videos (4%) or child pornography (3%). Bogaert's (1993) research emphasizes the central but generally ignored point that contact with sexually explicit material is a self-regulated choice which may be exercised or declined by individuals and that experience with sexually explicit materials should be studied in such a context by sexual scientists. When ecologically valid opportunities to choose are given, as is the case in this single study, the modal choice was not to bother to see *any* sexually explicit material at all, and the *least* common choice was to view violent pornography or child sexual activity. Such findings place an important qualification on experimental research concerning the effects of sexually explicit stimuli, in which exposure to such stimuli is enforced on individuals (e.g., Check & Guloien, 1989; Zillmann, 1989).[1]

What lessons can be taken from attempts to assess the prevalence of sexually explicit materials and applied to inform research on Internet sexuality? First, the record strongly suggests that it is important to avoid moral panic and premature pronouncements about the saturation of society with Internet pornography. Wildly conflicting statements, often doubtful on their face, about the extraordinary amount of sexually explicit material that is available, the extraordinary amount of such material that is sold, and the extraordinary proportion of all e-commerce accounted for by sales of sexual material, are quickly accepted. Such claims can just as quickly turn into a source of scientific embarrassment when the data are closely examined. Second, it is instructive to note that a degree of precision is warranted in assessments of the prevalence of sexually explicit materials on the Internet. Categories of erotica, degrading pornography, and violent pornography are almost always collapsed into the single category of "pornography" reflecting a presumably homogeneous " . . . industry of misogyny" (Cowan et al., 1988, p. 309–310; see also Malamuth et al., 2001). Such collapsing of all sexually explicit materials into a single category of "pornography" eliminates our ability to map out the prevalence of different types of sexually explicit materials on the Internet, or to consider effects of different types of sexually explicit content on the Internet, in any meaningful fashion, even ignoring serious reliability and validity concerns articulated earlier. Finally, Bogaert's (1993) research reminds us that use of erotic or pornographic materials is an individual choice. Studies of prevalence of different types of sexually explicit material on the Internet must include studies of consumer preference for various types of sexually explicit content in free-choice settings.

What Do We Know About Antecedents and Consequences of Experience with Sexually Explicit Materials?

In working toward an understanding of Internet sexually explicit materials, it would be useful to consider research concerning personality characteristics that incline individuals to seek out sexually explicit media. It would also be useful to consider research findings concerning effects of contact with sexually explicit media on individuals who have chosen to consume such material.

With respect to antecedents of self-directed experience with sexually explicit media, perhaps the most comprehensive study of personality factors that incline individuals to seek out such materials was conducted by Bogaert (1993). Bogaert assessed a range of relevant individual differences in a sample of undergraduate men, including aggression, altruism, delinquency, dominance, hypermasculinity, Machiavellianism, psychoticism, sensation seeking, erotophobia-erotophilia, and attraction to sexual aggression. Men's sexual experience, past sexual media exposure, history of sexual aggression, and current sexual behavior were assessed as well. The men were then asked to choose which of a number of videos they would like to view. The videos were presented to participants with titles and descriptions which established them as involving common sexual acts, novel sexual acts, sexually insatiable females, sexual violence, and children engaging in sexual acts, or as nonviolent, nonsexual, or violent nonsexual video material. After statistically controlling for social desirability, *none* of the individual difference characteristics assessed were associated with men's tendencies to choose to see the sexually violent or common sexual acts videos. Choice of female sexual insatiability videos was associated with erotophilia; choice of child sexual videos, which was very rare (3% of all males chose to see this stimulus), was associated with history of exposure to sexual media and with the personality traits of aggression and dominance; and choice of novel sexual acts videos was associated with history of exposure to sexually explicit media. Attraction to sexual aggression (Malamuth, 1989a, 1989b) was not correlated with choices to view any of the categories of sexual media under study. (See Bogaert, 2001, for additional results).

A single study known to us is relevant to the question of the antecedents of self-regulated exposure to Internet sexuality. Barak et al. (1999) examined individual difference correlates of choosing to access sexually explicit Internet sites in a sample of university men. These investigators found *no* association of men's social desirability, sensation seeking, attitudes toward women, rape myth acceptance, hypermasculinity, or erotophobia-erotophilia with time spent surfing sexually explicit Internet sites. The only correlate of the time men spent surfing sexually explicit Internet sites was men's past experience with sexually explicit media.

Other research of some relevance to the question of the antecedents of consumption of sexually explicit materials tells us that convicted sex criminals are either less likely or at least not differentially likely to have experience with sexually explicit media (see Abel, Becker, & Mittleman, 1985; Becker & Stein, 1991; Gebhard, Gagnon, Pomeroy, & Christensen, 1965; Goldstein, 1973; Langevin, Lang, Wright, Hand, Frenzel, & Black, 1988; see Marshall, 1988, and Malamuth et al., 2001, for conflicting evidence) and that it is egalitarian and not sexist attitudes toward women which are correlated with viewing sexually explicit movies or videos in natural settings (Padgett, Brislen-Slutz, & Neal, 1989; Reis, 1986). Still other research indicates that in general, erotophilic individuals, who show dispositionally positive affective, evaluative, and approach responses to sexuality, are more likely than erotophobic individuals to choose to consume sexually explicit materials (Fisher, Byrne, Kelly, & White, 1988), and that male (vs. female) gender is associated with more frequent consumption of sexually explicit material (Kinsey, Pomery, Martin, & Gebhard, 1953; Fisher & Byrne, 1978).

With respect to research concerning the effects of exposure to sexually explicit media on individuals who have chosen to have contact with such material, research is limited. We do know that in two separate studies reported by Barak et al. (1999), amount of self-directed exposure to Internet sexually explicit sites had no significant effects on post-exposure measures of university men's rape myth acceptance, attitudes toward women, acceptance of women as managers, or on a measure of likelihood of sexual harassment. In another potentially relevant study, Malamuth et al. (2001) examined factors such as family violence, delinquency, attitudes supporting violence, sexual promiscuity, hostile masculinity, and pornography use—defined as amount of exposure to sexually explicit magazines—as correlates of sexual aggression against women, in a national sample of men enrolled in postsecondary education. The authors report that men who were highest in hostile masculinity, sexual promiscuity, and pornography use as defined in this research were most likely to report a history of sexual aggression against women. At the same time, however, the researchers note that ". . . we cannot conclude on the basis of these analyses that

pornography use is a cause or an outcome of sexual aggressive tendencies . . ." (Malamuth et al., 2001, p. 79). Characteristics of this research, including its cross-sectional design and coding of sexually explicit magazine use as "pornography," seriously limit the ability of this study to address the question of effects of self-directed exposure to different types of sexually explicit materials, on or off the Internet. Findings that individuals who seek out sexually explicit movies or videos in natural settings have egalitarian and not sexist attitudes toward women (e.g., Padgett et al., 1989; Reis, 1986), and findings for a lack of association of sexual criminality with exposure to sexually explicit media (Abel, Becker, & Mittleman, 1985; Becker & Stein, 1991; Gebhard et al., 1965; Goldstein, 1973; Kutchinsky, 1973, 1985, 1991; Langevin et al., 1988; see Marshall, 1988 for contrasting evidence) are also not consistent with a view that self-directed exposure to sexually explicit materials results in antiwoman attitudinal shifts or antisocial sexual behavior.

As an additional and crude estimate of consequences of exposure to sexually explicit Internet materials on individuals who seek contact with such content, in Figure 8.2.1 we plot rates of reported forcible rape in the United States from 1995 to 1999 (U.S. Federal Bureau of Investigation, 2001). This time interval is by all accounts a period of exponential growth in the availability and use of all forms of Internet sexually explicit materials (Cheney, 2000; Elmer-Dewitt, 1995; Freeman-Longo, 2000; Harmon & Boeringer, 1996; Mehta & Plaza, 1998; Rimm, 1995; Wysocki, 1998). Although open to a variety of interpretations, we note that the rate of reported forcible rape in the U.S. *fell* consistently and significantly throughout this time period of spectacular increase in access to and use of Internet sexually explicit materials of all kinds.

Although there is an enormous amount of research concerning the effects of experimentally enforced exposure to sexually explicit materials on individuals who have not chosen to see such materials (see Davis & Bauserman, 1993; Donnerstein, Linz, & Penrod, 1987; Fisher & Barak, 1991; Fisher & Grenier, 1994; Malamuth et al., 2001; Malamuth & Donnerstein, 1984; Zillmann & Bryant, 1989, for reviews of this lit-

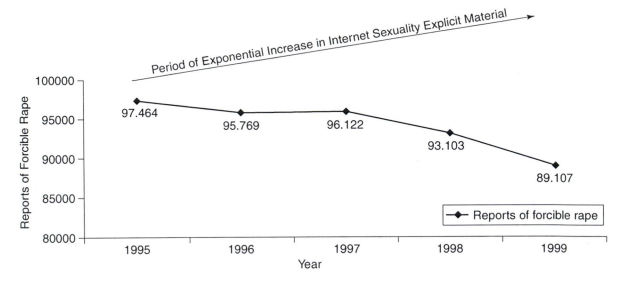

Figure 8.2.1 Reported cases of forcible rape (U.S. Federal Bureau of Investigation, 2001) during a period of exponential growth in availability and use of Internet sexually explicit material.

erature), extrapolating findings from such research is a risky proposition. Effects of Internet or other sexually explicit materials are almost certainly a joint function of the personality characteristics of the individual who seeks out such materials and of exposure to such materials per se (Bogaert, 1993; Check & Guloien, 1989; Fisher & Barak, 1991; Malamuth et al., 2001; Padgett et al., 1989; Reis, 1986). Experiments involving enforced exposure to sexually explicit materials ignore the influence of synergistic or buffering personality characteristics that might amplify or attenuate effects of exposure and which are correlated with the inclination to seek or to avoid sexually explicit material. Findings from enforced exposure experimental paradigms, therefore, cannot be generalized readily to assumptions about effects of self-directed, real world exposure to Internet sexually explicit materials.

What lessons can we carry forward from research concerning antecedents and consequences of exposure to sexually explicit materials to inform research concerning Internet sexuality?

First, we note that research on antecedents of self-directed exposure to sexually explicit materials is very limited, and that use of an ecologically valid research paradigm that examines individual difference correlates of choice of Internet sexually explicit materials is needed. Existing research (e.g., Barak et al., 1999; Bogaert, 1993; Fisher et al., 1988) has already identified a variety of individual difference correlates of choice of sexually explicit media, on and off the Internet, that are potentially highly relevant to moderating effects of exposure to such materials.

Second, we note that research concerning effects of exposure to sexually explicit materials on those who choose to consume them is also rare, and existing findings by and large fail to confirm fears of strong antisocial effects of self-directed exposure to sexually explicit media. A significant lesson to carry forward for emerging research on Internet sexuality involves the importance of conducting ecologically valid research concerning effects of self-regulated exposure to Internet sexually explicit materials on individuals who choose to consume them. Such research will be able to capture compound effects of the personality characteristics of those inclined to access Internet sexuality and of Internet sexually explicit materials per se.

A SOCIAL PSYCHOLOGICAL PERSPECTIVE ON INTERNET SEXUALLY EXPLICIT MATERIALS: CONCEPTUALIZING ANTECEDENTS AND CONSEQUENCES OF EXPERIENCE WITH INTERNET SEXUALITY

As sexual scientists confront the challenge of understanding antecedents and consequences of contact with Internet sexually explicit materials, we believe there is considerable advantage to be gained by applying social psychological theory to guide conceptual and research efforts. A number of relevant theories (e.g., Sexual Behavior Sequence, Byrne, 1977; Theory of Reasoned Action, Fishbein & Ajzen, 1975; Excitation Transfer Theory, Zillmann & Bryant, 1984; Social-Cognitive Theory, Bandura, 1986; Confluence Model, Malamuth et al., 2001) could serve as a basis for understanding factors which would incline an individual to access Internet sexually explicit materials, and could be extended as a basis for conjecture about how access to Internet sexually explicit materials will condition the individual's future sexual behavior. We have chosen the Sexual Behavior Sequence (Byrne, 1977, Byrne & Kelley, 1986; Fisher, 1986; Fisher & Barak, 2001) as a basis for conceptualizing antecedents and consequences of experience with Internet sexually explicit materials for a number of reasons. The Sexual Behavior Sequence focuses on understanding sexual stimuli; the arousal, affective, cognitive, and behavioral responses they evoke; and the effect of these responses in conditioning the future approach or avoidance of sexual stimuli and sexual behavior. As such, the Sexual Behavior Sequence provides a conceptually comprehensive heuristic guide for an initial attempt to understand some of the factors that will incline an individual to access Internet sexually explicit material and for understanding some of the internal psychological and external behavioral responses to such stimuli. In addition, the Sexual Behavior Sequence directly addresses the question of how the effects of experience with Internet sexuality may influence an individual's future sexual behavior. Although we believe that the Sexual Behavior Sequence is a conceptually comprehensive heuristic guide that addresses both antecedents and consequences of experience with Internet sexuality, we emphasize that it is utilized here only as a conceptual roadmap of constructs which are potentially important in the study of Internet sexuality and as a basis for hypothesis generation. Alternative models are available (e.g., Excitation Transfer Theory, Zillmann & Bryant, 1984; Confluence Model, Malamuth et al., 2001) and should be explored.

The Sexual Behavior Sequence

The Sexual Behavior Sequence (Byrne, 1977; Byrne & Kelley, 1986; Fisher, 1986) is a social psychological model of the antecedents and consequences of sexual behavior that can be applied to conceptualizing experience with Internet sexuality. As can be seen in Figure 8.2.2, the Sexual Behavior Sequence asserts that individuals respond to unconditioned and conditioned erotic cues with sexual arousal and affective and cognitive responses. Sexual arousal, affect, and cognitions may motivate and guide preparatory sexual behaviors that affect the likelihood of overt sexual behaviors. Overt sexual behaviors, according to the model, have subjectively positive or negative consequences that will influence the future probability of the responses that led to the sexual behavior in the first place, by way of a feedback loop specified by the model.

Sexual Stimuli—Sexual Arousal— Sexual Behavior

According to the Sexual Behavior Sequence, individuals respond to unconditioned sexual stimuli with physiological sexual arousal. Unconditioned erotic stimuli can include tactile stimulation of the genitals, exposure

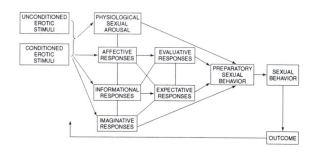

Fig. 8.2.2 The Sexual Behavior Sequence (Byrne, 1977).

to pheromones, and possibly, visual sexual cues such as exposure to the genitals or breasts or observation of copulatory behavior (Byrne, 1977; Fisher, 1986; Gallup, 1986). The Sexual Behavior Sequence also asserts that any other discriminable stimulus which is associated with an unconditioned erotic stimulus can become a conditioned erotic stimulus with the capacity to elicit physiological sexual arousal itself.

According to the Sexual Behavior Sequence, individuals who come into contact with erotic stimuli and who are sufficiently sexually aroused for a sufficient period of time are motivated to engage in preparatory sexual behavior that will increase the likelihood of overt sexual behavior. Preparatory sexual behaviors which increase the likelihood of overt sexual behavior can involve actions such as locking one's bedroom door and plugging in a vibrator, making sexual overtures to an opposite-sex or same-sex partner, or seeking sexual companionship in a singles bar or in an Internet chat room. If preparatory sexual behaviors are successful, sexual behavior will result, and sexual behaviors have outcomes that may be experienced as subjectively positive or negative events. Outcomes are assumed to feed back into the system to condition the future greater or lesser likelihood of the chain of events that led to the sexual behavior and outcome in question.

Considering only the erotic stimulus—physiological arousal—preparatory behavior—sexual behavior—outcome level of the Sexual Behavior Sequence, let us turn to the example of a neophyte male Internet user. Having discovered JJJ's Thumbnail Post (*http://www.pornno.com.gallerypost.shtml*) in the course of idle surfing, our Internet user has viewed text, images, and video clips depicting a variety of stimulus themes—including consensual heterosexual intercourse, bondage and discipline, interracial anal intercourse, urination, and cumshots, all depicted as discriminable stimulus accompaniments of unconditioned erotic stimuli such as copulatory behavior and breast and genital imagery. Our Internet explorer settles on a stimulus theme that he finds idiosyncratically to be arousing—cumshot still and moving images of a male ejaculating onto the face, hair, breasts, and vulva of a female. Over time, the Internet user finds that cumshot themes in general have become a conditioned erotic stimulus with the capacity to elicit high levels of

physiological sexual arousal and with the ability to motivate preparatory sexual behaviors, sexual behaviors, and outcomes. Whether or not the acquisition of the cumshot theme as a conditioned erotic stimulus will ever be translated into covert fantasy or overt behavior involving ejaculation onto a woman's face or body will be a function of affective and cognitive responses which are simultaneously evoked by the sexually explicit Internet stimulus category in question and whose roles are also specified by the Sexual Behavior Sequence.

Sexual Stimuli—Affective Responses— Sexual Behavior

The Sexual Behavior Sequence asserts that individuals respond to erotic stimuli with affective and evaluative responses as well as with physiological sexual arousal. According to the Sexual Behavior Sequence, affective and evaluative responses to sexual stimuli, along with physiological sexual arousal responses to such stimuli, will together influence the occurrence of preparatory sexual behavior, overt sexual behavior, and the subjective outcome of such behavior (see Figure 8.2.2).

From the perspective of the Sexual Behavior Sequence, individuals acquire affective and evaluative responses to erotic stimuli as a function of the association of erotic stimuli with rewarding or punishing experiences over the life span (Fisher, 1986; Fisher et al., 1988). An individual who has experienced predominantly rewarding experiences in association with sexuality is expected to develop a generalized trait disposition of erotophilia and should respond to sexual cues with positive affect and evaluations. An individual who has experienced predominantly punishing experiences in association with sexuality is expected to develop a generalized trait disposition of erotophobia and should respond to sexual cues with negative affect and evaluations. Positive affective and evaluative responses to sexual stimuli should incline the individual to engage in preparatory sexual behavior and sexual behavior and to experience the outcome of this sexual behavior as subjectively positive. Such a positive outcome will strengthen the future likelihood of further contact with similar sexual stimuli, the future likelihood of similar arousal and affective and evaluative responses, similar preparatory and overt sexual behaviors, and similar outcomes. In contrast, negative affective and evaluative responses to sexual stimuli should motivate the sexually stimulated individual to avoid the sort of preparatory sexual behavior and overt sexual behavior suggested by the sexual stimulus and to experience the sexual stimulus, and any arousal or behavior which it eventuates, as hedonically negative events that will condition future avoidance of sexual stimulation of the sort that triggered this sequence of responses.

According to the Sexual Behavior Sequence, then, experience with Internet sexually explicit materials will be a self-regulated activity that will take place in part as a function of an individual's erotophobic or erotophilic disposition to respond to Internet sexuality with positive or negative affect and evaluations. Erotophilic individuals should seek out and enjoy Internet sexually explicit materials, and may incorporate what is acquired from Internet sexually explicit materials into their preparatory and overt sexual behaviors, and should enjoy these behaviors, all else being equal. This sequence of responses, involving additional pairings of sexuality with positive affective responses, should also strengthen the erotophilic disposition which provoked it in the first place. Erotophobic individuals, in contrast, will experience contact with Internet sexually explicit materials as an emotionally negative event and will evaluate such materials negatively and avoid contact with them. By extension, erotophobic individuals will also avoid preparatory and overt sexual behaviors related to Internet sexually explicit materials. This sequence of responses, involving additional pairing of sexuality with negative affect, should strengthen the individual's erotophobic disposition and his or her inclination to avoid Internet sexually explicit materials in the future.

Let us return to our example of the Internet user who has acquired a sexual arousal response to the theme of ejaculation on a woman's face or body. Let us further assume, in accord with the Sexual Behavior Sequence, that the individual in question is erotophilic and that in fact it is his affective and evaluative positivity to sexuality which brought him to surf Internet sex sites and to acquire conditioned sexual arousal to cumshots in the first place. Sexual arousal and positive affective and evaluative responses to cumshot stimuli should, according to our model and all else being equal, affect the individual's preparatory sexual

behavior, sexual behavior, outcomes, and future probability of the sequence of events that provoked them. In the current case, the erotophilic individual likely has an erotophilic partner (for a review of evidence of assortative mating by erotophilic and erotophobic men and women, see Fisher et al., 1988), and the individual may be motivated to engage in a preparatory sexual behavior which involves discussion with a partner of incorporating an arousing new sexual activity—say, ejaculation onto her breasts—during sexual intercourse. Such discussion could be instrumental in the occurrence of a sexual behavior of this sort and could provoke a positive personal and dyadic outcome that would strengthen the future likelihood of this entire sequence of events. Alternatively, and almost certainly more realistically, the individual who is sexually aroused and affectively positive to the prospect of ejaculation on a partner's body might receive such a negative interpersonal reaction to either the discussion or performance of this behavior that the outcome would be profoundly negative and result in the future unlikelihood of anything remotely associated with cumshot activity. Or, the individual in question who is sexually stimulated by the cumshot theme might chose a preparatory behavior such as a generic sexual overture to a partner which results in a conventional sexual behavior such as sexual intercourse, accompanied by a covert sexual fantasy of cumshot activity. This personally rewarding outcome would condition the increased likelihood of this sequence of events in the future without involving potentially negative partner responses. For the individual who is aroused by the prospect of ejaculation onto a partner's body and who is affectively and evaluatively positive concerning this activity, the question of whether the overt or covert version or any version of this scenario will be enacted will depend heavily on the individual's cognitive responses to this category of sexual behavior, as specified by the Sexual Behavior Sequence and discussed following.

Sexual Stimuli—Cognitive Responses—Sexual Behavior

According to the Sexual Behavior Sequence, erotic stimuli evoke categories of cognitive responses that—together with arousal and affective responses—determine preparatory sexual behavior, overt sexual behavior, and the outcomes of such behavior. Cognitive responses to erotic stimuli include informational responses, expectative responses, and imaginative responses. Informational responses to sexual stimuli consist of beliefs about sexual activity, and expectative responses are subjective probability estimates concerning the outcomes of sexual activity. Imaginative responses to sexual stimulation involve script-like representations of entire sexual episodes which may be used to test out safely and in private contemplation a pattern of behavior that one is considering implementing, or which may be used to experience, solely in private contemplation, a behavior that one would never consider actually implementing.

From the perspective of the Sexual Behavior Sequence, information, expectancies, and imaginative responses will heavily affect an individual's experience with Internet sexually explicit materials. Consider our example of the erotophilic Internet surfer who has acquired sexual arousal responses to the stimulus category of ejaculation onto a female's face or body. From the perspective of the Sexual Behavior Sequence, the individual's informational, expectative, and imaginative responses to the prospect of ejaculation on a partner's face or body will determine the nature of his preparatory sexual behavior, sexual behavior, and outcomes. Assume, for example, that our protagonist is sexually aroused and affectively positive about the possibility of engaging in sexual activities that include ejaculation onto his partner. Assume as well that (a) the surfer in question believes that ejaculation onto his partner's breasts is a relatively reserved form of this behavior, as suggested by depictions he has seen on the Internet (an informational response); (b) the surfer in question believes that his partner would probably respond tolerantly to discussion of this activity and to its actual occurrence, as suggested by past experience with the partner (an expectative response); and (c) the surfer in question can imagine a sequence of cumshot activity behaviors producing a positive outcome for himself and his partner (an imaginative response). In such a case, contact with Internet sexually explicit stimuli may trigger overt experimentation with behavior and possibly a positive outcome and increased future likelihood of such behavior. If, in contrast, the individual's informa-

tional, expectative, and imaginative responses suggest that ejaculation onto the partner's breasts would almost certainly provoke negative responses which are vividly imagined, the individual might chose to confine his cumshot activity to covert fantasy accompaniment of conventional sexual activity as discussed earlier. Or, the surfer in question might choose to redirect his sexual fantasy to what he imagines to be a more acceptable behavior. In either case, it is the avoidance of an overt sexual behavior that would have a positive outcome and that would continue in the future.

All Together Now: Arousal, Affective, Cognitive, and Behavioral Responses to Internet Sexually Explicit Materials

From the perspective of the Sexual Behavior Sequence, exposure to Internet sexually explicit materials may trigger the acquisition of conditioned sexual arousal responses, affective and evaluative responses, informational and expective responses, and sexual fantasy responses. These internal psychological reactions to Internet sexually explicit stimuli will together determine the occurrence and nature of preparatory sexual behavior, overt sexual behavior, the outcome of such behavior, and the future probability of sexual behavior, including future contact with Internet sexually explicit materials. The Sexual Behavior Sequence thus conceptualizes experience with Internet sexually explicit material as a choice made by an active perceiver and interpreter of such material. The Sexual Behavior Sequence also emphasizes that the individual brings a lifetime learning history, involving emotional responses to sexuality, beliefs about sexual activity, and expectations and imagination concerning the outcomes of sexual behaviors, to experience with Internet sexuality. In contrast to implicit "Monkey see, monkey do" assumptions which seem to have guided much research on exposure to erotica and pornography (see Fisher & Barak, 1991), the Sexual Behavior Sequence conceptualizes contact with Internet sexually explicit material as a self-regulated event which will occur or not occur as a function of an individual's arousal, affective, and cognitive responses to sexuality. The individual's internal affective and cognitive responses to Internet sexually explicit materials will determine whether or not future contact with

Internet sexuality is sought or avoided, and will determine the sort of behavioral responses which are or are not provoked by experience with Internet sexually explicit materials. Finally, experience with Internet sexuality should also affect the future development of an individual's arousal, affective, and cognitive responses to sexuality and his or her future sexual behavior, most likely in a direction which is consistent with the individual's preexisting response tendencies in these areas. Understanding an individual's experience with Internet sexually explicit material requires consideration of multiple and simultaneous arousal, affective, and cognitive responses of the individual to sexual stimulation.

The Sexual Behavior Sequence can also be applied as a conceptual guide for clinical interventions designed to assist individuals who have self-designated or socially-designated problems with Internet sexuality, including excessive and interfering preoccupation with Internet sexually explicit materials, inappropriate behavior stemming from contact with Internet sexuality, or personally or socially problematic replacement of sexual activity on the Internet for sexual activity with a partner (Barak & King, 2000; Cooper, Putnam, Planchon, & Boies, 1999; Putnam, 2000; Schwartz & Southern, 2000). In such cases, diagnostic focus on arousal, affective, and cognitive factors that provoke or permit dysfunctional behavior might prove useful in understanding the problem and in formulating an intervention plan. Is the individual who is preoccupied with Internet sexually explicit materials in a way that is interfering with his or her work and relationships and finances involved in such maladaptive activity because Internet sexuality is more arousing to the individual than competing, noninterfering sources of sexual arousal? Is the individual more affectively positive to Internet sexuality than he or she is affectively negative to the consequences of excessive involvement? Is the individual unable to anticipate and imagine the individual consequences and social stigma occasioned by his or her behavior? And would interventions targeted at augmenting access to adaptive sources of sexual arousal, at increasing affective negativity to the consequences of his or her activity, and at encouraging the individual to imagine the negative reactions of employers and partners (e.g., Orzack & Ross, 2000;

Putnam, 2000), be effective in assisting the individual to avoid excessive and interfering use of Internet sexually explicit materials?

WHERE DO WE GO FROM HERE WITH INTERNET SEXUALLY EXPLICIT MATERIALS? A CONCEPTUALLY BASED RESEARCH AGENDA

In crafting an agenda for future research on Internet sexually explicit materials which integrates the issues discussed in this paper, we prioritize conceptually driven and ecologically valid research, guided by the Sexual Behavior Sequence and other relevant models. This agenda will focus on examining effects of preexisting arousal, affective, and cognitive responses to sexuality on self-regulated consumption of Internet sexually explicit materials in free-choice settings that model well the natural environment. This research agenda will also examine effects of self-regulated experience with Internet sexually explicit materials on individuals' arousal, affective, and cognitive responses to sexuality, and examine how effects on these internal responses may contribute to changes in individuals' covert sexual fantasy and overt sexual behavior over extended periods of time.

Based upon the Sexual Behavior Sequence and related research (Byrne, 1977; Fisher, 1986), we hypothesize that individuals with strong preexisting sexual arousal responses to sexually explicit materials, and strong preexisting positive affective and cognitive responses to sexuality, will engage in relatively greater self-regulated consumption of Internet sexually explicit materials (compared to individuals with preexisting weaker or more negative arousal, affective, and cognitive responses to sexuality). Based upon the current analysis, we also anticipate that experience with Internet sexuality will reinforce individuals' preexisting arousal, affective, and cognitive responses to sexuality. Those who approach Internet sexuality with strong arousal responses and positive affective and cognitive responses to sexuality will find these response tendencies strengthened. Those who approach Internet sexuality with weak arousal responses and negative affective and cognitive responses to sexuality will find these response dispositions made more pronounced. Finally, based on the Sexual Behavior Sequence (Byrne, 1977; Fisher, 1986), we expect that experience with Internet sexuality will affect individuals' covert imaginative and overt sexual behavior in a fashion that is consistent with his or her arousal, affective, and cognitive responses to sexuality. Individuals who approach Internet sexuality with strong arousal responses and positive affective and cognitive responses to sexuality will be more inclined to incorporate elements of Internet sexual scenarios into their covert and overt sexual behavior, all else being equal, and in accord with the expected outcomes of these behavioral choices. In contrast, individuals who approach Internet sexuality with weak arousal responses and negative affective and cognitive responses to sexuality will be unlikely to incorporate Internet sexual scenarios into their covert or overt sexual behavior.

By happy coincidence, existing Internet technology provides an exceedingly suitable methodology for executing the research agenda we have articulated. Assume, for example, that a researcher is able to create a panel of Internet users, representing both sexes, and sampling the age range from 18 to 65. Further assume that, after appropriate informed consent, the panel of Internet users completes a series of assessments of baseline sexual arousal responses to a range of sexually explicit stimuli, and a set of measures of affective—evaluative, informational—expectative, and imaginative responses to sexuality. Assume as well that the research subjects complete a profile of current sexual behavior and attitudinal and behavioral measures—such as attitudes toward women, rape myth acceptance, sexually coercive behaviors, and inappropriate and interfering utilization of Internet sexuality—which represent potential negative outcomes of self-regulated exposure to Internet sexually explicit materials. This battery of baseline assessments would be completed online. Participants would then be given free access to the Internet for a period of, say, 1 or 2 years, with informed consent to the proviso that software installed on their computers will sample Internet utilization at given intervals of time and will automatically and anonymously communicate these data to the researchers. Moreover, halfway through the period of study and at its conclusion the researchers will con-

duct repeat Internet-based assessments of arousal responses to sexually explicit stimuli and affective— evaluative, informational—expectative, and imaginative responses to sexuality. In addition, subjects will again complete assessments of sexual behavior, attitudes toward women, likelihood of rape, coercive sexual behavior, and inappropriate and interfering utilization of Internet sexuality at these intervals.

A research strategy with these characteristics would permit empirical study of such central questions as the self-regulation of experience with Internet sexually explicit materials, in relation to preexisting individual difference characteristics, and the mapping over extended periods of time of self-regulated experience with Internet sexually explicit materials by men and women across the age range. Such a research strategy would also permit prospective examination of the effects of self-regulated exposure to Internet sexuality over time on arousal, affective, cognitive, and behavioral responses, and on a range of possible antisocial attitudinal and behavioral outcomes of self-regulated experience with Internet sexually explicit materials. It is our hope that this research agenda will contribute to conceptually and empirically fruitful investigation which will inform understanding, policy, and practice concerning Internet sexuality in coming years.

NOTE

1. We refer to Bogaert's (1993) research as an ecologically valid approach, in relation to the fact that this research models well an individual's ability to choose, in real-world settings, whether to use or to avoid Internet sexually explicit materials. The fact that Bogaert's (1993) study utilized university undergraduates who were participating in an experiment is a potential limitation on our ability to generalize these findings.

REFERENCES

Abel, G. G., Becker, J. V., & Mittleman, M. S. (1985, July) *Sex offenders.* Paper presented at the 11th annual meeting of the International Academy of Sex Research, Seattle, WA.

Bandura, A. (1986). *Social foundations of thought and action: A social cognitive theory.* Englewood Cliffs, NJ: Prentice-Hall.

Barak, A., & Fisher, W. A. (1997). Effects of interactive computer erotica on men's attitudes and behavior toward women:

An experimental study. *Computers in Human Behavior, 13,* 353–369.

Barak, A., & Fisher, W. A. (2001). Toward an Internet-based, theoretically driven, innovative approach to sexuality education. *The Journal of Sex Research, 38,* 324–332.

Barak, A., Fisher, W. A., Belfry, S., & Lashambe, D. R. (1999). Sex, guys, and cyberspace: Effects of Internet pornography and individual differences on men's attitudes towards women. *Journal of Psychology and Human Sexuality, 11,* 63–91.

Barak, A., & King, S. A. (2000). The two faces of the Internet: Introduction to the special issue on the Internet and Sexuality. *CyberPsychology and Behavior, 3,* 517–520.

Barron, M., & Kimmel, M. (2000). Sexual violence in three pornographic media: Toward a sociological explanation. *The Journal of Sex Research, 37,* 161–168.

Becker J., & Stein, R. M. (1991). Is sexual erotica associated with sexual deviance in adolescent males? *International Journal of Law and Psychiatry, 14,* 85–95.

Blue Money. (1999, May 27) *The Guardian (Online),* p. 5.

Bogaert, A. F. (1993) *The sexual media: The role of individual differences.* Unpublished doctoral dissertation, University of Western Ontario, London, Ontario, Canada.

Bogaert, A. F. (2001). Personality, individual differences, and preferences for the sexual media. *Archives of Sexual Behavior, 30,* 29–53.

Byrne, D. (1977). Social psychology and the study of sexual behavior. *Personality and Social Psychology Bulletin, 3,* 3–30.

Byrne, D., & Kelley, K. (Eds.). (1986). *Alternative approaches to the study of sexual behavior.* Hillsdale, NJ: Erlbaum.

Check, J. V. P., & Guloien, T. H. (1989). Reported proclivity for coercive sex following repeated exposure to sexually violent pornography, non-violent dehumanising pornography, and erotica. In D. Zillmann & J. Bryant (Eds.), *Pornography: Research advances and policy considerations* (pp. 159–184). Hillsdale, NJ: Erlbaum.

Cheney, P. (2000, December 2). The triple-X crisis. Is pornography out of control? *The Globe and Mail,* pp. F4–F5.

Cooper, A., Putnam, D. E., Planchon, L. A., & Boies, S. C. (1999). Online sexual compulsivity: Getting tangled in the Net. *Sexual Addiction and Compulsivity, 6,* 79–104.

Cooper, A., Scherer, C. R., Bols, S. C., & Gordon, B. I. (1999). Sexuality on the Internet: From sexual exploration to pathological expression. *Professional Psychology: Research and Practice, 30,* 154–164.

Cowan, G., & Dunn, K. F. (1994). What themes in pornography lead to perceptions of the degradation of women? *The Journal of Sex Research, 31,* 11–21.

Cowan, G., Lee, C., Levy, D., & Snyder, D. (1988). Dominance and inequality in X-rated videocassettes. *Psychology of Women Quarterly, 12,* 299–311.

Davis, C. L., & Bauserman, R. (1993). Exposure to sexually explicit materials. An attitude change perspective. *Annual Review of Sex Research, 4,* 121–210.

Dietz, P. E., & Evans, B. (1982). Pornographic imagery and prevalence of paraphilia. *American Journal of Psychiatry, 139,* 1493–1495.

Donnerstein, E., & Berkowitz, L. (1981). Victim reactions in aggressive erotic films as a factor in violence against women. *Journal of Personality and Social Psychology, 41,* 710–724.

Donnerstein, E., Linz, D., & Penrod, S. (1987). *The question of pornography. Research findings and policy implications.* New York: Free Press.

Elmer-Dewitt, P. (1995). On a screen near you: Cyberporn. *Time, 146,* 1.

Eysenck, H. J. (1978). *Sex and personality.* London: Sphere.

Fishbein, M., & Ajzen, I. (1975). *Belief, attitude, intention, and behavior. An introduction to theory and research.* Reading, MA: Addison-Wesley.

Fisher, W. A. (1986). A psychological approach to human sexuality: The Sexual Behavior Sequence. In D. Byrne & K. Kelley (Eds.), *Alternative approaches to the study of sexual behavior* (pp. 313–172). Hillsdale, NJ: Erlbaum.

Fisher, W. A., & Barak, A. (1989). Sex education as a corrective. In D. Zillmann & J. Bryant (Eds.). *Pornography. Research advances and policy considerations* (pp 289–320). Hillsdale, NJ: Erlbaum.

Fisher, W. A., & Barak, A. (1991). Pornography, erotica, and behavior: More questions than answers. *International Journal of Law and Psychiatry, 14,* 65–83.

Fisher, W. A., & Barak, A. (2001). Online sex shops. Phenomenological, psychological, and ideological perspectives on Internet sexuality. *Cyberpsychology and Behavior, 3,* 575–590.

Fisher, W. A., & Byrne, D. (1978). Sex differences in response to erotica? Love versus lust. *Journal of Personality and Social Psychology, 36,* 117–125.

Fisher, W. A., Byrne, D., Kelley, K., & White, L. A. (1988). Erotophobia-erotophilia as a dimension of personality. *The Journal of Sex Research, 25,* 123–151.

Fisher, W. A., & Grenier, G. (1994). Violent pornography, antiwoman thoughts, and antiwoman acts: In search of reliable effects. *The Journal of Sex Research, 31,* 23–38.

Freeman-Longo, R. E. (2000). Children, teens, and sex on the Internet. *Sexual Addiction and Compulsivity, 7,* 75–90.

Freeman-Longo, R. E., & Blanchard, G. T. (1998). *Sexual abuse in America: Epidemic of the 21st century.* Brandon, VT: Safer Society Press.

Gallup, G. G., Jr. (1986). Unique features of human evolution in the context of evolution. In D. Byrne & K. Kelley (Eds.), *Alternative approaches to the study of sexual behavior* (pp. 13–42). Hillsdale, NJ: Erlbaum

Garcia, L., & Milano, L. (1991). A content analysis of erotic videos. *Journal of Psychology and Human Sexuality, 3,* 95–103.

Gebhard, P. H., Gagnon, J. H., Pomeroy, W. B., & Christensen, C. V. (1965). *Sex offenders.* New York: Harper and Row.

Goldstein, M. J. (1973). Exposure to erotic stimuli and sexual deviance. *Journal of Social Issues, 29,* 197–219.

Harmon, D., & Boeringer, S. B. (1996). A content analysis of Internet-accessible written pornographic depictions. Retrieved from http://www.acs.appstate.edu/~sbb/netporn. html.

Hoffman, D. L., & Novak, T. P. (1995). A detailed analysis of the conceptual, logical, and methodological flaws in the article, "Marketing pornography on the information superhighway." Retrieved January 7, 2002 from *http://www.2000. ogsm.vanderbilt.edu/rimm.cgi.*

Hyde, J. (1986). *Understanding human sexuality* (3rd ed.). New York: McGraw-Hill.

Kinsey, C., Pomery, W. B., Martin, C. E., & Gebhard, P. H. (1953). *Sexual behavior in the human female.* Philadelphia: Saunders.

Kutchinksy, B. (1973). The effect of easy availability of pornography on the incidence of sex crimes: The Danish experience. *Journal of Social Issues, 29,* 169–181.

Kutchinsky, B. (1985). Pornography and its effects in Denmark and the United States: A rejoinder and beyond. *Comparative Social Research, 8,* 301–330.

Kutchinshy, B. (1991). Pornography and rape: Theory and practice? Evidence from crime data in four countries where pornography is easily available. *International Journal of Law and Psychiatry, 14,* 47–64.

Langevin, R., Lang, R. A., Wright, P., Handy, L. Frenzel, R. R., & Black, E. L. (1989). Pornography and sexual offenses. *Annals of Sex Research, 1,* 335–362.

Malamuth, N. M. (1989a). The Attraction to Sexual Aggression Scale: Part 1. *The Journal of Sex Research, 26,* 26–49.

Malamuth, N. M. (1989b). The Attraction to Sexual Aggression Scale: Part 2. *The Journal of Sex Research, 26,* 324–354.

Malamuth, N. M., Addison, T., & Koss, M. (2001). Pornography and sexual aggression: Are there reliable effects? *Annual Review of Sex Research, 11,* 26–91.

Malamuth, N. M. & Donnerstein, E. (Eds.). (1984). *Pornography and sexual aggression.* Orlando, FL: Academic Press.

Malamuth, N. M., & Spinner, E. (1980). A longitudinal content analysis of sexual violence in the best-selling erotic magazines. *The Journal of Sex Research, 16,* 226–237.

Marshall, W. L. (1988). The use of sexually explicit stimuli by rapists, child molesters, and nonoffenders. *The Journal of Sex Research, 25,* 267–288.

Mehta, M. D., & Plaza, D. E. (1998). A content analysis of pornographic images on the Internet. Retrieved from *http://www.queensu.ca/cpu/mehta/pron.htm.*

Mosher, D. L. (1980). Three dimensions of depth of involvement in human sexual response. *The Journal of Sex Research, 16,* 1–42.

Mosher, D. L. (1988). Pornography defined: Sexual involvement theory, narrative context, and "goodness of fit." *Journal of Psychology and Human Sexuality, 1,* 67–85.

Orzack, M. H., & Ross, C. J. (2000). Should virtual sex be treated like other sex addictions? *Sexual Addiction & Compulsivity, 7,* 113–125.

Padgett, V. R., Brislen-Slutz, J. A., & Neal, J. A. (1989). Pornography, erotica, and attitudes towards women: The effects of repeated exposure. *The Journal of Sex Research, 26,* 479–491.

Palys, T. S. (1986). Testing the common wisdom: The social content of video pornography. *Canadian Psychology, 27,* 22–35.

Putnam, D. E. (2000). Initiation and maintenance of online sexual compulsivity. Implications for assessment and treatment. *CyberPsychology and Behavior, 3,* 553–564.

Reis, I. (1986). *Journey into sexuality: An exploratory voyage.* New York: Prentice-Hall.

Rimm, M. (1995). Marketing pornography on the information superhighway: A survey of 917,410 images, descriptions, short stories, and animations downloaded 8.5 million times by consumers in over 2000 cities in forty countries, provinces, and territories. *Georgetown Law Review, 83,* 1849–1934.

Schwartz, M. F., & Southern, F. (2000). Compulsive cybersex: The new tea room. *Sexual Addiction & Compulsivity, 7,* 127–144.

Scott, J., & Cuvelier, S. J. (1987). Violence in Playboy. magazine: A longitudinal analysis. *Archives of Sexual Behavior, 16,* 279–288.

Scott, J., & Cuvelier, S. J. (1993). Violence and sexual violence in pornography: Is it really increasing? *Archives of Sexual Behavior, 22,* 357–370.

Sherr-Klein, B. (Director). (1981). *Not a love story,* [Film]. Ottawa: National Film Board of Canada.

Smith, D. D. (1976). The social content of pornography. *Journal of Communications, 26,* 16–33.

Spenger, P. (1999, September 30). The porn pioneers. *The Guardian (Online),* pp. 2–3.

Snyder, M., & Ickes, W. (1985). Personality and social psychology. In G. Lindsey & E. Aronson (Eds.), *Handbook of social psychology* (Vol. II, 3rd ed., pp. 883–943). New York: Random House.

Sparrow, P., & Griffiths, M. D. (1997). Crime and IT: Hacking and pornography on the Internet. *Probation Journal, 44,* 144–147.

U.S. Attorney General's Commission. (1986). *Attorney General's Commission on Pornography: Final report.* Washington, DC: U.S. Department of Justice.

U.S. Federal Bureau of Investigation (2001). Retrieved from *http://www.fbi.gov* using a search for "forcible rape."

Winick, C. (1985). A content analysis of sexually explicit magazines sold in an adult bookstore. *The Journal of Sex Research, 21*, 206–210.

Wysocki, D. K. (1998). Let your fingers do the talking: Sex on an adult chatline. *Sexualities, 1*, 425–452.

Zillmann, D. (1989) Effects of prolonged consumption of pornography. In D. Zillmann & J. Bryant (Eds.), *Pornography: Research advances and policy considerations* (pp. 127–158). Hillsdale, NJ: Erlbaum.

Zillmann, D., & Bryant, J. (1984). Effects of massive exposure to pornography. In N. M. Malamuth & E. Donnerstein (Eds.), *Pornography and sexual aggression* (pp. 115–138). Orlando, FL: Academic Press.

Zillmann, D., & Bryant, J. (Eds.), (1989). *Pornography: Research advances and policy considerations.* Hillsdale, NJ: Erlbaum.

8.3 PORNOGRAPHY AND MEDIA
Toward a More Critical Analysis

Gail Dines and Robert Jensen

Because it is easy for discussions of pornography to drift off into the abstract, we start with the concrete and the visceral:

> After an intense three hours, the workshop on pornography is winding down. The forty women in the group work at a center that serves battered women and rape survivors. These are the women on the front lines, the ones who answer the twenty-four-hour hotline and work one-on-one with victims. They counsel women who have just been raped, help women who have been beaten, and nurture children who have been abused. They have heard it all and seen it all; no matter how brutal a story might be, these women have experienced or heard one even more brutal. There is no way to one-up these women on stories of male violence. But after three hours of information, analysis, and discussion of the commercial heterosexual pornography industry, many of these women are drained. A sadness hangs over the room.
>
> At the end of the session, one of the women who had been quiet starts to speak. Throughout the workshop she had held herself in tightly, her arms wrapped around her body. She talks for some time, and then apologizes for rambling. There is no need to apologize; she is articulating what many of the women seem to be feeling. She talks about her life, about what she has learned in the session and about how it has made her feel, and about her anger and sadness.
>
> Finally, she says: "This hurts. It just hurts so much."
>
> There is a moment of quiet as the words sink in. Slowly the conversation restarts and the women talk more about how they feel, how they will use the information, what it will mean to their work and in their lives. The session ends. But the words hang in the air.

It hurts.

It hurts to know that no matter who you are as a woman, you are reducible to a thing to be penetrated and that men will buy movies about that.

It hurts women, and men like it. Knowing that makes it difficult to avoid the hurt, even if one has found ways to cope with the injuries from male violence in other places. It is one thing to deal with acts, even extremely violent acts. It is another to know what thoughts, ideas, and fantasies lie behind those acts. In pornography, we are forced to confront the sexual imagination of a significant number of men.

In this essay, we analyze pornography as one would any media genre, by examining the system of production, the content, and the way it is used by consumers. We argue that the feminist critique of pornography, which grows out of the feminist movements to confront men's sexual violence and connects to a broad critique of the commercial sex industry, is the most compelling way to understand contemporary pornography. Finally, the study of pornography involves a critique not just of gender politics but also of racism and capitalism; it is a place where enmeshed systems of oppression can be seen clearly and confronted.

Before elaborating, some caveats and definitions. In this essay we use the term pornography to mean mass-marketed, graphically sexually explicit, heterosexual pornography in the contemporary United States—pornography that depicts actual (not simulated) sex between men and women (often with some woman-woman scenes) for a primarily male audience, the kind of material that one sees in the adult bookstores that exist in virtually every American city and can be purchased easily through the mail or obtained on the Internet. Although much of what we report here applies to pornography in other cultures, we make no cross-cultural claims; instead we examine the pornographic world in our society at this moment in history. We also do not address gay or lesbian pornography. Again, although some points in this essay are relevant to an examination of those genres, each genre requires a separate analysis.

STUDYING PORNOGRAPHY: THE "PORN WARS" AND BEYOND

Developing a critical media framework for the study of pornography requires an analysis of how pornography came to be of interest to academics and emerged as one of the most hotly debated topics in feminist media studies. Until the 1970s, debates over pornography typically usually involved liberal advocates of sexual freedom and conservative proponents of traditional sexual morality. The interested parties changed with the feminist critique of pornography, which emerged out of the larger struggle against patriarchal sexual violence during the second wave of the women's movement in the 1960s. Feminist critics argued that discussions of pornography should focus not on questions of sexual mores but on the harm to women, both those used in pornography and those against whom pornography is used. This argument led to what has become known as the "porn wars" in feminism.

Radical feminist activists and writers such as Andrea Dworkin (1981, 1988), Catharine MacKinnon (1987), Diana Russell (1993, 1998), and Laura Lederer (1980) argued that pornography eroticizes domination and subordination, objectifies women's bodies, and legitimizes sexual violence. These critics identified the harms connected to pornography, including the harm:

1. to the women and children used in the production of pornography;
2. to women and children who have pornography forced on them;
3. to women and children who are sexually assaulted by men who use pornography; and
4. in living in a culture in which pornography reinforces and sexualizes women's subordinate status (Dworkin & MacKinnon, 1988).

By rejecting traditional obscenity law and adopting a civil rights approach, the feminist critique sought to avoid censorship as a method of controlling pornography.

This radical feminist critique was rejected by some feminists, who argued that pornography was mere fantasy, a legitimate form of sexual expression, and/or an arena for female sexual agency, while others objected to the legislative initiatives on First Amendment grounds. Entire books have been written on this debate (Segal & McIntosh, 1993) and it is not our aim here to rehash the different positions. Rather, our intention in this essay is to articulate an approach to the study of pornography that is informed by radical feminism and cultural studies. While the academy has tended to set a radical feminist critique against a cultural studies approach, the two are compatible. Both approaches, in their founding moments, were concerned with social justice. Stuart Hall, one of the main contributors to the development of cultural studies in England, argued that cultural studies must have an activist agenda that involves "a practice which always thinks about its intervention in a world in which it would make some difference, in which it would have some effect" (Hall, 1982, p. 86). Radical feminism, even in its academic forms, has always taken as part of its mission the struggle to change patriarchal structures that subordinated, oppressed, and ultimately destroyed women.

The activist agenda that links both cultural studies and radical feminism has to be reasserted in light of the path that cultural studies has taken in the United States. In its journey across the ocean, cultural studies underwent many changes, one of which was the weakening of an agenda that sought to highlight the role media plays in supporting systems of domination. In its place is an almost obsessive interest in the text and reader agency that replaces a call for structural change in media production with a celebration of individual reader resistance. In British cultural studies, scholars were interested in the connections between media production, textual construction, and audience reception to foster a sense of critical political involvement (Blundell et al., 1993). Central to the activist agenda of cultural studies in Britain was the study of political economy, the very area that U.S. cultural studies have largely ignored. For McChesney, the failure of cultural studies scholars to ask questions about the politics of production has led to research that is "unimpressive, especially when viewed against the backdrop of the crucial political and intellectual questions surrounding communication in the present time" (McChesney, 2000, p. 109). Applying McChesney's critique to the study of pornography, we argue that the study of this genre needs to foreground a discussion on the politics of production before we can move to textual analysis or questions of audience response. When looking at production, McChesney argues that we need to study how "media and communication systems and content reinforce, challenge, or influence existing class and social relations" (McChesney, 2000, p. 110). Gender relations can be as important as class relations and, as radical feminists argue, the focus has to be on the lives of the women who are used in the actual making of pornography.

PRODUCTION

The most important thing to remember about the pornography industry is that it is an industry. In abstracted debates about pornography, amid talk about "sexual expression," we tend to forget that virtually all pornography is produced by a profit-driven industry that strives for maximal exploitation of labor, in this case primarily women. The systems of sexism, racism, capitalism, and First-World domination unite to produce a steady flow of female bodies to the pornography industry, domestically and from international trafficking in women (Barry, 1995; Giobbe, 1995).

In many books and articles by pro-pornography feminists, the area of production is rarely mentioned. When production is discussed, the industry often highlights a middle-class woman who chose pornography as a "career path," (most often Nina Hartley), or a woman who once performed in pornography before turning to the other side of the camera (such as Candida Royale), but these women are not representative of the thousands of women whose bodies are the raw material of the industry. We do not deny that some women stay in the sex industry for lengthy periods and make money—sometimes considerable amounts of money—especially when they successfully leverage visibility in pornography to gain higher wages while dancing in strip clubs. But focusing on these women is like arguing that worker-owned cooperatives are a good example of the capitalist mode of production. Yes, they exist, but the question is whether they are the norm.

One way of understanding the lived experiences of women in pornography is to look at the experiences of women who are prostituted. According to Evelina Giobbe, an activist and former prostituted woman, "prostitution is the foundation on which pornography is built . . . it is impossible to separate the two. The acts are identical, as is the population acted upon, except that in pornography, there is a permanent record of the abuse that is later marketed and sold as adult entertainment" (Giobbe, 1995, p. 314). Giobbe found that women in pornography and prostitution were driven primarily by financial need. Studies of prostitutes reveal that the average street prostitute sexually services about 1,500 men a year; the average starting age is fourteen; 60 to 70 percent of prostitutes were sexually abused as children, most often by family members; and the average age of victimization is ten (Baldwin, 1989, p. 123). Street prostitution is not the same endeavor as pornography in all respects, but like prostitution, pornography is the selling of women to a predominantly male clientele.

These comments do nothing to deny the agency of women or suggest that women in the sex industry are dupes. Critics of pornography and prostitution are often told they implicitly are denigrating or attacking prostituted women; nothing could be further from the truth. The radical feminist movements (distinct from conservative/religious movements) that critique the sex industry have always allied themselves with outreach groups for women. As is always the case, people make choices about their lives under conditions that include constraining and liberating factors. For example, students "choose" to take multiple-choice tests in class not necessarily because they believe the tests are a fair or sensible method of evaluation, but because they are willing to endure them on the path to earning a degree. Some may come to the conclusion that the tests actually are a meaningful measure of learning. To suggest to students that they should question their own acceptance of the exams is not to deny them agency, but to raise questions about the conditions under which they came to accept the exams. Any serious evaluation of these issues about choice and agency must acknowledge and highlight these constraints and possibilities. When we poll women in our classes and ask how many have given serious consideration to prostitution or pornography as a career they chuckle, making the obvious point that because they have other choices they do not include such a "choice" on their list of career options. That does not mean all women who perform in pornography are dupes; it simply acknowledges the conditions under which choices are made.

These choices that women make mean large profits for the pornography industry. About $10 billion a year is spent on pornography in the United States (Lane, 2000, p. xiv); estimates for worldwide sales are as high as $56 billion (*Forbes,* June 14, 1999, p. 214). Sales and rentals of pornographic videos in the United States total more than $4 billion a year, and there were 11,000 new pornographic videos released in 2000 (*Adult Video News,* December 2000, pp. 32–35). The market seems to absorb almost everything produced. When we interviewed adult-bookstore clerks and managers and asked them "what sells," they said, simply, "everything." The United States is a pornography-saturated culture.

In the twenty-first century, that saturation is achieved in part through the computer. At a panel on the Internet, entertainment executives focused on the perplexing question of why most dot-coms fail while pornography sites boom. Larry Kasanoff, chairman and CEO of the Los Angeles-based Threshold Entertainment asked:

> Why was no one talking about the adult entertainment business? In other words, why not talk about one segment of online entertainment that has flourished where others have failed . . . [Pornography was first] in cable TV, it was first in home video and [it's first] on the Internet . . . so you know what? Porn is great for all of us. We should all study it. (*Brandweek,* October 30, 2000, p. 48)

This is not the first time pornography has been a leading innovator in developing new technologies. It has been credited with helping to drive the evolution of the camera at the turn of the twentieth century, the home video business, cable TV, and DVDs (*Video Age International,* November 1, 2000, p. 3). *Playboy* was a major player in the development of the pornography Internet industry; its Web site has been around since 1994, making it one of the first national magazines to go digital. In August 1999, the site partnered with TheKnot.com, a New York based online wedding resource, to create *Playboy* BachelorParty.com, a complete online guide to help future grooms (lucky brides!). The pornographers are well aware of their power. As the operator of Bondagemistress.com succinctly puts it, "Technology is driven by adult entertainment . . . because sex then sells the technology" (*PC/Computing,* January 24, 2000, p. 64). Businesses that fail to follow this strategy pay a heavy price. For example, many entertainment analysts maintain that

Sony, by refusing to license its Betamax technology to pornographers, allowed VHS to monopolize the market by the early 1980s.

Studies of online pornography demonstrate that significant profits can be made in this business. Datamonitor, a research company based in New York and London, found that in 1998, nearly $1 billion was spent by users accessing pornography through an estimated 50,000 pornography-specific sites worldwide, an amount that is expected to triple by 2003. Off-line, pornography accounts for 69 percent of the current $1.4 billion domestic cable TV pay-per-view market, compared with 4 percent for video games and 2 percent for sports, according to one study (*Brandweek,* October 30, 2000, p. 48).

As if speaking to the pro-pornography camp, Andrew Edmond, president and CEO of Flying Crocodile, a $20 million pornography Internet business, has said that "a lot of people [outside adult entertainment], get distracted from the business model by [the sex]. It is just as sophisticated and multilayered as any other market place. We operate just like any Fortune 500 company" (*Brandweek,* October 30, 2000, p. 48).

Indeed, many of these Fortune 500 companies have links to the pornography industry. General Motors, the world's largest company, now sells more pornography films than Larry Flynt. According to the *New York Times,* "the 8.7 million Americans who subscribe to DirecTV, a General Motors subsidiary, buy nearly $200 million a year in pay-per-view sex films from satellite" (*New York Times,* October 23, 2000, p. 1). The *Times* also reports that AT&T, the nation's biggest communication company, offers to subscribers of its broadband cable service a hard-core pornography channel called Hot Network and owns a company that sells pornographic videos to nearly a million hotel rooms.

The second largest satellite provider, EchoStar Communications Corp., makes more money selling hard-core pornographic movies through its satellite subsidiary than all of *Playboy* holdings combined (*New York Times,* October 23, 2000, p. 1). The chief financial backer is Rupert Murdoch, CEO of News Corp. and owner of Fox Television Network, Twentieth Century Fox, the *New York Post,* and the LA Dodgers. Frontier Media, one of the most popular Web properties that features links to sites such as "Virgin Sluts," and "See Teens Have Sex," does business with In Demand, the nation's largest pay-per-view distributor, which is owned in part by AT&T, Time Warner, Advance-Newhouse, Cox Communications, and Comcast. The financial connections between mainstream companies and pornography highlight the degree to which pornography is not a marginalized industry but rather a major player in the development of sophisticated, multibillion-dollar new media technologies. Where all this will end is unclear because we have newer and newer technologies that no doubt will use pornography to make them user friendly. Virtual reality is just around the corner and already the pornographers are investing in its development.

The analysis of the production of pornography shows us that it is a multibillion-dollar industry controlled largely by men and dependent upon the bodies of women. We can extrapolate a number of assumptions about the text from this reality but, as Kellner points out, it is not enough to assume content from the politics of production. What is needed is an analysis of the text to "fully grasp the nature and effects of media culture" (Kellner, 1995, p. 10).

TEXT

Despite the rise of pornography on the computer, video pornography is still the primary distribution vehicle for sexually explicit material in the United States and thus is the focus of this discussion of content.

Pornographic videos range from collections of homemade footage (amateur), to cheaply made movies that string together sexual scenes with no storyline (gonzo), to efforts with larger budgets that approach Hollywood production values. There are many genres of pornography, including bisexual, transsexual, lesbian, and gay material. Bondage-and-domination pornography is sold in most stores as a separate category. Within heterosexual video pornography are a variety of subgenres: tapes featuring primarily oral or anal sex, various interracial combinations that usually play on overtly racist stereotypes, women who are depicted as being under the age of consent, and pregnant women. It is no exaggeration to say that any relationship of unequal power will be sexualized in pornography, including mental and physical disability (Elman, 1997).

Our analysis is based on a qualitative analysis of fifteen videotapes produced in 2000 and 2001, building on a similar study conducted in 1996 (Jensen & Dines, 1998). With such a small selection of tapes it is impossible to get a truly representative sample, but we specifically looked at videotapes that would be considered "mainstream" in the pornography industry; because the feminist antipornography movement is often criticized for focusing on the most violent material, we wanted to avoid being dismissed in that fashion. We visited pornographic stores and asked employees to guide us to the most commonly rented and purchased heterosexual tapes. So, for the purposes of our study, we let the market define pornography as what they sell in pornography shops, the material produced for the sexual stimulation of the mostly male clientele.

In a qualitative project such as this, the goal is not to make claims that can be generalized in "scientific" fashion to all of pornography. Instead of asserting "this is what all pornography looks like," we simply claim that "when pornography looks like this (and research suggests much of it does), this is what we think is going on." The goal is not definitive statements about an entire industry's products, but observations that can open up discussion about the industry and the sexual ideology of pornography.

It is easy to identify the main themes of pornographic videotapes: (1) All women always want sex from men; (2) women like all the sexual acts that men perform or demand, and; (3) any woman who does not at first realize this can be easily persuaded with a little force. Such force is rarely necessary, however, for most of the women in pornography are the "nymphomaniacs" men fantasize about: always on the lookout for sexual encounters and hyperorgasmic during sex. In pornographic videos everyone—men and women—is portrayed as always sexual, but there are crucial differences. In virtually all pornography, men are the sexual subjects, in control of the action and dictating the terms of the sex. Women are the sexual objects, whose job is to fulfill male desire. Women also tend to be more hypersexualized than men, that is, more quickly sent into a sexual frenzy.

Descriptions of two videos will illustrate these general points and provide examples of some of the specific conventions of pornography. The first is from "Hustler XXX Video #5," a compilation of five unrelated sex scenes. The "No Limits" segment begins with the camera panning a woman in lingerie and high heels as she does a striptease. After she describes her fantasy about multiple partners, four men enter the scene and she begins performing oral sex on them one by one while they masturbate and occasionally slap her with their penises. They then lift her onto a couch and one man enters her vaginally from behind with other men standing in front of her receiving oral sex. This basic pattern continues as the men switch positions, including vaginal and anal intercourse. The men receiving oral sex often hold the woman's head and thrust into her mouth. As one man moves between vaginal and anal penetration, the woman looks to be in pain, although it is difficult to know exactly what her facial expressions signal. He attempts to touch her clitoris, but she reaches down to push his hand away. He does it again, and she pushes it away again. At this point, she seems on the verge of crying. The scene then moves to "double penetration," in which two men enter her (vaginally and anally) at the same time. Finally, two of the men pick her up by the hair and guide her to the floor, where on her knees she performs oral sex on them all. She uses her hands and mouth to bring all of them to orgasm, and one by one they ejaculate into her mouth and on her face. As the camera closes in on her face, she smiles.

"Delusional" is a release from the Vivid studio, whose videos are considered the upscale end of the hardcore market. The plot concerns Lindsay, who, after discovering her husband cheating on her, has been slow to get into another relationship, saying she is waiting for a sensitive man. A case of mistaken identity leads to her first step back into sex with a woman, which leads to another sexual encounter with the woman and a man. In the final sex scene, the lead male character, Randy, professes his love for Lindsay: "I just want to look out for you." They embrace and after three minutes of kissing and removing their clothes, Lindsay begins oral sex on Randy while on her knees on the couch, and he then performs oral sex on her while she lies on the couch. They then have intercourse, with Lindsay saying, "Fuck me, fuck me, please" and "I have two fingers in my ass—do you like that?" This leads to the usual progression of positions: She is on top of him while he sits on the couch, and then he enters her vaginally from behind before he asks, "Do you want me to fuck you in the ass?" She answers, "Stick it in my ass." After two minutes of anal intercourse, the scene ends with him masturbating and ejaculating on her breasts.

These sexual scripts—vaginal and anal penetration, a focus on women performing oral sex on men, and ejaculations onto women—are standard in contemporary heterosexual video pornography. The participants move through the various positions with little variation. In most videos there are woman-woman scenes, filmed in similar style, usually with dildos to replace the missing penis. Scenes like these are typical of the range of the typical "mainstream" hardcore videos. The Hustler tape represents the rougher end of the mainstream market; although there is no overt violence, the woman in the tape is manipulated, pushed, pulled, and positioned to provide maximal male pleasure. Some of the penetration seems to be painful for her, and no attempt is made to edit out such expressions. The Vivid video attempts a coherent storyline and a sense of intimacy. But concentrating on those differences can obscure the similarities in representational conventions that make it clear that pornography is created to satisfy male sexual desire. Both videos represent a predictable pornographic mindset in which male pleasure defines sex and female pleasure is a derivate of male pleasure.

One example of this mindset is evident in the way oral sex is performed by men and by women. First, the scenes of men performing cunnilingus, if they appeared at all, were much shorter in duration than those of women performing fellatio. Men remained unemotional and unresponsive while performing cunnilingus, while women performing fellatio responded as if having a penis in their mouths brought them as much satisfaction as it did the man. Also, cunnilingus scenes almost always were set up in such a way as to maximize visibility of the woman's vagina; men usually position their heads off to the side, rather than directly over the vagina. Fellatio scenes, on the other hand, are constructed and photographed to center on the woman's technique of providing pleasure for the man.

During intercourse, sexual positions are used to maximize visibility of women's bodies. For example, in describing one of these positions (called the "reverse cowgirl," in which the woman is on top of a man facing away from him) a pornographic video director has said: "Very unnatural position. The girls hate it. It kills their legs, you know. But it shoots beautifully, because everything's opened up to the camera. It's very convenient" (Stoller & Levine, 1993, p. 133). The male body was not scrutinized in this way. The camera did not linger on the male body, nor did men present their bodies for the viewer. Men removed their clothes only when necessary for sex, and the penis was not explored with the obsession that the camera investigated the vagina. The camera rarely focused on the penis, except at the point of ejaculation, when recording the evidence of the male's pleasure was crucial.

That universal component of the pornographic script—the ejaculation onto women called the money, cum, or pop shot—offers insight into the ideology of pornography. What does the cum shot mean? One possible answer comes from "Taboo VIII," a video from the earlier Jensen and Dines study, in which a man refuses the request of a woman who he feels is untrustworthy to have intercourse and tells her, "I don't fuck sluts. I jerk off on them. Take it or leave it." He then ejaculates onto her breasts. If this is an accurate description of the meaning of the cum shot, then ejaculating onto a woman is a method by which she is turned into a slut, something—not someone—whose purpose is to be sexual with men. That assessment was echoed by a veteran pornographic director and actor, who said: "I'd like to really show what I believe the men want to see: violence against women. I firmly believe that we serve a purpose by showing that. The most violent we can get is the cum shot in the face. Men get off behind that, because they get even with the women they can't have. We try to inundate the world with orgasms in the face" (Stoller & Levine, 1993, p. 22).

With this analysis in mind, we ask a simple question: Is pornography pornographic? That is, is the material we collected at the pornography store porno-graphic in the critical feminist sense, a site of the social subordination of women? To answer that, we borrow from Andrea Dworkin's (1988, pp. 266–67) discussion of what we call the elements of the porno-graphic:

1. Objectification: when "a human being, through social means, is made less than human, turned into a thing or commodity, bought and sold."
2. Hierarchy: a question of power, with "a group on top (men) and a group on the bottom (women)."
3. Submission: when acts of obedience and com-pliance become necessary for survival, mem-bers of oppressed groups learn to anticipate the orders and desires of those who have power over them, and their compliance is then used by the dominant group to justify its dominance.
4. Violence: when it becomes "systematic, en-demic enough to be unremarkable and norma-tive, usually taken as an implicit right of the one committing the violence."

In the videos we analyzed, the first three elements were present throughout. The objectification of women in pornography is a foundation of the genre, and the gender hierarchy that pervades the wider cul-ture is, if anything, more intense in the pornographic world. Acts of submission are common in even the high-end tapes, though more obvious in the coarser material described earlier.

As indicated, most mainstream pornography does not include graphic depictions of violence, which leads many to assert that such pornography is not vio-lent. Yet there is a subtle violence throughout. Slap-ping and pulling hair are common. Women's bodies are jerked around to accommodate male desire. And there is violence in the kind of sexual intercourse that is common in pornography—the hard, repetitious pounding by the man into the woman for several min-utes at a time, sometimes vaginally and anally at the same time. Although women in pornography are expected to simulate an orgasmic state during all sex-ual activity, it is not unusual for women to stop the moaning during anal sex or double penetration. In

several videos, it seemed clear that the women were in pain and had to focus on carefully positioning their bodies to get through the scene. This is violent treat-ment of women's bodies.

Such routine, normative violence can be seen in the video "Blow Bang #4." The video includes eight different scenes in which a woman is on her knees in the middle of a group of three to eight men and performs oral sex on them. At the end of each scene, each of the men ejaculates onto the woman's face or into her mouth. To borrow from the description on the video box, the video consists of: "Dirty little bitches surrounded by hard throbbing cocks . . . and they like it."

In one of the scenes, a young woman dressed as a cheerleader is surrounded by six men. For about seven minutes, "Dynamite" (the name she gives on tape) methodically moves from man to man while they offer insults that start with "you little cheerleading slut" and become harsher. For another minute and a half, she sits upside down on a couch, her head hanging over the edge, while men thrust into her mouth, causing her to gag. She strikes the pose of the bad girl to the end. "You like coming on my pretty little face, don't you," she says, as they ejaculate on her face and in her mouth for the final two minutes of the scene. As the sixth man ejaculates onto her face, now covered with semen, Dynamite closes her eyes tightly and gri-maces. For a moment, her face changes; it is difficult to read her emotions, but it appears she may cry. After the last man ejaculates, she regains her composure and smiles. Then the narrator off camera hands her the pom-pom she had been holding at the beginning of the tape and says, "Here's your little cum mop, sweet-heart—mop up." Dynamite buries her face in the pom-pom. The screen fades, and she is gone.

Analyzing the pornographic text provides us with an understanding of the ways pornography, as both a form of representation and a practice, strengthens rather than subverts dominant patriarchal systems. Although one cannot read all the conditions of pro-duction from the text, it is crucial to remember that the video documents actual events; all accounts of the industry, including those favorable to it, make it clear that the cameras record actual sexual activity, not something staged. Put simply: the thrusting into

Dynamite's throat and her body's reaction happened in the world, not just on screen.

The last domain of analysis for a cultural studies approach is an examination of consumption, for, as Kellner argues, "to carry though a full cultural studies analysis, one must examine how diverse audiences actually read media texts, and attempt to determine what effects they have on audience thought and behavior" (Kellner, 1995, p. 11).

CONSUMPTION

No matter what the effects of pornography on men's behavior might be, it is important to ask a simple question: What does it mean that we live in a world in which men will buy these kinds of books, magazines, videos, and computer programs to spark their sexual fantasies and help them masturbate? The simple fact that billions of dollars of such material is sold every year, that in one year 11,000 new tapes are made that show men ejaculating onto women, tells us something about the world we live in.

But beyond basic consumption, we must ask questions about how men use pornography, about its effects on behavior. Does pornography, particularly the material that explicitly eroticizes violence, result in sexual violence against women, children, and other vulnerable people? Pornography's supporters and some researchers argue there is no conclusive evidence for such a claim. Other researchers contend the evidence points to certain effects with some groups of men (Malamuth, Addison, & Koss, 2000). No one argues that pornography is the sole causal factor in rape; sexual assault obviously occurs without pornography use. The question is whether the use of pornography can be considered a sufficient condition for triggering a sexual assault. In her review of laboratory studies and the testimony of women and men, Diana Russell argues that pornography is a causal factor in the way that it can: (1) predispose some males to desire rape or intensify this desire; (2) undermine some males' internal inhibitions against acting out rape desires; (3) undermine some males' social inhibitions against acting out rape desires; and (4) undermine some potential victims' abilities to avoid or resist rape (Russell, 1998, p. 121).

One underlying question is the level of certainty needed in establishing a casual link before society can or should act (Boyle, 2000). The limitations of social science and laboratory research suggest that definitive proof of a causal relationship between pornography and violence—at least at the level necessary to satisfy most social scientists and policy makers—is beyond the capabilities of the methods. Many feminists have argued that attention to the lived experience of men and women—both those who use pornography and those against whom pornography is used—makes the connection clear and provides the evidence necessary for collective action.

So, while acknowledging the complex theoretical and methodological debates around media effects and making no assertions involving causality in a strict sense, we will use narratives to describe the ways in which pornography is *implicated* in sexual violence in this culture. Pornography alone doesn't "make men do it." Rather, pornography is part of a world in which men do it. And we can look to people's stories about pornography use to understand that. Through the public testimony of women, interviews with pornography users and sex offenders, and other researchers' work, the following conclusions should be uncontroversial:

1. pornography can be an important factor in shaping a male-dominant view of sexuality;
2. pornography can be used to initiate victims and break down their resistance to sexual activity;
3. pornography can contribute to a user's difficulty in separating sexual fantasy and reality; and
4. pornography can provide a training manual for abusers.

How is pornography an important part of shaping sexual views? Here we switch to the voice of Robert alone:

I saw my first sexually explicit magazine in grade school. My friends and I begged, borrowed, and stole pornography throughout our childhood, hiding it in attics and garages and bedroom closets. Pornography was the first place I learned about the mechanics of sex—it was not the only place I heard about sex, but it was the primary curriculum for my sex education.

I continued to use pornography sporadically through my teens and twenties. I was not an obsessive user. I was a fairly normal kid and young adult. Most of the men I knew used pornography in the same way. And it is one of the ways in which we learned what sex was about, and what women were for. I am not a violent person; as a teen and young adult I was less macho and traditionally male (less aggressive, competitive, etc.). But I did learn to understand sex, and my relationship to women, in large part from pornography. Put more bluntly, pornography was one of the places where I learned to fuck women.

For some men, pornography is more central in their lives. It becomes a way to groom young people for sexual abuse, and it makes it difficult to separate sexual fantasy from reality, as this account from an interview subject in a study of convicted sex offenders and self-identified pornography users shows (Jensen, 1998). One man began grooming his stepdaughter for abuse when she was eight years old. He used pornographic videos to break down her resistance and persuade her that sex between a parent and child was acceptable. And he played the videos while he abused her:

> [The movies] played a big role, because I was fantasizing that . . . my stepdaughter and myself were actually engaging in the same behavior that was on the tape. So, it was more like I was having my own private orgy right there, with the tape, too. And also, it was something for my daughter to concentrate on. It made it more exciting for me.

When he would have sex with her without the videos,

> I'd be thinking about some women I saw in a video. Because if I was to open my eyes and see my stepdaughter laying there while I was abusing her, you know, that wouldn't have been very exciting for me. You know, that would bring me back to the painful reality that I'm a child molester, where [instead] I'm in this reality of I'm making love or having intercourse with this beautiful woman from the video. . . . It was just this beautiful person who had a beautiful body, and she was willing to do anything I asked.

Finally, one woman's story, told during public hearings on an antipornography ordinance in Min-

neapolis, illustrates how men sometimes model behavior they see in pornography. This woman described her husband's increasing interest in pornography as their marriage progressed. Out of a sense of duty, she accompanied him to pornographic movies and sex shows, but objected when he wanted to live out some of the pornography-based fantasies he had about group sex:

> He told me if I loved him I would do this. And that, as I could see from the things that he read me in the magazines initially, a lot of times women didn't like it, but if I tried it enough I would probably like it and I would learn to like it. And he would read me stories where women learned to like it. . . . To prevent more of these group situations, which I found very humiliating and very destructive to my self-esteem and my feeling of self-worth as a person, to prevent these I agreed with him to act out in privacy a lot of those scenarios that he read to me. A lot of them depicting bondage and different sexual acts that I found very humiliating. About this time when things were getting really terrible and I was feeling suicidal and very worthless as a person, at that time any dreams that I had of a career in medicine were just totally washed away. I could not think of myself anymore as a human being. . . . He would read from pornography like a textbook, like a journal. In fact, when he asked me to be bound, when he finally convinced me to do it, he read in the magazine how to tie the knots and how to bind me in a way that I couldn't get out. And most of the scenes . . . where I had to dress up or go through different fantasies were the exact scenes that he had read in the magazines. (MacKinnon & Dworkin, 1997, pp. 110–14)

Numerous women have testified to this type of experience with pornography. Again, these accounts do not prove that pornography causes abuse—they only make it clear that pornography is part of some abuse.

CONCLUSION

Linking a radical feminist critique with a critical cultural studies approach that foregrounds political economy highlights the ways in which pornography is a form of violence against women. Political economy, like radical feminism, is concerned with "commercial and material issues and . . . with issues of social justice" (McChesney, 2000, p. 115). Both radical feminism and critical cultural studies are radical movements that cut to the heart of systems of domination and hence rarely are welcomed by the official culture. Instead, they are attacked in various ways, depending on the time and place, and the perceived threat to that official culture.

This should not be surprising, given the roots of the feminist critique of pornography, and feminism more generally, in women's accounts of their lives that challenge official versions of reality. The original work of analysts such as Dworkin (1981) grew out of those stories that real women told each other, and the movement then took those stories to the public in the testimony for various attempts at passing the civil rights ordinance (MacKinnon & Dworkin, 1997). Other kinds of evidence were used in these political struggles, but there is a lesson for feminism, and perhaps for liberatory movements more generally, in this. One key source of the power of the antipornography critique is that it is rooted in, and has never lost touch with, the lives of ordinary people. Any analysis has to be built on more than just narratives, but those narratives remain at the core.

On the surface, the fate of the radical feminist critique of pornography seems rather grim. The movement's civil rights ordinance has, for the time being, been defeated in legislative and judicial arenas (*American Booksellers Association v. Hudnut*). In the academy, pro-pornography/anticensorship perspectives dominate the discussion (e.g., Strossen, 1995). Economically, the pornography industry is healthier than ever. In public discourse, the only antipornography position that gets serious attention in the mainstream is antifeminist, usually grounded in conservative religious objections that include not only objections to pornography but attacks on lesbian/gay rights and rejection of any conception of sexuality outside heterosexual marriage.

In that milieu, it would be easy to conclude that the critique has lost out, and that the political movement can be pronounced dead. But that obituary is premature. No social movement should expect to win its objectives overnight; no final determination of the success of a political project that is barely two decades old is possible.

The success of the critique is, for the moment, below the surface, precisely because the official culture leaves little space for its discussion and the social movement that gave voice to those views is currently in hibernation. In our experiences of discussing the feminist critique with students and members of the general public (men and women, but primarily women) at lectures and workshops, the critique resonates as much as ever with people for a simple reason: It helps many people understand their experiences. To assert that does not mean it explains *all* people's experiences; given individual variation, no social/political analysis ever does that. Instead, we simply observe that a significant percentage of women find it helpful to use the feminist critique not only to understand the use of pornography by men in their lives but also the larger sexual system in which they live.

REFERENCES

American Booksellers Association v. Hudnut, ordinance judged invalid, 598 F.Supp. 1316 (S.D. Ind. 1984); judgment affirmed, 771 F.2d 323 (7th Cir. 1985); judgment affirmed, 106 S.Ct. 1172 (1986); petition for rehearing denied, 106 S.Ct. 1664 (1986).

Baldwin, M. (1989). "Pornography and the Traffic in Women," *Yale Journal of Law and Feminism* 1(1), 111–55.

Barry, K. (1995). *The Prostitution of Sexuality.* New York: New York University Press.

Blundell, V. et al. (Eds.). (1993). *Relocating Cultural Studies.* London: Routledge

Boyle, K. (2000). "The Pornography Debates: Beyond Cause and Effect," *Women's Studies International Forum* 23(2), 187–95.

Dines, G., Jensen R., & Russo A. (1998). *Pornography: The Production and Consumption of Inequality.* New York: Routledge.

Dworkin, A. (1981). *Pornography: Men Possessing Women.* New York: Perigee. (Reprint edition, 1989, Plume.)

Dworkin, A. (1988). *Letters from a War Zone.* London: Secker & Warburg. (Reprint edition, 1989, Dutton.)

Dworkin, A., & MacKinnon, C. A. (1988). *Pornography and Civil Rights: A New Day for Women's Equality.* Minneapolis: Organizing Against Pornography. (Also available online at http://www.nostatusquo.com/ACLU/dworkin/other/ordinance/newday/TOC.htm.)

Elman, R. A. (1997). "Disability Pornography: The Fetishization of Women's Vulnerabilities," *Violence Against Women* 3(3), 257–70.

Giobbe, E. (1995). Surviving Commercial Sexual Exploitation. In G. Dines & J. Humez (Eds.), *Gender, Race and Class in Media: A Text-Reader* (pp. 314–18). Thousand Oaks, Calif.: Sage.

Hall, S. (1982). The Rediscovery of "Ideology": Return of the Repressed in Media Studies. In M. Gurevitch et al. (Eds.), *Culture, Society and the Media* (pp. 56–90). London: Methuen.

Jensen, R. (1998). Using Pornography. In G. Dines, R. Jensen, & A. Russo (Eds.), *Pornography: The Production and Consumption of Inequality* (pp. 101–46). New York: Routledge.

Jensen, R., & Dines, G. (1998). The Content of Mass-Marketed Pornography. In G. Dines, R. Jensen, & A. Russo (Eds.), *Pornography: The Production and Consumption of Inequality* (pp. 65–100). New York: Routledge.

Kellner, D. (1995). Cultural Studies, Multiculturalism and Media Culture. In G. Dines & J. Humez (Eds.), *Gender, Race and Class in Media: A Text-Reader* (pp. 5–17). Thousand Oaks, Calif.: Sage.

Lane, F. S. (2000). *Obscene Profits: The Entrepreneurs of Pornography in the Cyber Age*. New York: Routledge.

Lederer, L. (Ed.) (1980). *Take Back the Night: Women and Pornography*. New York: William Morrow.

MacKinnon, C. A. (1987). *Feminism Unmodified: Discourses on Life and Law*. Cambridge, Mass.: Harvard University Press.

MacKinnon, C. A., & Dworkin, A. (1997). *In Harm's Way: The Pornography Civil Rights Hearings*. Cambridge, Mass.: Harvard University Press.

Malamuth, N. M., Addison A., & Koss, M. (2000). "Pornography and Sexual Aggression: Are There Reliable Effects and Can We Understand Them?" *Annual Review of Sex Research* 11, 26–91.

McChesney, R. (2000). "The Political Economy of Communication and the Future of the Field," *Media, Culture & Society, 22*, 109–16.

Russell, D. E. H. (1993). *Making Violence Sexy: Feminist Views on Pornography*. Buckingham: Open University Press.

Russell, D. E. H. (1998). *Dangerous Relationships: Pornography, Misogyny, and Rape*. Thousand Oaks, Calif.: Sage.

Segal, L., & McIntosh, M. (Eds.). (1993). *Sex Exposed: Sexuality and the Pornography Debate*. New Brunswick, N.J.: Rutgers University Press.

Stoller, R. J., & Levine, I. S. (1993). *Coming Attractions: The Making of an X-Rated Video*. New Haven, Conn.: Yale University Press.

Strossen, N. (1995). *Defending Pornography: Free Speech, Sex, and the Fight for Women's Rights*. New York: Scribner's.

8.4 CREATING A SCENE
The Work of Performing Sex

Sharon A. Abbott

Much has been written about pornography, although very little of it originates from the perspectives of those within the industry. Most academic studies involve "outsider" (people outside of the industry) views of the meanings and consequences of porn. The experiences and observations of those involved in the industry, the "insiders," are ignored in social science research. As a result, pornography research has been conducted without a consideration of the work identity and work culture of participants in the industry.

To achieve a more sound understanding of the pornography industry, it is necessary to investigate the work of performing sex from the insider perspective. From this perspective, it is possible to examine facets of sex work such as the norms that govern the production process, participants' attitudes toward their jobs, the influence of sex work on intimate relationships, and the routinization of erotic labor. With this goal in mind, I have done extensive fieldwork in the pornography industry in the United States. Since 1996, I have

Original for this volume.

conducted nearly a hundred interviews with members of the pornography industry, including actresses, actors, directors, producers, company owners, camera crews, sound technicians, makeup artists, and caterers. In addition, I have observed the filming of thirty porn videos, attended industry functions, and toured production and distribution companies. Most of the fieldwork was conducted in the Los Angeles area, where the majority (85 percent) of pornography is produced in the United States.

THE WORK OF PORNOGRAPHY PRODUCTION

The production of pornography is a unique form of work because of the high degree of convergence between labor and self. This is particularly true for the talent (as actresses and actors are known within the industry), whose bodies and sexual expressions become the means of work. As a form of *expressive work,* the production process requires a high degree of cooperation among participants. Being cooperative is a necessity to earn a reputation in the industry as someone who is professional and competent. This reputation serves to secure future work because most actresses and actors do not hold exclusive contracts with any one company. Instead, talent operate as freelance employees, taking jobs with many companies and using connections with co-workers to secure future work.

The shooting of a pornography video is influenced by a number of factors, including the vision of the director, the budget, and the type of production company generating the product. Broadly, porn productions can be divided into three main categories: amateur, pro-amateur or gonzo, and professional. Amateur productions are typically shot in private locations (e.g., homes), and are sent to a distributor for marketing and sales. In the ideal form, amateur productions do not use paid talent, but rather capture unscripted sexual activities between "real" people. There is no pretense regarding the quality of the product; viewers are drawn to the "homemade" feel of the production.

In contrast, pro-amateur and professional videos are produced by companies using hired talent and experienced film crews. They are distinguishable from one another by company size, production budget, and availability of recognizable or "A list" talent. Professional features are known to have more popular and attractive actresses and actors, better production quality, more advertisements for big budget productions, and more glamorous box covers. Pro-amateur productions are intended to fill the wide gap between amateur and professional videos.

Pro-amateur and professional productions are filmed in studios or at private locations rented by the day. The studios are most often located in neighborhoods of small businesses and family houses. A typical set consists of a main floor with several rooms, a kitchen, at least one bathroom with a shower, an office, and a makeup room. The sets are arranged and decorated according to the script prior to the beginning of filming. Common set designs include bedrooms, bars, and offices—the settings typical of the porn formula.

Production sets may be either "open" or "closed" based on the preference of the lead actress and actor. A closed set allows only necessary members to be present during the filming of a sex scene. These necessary members include the talent, the director, the camera crew, and the sound technician. Even on open sets, however, it was rare in my experience to have visitors or extraneous members present. During the filming of a sex scene, other actresses and actors would wait in neutral areas, such as the kitchen or living room. I originally speculated that this practice originated out of respect for co-workers. I later learned that it instead reflects a general boredom with the work of porn production. There was no sexual turn-on from watching each others' performances.

In Los Angeles, production companies can also make use of the many private homes available for daily rental by the entertainment industry. Homes that are most desirable for porn productions are those with pools, private outdoor areas, large central rooms, and interiors decorated with minimal personal effects. The desire for nondescript interiors is linked to a practice known as "piggybacking a shoot." As a money-saving technique, companies will often shoot two videos at the same location within the same three-day period.

The productions are then released on different months and with different titles. This is financially advantageous to a production company due to cost savings in daily fees for the makeup artist, location, caterers, and film crew. By doubling up on the filming schedule, the production company pays one set of fees for two productions. Nondescript homes assist this practice by providing a neutral backdrop for several productions. This neutrality is coupled with a prescribed porn formula; most videos include a female masturbation sequence, a woman-to-woman scene, a scene of penile-vaginal intercourse, a group scene, and a scene including oral sex. As a result, most porno videos have a similar look and feel.

The people involved backstage in the production process (directors, camera crews, sound technicians, caterers, production assistants, and makeup artists) often work sixteen to twenty hours a day during the shoot. Actresses and actors usually arrive a few hours before their scenes to complete all necessary paperwork. Paperwork includes signing a model release form, offering verification of age, and demonstrating proof of HIV-negative status. All talent in heterosexual commercial porn must be tested for HIV antibodies every thirty days and must bring documentation of the test results to each shoot. After completing paperwork, actresses will have their hair and makeup done, and costumes, if used in the production, will be assigned. Talent are given scripts and asked to learn the dialogue in their scenes, although this is given relatively low priority. There are no rehearsals in porn, and improvisation is common.

Although each individual production has its own nuances, most share general similarities. Much like the mainstream industry, participants characterized the production process as "hurry up and wait." They were expected to be ready for their scenes at a scheduled time, although it was understood that the schedule was usually off by several hours. Between the filming of dialogue and sex scenes, there is a great deal of "hanging out" time. Participants often lounge in the kitchen or by the pool, gossiping about others in the industry. Food plays a central role on production sets, as meals are used to break the monotony of the day and to bring participants together to socialize. People hang out in the kitchen, and because of this, the caterer becomes an integral part of the production process. The ready availability of food and television fill the empty hours between scenes.

PERFORMING SEX

From the outsider perspective, the most titillating or intriguing part of the work of pornography participants is the filming of sexual scenes. Ironically, this is the aspect of porn work that is the most routine, mundane, and scripted. While the home viewer is encouraged to see the performance as highly sexualized, on production sets, the work is desexualized in a number of ways. Porn sets are brightly lit and sterile, camera crews and directors concentrate on the production quality of the video rather than the actions of the participants, and talent imitate sexual encounters they assume capture the fantasies of the intended audience. Routine practices on sets further encourage the notion that porn sex is a performance and a job. For example, there is very little interaction between participants prior to the beginning of a scene. There may be some minor flirting, but typically no contact. Most frequently, actresses and actors are hanging out in different rooms before being called into a scene. Nothing in their behavior mirrors the type of exchanges you would expect to see from two individuals about to have sex in the "outside" world.

A typical sex scene that will result in fifteen minutes in the final video takes about an hour and a half to shoot. During that time, there may be as many as eight breaks to change the camera position or the lighting. Typically, any sexual interaction between the participants will stop during these breaks, although actors will usually masturbate to maintain their erections. Male masturbation is routine and considered a work necessity. To be successful at porn work, and to secure future projects, actors must prove that they are reliable sexual performers. In addition to maintaining erections, actors must also be able to ejaculate on command. Directors will usually tell actors a few minutes in advance that they are ready to wrap up a scene. Often this was conveyed through a simple statement such as "We have enough tape, so whenever you are ready to go, that would be great." At this point, actors know that they should beginning building toward climax. The external ejaculation sequence is known as the "money shot" because actors are not paid unless they can complete the scene.

The norms governing interaction between participants on sets arise, in part, from a recognition that many actresses and actors are in relationships they consider monogamous (that is, no sex other than work sex). As Stephen explains:

> There is a sexual element to all of it, but wouldn't you be bothered by someone touching you every five minutes? Wait a couple minutes before the scene, before they turn it on [sexual advances], so it's really strange, cause it's almost a civil thing.

Couples working in the industry need to make special arrangements for negotiating sex on the job. Tim, an actor married to an actress, explains how they have decided to deal with this issue:

> I call it the two minute zone, what it really is, is if I'm in a relationship with her [his wife] and possibly the actress I'm going to work for is in a relationship, anything prior to the sexual encounter is considered a no-no. It's like extra points. I mean, there have to be guidelines. If I were to take an actress into a bathroom and have sex with her before my sex scene, that's cheating on my wife essentially. Even though it sounds funny, we're all in there fucking, but there it is. So, I call it the two minute zone, that's essentially two minutes before I am supposed to do it, that's when I start my caressing or my just being warm to her. And a lot of women find that professional.

While not everybody referred to this norm in the same terms, some unspoken version of it was widely followed on all the sets I visited.

Although the sex in a professional or pro-amateur feature is scripted and directed, the actresses and actors must nevertheless create a convincing performance. A key aspect of this performance requires exaggerating sexual enjoyment and coordinating the performance of other actors or actresses in the scene. For example, Niles explains:

> The ticket to my success and the reason why women like me is I can make it look like a whole lot of shit is going on, but in reality, I'm not putting it through the same rigorous workout. So once you learn that, you're making the director happy because you look like a steam engine, and making her happy because even though you look like a steam engine, you are in no way pounding her like a fucking V8 cylinder, so she is happy with you, the performance looks good, an all around takeoff. I put a high percent effort into making the performance look good. I still always consider it a performance.

For the scene to be sexually arousing, talent suggested that there needed to be some connection between the participants, a type of "chemistry" or "heat" that could be perceived by the anticipated audience. As one actress stated,

> I'm there to create passion, I'm there to create heat, I'm there to create what I consider to be a good sex scene, and what I consider to be a good sex scene is contact between me and the other person. And not just physical contact, but eye contact. There's a bit of emotional contact. I would be lying if I said, like so many actresses in the mainstream say, that I didn't fall in love a little bit with the person I'm performing with.

This chemistry makes the work more enjoyable for some participants and enhances the performance.

While the sexual enjoyment is exaggerated for the video, most actresses suggest that they do feel some sense of sexual enjoyment from their work. Enjoyment, however, rarely translates into orgasms. The positioning of the cameras and the frequent breaks makes sexual buildup impossible. As one actress put it, "You just can't eat good pussy on film." Instead, the pleasure described by participants was usually linked to work conditions. For example, many reported that a good relationship between themselves and the other participant(s) increased their sexual pleasure. Popular actresses and actors at the higher levels are able to choose with whom they want to work. Many actresses reported that they liked working with the same set of actors, as they felt more comfortable with each one over time, and knew what the other person liked. Because the pool of available actors is so small (about 20 actors to about 200 actresses), actresses were given the opportunities to foster these work relationships. Working with "nice guys," having an "easy scene" (no anal), and getting through a scene quickly were also reported to increase satisfaction.

Both actresses and actors reported that, as professionals, they were very concerned with their performances in the final product. Interestingly, these specific concerns illustrate a gender split within the industry. Actresses are far more concerned with their appearances, and actors with their sexual performances. For example, Sola suggests that during filming she is worried about body fat, ingrown hairs, and hygiene. As she argues:

> You are trying to look the best for the camera. You don't want to have a roll of fat or tits bouncing in a way that they look fake.

Similarly, in response to the question "What do you typically think about during filming?" Lori answered:

> One of them is where is the camera and how am I appearing to the camera. There are certain angles that look great with me, and there are certain angles that don't look great with me. I really like to look as good as I can that's part of it . . . So, yeah, there are one or two things that I'll keep in mind. What I'm thinking about is making a better performance so you can whack off.

There are several explanations for why actresses would be more concerned with their appearance. Many theorists have documented that norms governing appearance strongly influence women's lives, and most women are highly concerned with meeting these norms. Schur further argues that men's and women's preoccupation with women's appearance results in the commodification of female sexuality. As socialized women in this culture, actresses have been trained to feel self-worth in regard to their physical appearance. Actresses' careers are also more influenced by their appearance, suggesting an additional need to focus on their looks. The link between appearances and work success is supported by industry practices. Pay and recognition are dependent on beauty. Furthermore, many porn actresses dance in strip clubs for additional money. More attractive and slim actresses are able to command higher fees. Appearances, therefore, have economic consequences.

Actors more than actresses reported experiencing tension or apprehension in regard to their performances. Most of this tension surrounded their ability to perform sexuality on set. This concern extends even to the preparation time prior to a scene. For example, Tim explains:

> So when my career, when it got stale for me, that's when I start going "God, she doesn't like me, can I get a boner?" And so the director told me, he goes, "Every time you drive to a set, do you even think about whether you get a boner or not?" And at the time, I used to think yeah, I do. I'm driving there going, "Can I do this?" Now that I know what I am doing, it's no question. There's just no question in my mind. I don't even think about it. I just want to get there and I've learned how to master every possible scenario there is. There's nothing, and I've done extreme things I never used to do before just to test myself, just to see if I do have that mental staying power. Cause that's really what it boils down to, mental staying power.

For actors, a successful performance is also based on "real" sexual arousal, at least in regard to achieving erections. Actors often reported that they needed to get into a particular state of mind in order to perform, often referred to as their "groove" or "zone," or as Tim stated, his "staying power." When asked what makes a good actor, one producer suggested it was his ability to delve into his fantasies. Many respondents suggested that actors who "can't make it" lack the ability to recess into this fantasy space.

Actors also use personal fantasies of fetishes to achieve this state of sexual arousal. For example, Stephen reported:

> I think of my ex's legs. The back of her legs. Even though she totally screwed me over, I still get hot. I just need to think of her, and I can get there.

These fetishes can also help if an actor is not interested in a particular actress. When asked if he could "fake it" with someone he was not interested in, Jon replied:

> Early in your career that happens, but once you set your standards . . . now I get my choice, and I know who's out there and I know who's what, But normally, I have fetishes. I have a foot fetish, and I also have an oral fetish, so I said, as long as she's got feet, I'm not going to have a problem, and I don't work with paraplegics.

Shortly after our interview, I had a chance to watch Jon film a scene. During breaks in the filming, he would caress and lick the actress's feet. At one point, she turned to the director and me (we were sitting behind the video monitor in the corner of the room), and exclaimed: "All these body parts, and all he wants is my dirty feet." Like most actresses I observed, she seemed tolerant of this interaction since it was necessary to keep Jon aroused (and thus, to complete the scene).

The performance created by actresses and actors is encouraged and supported by directors, producers, and crew. Directors in particular must coordinate efforts with actresses and actors to produce a good scene. This involves understanding the dynamics or chemistry between participants, having a sense of what is being shot (how it appears on camera), and perceiving how the scene will be received by the anticipated audience To do their jobs competently, camera crews, directors, editors, and sound technicians are expected to be disinterested in the content of the production. Many respondents claimed that they had become desensitized to sexual imagery through continuous exposure. As one director responded, "I couldn't do my job if I was turned on all the time."

AT-HOME SEX VERSUS WORK SEX

Performing sex for work has encouraged those in the porn industry to make distinctions between sex on the job (work sex), and sex in their private lives (at-home sex). Respondents articulated several differences between the two. Work sex is a performance. It is exaggerated, faked, scripted, and routine. It may or may not be arousing. At-home sex, in contrast, is real, intimate, spontaneous, pleasurable, and genuine. Even couples working in the industry distinguished between the sex they have together on sets and the sex they have in their nonworking time.

Despite these distinctions, the work of actresses and actors has an undeniable effect on their intimate relationships. Most commonly, talent explained that performing sexually on set temporarily rendered them incapable, unwilling, or disinterested in engaging in sex at home. When asked if working several days in a row affects their personal sex life, one actress answered:

Sometimes it does, sometimes it doesn't. Last week, I was working an awful lot. As a matter of fact,

Thursday was the last day of eight days in a row for me, that's a lot. . . . After eight days, I tell you, I was really sore. The sixth day, I had a three-hour hard core scene in the evening. Three hours of actually getting penetrated, with an actor who was very well endowed, lots of them are, that's part of why they are there, and of course, he was wearing a condom. . . . That eight-day stretch, I was not neglecting my partner, but we weren't having penetrative sex. I couldn't.

In addition to feeling sore after a day of filming, some actresses also reported that sex within their relationships was also influenced by upcoming jobs. For example, Brianna explains:

I say, "Honey, I gotta do it twice tomorrow, and if we do it now, I'm not going to be able to do it twice tomorrow." This is how I make my living, and he is completely understanding of that.

In these situations, couples may need to form new expectations or engage in nonpenetrative sexual behaviors. As Rita reported:

There are times I am just out of commission at the moment. I care enough about the person I am with to make sure that they are receiving satisfaction though. Sex is also holding somebody's hand, or giving someone a hug, touching them, caressing them, kissing. I understand that men like to have orgasms, and I am not stupid enough to think I can neglect my personal sex life in favor of my career.

Similarly, Meka explains:

He is monogamous with me and I am monogamous with him, except for what I do for a living, and he is completely capable of making that separation, always has been. He is supportive when I come home in a bad mood, which, hey, it happens, it's not all fun and games, he'll draw me a bath and give me a massage. He'll snuggle with me and he's not expecting me to say, "okay, let's have sex now," because I've had a bad day and my day deals with sex.

Success in these arrangements requires having a supportive and understanding partner.

Actors also reported a diminished interest in sex at home after a day of sex at work. For example, one actor I interviewed on a production set had two scenes scheduled that day, one in the late morning and one in the afternoon. His negotiations of sex at home were eased because his wife was familiar with the work. She had been an actress when they were first married, but had recently left the industry. Asked how a day of filming affects their relationship, he responded:

> I can assure you my wife won't be looking for any [sex] tonight! She understands though. I imagine it is more difficult if you are with someone who doesn't know the business.

Other actors argued that it was easier to stay single so that they would not have to deal with sexual pressures in their intimate lives.

Couples with both partners working in the industry also reported negotiating a balance between their personal and professional sexuality. For example, Nesa and Kyle, a girlfriend and boyfriend acting pair, explained that their personal sexual relationship was often influenced by their schedules for the week. As one of the most popular actors in the industry at the time, Kyle would frequently shoot for several days in a row. Nesa held an exclusive contract with a pro-amateur company, and was required to do several dancing (stripping) assignments each month. The couple complained that they were often exhausted and that, although they valued spending their free time together, having sex was not a central feature in their relationship. This exhaustion is familiar to many working couples who are drained by the demands of their careers.

Some couples, however, told of problems that can arise when one partner performs sex for a living. In these situations, it appears that the constructed dichotomy between home and work sex was not fully appreciated by both members. For example, in a conversation with an actress and her husband-manager, the actress commented that her husband expressed disappointment that she was not like her screen persona at home. As she explains:

> I just can't, it is not real. I don't want it to be like that between us. He does and he doesn't understand that. I have given him a [screen name] blowjob once, but I can't make love.

Her husband's desire for her to perform at home is especially interesting because he takes credit for inventing and naming her screen persona. Ironically, he has created a fantasy from which he is now excluded.

This collapse between fantasy images and real individuals was evident in the descriptions from actresses regarding their experiences dating men outside of the business. Amelia's statement characterizes this situation:

> I've been on quite a few dates with men who knew who I was, knew who I am, and they expected that because of what I did for a living, that I was going to jump into bed with them that night. Well, there are a few sorely disappointed men out there. It's interesting, because of situations like that, I've gotten to the point where I will not go on a date unless I am interested in them sexually because if we're just going to be friends, no, it is never just friends, it really isn't. You're constantly bombarded with sexual come-ons because of the nature of what we do.

As a result, many of those in the industry choose to date others in the business, assuming that they would better understand the unique aspects of porn work. Similar to other deviant subcultures, participants come to serve multiple roles as friends, co-workers, relationship partners, and business associates.

The sexual expectations that surround porn actresses also influence their career trajectories. Actresses are more likely than actors to work intermittently in the industry. Respondents suggest that this pattern exists because women leave the business to pursue personal relationships. When the relationships fail, women return to porn work. These arrangements, however, may be confounded by cultural expectations and a gender double standard. As Danielle explains:

> When you first meet a guy, they think it is hot, like you really know what you are doing. But as soon as you are together, it's like suddenly not so cool you are having sex with hundreds of men. So girls leave the industry, but he doesn't forget. Now suddenly she is the slut he had to save. There is no way for the relationship to work. Soon enough, she'll be back.

Other actresses told of problems encountered after leaving the industry to concentrate on their intimate relationships. For example, Rita left for a period of one year after meeting a man who wanted her to stop working and promised to support her. She provides her reason for leaving the relationship and returning to the industry:

> When I got out of it [the industry] and got into this relationship and we started living together, it became clear that I was very much his beck and call girl, and whenever he wanted to bring clients home, it was my responsibility to be little Miss Housewife. I'm not that kind of person, and it took that relationship to learn to accept that.

Unwilling to give up the freedom and independence she had while in the industry, Rita eventually left her relationship and returned to sex work.

In contrast, nearly all of the actors I interviewed were single. There are several possible explanations for this. First, because there are fewer actors than actresses, actors typically work on more projects in any given month than their female co-workers. The extended hours and travel time may prohibit the feasibility of maintaining a relationship. Second, part of the image of a successful porn actor is that he is independent and interested, continuously, in sex. Being single supports this image more than if an actor is known to be in a committed relationship. Third, some respondents suggested that a man outside the industry would be more willing to date an actress than a woman would be to date an actor. According to this argument, actors experience greater stigma due to women's assumed interest in committed monogamous relationships. As Dane explains:

> No woman in her right mind, no lawyer, doctor, accountant, is going to say that's the man I want, he's fucking everybody. Women are a lot more single-minded than that, they need monogamy more than that. Most of the men, when they get into relationships, they're with women in the business.

Finally, traditionally constructed sexual scripts might suggest that actors are less interested in relationships because they have the guarantee of sex on the job. As one actor argues, "I don't need it at home if I am getting enough at work."

THE CREATION OF A PORN PERSONA

To assist in the separation of work sex and home sex, actresses and actors create porn personas or personalities that can provide a separation from their "real" selves. This phenomenon, however, is not unique to the porn industry. The dramaturgical perspective claims that all individuals create identities (or multiple versions of self) that are performed for different audiences. Individuals present themselves to different audiences based on audience expectations. Those involved in the porn industry similarly possess multiple versions of themselves, although porn actresses and actors must also create a sexualized identity for their work performances. The created sexual persona is typically a fabricated or exaggerated version of self. Respondents report that there are several dynamics involved in creating a good persona. Porn personas must be desirable, convey the impression that the work is enjoyable, and portray sex as authentic and pleasurable. Perhaps most importantly, however, the created persons must feed the fantasies of the imagined viewer.

Actresses and actors state that the type of persona they constructed for themselves was influenced by the type of audience they wished to attract. For example, one actor who described himself as a "young, attorney" type selected this image to appeal to viewers of professional features. Another actress explained that she chose a stage name that conjured images of "wild, out-of-control women" to appeal to fans attracted to stronger and sexually aggressive women. Names often suggest a desire for certain sexual activities (e.g., Janet Jackme), geographical location (e.g., Steven St. Croix), ethnicity (e.g., Kobi Tai), and personality (e.g., Kitty Yung).

Similar to erotic dancers, porn actresses and actors create personas they believe are appealing to audiences. For example, as Ronai and Ellis argue, many strippers portray exaggerated stereotypes to get bigger tips from certain customers. Similarly, Frank (1998) asserts that strippers sell their "selves" or identities, which are created in part to generate and sustain male desires. These identities are re-created to attract different admirers and/or for various situations. Similarly, actresses and actors sell their sexual performance for an imagined audience, using various personas to attract a range of viewers.

Although personas are created identities, respondents suggest that there are often some authentic aspects to them. For example, many reported that their camera personas developed out of some part of their personalities. Often their created personas exaggerated certain characteristics that they believed were the best, or most desirable, parts of themselves. Aliza explains:

> [Her performance name] is way wilder than I am, she is more raw, more in your face. There is about 50 percent of me in her, and maybe 10 percent of her in me.

Although many respondents suggested their personas reflected themselves, none suggested they were identical. Rather, they distinguished between the identities, suggesting that on-screen identities were "bigger," "louder," "raunchier," and "sexier."

The fact that actresses and actors create personas is not unknown to the audience (i.e., the consumers), although these glimpses behind the curtain are often orchestrated by the industry. For example, X-rated magazines and industry publications such as *Adult Video News* (*AVN*) offer "behind the scenes" pictures of the filming of professional and pro-amateur videos, revealing the constructed nature of the productions. In addition, "candid" interviews with performers often hint at the "real" person behind the on-screen persona. Some interviews have even provided the rationale for developing a certain type of persona. For example, one actress reported to *AVN:*

> I want my persona to be different from the rest of the girls. I don't want to be "the quiet one"; I want to be "the mean one." I want to be the bitch. I want to be the girl that roughhouses with the guys and tells them to fuck me, because if they don't, I'm going to slit their throats or something.

The article proceeds to state that while the actress appears soft spoken, she was very active in the New York City's SM scene, and a fan of porn prior to entering the industry, thus supporting her chosen persona. In doing so, the article suggested that the persona better mirrors her true self than her everyday appearance. Many respondents claimed that these "real life" exposes were merely second-level support for their constructed persona. The "true self" remains separate and hidden.

The creation of screen personas was seen by many respondents as a career necessity. Disguising their real identities also helps prevent unwanted contact with "sickos" and assists in preserving their personal privacy. Created personas also serve as a reminder that the work of porn production is a performance. Similar to the norms created to differentiate between "home sex" and "work sex," created personas serve to protect the core self by reminding the participant that porn work is a created, fantasy-based performance.

Not all respondents believed that the split between created persona and true self was completely possible. For example, Rachel suggests some of the possible problems with the creation of alternative selves:

> Don't try to fool yourself into thinking that just because you call yourself something else, that you are something else. This whole thing about trying to separate this on-screen persona from this off-screen person, good story, but you are signing your real name to those contracts, you're doing the job, and if you didn't have something in your psyche that made you want to do this, that on-screen persona wouldn't exist. This whole trying to turn it on and off is going to drive you insane. But if you accept the fact that you are a woman who enjoys being sexual in front of people, who is an exhibitionist, and who enjoys the attention that you are getting, etcetera, and realize that you can have a long career in this business with a much saner mind.

Similarly, Nicola, an actress in the industry for twelve years, suggests that actors can become disassociated because of their jobs. She claims:

> It is an unhealthy split between their dicks and their hearts. The fantasies have to get weirder and weirder. It is a real harm to male sexuality. At best, it is a very lonely thing.

Rachel and Nicola's comments suggest some of the possible problems associated with performing sex for a living, such as detachment or alienation, inability to acknowledge the similarities between on-screen and off-screen personas, and the loss of intimacy as a result of these performances. Other respondents echoed their concerns, but suggested means to care for themselves, including taking time off from their careers, maintaining relationships outside of the industry, and taking pride in their ability to do their job successfully. Many of these same strategies are used by people in other professions requiring a high degree of emotional labor, such as service workers.

CONCLUSION

The work of porn production thus becomes routinized in a number of ways. The productions are made as cheaply as possible and adhere to a widely accepted formula. The sex scenes are orchestrated in such a way as to produce a good scene for the video but a mediocre sexual experience for the participants. The creation of personas, supported by industry productions, serves to separate the performances of actresses and actors from their true selves. On multiple levels, the audience is given fabricated versions of constructed personas. In addition, the norms on production sets, as well as the design of the sets themselves, desexualize and normalize the work for the participants both in front of and behind the camera. Nevertheless, most participants suggest that they are able to find pleasure in their jobs. The aspects of work satisfaction include such things as co-worker relations and a sense of competency about their jobs.

This reality exists in sharp contrast with outsider views of the industry. Outsiders include those most interested in pornography: consumers, scholars, feminists, and politicians. Publications for porn consumers encourage the idea that porn work is excessively titillating and that porn participants are highly sexualized both on and off camera. Academic research typically assumes that the content of pornography is purposeful and significant. Numerous studies have addressed the possible consequences of viewing porn, while neglecting the conditions under which it is produced. In addition, feminist theorists have long questioned the effect of engaging in sex work on an individual's life. Many have speculated that women are damaged from their participation in an industry that is sexually exploitative. Their writings fail to account for the lived experiences of those in the industry that have actively worked to protect themselves from the consequences of performing sex.

By exploring at the porn industry from an insider perspective, it is possible to uncover a deeper understanding of work of pornography. Discussions can move from topics of content and consequences to a better appreciation for the experiences of those involved in this type of sex work. In doing so, we can achieve a better sociological understanding of pornography as a product, a subculture, and an industry.

REFERENCES

Schlenker, Barry R. (1980). *Impression Management.* Belmont, CA: Brooks/Cole Publishing Company.

Ronai, Carol Rambo and Carolyn Ellis. (1989). "Turn-ons for Money: Interactional Strategies of the Table Dancer." *Journal of Contemporary Ethnography 18,* 271–298.

Frank, Katherine. (1998). "The Production of Identity and the Negotiation of Intimacy in a Gentleman's Club." *Sexualities 1 (2),* 175–201.

Kernes, Mark. (1996). "Madelyn Knight: Vivid's New Tough and Gritty Kitty." *Adult Video News,* May 28.

PART FOUR

SEXUALITY
AS POLITICS

CHAPTER NINE

SEXUAL VIOLENCE

That violence is associated with sexuality is not inevitable; it need not be the case. But about 15 percent of college women report having been sexually assaulted; more than half of these assaults were by a person the woman was dating. Some studies have estimated the rates to be significantly higher, nearly double (27 percent) that of the study undertaken by Mary Koss and her colleagues.[1] And, although some pundits have expressed outrage that feminists have transformed college aged women into "victims," it is more accurate to express outrage that predatory males have turned college women into victims of sexual assault. The fact that significant numbers of college women are forced to change their behaviors because of the behaviors of these men—where they study, how late they stay in the library, which parties they go to, whom they date—is the outrage.

Among adults, women and men report quite different rates of forced sex. While 96.1 percent of men and 77.2 percent of women say they have never been forced to have sex against their will, those who have been forced display dramatic differences. Just slightly more than 1 percent of men (1.3 percent), but over one-fifth of all women (21.6 percent) were forced to have sex by the opposite sex; only about 2 percent of men (1.9 percent) and just 0.3 percent of women were forced by someone of the same sex. Men continue to be the principal sexual predators. Several studies estimate the likelihood that a woman will be the victim of a completed rape to be about one in five. The figure for an attempted rape is nearly double that.[2]

The essays in this section address the relationship between violence and sex. Carole Sheffield describes a matrix of rape, assault, and battery that constitutes what she calls "sexual terrorism."

In a wide-ranging survey using techniques she developed studying other cultures, anthropologist Peggy Reeves Sanday explores the differences between campuses that are "rape prone" and "rape free." Psychologists Susan Hickman and Charlene Muehlenhard describe the variety of evasive and precautionary behaviors that women engage in on either type of campus to ensure that they don't become victims of sexual assault. Fred Pelka describes his own experience of being raped by another man.

1. Koss, M., Dinero, P. T., Seibel, C. A., and Cox, S. L. "Stranger and Acquaintance Rape: Are There Differences in the Victim's Experience?" in *Psychology of Women Quarterly* 12(1), 1988. pp. 1–24.

2. Laumann, E. et al., *The Social Organization of Sexuality,* p. 336; see also Koss, M. et al., *No Safe Haven.*

9.1 College Women's Fears and Precautionary Behaviors Relating to Acquaintance Rape and Stranger Rape

Susan E. Hickman and Charlene L. Muehlenhard

Past research on women's fear of rape has focused on women's fears relating to stranger rape, even though most rapes are acquaintance rapes. In this study, 139 undergraduate women completed a questionnaire concerning their fears, precautionary behaviors, and beliefs relating to acquaintance and stranger rape. Women reported being more fearful of rape by strangers than by acquaintances, and they reported engaging in more precautionary behaviors because of fear of stranger rape than of acquaintance rape. When asked to self-generate situations in which they feared rape, they generated more situations in which they feared stranger rape than acquaintance rape. Paradoxically, they estimated that acquaintance rape was more common. Precautionary behaviors were best predicted by level of fear. A history of acquaintance rape had no effect on women's responses. Theoretical and educational implications are discussed.

I have never been free of the fear of rape. From a very early age I, like most women, have thought of rape as part of my natural environment—something to be feared and prayed against like fire or lightning. I never asked why men raped: I simply thought it one of the many mysteries of human nature.

—*Susan Griffin*

Most women live their lives in fear of becoming a victim of rape (Brownmiller, 1975; Griffin, 1971; Warr, 1985). This fear is not unfounded. Approximately 15% to 24% of the women surveyed in various studies report being raped (Koss, 1993; Koss, Gidyez, & Wisniewski, 1987; Koss, Woodruff, & Koss, 1990; Russell, 1984). Russell (1984) estimated that women have a 26% probability of being the victim of a completed rape at some point in their lives; when completed *and attempted* rapes are included, this probability rises to 46%.

The fear of being victimized causes women to restrict their behavior in numerous situations (Gordon & Riger, 1989; Riger & Gordon, 1981; Softas-Nall, Bardos, & Fakinos, 1993; Warr, 1985). In a 1977 study of women in urban neighborhoods, 41% of the respondents reported frequently using isolation tactics intended to prevent exposure to risk, such as not going out on the street at night; 74% reported frequently using street-savvy tactics intended to reduce risk when exposed to danger, such as wearing shoes that permit them to run (Riger & Gordon, 1981). Women's level of fear was the best predictor of engaging in isolation and street-savvy tactics. In a 1981 mail survey of Seattle residents, 42% of the women sampled reported avoiding going out alone, 67% reported avoiding certain places in the city, and 27% reported refusing to answer their door. Women who reported higher levels of fear of rape were more likely to take such precautions (Warr, 1985). Similarly, a study of Greek women found that 71% of the women sampled reported avoiding going out late at night and 78% avoided certain places in the city because of their fear of becoming a victim of a crime. They reported that they were more fearful of being raped than becoming the victim of any other crime, including murder (Sof-tas-Nall et al., 1993).

Fear of Acquaintance Rape

For the purposes of this article, acquaintance rape is defined as occurring when a woman is raped by someone known to her, ranging from a man she has just met to a close friend or boyfriend. In contrast, stranger rape occurs when a woman is raped by someone she does not know (Bechhofer & Parrot, 1991). Acquaintance rape accounts for approximately 80% to 90% of all rapes (Koss, Dinero, Seibel, & Cox, 1988; Russell, 1984).

Currently, published research on women's fear of rape makes no distinction between fears relating to acquaintance rape and fears relating to stranger rape. When researchers ask about rape without specifically mentioning acquaintance or stranger rape, two thirds of the women who volunteer information that they have been raped report being raped by a stranger, not an acquaintance (Hindelang & Davis, 1977), despite evidence that the vast majority of rapes are acquaintance rapes. Moreover, questions asked in studies about women's fear of rape have focused on situations in which the rapist would typically be a stranger, such as going out alone at night (Heath & Davidson, 1988; Kelly & DeKeseredy, 1994; Riger & Gordon, 1981; Softas-Nall et al., 1993; Warr, 1985). Hence, most of the literature on fear of rape pertains primarily to stranger rape.

There are differences between acquaintance and stranger rape, however. Most obviously, there is a difference in the relationship between the rapist and victim. In acquaintance rape, a relationship of some sort (e.g., a dating relationship, friendship, or working relationship) has already been established, and the woman has often entered into the relationship voluntarily. Stranger rape, in contrast, does not involve any prior interaction with the rapist and therefore is less likely to call into question the woman's behavior, judgment, or social competence (Katz, 1991). Acquaintance and stranger rapes also occur in different circumstances. "Date and acquaintance rape occur in a social context where consensual sex is a possibility; in stranger rape, sex is generally out of context" (Bechhofer & Parrot,

1991, p. 10). Furthermore, although acquaintance and stranger rape can both be used to express power and anger (Groth & Birnbaum, 1990), some acquaintance rapes may result from miscommunication or misperception (Abbey, 1991; Bechhofer & Parrot, 1991; Parrot, 1988; Warshaw, 1994) or from the rapist's feelings of entitlement based on the nature of the relationship (Muehlenhard, Goggins, Jones, & Satterfield, 1991; Russell, 1982/1990; Shotland & Goodstein, 1992). As a result of the different circumstances and motivations associated with stranger and acquaintance rape, it is probable that women would take different precautions to protect themselves from acquaintance rape than they would to protect themselves from stranger rape. It is also likely that women have different fears relating to the two kinds of rape.

Predictors of Precautionary Behaviors

Several interrelated factors can affect a person's precautionary behaviors relating to a threat such as rape. These include fear, perceived personal vulnerability, perceived trauma, perceived controllability, and previous personal experience (Heath & Davidson, 1988; Weinstein, 1988, 1989; Weinstein & Nicolich, 1993). Fear or worry about a situation can increase a person's precautionary behaviors, serving as either a direct or indirect motivator to engage in precautionary behaviors (Weinstein, 1988, 1989). Perceptions of personal vulnerability to the threat as well as the perceived trauma of the event can also affect the adoption of precautionary behaviors (Weinstein, 1988, 1989; Weinstein & Nicolich, 1993). Additionally, one's sense of control over an event can influence the adoption of precautions. In a 1988 study, Heath and Davidson found that women who believed that rape was uncontrollable showed higher levels of fear of rape than did women who believed rape was controllable; they also reported taking fewer precautions to protect themselves from rape than did women who viewed rape as more controllable. The authors theorized that learned helplessness contributes to this observed pattern. Finally, personal experience has been found to affect precautionary behavior in victims of rape. In one study, over half the women surveyed reported that after being raped, "they felt restricted and would venture out only with friends" (Nadelson, Notman, Zackson, & Gornick, 1982, p. 1268). Numerous other studies have found that a woman's fear of rape often increases after being raped (Burgess & Holmstrom, 1974; Calhoun, Atkeson, & Resick, 1982; Cohen & Roth, 1987; Kilpatrick, Resick, & Veronen, 1981; Kilpatrick, Veronen, & Resick, 1979; Santiago, McCall-Perez, Gorcey, & Beigel, 1985; Scheppele & Bart, 1983; Veronen, Kilpatrick, Calhoun, & Atkeson, 1986), which may prompt increases in precautionary behaviors. It is possible that all these variables affect women's precautionary behaviors relating to rape.

The Present Study

The present study investigates college women's fears of acquaintance and stranger rape. We were interested in how two variables—level of acquaintance (acquaintance rape or stranger rape, a within-subjects variable) and history of acquaintance rape (whether women had ever experienced acquaintance rape, a between-subjects variable)—affected the following four sets of variables:

1. The extent to which women worry about acquaintance and stranger rape in various situations.
2. The extent to which women engage in precautionary behaviors due to fears of acquaintance and stranger rape.
3. When women are asked to self-generate descriptions of situations in which they fear rape, the numbers of these situations related to acquaintance and stranger rape.
4. Women's beliefs about acquaintance and stranger rape, including their beliefs about the probability that they will experience each type of rape in the future, the probability that the average college woman will experience each type of rape in the future, the percentages of all rapes that are acquaintance and stranger rapes, how much control they have over each type of rape, and the degree of trauma associated with each type of rape.

Additionally, we were interested in the following question:

5. What are the best predictors of women's engaging in precautionary behaviors to protect themselves from acquaintance rape and stranger rape: fear of rape, beliefs about the likelihood of being raped, feelings of control regarding rape, beliefs about the trauma associated with rape, or a history of acquaintance rape?

Because we conducted five sets of analyses, we used a Bonferroni procedure to set alpha to $.05/5 = .01$.

METHOD
Pilot Study
Purpose

The purpose of the pilot study was to generate items for the final questionnaire. We wanted to elicit women's ideas about situations in which they feared acquaintance and stranger rape and identify precautions they took to avoid acquaintance and stranger rape.

Participants

The pilot participants were 30 female introductory psychology students from the University of Kansas, a large Midwestern public university located in a small city. Their participation was solicited through posted sign-up sheets that did not mention the topic of the study. Each respondent received credit toward a course research requirement.

Questionnaire

Participants were asked the following questions regarding their fears about rape: "What types of situations/circumstances, if any, make you afraid of being raped by someone you know?"; "In what ways, if any, do you change/restrict/modify your behavior because of fears of being raped by someone you know?"; "Are there any precautions against acquaintance rape you currently take that you feel you could stop taking in a world where acquaintance rape did not exist?" Parallel questions were asked about stranger rape. The order of the questions was counterbalanced across participants.

Procedure

After signing consent forms, participants completed the questionnaires anonymously, seated in alternate seats to protect their privacy. When they were finished, they were given information about the purpose of the study as well as phone numbers of the researchers and local counseling centers and crisis lines.

Results

Participants' responses to the pilot questions were compiled into lists of situations in which women feared acquaintance or stranger rape, as well as lists of precautions taken to guard against acquaintance and stranger rape. Situations and behaviors that appeared most frequently were used to construct items for the questionnaire used in the next phase of the study.

Main Study Participants

The participants for the main part of the study were 151 female introductory psychology students at the University of Kansas. Their demographics were as follows: 84.1% European American/White, 6.0% African American, 6.0% international students, 2.0% Asian Americans, 1.3% Hispanic Americans, 0.6% biracial; 76.5% first year in college, 15.8% second year, 5.0% third year, 1.4% fourth year, 1.4% fifth year and beyond; mean age = 19.0 years. Participation was solicited in the same manner as previously described, and the women received research credit for participating. Twelve women were dropped because of incomplete questionnaires or failed validity checks, to be described later, leaving a final sample of 139.

Measures

Cover Sheet

Women were asked to complete a set of demographic questions and then to list situations (if any) in which they were fearful of being raped. Our intent was to assess what kinds of situations aroused their fear of rape before any questions were asked that might have biased their answers.

Definitions

The women were provided with definitions of an acquaintance, a stranger, acquaintance rape, and stranger rape to ensure that they were all using the same definitions in answering subsequent questions. An acquaintance was defined as "a guy you DO know, from guys you've just met to close friends/boyfriends. This includes boyfriends, friends, family members, dates, teachers, neighbors, spouses, someone you've just met, coworkers, supervisors, bosses, etc." A stranger was defined as "a guy you DO NOT know. That is, either a total stranger or a guy you've seen before but never met." Acquaintance rape was defined as "when someone is raped by an acquaintance," and stranger rape was defined as "when someone is raped by a stranger." The women were then instructed to return to the situations they had listed on the cover sheet and to indicate for each situation whether they were fearful of being raped by a stranger, an acquaintance, or either.

Questions About Precautionary Behaviors

These questions concerned women's precautionary behaviors related to their fear of rape. There were two parallel sets of questions: one for behaviors relating to acquaintance rape and one for behaviors relating to stranger rape. The order of these two sets of questions was counterbalanced across participants. The set of questions on acquaintance rape began with the stem, "Because I am afraid of acquaintance rape . . ."; a list of 29 behaviors followed this stem. Items included, "I avoid flirting with guys I **know**," and "I say something if a guy I **know** comes on too strong." The questions on stranger rape were parallel to those on acquaintance rape; for example, the items above were reworded to read, "I avoid flirting with guys I **don't know**," and "I say something if a guy I **don't know** comes on too strong." For both sets of questions, respondents were asked to rate how frequently they engaged in these behaviors on a 5-point Likert scale ranging from 1 = *not at all/never* to 5 = *a lot/always*. A validity check instructing women to answer with a specific number was included in each set of questions to ensure that they were reading the items carefully and were not answering randomly. Those who answered incorrectly were eliminated from the study.

Questions About Worry in Various Situations

There were two parallel sets of questions concerning situations in which women might worry about rape, one for acquaintance rape and one for stranger rape. The order of these sets was counterbalanced across participants. In each set, women were asked 24 questions about how much they worry about being raped by an acquaintance or stranger in specific situations. If they had never been in that situation, they were asked to imagine themselves in that situation and to answer on that basis. For example, in the acquaintance rape question set they were asked, "When you are being followed by a guy you **know,** how much do you worry about being raped by him?" They responded using a 5-point Likert scale ranging from 1 = *not at all* to 5 = *very much.* In each set of questions, a validity check was again included in which the women were instructed to answer with a specific number.

Questions About Beliefs and Experiences

The women were asked a series of questions concerning their beliefs and experiences pertaining to acquaintance and stranger rape. They were asked to rate on a 5-point Likert scale, ranging from 1 = *none* to 5 = *a lot,* how much control they thought they had over being raped by an acquaintance. They were also asked to rate on a 5-point Likert scale, ranging from 1 = *not at all traumatic* to 5 = *very traumatic,* how traumatic they thought it would be to be raped by an acquaintance. Finally, they were asked to estimate how likely it is that they would be raped by an acquaintance in the future, how likely it is that the average college woman would be raped by an acquaintance in the future, and what percentage of rapes are acquaintance rape. Their estimates could range from 0% to 100%. Parallel questions were asked about stranger rape.

Rape-History Questions

Women were asked two questions to assess if they had ever been raped: "Have you had sexual intercourse (oral, anal, or vaginal) with a guy when you didn't want to because you were incapable of giving consent or resisting due to alcohol, drugs, etc.?" and "Have you ever had sexual intercourse (oral, anal, or vaginal) when you didn't want to because a guy threatened or used some degree of physical force (twisting your arm, holding you down, etc.) to make you?" These two questions were used to determine women's rape-history sta-

tus; they are modifications of questions from the Sexual Experiences Survey (Koss et al., 1987). Similar to Russell (1984) we did not specify a time frame for these experiences. Women who answered "no" to these questions were instructed to skip ahead to the next section. Women who answered "yes" to either or both questions were asked how many "guys" were involved in the situation(s). Those who said "one" were asked if he was an acquaintance or a stranger, how well they knew him, and their relationship with him, if any. If more than one "guy" was involved, they were asked similar questions about the "guys" involved.

Procedure

The questionnaires were administered in groups with the women seated in alternate desks to protect their privacy. After they read and signed the consent forms, they completed the questionnaires anonymously. Afterward, the research assistants distributed and read aloud a debriefing script about the purpose of the study data on the prevalence of acquaintance and stranger rape, and phone numbers of the researchers and local counseling centers and crisis lines.

RESULTS

Descriptive Statistics

In this sample, 28.1% (*n* = 39) of the women had been raped. Of these women, 84.6% (*n* = 33; 23.7% of the entire sample) had been raped by one or more acquaintances, 2.6% (*n* = 1; 0.7% of the entire sample) had been raped by a stranger, and 12.8% (*n* = 5; 3.6% of the entire sample) had been raped by one or more strangers and acquaintances.

Preliminary Factor Analyses

Prior to comparing women's situational fears and precautionary behaviors related to acquaintance and stranger rape, we factor analyzed the participants' situational and behavioral ratings. There were two purposes for conducting these exploratory factor analyses: investigating how items related to each other, and then using these results to create subscales to be used in subsequent analyses.

Each of the situational items had been rated on a scale ranging from 1 = *not at all* to 5 = *very much.*

Similarly, the behavioral items had been rated on a scale ranging from 1 = *not at all/never* to 5 = *a lot/always*. Participants had completed two versions of each set of questions, one concerning acquaintance rape and one concerning stranger rape. We used either the stranger or acquaintance rape data from each participant for the factor analysis because using the same person's stranger and acquaintance data would have violated the assumption of independence. If a participant received the acquaintance rape version of the questions first, her acquaintance data were used in the factor analysis, and if a participant received the stranger rape version of the questions first, her stranger data were used in the factor analysis. Thus, there were 139 research participants in the analysis, providing a sufficient variable-to-subject ratio (Kline, 1994). A principal-components factor analysis with varimax rotation was conducted for items regarding situations in which women worry about rape; a similar analysis was conducted for items regarding precautionary behaviors women engage in because of their fear of rape. Three factors emerged for the questions concerning women's fear of rape in different situations (see Table 9.1.1). Six factors emerged for the questions concerning women's precautionary behaviors (see Table 9.1.2).

These factors were used to derive subscales. Items were dropped from the subscales if they cross-loaded on more than one factor, did not load highly on any factor, or did not fit conceptually with the other items on that factor. The dropped items are presented at the end of each table. Two subscales were derived from each factor: one for acquaintance rape and one for stranger rape. Cronbach's alpha reliability coefficients are presented in Table 9.1.1 and 9.1.2. A participant's subscale scores equaled the mean of her responses to the items on that subscale. These subscale scores were used as dependent variables in subsequent analyses.

Assessing the Impact of Level of Acquaintance, Order, and a History of Acquaintance Rape

For each analysis in this section, level of acquaintance had two levels, acquaintance and stranger, except where noted. Order had two levels reflecting the two versions of the questionnaire; half the participants had completed the acquaintance rape questions first (the AS order), and half had completed the stranger rape questions first (the SA order). History of acquaintance rape had two levels, women who had never been raped ($n = 100$) and women who had been raped by an acquaintance but not a stranger ($n = 33$). The six women who had been raped by a stranger ($n = 1$) or by both a stranger and an acquaintance ($n = 5$) were dropped from these analyses because of their small numbers, which would make accurately assessing the impact of being raped by a stranger impossible.[1]

We conducted four sets of analyses. In order to address Research Question 1, we conducted a 2 within-subjects (level of acquaintance) × 2 between-subjects (order) × 2 between-subjects (history of acquaintance rape) multivariate analysis of variance (MANOVA) with the dependent variables being women's subscale scores of worry about rape in different situations. For Research Question 2, we conducted a 2 within-subjects (level of acquaintance) × 2 between-subjects (order) × 2 between-subjects (history of acquaintance rape) MANOVA with subscale scores of precautionary behaviors as the dependent variables. For Research Question 3, we conducted a 3 within-subjects (level of acquaintance) × 2 between-subjects (order) × 2 between-subjects (history of acquaintance rape) analysis of variance (ANOVA). For this research question only, level of acquaintance had three levels: Some of the self-generated situations in which women feared rape were relevant to *acquaintance* rape, some were relevant to *stranger* rape, and some were relevant to *either* acquaintance or stranger rape. The dependent variables were the number of situations each woman had generated in each of these categories. For Research Question 4, we conducted a 2 within-subjects (level of acquaintance) × 2 between-subjects (order) × 2 between-subjects (history of acquaintance rape) MANOVA with beliefs about rape as the dependent variables.

In three of the four analyses, order was not significant either as a main effect or in an interaction. The only significant order effect was for questions regarding precautionary behaviors. Participants' ratings of precautionary behaviors were somewhat higher overall in the AS order, $F(1, 129) = 12.51$, $p < .001$, than in the SA order. There was no interaction; partici-

Table 9.1.1 Subscales Derived from Factor Analysis of Situations in Which Women Worry About Being Raped

Being alone with men	(12.83)[a]	(.83/.80)[b]

When you are being followed by a guy you know/don't know

When a guy you know/don't know comes over to your place without a specific reason

When you are alone with a guy you know/don't know

When you accept a ride from a guy you know/don't know

When you accept a ride from a group of guys you know/don't know

Being with aggressive men	(2.19)[a]	(.92/.86)[b]

When a guy you know/don't know invades your personal space

When a guy you know/don't know doesn't show respect for you

When a guy you know/don't know doesn't accept "no" for an answer

When there is an unequal distribution of power between you and a guy you know/don't know

When guys you know/don't know are condescending, rude, or try to belittle you with their actions or speech

When a guy you know/don't know ignores your signals

When a guy you know/don't know touches you when you don't want to be touched

When you are with a guy you know/don't know who has a reputation for being forceful sexually

Drinking situations	(1.29)[a]	(.87/.89)[b]

When you are around guys you know/don't know who are drinking

When you are drinking around guys you know/don't know

When you are at a party where people are drinking

When you are at a bar

Items dropped from subscales[c]

When a guy you know/don't know wants more from you sexually than you are comfortable with

When a guy you know/don't know touches or grabs you

When you are about to be picked up for a date by a guy you know/don't know (blind date)

When you are with a guy you know/don't know who has a reputation for sleeping around a lot

When you are working alone with a guy you know/don't know

When a guy you know/don't know moves too fast sexually with you

When a guy you know/don't know tells sexual jokes or says sexual things

Notes: [a]The eigenvalue for the factor. [b]Numbers before and after the slash represent Cronbach's alphas for this subscale when women responded thinking about acquaintance rape and stranger rape, respectively. [c]These items were not included on any subscale because they cross-loaded on more than one factor, did not load highly on any factor, or did not fit conceptually with the factor on which they loaded.

pants' ratings of precautions related to acquaintance and stranger rape were affected equally—there was no differential effect. Fortunately, we had counterbalanced to control for possible order effects. Therefore, we collapsed data across both orders for subsequent analyses.

In all four analyses, history of acquaintance rape was never significant either as a main effect or in an interaction. Therefore, history of acquaintance rape was dropped from further analyses. In order to investigate history of acquaintance rape, we had dropped the six women raped by strangers or by both acquaintances and strangers. Because we were no longer including this variable and because we wanted the results to generalize to all women rather than only to women who had not been raped by a stranger, we reran all four

Table 9.1.2 Subscales Derived from Factor Analysis of Precautionary Behaviors Women Engage in Because of a Fear of Rape

Wariness around men	(10.02)[a]	(.83/.82)[b]
I keep my guard up around guys I know/don't know		
I distrust guys that I know/don't know		
I avoid guys I know/don't know who have a reputation for sleeping around		
I avoid being alone with a guy I know/don't know in his home or room		
I avoid going on dates with guys I know/don't know		
I avoid talking about sex with guys I know/don't know		
I avoid accepting help with my car from guys I know/don't know		
I avoid accepting drinks from guys I know/don't know		
I avoid accepting a place to stay overnight from guys I know/don't know		
I try to stay in public places when I'm out with guys I know/don't know		
Dealing with aggressive men	(2.24)[a]	(.79/.70)[b]
I say something if a guy I know/don't know comes on too strong		
I try to leave if a guy I know/don't know comes on too strong		
I avoid spending time alone with guys I know/don't know who make me uncomfortable		
I try to stay in control of the situation when I'm with guys I know/don't know		
Avoiding mixed signals	(1.87)[a]	(.76/.82)[b]
I stay in groups at bars (because of a fear of acquaintance rape/stranger rape)		
I watch what I wear around guys I know/don't know		
I stay in groups at parties (because of a fear of acquaintance rape/stranger rape)		
I avoid flirting with guys I know/don't know		
Avoiding outdoor behaviors	(1.65)[a]	(.96/.87)[b]
I avoid walking alone at night (because of a fear of acquaintance rape/stranger rape)		
I avoid walking through parking lots (because of a fear of acquaintance rape/stranger rape)		
Defensive behaviors	(1.37)[a]	(.66/.65)[b]
I carry mace/tear gas to use if attacked by a guy I know/don't know		
I carry something to use as a weapon (lit cigarette, keys, etc.) to use if attacked by someone I know/don't know		
I carry a whistle/personal safety alarm to use if attacked by guys I know/don't know		
Caution in drinking situations	(1.25)[a]	(.76/.84)[b]
I refrain from drinking around guys I know/don't know		
I avoid getting drunk at parties (because of a fear of acquaintance rape/stranger rape)		
Items dropped from subscales[c]		
I try not to miscommunicate my intentions with guys I know/don't know		
I avoid working alone with male coworkers I know/don't know		
I have taken a self-defense class to protect myself from guys I know/don't know		
I avoid being alone with guys I know/don't know who make passes at me		

Note: [a]The eigenvalue for the factors. [b]Numbers before and after the slash represent Cronbach's alphas for this subscale when women responded thinking about acquaintance rape and stranger rape, respectively. [c]These items were not included on any subscale because they cross-loaded on more than one factor, did not load highly on any factor, or did not fit conceptually with the factors on which they loaded.

analyses using the entire sample of women and using level of acquaintance as the only independent variable.

Women's Worry About Acquaintance and Stranger Rape in Various Situations

To answer Research Question 1, a within-subjects MANOVA was performed on participants' subscale scores involving situations that might elicit worry about rape. The independent variable was level of acquaintance (acquaintance or stranger) and the dependent variables were subscale scores for the three situational subscales derived from the factor analyses. The results were highly significant, $F(1, 138) = 944.01, p < .0001$. Subsequent ANOVAs revealed that women worried significantly more about rape in all three situations involving strangers than in similar situations involving acquaintances (see Table 9.1.3).

Women's Precautionary Behaviors Related to Acquaintance and Stranger Rape

To answer Research Question 2, a within-subjects MANOVA was performed on questions relating to precautionary behaviors women engage in due to their fear of rape. The independent variable was level of acquaintance, and the dependent variables were subscale scores for the six precautionary behaviors. Results were highly significant, $F(1, 138) = 551.03$, $p < .0001$. Subsequent ANOVAs revealed that women reported engaging in more precautionary behaviors because of their fear of stranger rape than because of their fear of acquaintance rape (see Table 9.1.3).

Self-Generated Situations

To address Research Question 3, participants had been asked to generate situations in which they feared rape and then to code these situations to indicate whom they feared in each situation: an acquaintance, a stranger, or either. The number of situations generated ranged from 0 to 8, with a mean of 3.16. An ANOVA was conducted in which the independent variable was level of acquaintance (acquaintance, stranger, or either) and the dependent variable was the number of self-generated situations. There were significant differences in the types of situations the

Table 9.1.3 Mean Ratings of Worry in Situations and Precautionary Behaviors Taken Due to Fears of Acquaintance and Stranger Rape

	Level of acquaintance		
Subscales	Acquaintance	Stranger	F
Levels of worry about rape in various situations[a]			
Being Alone With Men	2.25 (1.03)	4.43 (0.75)	1295.57
Being With Aggressive Men	2.02 (1.01)	3.37 (1.04)	206.73
Drinking Situations	2.04 (1.04)	3.30 (1.11)	366.20
Precautionary behaviors[b]			
Wariness Around Men	2.12 (0.93)	3.81 (1.06)	930.45
Dealing With Aggressive Men	1.79 (0.79)	3.49 (1.11)	60.58
Avoiding Mixed Signals	2.06 (1.19)	3.26 (1.36)	183.26
Avoiding Outdoor Behaviors	2.81 (1.33)	3.89 (1.10)	155.30
Defensive Behaviors	2.13 (0.98)	4.52 (0.75)	81.32
Caution in Drinking Situations	3.97 (1.17)	4.30 (1.01)	111.64

Note: $N = 139$. Numbers in parentheses are standard deviations. All $ps < .0001$.

[a]Ratings of how worried about rape women were in acquaintance and stranger situations were rated on a scale ranging from $1 = not\ at\ all$ to $5 = very\ much$. [b]Ratings of precautionary behaviors engaged in due to a fear of rape were rated on a scale ranging from $1 = not\ at\ all/never$ to $5 = a\ lot/always$.

women generated, $F (2, 130) = 64.82, p < .0001$. Post hoc ANOVAs revealed that women self-generated significantly more situations in which they feared being raped by a stranger ($M = 1.90$) than situations in which they feared being raped by an acquaintance ($M = 0.64$), $F (1, 131) = 91.13, p < .0001$, or by either a stranger or acquaintance ($M = 0.62$), $F (1, 131) = 80.38, p < .0001$; the latter two means did not differ significantly from each other. Thus, when women thought about situations in which they fear being raped, they thought primarily about stranger rape.

Beliefs About Acquaintance and Stranger Rape

To answer Research Question 4, a within-subjects MANOVA was conducted on women's beliefs about rape. The independent variable was level of acquaintance (acquaintance or stranger), and the dependent variables were women's ratings regarding their beliefs about rape. Results were significant, $F (1, 120) = 45.59, p < .0001$. Thus, the MANOVA was followed by ANOVAs.

Frequency Estimates

Participants were asked to estimate the percentage of rapes that were acquaintance rapes and the percentage that were stranger rapes. Women whose estimates did not sum to 100% ($n = 18$) were excluded from this analysis. Women estimated that significantly more rapes were acquaintance rapes (65.36%) than stranger rapes (34.64%), $F(1, 120) = 89.87, p < .0001$.

Likelihood of Being Raped

Women estimated that they have a 28.5% probability of being raped by a stranger and a 24.9% probability of being raped by an acquaintance in the future, $F (1, 137) = 4.1, p = .0431$, not significant at the .01 level. However, they estimated that the average college woman has a significantly greater probability of being raped in the future by an acquaintance (50.0%) than by a stranger (42.9%), $F (1, 138) = 17.31, p < .0001$.

To explore these results further, a 2 × 2 within-subjects ANOVA was performed with level of acquaintance and who is at risk (the respondent herself or the average college woman) as the independent variables and the probability of being raped in the future, ranging from 0% to 100%, as the dependent

variable. Participants believed that the average college woman has a greater chance of being raped in the future by either a stranger or an acquaintance than they themselves do, $F (1, 137) = 128.20, p < .0001$. There was no main effect for level of acquaintance, but there was an interaction, $F (1, 137) = 36.57, p < .0001$, with participants rating the average college woman, but not themselves, as more vulnerable to acquaintance rape than to stranger rape.

Control

A within-subjects ANOVA was performed with level of acquaintance as the independent variable and women's beliefs about the controllability of rape as the dependent variable. Women thought they had more control over being raped by an acquaintance ($M = 3.61$) than they did over being raped by a stranger ($M = 2.37$), $F (1, 138) = 131.56, p < .0001$.

Trauma

A within-subjects ANOVA was performed with level of acquaintance as the independent variable and women's beliefs about how traumatic it would be to be raped as the dependent variable. Women indicated that they thought it would be as traumatic to be raped by an acquaintance ($M = 4.76$) as by a stranger ($M = 4.82$), $F (1, 138) = 0.94, p = .33$.

Predictors of Precautionary Behaviors

To address Research Question 5, we conducted two simultaneous multiple regression analyses, one for predictors of precautionary behaviors related to acquaintance rape and one for predictors of precautionary behaviors related to stranger rape. In each analysis, the dependent variable was the mean of all the precautionary behavior items for acquaintance rape or stranger rape, respectively; predictor variables were rape history, personal likelihood, trauma, control, and the mean of all the fear items for acquaintance rape or stranger rape, respectively. Because we wanted single indicators of precautionary behaviors and fear, we averaged across all the items on the original scales rather than using the subscale scores. Cronbach's alphas for these newly created variables were .94 for fear of acquaintance rape, .93 for fear of stranger rape, .89 for precautionary behaviors related to acquaintance rape, and .90 for precautionary behaviors related to stranger rape. Pearson's correlations between the dependent variable (precautionary behaviors) and the predictor variables (rape history, personal likelihood, trauma, control, and fear of rape) for acquaintance rape and stranger rape items were calculated to assess the relationship between variables (see Table 9.1.4).

Fear of acquaintance rape was the only significant predictor of precautionary behaviors related to acquaintance rape ($\beta = 0.595$, $p < .0001$). Perceived trauma of being raped by an acquaintance ($\beta = 0.031$, $p = .68$), perceptions of control over being raped by an acquaintance ($\beta = -0.082$, $p = .29$), estimated probability of being raped by an acquaintance ($\beta = 0.000$, $p = .99$), and history of acquaintance rape ($\beta = -0.049$, $p = .52$) did not significantly predict engaging in precautionary behaviors related to acquaintance rape.

Fear of stranger rape was also the only significant predictor of precautionary behaviors related to stranger rape ($\beta = 0.621$, $p = .0001$). Perceived trauma of being raped by a stranger ($\beta = 0.026$, $p = .72$), perceptions of control over being raped by a stranger ($\beta = 0.079$, $p = .28$), estimated probability of being raped by a stranger ($\beta = 0.030$, $p = .69$), and history of acquaintance rape ($\beta = -0.122$, $p = .09$) did not significantly predict engaging in precautionary behaviors related to stranger rape. Additional multiple regressions using likelihood, trauma, control, and history of acquaintance rape as predictor variables and fear of rape as the dependent variable revealed that none of

these variables significantly predicted fear of either acquaintance rape or stranger rape.

DISCUSSION

Fears and Precautionary Behaviors

The fear of rape is widespread and restricts women's behaviors. All of the women in this study reported being fearful of acquaintance and stranger rape in at least some situations, and all said that they take at least some precautions to protect themselves from both types of rape. Women were more fearful of being raped by a stranger than by an acquaintance, however, even if they had a history of acquaintance rape but not stranger rape. Women also reported taking more precautions to guard themselves against being raped by a stranger than by an acquaintance, and they were more likely to self-generate situations in which they feared stranger rape. This is striking in light of the facts that the vast majority of rapes are acquaintance rapes and that the women themselves estimated that over 65% of all rapes occur between acquaintances. Their knowledge about rape did not match their worries or precautionary behaviors relating to rape.

Relationship Between Fears and Precautionary Behaviors

Several researchers have concluded that women engage in precautionary behaviors because of their fear of rape. Interestingly, they did not ask women questions specifically about precautions taken because

Table 9.1.4 Correlations Between Precautionary Behaviors, Fears, Beliefs About Rape, and History of Acquaintance Rape

Variable	Precautions	Fear	Likelihood	Trauma	Control	History
Precautions	—	.59***	.13	.06	−.18*	−.05
Fear	.41***	—	.24**	.07	−.22*	−.02
Likelihood	.13	.21*	—	−.05	−.24**	.22*
Trauma	.02	.05	.03	—	.09	−.02
Control	.02	−.16	−.15	.02	—	−.16
History	−.12	.02	.10	.03	-.20*	—

Note: Numbers above the diagonal represent correlations for acquaintance-rape items. Numbers below the diagonal represent correlations for stranger-rape items, except History, which refers to history of acquaintance rape (see Note 1).

*$p < .05$; **$p < .01$; ***$p < .0001$.

of their fear of rape. For example, Riger and Gordon (1981) and Warr (1985) asked women about their precautionary behaviors and about their fear of various crimes, including rape, but they did not ask women what precautionary behaviors they engaged in *because* of their fear of rape. In this study, we addressed this issue specifically, asking women to indicate how often they engage in various precautionary behaviors "Because I am afraid of acquaintance rape" or "Because I am afraid of stranger rape." We also found statistical evidence for this relationship: In a multiple regression analysis, women's fear of rape predicted their level of precautionary behaviors better than did their acquaintance rape history, ratings of trauma associated with rape, feelings of control regarding rape, or beliefs about the likelihood of being raped.

It is probable, however, that the relationship between fears and precautions is complex; this relationship may be bidirectional and may differ across women. Fear may cause some women to engage in more precautionary behaviors but cause others to avoid thinking about rape and thus to engage in fewer precautionary behaviors. In turn, engaging in precautionary behaviors may increase or decrease levels of fear. Moreover, the relationship between fear and precautionary behaviors may be affected by perceptions of control over rape (see Heath & Davidson, 1988). Further research is needed in this area.

Possible Explanations for Observed Differences in Reaction to Acquaintance Rape and Stranger Rape

Perceptions of Personal Vulnerability

Although the women in this study knew that acquaintance rape was more common than stranger rape, and although they estimated that the average college woman has a greater chance of being raped by an acquaintance than by a stranger, they estimated that they themselves had a similar chance of being raped by a stranger or by an acquaintance. They estimated that they had a 24.88% probability of being raped by an acquaintance and a 28.48% probability of being raped by a stranger. In a community sample of women, Russell (1984) found that although 24% had been raped, only 3% had been raped by strangers.

Thus, women in our sample vastly overestimated the risk of stranger rape, which may in part explain why they were so fearful of stranger rape.

Interestingly, the women believed that they had less of a chance of being raped by either a stranger or an acquaintance than did the average college woman. The theory of unique invulnerability offers one possible explanation for this apparent incongruity. Unique invulnerability is the tendency of both adults and adolescents to underestimate their own risk for negative outcomes in comparison with their peers, including their risk of being victimized (Perloff, 1983; Perloff & Fetzer, 1986; Quadrel, Fischhoff, & Davis, 1993; Weinstein, 1980; Weinstein & Lachendro, 1982). This sense of unique invulnerability may be related to people's fundamental assumptions that the world is benevolent and meaningful and that the self is worthy (Janoff-Bulman, 1992; Janoff-Bulman & Schwartzberg, 1991). In a benevolent, meaningful world, bad things do not happen to good people, so the worthy self is not in danger. Unique invulnerability may also result from downward social comparisons in which individuals compare themselves favorably with others who are less fortunate or more at risk, allowing themselves to maintain an illusion of invulnerability (Perloff & Fetzer, 1986). A sense of unique invulnerability may enable women to underestimate their own risk for rape in comparison with their peers.

Control

Women reported feeling that they had more control over acquaintance rape than stranger rape. This sense of control may explain why women reported less fear and fewer precautionary behaviors related to acquaintance rape than to stranger rape. Why do women feel a greater sense of control over acquaintance rape than over stranger rape? Perhaps they feel able to judge the trustworthiness of men they know. As one pilot study participant wrote, "I trust my own judgement of others. . . . I make sure I know enough about a person so that acquaintance rape is not a worry for me."

Trauma

The women did not fear stranger rape more than acquaintance rape because they regarded stranger rape as more traumatic. The common stereotype is that acquaintance rape is less traumatic than stranger rape; however, the respondents rated both kinds of rape as highly traumatic. Research supports this belief (Koss et al., 1988; see Resick, 1993, for a recent review). There was little variability in participants' ratings of the trauma associated with both kinds of rape, which may explain why perceptions of trauma did not significantly predict fears or precautionary behaviors.

Personal Experience

Although one of the more commonly observed consequences of rape is an increased level of fear (Burgess & Holmstrom, 1974; Calhoun et al., 1982; Cohen & Roth, 1987; Kilpatrick et al., 1979, 1981; Nadelson et al., 1982; Santiago et al., 1985; Scheppele & Bart, 1983; Veronen et al., 1986), a history of acquaintance rape had little impact on participant responses in this study. Women who had been raped by an acquaintance and women who had not been raped showed no significant differences on questions concerning worry, precautionary behaviors, or beliefs related to acquaintance or stranger rape.

One possible explanation for this discrepancy with other studies involves sampling. The present study involved undergraduate college women. Rape victims identified in this study may or may not have labeled their experiences as rape and reported them to a rape crisis center or to the police. The majority of past studies on rape victims' fears of rape used samples from rape crisis centers (Calhoun et al., 1982; Kilpatrick et al., 1979, 1981; Nadelson et al., 1982; Santiago et al., 1985) or samples obtained by placing advertisements that specifically solicited women who had been raped (Cohen & Roth, 1987; Santiago et al., 1985). Thus, these studies included only women who considered themselves to be victims of rape and who sought help from a rape crisis center or volunteered for a study about rape. These rape victims and the rape victims in the present study could have differed in the nature of their experiences or in their interpretation of those experiences, which could in turn account for the differences in their fears related to rape. Additionally, we did not assess the perceived severity of the rape or the amount of time that had passed since the rape. Both these factors could affect victim's responses (Weinstein, 1989).

In addition to a history of rape, women have other kinds of experiences that might help explain the discrepancy between their knowledge about rape and their worries and precautionary behaviors relating to rape. In a study of Canadian University undergraduate women, DeKeseredy, Schwartz, and Tait (1993) found that 84.1% of their sample reported having one or more experiences with an uncomfortable advance from a male stranger in a public setting or an obscene phone call. As they pointed out, it is impossible for women to know whether these encounters will lead to rape. Only in hindsight can they be judged as relatively harmless. It may be that a larger percentage of women's encounters with strangers than with acquaintances are frightening, leading to more fears and precautionary behaviors relating to stranger rape than to acquaintance rape. Women may also have other kinds of victimization experiences, such as verbal sexual coercion and attempted rape, which might affect their level of worry, precautionary behaviors, and beliefs about rape (Norris, Nurius, & Dimeff, 1996).

Women also have vicarious experiences with rape through the media, which present a distorted picture of rape. The media tend to avoid "the representative rape in favor of the most lurid, in order to capture their readers' attention" (Gordon & Riger, 1989, p. 69). Additionally, the media rely on police reports for their information about the occurrence of rapes; because acquaintance rape is vastly underreported, the media disproportionately report stranger rape (Gordon & Riger, 1989; Koss et al., 1988; Russell, 1984). The result is that women are primed to fear stranger rape, not the more common acquaintance rape.

Implications

Theoretical Implications

In Griffin's (1971) article, "Rape: The All-American Crime," she contended that men are rewarded for being both sexually aggressive and protective of women. "This dichotomy implies that men fall into one of two categories: those who rape and those who protect" (p. 30). Brownmiller (1975) suggested that women are socialized to believe that familiar men are protectors and unfamiliar men—strangers—are to be feared. The findings of this study suggest that women do indeed believe in these artificial categories about whom to fear.

In reality, the majority of rapes are committed by acquaintances (Koss et al., 1988; Russell, 1984), the very men women trust to protect them. In the present sample, over 27% of the women had been victims of acquaintance rape; fewer than 5% had been victims of stranger rape. Ironically, women should logically be more fearful of acquaintances—the same men whom many women trust. But to advocate that women be fearful of acquaintances is unrealistic and probably unhealthy for the women. As feminist writer Catharine MacKinnon stated, "The Stanford police tell us 'A little fear is a good thing right now.' I think we do not need more fear. We need to make fear unnecessary" (1987, p. 83).

Educational Implications

The dilemma in doing educational programming for women in this area is that there is no ideal level of fear that we should recommend to women. We do not want to make any judgments about how afraid women ought be, nor do we wish to suggest that women should take certain precautions in order to protect themselves. Precautions are restrictive, as is fear. But to advocate that women not be fearful of rape or that women take no precautions against rape may place women at risk. Clearly, it is a lose-lose situation for women. We can only conclude that the solution lies in focusing educational efforts on the people who can stop rape: men. They need to be taught starting at an early age that acquaintance rape is unacceptable and that it is a crime. Although women should be educated about rape and prevention-strategy options so that they can recognize and cope with such situations if they arise (Nurius & Norris, 1996), rape educators need to focus on and involve men in their efforts to put an end to rape (Warshaw, 1994). Furthermore, at every level, ranging from individuals' beliefs to the media and the law, we need to challenge ideas and stereotypes that perpetuate rape.

Directions for Future Study

Because of the exploratory nature of this study, we used a broad definition of "acquaintance," ranging from someone a woman just met to a close friend or boyfriend. We do not know whom participants were thinking of in answering our questions about acquaintance rape. It is probable that women would answer the questions quite differently if they were thinking of their boyfriend than if they were thinking of someone they just met. Further study is needed to determine if women differentially fear acquaintances and how this fear affects their precautionary behaviors.

A between-subjects design would be useful to evaluate women's fears of acquaintance rape without the implicit comparison with stranger rape and vice versa. Also, it is unclear whether women's reported precautionary behaviors are similar to their actual precautionary behaviors. Further study is needed to address these questions.

Conclusions

Although the women in this study reported experiencing higher levels of worry about stranger rape and taking more precautions because of a fear of stranger rape, it is important to realize that these women still reported being fearful of acquaintance rape and taking precautions against acquaintance rape. The fear of rape, be it by a stranger or acquaintance, is oppressive. We must work toward a future in which rape is not a fear for women. Only then can women feel safe among both friends and strangers and be fully free to live life as they choose.

NOTE

1. Because the purpose of this study was to assess fear of acquaintance rape separately from fear of stranger rape, it was important to look separately at women who had been raped by acquaintances strangers, or both. The number of women raped by a stranger but not an acquaintance ($n = 1$) or by both a stranger and an acquaintance ($n = 5$) did not allow us to generalize based on such small cell sizes. Thus, when investigating rape history, we were able to assess only history of acquaintance rape. In analyses involving rape history, we dropped the six women who had been raped by strangers. In other analyses, however, we included the entire sample.

REFERENCES

Abbey, A. (1991). Misperception as an antecedent of acquaintance rape: A consequence of ambiguity in communication between women and men. In A. Parrot & L. Bechhofer

(Eds.), *Acquaintance rape. The hidden crime* (pp. 96–112). New York: Wiley.

Bechhofer, L., & Parrot, A. (1991). What is acquaintance rape? In A. Parrot & L. Bechhofer (Eds.), *Acquaintance rape: The hidden crime* (pp. 9–25). New York: Wiley.

Brownmiller, S. (1975). *Against our will: Men, women and rape.* New York: Bantum.

Burgess, A. W., & Holmstrom, L. L. (1974). *Rape: Victims of crisis.* Bowle, MD: Robert J. Badly

Calhoun, K. S., Atkoson, B. M., & Besick, P. A. (1982). A longitudinal examination of fear reactions in victims of rape. *Journal of Counseling Psychology, 29,* 655–661.

Cohen, L. J., & Roth, S. (1987). The psychological aftermath of rape: Long-term effects and individual differences in recovery. *Journal of Social and Clinical Psychology, 5,* 525–534.

DeKeseredy, W. S., Schwartz, M. D., & Tait, K. (1993). Sexual assault and stranger aggression on a Canadian university campus. *Sex Roles, 28,* 263–277.

Gordon, M. T., & Riger, S. (1989). *The female fear.* New York: Free Press.

Griffin, S. (1971). Rape: The all-American crime. *Ramparts, 10,* 26–36.

Groth, A. N., & Birnbaum, H. J. (1990). Men who rape: *The psychology of the offender.* New York: Plenum.

Heath, L., & Davidson, L. (1988). Dealing with the threat of rape: Reactance or learned helplessness? *Journal of Applied Social Psychology, 18,* 1334–1351.

Hindelang, M. J., & Davis, B. J. (1977). Forcible rape in the United States: A statistical profile. In D. Chappell, R. Geis, & G. Geis (Eds.), *Forcible rape: The crime, victim, and the offender* (pp 7–114). New York: Columbia University Press.

Janoff-Bulman, R. (1992). Shattered assumptions: *Towards a new psychology of trauma.* New York: Free Press.

Janoff-Bulman, R., & Schwartzberg, S. S. (1991). Toward a general model of personal change. In C. R. Snyder & D. R. Forsyth (Eds.), *Handbook of social and clinical psychology.* New York: Pergamon.

Katz, B. L. (1991). The psychological impact of stranger versus nonstranger rape on victims' recovery. In A. Parrot & L. Bechhofer (Eds.), *Acquaintance rape: The hidden crime* (pp. 251–269). New York: Wiley.

Kelly, K. D., & DeKeseredy, W. S. (1994). Women's fear of crime and abuse in college and university dating relationships. *Violence and Victims, 9,* 17–30.

Kilpatrick, D. G., Resick, P. A., & Veronen, L. J. (1981). Effects of a rape experience: A longitudinal study. *Journal of Social Issues, 37*(4), 105–122.

Kilpatrick, D. G., Veronen, L. J., & Resick, P. A. (1979). The aftermath of rape: Recent empirical findings. *American Journal of Orthopsychiatry, 49,* 658–669.

Kline, P. (1994). *An easy guide to factor analysis.* London: Routledge.

Koss, M. P. (1993). Detecting the scope of rape: A review of prevalence research methods. *Journal of Interpersonal Violence, 8,* 198–222.

Koss, M. P., Dinero, T. E., Seibel, C. A., Cox, S. L. (1988). Stranger and acquaintance rape: Are there differences in the victim's experience? *Psychology of Women Quarterly, 12,* 1–24.

Koss, M. P., Gidyez, C. A., & Wisniewski, N. (1987). The scope of rape: Incidence and prevalence of sexual aggression and victimization in a national sample of higher education students. *Journal of Consulting and Clinical Psychology, 55,* 162–170.

Koss, M. P., Woodruff, W. J., & Koss, P. G. (1990). Relation of criminal victimization to health perceptions among women medical patients. *Journal of Consulting and Clinical Psychology, 58,* 147–152.

MacKinnon, C. A. (1987). *Feminism unmodified: Discourses on life and law.* Cambridge, MA: Harvard University Press.

Muehlenhard, C. L., Goggins, M., Jones, J., & Satterfield, A. (1991). Sexual violence and coercion in close relationships. In K. McKinney & S. Sprecher (Eds.), *Sexuality in close relationships* (pp. 155–175). Hillsdale, NJ: Erlbaum.

Nadelson, C. C., Notman, M. T., Zackson, H., & Gornick, J. (1982). A follow-up study of rape victims. *American Journal of Psychiatry, 139,* 1266–1270.

Norris, J., Nurius, P. S., & Dimeff, L. A. (1996). Through her eyes: Factors affecting women's perception of and resistance to acquaintance sexual aggression threat. *Psychology of Women Quarterly, 20,* 123–145.

Nurius, P. S., & Norris, J. (1996). A cognitive ecological model of women's response to male sexual coercion in dating. *Journal of Psychology and Human Sexuality, 8*(1/2), 117–139.

Parrot, A. (1988). *Coping with date rape and acquaintance rape.* New York: Rosen.

Perloff, L. S. (1983). Perceptions of vulnerability to victimization. *Journal of Social Issues, 39*(2), 41–67.

Perloff, L. S., & Fetzer, B. K. (1986). Self-other judgements and perceived vulnerability to victimization. *Journal of Personality and Social Psychology, 50,* 502–510.

Quadrel, M. J., Fischhoff, B., & Davis, W. (1993). Adolescent (In)vulnerability. *American Psychologist, 48,* 102–116.

Resick, P. A. (1993). The psychological impact of rape. *Journal of Interpersonal Violence, 8,* 223–255.

Riger, S., & Gordon, M. T. (1981). The fear of rape: A study in social control. *Journal of Social Issues, 37*(4), 71–92.

Russell, D. E. H. (1984). *Sexual exploitation: Rape, child sexual abuse, and workplace harassment.* Beverly Hills, CA: Sage.

Russell, D. E. H. (1990). *Rape in marriage* (rev. ed.). Bloomington, IN: Indiana University Press. (Original work published 1982).

Santiago, J. M., McCall-Perez, F., Gorcey, M., & Beigel, A. (1985). Long-term psychological effects of rape in 35 rape victims. *American Journal of Psychiatry, 142,* 1338–1340.

Scheppele, K. L., & Bart, P. B. (1983). Through women's eyes: Defining danger in the wake of sexual assault. *Journal of Social Issues, 39*(2), 63–81.

Shotland, R. L., & Goodstein, L. (1992). Sexual precedence reduces the perceived legitimacy of sexual refusal: An examination of attribution concerning date rape and consensual sex. *Personality and Social Psychology Bulletin, 18,* 756–764.

Softas-Nall, B., Bardos, A. N., & Fakinos, M. (1993, April). *Fear of rape and its impact. An empirical study with Greek women.* Poster presented at the Kansas Series in Clinical Psychology on Women's Psychological and Physical Health: A Scholarly and Social Agenda, Lawrence, KS.

Veronen, L. J., Kilpatrick, D. G., Calhoun, K. S., & Atkeson, B. M. (1986). Assessment of fear reactions in sexual assault victims: A factor-analytic study of the Veronen-Kilpatrick Modified Fear Survey. *Behavioral Assessment, 8,* 271–283.

Warr, M. (1985). Fear of rape among urban women. *Social Problems, 32,* 238–250.

Warshaw, R. (1994). *I never called it rape* (2nd ed.). New York: Harper & Row.

Weinstein, N. D. (1980). Unrealistic optimism about future life events. *Journal of Personality and Social Psychology, 39,* 806–820.

Weinstein, N. D. (1988). The precaution adoption process. *Health Psychology, 7,* 355–386.

Weinstein, N. D. (1989). Effects of personal experience on self-protective behavior. *Psychological Bulletin, 105,* 31–50.

Weinstein, N. D., & Lachendro, E. (1982). Egocentrism as a source of unrealistic optimism. *Personality and Social Psychology Bulletin, 8,* 195–200.

Weinstein, N. D., & Nicolich, M. (1993). Correct and incorrect interpretations of correlations between risk perceptions and risk behaviors. *Health Psychology, 12,* 235–245.

9.2 SEXUAL TERRORISM

Carole J. Sheffield

No two of us think alike about it, and yet it is clear to me, that question underlies the whole movement, and our little skirmishing for better laws, and the right to vote, will yet be swallowed up in the real question, viz: Has a woman a right to herself? It is very little to me to have the right to vote, to own property, etc., if I may not keep my body, and its uses, in my absolute right. Not one wife in a thousand can do that now.

—*Lucy Stone, in a letter to Antoinette Brown,*
July 11, 1855

THE RIGHT OF MEN TO control the female body is a cornerstone of patriarchy. It is expressed by their efforts to control pregnancy and childbirth and to define female health care in general. Male opposition to abortion is rooted in opposition to female autonomy. Violence and the threat of violence against females represent the need of patriarchy to deny that a woman's body is her own property and that no one should have access to it without her consent. Violence and its corollary, fear, serve to terrorize females and to maintain the patriarchal definition of woman's place.

The word *terrorism* invokes images of furtive organizations of the far right or left, whose members blow up buildings and cars, hijack airplanes, and murder innocent people in some country other than ours. But there is a different kind of terrorism, one that so pervades our culture that we have learned to live with it as though it were the natural order of things. Its target is females—of all ages, races, and classes. It is the common characteristic of rape, wife battery, incest, pornography, harassment, and all forms of sexual vio-

From *Women: A Feminist Perspective,* 5th ed., edited by Jo Freeman, 1995, Mayfield Publishing Co. © Carole J. Sheffield.

lence. I call it *sexual terrorism* because it is a system by which males frighten and, by frightening, control and dominate females.

The concept of terrorism captured my attention in an "ordinary" event. One afternoon I collected my laundry and went to a nearby laundromat. The place is located in a small shopping center on a very busy highway. After I had loaded and started the machines, I became acutely aware of my environment. It was just after 6:00 P.M. and dark, the other stores were closed, the laundromat was brightly lit, and my car was the only one in the lot. Anyone passing by could readily see that I was alone and isolated. Knowing that rape is often a crime of opportunity, I became terrified. I wanted to leave and find a laundromat that was busier, but my clothes were well into the wash cycle, and, besides, I felt I was being "silly," "paranoid." The feeling of terror persisted, so I sat in my car, windows up and doors locked. When the wash was completed, I dashed in, threw the clothes into the dryer, and ran back out to my car. When the clothes were dry, I tossed them recklessly into the basket and hurriedly drove away to fold them in the security of my home.

Although I was not victimized in a direct, physical way or by objective or measurable standards, I felt victimized. It was, for me, a terrifying experience. I felt controlled by an invisible force. I was angry that something as commonplace as doing laundry after a day's work jeopardized my well-being. Mostly I was angry at being unfree: a hostage of a culture that, for the most part, encourages violence against females, instructs men in the methodology of sexual violence, and provides them with ready justification for their violence. I was angry that I could be victimized by being "in the wrong place at the wrong time." The essence of terrorism is that one never knows when is the wrong time and where is the wrong place.

Following my experience at the laundromat, I talked with my students about terrorization. Women students began to open up and reveal terrors that they had kept secret because of embarrassment: fears of jogging alone, shopping alone, going to the movies alone. One woman recalled feelings of terror in her adolescence when she did child care for extra money. Nothing had ever happened, and she had not been afraid of anyone in particular, but she had felt a vague

terror when being driven home late at night by the man of the house.

The male students listened incredulously and then demanded equal time. The harder they tried, the more they realized how very different—qualitatively, quantitatively, and contextually—their fears were. All agreed that, while they experienced fear in a violent society, they did not experience terror, nor did they experience fear of rape or sexual mutilation. They felt more in control, either from a psychophysical sense of security that they could defend themselves or from a confidence in being able to determine wrong places and times. All the women admitted feeling fear and anxiety when walking to their cars on the campus, especially after an evening class or activity. None of the men experienced fear on campus at any time. The men could be rather specific in describing where they were afraid: in Harlem, for example, or in certain parts of downtown Newark, New Jersey—places that have a reputation for violence. But either they could avoid these places or they felt capable of self-protective action. Above all, male students said that they *never* feared being attacked simply because they were male. They *never* feared going to a movie or to a mall alone. Their daily activities were not characterized by a concern for their physical integrity.

The differences between men's and women's experiences of fear underscore the meaning of sexual terrorism: that women's lives are bounded by both the reality of pervasive sexual danger and the fear that reality engenders. In her study of rape, Susan Brownmiller argues that rape is "nothing more or less than a conscious process of intimidation by which all men keep all women in a state of fear."[1] In their study *The Female Fear*, Margaret T. Gordon and Stephanie Riger found that one-third of women said they worry at least once a month about being raped. Many said they worry daily about the possibility of being raped. When they think about rape, they feel terrified and somewhat paralyzed. A third of women indicated that the fear of rape is "part of the background" of their lives and "one of those things that's always there." Another third claimed they never worried about rape but reported taking precautions, "sometimes elaborate ones," to try to avoid being raped.[2] Indeed, women's attempts to avoid sexual intrusion take many forms.

To varying degrees, women change and restrict their behavior, life-styles, and physical appearances. They will pay higher costs for housing and transportation and even make educational and career choices to attempt to minimize sexual victimization.

Sexual terrorism includes nonviolent sexual intimidation and the threat of violence as well as overt sexual violence. For example, although an act of rape, an unnecessary hysterectomy, and the publishing of *Playboy* magazine appear to be quite different, they are in fact more similar than dissimilar. Each is based on fear, hostility, and a need to dominate women. Rape is an act of aggression and possession. Unnecessary hysterectomies are extraordinary abuses of power rooted in men's concept of women as primarily reproductive beings and in their need to assert power over that reproduction. *Playboy,* like all forms of pornography, attempts to control women through the power of definition. Male pornographers define women's sexuality for their male customers. The basis of pornography is men's fantasies about women's sexuality.

COMPONENTS OF SEXUAL TERRORISM

The literature on terrorism does not provide a precise definition.[3] Mine is taken from Hacker, who says that "terrorism aims to frighten, and by frightening, to dominate and control."[4] Writers agree more readily on the characteristics and functions of terrorism than on a definition. This analysis will focus on five components to illuminate the similarities and distinctions between sexual terrorism and political terrorism. The five components are ideology, propaganda, indiscriminate and amoral violence, voluntary compliance, and society's perception of the terrorist and the terrorized.

An *ideology* is an integrated set of beliefs about the world that explains the way things are and provides a vision of how they ought to be. Patriarchy, meaning the "rule of the fathers," is the ideological foundation of sexism in our society. It asserts the superiority of males and the inferiority of females. It also provides the rationale for sexual terrorism. The taproot of patriarchy is the masculine/warrior ideal. Masculinity must include not only a proclivity for violence but also all those characteristics claimed by warriors: aggression, control, emotional reserve, rationality, sexual potency,

etc. Marc Feigen Fasteau, in *The Male Machine,* argues that "men are brought up with the idea that there ought to be some part of them, under control until released by necessity, that thrives on violence. This capacity, even affinity, for violence, lurking beneath the surface of every real man, is supposed to represent the primal untamed base of masculinity."[5]

Propaganda is the methodical dissemination of information for the purpose of promoting a particular ideology. Propaganda, by definition, is biased or even false information. Its purpose is to present one point of view on a subject and to discredit opposing points of view. Propaganda is essential to the conduct of terrorism. According to Francis Watson, in *Political Terrorism: The Threat and the Response,* "Terrorism must not be defined only in terms of violence, but also in terms of propaganda. The two are in operation together. Violence of terrorism is a coercive means for attempting to influence the thinking and actions of people. Propaganda is a persuasive means for doing the same thing."[6] The propaganda of sexual terrorism is found in all expressions of the popular culture: films, television, music, literature, advertising, pornography. The propaganda of sexual terrorism is also found in the ideas of patriarchy expressed in science, medicine, and psychology.

The third component, which is common to all forms of political terrorism, consists of "indiscriminateness, unpredictability, arbitrariness, ruthless destructiveness and amorality."[7] Indiscriminate violence and amorality are also at the heart of sexual terrorism. Every female is a potential target of violence—at any age, at any time, in any place. Further, as we shall see, amorality pervades sexual violence. Child molesters, incestuous fathers, wife beaters, and rapists often do not understand that they have done anything wrong. Their views are routinely shared by police officers, lawyers, and judges, and crimes of sexual violence are rarely punished in American society.

The fourth component of the theory of terrorism is voluntary compliance. The institutionalization of a system of terror requires the development of mechanisms other than sustained violence to achieve its goals. Violence must be employed to maintain terrorism, but sustained violence can be costly and debilitating. Therefore, strategies for ensuring a significant degree of voluntary compliance must be developed. Sexual terrorism is maintained to a great extent by an elaborate system of sex-role socialization that in effect instructs men to be terrorists in the name of masculinity and women to be victims in the name of femininity.

Sexual and political terrorism differ in the final component, perceptions of the terrorist and the victim. In political terrorism we know who is the terrorist and who is the victim. We may condemn or condone the terrorist, depending on our political views, but we sympathize with the victim. In sexual terrorism, however, we blame the victim and excuse the offender. We believe that the offender either is "sick" and therefore in need of our compassion or is acting out normal male impulses.

TYPES OF SEXUAL TERRORISM

While the discussion that follows focuses on four types of sexual terrorism—rape, wife abuse, sexual abuse of children, and sexual harassment—recent feminist research has documented other forms of sexual terrorism, including threats of violence, flashing, street hassling, obscene phone calls, stalking, coercive sex, pornography, prostitution, sexual slavery, and femicide. What women experience as sexually intrusive and violent is not necessarily reflected in our legal codes, and those acts that are recognized as criminal are often not understood specifically as crimes against women—as acts of sexual violence.

Acts of sexual terrorism include many forms of intrusion that society accepts as common and are therefore trivialized. For example, a recent study of women's experiences of obscene phone calls found that women respondents overwhelmingly found these calls to be a form of sexual intimidation and harassment.[8] While obscene phone calls are illegal, only in rare cases do women report them and the police take them seriously. In contrast, some forms of sexual terrorism are so extraordinary that they are regarded not only as aberrant but also as incomprehensible. The execution of fourteen women students at the University of Montreal on December 6, 1989, is one example of this. Separating the men from the women in a classroom and shouting, "You're all fucking feminists,"

twenty-five-year-old Marc Lepine systematically murdered fourteen women. In his suicide letter, claiming that "the feminists have always enraged me," Lepine recognized his crime as a political act.[9] For many women, this one act of sexual terrorism galvanized attention to the phenomenon of the murder of women because they are women. "Femicide," according to Jane Caputi and Diane E. H. Russell, describes "the murders of women by men motivated by hatred, contempt, pleasure, or a sense of ownership of women."[10] Most femicide, unlike the Montreal massacre, is committed by a male acquaintance, friend, or relative. In *Surviving Sexual Violence,* Liz Kelly argues that sexual violence must be understood as a continuum—that is, "a continuous series of events that pass into one another" united by a "basic common character."[11] Viewing sexual violence in this way furthers an understanding of both the "ordinary" and "extraordinary" forms of sexual terrorism and the range of abuse that women experience in their lifetimes.

Many types of sexual terrorism are crimes, yet when we look at the history of these acts, we see that they came to be considered criminal not so much to protect women as to adjust power relationships among men. Rape was originally a violation of a father's or husband's property rights; consequently, a husband by definition could not rape his wife. Wife beating was condoned by the law and still is condemned in name only. Although proscriptions against incest exist, society assumes a more serious posture toward men who sexually abuse other men's daughters. Sexual harassment is not a crime, and only recently has it been declared an actionable civil offense. Crimes of sexual violence are characterized by ambiguity and diversity in definition and interpretation. Because each state and territory has a separate system of law in addition to the federal system, crimes and punishments are assessed differently throughout the country.

Rape

Rape statutes have been reformed in the past decade, largely to remove the exemption for wife rape and to use gender-neutral language. The essence of the definition of rape, however, remains the same: sexual penetration (typically defined as penile-vaginal, but may include oral and anal sodomy or penetration by fingers or other objects) of a female by force or threat of force, against her will and without her consent.[12]

Traditional views of rape are shaped by male views of sexuality and by men's fear of being unjustly accused. Deborah Rhode argues, in *Justice and Gender,* that this reflects a "sexual schizophrenia." That is, forced sexual intercourse by a stranger against a chaste woman is unquestionably regarded as a heinous crime, whereas coercive sex that does not fit this model is largely denied.[13] Since most women are raped by men they know, this construction excludes many forms of rape.

Because rape is considered a sexual act, evidence of force and resistance is often necessary to establish the nonconsent needed to convict rapists. Such proof is not demanded of a victim of any other crime. If females do not resist rape as much as possible, "consent" is assumed.

By 1990, forty-two states had adopted laws criminalizing rape in marriage: sixteen states recognize that wife rape is a crime and provide no exemptions; twenty-six states penalize wife rape but allow for some exemptions under which husbands cannot be prosecuted for raping their wives. Eight states do not recognize wife rape as a crime.[14] In spite of statutory reform, wife rape remains a greatly misunderstood phenomenon, and the magnitude of sexual abuse by husbands is not known. In Diana E. H. Russell's pioneering study on rape in marriage, 14 percent of the female respondents reported having been raped by their husbands.[15] The prevalence of wife rape, however, is believed to be much higher; approximately 40 percent of women in battered women's shelters also report having been raped by their husbands.[16] Victims of wife rape, according to one study, are at a greater risk of being murdered by their husbands, or of murdering them, than women who are physically but not sexually assaulted.[17]

Wife Abuse

For centuries it has been assumed that a husband had the right to punish or discipline his wife with physical force. The popular expression "rule of thumb" originated from English common law, which allowed a husband to beat his wife with a whip or stick no bigger in diameter than his thumb. The husband's prerogative was incorporated into American law. Several states once had statutes that essentially allowed a man to beat his wife without interference from the courts.[18]

In 1871, in the landmark case of *Fulgham v. State,* an Alabama court ruled that "the privilege, ancient though it be, to beat her with a stick, to pull her hair, choke her, spit in her face or kick her about the floor or to inflict upon her other like indignities, is not now acknowledged by our law."[19] The law, however, has been ambiguous and often contradictory on the issue of wife abuse. While the courts established that a man had no right to beat his wife, it also held that a woman could not press charges against her abusive husband. In 1910, the U.S. Supreme Court ruled that a wife could not charge her husband with assault and battery because it "would open the doors of the court to accusations of all sorts of one spouse against the other and bring into public notice complaints for assaults, slander and libel."[20] The courts virtually condoned violence for the purpose of maintaining peace.

Laws and public attitudes about the illegality of wife abuse and the rights of the victim have been slowly evolving. During the 1980s, there was a proliferation of new laws designed to address the needs of victims of domestic violence and to reform police and judicial responses to wife abuse. These measures include temporary or permanent protection orders, state-funded or state-assisted shelters, state-mandated data collection, and proarrest or mandatory arrest policies.[21] Most states, however, continue to define domestic violence as a misdemeanor crime, carrying jail sentences of less than one year. Felony crimes are punishable by more than one year in jail, and police officers tend to arrest more often for felony offenses. The distinction between misdemeanor and felony crimes is also based on the use of weapons and the infliction of serious injuries.[22] While wife abuse is still considered a misdemeanor crime, a National Crime Survey revealed that at least 50 percent of the domestic "simple assaults" involved bodily injury as serious as or more serious than 90 percent of all rapes, robberies, and aggravated assaults.[23]

Sexual Abuse of Children

Defining sexual abuse of children is very difficult. The laws are complex and often contradictory. Generally, sexual abuse of children includes statutory rape, molestation, carnal knowledge, indecent liberties, impairing the morals of a minor, child abuse, child neglect, and incest. Each of these is defined, interpreted, and punished differently in each state.

The philosophy underlying statutory-rape laws is that a child below a certain age—arbitrarily fixed by law—is not able to give meaningful consent. Therefore, sexual intercourse with a female below a certain age, even with consent, is rape. Punishment for statutory rape, although rarely imposed, can be as high as life imprisonment. Coexistent with laws on statutory rape are laws on criminal incest. Incest is generally interpreted as sexual activity, most often intercourse, with a blood relative. The difference, then, between statutory rape and incest is the relation of the offender to the child. Statutory rape is committed by someone outside the family; incest, by a member of the family. The penalty for incest, also rarely imposed, is usually no more than ten years in prison. This contrast suggests that sexual abuse of children is tolerated when it occurs within the family and that unqualified protection of children from sexual assault is not the intent of the law.

Sexual Harassment

Sexual harassment is a new term for an old phenomenon. The research on sexual harassment, as well as the legal interpretation, centers on acts of sexual coercion or intimidation on the job and at school. Lin Farley, in *Sexual Shakedown: The Sexual Harassment of Women on the Job,* describes sexual harassment as "unsolicited nonreciprocal male behavior that asserts a woman's sex role over her function as a worker. It can be any or all of the following: staring at, commenting upon, or touching a woman's body; requests for acquiescence in sexual behavior; repeated nonreciprocated propositions for dates; demands for sexual intercourse; and rape."[24]

In 1980 the Equal Employment Opportunity Commission issued federal guidelines that defined sexual harassment as any behavior that "has the purpose or effect of unreasonably interfering with an individual's work performance or creating an intimidating or hostile or offensive environment." Such behavior can include "unwelcome sexual advances, requests for sexual favors, and other verbal or physical conduct of a sexual nature."[25] It was not until six years later, however, that the Supreme Court, in *Meritor Savings Bank FSB v. Vinson,* ruled that sexual harassment was a form of sex discrimination under Title VII of the Civil Rights Act of 1964.[26]

In October 1991 national attention was focused on the issue of sexual harassment as a result of allegations made against Supreme Court Justice nominee Clarence Thomas by Professor Anita Hill. (Thomas was subsequently confirmed as a Supreme Court justice by a vote of fifty-two to forty-eight.) While there was a blizzard of media attention about sexual harassment, what emerged most clearly from the confirmation hearings was that the chasm between women's experiences of sexual harassment and an understanding of the phenomenon by society in general had not been bridged. Perhaps most misunderstood was the fact that Professor Hill's experience and her reaction to it were typical of sexually harassed women.[27]

CHARACTERISTICS OF SEXUAL TERRORISM

Those forms of sexual terrorism that are crimes share several common characteristics. Each will be addressed separately, but in the real world these characteristics are linked together and form a vicious circle, which functions to mask the reality of sexual terrorism and thus to perpetuate the system of oppression of females. Crimes of violence against females (1) cut across socio-economic lines; (2) are the crimes least likely to be reported; (3) when reported, are the crimes least likely to be brought to trial or to result in conviction; (4) are often blamed on the victim; (5) are generally not taken seriously; and (6) fuse dominance and sexuality.

Violence Against Females Cuts Across Socioeconomic Lines

The question "Who is the typical rapist, wife beater, incest offender, etc.?" is raised constantly. The answer is simple: men. Female sexual offenders are exceedingly rare. The men who commit acts of sexual terrorism are of all ages, races, and religions; they come from all communities, income levels, and educational levels; they are married, single, separated, and divorced. The "typical" sexually abusive male does not exist.

One of the most common assumptions about sexual violence is that it occurs primarily among the poor, uneducated, and predominantly nonwhite populations. Actually, violence committed by the poor and nonwhite is simply more visible because of their lack of resources to secure the privacy that the middle and upper classes can purchase. Most rapes, indeed, most incidents of sexual assault, are not reported, and therefore the picture drawn from police records must be viewed as very sketchy.

The data on sexual harassment in work situations indicates that it occurs among all job categories and pay ranges. Sexual harassment is committed by academic men, who are among the most highly educated members of society. In a 1991 *New York Times* poll, five out of ten men said they had said or done something that "could have been construed by a female colleague as harassment."[28]

All the studies on wife abuse testify to the fact that wife beating crosses socioeconomic lines. Wife beaters include high government officials, members of the armed forces, businessmen, policemen, physicians, lawyers, clergy, blue-collar workers, and the unemployed.[29] According to Maria Roy, founder and director of New York's Abused Women's Aid in Crisis, "We see abuse of women on all levels of income, age, occupation, and social standing. I've had four women come in recently whose husbands are Ph.D.s—two of them professors at top universities. Another abused woman is married to a very prominent attorney. We counseled battered wives whose husbands are doctors, psychiatrists, even clergymen."[30]

Similarly, in Vincent De Francis's classic study of 250 cases of sexual crimes committed against children, a major finding was that incidents of sexual assault against children cut across class lines.[31] Since sexual violence is not "nice," we prefer to believe that nice men do not commit these acts and that nice girls and women are not victims. Our refusal to accept the fact that violence against females is widespread throughout society strongly inhibits our ability to develop meaningful strategies to eliminate it. Moreover, because of underreporting, it is difficult to ascertain exactly how widespread it is.

Crimes of Sexual Violence Are the Least Likely to Be Reported

Underreporting is common for all crimes against females. There are two national sources for data on crime in the United States: the annual Uniform Crime Reports (UCR) of the Federal Bureau of Investigation, which collects information from police departments, and the National Crime Survey (NCS), conducted by the U.S. Department of Justice, which collects data on personal and household criminal victimizations from a nationally representative sample of households.

The FBI recognizes that rape is seriously underreported by as much as 80 to 90 percent. According to FBI data for 1990, 102,555 rapes were reported.[32] The FBI Uniform Crime Report for 1990 estimates that a forcible rape occurs every five minutes.[33] This estimate is based on reported rapes; accounting for the high rate of underreporting, the FBI estimates that a rape occurs every two minutes. The number of forcible rapes reported to the police has been increasing every year. Since 1986, the rape rate has risen 10 percent.[34]

The National Crime Survey (renamed in 1991 as the National Crime Victimization Survey) data for 1990 reports 130,260 rapes.[35] This data is only slightly higher than FBI data; researchers argue that NCS data has serious drawbacks as well.[36] Just as victims are reluctant to report a rape to the police, many are also reluctant to reveal their victimization to an NCS interviewer. In fact, the NCS does not ask directly about rape (although it will in the future). A respondent may volunteer the information when asked questions about bodily harm. The NCS also excludes children under twelve, thus providing no data on childhood sexual assault.

In April 1992 the National Victim Center and the Crime Victims Research and Treatment Center released a report entitled "Rape in America," which summarized two nationwide studies: the National Women's Study, a three-year longitudinal survey of a national probability sample of 4,008 adult women, and the State of Services for Victims of Rape, which surveyed 370 agencies that provide rape crisis assistance.[37] The National Women's Study sought information about the incidence of rape and information about a number of health issues related to rape, including depression, posttraumatic stress disorder, suicide attempts, and alcohol- and drug-related problems.

The results of the National Women's Study confirm a belief held by many experts that the UCR and NCS data seriously underrepresents the occurrence of rape. According to the National Women's Study, 683,000 adult women were raped during a twelve-month period from the fall of 1989 to the fall of 1990.[38] This data is significantly higher than UCR and NCS data for approximately the same period. Moreover, since rapes of female children and adolescents under the age of eighteen and rapes of boys or men were not included in the study, the 683,000 rapes of adult women do not reflect an accurate picture of all rapes that occurred during that period. The data in this study also confirms the claim that acquaintance rape is far more pervasive than stranger rape. While 22 percent of victims were raped by someone unknown to them, 36 percent were raped by family members: 9 percent by husbands or ex-husbands, 11 percent by fathers or stepfathers, 16 percent by other relatives. Ten percent were raped by a boyfriend or ex-boyfriend and 29 percent by nonrelatives such as friends or neighbors (3 percent were not sure or refused to answer).[39]

Perhaps the most significant finding of the National Women's Study is that rape in the United States is "a tragedy of youth."[40] The study found that 29 percent of rapes occurred to female victims under the age of eleven, 32 percent occurred to females between the ages of eleven and seventeen, and 22 percent occurred to females between the ages of eighteen and twenty-four.[41] Other research suggests that one in four women will be the victim of rape or an attempted rape by the time they are in their midtwenties, and at least three-quarters of those assaults will be committed by men known to the victims.[42] Lifetime probability for rape victimization is as high as 50 percent; that is, one out of two women will be sexually assaulted at least once in her lifetime.[43]

The FBI's Uniform Crime Report indexes 10 million reported crimes a year but does not collect statistics on wife abuse. Since statutes in most states do not identify wife beating as a distinct crime, incidents of wife abuse are usually classified under "assault and battery" and "disputes." Estimates that 50 percent of American wives are battered every year are not uncommon in the literature.[44] Recent evidence shows that violence against wives becomes greatest at and after separation.[45] Divorced and separated women account for 75 percent of all battered women and report being battered fourteen times as often as women still living with their partners.[46] These women are also at the highest risk of being murdered by their former husbands. Thirty-three percent of all women murdered in the United States between 1976 and 1987 were murdered by their husbands.[47]

"The problem of sexual abuse of children is of unknown national dimensions," according to Vincent De Francis, "but findings strongly point to the probability of an enormous national incidence many times larger than the reported incidence of the physical abuse of children."[48] He discussed the existence of a wide gap between the reported incidence and the actual occurrence of sexual assaults against children and suggested that "the reported incidence represents the top edge of the moon as it rises over the mountain."[49] Research definitions as to what constitutes sexual abuse and research methodologies vary widely, resulting in reported rates ranging from 6 percent to 62 percent for female children and 3 percent to 31 percent for male children.[50] David Finkelhor suggests that the lowest figures support the claim that child sexual abuse is far from a rare occurrence and that the higher reported rates suggest a "problem of epidemic proportions."[51]

In a study of 126 African-American women and 122 white women in Los Angeles County, 62 percent reported at least one experience of sexual abuse before the age of eighteen.[52] The same men who beat their wives often abuse their children. Researchers have found that "the worse the wife-beating, the worse the child abuse."[53] It is estimated that fathers may sexually abuse children in 25 percent to 33 percent of all domestic abuse cases. There is also a strong correlation between child abuse and the frequency of marital rape, particularly where weapons are involved.[54]

Incest, according to author and researcher Florence Rush, is the *Best Kept Secret.*[55] The estimates, however speculative, are frightening. In a representative sample of 930 women in San Francisco, Diana E. H. Russell found that 16 percent of the women had been sexually abused by a relative before the age of eighteen and 4.5 percent had been sexually abused by their fathers (also before the age of eighteen).[56] Extrapolating to the general population, this research suggests that 160,000 women per million may have been sexually abused before the age of eighteen, and 45,000 women per million may have been sexually abused by their fathers.[57]

Accurate data on the incidence of sexual harassment is impossible to obtain. Women have traditionally accepted sexual innuendo as a fact of life and only recently have begun to report and analyze the dimensions of sexual coercion in the workplace. Research indicates that sexual harassment is pervasive. In 1978 Lin Farley found that accounts of sexual harassment within the federal government, the country's largest single employer, were extensive.[58] In 1988 the U.S. Merit Systems Protection Board released an updated study that showed that 85 percent of working women experience harassing behavior at some point in their lives.[59]

In 1976 over nine thousand women responded to a survey on sexual harassment conducted by *Redbook* magazine. More than 92 percent reported sexual harassment as a problem, a majority of the respondents described it as serious, and nine out of ten reported that they had personally experienced one or more forms of unwanted sexual attentions on the job.[60] The Ad Hoc Group on Equal Rights for Women attempted to gather data on sexual harassment at the United Nations. Their questionnaire was confiscated by UN officials, but 875 staff members had already responded; 73 percent were women, and more than half of them said that they had personally experienced or were aware of incidents of sexual harassment at the UN.[61] In May 1975, the Women's Section of the Human Affairs Program at Cornell University in Ithaca, New York, distributed the first questionnaire on sexual harassment. Of the 155 respondents, 92 percent identified sexual harassment as a serious problem, 70 percent had personally experienced some form of sexual harassment, and 56 percent reported incidents of physical harassment.[62] A 1991 *New York Times*/CBS poll found that four out of

ten women experienced sexual harassment at work, yet only 4 percent reported it.[63]

In *The Lecherous Professor,* Billie Wright Dziech and Linda Weiner note that the low reportage of sexual harassment in higher education is due to the victims' deliberate avoidance of institutional processes and remedies.[64] A pilot study conducted by the National Advisory Council on Women's Educational Programs on Sexual Harassment in Academia concluded:

> The sexual harassment of postsecondary students is an increasingly visible problem of great, but as yet unascertained, dimensions. Once regarded as an isolated, purely personal problem, it has gained civil rights credibility as its scale and consequences have become known, and is correctly viewed as a form of illegal sex-based discrimination.[65]

Crimes of Violence Against Females Have the Lowest Conviction Rates

The common denominator in the underreporting of all sexual assaults is fear. Females have been well trained in silence and passivity. Early and sustained sex-role socialization teaches that women are responsible for the sexual behavior of men and that women cannot be trusted. These beliefs operate together. They function to keep women silent about their victimization and to keep other people from believing women when they do come forward. The victim's fear that she will not be believed and, as a consequence, that the offender will not be punished is not unrealistic. Sex offenders are rarely punished in our society.

Rape has the lowest conviction rate of all violent crimes. The likelihood of a rape complaint ending in conviction is 2 to 5 percent.[66] While the intent of rape reform legislation was to shift the emphasis from the victim's experiences to the perpetrator's acts,[67] prosecutions are less likely to be pursued if the victim and perpetrator are acquainted, and juries are less likely to return a conviction in cases where the victim's behavior or *alleged behavior* (emphasis mine) departed from traditional sex-role expectations.[68]

Data on prosecution and conviction of wife beaters is practically nonexistent. This is despite the fact that battery is, according to the U.S. Surgeon General, the "single largest cause of injury to women in the U.S." and accounts for one-fifth of all emergency room visits by women.[69] Police departments have generally tried to conciliate rather than arrest. Guided by the "stitch rule," arrests were made only when the victim's injuries required stitches. Police routinely instructed the parties to "break it up" or "talk it out" or asked the abuser to "take a walk and cool off." Male police officers, often identifying with the male abuser, routinely failed to advise women of their rights to file a complaint.[70]

As a result of sustained political activism on behalf of abused women, many states have revised their police training and have instituted pro- or even mandatory arrest policies. In 1984 the Attorney General's Task Force on Family Violence argued that the legal response to such violence be predicated on the abusive act and not on the relationship between the victim and the abuser.[71] A key issue, however, is the implementation of such reform. The record shows that the criminal justice system has responded inconsistently.[72]

Studies in the late 1970s and 1980s showed that batterers receive minimal fines and suspended sentences. In one study of 350 abused wives, none of the husbands served time in jail.[73] And while the result of pro- and mandatory arrest policies is a larger number of domestic violence cases entering the judicial system,[74] "there is considerable evidence that judges have yet to abandon the historical view of wife abuse."[75] In 1981 a Kansas judge suspended the fine of a convicted assailant on the condition that he buy his wife a box of candy.[76] In 1984 a Colorado judge sentenced a man to two years on work release for fatally shooting his wife five times in the face. Although the sentence was less than the minimum required by law, the judge found that the wife had "provoked" her husband by leaving him.[77] Recent task force reports on gender bias in the courts reveal a pattern of nonenforcement of protective orders, trivialization of complaints, and disbelief of females when there is no visible evidence of severe injuries.[78] In 1987 a Massachusetts trial judge scolded a battered women for wasting his time with her request for a protective order. If she and her husband wanted to "gnaw" on each other, "fine," but they "shouldn't do it at taxpayers' expense." The husband later killed his wife, and taxpayers paid for a murder trial.[79]

The lack of support and protection from the criminal justice system intensifies the double bind of bat-

tered women. Leaving the batterer significantly increases the risk of serious injury or death, while staying significantly increases the psychological terrorism and frequency of abuse. According to former Detroit Police Commander James Bannon, "You can readily understand why the women ultimately take the law into their own hands or despair of finding relief at all. *Or why the male feels protected by the system in his use of violence*" (emphasis mine).[80]

In his study of child sexual abuse, Vincent De Francis found that plea bargaining and dismissal of cases were the norm. The study sample consisted of 173 cases brought to prosecution. Of these, 44 percent (seventy-six cases) were dismissed, 22 percent (thirty-eight cases) voluntarily accepted a lesser plea, 11 percent (six cases) were found guilty of a lesser charge, and 2 percent (four cases) were found guilty as charged. Of the remaining thirty-five cases, either they were pending (fifteen) or terminated because the offender was committed to a mental institution (five) or because the offender absconded (seven), or no information was available (eight). Of the fifty-three offenders who were convicted or pleaded guilty, thirty offenders escaped a jail sentence. Twenty-one received suspended sentences and were placed on probation, seven received suspended sentences without probation, and two were fined a sum of money. The other 45 percent (twenty-three offenders) received prison terms from under six months to three years; five were given indeterminate sentences—that is, a minimum term of one year and a maximum term subject to the discretion of the state board of parole.[81]

In Diana E. H. Russell's study of 930 women, 648 cases of child sexual abuse were disclosed. Thirty cases—5 percent—were reported to the police; four were cases of incestuous abuse, and twenty-six were extrafamilial child sexual abuse. Only seven cases resulted in conviction.[82]

Most of the victims of sexual harassment in the Cornell University study were unwilling to use available procedures, such as grievances, to remedy their complaints, because they believed that nothing would be done. Their perception is based on reality; of the 12 percent who did complain, over half found that nothing was done in their cases.[83] The low adjudication and punishment rates of sexual-harassment cases are particularly revealing in light of the fact that the offender is known and identifiable and that there is no fear of "mistaken identity," as there is in rape cases. While offenders accused of familial violence—incest and wife abuse—are also known, concern with keeping the family intact affects prosecution rates.

Blaming the Victim of Sexual Violence Is Pervasive

The data on conviction rates of men who have committed acts of violence against females must be understood in the context of attitudes about women. Our male-dominated society evokes powerful myths to justify male violence against females and to ensure that these acts will rarely be punished. Victims of sexual violence are almost always suspect. We have developed an intricate network of beliefs and attitudes that perpetuate the idea that "victims of sex crimes have a hidden psychological need to be victimized."[84] We tend to believe either that the female willingly participated in her victimization or that she outright lied about it. Either way, we blame the victim and excuse or condone the offender.

Consider, for example, the operative myths about rape, wife battery, incest, and sexual harassment.

Rape

All women want to be raped.
No woman can be raped if she doesn't want it (you-can't-thread-a-moving-needle argument).
She asked for it.
She changed her mind afterward.
When she says no, she means yes.
If you are going to be raped, you might as well relax and enjoy it.

Wife Abuse

Some women need to be beaten.
A good kick in the ass will straighten her out.
She needs a punch in the mouth every so often to keep her in line.
She must have done something to provoke him.

Incest

The child was the seducer.
The child imagined it.

Sexual Harassment

She was seductive.
She misunderstood. I was just being friendly.

Underlying all the myths about victims of sexual violence is the belief that the victim causes and is responsible for her own victimization. In the National Women's Study, 69 percent of the rape victims were afraid that they would be blamed for their rape, 71 percent did not want their family to know they had been sexually abused, and 68 percent did not want people outside of their family knowing of their victimization.[85] Diana Scully studied convicted rapists and found that these men both believed in the rape myths and used them to justify their own behavior.[86] Underlying the attitudes about the male offender is the belief that he could not help himself: that is, he was ruled by his biology and/or he was seduced. The victim becomes the offender, and the offender becomes the victim. These two processes, blaming the victim and absolving the offender, protect the patriarchal view of the world by rationalizing sexual violence. Sexual violence by a normal male against an innocent female is unthinkable; therefore, she must have done something wrong or it would not have happened. This view was expressed by a Wisconsin judge who sentenced a twenty-four-year-old man to ninety days' work release for sexually assaulting a five-year-old girl. The judge, claiming that the child was an "unusually promiscuous young lady," stated that "no way do I believe that [the defendant] initiated sexual contact."[87] Making a victim believe she is at fault erases not only the individual offender's culpability but also the responsibility of the society as a whole. Sexual violence remains an individual problem, not a sociopolitical one.

One need only read the testimony of victims of sexual violence to see the powerful effects of blaming the victim. From the National Advisory Council on Women's Educational Programs Report on Sexual Harassment of Students:

I was ashamed, thought it was my fault, and was worried that the school would take action against me (for "unearned" grades) if they found out about it.

This happened seventeen years ago, and you are the first person I've been able to discuss it with in all that time. He's still at _____ , and probably still doing it.

I'm afraid to tell anyone here about it, and I'm just hoping to get through the year so I can leave.[88]

From *Wife-Beating: The Silent Crisis,* Judge Stewart Oneglia comments,

Many women find it shameful to admit they don't have a good marriage. The battered wife wraps her bloody head in a towel, goes to the hospital, and explains to the doctor she fell down the stairs. After a few years of the husband telling her he beats her because she is ugly, stupid, or incompetent, she is so psychologically destroyed that she believes it.

A battered woman from Boston relates,

I actually thought if I only learned to cook better or keep a cleaner house, everything would be okay. I put up with the beatings for five years before I got desperate enough to get help.[89]

Another battered woman said,

When I came to, I wanted to die, the guilt and depression were so bad. Your whole sense of worth is tied up with being a successful wife and having a happy marriage. If your husband beats you, then your marriage is a failure, and you're a failure. It's so horribly the opposite of how it is supposed to be.[90]

Katherine Brady shared her experience as an incest survivor in *Father's Days: A True Story of Incest.* She concluded her story with the following:

I've learned a great deal by telling my story. I hope other incest victims may experience a similar journey of discovery by reading it. If nothing else, I would wish them to hear in this tale the two things I needed most, but had to wait years to hear: "You are not alone and you are not to blame."[91]

Sexual Violence Is Not Taken Seriously

Another characteristic of sexual violence is that these crimes are not taken seriously. Society manifests this attitude by simply denying the existence of sexual violence, denying the gravity of these acts, joking about them, and attempting to legitimate them.

Many offenders echo the societal norm by expressing genuine surprise when they are confronted by authorities. This seems to be particularly true in cases of sexual abuse of children, wife beating, and sexual harassment. In her study of incest, Florence Rush found that child molesters very often do not understand that they have done anything wrong. Many men still believe that they have an inalienable right to rule "their women." Batterers, for example, often cite their right to discipline their wives; incestuous fathers cite their right to instruct their daughters in sexuality. These men are acting on the belief that women are the property of men.

The concept of females as the property of men extends beyond the family unit, as the evidence on sexual harassment indicates. "Are you telling me that this kind of horsing around may constitute an actionable offense?" queried a character on a television special on sexual harassment.[92] This represents the typical response of a man accused of sexual harassment. Men have been taught that they are the hunters, and women—all women—are fair game. The mythology about the workaday world abounds with sexual innuendo. Concepts of "sleazy" (i.e., sexually accessible) nurses and dumb, big-breasted, blond secretaries are standard fare for comedy routines. When the existence of sexual violence can no longer be denied, a common response is to joke about it in order to belittle it. "If you are going to be raped, you might as well enjoy it" clearly belittles the violence of rape. The public still laughs when Ralph threatens Alice with "One of these days, POW—right in the kisser." Recently, a television talk-show host remarked that "incest is a game the whole family can play." The audience laughed uproariously.

Sexual Violence Is About Violence, Power, and Sex

The final characteristic common to all forms of violence against females is perhaps the most difficult to comprehend. During the past decade, many researchers argued (as I did in earlier versions of this article) that sexual violence is not about sex but about violence. I now believe, however, that the "either-or" dichotomy—either sexual violence is about sex or it's about violence—is false and misleading. Male supremacy identifies females as having a basic "flaw"— a trait that distinguishes males and females and legitimates women's inferior status. This "flaw" is female sexuality: it is tempting and seductive and therefore disruptive, capable of reproducing life itself and therefore powerful.[93] Through sexual terrorism men seek to bring this force under control. The site of the struggle is the female body and female sexuality.

Timothy Beneke, in *Men on Rape,* argues that "not every man is a rapist but every man who grows up in America and learns American English learns all too much to think like a rapist" and that "for a man, rape has plenty to do with sex."[94] Twenty years of research and activism have documented that women largely experience rape, battery, incest, and sexual harassment as violence. That women and men often have vastly different experiences is not surprising. Under patriarchy men are entitled to sex; it is a primary vehicle by which they establish and signal their masculinity. From the male perspective, female sexuality is a commodity, something they must take, dominate, or own. Our popular culture routinely celebrates this particular notion of masculinity. Women are permitted to have sex, but only in marriage (the patriarchal ideal), or at least in love relationships. Women earn their femininity by managing their sexuality and keeping it in trust for a potential husband. The double standard of sexuality leads inevitably to coercion and sexual violence.

Many believe that re-visioning rape as violence not only accurately reflects many women's experiences but also is a more productive strategy for reforming legislation and transforming public attitudes. While arguing that "theoretically and strategically" the "rape as violence" position is the better one, attorney and author Susan Estrich points out that such an approach obscures the reality that the majority of rapes are coerced or forced but unaccompanied by conventional violence.[95] In fact, one consequence of this approach is that it precludes protest from women who experience sexual intrusions in ways not typically seen as violent.

It is argued that in sexual harassment the motive is power, not sex. There is a wide consensus that sexual harassment is intended to "keep women in their place." Yet, the means by which this is attempted or accomplished are sexual: rude comments about sex or about a woman's body, pornographic gestures or posters, demands for sexual favors, rape, etc. Clearly, to the harassers, a woman's place is a largely sexual

one; her very presence in the workplace sexualizes it. In the accounts of women's experiences with sexual harassment in *Sexual Harassment: Women Speak Out,*[96] themes of sexual power and sexual humiliation resonate in each essay.

In wife battery the acts of violence are intended to inflict harm on the woman and ultimately to control her, but the message of the violence is explicitly sexual. For example, the most common parts of a woman's body attacked during battering are her face and her breasts—both symbols of her sexuality and her attractiveness to men. During pregnancy, the focus of the attack often shifts to the abdomen—a symbol of her reproductive power. In addressing the "either-or" debate in the sexual abuse of children, David Finkelhor points out "sex is always in the service of other needs. Just because it is infused with nonsexual motives does not make child sexual abuse different from other kinds of behavior that we readily call 'sexual'."[97]

CONCLUSION

The dynamic that underscores all manifestations of sexual terrorism is misogyny—the hatred of women. Violence against women is power expressed sexually. It is violence eroticized. Diana E. H. Russell argues that "we are socialized to sexualize power, intimacy, and affection, and sometimes hatred and contempt as well."[98] For women in the United States, sexual violence and its threat are central issues in their daily lives. Both violence and fear are functional. Without the power to intimidate and punish women sexually, the domination of women in all spheres of society— political, social, and economic—could not exist.

NOTES

1. Susan Brownmiller, *Against Our Will: Men, Women and Rape* (New York: Simon and Schuster, 1975), 5.

2. Gordon and Riger, 22.

3. Yonah Alexander, "Terrorism and the Mass Media: Some Considerations," in Yonah Alexander, David Carlton, and Paul Wilkinson (eds.), *Terrorism: Theory and Practice* (Boulder, CO: Westview Press, 1979), 159; Ernest Evans, *Calling a Truce to Terrorism: The American Response to International Terrorism* (Westport, CT: Greenwood Press, 1979), 3;

Charmers Johnson, "Perspectives on Terrorism," in Walter Laquer (ed.), *The Terrorism Reader* (Philadelphia: Temple University Press, 1978), 273; Thomas P. Thornton, "Terror as a Weapon of Political Agitation," in Harry Eckstein (ed.), *The Internal War* (New York: Free Press, 1964), 73; Eugene Walter, *Terror and Resistance* (New York: Oxford University Press, 1969), 6; Francis M. Watson, *Political Terrorism: The Threat and the Response* (Washington, DC: R. B. Luce Co., 1976), 15; Paul Wilkinson, *Political Terrorism* (New York: John Wiley and Sons, 1974), 11.

4. Frederick F. Hacker, *Crusaders, Criminals and Crazies: Terrorism in Our Time* (New York: W. W. Norton and Co., 1976), xi.

5. Marc Feigen Fasteau, *The Male Machine* (New York: McGraw-Hill Book Co., 1974), 144.

6. Watson, 15.

7. Wilkinson, 17.

8. Sheffield, "Obscene Phone Calls," 487.

9. Malette and Chalouh, 100.

10. Caputi and Russell, 34.

11. Kelly, 76.

12. Estrich, 8; UCR, 43; Koss and Harvey, 4.

13. Rhode, 245.

14. Russell, *Rape in Marriage*, 21–22.

15. Ibid., xxii.

16. Ibid., xxvi.

17. Campbell, 340.

18. *Bradley v. State. I Miss.* (7 Walker) 150 (1824); *State v. Black,* 60 N.C. (Win.) 266 (1864).

19. *Fulgham v. State,* 46 Ala. 143 (1871).

20. *Thompson v. Thompson,* 218 U.S. 611 (1910).

21. SchWeber and Feinman, 30.

22. *Arrest in Domestic Violence Cases: A State by State Summary* (New York: National Center on Women and Family Law, Inc., 1987), 1.

23. Langan and Innes, 1.

24. Lin Farley, *Sexual Shakedown: The Sexual Harassment of Women on the Job* (New York: McGraw-Hill Book Co., 1978), 14–15.

25. U.S. House of Representatives, 1980: 8.

26. *Meritor Savings Bank FSB v. Vinson,* 477 U.S. 57 (1986).

27. Lewin, A22; *Sexual Harassment: Research and Resources. A Report in Progress* (New York: The National Council for Research on Women, 1991), 10–13.

28. Kolbert, 1.

29. Roger Langley and Richard C. Levy, *Wife-Beating: The Silent Crisis* (New York: E. P. Dutton, 1977), 43.

30. Ibid., 44.

31. Vincent De Francis, *Protecting the Child Victim of Sex Crimes Committed by Adults* (Denver: American Humane Society, 1969), vii.

32. UCR, 1991, 16.

33. Ibid., 7.

34. Ibid., 16.

35. *Criminal Victimization in the United States,* 1990, 5.

36. Koss and Harvey, 11–17.

37. *Rape in America,* 1.

38. Ibid., 2.

39. Ibid., 4.

40. Ibid., 3.

41. Ibid.

42. Parrot and Bechofer, ix.

43. Crites, 36.

44. Langley and Levy, 3.

45. Zorza, 423.

46. Harlow, 5.

47. Caputi and Russell, 35.

48. De Francis, vii.

49. Ibid.

50. Finkelhor, *Sourcebook,* 19.

51. Ibid.

52. Russell, *Secret Trauma,* 69.

53. Bowker et al., 164.

54. Ibid.

55. Florence Rush, *The Best Kept Secret* (Englewood Cliffs, NJ: Prentice-Hall, 1980), 5.

56. Russell, *Secret Trauma,* 10.

57. Ibid.

58. Farley, 31.

59. Rhode, 232.

60. Ibid., 20.

61. Ibid., 21.

62. Ibid., 20.

63. Kolbert, A17.

64. Dziech and Weiner, xxi.

65. Frank J. Till, *Sexual Harassment: A Report on the Sexual Harassment of Students* (Washington, DC: National Advisory Council on Women's Educational Programs, 1980), 3.

66. Rhode, 246.

67. Koss and Harvey, 5.

68. LaFree, 240.

69. Zorza, 243.

70. Rhode, 239.

71. *Attorney General's Task Force,* 4.

72. Ibid.

73. Rhode, 241.

74. Goolkasian, 3.

75. Crites, 41.

76. Ibid., 45.

77. Ibid.

78. Schafran, 280, 283–84.

79. Goodman, 13.

80. James Bannon, as quoted in Del Martin, *Battered Wives* (New York: Pocket Books, 1977), 115.

81. De Francis, 190–91.

82. Russell, *Secret Trauma,* 85.

83. Farley, 22.

84. Georgia Dullea, "Child Prostitution: Causes Are Sought" (*New York Times,* Sept. 4, 1979), p. C11.

85. *Rape in America,* 4.

86. Scully, 58.

87. Stanko, 95.

88. Till, 28.

89. Ibid., 115.

90. Ibid., 116.

91. Katherine Brady, *Father's Days: A True Story of Incest* (New York: Dell Publishing Co., 1981), 253.

92. Till, 4.

93. Sheffield, "Social Control," 172.

94. Timothy Beneke, *Men on Rape: What They Have to Say About Sexual Violence* (New York: St. Martin's Press, 1982), 16.

95. Estrich, 83.

96. Sumrall and Taylor.

97. Finkelhor, *New Theory,* 34.

98. Russell, *Secret Trauma,* 393.

RESOURCES

Attorney General's Task Force on Family Violence, Final Report. Washington, DC, 1984.

Lee H. Bowker, Michelle Arbitell, and J. Richard McFerron. "On the Relationship Between Wife Beating and Child Abuse," in Kersti Yllo and Michele Bograd (eds.), *Feminist Perspectives on Wife Abuse.* Newbury Park, CA: Sage Publications, Inc., 1988.

Jacquelyn C. Campbell. "Women's Responses to Sexual Abuse in Intimate Relationships." *Health Care for Women International* 8 (1989).

Jane Caputi and Diana E. H. Russell. "Femicide: Speaking the Unspeakable," in "Everyday Violence Against Women, Special Report." *Ms.* 1, no. 2 (1990).

Crime in the United States: Uniform Crime Reports, 1990. Washington, DC: U.S. Department of Justice, 1991.

Criminal Victimization in the United States, 1990. Washington, DC: U.S. Department of Justice, 1992.

Laura L. Crites. "Wife Abuse: The Judicial Record," in Laura L. Crites and Winifred L. Hepperle, *Women, the Courts and Equality.* Beverly Hills, CA: Sage Publications, Inc., 1987.

Billie Wright Dziech and Linda Weiner. *The Lecherous Professor: Sexual Harassment on Campus* (2nd ed.). Chicago: University of Illinois Press, 1990.

Susan Estrich. *Real Rape.* Cambridge, MA: Harvard University Press, 1987.

David Finkelhor. *A Sourcebook on Child Sexual Abuse.* Beverly Hills, CA: Sage Publications, Inc., 1986.

David Finkelhor (ed.). *Child Sexual Abuse: New Theory and Research.* New York: The Free Press, 1984.

David Finkelhor and Kersti Yllo. *License to Rape: Sexual Abuse of Wives.* New York: The Free Press, 1985.

Ellen Goodman. "My Equal Rights Winners." *Boston Globe,* Aug. 25, 1987, p. 13.

Gail A. Goolkasian. "Confronting Domestic Violence: The Role of the Criminal Court Judges." Washington, DC: U.S. Department of Justice, National Institute of Justice, 1986.

Margaret T. Gordon and Stephanie Riger. *The Female Fear.* New York: The Free Press, 1989.

Caroline Wolf Harlow. "Female Victims of Violent Crime." Washington, DC: U.S. Department of Justice, 1991.

Liz Kelly. *Surviving Sexual Violence.* Minneapolis: University of Minnesota Press, 1988.

Elizabeth Kolbert. "Sexual Harassment at Work Is Pervasive, Survey Suggests." *New York Times,* Oct. 11, 1991, pp. 1, A17.

Mary P. Koss and Mary R. Harvey. *The Rape Victim: Clinical and Community Interventions* (2nd ed.). Newbury Park, CA: Sage Publications, Inc., 1991.

Gary D. LaFree. *Rape and Criminal Justice: The Social Construction of Sexual Assault.* Belmont, CA: Wadsworth Publishing Co., 1989.

Patrick A. Langan and Christopher Innes. "Preventing Domestic Violence Against Women." Washington, DC: U.S. Department of Justice, Bureau of Justice Statistics, 1986.

Tamar Lewin. "Law on Sex Harassment Is Recent and Evolving." *New York Times,* Oct. 8, 1991, p. A22.

Louise Malette and Marie Chalouh. *The Montreal Massacre.* Translated by Marlene Wildeman. Charlottetown, Prince Edward Island: Gynergy Books, 1991.

Andrea Parrot and Laurie Bechofer. *Acquaintance Rape: The Hidden Crime.* New York: John Wiley and Sons, Inc., 1991.

Rape in America: A Report to the Nation. Prepared by the National Victim Center and the Crime Victims Research and Treatment Center, New York, Apr. 23, 1992.

Deborah L. Rhode. *Justice and Gender: Sex Discrimination and the Law.* Cambridge, MA: Harvard University Press, 1989.

Diana E. H. Russell. *Rape in Marriage* (2nd ed.). Indianapolis: Indiana University Press, 1990.

Diana E. H. Russell. *The Secret Trauma: Incest in the Lives of Girls and Women.* New York: Basic Books, Inc., 1986.

Lynn Hecht Schafran. "Documenting Gender Bias in the Courts: The Task Force Approach." *Judicature* 70 (1987): 280, 283–84.

Claudine SchWeber and Clarice Feinman, eds. *Criminal Justice Politics and Women: The Aftermath of Legally Mandated Change.* New York: The Haworth Press, 1985.

Diana Scully. *Understanding Sexual Violence: A Study of Convicted Rapists.* Boston: Unwin Hyman, Inc., 1990.

Carole Sheffield. "The Invisible Intruder: Women's Experiences of Obscene Phone Calls." *Gender and Society* 3, no. 4 (1989): 483–88.

Carole Sheffield. "Sexual Terrorism: The Social Control of Women," in Beth B. Hess and Myra Marx Feree (eds.), *Analyzing Gender: A Handbook of Social Science Research.* Beverly Hills, CA: Sage Publications, Inc., 1987.

Elizabeth A. Stanko. *Intimate Intrusions: Women's Experiences of Male Violence.* London: Routledge and Kegan Paul, 1985.

Amber Coverdale Sumrall and Dena Taylor. *Sexual Harassment: Women Speak Out.* Freedom, CA: The Crossing Press, 1992.

U.S. House of Representatives. Hearings on Sexual Harassment in the Federal Government, Committee on the Post Office and Civil Service, Subcommittee on Investigations. Washington, DC: U.S. Government Printing Office, 1980.

Joan Zorza. "Woman Battering: A Major Cause of Homelessness." *Clearinghouse Review* (Special Issue) 24, no. 4 (1991): 421–29.

9.3 RAPED
A Male Survivor Breaks His Silence

Fred Pelka

The man who raped me had a remarkable self-assurance which could only have come from practice. He picked me up just outside Cleveland, heading east in a van filled with construction equipment. That early morning in May I'd already spent a sleepless twenty-four hours trying to hitchhike from Oxford, Mississippi, to Buffalo, New York, so it felt good when I was offered a ride through the western fringe of Pennsylvania. First, though, the driver told me he needed to stop along the way, to pick up some building supplies. We drove to a country club undergoing renovation, where I hung out with his co-workers while he signed for several boxes of equipment which we carried back to his van. Getting back onto the turnpike he told me about one more stop he had to make.

As a man, I've been socialized never to admit to being vulnerable, to discuss those moments when I wasn't in control. I know also how women and children are routinely punished when they speak out about abuse, how they are blamed for their own victimization. The examples are endless: Witness the contempt with which Anita Hill was treated. For these reasons and more I'm still reticent, years after it happened, to recount what happened to me that day in Ohio. This chapter marks the first time in fifteen years I have publicly discussed it under my own name.

The second building seemed deserted. We went up a flight of stairs, down a corridor into a side room. I looked around for the equipment he'd mentioned, and noticed him locking the door behind us. He slugged me before I could react, forced me down with his hands around my throat. As I began to lose consciousness I heard him say, "If you scream, if you make one wrong move, I'll kill you."

The police told me later that the man who raped me was a suspect in the rapes of at least six other young men. During the assault his mood swung from vicious,

---

when he promised to strangle me or break my neck, to self-pity, when he wept because we were both among "the wounded ones." In that enormous calm that comes after the acceptance of death, I wondered who would find my body.

Most rapes don't happen like this. Most victims know their attacker(s)—he is a neighbor, friend, husband, or father, a teacher, minister or doctor. The vast majority of rapes are committed by men against women and children, and the FBI estimates that anywhere from 80 to 90 percent go unreported. Rape is an integral part of our culture, and fully one third of all women in this country will be raped at some point in their lives. But this sexist violence does occasionally spill over onto boys and men. The National Crime Survey for 1989 estimated that one in twelve rape survivors is male.

For all this, nobody really knows how many men are raped each year, or how many boys are sexually abused. One study at the University of New Hampshire found that one in eleven young men surveyed had been sexually abused before their eighteenth birthday. I've seen articles which speculate that anywhere from one in nine to one in seven men will be raped or sexually abused in their lifetime, most often by other males, but these are little more than guesses.

"Since rape is generally misconstrued to be a sexually motivated crime," writes Dr. A. Nicholas Groth and Anne Wolbert Burgess, "it is generally assumed that males are unlikely targets of such victimization, and then when it does occur, it reflects a homosexual orientation on the part of the offender. However, the causes of male rape that we have had an opportunity to study do not lend much support to either assumption." Groth and Burgess interviewed men in the community who had been raped, and men who admitted to raping other men, and published their findings in the *American Journal of Psychiatry*. In half the cases they studied, the gender of the victim "did not appear to be of specific significance" to the rapist. "Their victims included males and females, adults and children," and "may symbolize . . . something they want to conquer or defeat. The assault is an act of retaliation, an expression of power, and an assertion of their strength or manhood."

In their article, Burgess and Groth dispute some of the prevalent myths about male rape. The first is that men simply don't get raped, at least not outside prison. Of course, if men don't get raped then what happened to me either wasn't rape (the police asking, "Did you come?"), or I'm not a man (my male friends wanting to know how I could "let something like this" happen to me). The second myth—that all men who are raped or rape other men are gay—is a product of our culture's homophobia, and our ignorance of the realities of sexual violence. Most people find it difficult to understand why a straight man would rape another straight man. But if you see rape as a way of exerting control, of confirming your own power by disempowering others, then it makes perfect sense. If it makes you feel powerful and macho to force sex on a woman or child, think of how much more powerful you feel raping another man.

"I have a special place," the man who raped me said after a long while. "It's out in the country, where we can make all the noise we want." It seemed obvious what would happen to me once we arrived at "his special place," but I knew there was no hope for my survival as long as we stayed in that room. So I agreed to go with him to "the country." I promised not to try to escape. It is perhaps an indication of his fragile hold on reality that he believed me.

We walked back to his van and drove away. I waited until I saw some people, then jumped as we slowed to make a turn, rolling as I hit the pavement. I ran into the nearest building—a restaurant—just as patrons were finishing their lunch. Conversation stopped, and I was confronted by a roomful of people, forks raised in mid-bite, staring.

"I think you'd better call the police," I told the waitress. This was all I could say, placing my hands flat on the counter between us to control their trembling. She poured me a cup of black coffee. And then the police arrived.

The two detectives assigned to my case conformed to the standard good cop/bad cop archetype. The good cop told me how upset he'd seen "girls" become after being raped. "But you're a man, this shouldn't bother you." Later on he told me that the best thing to do would be to pull up my pants "and forget it ever happened." The bad cop asked me why my hair was so long, what was I doing hitchhiking at seven o'clock in the morning? Why were my clothes so dirty? Did I do drugs? Was I a troublemaker?

I used to be puzzled at how the bad cop obviously didn't believe me, in spite of the fact that, by his own account, in the months before my assault six other men had come to him with similar stories. Then I heard of the Dahmer case in Milwaukee, how in May 1991 Dahmer's neighbors saw him chasing a naked fourteen-year-old boy, bleeding from the anus, through the alley behind their building. The responding officers returned the boy to Dahmer's apartment, where Dahmer explained that this was just a lover's spat, which the police believed in spite of the youth's apparent age, and the photos scattered on Dahmer's floor of murdered and mutilated boys and men. The police reassured a neighbor who called again, saying that everything was all right—this at the very moment Dahmer was murdering Konerak Sinthasomphone. Afterwards Dahmer dismembered Sinthasomphone's body.

Sinthasomphone was one of at least seventeen boys and men raped and murdered by Dahmer, their body parts stored in vats and freezers in his apartment. It was reported that his first assaults were committed in Ohio, so I had to brace myself before I could look at Jeffrey Dahmer's photo in the paper. At first I was relieved to find that he was not the man who raped me. Then I thought how this meant my assailant is likely still out there, looking for more "wounded ones."

Because I gave them such detailed information— the country club, the name painted on the side of his van—the detectives were able to locate my assailant not too many hours after I was brought into their precinct. The good cop asked, after I identified the rapist, whether I wanted to press charges. He explained how I'd have to return to Ohio to appear before a grand jury, and then return again for the trial, how the newspapers would publish my name, how little chance there was of a conviction.

"He says you seduced him," the good cop said. "So it's your word against his."

The bad cop glared at me when I told them there was no way I wanted any of this to be made public. "You mean," he fumed, "I wasted my whole afternoon on this shit?" Standing in front of me with an expres-

sion of disgust, he asked, "How do you think this makes me feel?"

By then it was getting dark. I hitchhiked the remaining 200 miles home, studying every movement of every man who offered me a ride. I arrived at my apartment after midnight, walking the last ten miles.

In the weeks that followed the assault, every stupid, insensitive thing I'd ever said about rape came back to haunt me. A friend of mine had been attacked several months earlier, also while hitchhiking. She told me just a few hours after it happened how she'd missed her bus, and didn't want to be late to work. She said the man offering her a lift seemed normal enough, even "nice."

"You should've waited for the next bus," I lectured. Today I cringe at my arrogance. Hitchhiking, like walking alone after dark, or feeling safe on a date, at work, at home, is another perquisite to which only men are entitled. How dare she not understand the limits of her freedom?

While women tell me that the possibility of rape is never far from their minds, most men never give it a first, let alone a second, thought. This may explain why they react so negatively to accounts by male survivors. To see rape as "a women's issue" is a form of male privilege most men would prefer not to surrender. They would rather believe that they can move with immunity through the toxic atmosphere of violence and fear they and their compatriots create. Being a male survivor meant I'd lost some of that immunity. No wonder I felt as if I'd been poisoned, as if I were drowning.

For years I pretended, as per the good cop's recommendation, that nothing had happened, secretly feeling that I was somehow responsible, somehow less masculine. The turning point came with the media storm that swirled up around the Big Dan rape in New Bedford, Massachusetts. The movie "The Accused" is based on that incident—a woman assaulted in a bar while other men looked on and cheered. Naive as I was, I figured this was a pretty clear-cut case. Where the police might have doubted my will to resist (no broken bones, no massive lacerations), here was a victim overpowered by half a dozen men. How could anyone doubt that she had been brutalized? Yet, during the trial, *The Boston Herald* ran the front page headline "SHE LED US

ON!" I realized then that, even had I been murdered, someone would have inevitably questioned my complicity: "He probably liked rough sex."

It's just this sort of victim-blaming that discourages survivors from reporting their trauma, or seeking treatment, but there are other factors which may discourage males in particular. Homophobia for one: The sort of gender McCarthyism that labels any man a faggot who cannot or will not conform to accepted norms of masculine feeling or behavior. Men who rape other men capitalize on this, knowing that straight victims don't want to appear gay, and gay victims might fear coming out of the closet. Groth and Burgess report, for instance, that "a major strategy used by some offenders . . . is to get the victim to ejaculate." This "strategy" was attempted in roughly half the cases they studied, and in half of those the rapist succeeded in ejaculating his victim. This confuses the victim, who often misidentifies ejaculation with orgasm. It confirms for the rapist the old canard about how victims "really want it." And, as Groth and Burgess say, it leaves the survivor "discouraged from reporting the assault for fear his sexuality may be suspect."

For male survivors of child sexual abuse there is also the unfortunate theory that boys who are abused inevitably grow up to be men who rape. One survivor told me it was for this reason he had decided never to be a father. Not that he'd ever wanted to abuse children, nor was there any evidence he ever would. He eventually came to realize that because some rapists are themselves survivors doesn't mean that all male survivors of child sexual abuse turn out to be rapists.

Finally, rape-crisis centers, the only institutions in our society founded expressly to help rape survivors, are identified by some men as hotbeds of feminism, and many men take "feminist" to mean "man-hating." It's true that the vast majority of rape crisis counselors are women, that the entire stop-rape movement is an extension of the women's movement. For the record, though, I have never felt any hostility in response when calling a rape-crisis center, this in spite of the fact that RCCs are often plagued by "hotline abusers"—men who call to masturbate to the sound of a female voice.

On the other hand, I've run across a good deal of hostility towards women from male survivors with whom I've talked. One man told me how certain he

was that the counselors at his local RCC hated men, even though, by his own admission, he'd never called, and knew no one who had. A while back I attended a survivors' conference organized by a Boston women's group, attended by several hundred women and maybe a dozen men. One of these men stood up during a plenary session to shout at the women on the podium. As an incest survivor, he said, he felt "marginalized" and "oppressed" by the way the conference was run, despite the fact that a number of the workshops were specifically geared toward males, and that a keynote speaker received a standing ovation when he described his work with boys and men. Some male survivors even blame women for the denial and homophobia they encounter after their assault. They openly resent the (pitifully few) resources available to female survivors, as if any help women receive is at the expense of men. Even Geraldo has picked up this theme: His show on male survivors ended with an attack on rape crisis centers for their alleged refusal to acknowledge male victimization.

This hostility has been exacerbated by the so-called men's movement, the Robert Bly/mythopoetic crowd, with their "Wild Man" and "Inner Warrior" archetypes. These men say a lot of absurd things about sexual violence, not the least of which is that "just as many men get raped as women." This last statement is often repeated by Chris Harding, editor of *Wingspan*, which *The Boston Globe* calls "the bible of the new men's movement." Harding is generally quick to add that most of these rapes "occur in prison"—a statement which is as inaccurate as it is pernicious, assuming as it does that a disproportionate number of male rapes are committed by working-class and minority men. The men's movement claims that rape is a "gender-neutral issue," and thus has nothing to do with sexism.

What is ironic about all this is that what little acknowledgment there is of male victimization generally comes from the *women's* stop-rape movement. To the extent that male survivors *can* tell their stories, it is because of the foundation laid by feminists. So this woman-bashing is as ungrateful as it is gratuitous.

One source of confusion appears to be the distinction between victimization and oppression. Male survivors charge that feminists see rape as a "man vs. woman" issue, emphasizing the central role male violence plays in stunting and destroying women's lives, and they're right. The distinction is that while many women, and some men, are victimized by rape, all women are oppressed by it, and any victimization of women occurs in a context of oppression most men simply do not understand. Rape for men is usually a bizarre, outrageous tear in the fabric of reality. For women, rape is often a confirmation of relative powerlessness, of men's contempt for women, and its trauma is reinforced every day in a thousand obvious and subtle ways.

For myself, I don't need for rape to be gender neutral to feel validated as a male survivor. And I certainly don't need to denigrate women, or to attack feminists, to explain why I was abused by the (male) police, ridiculed by my (male) friends, and marginalized by the (male dominated) society around me. It is precisely because we have been "reduced" to the status of *women* that other men find us so difficult to deal with. It was obvious to me at the police station that I was held in contempt because I was a *victim*—feminine, hence perceived as less masculine. Had I been an accused criminal, even a rapist, chances are I would have been treated with more respect, because I would have been seen as more of a man. To cross that line, to become victims of the violence which works to circumscribe the lives of women, marks us somehow as traitors to

our gender. Being a male rape survivor means I no longer fit our culture's neat but specious definition of masculinity, as one empowered, one always in control. Rather than continue to deny our experience, male survivors need to challenge that definition.

As Diana E. H. Russell says in *The Politics of Rape,* "Women must start talking about rape: Their experiences, their fears, their thoughts. The silence about rape must be broken."

The same must be true for men. And so I offer this article as my first contribution to that effort.

I've been back to northern Ohio exactly once in the fifteen years following that day. Seven years ago I was traveling from Boston to Chicago with a car full of friends. It was early morning, and I was sleeping in the back seat when we pulled off the highway, and steered onto a street that looked oddly, disturbingly familiar. Rubbing my eyes, I felt an unsettling sense of deja vu. And then I remembered.

"Time for some coffee," the driver said, and I wondered then if we would eat breakfast at that same restaurant, if I would meet that same waitress. We didn't, and I chose not to tell my companions what had happened to me all those years ago.

Today I think I might be less disconcerted. Today I think I just might have told them what happened.

9.4 Rape-Prone Versus Rape-Free Campus Cultures

Peggy Reeves Sanday

In *Fraternity Gang Rape* (Sanday 1990) I describe the discourse, rituals, sexual ideology, and practices that make some fraternity environments rape prone. The reaction of fraternity brothers to the book was decidedly mixed. Individuals in some chapters were motivated to rethink their initiation ritual and party behavior. In sarcastic opinion pieces written for campus

newspapers others dismissed the book on the grounds that I was "out to get" fraternities. As recently as December 1995, a young man wrote a Letter to the Editor of *The Washington Post* criticizing me for allegedly connecting hate speech and sexual crimes on college campuses with "single-sex organizations." Having set me up as the avenging witch, this young man then blames me for perpetuating the problem. My "[a]cross-the-board generalizations," he claims "only make it more difficult for supportive men to become involved and stay active in the fight against these attacks."

It is one of the tragedies of today's ideological warfare that this writer finds such an easy excuse to exempt himself from participating in the struggle to end violence against women. To make matters worse, his rationalization for opting out is based on a trumped up charge. In the Introduction to my book, I carefully note that I am dealing with only "a few of the many fraternities at U. and on several other campuses." I state the case very clearly:

> The sexual aggression evident in these particular cases does not mean that sexual aggression is restricted to fraternities or that all fraternities indulge in sexual aggression. Sexist attitudes and the phallo-centric mentality associated with "pulling train" have a long history in Western society. For example, venting homoerotic desire in the gang rape of women who are treated as male property is the subject of several biblical stories. Susan Brownmiller describes instances of gang rape by men in war and in street gangs. Male bonding that rejects women and com-modifies sex is evident in many other social contexts outside of universities. Thus, it would be wrong to place blame solely on fraternities. However, it is a fact also that most of the reported incidents of "pulling train" on campus have been associated with fraternities (Sanday 1990:19).

As an anthropologist interested in the particulars of sexual ideologies cross-culturally, I am very wary of generalizations of any sort. In 1975 I was very disturbed to read Susan Brownmiller's claim in the opening chapter of *Against Our Will* (1975:15) that rape is "a conscious process of intimidation by which all men keep all women in a state of fear." This statement was inconsistent with the compelling argument she presents in subsequent chapters that rape is culturally constructed and my own subsequent research on the socio-cultural context of rape cross-culturally, which provided evidence of rape-free as well as rape-prone societies.

The articles in this issue of *Violence Against Women* present three empirically based articles on the relationship between all-male organizations on college campuses and sexual assault. The article by Schwartz and Nogrady confirm the finding reported by Koss and Gaines (1993) that fraternity membership does not predict self-reported sexual assault. The very different results reported by Boeringer, however, suggest that we need to be careful in jumping to wholesale conclusions regarding the role of all-male organizations. The results reported by Crosset et. al. demonstrating that varsity athletes are over-represented in allegations of sexual assault reported in campus judicial affairs records are consistent with other studies of the role of male athletes (see Koss and Gaines 1993).

The research reported by Schwartz and Nogrady and Boeringer is of interest to me as an ethnographer for the amplification of the cultural context of sexual assault on college campuses. Their different results are surprising only if we assume that fraternities are culturally homogeneous. From the view point of a cultural anthropologist such an assumption is unwarranted unless we can show that the same templates for behavior are present in all fraternities. The question of variation both in campus cultures and fraternities is the subject of this paper. In the following, I will briefly summarize what we know about rape-prone fraternity cultures and contrast this information with what a rape-free context might look like. Since the available data are sparse my goal here is mostly programmatic, namely to encourage studies of intra-campus and cross-campus variation in the rates and correlates of sexual assault.

RAPE-PRONE CAMPUS ENVIRONMENTS

The concept of rape-free versus rape-prone comes from my study of 95 band and tribal societies in which I concluded that 47% were rape free and 18% were rape prone (Sanday 1981). For this study I defined a rape-prone society as one in which the incidence of rape is reported by observers to be high, or rape is excused as a ceremonial expression of masculinity, or rape is an act by which men are allowed to punish or threaten women. I defined a rape-free society as one in which the act of rape is either infrequent or does not occur. I used the term "rape free" not to suggest that rape was entirely absent in a given society but as a label to indicate that sexual aggression is socially disapproved and punished severely. Thus, while there may be some men in all societies who might be potential rapists, there is abundant evidence from many societies that sexual aggression is rarely expressed.

Rape in tribal societies is part of a cultural configuration that includes interpersonal violence, male dominance, and sexual separation. Phallocentrism is a dominant psycho-sexual symbol in these societies and men "use the penis to dominate their women" as Yolanda and Robert Murphy say about the Mundurucu (Sanday 1981:25). Rape-prone behavior is associated with environmental insecurity and females are turned into objects to be controlled as men struggle to retain or to gain control of their environment. Behaviors and attitudes prevail that separate the sexes and force men into a posture of proving their manhood. Sexual violence is one of the ways in which men remind themselves that they are superior. As such, rape is part of a broader struggle for control in the face of difficult circumstances. Where men are in harmony with their environment, rape is usually absent.

In *Fraternity Gang Rape* I suggest that rape-prone attitudes and behavior on American campuses are adopted by insecure young men who bond through homophobia and "getting sex." The homoeroticism of their bonding leads them to display their masculinity through heterosexist displays of sexual performance. The phallus becomes the dominant symbol of discourse. A fraternity brother described to me the way in which he felt accepted by the brothers while he was a pledge.

> We . . . liked to share ridiculously exaggerated sexual boasting, such as our mythical "Sixteen Kilometer Flesh- Weapon." . . . By including me in this perpetual, hysterical banter and sharing laughter with me, they showed their affection for me. I felt happy, confident, and loved. This really helped my feelings of loneliness and my fear of being sexually unappealing. We managed to give ourselves a satisfying substitute for sexual relations. We acted out all of the sexual tensions between us as brothers on a verbal level. Women, women everywhere, feminists, homosexuality, etc., all provided the material for the jokes (Sanday 1990:140–41).

Getting their information about women and sex from pornography, some brothers don't see anything wrong with forcing a woman, especially if she's drunk. After the 1983 case of alleged gang rape I describe in the book one of the participants, a virgin at the time, told a news reporter:

> We have this Select TV in the house, and there's soft porn on every midnight. All the guys watch it and talk about it and stuff, and [gang banging] didn't seem that odd because it's something that you see and hear about all the time. I've heard stories from other fraternities about group sex and trains and stuff like that. It was just like, you know, so this is what I've heard about, this is what it's like. . . . (Sanday 1990:34).

Watching their buddies have sex is another favorite activity in rape-prone campus environments. A woman is targeted at a party and brothers are informed who hide out on the roof outside the window, or secret themselves in a closet, or look through holes in the wall. Since the goal is to supply a live pornography show for their buddies, the perpetrators in these cases may easily overlook a woman's ability to consent. They certainly don't seek her consent to being watched. It is assumed that if she came to the house to party she is prepared for anything that might happen, especially if she gets drunk. On some campuses I have been told that this practice is called "beaching" or "whaling."

Taking advantage of a drunk woman is widely accepted. As a group of brothers said in a taped conversation in which they discussed the young woman in the 1983 case:

> "She was drugged."
> "She drugged herself."
> "Yeah, she was responsible for her condition, and that just leaves her wide open . . . so to speak."
> [laughter] (Sanday 1990:119)

In a 1990 talk show on which I appeared with the victim of gang rape a young man from a local university called up and admitted that the goal of all parties at his fraternity was "To get em drunk and go for it." In 1991, I read an article entitled, "Men, Alcohol, and Manipulation," in a campus newspaper from still another university. The author reported hearing several members of a fraternity talking with the bartender about an upcoming social event as follows:

BROTHER 1   "Hey, don't forget—make the women's drinks really strong."

BARTENDER   "Yeah, I won't forget. Just like usual."

BROTHER 2   "We need to get them good and drunk."

BARTENDER   "Don't worry, we'll take care of it."

BROTHER 3   "That'll loosen up some of those inhibitions."

This is the kind of discourse I would classify as rape prone.

Getting a woman drunk to have sex in a show staged for one's buddies is tragically evident in the testimony heard in the St. Johns' sex case tried in Queens, New York, in 1991–92. This case involved six members of the St. Johns University lacrosse team who were indicted for acts ranging from unlawful imprisonment and sexual abuse to sodomy. A seventh defendant pleaded guilty and agreed to testify for immunity (see Sanday 1996 for a description of the case and the subsequent trial). From the testimony in the case and interviews with the complainant and members of the prosecution team, I reconstructed the following scenario.

A young, naive woman student, whom I call Angela (pseudonym), accepted a ride home from school from a male friend, Michael. On the way, he stopped at the house he shares with members of the St. Johns lacrosse team to get gas money and invited her inside. At first she refused to go in but upon his insistence accepted the invitation. Inside she met his roommates. Left alone in the third floor bedroom, she accepted a drink from Michael.

> The drink tasted terrible. It was bitter and stung her throat. When she asked what was in it, Michael said he put a little vodka in it. When she explained that she never drank, because drinking made her sick, Michael didn't listen. Then she tried to tell him that she hadn't eaten anything since lunch, but, this did not move him. "Vodka is a before dinner drink," he explained, insisting that she drink it.
>
> Finally, she gave into his pressure and downed the contents of the first cup in a few gulps because of the bitter taste. When she finished, Michael went over to the refrigerator and brought back a large container, which he said was orange soda with vodka. He placed the container on the floor beside her feet. When Michael poured another cup, she told him,

> "But Michael, I couldn't finish the first one. I don't think I will be able to finish another." Michael said again: "It's only vodka. It can't do anything to you, Angela." He also said, "You know, Angela, in college everyone does something, something wild they can look back on."
>
> "Something wild?" Angela asked quizzically.
>
> "Something wild," Michael said again. "Something you can look back on and talk about later in life." With the beer can that he was holding in his hand but never drank from, he hit her cup and said, "Here's to college life."
>
> Later, Angela blamed herself for accepting the drinks from Michael. She was caught between wanting to please the host and wanting to assert her own needs. She had tried to please him by finishing the first drink. Now, she drank the second.
>
> Then, he poured a third drink. When she balked at drinking this one, he started getting upset and annoyed. He told her it was a special drink, made just for her. He accused her of making him waste it. He started pushing the drink up to her mouth. He put his hands over the cup and pushed it to her lips. He said, "Oh Angela, don't make me waste it. It's only vodka. A little vodka can't do anything to you."
>
> By now, Angela felt dizzy and her hands were shaking. She felt lost, unable to move. She had spent a lifetime doing what she was told to avoid being punished. Here was Michael upset with her because she didn't want the drink he had made for her. She thought to herself, "If he wants me to drink it, I'll drink it for him." After she drank most of the third cup, Michael went to put the container back. Her head was spinning and she began to feel really sick, like she was going to vomit. She tried to tell Michael that she was sick, but he didn't seem interested in how she was feeling.
>
> Michael sat next to her and massaged her shoulder. She would never forget his pseudo-seductive voice. She hardly knew him, and here he was talking to her like he really cared for her. It was so obviously a put on, she was shocked by the insincerity. He kept telling her, "You need to relax. You are too tense. If you relax, you will feel better." She tried to get up but she was too weak and she fell back down (Sanday 1996:11–12).

Testimony in the case revealed that after Angela passed out from Michael's drinks, three house members stood on the landing and watched as Michael engaged in oral sodomy. After Michael left the house, these three took their turns while visitors invited over from another lacrosse team house watched. At the trial these visitors testified that they left the room when Angela woke up and started screaming. One of the lead prosecutors speculated that they left because they realized only then that she was not consenting. They did not understand that the law applies to using drugs and alcohol as it does to using force.

CROSS-CAMPUS VARIATION IN RAPE AND SEXUAL COERCION

In his paper, Boeringer reports that 55.7% of the males in his study at a large southeastern university obtained sex by verbal harassment (i.e., "threatening to end a relationship unless the victim consents to sex, falsely professing love, or telling the victim lies to render her more sexually receptive," the variable labelled Coercion). One-quarter of the males in Boeringer's study reported using drugs or alcohol to obtain sex (Drugs/Alcohol) and 8.6% of the sample reported at least one use of force or threatened force to obtain sex (Rape).

Schwartz and Nogrady found a much lower incidence of sexual coercion and assault at their research site, a large midwestern university. These authors (private communication) reported that 18.1% of the 116 males in their sample reported some form of unwanted sex: sex by pressure (6.9%); forced sex play/attempted rape (5.2%); or completed rape (6.0%). Of the 177 women interviewed 58.6% reported some form of unwanted sex; sex by pressure (24.1%); forced sex play/attempted rape (14.4%); and completed rape (20.1%).

The effect of fraternities is quite different on the two campuses. Boeringer found that fraternity men reported a higher overall use of coercion short of physical force to obtain sex. According to Boeringer, "fraternity members engage in significantly greater levels of sexual assault through drugging or intoxicating women to render them incapable of consent or refusal" (p. 9). Fraternity members are also more likely than independents to use "nonassaultative sexual coercion," or verbal pressure. "While not criminal in nature," Boeringer points out, "these verbally coercive tactics are nonetheless disturbing in that they suggest a more adversarial view of sexuality in which one should use deceit and guile to 'win favors' from a woman" (p. 10). From his study, Boeringer concludes that "fraternity members are disproportionately involved in some forms of campus sexual aggression." Like the prosecutor in the St. John's case mentioned above, he suggests that in all likelihood the process of "working a yes out" which I describe (Sanday 1990:113) is viewed by fraternity members as a "safer path to gaining sexual access to a reluctant, non-consenting woman than use of physical force" (p. 12).

Schwartz and Nogrady find no effect of fraternity membership. The most important predictor of sexual victimization in their study involves alcohol. It is not drinking per se that they found important, but whether or not a male perceives that his friends approve of getting a woman drunk for the purpose of having sex (the APPROVE variable). Also important is whether a male reports that he has friends that actually engage in this behavior (the GETDRUNK variable). The drinking variable that is the most influential in predicting a man's reported sexual assault is the intensity of his drinking, that is the number of drinks he consumes when he goes out drinking (DRINKS). Thus, the authors conclude that "the level of the perceived male peer support system for exploiting women through alcohol, plus the amount of alcohol actually consumed by men when they drink, are the primary predictors of whether they will report themselves as sexual victimizers of women."

The differences reported by Boeringer and Schwartz and Nogrady suggest not only that fraternities vary with respect to rape-prone behaviors but also that campuses vary with respect to overall rates of sexual assault. The latter result suggests that we need to look at cross-campus variation as well as at intra-campus variation. There are several problems that need to be addressed before either intra- or cross-campus variation can be established. First, in studying intra-campus variation we must be careful in reaching conclusions about the effect of such factors as drinking intensity or fraternity membership because the dependent variable is frequently lifetime prevalence rates rather than incidence in the past year.

Regarding cross-campus variation, there is the problem of comparability of studies. Boeringer (private communication), for example, measures prevalence rates in his study, while Schwartz and Nogrady (private communication) measure incidence. Since incidence rates are always lower, we cannot conclude that the campuses studied by these authors are that much different. Additionally, as noted by Schwartz and Nogrady as well as by Koss (1993), victimization rates from one study to another may not be comparable because of different methodologies, definitions, questions, and sampling procedures.

Nevertheless, some trends can be noticed. The available evidence against variation is seen in the fact that Koss's 15% completed rape prevalence rate in the national study of 32 campuses is replicated by other studies of college students on particular campuses. Koss and Cook (1993:109) note, for example, that estimates of completed rape frequency in the 12% range have been reported for two campuses and estimates "as high or higher than 12% for unwanted intercourse have been reported in more than 10 additional studies lacking representative sampling methods." According to these authors "there are no studies that have reported substantially lower or higher rates of rape among college students."

Evidence for variation comes from Koss's analysis of the relationship of prevalence rates to the institutional parameters used to design the sample (Koss 1988:11–12). She found that rates varied by region and by governance of the institution. Rates were twice as high at private colleges and major universities (14% and 17% respectively) than they were at religiously affiliated institutions (7%).

Ethnicity of the respondent (but, interestingly not the respondent's family income) was also associated with prevalence rates. More white women (16%) reported victimization than did Hispanic (12%), Black (10%), or Asian women (7%). These figures were almost reversed for men. Rape was reported by 4% of white men, 10% of black men, 7% of Hispanic men, and 2% of Asian men. Prevalence rates reported by men also differed by region of the country. More men in the Southeast region (6%) admitted to raping compared with men in the Plains states (3%) and those in the West (2%) (Koss 1988:12).

Intriguing evidence for cross-campus variation in rape rates and related variables comes from Koss's national study of 32 campuses. Using Koss's data I looked at prevalence and incidence rates for each of 30 campuses in her study (2 campuses were excluded because of the amount of missing information.) The results show a wide discrepancy when campuses are compared. For example the campus percentages of males admitting that they have used alcohol or force to obtain sex (Koss's 1988:11 rape variable) range from 0% to 10%. Campus percentages of males who admit to perpetrating unwanted sex in the past year (as opposed to since the age of 14) range from 6% to 22%. The latter percentages are higher because I computed them using all the sexual experience questions (excluding the two authority questions). Since the latter percentages are based on a question that measures incidence ("How many times in the past school year?") the results provide a measure of an dependent variable that can be compared with drinking intensity.

The Koss survey includes two questions that might be taken as measures of drinking intensity. Both questions are asked in such a fashion as to measure drinking intensity in the past year. One asks "How often do you drink to the point of intoxication or drunkenness?"; the other asks "On a typical drinking occasion, how much do you usually drink?" The campus percentages of males checking the most extreme categories of the first question (1–2 or more times a week) ranges from 1% to 24%. The campus percentages of males checking the most extreme categories of the second question (more than 5 or 6 cans of beer or other alcoholic beverages) ranges from 6% to 71%. Since all studies—Schwartz, Boeringer, Koss and Gaines (1993)—are unanimous on the effect of drinking this information, perhaps more than any other, is suggestive of variation in the rape prone nature of campus environments.

THE CONCEPT OF A RAPE-FREE SOCIETY

Assuming that we could identify campuses on which both males and females reported a low incidence of rape and/or unwanted sex, the next question would be whether there is a significant difference in the sexual culture on these campuses compared to the more rape prone campuses. My cross-cultural research which demonstrated differences in the character of heterosexual interaction in rape free as opposed to rape prone societies would suggest that the answer to this question is yes. The outstanding feature of rape-free societies is the ceremonial importance of women and the respect accorded the contribution women make to social continuity, a respect which places men and women in relatively balanced power spheres. Rape-free societies are characterized by sexual equality and the notion that the sexes are complementary. Although the sexes may not perform the same duties or have the same rights or privileges, each is indispensable to the activities of the other.

Since 1981 when this research was published, I spent approximately twenty-four months (extended over a period of fourteen years) doing ethnographic research among the Minangkabau, a rape-free Indonesian society. I chose the Minangkabau because of social factors that conformed with my profile of rape-free societies. The Minangkabau are the largest and most modern matrilineal society in the world today. Women play an undisputed role in Minangkabau symbol system and daily life, especially in the villages. Among the most populous of the ethnic groups of Indonesia, the Minangkabau are not an isolated tribal society in some far off corner of the world. Banks, universities, modern governmental buildings are found in two of the major cities of West Sumatra, the traditional homeland of the Minangkabau people. At the major universities, it is not uncommon to find Minangkabau Ph.D's trained in the U.S. People own cars and travel by bus throughout the province. Most children go to local schools, and many increasingly attend college.

The challenge facing me when I went to West Sumatra was first to find out whether the incidence of rape was low and if so to crack the cultural code that made it so. In the early years there was ample evidence from police reports and from interviews conducted all over the province that this was a rape free society. Ethnographic research conducted in several villages provided confirmation. This research demonstrated that women are the mainstays of village life. The all important family rice fields are inherited through the female line. Husbands live in their wives houses. It is believed that this is the way it should be, because otherwise in the event of a divorce women and children would be left destitute. The main reason given for the matrilineal inheritance of property is that

since women bear the infant and raise the child it is in keeping with the laws of nature to give women control of the ancestral property so that they will have the wherewithal to house and nurture the young.

Missing from the Minangkabau conception of sexuality is any show of interest in sex for the sake of sex alone. Sex is neither a commodity nor a notch in the male belt in this society. A man's sense of himself is not predicated by his sexual functioning. Although aggression is present, it is not linked to sex nor is it deemed a manly trait. The Minangkabau have yet to discover sex as a commodity or turn it into a fetish.

There is a cultural category for rape, which is defined as "forced sex" and is punishable by law. Rape is conceived as something that happens in the wild which places men who rape beyond the pale of society. In answer to my questions regarding the relative absence of rape among them compared to the United States, Minangkabau informants replied that rape was impossible in their society because custom, law, and religion forbade it and punished it severely. In the years that I worked in West Sumatra, I heard of only two cases of rape in the village where I lived. One case involved a group of males who ganged up on a young, retarded woman. In this case the leader of the group hanged himself the next day out of fear of avenging villagers. The rest of the assailants went to jail. The second case involved a local woman and a Japanese soldier during the Japanese occupation of the second world war and after. To this day people remember the case and talk about the horror of the Japanese occupation.

In the past few years, Indonesia's entrance into the global economy has been accompanied by an amazing shift in the eroticization of popular culture seen on TV. In 1995 the signs that this culture was filtering into Minangkabau villages were very evident. To the extent that commodification and eroticization breaks down the cultural supports for its matrilineal social system, the Minangkabau sexual culture will also change. Indeed, today in the provincial capital some argue that the Minangkabau are not rape free.

During my last field trip in 1995, I heard of many more reports of rape in the provincial capital. In the early 1990's, for example, there was a widely publicized acquaintance gang rape of a young woman by a group of boys. Interviewing court officers in the capital, I was told that this was the only case of its kind. Compared with similar cases in the U.S., such as the St. Johns case, the outcome was still very different. While the St. Johns defendants were either acquitted or got probation after pleading guilty, all the defendants in the Sumatran case were convicted and sent to jail. But, one may well ask whether the criminal justice system will continue to convict defendants as tolerance for sexual coercion begins to permeate popular beliefs.

RAPE-FREE CAMPUS CULTURES

A rape-free campus is relatively easy to imagine, but hard to find. Based on anecdotal information one candidate comes to mind. On this campus everyone, administrators, faculty, and students are on a first-name basis, which makes the atmosphere more egalitarian than most campuses. Decision making is by consensus and interpersonal interaction is guided by an ethic of respect for the individual. Those who are disrespectful of others are ostracized as campus life is motivated by a strong sense of community and the common good. No one group (such as fraternities, males, or athletes) dominates the social scene. Sexual assault is a serious offense treated with suspension or expulsion. Homophobic, racist, and sexist attitudes are virtually nonexistent. Individuals bond together in groups not to turn against others but because they are drawn together by mutual interests. Interviews suggest that the incidence of unwanted sex on this campus is low, however this must be corroborated by a campus-wide survey.

For information on a rape free fraternity culture I turn to a description offered by a student who wrote a mini-ethnography on his fraternity for a class project. Corroboration of his description was offered by another brother in the same fraternity who read the ethnography and added additional information. In the following, the fraternity is referred to by the pseudonym QRS. With their permission, the fraternity brothers are identified by name.

Noel Morrison and Josh Marcus recognize that fraternities on their campus (called U.) "propagate sexist attitudes and provide a breeding ground for insecure acts of sexism, racism, and homophobia." According to Noel, U.'s fraternities "tend to be self-segregating entities which seek to maintain the inferior social position of women and minority students through exclusion" and social intolerance. QRS, however, consciously fights against this norm.

QRS is one of the oldest fraternities at U., going back at least 100 years. It was like all other fraternities at U. until 1977 when it was almost forced to disband due to insufficient numbers. At that time, a group of nine first year males pledged as a group knowing that their numbers would give them control of house decisions. They exercised this control by rewriting the house constitution and initiation rituals. Today the brothers are proud to say that they are "not a real fraternity." Interestingly, although both Joel and Noel treasure their lives in QRS (because of the fun, companionship of respected friends, and community the house offers), both feel that fraternities should be abolished.

Partly as a defense mechanism and partly to underscore their difference, QRS brothers stigmatize members of other fraternities as "jarheads." The word "jarhead" is used to refer to the "loud, obnoxious, sexist, racist, homophobic" members of U.'s fraternities. Most of the brothers in QRS do not participate in the campus inter-fraternity council and prefer to see themselves as "a group of friends," rather than as a fraternity, and their house as "a place to have concerts." Parties are always open to anyone and are either free to everyone or everyone pays, contrary to parties at other houses in which men pay and women are admitted for free.

At QRS heavy drinking is not a requisite for membership and is not a part of initiation. There are no drinking games and binge drinking does not occur. While some brothers drink to get drunk more than once a week, most don't. At parties there are always brothers who watch out for women or house members who have had too much to drink. Josh stressed that "it is clearly not acceptable for someone to take advantage of a drunk woman, because that's rape." There is no talk in the house about getting a girl drunk to have sex, he says. Members are very aware that where there is heavy drinking someone can be taken advantage of. If a female passes out or is very drunk she is watched or escorted home. Both Josh and Noel remember an incident during a party in the fraternity next door, in which several members of QRS came to the aid of a young woman whose shirt was above her waist and who had passed out on their porch, left there perhaps by friends from the party who had deserted her. Their intervention may have saved her life. When they were unable to get her to talk, they took her to the emergency room of a nearby hospital only to learn that she was in a coma and her heart had stopped. Fortunately, they were in time and she responded to treatment.

Women are not seen as sex objects in the house, but as friends. Unlike other fraternities at U., there is no distinction drawn between "girlfriends" and friends and there are no "party girls." Noel says that when he was rushing he would often hear women referred to as "sluts" in other fraternities. However, at QRS this is unheard of. According to Josh, a brother who acted "inappropriately" with a woman would be severely reprimanded, perhaps even expelled from the fraternity. The brothers are not afraid of strong women. There are women's studies students who are regulars at the house, along with outspoken feminists and activists. Noel quotes one of them:

> I guess there's a few brothers who make sexist jokes, but I don't know how seriously people take them. I remember last year in the middle of midterms I was studying late at night and was feeling sick and tired, and in a span of about five minutes, four people offered their beds to me, not as a sexual thing at all, but just because they cared.

One QRS brother started the Men's Association for Change and Openness (MAChO) and is an active participant in U's student peer-counseling group for sexual health. One brother displays a "Refuse and Resist" sticker on his door, proclaiming, "Date rape: cut it out or cut it off." In a 1993 pamphlet advertising QRS as the site of the National Anarchist gathering, the brothers wrote "Although QRS is a frat, it is generally a friendly place, along with being a safe haven for women."

Most interesting about QRS is its acceptance of homosexuality, and bisexuality. Homophobia does not become the basis for males to prove their virility to one another. Because of its openness about sex and acceptance of homosexuality, QRS has earned the reputation on campus of being "the gay frat" or "faggot house." Josh comments on this reputation and what it means to him:

> QRS's attitudes about homosexuality are complex, but fundamentally tolerant and respectful. Some brothers revel in rumors that we are the "gay frat." It is rumored that a few years ago a few of the brothers were involved sexually, and one of our most involved alumni is homosexual.

Although most fraternities have had or have a few homosexual brothers, this honest acceptance of homosexuality is unusual. QRS brothers are proud of being called the "gay frat." Evidence of this is the humorous statement in the letters given prospective pledges offering bids, which ends with the phrase "we are all gay."

CONCLUSION

The first step in the struggle against "hidden rape," which began in the late sixties with consciousness raising groups (see Sanday 1996, Chapter 8) was to recognize the problem and speak out against it. The next step was to change outmoded rape laws and assess the causes and frequency of sexual violence against women. Mary Koss's national survey of 1985 demonstrated that one-in-four women will experience rape or attempted rape in her lifetime. Since the eighties many other surveys have replicated her findings. The search for causes has been the subject of numerous studies, including those represented in this volume.

The next step is to go beyond the causes and study solutions. One approach would be to find naturally occurring rape free environments on today's college campuses. QRS is one example. No rape-free campuses have been identified by research, yet I have heard descriptions from students that lead me to believe that such campuses exist. Identifying such campuses and seeking out environments like QRS is the next step for research. In this paper I have identified the kinds of problems such research must address. First, it is necessary to obtain incidence as well as prevalence data. Secondly, we need more subtle measures of the kinds of socio-cultural correlates that have been discussed in this paper: drinking intensity; using pornography to learn about sex rather than talking with one's partner; bragging about sexual conquests; setting women up to display one's masculinity to other men; heterosexism; homophobia; and using pornography as a guide to female sexuality. Finally, we need to develop a consensus on the criteria for labelling a campus either rape free or rape prone. If at least one-in-five women on a given campus say they have experienced unwanted sex in the last year, I would label the campus rape prone. However, others may want to propose different criteria. Once a consensus is reached, the movement to make our campuses safe for women might include identifying rape-free and rape-prone campuses.

NOTE

This article has benefited from the comments of Mary P. Koss. I am also grateful to Koss for supplying me with the data on her 1986 study of 32 campuses. Martin D. Schwartz and Scot B. Boerginer graciously supplied me with additional data from their studies and answered my many questions. Noel Morrison played an important role by giving me permission to summarize his description of his fraternity. John Marcus, a brother in the same fraternity, was also helpful in corroborating Noel's observations and supplying a few of his own.

REFERENCES

Brownmiller, S. (1975). *Against Our Will: Men Women and Rape.* New York: Simon and Schuster.

Koss, M. P. (1988). Hidden Rape: Sexual Aggression and Victimization in a National Sample of Students in Higher Education. In A. W. Burgess (ed.), *Rape and Sexual Assault II* (pp. 3–25). New York: Garland.

Koss, M. P. (1993). *Rape: Scope, Impact, Interventions, and Public Policy Responses.* American Psychologist. October 1062–1069.

Koss, M. P. & S. L. Cook. (1993). Facing the Facts: Date and Acquaintance Rape Are Significant Problems for Women. In R. J. Gelles and D. R. Loseke (eds.), *Current Controversies on Family Violence* (104–119). Newbury Park, CA: Sage.

Koss, M. P. & Gaines, J. A. (1993). "The Prediction of Sexual Aggression by Alcohol Use, Athletic Participation, and Fraternity Affiliation," *Journal of Interpersonal Violence* 8, 94–108.

Sanday, P. R. (1981). "The Socio-Cultural Context of Rape: A Cross-Cultural Study," *Journal of Social Issues,* 37, 5–27.

Sanday, P. R. (1990). *Fraternity Gang Rape: Sex, Brotherhood and Privilege on Campus.* New York: New York University Press.

Sanday, P. R. (1996). *A Woman Scorned: Acquaintance Rape on Trial.* New York: Doubleday.

CHAPTER TEN

SEX EDUCATION AND SEXUAL HEALTH

No book about sexuality would be complete without a discussion of sexual health issues and sex education. But even these topics are fraught with danger. As Judith Levine points out in her controversial book *Harmful to Minors,* the very act of teaching children about human sexuality is considered "harmful" to them. Most school curricula cannot teach about sex under the mistaken notion that the more you know, the more you will do. (There is no evidence for this; in fact, rates of sexual activity decline slightly among those who have comprehensive sex education in school.) What Levine demonstrates so convincingly is that the harm—unwanted pregnancies, higher rates of STDs—comes from shielding children from sexual information, not exposing them to it.

The other essays in this section explore varieties of sex education. Peggy Kleinplatz examines educational videos and finds that they are conveying far more than simply information about birds and bees. Rebecca Plante's essay follows a peer-sexuality education program as it attempts to encourage certain sexual expressions and discourage others. Richard Parker reviews how AIDS has been interpreted around the world.

10.1 NO-SEX EDUCATION
From "Chastity" to "Abstinence"

Judith Levine

There is mainstream sex ed and there is right-wing sex ed. But there is no left-wing sex education in America. Everyone calls themselves "abstinence educators." Everyone.

—Leslie Kantor, education director, Sex Information and Education Council of America (1997)

In 1981, the freshman Alabama Republican Senator, a Baptist with the apocalyptic given name of Jeremiah, came up with a way to wrestle down teen pregnancy at the same time as vanquishing what he believed were twin moral scourges: teen sex and abortion. In place of several successful national programs that provided birth-control services and counseling to young women, Jeremiah Denton's Adolescent Family Life Act (AFLA) proposed to stop teen sex by deploying nothing more than propaganda. AFLA would fund school and community programs "to promote self-discipline and other prudent approaches" to adolescent sex. Opponents quickly dubbed his innovation chastity education.

At first, the press and the public reactions were bemused. "Amazing," commented Zonker in Garry Trudeau's "Doonesbury," as he and Mike Doonesbury sat on their front porch on the comics pages, contemplating what the chastity bill might mean. ID checks outside Brooke Shields movies? Government-sponsored sound trucks cruising around on Saturday nights blaring *Cut that out!?* "Wow," said Zonker, stupefied by the thought.

But when Orrin Hatch, the powerful Utah Republican chair of the Labor and Human Resources Committee, signed on as AFLA's cosponsor, the bill suddenly gained gravitas. "This benighted piece of legislation is called the 'chastity law,' but it is no joke," said a *New York Times* editorial condemning the bill at the time.[1]

No joke indeed. AFLA was the first federal law specifically written to fund sex education, and it is still on the books. It has not yet accomplished its ambitious goals of eradicating teen sex, teen pregnancy, and abortion in one swipe. But for a triumphal New Right recently installed in Washington, under its imperial president, Ronald Reagan, the new law was a major victory. For young people's sexual autonomy and safety, though, it was a great blow—the first of a pummeling that has not yet ceased.

Over the next two decades, large, well-funded national conservative organizations with a loyal infantry of volunteers marched through school district after school district, firing at teachers and programs that informed students about their bodies and their sexual feelings, about contraception and abortion. These attacks met with only spotty resistance. Sex ed was a political backwater to begin with; hardly anyone paid attention to it. Unlike its opponents, sex ed's champions had a couple of national organizations but no national movement, no coherent cultural-political agenda. As the sociologist Janice Irvine points out, neither feminists nor the political Left rallied to the cause; gays and lesbians joined the fray only in the 1990s, when attacks began to focus more directly and hostilely on them. The most progressive and politically savvy sex educators were working outside the public schools, so they had limited say in public policy and little direct effect on the majority of kids. At the grass roots, the visible forces against sex ed were usually minuscule, often one or two ferocious parents and their pastor. But local defenses were feebler, and the already

puny garrisons of comprehensive sexuality education began to fall.

Twenty years later, the Right has all but won the sex-education wars. In 1997, the U.S. Congress committed a quarter billion dollars over five years' time to finance more education in chastity, whose name had been replaced by the less churchy, more twelve-steppish *abstinence*.[2] As part of the omnibus "welfare reform bill," the government's Maternal and Child Health Bureau extended grants to the states for programs whose "exclusive purpose [is] teaching the social, psychological, and health gains to be realized by abstaining from sexual activity." In a country where only one in ten school-children receives more than forty hours of sex ed in any year,[3] the regulations prohibit funded organizations from instructing kids about contraception or condoms except in terms of their failures. In a country where 90 percent of adults have sex before marriage and as many as 10 percent are gay or lesbian, the law underwrites one message and one message only: that "a mutually faithful monogamous relationship in the context of marriage is the expected standard of human sexual activity." Nonmarital sex, educators are required to tell children, "is likely to have harmful psychological and physical effects."[4]

At first, there was a flurry of opposition to the welfare regulations. But every state eventually took the money. In many states, the dollars went largely to curriculum developers outside schools. But over the decade, right-wing propaganda and political action had been pushing public-school sex ed steadily toward chastity. Now that push was compounded by the financial pull from Washington, and the process lurched forward. By 1999, fully a third of public school districts were using abstinence-only curricula in their classrooms.[5] Of a nationwide sample of sex-ed instructors surveyed by the Alan Guttmacher Institute, 41 percent cited abstinence as the most important message they wanted to convey to their students, compared with 25 percent in 1988. In the same dozen years the number of sex-ed teachers who talked exclusively about abstinence in their classes rose elevenfold, to nearly 25 percent from only 2 percent. The study's findings suggested "steep declines . . . in teacher support for coverage of many topics including birth control, abortion, information on obtaining contraceptive and STD services, and sexual orientation," commented one report. "Moreover, the proportion of teachers actually addressing these topics also declined."[6]

Today, the embrace of abstinence appears nearly unanimous. The only thing left to debate is whether abstinence is the *only* thing to teach. The Planned Parenthood Federation, for decades the Right's designated agent of Satan on earth, almost immediately rolled into bed with the abstinence mongers; only a few courageous chapters, such as Greater Northern New Jersey and New York City, buck the tide. Although it has been America's flagship advocate and a valiant defender of comprehensive sexuality education since 1964, the Sex Information and Education Council of the United States also publicly pledged allegiance to abstinence. "SIECUS supports abstinence. I repeat: SIECUS supports abstinence," began a typical mid-1990s speech by then-president Debra Haffner. "But SIECUS does not support teaching young people only about abstinence." Even Advocates for Youth, perhaps the single most progressive independent sexuality educator and sex-ed proponent in the country (in 1997 it told states to reject the welfare money "four-square"), now touts abstinence along with the more liberal messages in its publications. Today comprehensive sexuality education calls itself abstinence-plus education, to distinguish itself from abstinence-only.

Parents, when asked, overwhelmingly rise in favor of sexuality education covering a wide variety of topics, including contraception and even abortion and sexual orientation.[7] But, no doubt motivated by fear of AIDS, they like abstinence too. Of a national sample of parents surveyed in 2000 by the Kaiser Family Foundation, 98 percent put HIV/AIDS prevention on the list of desired topics to be taught in school, with abstinence following close behind, at 97 percent.

The idea that sex is a normative—and, heaven forfend, positive—part of adolescent life is unutterable in America's public forum. "There is mainstream sex ed and there is right-wing sex ed," said Leslie Kantor in 1997, when she was traveling the nation in her work for SIECUS. "But there is no left-wing sex education in America." She included her own organization in that characterization. Just fifteen years after Joyce Purnick's newspaper denounced the idea of chastity as antediluvian, the *New York Times* columnist felt compelled to insert a caveat into her critique of the new abstinence-only regulations. "Obviously," she began, "nobody from the Christian right to the liberal left objects to . . . encouraging sexual abstinence."[8]

There are two problems with this consensus. First, around the globe, most people begin to engage in sexual intercourse or its equivalent homosexual intimacies during their teen years. And second, there is no evidence that lessons in abstinence, either alone or accompanied by a fuller complement of sexuality and health information, actually hold teens off from sexual intercourse for more than a matter of months.

On the one hand, it seems obvious that American adults would preach to children not to have sex. The majority of them always have. But the logic that it is necessary and good to offer abstinence as one of several sexual "options"—the rationale given by the abstinencepius (formerly comprehensive) educators—is more apparent than real. When asked a few years ago why her new curriculum's title has prominently featured the word *abstinence*, a progressive sex educator (who has herself worked to build a dike against the deluge abstinence ed) said, "Because it is one way teens can choose to deal with sex." Her interlocutor, a saber-tongued sex therapist replied. "Right. So's suicide." Abstinence education is not practical. It is ideological.

NO SEX, PLEASE. WE'RE SEX EDUCATORS

Of course Orrin Hatch and Jeremiah Denton did not invent sex education as an instrument of sex prevention. Throughout history, wrote Patricia Campbell in a historical survey of sex-education texts, "whether the tone is pompous or jazzy, the intent is always to teach young people] the currently approved sexual behavior for their age group."[9] And the currently approved sexual behavior for any child's age group in almost any era has been no sexual behavior at all.

"[Sex instruction] should emphasize the perils of illicit coitus, moral and physical, without which . . . the instruction would be likely to have little deterrent effect," wrote one of the "progressive" fathers of the sex instruction in 1906, laying out the goals of his discipline.[10] By 1922, when the federal government undertook to publish its own sex-ed guide, *High Schools and Sex Education,* it practically eliminated sexuality from the courses altogether. Its accompanying medical examination forms, for instance, presumably employed to elicit some intelligence about the students' sex lives, steered clear of the subject and probed instead for such crucial information as "Do you masticate thoroughly?"[11] Evelyn Duvall's 1950s megaseller, *Facts of Life and Love for Teenagers,* rehearsed the stifling protocols of approved teen social behavior for decades to come in more detail: "When they reach the box office, Mary steps back and looks at the display cards while John buys the tickets." But life and love for teenagers meant "dating," which emphatically did not mean sex. At the end of the evening, Mary "is careful not to linger at the door."[12]

The founder of modern progressive sex education, Dr. Mary S. Calderone pulled back from saying "no" but persisted in saying "wait." Addressing Vassar College's all-female class of 1964, Calderone president of Planned Parenthood, world-renowned birth-control advocate, and soon-to-be charter president of SIECUS, neither moralized nor trafficked in fear. Yet she promised a youthful freedom and adult satisfaction that could be gained only by eschewing premarital sex. Hold off now, she told the students, and you will have "time . . . to grow up into the woman you were meant to be." The rigors of self-restraint would be repaid in more emotionally and sexually rewarding marriages, she said.[13]

Although her counsel seems moderate now, Calderone and her fellow sex-education advocates suffered bloodthirsty attacks from the Right, who smeared them with McCarthyist and anti-Semitic innuendo and implicated them in undermining the American way of life itself. "The struggle continues between those who believe in parental responsibility and those who seek to seize control of the thinking of America's youth," declared the deep-voiced narrator of an anti-sex-education filmstrip produced by the John Birch Society. "The future of your children and your nation is at stake."[14]

Calderone's disciples, who would become the founding generation of modern progressive and mainstream sex educators, were the first to hint that sex, if not always approved, was nonetheless normative teen behavior. A few were unabashed child-sexual liberationists. "Sex is a natural appetite. If you're old enough to want to have sex, you're old enough to have it," proclaimed Heidi Handman and Peter Brennan, in their 1974 *Sex Handbook: Information and Help for Minors.*[15] Psychologist Sol Gordon produced a stack of books that were not as radical as Handman and Brennan's but also respected young people's ability to make their own decisions. In *You* (1975), Gordon answered the perennial question "Are you ready [for sex]?" with more queries: "Are you mature? Are you in love? Are you using birth control?"[16]

Reading these books, one is struck by the total absence of the word *abstinence,* which did not enter the popular lexicon until the early 1980s (a Lexis-Nexis search of all U.S. magazines and newspapers brought up two citations in 1980, both of which were stories about the pope). Mainstream sex ed in the 1970s was still flogging the no-sex message, but books like Gordon's also represented an important strain of liberalism regarding child sexuality.

CHASTITY

Indeed, the 1970s were a banner decade for youthful sexual autonomy, not only in the streets and rock clubs, but also in schools, clinics, and the highest courts of the land. Following *Roe v. Wade* (1973), liberals and feminists won a steady series of court cases guaranteeing poor and teenage women's rights to birth control information and services, and Washington and the states responded by establishing major programs to provide them.[17] This proliferation of clinics reporting to the government had an unexpected result, noted by the public-health historian Constance Nathanson: suddenly, there were mountains of data on teen sex, contraception, and pregnancy and its termination—information previously available only about the poor. The liberal family-planning establishment thought it could deploy the new data to gain support for its cause. So did the Right.

Then in 1976, some statistics dripping with propaganda potential arrived. The pro-family-planning Alan Guttmacher Institute released *Eleven Million Teenagers,* a report announcing a national "epidemic" of teen pregnancy. "Unwanted pregnancy is happening to our young women, not only among the poor and minority groups, but in all socioeconomic groups," the institute's president told Congress. "If I had a daughter, I would say [it was happening] to 'our' daughters."[18]

This was not accurate.[19] First of all, unwanted pregnancy, for the most part, was not happening to the daughters of demographers, doctors, and Washington bureaucrats. Now as then, more than 80 percent of America's teen mothers come from poor households.[20] And even among these young women, there was no epidemic. Eleven million referred to the number of people under eighteen who had had intercourse at least once. Teen pregnancies actually numbered fewer than a million a year, and of those teen mothers, six in ten were legal adults, eighteen or nineteen years old.[21] Yes, unmarried teens were having more sex in the 1970s than they'd had in the decades before.[22] But teen motherhood had hit its twentieth-century zenith in the mid-1950s, when one in ten girls between fifteen and nineteen years of age gave birth. Since then, the rate has steadily dropped.[23]

Still, the idea of the teen-pregnancy epidemic focused public anxiety about teenage girls' newly unfettered sex lives. Politically, it served both liberals and conservatives—the former arguing for reproductive health services and education for sexually active youths, the latter trying to rein in the services, the education, and most definitely the sex.

The 1980 national elections gave conservatives their chance. Voters returned Republican control to the Senate, a Democratic stronghold for the previous twenty-eight years, and installed Ronald Reagan in the Oval Office. The new president appointed to every office related to sex education, contraception, or abortion someone who opposed all of the above.[24] "These people provided for the anti-abortion movement a forum in government that it had never had," said Susan Cohen, now a senior policy analyst at the Guttmacher Institute. For the reproductive-rights movement, added Bill Hamilton, then lobbying for the Planned Parenthood Federation, the 1980 elections

were "a cataclysmic setback." For comprehensive sex education, it was the beginning of the end.

A few months into the 97th Congress, Orrin Hatch honored the president's request to demolish Title X of the Public Health Services Act of 1970, which provided contraceptive services to poor and young women. What Hatch planned to do was reduce the program's appropriation by a quarter and repackage the whole thing into block grants to the states. Bundled in with rodent control and water fluoridation and without a mandate that the legislatures commit any money to reproductive services, Title X might well cease to serve its reproductive-services mandate.[25]

Meanwhile, down the hall, the anti-abortion zealot Jeremiah Denton was chairing the subcommittee on human services of Hatch's Labor and Human Resources Committee and contemplating his role in history. With the help of some friends, including Catholic birth-control advocate Eunice Shriver, sister of Ted Kennedy, he arrived at S. 1090, the Adolescent Family Life Act. Soon, Hatch was on board, too.

AFLA was a trident: One prong promoted adoption as the "positive" alternative to unwed motherhood or abortion, although at that time 96 percent of pregnant adolescents were rejecting adoption as a cruel and unnecessary option.[26] Another prong prohibited government funds to any agency whose workers even uttered the word *abortion* to a teenager, much less performed the operation. "Chastity education" was the central, most controversial prong.

But public controversy and press ridicule, from the political cartoons of small city papers to the editorial pages of the *New York Times* and the *Washington Post,* seemed barely to ruffle Capitol Hill's confident new majority. With the National Right to Life and the American Life League barnstorming in the background and the family planners distracted in the rush to save Title X, S. 1090 zipped through the Senate. When it came up during the final budget reconciliation, California Democrat Henry Waxman, chair of the Commerce Committee's subcommittee on public health and Title X's most active defender, was forced to make a trade with Hatch and Denton. Waxman could keep Title X, but only with AFLA tied to it like a string of clattering cans.

"AFLA was the anti-abortion answer to Title X

Family Planning," Judy DeSarno, president and CEO of the National Family Planning and Reproductive Health Association, summed it up seventeen years later. At the time, she added, most of the family-planning community was relieved. Had Title X been lost, millions of poor women would have gotten no reproductive health services at all, she said. "It was unfortunate," added Cohen of the Guttmacher Institute, "but the important thing is that the real preventive program has been able to survive over the last decade-plus, and AFLA has not really hurt that program."

Others disagreed strongly with the assessment that AFLA was doing little harm. Among the detractors were the lawyers at the American Civil Liberties Union's Reproductive Freedom Project, who believed that while the legislation might not hurt Title X, it would hurt sex education—and the First Amendment. In 1983, in *Kendrick v. Bowen,* they argued that the sex-education portion of the law was a Trojan horse smuggling the values of the Christian Right, particularly its unbending opposition to abortion, to public-school children at public expense. AFLA, they said, was a violation of the constitutional separation of church and state.[27]

The Supreme Court finally decided, ten years later, that AFLA was constitutional as written—"facially"—but that in practice the government was indeed promoting certain religions and discriminating against others. The bench appointed the ACLU to monitor the law's administration, which it unofficially had been doing throughout the litigation.

But, many now believe, it was too late. Some of the biggest federal grant recipients, including Sex Respect and Teen-Aid, had already turned their taxpayer-funded church-developed anti-sex-education curricula into big for-profit businesses. Respect Inc., which received more than $1.6 million in federal and state grants during the 1980s,[28] claimed in the early 1990s that its curricula were in use in one-quarter of American school districts.[29] Teen-Aid, which received AFLA grants amounting to $784,683 between 1987 and 1991,[30] became one of the major publishers of abstinence-only programs, which teach little more than "just say no."

This bankrolling—and the substitution of federal funds for contraception with dollars for chastity—was anything but surreptitious. AFLA "was written expressly for the purpose of diverting [federal] money that would otherwise go to Planned Parenthood into groups with traditional values," a *Conservative Digest* writer reported. "That noble purpose has certainly been fulfilled here. If it hadn't been for the seed money provided by the government, 'Sex Respect' might still be just an idea sitting in a graduate student's thesis."[31] Said former SIECUS spokesman Daniel Daley in 1997, "In those first years of AFLA, this money went directly from the government to Christian fundamentalist groups, who built the infrastructure of the organizations that are the most vehement opponents of comprehensive sexuality education today." Also born during that time was the discourse of teen sex that shapes policy to this day.

"THE PROBLEM OF PREMARITAL ADOLESCENT SEXUAL RELATIONS"

In his July 1981 committee report on S. 1090, Denton quoted the statistics promulgated by the Guttmacher Institute[32] (he was probably unaware the organization was named for one of history's great champions of abortion rights). The senator declared that the government should address the "needs of pregnant adolescents" and proposed a prescription that the entire family-planning profession could applaud: *more prevention.*

But prevention of what? Poverty? Teen pregnancy? Unwed motherhood? Abortion? Denton claimed he could eradicate all of the above by preventing what he saw as the cause of them all: *teen sex.* In what would become the central maneuver in the conservative rhetoric of teen sexuality over the next decades, Denton collapsed four separate events—sex, pregnancy, birth, and abortion—into one "widespread problem." He attributed "serious medical, social, and economic consequences" to all four and then wrapped them into one whopper: *the problem of premarital adolescent sexual relations.*[33]

This "problem" had been exacerbated by a decade of social policy, which he and Hatch summed up in a letter to the *New York Times* as "$1.5 billion of taxpayers' money [spent] on 'family planning.'"[34] Contraception and abortion, they reasoned, had led to teen sex, which led to pregnancy. The logical sleight of hand was impressive: contraception and abortion caused teen pregnancy.

But the real trouble, as the sponsors saw it, was not just adolescent sex. It was sex behind Mom and Dad's back. "The deep pocket of government has funded this intervention between parents and their children in schools and clinics for 10 years," wrote Hatch and Denton. "[I]t is little wonder that problems of adolescent sexual activity grow worse."[35] In other words, clinics that offered confidential services to adolescents, as the Supreme Court had ordered in 1977, were ripping the family apart by promoting children's liberation at the expense of a newly articulated subset of family values, "parental rights."[36] (Later, in conservative parlance, "parents" would become "families," implying a harmonious and cooperative unit without gender or generational conflict.)

For a decade, whether out of grudging realism or genuine support for the rights of young women, policymakers had gone along with the liberal family-planning establishment in regarding minorage clients as independent actors in their own sexual lives. But by the 1980s, with AFLA inscribed as statute and political pressure rising from the Right, a time-tested theme was revived: parents should control all aspects of their kids' sexuality. "I am not opposed to family planning when we are planning families," Denton told the press. "However, unemancipated minors do not plan families."[37]

Family planning had long been a euphemism for contraception, which was a trope for modern, conscious, technologically enhanced sexual activity. To family planners, prevention had meant the prevention of unplanned pregnancy. Now prevention was the prevention of sex, and it would be accomplished not by the Pill but by diatribe and ideology. AFLA installed sex education under the aegis of "family life." And in the ideal family, parents kept their children safe by denying their sexuality and their autonomy, and children could feel safe by accepting the limits of childhood.

"ABSTINENCE" TRIUMPHANT

Sexuality was "family life." And only families—that is, heterosexual married mommies and daddies—

could have sex. In 1996, the man who brought extramarital fellatio and erotic cigar play to prime-time television signed into law a provision that would fiscally ex-communicate sex educators who did not hew to this credo: Section 501(b): Abstinence Education, of the Social Security Act of 1997. To receive money from Washington, states would have to match each federal dollar with two from their own coffers that might otherwise go to more catholic programs. Not only was the federal government encouraging abstinence-only; it was discouraging everything else.

The abstinence-only funding regulations were the platinum standard of conservative ideology about sexuality and the family. And like the AFLA-funded curricula that inspired them, their absoluteness made them easy for most Americans to dislike.[38] So at first, a number of health and education departments balked at using their limited dollars to preach abstinence in schools where half the kids were already having sex, and some already had babies or HIV. Some youth, sex-ed, and reproductive-rights advocates (most vocally Advocates for Youth) extolled their state bureaucracies to turn down the money. But many states already had similar, if not equally restrictive, laws. Of the twenty-three requiring sex education, fewer than half prescribed lessons on contraception, and all mandated instructing on abstinence.[39]

In the end, every state applied for the federal abstinence-only money in the first year, and all but two took it.[40] Five states passed laws requiring that sexuality education programs teach abstinence-only as the standard for school-age children.[41] In 2000, under the sponsorship of Oklahoma archconservative Republican representative Ernest Istook, the language of AFLA was brought into conformity with that of the welfare law, and an additional twenty million dollars were appropriated to fund AFLA's now seamlessly doctrinaire grant making. Organizations such as Advocates for Youth, SIECUS, and the National Coalition Against Censorship began campaigning that year to block the reappropriation of abstinence-only funding in 2001. But with George W. Bush in the White House and few Congress members willing to squander political capital opposing it, the program's healthy survival is almost assured.

In one way, the wide support for abstinence makes sense. Americans are still convinced that teen pregnancy is pandemic, and in a time of sex-borne death, containing the exchange of adolescent body fluids is an attractive notion to parents,[42] educators, and even to kids themselves.

In another way, however, it is senseless, and for the simplest of reasons: Comprehensive, nonabstinence sex education works. And abstinence education does not. In many European countries, where teens have as much sex as in America, sex ed starts in the earliest grades. It is informed by a no-nonsense, even enthusiastic, attitude toward the sexual; it is explicit; and it doesn't teach abstinence. Rates of unwanted teen pregnancy, abortion, and AIDS in every Western European country are a fraction of our own; the average age of first intercourse is about the same as in the United States.[43]

Abstinence programs, on the other hand, do not change students' attitudes for long, and they change behavior hardly a whit. By 1997, six studies had been published in the scientific literature showing that these classes did not accomplish their goal: to get kids to delay intercourse.[44] In one case, male students enrolled in a chastity-only course actually had more sex than those in the control group.[45] Following the implementation of the welfare rules, a study of 659 African American Philadelphia sixth- and seventh-graders, published in the *Journal of the American Medical Association,* returned the same verdict. A year after the classes, the kids who had undergone an abstinence-only program were engaging in intercourse in the same numbers (about a fifth) as kids who had received lessons stressing condom use, with the dangerous difference that the first group hadn't been taught anything about safe sex.[46] "It is difficult to understand the logic behind the decision to earmark funds specifically for abstinence programs," commented *JAMA*'s editors.[47] A consensus statement on AIDS prevention by the National Institutes of Health delivered an even more damning indictment: abstinence-only education was potentially lethal. The "approach places policy in direct conflict with science and ignores overwhelming evidence that other programs would be effective," concluded the group, whose members included many of the country's top

AIDS experts. "[A]bstinence-only programs cannot be justified in the face of effective programs and given the fact that we face an international emergency in the AIDS epidemic."[48]

If it is difficult to understand the logic behind abstinence-only policy, it may be instructive to know that its proponents were proudly unswayed by logic. Although the law's impetus came in part from the continuing concern over nonmarital births, the House staffers who worked on the legislation admitted, in the commentary circulated in Congress, that "there is little evidence . . . that any particular policy or program will reduce the frequency of non-marital births."[49] Now, this is not true: any number of policies, from contraceptive education to college scholarships for women, can reduce the frequency of nonmarital teen births. But the welfare law was not really intended to reduce teen births anyway. It was intended to make a statement: "to put Congress on the side of the social tradition . . . that sex should be confined to married couples." Like missionaries forcing the indigenous people to throw off their own gods and adopt the new dogma whole, the authors expected—indeed, seemed almost to relish—popular resistance to their ideas. "That both the practices and standards in many communities across the country clash with the standard required by the law," they wrote, "is precisely the point."[50]

Comprehensive educators, on the other hand, claim to be guided by reliable data, not ideology, or at least not conservative, antisexual ideology. So what was driving them to adopt abstinence?

Advocates were tired. They were worn down and in some cases financially broken by a decade of furious battering from the organized Christian Right, including hundreds of direct personal threats of divine retribution or its equivalent by human hands. (In one campaign, the conservative Concerned Women for America generated thirty thousand missives to Congress accusing SIECUS of supporting pedophilia and baby killing. "You will burn in the lake of fire," was only one of thousands sent directly to SIECUS president Haffner.) Classroom teachers were under increasing surveillance, which made them more cautious. Some got rid of the anonymous question box into which students used to place embarrassing queries, knowing they'd get straight responses; now, this was too dangerously unpredictable. Some told me their principals advised sending students who asked embarrassing questions that indicated they were sexually active off to the guidance counselor for a tête-à-tête (implying that sex is not only private but also a psychological and social problem). More and more dropped discussion of the controversial subjects, such as abortion, or stopped informing students about where they could get birth control.[51] In 1998 SIECUS published a handbook called *Filling the Gaps: Hard to Teach Topics in Sexuality Education.* The topics included safer sex, condoms, sexual orientation, diversity, pregnancy options, sexual behavior, sex and society, and (incongruously, but presumably because it could not be left off any list) abstinence. The "gaps," in short, were everything but sexual plumbing and disease.

But even those who continued to teach the "gaps" pitched abstinence too, whether they believed it was worthwhile or not. "The fact is, we all have to pay homage to abstinence before we can say anything else. Professionally, it is almost suicidal not to," Leslie Kantor, education vice-president of Planned Parenthood of New York City, told me ruefully. "The vast majority of adolescents in America and across the globe enter into sexual relations during their teen years. This is just a fact, and to talk about anything else is simply wasting time. [Nevertheless,] if you are not seen as a supporter of abstinence . . . you are not likely, if you are a teacher, to keep your job, and if you're from the outside, you won't get in to do any sexuality education at all."

The titles of the comprehensive curricula were white flags spelling out this surrender. "Living Smart: Understanding Sexuality," put out by ETR Associates, the nation's largest mainstream sex-education publisher, became "Sex Can Wait: An Abstinence-Based Sexuality Curriculum for Middle School." Planned Parenthood's 1986 "Positive Images: A New Approach to Contraceptive Education" was born again as "The New Positive Images: Teaching Abstinence, Contraception, and Sexual Health," even though the content is about as scant on abstinence lessons as its predecessor. A pamphlet on birth control education published in 2000 by the National Campaign to Prevent Teen Pregnancy was called *The Next Best Thing.* The title implied that contraception was the next best thing to abstinence, which the campaign had adopted from the start as the optimal defense against unwanted pregnancy. But to a skeptical observer it might signal the campaign's decision to champion the next-best method of sex education, because the best had become politically untenable.

Discouragement and realpolitik—these motivated the gradual retreat of the comprehensive sex educators. But there might have been something else operating, if not on the organizational level, then on the personal. By the 1990s, the sexual revolutionaries were parents, and, especially with AIDS in the picture, they were getting scared for their kids. "It's precisely because many of us experimented with sex at an early age that we know how problematic it can be," wrote New Mexico physician Victor Strasburger in the best-selling advice book *Getting Your Kids to Say "No" in the '90s When You Said "Yes" in the '60s.* "It's only now, when we are parents ourselves, that we are willing to acknowledge that perhaps we might have made a mistake in beginning to have sexual intercourse at too young an age."[52] He did not elaborate on the "problems" or the effects of that "mistake." Fourteen years after his book *You,* Sol Gordon and his wife, Judith, wrote *Raising a Child Conservatively in a Sexually Permissive World,* which stolidly repudiated their former relativist stance on sexual readiness. "We think that young people should not engage in sexual intercourse until they are at least eighteen and off to college, working or living on their own," they advised.[53] (In the title of a later edition—as new marketing strategy or sign of remorse?—the authors changed the word *conservatively* to *responsibly.*)

Unlike the Gordons' earlier books, *Raising a Child* spoke not to teens themselves but to parents, now the designated guardians of their children's sexual lives. And like Hatch and Denton and the writers of the welfare regulations, these authors were speaking directly to parental fears. Those fears must surely have accounted for the lack of resistance among parents who supported comprehensive sex ed when those few (and it was almost invariably a very few) detractors started showing up at school board meetings. When educators Peter Scales and Martha Roper assayed the sex-ed battlefield in 1996, they discovered that "out of the glare of publicity, most 'opponents' and 'supporters' of sexuality education share many of the same basic values and hopes for children."[54]

They also shared the same anxieties. And progressive sex educators, most of whom were parents as well as professionals, had anxieties too. A joke circulating among them in the mid-1990s told the story:

Q   What's a conservative?
A   A liberal with a teenage daughter.

ABSTINENCE-ONLY: FEAR AND FREEDOM

Here, according to the popular conservative-Christian-authored *Sex Respect,* are a few of the hazards of nonmarital sex:

> Pregnancy, AIDS, guilt, herpes, disappointing parents, chlamydia, inability to concentrate on school, syphilis, embarrassment, abortion, shotgun wedding, gonorrhea, selfishness, pelvic inflammatory disease, heartbreak, infertility, loneliness, cervical cancer, poverty, loss of self-esteem, loss of reputation, being used, suicide, substance abuse, melancholy, loss of faith, possessiveness, diminished ability to communicate, isolation, fewer friendships formed, rebellion against other familial standards, alienation, loss of self-mastery, distrust of [other] sex, viewing others as sex objects, difficulty with long-term commitments, various other sexually transmitted diseases, aggressions toward women, ectopic pregnancy, sexual violence, loss of sense of responsibility toward others, loss of honesty, jealousy, depression, death."[55]

"Sadness, not happiness, causes teen sex," declares a pamphlet published by the same company, and "teen sex causes sadness." The "Safe Sex" program marketed by the politically influential pro-abstinence, antichoice Medical Institute for Sexual Health, or MISH, packs seventy-five full-color slides of diseased genitals.[56] And in the film *No Second Chance* a student asks the school nurse, "What if I want to have sex before I get married?" She answers: "Well, I guess you'll just have to be prepared to die."[57] It is not for nothing that the comprehensive educators call these fear-based programs.

But the writers of the abstinence-only curricula had a credibility problem. Every kid knows that Mom and Dad, if they were like more than 90 percent of baby boomer adults, did it before they tied the knot, that they took the Pill, had abortions, and came through it alive, well, and seemingly unharmed (unless premarital sex caused baldness and a deafness to decent music). To overcome the consumer's skepticism, not only did abstinence educators need to instill in kids a reason to run from the lures of sex; they also had to point them *toward* something worth having. So, believing that teen sex is a form of self-destruction, the abstinence-only people (who are also antichoice activists) ask kids to "choose life," not necessarily their current lives but better lives further down the road. "Our goal should be to instill hope for their futures: future marriages, spouses, and families," read the MISH guidelines (sounding not so different from Mary Calderone addressing the Vassar women).[58]

Thus, in alternately bleak and hearty language, the Christian curricula coach their students to wrestle against desire. It is a match worthy of Saint Augustine himself. "At one time in adolescence I was burning to find satisfaction in hellish pleasures," confessed the tortured supplicant. "If only someone could have imposed restraint on my disorder."[59] Abstinence is not easy, yet the goal is attainable, the abstinence-only educators cheer. And if you don't succeed at first, you get another chance: you can pledge "secondary virginity." If only Augustine had taken "Sex Respect." With that option, he might have finessed his famous dilemma: the yearning to be chaste, but not yet.

Of course, like the young Augustine, the modern teenager isn't usually thinking that far ahead. When neither stick nor carrot does the trick (disease and death seem improbable, and future happiness vague and remote) there has to be a sweeter, more immediate promise held before the students' noses. Chastity's advocates came up with a gold ring that glitters for both kids and parents: "freedom."

"Adolescent sexual abstinence offers the freedom to develop respect for oneself and others, use energy to accomplish life goals, be creative in expressing feelings, develop necessary communication skills, develop self-appreciation, achieve financial stability before having a family, and establish greater trust in marriage," says MISH.[60] In *Sex Respect,* one version is subtitled "The Option of True

Sexual Freedom." And Teen-Aid claims: "Saving sex brings freedom."

The only "freedom" reserved for skepticism in these texts is "reproductive freedom," put between quotes by Teen-Aid's authors, who also note the feminist provenance of the idea and list it among the "myths of premarital sex" that students are encouraged to challenge. ("*Consider:* Who waits anxiously each month for her period? Whose lifestyle is drastically changed?") "Men" are directed to ponder, "Where is the freedom in worrying about getting a girl pregnant?"[61] As is common in abstinence ed, the gender-unequal burdens of sex are acknowledged, but claims to gender equality are dismissed, even denigrated—here, with the implication that feminists are fighting for pie in the sky and that "men" do best honoring their paternalistic obligation to "girls" by respecting their purity.

The idea of freedom, soaring like an aria over the ostinato of sexual peril, was a stroke of marketing brilliance, resonating with a major theme of American history and advertising. Freedom can mean anything from universal suffrage to a choice of twenty-seven flavors of Snapple, and bondage anything from chattel slavery to the discomfort of bulky sanitary pads. But as Aunt Lydia told the women whose lives were consecrated to breeding babies for the ruling classes in Margaret Atwood's dystopic-futurist novel *The Handmaid's Tale,* "There is more than one kind of freedom. Freedom to and freedom from." Referring to the democratic, gender-egalitarian period before the totalitarian theocracy that cannily resembles the one radical Christians might like to create in the United States, Lydia says, "In the days of anarchy, it was freedom to. Now you are being given freedom from. Don't underrate it."[62] The narrator, even as she cowers behind the fear that the aunts' protection has begun to instill in her, longs for the confusing but exhilarating "freedom to."

Like their fictional counterparts, the cleverest marketers of abstinence seem to intuit that teens vacillate between the attractions of the two kinds of freedom. With the popular culture pulling for "freedom to" engage in sex, and their teachers holding out "freedom from" all the sexual and emotional fuss and muss implied in growing up, students are by turns im-

pressed by and dismissive of the dangers hyperbolized in abstinence education. Like advertising, which must continually jack up its seduction just to stay visible as other advertising proliferates, abstinence education had to make sex scarier and scarier and, at the same time, chastity sweeter. By neglecting the other information about pleasure that good sex ed could offer, fear and freedom had a fighting chance against teenage desire.

FAMILY LIFE

If abstinence offers kids the freedom from growing up, it tenders to parents an equally impossible corollary, freedom from watching their kids grow up. That promise is fully consonant with what conservative parents want for themselves and their children, and sometimes it is fulfilled, at least temporarily. A woman I met at a convention of the conservative Christian organization Concerned Women for America told me that her fifteen-year-old daughter's "crisis pregnancy" turned out to be "a blessing." In renouncing her sexual relationship and pledging herself to "secondary virginity," the girl reconnected with her family. During her confinement, before she gave the baby up for adoption, she spent time with her mother, shopping, talking, and praying; she played with her sisters, went to church midweek with her father. Literally unsteady on her feet, alienated from the pleasures that had pulled her toward her boyfriend and away from family and church, she was now thrown back to childlike dependence and gratitude, precisely at the age when she might otherwise have spurned her parents' best-meant solicitations in order to fly on her own.

For more moderate or liberal parents, the wish for such a "freedom" is more conflicted. The majority of American adults champion sexuality education at school: the very first Gallup Poll, in 1943, found 68 percent of parents favoring it,[63] and even the heaviest right-wing fire in the 1980s and 1990s didn't manage to blast away the base of that support, which consistently bested 80 percent.[64] But parents also embrace abstinence. Most concede that their kids will probably have sex in their teens, in other words, but surveying the dangers their children face, also wish they wouldn't.

Abstinence-plus speaks to these mothers and fathers. The *plus* addresses the rational concession that sex will happen. But the *abstinence* connects powerfully to that deep parental wish: to protect and "keep" their children by guarding their childhood. In this sense, abstinence is about reversing, or at least holding back, the coming of age, which for parents is a story of loss, as their children establish passionate connections with people and values outside the family.

Even for parents who revel in their children's emerging sexuality, it can mean loss. A strong feminist advocate of sexual freedom described watching her son, then about seventeen, standing side by side with his girlfriend at her living room window. "They were not hugging or kissing, but every part of their bodies was touching," she recalled. "The light from the window was all around them, but there was no light between them. Immediately, I knew they had made love." Twenty years later, the memory still brought a wistful softness to her face. "I went to the kitchen and burst into tears, because I knew I was no longer the most important woman in my son's life."

In some advertising copy in 1997, SIECUS president Debra Haffner criticized abstinence-only education as a kind of child neglect. "When we treat sexuality as adults-only," she said, "we abandon teenagers to learn about their sexuality on their own, by trial and error."[65] Her point was correct and crucial: accurate, positively communicated, and effectively transmitted information about sexuality makes the going happier, easier, and far less dangerous for young people. Abstinence-only education falsely promises parents it can eliminate the awfulness of watching children try and fail (because by the time they get to sex, they will be adults and able to handle it). But comprehensive education may also encourage a similarly unrealistic, but profoundly held, parental hope: that teen sexuality can be rational, protected, and heartbreak-free.

"The nature of teen romance is that it is tortured, and then it ends," the writer and former sex educator Sharon Thompson commented, laughing sympathetically. Thompson sees not only the avoidance of romantic pitfalls but also the knocks themselves as potentially "educative." She advocates "romance education," but she also knows that adults can't save their kids from *le chagrin d'amour*. Contrary to the impli-

cation in Haffner's plea that adults not "abandon" teens to sexual trial and error, the fact is that sexual relationships are by definition what teenagers do on their own, and the only way for teens to learn about them is to try—which usually means failing, too. "Maturity," including sexual maturity, cannot be attained without practice, and in sex as in skiing, practice is risky.

Haffner's statement fits with the contemporary belief that parents can be involved in every aspect of their children's lives, from soccer to sex. It is not surprising that this should be the direction in which sex education is turning. In the 1980s, sexuality ed was renamed family life education, even by Planned Parenthood, sending the message that sex belongs in the context of the heterosexual reproductive family. Along with sexual responsibility, students in many family-life courses learn the skills of householder and parent, the definitions of adulthood in centuries past. One course included a lesson on filling out a tax return. In almost all programs, parental consent forms are distributed at the start of the course. A tactic initially used to defuse community opposition, these forms also stack up as de facto acquiescence by sex educators to a parental "right" of control over their children's sexuality.

The comprehensive, who have long encouraged parents to talk frankly with children from early on, also have recognized that many won't or can't. Now, however, that balanced understanding is subtly drifting—with the gale force of political pressure from the Right behind it—toward more reliance on parents. With it have come many programs to educate them on how to be "the primary sex educators of their children," as the phrase always goes.

"Parent education" is a fine idea. But because the political goal is more about some liberal version of family values than it is about creating the highest-quality education, some of the courses get their priorities mixed up. One such curriculum is "Can We Talk?" a four-session video and discussion program for parents created by the visually inventive Dominic Capello under the sponsorship of the National Education Association and the Health Information Network. After a training session for educators, I expressed my concern to Capello that there seemed to be little guidance to parents about what they should say and that they there-fore might well say inaccurate and bigoted things to their children—that masturbation causes blindness, for instance, or that Pop will beat you black and blue if you come home pregnant. "There's plenty of information in there," he countered, pointing to the twenty pages (with lots of white space and pictures) on puberty, reproduction, pregnancy AIDS, and anatomy in the three-ring binder parent participants receive. (I sug-gested that in the next edition he add the clitoris to the list of relevant female body parts.) "But this is a first step," said Capello, an openly gay man who started his career as an art director for a radical queer magazine. "We're trying to help parents learn to communicate their values"—whatever those values may be.

Allies of comprehensive sexuality education have not ceased agitating for higher professionalism among sexuality educators (who are now, likely as not, the gym teacher or other reluctant draftee), through more rigorous training and accreditation. They have contin-ued to lobby for compulsory school-based comprehen-sive sex ed taught by trained instructors. Yet the in-creasing propaganda and programmatic creep toward the kitchen table, at the very moment schoolteachers are being gagged in the classroom, amounts to a capit-ulation to the Right's agenda. Parent education, even well-trained parent education, affirms the new ortho-doxy that parents possess the sex-educational will and competence whose very absence mobilized the founders of sex instruction nearly a century ago.

These recent moves toward parent education be-speak a contradiction inside sex ed. On the one hand, they are consistent with the historical conservatism of the discipline, which has always consigned sex to mar-riage and aimed to strengthen parental authority. On the other, they represent a retreat from the critique of the family implicit in school-based sexuality educa-tion, which endorses the sexual-intellectual autonomy of children and suggests that the family, with its hierar-chical structure, its neuroses, ignorance, and taboos, is *not* the best sex educator after all.

SUCCESSES AND FAILURES

After rising steadily from 1970, the rate of teen inter-course in America dropped a smidgen in the 1990s,[66]

while the teen pregnancy and birth rates slid, by 17 percent and 19 percent, respectively (these were still the highest in the developed world, about compa-rable with Bulgaria).[67] Unsurprisingly, many link these two facts to a spreading conservatism among kids, including the embrace of virginity. The renewed popularity of virginity has been attributed to absti-nence education.

Examined more closely, however, the causal rela-tionship between abstinence education and a reduc-tion in teen pregnancy is, at best, small. A major analysis by the Alan Guttmacher Institute attributes about a fourth of the decline to delayed intercourse but three-quarters to improved contraceptive use among sexually experienced teenagers.[68] In Europe, where kids have as much sex as they do in America, teen pregnancy rates are about a fourth as high as ours.[69]

In the Netherlands, where celibacy is not taught, contraception is free through the national health ser-vice, and condoms are widely available in vending machines, "teenage pregnancy seems virtually elimi-nated as a health and social problem," according to Dr. Simone Buitendijk of the Dutch Institute for Applied Scientific Research. Fewer than 1 percent of Dutch fif-teen- to seventeen-year-olds become pregnant each year.[70] "The pragmatic European approach to teenage sexual activity, expressed in the form of widespread provision of confidential and accessible contraceptive services to adolescents, is . . . a central factor in ex-plaining the more rapid declines in teenage childbear-ing in northern and western European countries, in contrast to slower decreases in the United States," commented the authors of another, cross-national Guttmacher study.[71]

There may even be an inverse relationship between abstinence education and declining rates of pregnancy. For one thing, because many abstinence programs teach kids that refraining from intercourse is the only surefire way to prevent pregnancy and vastly exagger-ate the failures of contraception and condoms, students get the impression that birth control and STD preven-tion methods don't work. So they shrug off using them or don't know how to use them. Contraception educa-tion, on the other hand, works: teens who learn about birth control and condoms are 70 to 80 percent more likely to protect themselves if they have intercourse than kids who are not given such lessons.[72]

More fundamentally, though, it is a truth universally acknowledged among social scientists that attitude is one thing and behavior quite another. In one major recent government survey, only about a quarter of kids who hadn't yet had intercourse expected to do so while they were still in their teens. In reality, twice as many do.[73] Good intentions, moreover, are the paving-stones on the road to what public-health professionals call bad outcomes. In this case, the outcome proves another sad truth: "good girls get caught." A good girl, by definition, is not a girl with condoms and lube in her backpack. As Planned Parenthood's curriculum "Positive Images" points out, "'Abstinence' often fails, i.e., people who *intended* to be abstinent have sexual intercourse and don't use either a contraceptive or a condom."[74]

In a recent analysis of the massive National Longitudinal Study of Adolescent Health, Columbia University sociologist Peter Bearman looked at the success of "chastity pledges." The pledges, usually taken publicly as part of a Christian fundamentalist virginity movement, have indeed given several million teens the personal gumption and peer support to postpone intercourse—on average, eighteen months longer than nonpledgers. But in the end, such pledges are counterproductive to developing habits of lifetime sexual responsibility. When they broke the promise, as almost all did, these fallen angels were less effective contraceptors than their peers who had become active earlier.[75] The study of Philadelphia middle schoolers reported in *JAMA* educed the same results. When the abstinence-only students engaged in intercourse a year later, a third of them did so without protection. Fewer than one-tenth of the group who had been taught about condoms took that risk.[76]

Another little-publicized fillip in the statistics is this: when analysts at the Centers for Disease Control looked more closely at the diminishing teen-sex rates, they found that boys were having less intercourse (15 percent less from 1991 to 1997), but girls' rates hadn't slowed.[77] The practice that had declined among girls was *unprotected* intercourse.[78] Condom use, not chastity, more plausibly explains the encouraging news about declining teen pregnancy.[79]

In the end, sex education classes may be no more responsible for any sexual "outcomes" than the larger culture in which the classes are embedded. Advocates for Youth, which leads annual summer tours of the European sex-ed field for American educators, has observed that the Continent's relatively low rates of teen pregnancy, abortion, and sexually transmitted diseases are rooted most of all in Europeans' attitudes about sex. "Adults see intimate sexual relationships as normal and natural for older adolescents, a positive component of emotionally healthy maturation," a brief report of the early tours' lessons said. "At the same time, young people believe it is 'stupid and irresponsible' to have sex without protection and use the maxim, 'safe sex or no sex.' The morality of sexual behavior is weighed through an individual ethic that includes the values of responsibility, love, respect, tolerance, and equity."[80]

Of course, inculcating values is a large part of what sex education is and has always been about. The Right is less shy than the Left about saying this. Sadly, of the lofty list above, tolerance and equity are not exactly majority values among American teens. But, Bear-man found, neither are love and respect expressed through chastity. Indeed, an interesting thing about chastity pledges is that virginity must remain a minority value, and the pledgers a countercultural clique, in order to succeed. As soon as more than about 30 percent of a school's students climb on, the pledged virgins start falling off the wagon.[81]

At any rate, most mainstream professional organizations have deduced that declining rates of teen pregnancy can be attributed to a combination of abstinence messages and contraceptive and safe-sex information; in 1999 the American Medical Association and other prominent organizations endorsed abstinence-plus education. And to be sure, for many of these social-sexual changes the comprehensive, or abstinence-plus curricula, can take credit. Still, there is evidence that the most impressive gains of such programs lie in the "pluses": students' tolerance toward sexual difference, increased contraceptive and condom use, and improved sexual negotiation skills.[82]

So how do the abstinence-plusers score in the main event, achieving abstinence from intercourse? Kids who get a taste of the full menu of sex-ed topics postpone intercourse longer than those who receive no such classes. But on a measure of virginity-guarding months, the ab-plusers have done almost as pitifully as the ab-onlys. According to the evaluation of one "plus" plan, the length of time students held off intercourse averaged seven months.[83] A kid who resists on New Year's Eve, in other words, succumbs on the Fourth of July.

"CRIMINAL" ACTIVITIES

As the decades plod on, some public-school comprehensive sex educators work harder, taking risks to teach what needs to be taught. Others toe the line and feel discouraged. Some quit their jobs to move to alternative institutions—churches, community, gay and lesbian, or AIDS-education groups, progressive chapters of moderate national organizations like Planned Parenthood, or rare innovative outfits like New Jersey's Network for Family Life Education, which puts out the excellent teen-run publication and Web site Sxetc.com.

But nationally influential progressive sex educators are a dwindling crew: Some "outsider" educators, seeing their ideas pushed further and further to the margins, have broached the possibility of shifting sex ed out of the public schools altogether in favor of invigorating public-service media and community-based educational strategies—an idea that others, including me, criticize as misguided.

Some formerly committed teachers have lined up at the abstinence-only trough, ethics be damned. A Minneapolis sex-ed consultant told me boldly one morning in 1998 that "we've been doing sex ed wrong for the past fifteen years." How so? "We say sex is bad for kids, and it isn't." The interview was rushed, because that afternoon she was slated to do a teacher-training workshop—on the city's new abstinence-only curricula. Huh? "It helps me get more business in town," the educator explained. If a woman with these beliefs was now concealing them in order to preach the gospel of chastity to young teachers, I despaired of the next generation of sex educators, not to mention their students.

The Minneapolis teacher was an extreme example of a slow but sure surrender by a significant portion of the sex-ed mainstream to the demands of a brazen right-wing minority. But not that extreme. In the fall of 2000, the super-mainstream National Campaign to Prevent Teen Pregnancy, in Washington, D.C., placed free public-service advertisements in youth-directed publications such as *Teen People* and *Vibe*. Each ad featured a photo of a teenager (ethnic and stylistic diversity dutifully respected) with a large word emblazoned across it: NOBODY, USELESS, CHEAP, DIRTY, REJECT, PRICK. Smaller, far less legible type softened these smears: "Now that I'm home with a baby, NOBODY calls me anymore"; "All it took was one PRICK to get my girlfriend pregnant. At least that's what her friends say." (The prick apparently was not the boy in the picture.)

Some people in the field, including Advocates for Youth president James Wagoner, were outraged by the resurrection of these ugly stereotypes of sexually active or pregnant teens and charged the campaign with blaming teens, whom "society" has denied "access to information and confidential sexual health services—and a true stake in the future." But in one of its mailings, the National Campaign held up as a shield the encomia of teens who (spontaneously?) wrote in to praise the advertisements. "They don't glamorize sex," one correspondent said. "They simply show the reality."

Yes, this campaign did show the reality at the turn of the twenty-first century: shame and blame still surround teen sexuality, and its prosecutors are not Bible-thumpers but "responsible" sex educators and teens themselves. The Right also indicted the ads, by the way, for neglecting to pitch abstinence. But Focus on the Family could have blown them up and plastered them across the stage at their 2001 national convention. A pretty, pouty Latina with CHEAP slashed across her bare belly in big bright letters, a brown-skinned boy in a backward cap with the scarlet letters USELESS labeling him—these, better than anything their public-relations firms could have produced, proclaimed the conservative activists' good news: Victory!

The Right won, but the mainstream let it. Comprehensive sex educators had the upper hand in the 1970s, and starting in the 1980s, they allowed their enemies to seize more and more territory, until the Right controlled the law, the language, and the cultural consensus. Sad as the comprehensive sex educators' story is, they must share some of the blame for what the abstinence-only movement has wrought in the lives of the young. Commenting on its failure to defend explicit sexuality education during an avalanche of new HIV infection among teenagers, Sharon Thompson said, "We will look back at this time and indict the sex-education community as criminal. It's like being in a nuclear power plant that has a leak, and not telling anybody."

NOTES

1. Joyce Purnick, "Where Chastity Is Not Virtuous," *New York Times,* May 25, 1981, A14.

2. My suspicion is the word *abstinance* migrated into sex ed from the hugely popular movement of twelve-step anti-"addiction" programs based on the model of Alcoholics Anonymous, which preached that only complete renunciation and daily recommitment could bring a bad habit under control.

3. *Guidelines for Comprehensive Sexuality Education* (New York: Sex Information and Education Council of the U.S., 1994), 1.

4. Social Security Act, Title V, Section 510 (1997), Maternal and Child Health Bureau, U.S. Department of Health and Human Services.

5. David J. Landry, Lisa Kaeser, and Cory L. Richards, "Abstinence Promotion and the Provision of Information about Contraception in Public School District Sexuality Education Policies," *Family Planning Perspectives* 31, no. 6 (November/December 1999): 280–86; Kaiser Family Foundation, "Most Secondary Schools Take a More Comprehensive Approach to Sex Education," press release, December 14, 1999.

6. "Changes in Sexuality Education from 1988–1999," SEICUS, *SHOP Talk Bulletin* 5, no. 16 (October 13, 2000).

7. Diana Jean Schemo, "Survey Finds Parents Favor More Detailed Sex Education," *New York Times,* October 4, 2000, A1.

8. Joyce Purnick, "Welfare Bill: Legislating Morality?" *New York Times,* August 19, 1996, "Metro Matters," B1.

9. Patricia Campbell, *Sex Education Books for Young Adults 1892–1979* (New York: R. R. Bowker Co., 1979), viii.

10. F. Valentine, "Education in Sexual Subjects," *New York Medical Journal* 83 (1906): 276–78.

11. Benjamin C. Gruenberg, *High Schools and Sex Education: A Manual of Suggestions of Education Related to Sex* (Washington, D.C.: U.S. Public Health Service and U.S. Bureau of Education, 1922), 95.

12. Evelyn Duvall, *Facts of Life and Love for Teenagers,* as quoted in Campbell, *Sex Education Books for Young Adults,* 87.

13. Mary S. Calderone, "A Distinguished Doctor Talks to Vassar College Freshmen about Love and Sex," *Redbook,* February 1964 (reprint).

14. *Sex Education: Conditioning for Immorality,* filmstrip, John Birch Society, released around 1969 (n.d.).

15. Handman and Brennan, *Sex Handbook,* 170.

16. Sol Gordon, *You: The Psychology of Surviving and Enhancing Your Social Life, Love Life, Sex Life, School Life, Home Life, Work Life, Emotional Life, Creative Life, Spiritual Life, Style of Life Life* (New York: Times Books, 1975).

17. In 1972, worried that young single women's kids would end up on the dole, Congress required all welfare departments to offer birth control services to minors. The Supreme Court ruled in *Carey v. Population Services International* (1977) that teens had a privacy right to purchase contraception; in 1977 and 1979, when Congress reauthorized Title X of the Public Health Services Act of 1970, providing health care to the poor, it singled out adolescents as a specific group in need of contraceptive services.

18. Guttmacher Report, quoted in Constance A. Nathanson, *Dangerous Passages: The Social Control of Sexuality in Women's Adolescence* (Philadelphia: Temple University Press, 1991), 47.

19. The history of family planning and concomitant legislation before the Adolescent Family Life Act draws from Nathanson, *Dangerous Passages*; Rosalind Pollack Petchesky, *Abortion and Women's Choice: The State, Sexuality, and Reproductive Freedom,* rev. ed. (Boston: Northeastern University Press, 1990); and Luker, *Dubious Conceptions,* as well as interviews with birth control professionals, lawyers, and women's movement activists from the 1970s and 1980s.

20. Alan Guttmacher Institute, *Sex and America's Teenagers* (New York: the institute, 1994), 58. Luker notes that many are also discouraged at school or already dropouts and that motherhood does not diminish such a young woman's standard of living: they are poor when they have children, and they stay poor (Luker, *Dubious Conceptions,* 106–8).

21. This number represented about 50 percent of the fifteen- to nineteen-year-olds, the same percentage who are now sexually active. Alan Guttmacher Institute, *Eleven Million Teenagers: What Can Be Done about the Epidemic of Adolescent Pregnancies in the United States* (New York: Planned Parenthood Federation on America, 1976), 9–11.

22. Nathanson, *Dangerous Passages,* 60.

23. Luker, *Dubious Conceptions,* 8.

24. For surgeon general, Reagan nominated Everett Koop, who had appeared in an anti-abortion propaganda video standing in a field of dead fetuses. But Koop turned out not to be the antichoice puppet the Right to Life had hoped for. Keeping his views on abortion to himself, he became a tireless crusader for frank AIDS education.

25. "Block-granting" Title X into the Maternal and Child Health Bureau had been proposed during the Nixon administration too but failed.

26. African American communities had always kept such babies close to home. Ricki Solinger, *Wake Up Little Susie* (New York: Routledge, 1992).

27. *Kendrick v. Bowen* (Civil A. No. 83-3175), "Federal Supplement," 1548. Patricia Donovan, "The Adolescent Family Life Act and the Promotion of Religious Doctrine," *Family Planning Perspectives* 4, no. 4 (September/October 1984): 222.

28. The anti-ERA Illinois Committee on the Status of Women received grants of over $600,000 to develop and evaluate the workbook *Sex Respect* (ACLU "Kendrick I," List of Grantees), authored by former Catholic schoolteacher and anti-abortion activist Colleen Kelly Mast, and another $350,000 for *Facing Reality,* the workbook of its companion curriculum (*Teaching Fear: The Religious Right's Campaign against Sexuality Education* (Washington, D.C.: People for the American Way, June 1994), 10).

29. This figure has also been cited for the number of school districts employing any abstinence-only curriculum, "States Slow to Take U.S. Aid to Teach Sexual Abstinence," *New York Times,* May 8, 1997, 22.

30. During that time, the average grant for other organizations the size of Teen-Aid or Respect Inc. was less than half of Teen-Aid's and less than a third of Respect's. Department of Health and Human Services, Public Health Service, "Adolescent Family Life Demonstration Grants Amounts Awarded 1982–1996," Office of Adolescent Pregnancy Prevention document, Washington, D.C., 1996.

31. *Teaching Fear,* 11.

32. The statistics available at the time from the institute were that about 780,000, or 39 percent, of 2 million then-fourteen-year-old girls would have at least one pregnancy in their teen years; 420,000 would give birth; 300,000 would have abortions.

33. U.S. Senate, Jeremiah Denton, *Adolescent Family Life,* S. Rept. 97-161, July 8, 1981, 2; emphasis added.

34. "To Attack the Problems of Adolescent Sexuality," *New York Times,* June 15, 1981, A22.

35. "To Attack the Problems of Adolescent Sexuality."

36. A few years earlier, the Family Protection Act (H.R. 7955), a blueprint of the Right's agenda to come and also cosponsored by Hatch, proposed defunding all state protections of children and women independent of their fathers and husbands, including child-abuse and domestic-abuse programs. It did not pass.

37. Bernard Weinraub, "Reagan Aide Backs Birth-Aid Education," *New York Times,* June 24, 1981, C12.

38. A SIECUS-Advocates for Children Survey in 1999 found that 70 percent opposed the federal abstinence-only standards and thought they were unrealistic in light of kids' actual sexual behavior. SIECUS, *SHOP Talk Bulletin* 4 (June 11, 1999).

39. "State Sexuality and HIV/STD Education Regulations," National Abortion Rights Action League fact sheet, February 1997.

40. "Sex Education That Teaches Abstinence Wins Support," Associated Press, *New York Times,* July 23, 1997.

41. "Between the Lines: States' Implementation of the Federal Government's Section 510(b) Abstinence Education Program in Fiscal Year 1998," SIECUS report, Washington, D.C., 1999.

42. Six in ten believe that sexual intercourse in the teen years was always wrong, and nine out of ten wanted their kids to be taught about abstinence at school. Yet eight in ten also wanted them to learn about contraception and preventing sexually transmitted diseases. SIECUS, *SHOP Talk Bulletin* 4 (June 11, 1999).

43. "Adolescent Sexual Health in Europe & the U.S.— Why the Difference?" 2d ed., Advocates for Youth report, Washington, D.C., 2000.

44. Douglas Kirby, "No Easy Answers: Research Findings on Programs to Reduce Teen Pregnancy," National Campaign to Prevent Teen Pregnancy report, Washington, D.C., 1997.

45. Marl W. Roosa and F. Scott Christopher, "An Evaluation of an Abstinence-Only Adolescent Pregnancy Prevention Program: Is 'Just Say No' Enough?" *Family Relations* 39 (January 1990): 68–72.

46. John B. Jemmott III, Loretta Sweet Jemmott, and Geoffrey T. Fong, "Abstinence and Safer Sex: HIV Risk-Reduction Interventions for African American Adolescents," *Journal of the American Medical Association* 279, no. 19 (May 20, 1998): 1529–36.

47. Ralph J. DiClemente, Editorial: "Preventing Sexually Transmitted Infections among Adolescents," *Journal of the American Medical Association* 279, no. 19 (May 20, 1998).

48. National Institutes of Health Consensus Development Conference Statement, *Interventions to Prevent HIV Risk Behaviors,* February 11–13, 1997 (Bethesda, Md.: NIH), 15.

49. Ron Haskins and Carol Statuto Bevan, "Implementing the Abstinence Education Provision of the Welfare Reform Legislation," U.S. House of Representatives memo, November 8, 1996, 1.

50. Haskins and Bevan, "Implementing the Abstinence Education Provision," 8–9.

51. "Changes in Sexuality Education from 1988–1999."

52. Victor Strasburger, *Getting Your Kids to Say "No" in the '90s When You Said "Yes" in the '60s* (New York: Simon and Schuster, 1993), 87–88.

53. Sol Gordon and Judith Gordon, *Raising a Child Conservatively in a Sexually Permissive World* (New York: Simon and Schuster, 1989), 101.

54. Peter C. Scales and Martha R. Roper, "Challenges to Sexuality Education in the Schools," in *The Sexuality Education Challenge: Promoting Healthy Sexuality in Young People,* ed. Judy C. Drolet and Kay Clark (Santa Cruz, Calif.: ETR Associates, 1994), 79.

55. Colleen Kelly Mast, *Sex Respect: Parent-Teacher Guide* (Bradley, Ill.: Respect Inc., n.d.), 45.

56. Other educators have pointed out the implicit inaccuracy of the impression these slides leave: unfortunately, one of the most common STDs, chlamydia, is asymptomatic.

57. *Teaching Fear,* 8.

58. Medical Institute for Sexual Health, *National Guidelines for Sexuality and Character Education* (Austin, Tex.: Medical Institute for Sexual Health, 1996), 82.

59. Saint Augustine, *Confessions* (Oxford: Oxford University Press, 1991), 24–25.

60. Medical Institute for Sexual Health, "National Guidelines," 89.

61. "HIV: You Can Live without It!" (Spokane, Wash.: Teen-Aid, Inc., 1998), 33.

62. Margaret Atwood, *The Handmaid's Tale* (New York: Houghton Mifflin, 1986), 24.

63. Scales and Roper, "Challenges to Sexuality Education," 70.

64. Irving R. Dickman, *Winning the Battle for Sex Education,* pamphlet (New York: SIECUS, 1982); Debra Haffner and Diane de Mauro, *Winning the Battle: Developing Support for Sexuality and HIV/AIDS Education,* pamphlet (New York: SIECUS, 1991); *Teaching Fear.*

65. The ad ran in the *New York Times,* April 22, 1997, the *Los Angeles Times,* April 28, 1997, as well as the West Coast editions of *Time, Newsweek,* and *People* during that month.

66. "Trends in Sexual Risk Behaviors among High School Students—U.S. 1991–97," *Morbidity and Mortality Weekly Report* 47 (September 18, 1998): 749–52. Teens may be doing better than adults. "Most Adults in the United States Who Have Multiple Sexual Partners Do Not Use Condoms Consistently," *Family Planning Perspectives* 26 (January/February 1994): 42–43.

67. Susheela Singh and Jacqueline E. Darroch, "Adolescent Pregnancy and Childbearing: Levels and Trends in the Developed Countries," *Family Planning Perspectives* 32 (2000): 14–23. Centers for Disease Control and Prevention National Center for Health Statistics, *National Vital Statistics Report* 4, no. 4 (2001).

68. About three-quarters of girls use a method the first time; as many as two-thirds of teens say they use condoms regularly—three times the rate in 1970. Long-acting birth control injections and implants have also gained popularity among teens. "Why Is Teenage Pregnancy Declining? The Roles of Abstinence, Sexual Activity and Contraceptive Use," Alan Guttmacher Institute Occasional Report, 1999.

69. Singh and Darroch, "Adolescent Pregnancy and Childbearing."

70. "Teen Pregnancy 'Virtually Eliminated' in the Netherlands," Reuters Health/London news story (accessed through Medscape), March 2, 2001.

71. "United States and the Russian Federation Lead the Developed World in Teenage Pregnancy Rates," Alan Guttmacher Institute press release, February 24, 2000.

72. J. Mauldon and K. Luker, "The Effects of Contraceptive Education on Method Use at First Intercourse," *Family Planning Perspectives* (January/February 1996): 19.

73. J. C. Abma et al., "Fertility, Family Planning, and Women's Health: New Data from the 1995 National Survey of Family Growth," *Vital Health Statistics* 23, no. 19 (1997).

74. Peggy Brick et al., *The New Positive Images: Teaching Abstinence, Contraception and Sexual Health* (Hackensack, N.J.: Planned Parenthood of Greater Northern New Jersey, 1996), 31.

75. Peter Bearman, paper presented at Planned Parenthood New York City's conference Adolescent Sexual Health: New Data and Implications for Services and Programs, October 26, 1998; Diana Jean Schemo, "Virginity Pledges by Teenagers Can Be Highly Effective, Federal Study Finds," *New York Times,* January 4, 2001.

76. Lantier, "Do Abstinence Lessons Lessen Sex?"

77. "Trends in Sexual Risk Behaviors among High School Students—United States 1991–1997," *Morbidity and Mortality Weekly Reports* 47 (September 18, 1998): 749–52.

78. Abma et al., "Fertility, Family Planning, and Women's Health."

79. It is important to point out that, in spite of these declines, nearly two-thirds of teen births resulted from unintended pregnancies. Abma et al., "Fertility, Family Planning, and Women's Health."

80. "Adolescent Sexual Health in the U.S. and Europe—Why the Difference?" Advocates for Youth fact sheet, Washington, D.C., 2000.

81. Schemo, "Virginity Pledges by Teenages."

82. It is impossible to find a forthright statement that abstinence-plus education meaningfully delays teen sexual intercourse. Its evaluators have been able to find out only that, for instance, if you want to delay intercourse, you should start classes before kids start "experimenting with sexual behaviours." And all studies show that sex ed does not encourage earlier intercourse. J. J. Frost and J. D. Forrest, "Understanding the Impact of Effective Teenage Pregnancy Prevention Programs," *Family Planning Perspectives* 27 (1995): 188–96; D. Kirby et al., "School Based Programs to Reduce Sexual Risk Behaviors: A Review of Effectiveness," *Public Health Reports* 190 (1997): 339–60; A. Grunseit and S. Kippax, *Effects of Sex Education on Young People's Sexual Behavior* (Geneva: World Health Organization, 1993).

83. S. Zabin and M. B. Hirsch, *Evaluation of Pregnancy Prevention Programs in the School Context* (Lexington, Mass.: D.C. Health/Lexington Books, 1988); Institute of Medicine, *The Best Intentions: Unintended Pregnancy and Well-Being of Children and Families* (Washington, D.C.: National Academy Press, 1995).

10.2 EDUCATIONAL SEX VIDEOS
What Are They Teaching?

Peggy J. Kleinplatz

CONSUMER DEMAND FOR "EDUCATIONAL" SEX VIDEOS

Why are educational sex videos quite so popular? Video sales benefit from the void created by the absence of accurate sexual information in our society and the lack of open communication on the subject. The scarcity of comprehensive sexuality education for young people forces us to depend on unreliable, and often inaccurate, sources of sexuality information as we grow up. For as long as sexuality remains shrouded in darkness and blanketed by ignorance, consumers will continue to grasp for information in whatever way they can. Everyone wants to know how to be a better lover. The emphasis has generally been on sexual skills and technical expertise as though that is what leads to sexual fulfilment. Sex videos seem to provide a safe, easy avenue for satisfying one's curiosity and for obtaining simple, easy to follow instructions with no intimate communication required. Much of the educational sex video industry capitalizes on sexual insecurities, fears and myths, and sells consumers the promise of a new and improved sex life without having to disclose one's ignorance, particular preferences and desires or to ask questions of one's partners. These videos attempt to fill the vacuum of silence and to offer instant solutions to sexual problems and dysfunctions. They provide hope for those who wish to be just like everybody else or to have greater sex.

WHAT DO "EDUCATIONAL" SEX VIDEOS ACTUALLY PROVIDE? SEX EQUALS INTERCOURSE

Unfortunately, what educational sex videos frequently tend to offer is reinforcement of traditional notions, myths, stereotypes and a fantasy model of sex (Zilbergeld, 1992). For example, many videos demonstrate a variety of different positions for intercourse, discuss the advantages and disadvantages of each major coital position and focus upon them at length. In so doing, they subtly communicate the message that sex equals intercourse. This message is reinforced by the sequence of sexual acts which are arranged so that they culminate in intercourse. Other sexual acts continue to be portrayed as preliminaries, notwithstanding lip-service (or narrative voice-overs) to the contrary. Real sex is just not seen as complete without intercourse. The idea that intercourse is the ultimate end of sex is further supported in videos which deal with sexual difficulties (e.g., "Loving Better: Sexual Problems," Kule, 1992, "You Can Last Longer," Schoen, 1992). Sexual problems tend to be defined as whatever obstructs or interferes with coitus (as opposed to sexual pleasure per se). Even in those videos wherein intercourse is not explicitly defined as the goal in overcoming sexual problems (e.g., "Becoming Orgasmic," Schoen, 1993), intercourse is performed as the finale. This implies that the ultimate criterion for sexual well-being is the ability to engage in satisfying intercourse. Some videos go even further, (e.g., "The Lover's Guide: Making Sex Even Better," Stanway, 1991), harkening back to the 1950s by stating that the ideal form of sexual fulfilment is simultaneous orgasm during intercourse.

GREAT SEX EQUALS TECHNICAL PROFICIENCY: INSTRUCTIONS VERSUS EDUCATION

By focusing so heavily upon technique, many videos suggest that sex equals performance. They offer

---

From *Canadian Journal of Human Sexuality* 6(1): 39–43. Copyright © 1997 by SIECCAN. Reprinted by permission of SIEC-CAN and Peggy J. Kleinplatz.

mechanical instructions rather than sexuality education. They describe and demonstrate correct technique and form for engaging in intercourse, manual, oral and anal stimulation, and occasionally, self-pleasuring. This tends to perpetuate the belief that there is a right way to do "it," as opposed to fostering sexual exploration, communication and pluralism. It is implicit that to be a good lover is to be a skillful lover. Eroticism is equated with technical mastery. Even when the narrator is stating that sex should be fun, there is a striking contrast with the visual content in which a normative performance standard is upheld (e.g., "The Better Sex Video: Sex Techniques," Learning Corp., 1991). The message that emerges is that sex is to be goal-oriented toward intercourse and orgasm, rather than for expression of intimacy or for pleasure per se.

GREAT SEX IS FOR A PRIVILEGED FEW

Many videos tend to imply that sex is to be reserved for a select, limited few—the elite. The actors chosen to star in such videos are generally stereotypically beautiful and come complete with plastic, Ken and Barbie doll looks (Britton & Royalle, 1994, Guldner, 1992). Their presence signals the assumption that to be sexually desirable means to be youthful, white, heterosexual, able-bodied, gorgeous, etc. The women typically have slim bodies with large breasts, while the men have strikingly large penises. Even the "real-life" lovers (rather than actors) featured in the "Videos for Lovers" series (Kapelow & Kapelow, 1993) are far from ordinary. Most of those portrayed in educational sex videos are more likely to intimidate viewers already struggling with poor body images and feelings of inadequacy, than to encourage or reassure them. Notable exceptions include "Becoming Orgasmic" (Schoen, 1993) and "Sex After 50" (Barbach, 1991) in which the actors chosen are appealing, attractive and personable—characters with whom viewers will be able to relate—without being untouchably stunning. Furthermore, certain videos often portray sex occurring in luxurious, expensive settings. They thereby suggest that great sex requires wealth and an extraordinary physical environment (as opposed to deep sharing, openness, trust, vulnerability and intimacy). For "average" couples, hot sex must remain the stuff

of fantasy, out of reach. Playboy's "Secrets of Making Love" (Playboy, 1991) deserves to be singled out for special mention. This video shows couples engaging in sex in limousines, swimming pools, at secluded rooftop restaurants (near strolling musicians) and in a rowboat floating leisurely on a lake. It then recommends a trip to Maui or hiring a geisha as a means of treating sexual boredom. Such approaches may be interesting, but are misleading and not very practical. Gimmicks and lavish surroundings may provide the occasional diversion, but will not solve sexual desire problems. In contrast, "Making Love Better" (Bolt, 1996) offers a more inspiring, if less glamorous, seduction scene. It portrays two presumably tired parents making contact while picking up their children's toys together. It suggests that the possibility of sexual renewal may lie in making a point of sharing everyday experiences with one another.

GENDER ROLE MYTHS AND SEXUAL EXCITEMENT

A variety of other myths involving gender roles, romance and sexual excitement are reinforced in educational sex videos. For example, women should refrain from dressing provocatively in dating so that men won't get the "wrong messages." If you want to get in the mood, try some alcohol ("The Lovers' Guide: Making Sex Even Better," Stanway, 1991). To prevent sex from getting stale, women should perform striptease routines for their partners ("Playboy's Secrets of Making Love," Playboy, 1991). Sex requires an erect penis and usually begins with an erection. A noteworthy exception is "Sex: A Lifelong Pleasure: Enjoying Sex" (Brouwer & Balian, 1991) in which a woman is shown stroking her partner's soft penis. Both are clearly enjoying her caresses as his erections wax and wane throughout their sexual contact.

SEX SHOULD BE "NATURAL AND SPONTANEOUS"

The myth that sex ought to be "natural and spontaneous" is ubiquitous in educational sex videos. Hot sex occurs over breakfast, first thing in the morning, when he lifts her onto the (immaculate) kitchen counter or bends her over the sink while she moans and groans. Aside from the marketing of unabashed pornography dignified and masquerading as educational materials (Guldner, 1992), where are the children spilling cereal on the floor? Why is there no one worrying about being late for work or even about privacy? Who arranged for the baby-sitter? Sex therapists frequently suggest to clients that there can be something very romantic and sexy about anticipation about partners' making time for one another about saying, in effect, "You are a priority for me and I want for us to be together," despite the demands of other responsibilities. These videos hinder rather than bolster our efforts. If planning sex is portrayed as incompatible with sexual passion, it follows that there is a dearth of contraceptives and safer sex. The filmmakers have overlooked an invaluable opportunity to include safer sex guidelines, to encourage and to eroticize safer sex practices. The conventional sexual script suggests that all talk of risks and responsibility prohibits exciting sex. The possibility of fashioning an alternate sexual script by incorporating and modelling communication, negotiation and implementation of safer sex in action has been lost. It seems a waste to set out to create "educational" sex materials and to omit such a critical aspect of sex in the 1990s. Once again, a notable exception is "Sex: A Lifelong Pleasure: Harmony" (Brouwer & Balian, 1992) in which condoms are introduced as a routine element of gentle, caring, sex play.

DO "EDUCATIONAL" SEX VIDEOS PROVIDE ANYTHING VALUABLE?

For those who are bored with their routine, mundane sex lives, videos offer variations for experimentation, play and to add diversity. These options are presented as legitimate alternatives to missionary-style, heterosexual intercourse. Videos give permission to try new positions, oral, anal and manual stimulation, to caress oneself alone (or in some cases, with a partner), to play with sex toys, and to venture into new settings. They illustrate how to perform these new acts, teaching and modelling them clearly and smoothly for uninformed, inhibited and eager viewers alike. A few of the better

videos provide an important and appealing alternative to traditional definitions of sexuality (e.g., "Making Love Better," Bolt, 1996 "Sex: A Lifelong Pleasure," Brouwer & Balian, 1991, 1992 "Selfloving," Dodson, 1993 "Becoming Orgasmic," Schoen, 1993). They challenge presumptions, dispel myths and offer accurate information about sexuality. There is an emphasis on sensuality rather than only upon genital stimulation, pleasure and enjoyment over skill; the excitement of desire building instead of being instantaneously quelled for tension relief; playfulness, curiosity and exploration versus determining the "right" way to bring a partner to orgasm. The characters featured seem to be credible and realistic, not simply cardboard cutouts. Their discomforts are approached respectfully and suggest that the viewer is not alone in facing sexual difficulties. In "Becoming Orgasmic" (Schoen, 1993) and "Sex: A Lifelong Pleasure" (Brouwer & Balian, 1991, 1992), the principals seem genuinely comfortable and caring with one another. Their warmth, mutuality and intimacy are evident. There is a strong focus on communication and upon connecting beyond the genitals. In "Making Love Better" (Bolt, 1996), the couples are oriented towards satisfaction rather than performance. The principals and narrators emphasis the centrality of consideration, emotional sensitivity, openness and trust in developing and sustaining sexual intimacy. In "Selfloving" (Dodson, 1993), the women shown are actual participants in Dodson's workshops rather than actors. A variety of ages, shapes, sizes and sexual preferences are exhibited. The existence of an entire spectrum of different kinds of sexual responses is displayed. The tone is affirming and empowering rather than prescriptive (Britton & Royalle, 1994). The sense of freedom and real eroticism is palpable. As summarized by D'Ardenne and Riley (1993), "Educational videos have an important role in disseminating information, changing attitudes [. . .] and informing the sexual majority about sexual minority behaviour" (p. 4). Educational sex videos may occasionally offer an additional benefit. In his introduction to "Making Love Better" (Bolt, 1996), Dr. Gerald Weeks suggests that viewers ask themselves the following three questions: "What did I learn about myself from this film? What would I like to tell my partner about my emotional and sexual needs? What could we do as a couple to deepen or enrich our sexual relationship and our overall level of intimacy?" Indeed, his guidelines may promote sexual awareness, exploration and dialogue among viewers of this or any educational sex video, regardless of its merits or lack thereof.

RECOMMENDATIONS AND CONCLUSIONS

Unfortunately, at this time, most educational sex videos are not available to the general public for rental, but primarily for purchase. It is almost impossible for the consumer to ascertain if the video is worth buying in advance. Once the video is at home, how is the consumer to assess the value of the material? The consumer is advised to attend to whatever feelings arise in him/her in response to watching the video. If while watching the video, the viewer is thinking, "Yeah! Isn't that interesting. I could try that. It looks like fun. So that's how you do it! I'd like to show that to my partner," then the video has fulfilled its intended purpose. The video has provided information, contributed to a sense of excitement, arousal, competence and has perhaps even stimulated creativity. However, if the viewer feels inadequate, unattractive, fearful, bored, turned off, repulsed, alienated, marginalized, pressured, etc., it is time to disregard and to discard the video. For counsellors and therapists, it may be possible to preview videocassettes before deciding on a purchase. Videos can be used in therapy to supplement more traditional forms of bibliotherapy. They may be particularly advantageous in working with non-literate clients. Videos may serve to initiate and stimulate communication about sexuality among couples (Crooks & Baur, 1993). Therapists may wish to recommend their use for that purpose. However, given the unfortunate quality of many videos and their aforementioned deficiencies, books remain a better option in most instances. Perhaps the eventual selection of educational sex videos will broaden and improve, thereby allowing consumers and professional sexologists access to more useful, informative and affirming materials. At present, the messages and images conveyed in most videos are so stereotypical, mechanical and limiting that they may do more harm than good. Perhaps with widespread availability of comprehensive sexuality education, such videos could one day become obsolete.

REFERENCES

Barbach, L. (1991). *Sex after 50* [Film]. Pompano Beach, FL.: Sex After 50, Inc.

Bolt, N. (Producer). (1996). *Making love better* [Film]. Markham, ON: PromoVision Marketing Corporation.

Britton, P.O., & Royalle, C. (1994). Sexual enhancement videos: A sexologist and a filmmaker review five titles. *Contemporary Sexuality, 28,* 1–2, 17–19.

Brouwer, C., & Balian, H. (Producers). (1991). *Sex: A lifelong pleasure: Enjoying sex* [Film]. Huntington, NY: Focus International.

Brouwer, C., & Balian, H. (Producers). (1992). *Sex: A lifelong pleasure: Harmony* [Film]. Huntington, NY: Focus International.

Crooks, R., & Baur, K. (1993). *Our sexuality.* Redwood City, CA: Benjamin/Cummings.

D'Ardenne, P., & Riley, A.J. (1993). (Editorial). *Sexual and Marital Therapy, 8,* 3–4.

Dodson, B. (1993). *Selfloving: Video portrait of a women's sexuality seminar* [Film]. New York: Femme Distribution.

Guldner, C. (1992). Review of films for use in sex therapy. *Canadian Journal of Human Sexuality, 1,* 89–92.

Kapelow, L., & Kapelow, S. (Producers). (1993). *Videos for lovers: Behind the bedroom door* [Film]. Pompano Beach FL: Educational Video Corp.

Kule, S. (1992). *Loving better: Sexual problems* [Film]. Wantagh, NY. Mandolay Productions.

Learning Corp. (Producers). (1991). *The better sex video: Better sexual techniques* [Film]. Huntington, NY: Focus International.

Learning Corp. (Producers). (1991). *The better sex video: Advanced sexual techniques* [Film]. Huntington, NY: Focus International.

Playboy. (Producers) (1991). *Playboy's secrets of making love* [Film]. N.p.: The Sharper Image.

Schoen, M. (1992). *You can last longer: Solutions for ejaculatory control* [Film] Huntington, NY: Focus International.

Schoen, M. (Producer). (1993). *Becoming orgasmic: A sexual growth program for women* [Film]. Huntington, NY: Focus International.

Stanway, A. (1991). *The lovers' guide: Making sex even better* [Film]. N.p.: Pickwick Video Ltd.

Zilbergeld, B. (1992). *The new male sexuality.* New York: Bantam.

10.3 SEXUALITY AND SUBVERSION
University Peer Sexuality Educators and the Possibilities for Change

Rebecca F. Plante

ONE DAY IN late January, after the autumn training quarter, some peer sexuality educators (PSEs) were talking before class began. Laura Sorensen, PSE supervisor, told the students about restrictions on her and Maria Scott, the other supervisor. As campus health services professionals, their behaviour was scrutinized. As paraprofessional staff, PSEs were similarly bound. For example, every programme PSEs provided had to begin with the statement that 'abstinence is the safest sex'.

Sorensen suggested that if the PSEs wanted more freedom, they could form a group external to the organized programme. By operating as just another student group, they could plan more 'radical' activities. One PSE asked, 'But what would we do?' Another responded, 'Anything we want.' One PSE, Trixie, suggested that everyone who was interested should stay after class to discuss forming a group.

So the 'Sexual Health Information Network' (SHIN) was born, formed by what turned out to be a core group of PSEs: Debra, Jennifer, Christine, Jill, Mike, Trixie, Carlin, Samantha and Ed. Although the group was suggested by a professional in an offhand way, every step toward success or failure was taken by students. SHIN wanted to provide explicit campus sexuality education, otherwise frowned on by administrators and staff at health services. The group wanted to challenge the university, challenge the institutional version of sexuality education, challenge accepted policies about such education at the university.

SETTING THE SCENE:
PROGRAMME, METHODS AND FOCUS

University sexuality information usually occurs via health services, academic departments or, rarely, via peer education. Trained students go into classrooms and campus housing to provide programming to their peers. However, peer education is situated in the broader context of institutionalized sexuality education, which has always been controversial.

Research on sexuality education in colleges and universities is limited to assessment of departments' teaching interventions (e.g. Brasseur, 1983; Pollis, 1986; Gingiss and Hamilton, 1989; Cohen et al., 1994). One journal produced a special issue on peer education, merely detailing how to implement peer education of all types (*Journal of American College Health*, 41, 1993). Critical analysis of peer sexuality education programmes is nonexistent (Fennell, 1993).

This chapter revolves around a PSE programme (in existence since 1988) at a large, public university in the south-eastern United States. The central focus of this study, part of a larger examination, is how PSEs challenge institutionalized sexuality discourses and policies.

This university's policies about sexuality education are not written in stone. One administrator said, 'I wouldn't say that the university—whoever that is—feels like we need to do so much in the area of sex education. I think [sexuality education] could fall off the face of the earth, stop tomorrow, and nobody would notice.'

However, the three administrators I interviewed are unlikely to disturb the PSE programme unless it draws negative attention. One example, according to one administrator, would be complaints by parents, students or student (religious) groups about the content and conduct of PSE programmes:

If public opinion changed and we got a lot of letters . . . Let's say one of the PSEs does something really bizarre, we'd hear about it pretty fast. That stuff gets to the media pretty fast, and then we would have to do something.

As peer sexuality educators, students are simultaneously consumers and producers of education. Peer education casts students as subjects of institutional discourses and policies, but also as objects, able to reproduce these ideologies. Sexuality becomes an instrumental element in the social appropriation of bodies: 'Sex is located at the point of intersection of the discipline of the body and the control of the population' (Foucault, 1980, p. 125).

Based on six months of intensive fieldwork, participant observation and interviews, I analyse a smaller group of PSEs. The 'Sexual Health Information Network' I focus on was started by PSEs in February 1994, and functioned until June 1994. Nine of its ten members were PSEs (there were 25 PSEs in the larger programme). Under informed consent, participants' names are changed.

THE SEXUAL HEALTH INFORMATION NETWORK

The students surprised me that day in January. In interviews, several PSEs confessed to being disappointed by their classmates. One thought fellow PSEs would be more radical, interested in more than just sexual health. When I became a PSE in another programme ten years ago, I felt similarly. After a month, it was clear that my colleagues were only there to learn how to teach and to satisfy education major requirements.

Enthusiastic at first, SHIN organizers developed outreach and programming ideas that surpassed PSE programmes (standard fare included contraception, AIDS and gay and lesbian issues). I was also excited, because I wanted to observe how sexualities are institutionalized, and to answer two Foucaultian questions: what form could student resistance to institutional policies take, and was resistance even possible?

Although SHIN was student-organized and student-run, it had to be sanctioned through institutional channels. Various avenues in the university were closed to unofficial groups—most importantly funding. A week after the initial discussion about starting a group, Trixie addressed the PSE class: 'Anyone

with activist concerns, anyone who wants campus involvement via campus channels, should join us', she said. Trixie considered herself an activist already. She worked for the local AIDS agency, delivering meals to clients and case-managing for a short time. Her classmates were used to hearing her ideas, since her soft voice often added a radical edge to class discussions.

Jennifer took charge of the steps necessary for official recognition. She was well integrated into the upper levels of the university's structure. Only a sophomore, Jennifer held a high position in student government and was vice-president of her sorority. She told the class that to petition for group formation, at least ten names and social security numbers needed to be signed to a form. 'We need to get money', Jennifer said. 'We're new, and we have to let the student affairs people know what our plans are, do a budget, and pick a group affiliation—maybe service?'

She circulated the form and some PSEs signed it, knowing their signatures did not obligate them to anything. Jennifer said the group would need an official name, a constitution, officers and a committee structure. Only Trixie realized the irony of forming a 'radical' group via official, university channels, but thought that it would be ironically appropriate to spend institutional money doing 'guerrilla sexuality education'. But the class wanted to know how this group would be different from the PSEs, and why they had to be completely separate from the programme. 'There are advantages to being perceived as a completely different entity', Trixie said.

'You could be a lot more political', Maria Scott said, implying that she and Trixie had discussed this previously. Maria and Trixie were acquainted outside the PSE class, because both were affiliated with the local AIDS group. 'Health services wouldn't approve of being political. You could be a lot more activist. As students, you can get away with it.'

'I'm attracted to controversial things', Trixie said. 'But I wouldn't want this to come down on the two of you [programme supervisors Laura and Maria]. Maybe you could just act as a steering committee.'

Maria said students have more luck changing policies than do professionals, citing student housing representatives' success in getting dormitory condom machines approved. If SHIN wanted to distribute condoms, however, it was 'sticky', Maria said, unless the group's members were all PSEs. The logic was apparently that PSEs in any context were 'experts', trained to use and distribute condoms.

After debating names like 'Sex' and 'Students Advocating Safer Sex Issues' the group called themselves 'Sexual Health Information Network'. They wanted a 'non-gendered' acronym—'SHIN'— and agreed that a non-threatening name could attract more people. They wanted to reach those who did not get PSE programmes, whether due to schedule conflicts, living off-campus or through fear of group discussions.

The palatable, mainstream name with 'health' in it was the first of the group's many concessions. In keeping with student senate policies, they appointed officers and committee heads, in spite of their small size and desire to be egalitarian. Everyone was an officer or a committee head, but this did not equalize things. The president organized the schedule, arranged for meeting space and ran meetings. Appointed committee members had designated duties, such as public relations, making contacts in residence halls and programme development.

STARTING THE GROUP: BECOMING INSTITUTIONALLY SANCTIONED

SHIN met on campus, in the student union of the institution whose approaches they sought to challenge. Initially, they met after class, to organize how to obtain official recognition. Once the student senate approved SHIN, core members emerged (Christine, Jill, Mike and Samantha; Debra, Ed and Carlin attended sporadically). Jennifer shepherded SHIN through the paperwork, then quit to run for student body president. She was ultimately much more interested in maintaining institutional powers and policies than in challenging them.

SHIN selected officers, in keeping with institutional mandates for funded campus groups. Debra agreed to be scribe; Jill, treasurer; and Mike, facilitator (president). Ed and Carlin volunteered to be the publicity committee. Perhaps recognizing that the group would not become an activist, subversive force, Trixie bowed out, saying that she could be an *ad hoc*

'information source', but she could not be truly involved.

Every activity SHIN envisioned needed the cooperation of campus entities, including the bus company, the student senate activities council and a dormitory. Like other campus groups (such as a political club), the student activities fund bankrolled SHIN. This fund came from fees paid by every student each quarter. Each SHIN member was essentially paying for the group's activities (while also paying to support other campus groups with less subversive goals). The university acted as treasurer and gatekeeper, ultimately determining which groups were funded.

None the less, Mike reiterated that SHIN was 'A student organization that could do things a bit more radical than what the PSEs could do, with no fallout on our advisers [Sorensen and Scott].' Mike had always felt constrained by the PSE policy of a disclaimer before every programme: 'As representatives of the health services, we advocate total abstinence as the safest sex.' He was the only PSE who departed from standard practice in his programmes—he talked openly about pleasure.

By the spring quarter, SHIN was meeting every Sunday evening. Most of their time was spent haggling over how to proceed—what kind of education to do and how and where to do it. Their goals for the spring quarter included a simple necessity—getting their name 'out to the public'. The members were surprised that I spent my Sunday evenings with them. They thought there was nothing interesting about what they were doing.

SHIN'S PROJECTS: WINTER QUARTER

SHIN members wanted to channel their 'activist concerns' into intervention and outreach that differed from the standard PSE programmes. They wanted to reach people who did not normally attend PSE programmes in dormitories or classes. Group members worked on three projects (during winter and spring quarters): informational placards on campus buses, a party/benefit at the local gay bar and a programme with the working title, 'How to Be a Better Lover'.

The idea for bus placards grew from the desire to reach students living off-campus. The campus bus service carried many students, including commuter students using satellite car parks and those travelling directly from their apartment complexes. The bus company regularly sold the space above the seats for announcements and advertisements. Everyone in SHIN was enthusiastic, citing examples of long bus rides with nothing to read, eyes searching for anything interesting to look at. But what would be printed on the bus cards? 'We should do brief, buzzword, sound-bite kinds of things', said Mike, using the language of postmodern political image-makers. 'We don't want to have so much going on that no one reads them.'

Ed volunteered to talk to the bus company and find out how to get cards printed and distributed. Samantha volunteered to design the first group of cards, focused on acquaintance rape. The others chose topics: Jill, gay and lesbian issues; Debra, STDs and women and AIDS; Christine, contraception; Mike, safer sex.

Before the winter quarter had ended, SHIN had discussed their progress. Ed reported that the bus cards would cost $20 each time they were circulated on the buses. Businesses used the cards as a way to get inexpensive, wide-scale advertising, but at those rates, SHIN would only be able to make cards five times each quarter. The group thought of several ways to operationalize this. Mike suggested that each placard author write a short editorial, to be published in the independent student newspaper. The editorial would be published at the beginning of each bus 'campaign' and would relate to the topic addressed by the bus cards.

The other project SHIN began to develop in the winter was to host a party at a local gay bar. The night would include drinking, dancing and free condoms with a safer sex information card from SHIN. Mike volunteered to call condom companies, focusing on the company that had won the contract to stock the future dormitory machines. He hoped that the opportunity for relevant publicity would inspire the condom company to provide the condoms to SHIN free of charge.

No one in SHIN thought about the overall impact of these efforts in any significant way. Each strategy—bus cards, editorials and a party—had been utilized by other local groups. A local AIDS group had hosted parties and benefits at the gay club, the local rape crisis centre had bought space on the buses and individuals

had written many editorials (including some protesting against the dormitory condom machines). It was unclear why the members of SHIN thought that any of these approaches were 'radical', as per the group's philosophy.

One radical suggestion, given that the audience was college students (85 per cent of whom are sexually active), was brushed aside. Carlin, who gave PSE programmes on 'intimacy without intercourse', asked why the group was doing nothing on abstinence, and Debra replied, 'Well, this is the "Sexual Health Information Network", so automatically, it's about sex . . . you know?'

SPRING QUARTER: NOTHING COMES TO FRUITION

Samantha opened the meeting by excitedly detailing the soundbites she had developed for her bus cards: 'Did you know that, legally, men cannot be raped?' and 'The average rapist rapes between 50 and 60 women before he is caught.' Samantha was a date-rape survivor and provided all the PSE programmes on rape. She also worked at the local rape crisis centre. She was very keen to get her cards onto the buses. All that remained now was for someone to design the card and submit the text, with payment, to the company which printed the cards.

No one discussed the implication of these cards, and what their connection was to acquaintance rape. What would the average reader do after digesting this information? Would the card about the number of women a 'rapist' rapes encourage a reader to view rape as something that (in reality) most often happens between acquaintances, or as something that a 'sick' minority of men do to strangers?

During this meeting, Mike broached the possibility of SHIN doing an 'interesting' programme, on sexual pleasure and techniques. The group was very excited by this idea. Samantha and Christine discussed whether they would be allowed to go into a dormitory and discuss how to be a better lover, in 'real', explicit terms. The dormitories were, on the whole, accustomed to PSE programmes, but none of these programmes specifically dealt with pleasure or doing 'technique a' with 'thing b' and 'part c'.

The possibility of moving beyond programmes with heavily factual, negatively consequential, health-related content was born. The week after Mike's suggestion, several members returned with more ideas about designing a programme on sexual pleasure and technique. Of all SHIN's projects, this programme was perhaps most closely related to their original (subversive) mandate: combining radical politics with activism, and using campus channels and resources to do so.

Each had a different idea about proceeding. Mike wanted to show excerpts from pornographic movies, to show techniques explicitly. Christine was more interested in informal discussion with programme participants, a sanctioned 'kiss and tell', where people described their best lovers and shared their techniques. Other SHIN members had no specific ideas, preferring to wait and wade through Mike and Christine's suggestions.

SHIN's programme-designing was hampered because nothing in their official curriculum had taught them how to design programmes. They also had no training specifically on 'sexual pleasure' or technique. Christine felt uncomfortable presenting herself as 'an expert' on sexual techniques. This would be the implied message if she addressed her peers, telling them how to put 'tab a' with 'slot b' in 'manner c'. Other SHIN members were worried about Mike's proposed approach as well. Samantha and Susan (the one non-PSE member, Samantha's room-mate) were wary of showing pornography, saying that it exploited women and was a 'male fantasy' of sex. At one point, they asked me what I thought.

'Do you want to risk getting arrested or seriously censured?' I said. 'Because I suspect that's the main risk you'd run if you showed explicit videos. Also, you might really offend some participants' sensibilities.' The policy on this was completely unclear. Mike said, 'But in my human sexuality class here, the professor showed some clips from these training videos, like the kind people buy from those upscale sex toy companies.' 'Did he get consent forms from you beforehand, or warn you somehow about what was going to happen?' I asked.

Mike did not remember what the professor had done. He asserted that similar clips, even from pornographic movies, would not offend someone who knowingly came to a programme on being a better lover (in other words, they would know what they were getting into before they arrived). But Mike wanted to present the programme in the lobby of one of the high-rise dormitories, to increase audience. He did not think that screening explicit sexual videos in such a public place would be problematic.

Beyond these sticky negotiations, SHIN had other planning difficulties. Mike thought SHIN members should present themselves as young Alex Comforts, offering tips, like *The Joy of Sex,* on how to improve sexual experiences. Christine was very uncomfortable with this idea, and again asked for my opinion. I said that being a good lover was more than the sum of its parts—that it was not as simple as knowing abstract techniques. I suggested they start planning by determining what their objectives were, and then design an effort that would meet those objectives.

While I was not surprised that SHIN asked my advice, I was in conflict about giving it. The footing was difficult: on one hand, I did not want to see SHIN get arrested or reprimanded for their actions, for violating university policies; on the other, I did not want to influence their behaviour or choices. But I could not plead programmatic ignorance when they questioned me, because all knew that I had led 'How to Be a Better Lover' programmes when I was a PSE.

Eventually, SHIN decided to combine some of a 'Sex and Self-Esteem' PSE programme with open discussion of technique-related activities (mostly connected to 'outercourse', oral sex and intercourse positions). Members wrote their goals for the first programme (listed verbatim):

1. Examine beliefs, attitudes, etc. that hinder good sex and try to think of attitudes that will reinforce good sex.
2. Examine whys in sex: why do you do it? why you don't? are you comfortable with sex and why or why not?
3. Figure out 'your' conditions for good sex and why.
4. Everyone is a sexual being. Piece your sexuality together in a positive way. Define.

5. Fantasies (why they're useful; they're okay to have).
6. We assume all sexual activity is OK, except with an unconsensual partner.
7. Put together a sourcebook (how to get help, think more about this).

The group wanted to accomplish these goals through various methods. Facilitators would depend heavily on do-it-yourself checklists and inventories, combined with audience participation. They considered the following: anatomy knowledge quizzes; a non-pornographic film clip; agree/disagree statements; a discussion about masturbation; assumption statements about sexuality; and anonymous index cards with details about what makes sexual activities uncomfortable (related to attitudes, beliefs and expectations). By the time the group decided the content and objectives, it was almost final exam study week.

The owner of the gay bar had offered to host a 'condom party' and to give some of the entry fee to SHIN, but Mike was unable to get any free condoms. No bus cards were ever printed or distributed. Attendance at SHIN meetings was low, with some members showing up for the first five minutes, reporting their lack of progress and then leaving. One week, only one person besides me attended.

A dorm had offered to promote the workshop on sexual pleasure while providing its lobby. One tentative date was cancelled because SHIN was unprepared. Rescheduling before finals week proved impossible, because of other commitments dorm personnel had made. Ultimately, the quarter and school year ended with no outward sign of SHIN's existence. The group had accomplished none of its plans, objectives or goals.

POSSIBILITIES AND CHANGES

The peer sexuality educators in SHIN never did any radical, subversive education. They did nothing that outwardly challenged the university's policies on sexuality education in spite of the fact that SHIN developed because of policy constraints on PSE programme administrators. Can sexuality education challenge typical ideologies about such education,

even when not provided by professionals and administrators? Szirom (1988, p. 56) argues that, 'Sex education as it is currently taught, rather than being a radical subject which challenges the status quo, in fact maintains the established order.' But can peer sexuality education become education that does not 'maintain the established [policies]'?

In an examination of sexuality education and policy issues in Britain and Europe, Meredith (1989, p. 3) quotes a sceptical sexuality education supporter: 'No sexually-liberating education can be provided within the context of what is in practice felt by many of its clients to be a repressive institution.' For PSEs, the 'repressive institution' is, in one sense, the university. Foucault asserts that specific knowledges are central to normalizing social life and institutions, including the knowledges produced by, in and around education. The possibilities for new languages and challenges are innately constrained by 'institutional practices, power relations' (Ball, 1990). The possibilities for PSEs are restricted by the institutional and political contexts in which their efforts occur. PSEs are thus impeded from doing anything other than maintaining the *status quo*.

According to Szirom (1988, p. 134), '[Sexuality education] continues to maintain an "objective" or "value free" position, which neither examines such issues as power within relationships, nor the sociopolitical context in which such relationships occur'. Some might argue that peer educators can operate outside this context, producing knowledges devoid of the influence of official discourses and policies. But my case suggests that context is too central; SHIN was officially sanctioned, was subject to university policies for group formation and budgeting and was operating fully within institutional confines. Ultimately, SHIN challenged no policies, did nothing 'radical' in public.

In this case study, subversion did not happen on an institutional scale. SHIN accomplished nothing except the reinscription of certain health promotion discourses and other sexuality discourses (specifically, the libertarian 'pleasure is the answer'). The group began and faded without notice; no one on campus ever knew what SHIN was. Why?

There are two strands of answers: institutional constraints and individual constraints. Funded by student activity fees, approved by the student senate and forced to appoint committees and officers, SHIN was subject to institutional policies. Even as a subversive response to the PSE programme, SHIN occurred within the confines of this system. SHIN was organized by PSEs after their training into the discursive strategies of health promotion and sexuality education. These disciplinary and institutional constraints impeded both the PSEs and SHIN.

Ultimately, though, it is probably impossible for peers to educate outside the borders of the institution. The history of university peer education in the United States includes underground, illegal student efforts (in the 1960s and 1970s), which were quickly quashed by and/or reappropriated by administrators (Sloane and Zimmer, 1993). What the peer educators were doing and not doing, and could and could not do, is contextualized by individual constraints via socialization into sexuality—through education, peers, family, media and religion.

But subversion on a small, individual scale did happen. Some individuals bucked socialization by becoming PSEs in the first place. Although Foucault would argue that we have not been repressed in talking about sexuality, many of the PSEs describe parental sexual silences. For them, training to talk about sexuality (in public, no less) was subversive. For most of the PSEs, the most subversive act was discarding socialized heterosexism during training. Some had never met gays, lesbians or bisexuals before the class.

So what form would resistance to institutional policies take? In terms of sexuality, resistance might be a turning away, a renouncing. Resistance might be refusing to believe that 'sex' is a universal, that 'sex' is pleasure, that 'liberated sex' can exist. Resistance would be a form of atheism: 'I do not believe in sexual pleasure; it does not exist.'

There is no room for atheism in peer sexuality education. There is only room for truths. Perhaps PSE is flawed because it is not really about sexuality or 'sex'. It is about health, 'facts', and 'problems with solutions'. Peer sexuality education operates within this context but also outside this context. Ultimately, peer sexuality educators are object and subject simultaneously.

REFERENCES

Ball, S. J. (1990). 'Introducing Monsieur Foucault', in S. J. Ball (ed.), *Foucault and Education: Disciplines and Knowledge.* London: Routledge, pp. 1–10.

Brasseur, J. (1983). 'An anonymous peer counseling system for use with pregnant students', *Journal of American College Health,* 32: 88.

Cohen, G., Byrne, C., Hay, J. and Schmuck, M. L. (1994). 'Assessing the impact of an interdisciplinary workshop in human sexuality', *Journal of Sex Education and Therapy,* 20(1): 56–68.

Fennell, R. (1993). 'A review of evaluations of peer education programs', *Journal of American College Health,* 41: 251–3.

Foucault, M. (1980). *Power/Knowledge: Selected Interviews and Other Writings 1972–1977.* New York: Pantheon.

Gingiss, P. L., and Hamilton, R. (1989). 'Teacher perspectives after implementing a human sexuality education program', *Journal of School Health,* 59(10): 427–31.

Gould, J. M. and Lomax, A. R. (eds) (1993). 'The evolution of peer education: where do we go from here?' [Special issue], *Journal of American College Health,* 41.

Meredith, P. (1989). *Sex Education: Political Issues in Britain and Europe.* London: Routledge.

Morris, R. W. (1994). *Values in Sexuality Education: A Philosophical Study.* Lanham, MD: University Press of America.

Pollis, C. A. (1986). 'Sensitive drawings of sexual activity in human sexuality textbooks: an analysis on communication and bias', *Journal of Homosexuality,* 13(1): 59–73.

Sloane, B. C. and Zimmer, C. G. (1993). 'The power of peer health education', *Journal of American College Health,* 41: 241–5.

Szirom, T. (1988). *Teaching Gender? Sex Education and Sexual Stereotypes.* Sydney, Australia: Allen & Unwin.

10.4 SEXUALITY, CULTURE, AND POWER IN HIV/AIDS RESEARCH

Richard Parker

INTRODUCTION

Like many other disciplines, anthropology largely failed to distinguish itself in its initial responses to the HIV/AIDS epidemics. Certain other social science disciplines—in particular, psychology—were quick to mobilize themselves internally during the mid-1980s in order to lobby the U.S. federal government for funding and to offer institutional responses to the epidemic through the foundation of HIV/AIDS research centers (typically based in academic departments of psychiatry or psychology and well-integrated into largely epidemiological research efforts). However, anthropologists for the most part contributed only irregularly to such early research mobilization, largely on the basis of their own individual research initiatives and publications rather than as part of a formal or organized research response. This is not to say that no important anthropological contributions were made to the study of HIV and AIDS during this time (e.g., Bolognone 1986; Conant 1988a,b; Feldman 1985; Feldman & Johnson 1986; Feldman et al 1987; E. Gorman 1986; M. Gorman 1986; Herdt 1987; Lang 1986; Nachmann & Dreyfuss 1986; Sindzingré & Jourdain 1987; Stall 1986; for further references to early anthropological work on HIV/AIDS, see Bolton et al 1991). But the dominant paradigm for the organization and conduct of AIDS research—both in the United States, where the epidemic was most intense at the time, and internationally, where its size and shape were only beginning to be perceived—was established in large part independently of anthropological contributions. The paradigm was characterized by a heavily biomedical emphasis and a largely individualistic bias in relation to the ways in which the social sciences might contribute meaningfully to the development and implementation of an HIV/AIDS research agenda.

This historical context proved to be especially important in shaping the dominant tendencies in the study of sexuality in relation to HIV and AIDS. One of the most immediate consequences of the HIV/AIDS epidemic was a remarkable increase in concern with (and funding for) research on sexuality—as well as a growing awareness of the extent to which the widespread neglect and even marginalization of sex research over much of the twentieth century had left virtually all countries largely unprepared to respond to an epidemic that appeared to be driven, above all else, through the sexual transmission of a viral infection (Herdt 1987; Herdt & Lindenbaum 1992). As policy makers and planners found themselves returning to the Kinsey surveys of sexual behavior—carried out in the United States more than fifty years earlier but now often invoked as if they applied to the historical present or, even more problematically, to the sexual practices found in radically different cultural traditions—new emphasis was placed on the urgent need for more adequate, current data on the nature of sexual behavior (see Turner et al 1989).

Indeed, much of the social science research activity that emerged in response to AIDS, not only during the mid- to late 1980s, but up to the present time, focuses on surveys of risk-related sexual behavior and on the knowledge, attitudes, and beliefs about sexuality that might be associated with the risk of HIV infection. Most of these studies have aimed to collect quantifiable data on numbers of sexual partners, the frequency of different sexual practices, previous experience with other sexually transmitted diseases, and any number of other similar issues that were understood to contribute to the spread of HIV infection (e.g., Carballo et al

1989; Chouinard & Albert 1989; Turner et al 1989; Cleland & Ferry 1995). On the basis of such data, the primary goal was to point the way for prevention policies and intervention programs designed to reduce behaviors associated with increased risk for HIV infection. By focusing on the links between empirical data on sexual behavior and largely psychological theories of individual behavior change (such as the Health Belief Model, the Theory of Reasoned Action, or the Stages of Change Model), it was assumed that more broad-based prevention programs could be developed in order to persuade individuals to change their behaviors in ways that would ultimately reduce the risk of HIV infection (e.g., Turner et al 1989).

Increasingly, however, as behavioral research and behavioral interventions began to be developed in a growing range of diverse social and cultural settings, the relative effectiveness of both the research instruments and intervention strategies came to be questioned, notably by anthropologists (see Herdt et al 1991, Parker et al 1991). The difficulties of translating or adapting research protocols for cross-cultural application quickly became apparent in the face of often radically different understandings of sexual expression and practices in different societies and cultures— and even in different subcultures within the same society (Bibeau 1991, Bolton et al 1991, Singer 1992, ten Brummelhuis & Herdt 1995, Clatts 1994, Herdt & Lindenbaum 1992, Parker 1994, Pollak 1988). The limitations of behavioral interventions based on information and reasoned persuasion as a stimulus for risk reduction also quickly became evident. In study after study, the finding that information in and of itself is insufficient to produce risk-reducing behavioral change was repeated, and the relative limitations of individual psychology as the basis for intervention and prevention programs became apparent (see Carrier & Magaña 1991, Clatts 1989, Herdt & Boxer 1992, Herdt et al 1991). By the late 1980s, therefore, on the basis of both research findings and practical experience around the world, it had become clear that a far more complex set of social, structural, and cultural factors mediate the structure of risk in every population group, and that the dynamics of individual psychology cannot be expected to fully explain, let alone produce, changes in sexual conduct without taking these broader issues into account (see Bolton & Singer 1992; Carrier 1989; Flowers 1988; Herdt & Lindenbaum 1992; Herdt et al 1991; Obbo 1988; Parker 1987, 1988; Schoepf et al 1988).

FROM BEHAVIORAL RISKS TO CULTURAL MEANINGS

Although anthropological work has played only a very limited role during the 1980s in the development of HIV/AIDS research agendas and initiatives focusing on sexual behavior, quite the opposite is the case for anthropology in the 1990s, in relation to finding the most important alternative approaches to research on sexuality and AIDS. While there has in fact been increasing convergence between these approaches over time, it is nonetheless possible to identify at least two major tendencies that, by the early 1990s, had begun to mount a serious challenge to the dominance of biomedically and epidemiologically driven behavioral research agendas for the study of HIV and AIDS, as well as to the psychological approach to sexuality described above.

On the one hand, particularly during the early 1990s, there was a growing focus on the interpretation of cultural meanings (as opposed to the calculus of behavioral frequencies) as central to a fuller understanding of both the sexual transmission of HIV in different social settings and the possibilities that might exist for responding to it through the design of more culturally appropriate prevention programs (Treichler 1999). On the other hand, emerging at the same time but gaining greater attention over the mid- to late 1990s, there was increasing concern with the impact of a range of wider structural factors that could be seen as shaping vulnerability to HIV infection as well as conditioning the possibilities for sexual risk reduction in specific social contexts (see Farmer 1992; Farmer et al 1996; Schoepf 1992a,b,c; Schoepf et al 1988; Treichler 1999).

By the early 1990s, a range of broader cultural factors began to be identified as centrally important to an adequate understanding of the social dimensions of HIV and AIDS. Furthermore, the limitations of traditional behavioral research approaches in public health had begun to become apparent, particularly with regard to the development of prevention and intervention activities (see Bolton & Singer 1992; Herdt & Lindenbaum 1992; Herdt et al 1991). Heavily influenced by developments within interactionist sociology and interpretive cultural anthropology, as well as by insights emerging from fields such as women's and gay and lesbian studies, attention turned to the broader set of social representations and cultural meanings that could be understood as shaping or constructing sexual experience in different contexts (Alonso & Koreck 1989; Carrier & Magaña 1991; Daniel & Parker 1993; Gorman 1991; Herdt & Boxer 1991, 1992; Obbo 1993; Schoepf 1992a,b). Stimulated by such social constructionist concerns, an important shift of emphasis began to take place from an earlier focus on individual psychology and individual subjectivity to a new concern with intersubjective cultural meanings related to sexuality (Brummelhuis & Herdt 1995; Gagnon & Parker 1995; Herdt & Lindenbaum 1992; Paiva 1995; Parker 1991; Parker & Aggleton 1999).

Fundamentally informed by anthropological approaches to other cultural phenomena (such as religious belief and political ideology), this new attention to sexual meanings emphasized their shared or collective character—their constitution not as the property of atomized or isolated individuals but rather of social persons who are integrated in the context of specific cultural settings (Herdt & Lindenbaum 1992). This new wave of anthropological research on HIV and AIDS thus sought to go beyond the calculation of behavioral frequencies. In order to examine and explicate what sexual practices mean to the persons involved, the significant contexts in which they take place, the social scripting of sexual encounters, and the diverse sexual cultures and subcultures that are present or emergent within different societies, the research also sought to go beyond the identification of statistical correlates aimed at explaining sexual risk behavior (e.g., Bolton & Singer 1992; ten Brummelhuis & Herdt 1995; Herdt & Lindenbaum 1992; Parker 1994, 1996a). It is perhaps not surprising that much of this work first emerged in cross-cultural research and in analyses of the situation in non-

Western settings in which the biomedical categories used in epidemiological analysis failed to be fully applicable (Carrier 1989; Parker 1987, 1988; Wilson 1995; de Zalduondo et al 1991). Increasingly, cultural analysis has also been applied when considering specific sexual cultures or subcultures in the industrialized West, offering important new insights even in settings where extensive behavioral research had already been carried out (see Alonso & Koreck 1989; Clatts 1995; Henriksson 1995; Irvine 1994; Kane & Mason 1992; Magaña 1991; Sobo 1993, 1995a).

The focus of much important research on sexuality in relation to HIV and AIDS over the course of the past decade has thus moved from behavior, in and of itself, to the cultural settings within which behavior takes place—and to the cultural symbols, meanings, and rules that organize it (see Bolton 1992; González Block & Liguori 1992; Henriksson 1995; Henriksson & Mansson 1995; Herdt 1997a,b,c; Herdt & Boxer 1991, 1992; Hogsborg & Aaby 1992; Kendall 1995; Lyttleton 2000; Paiva 1995, 2000; Setel 1999). Special emphasis has been given to analyzing indigenous cultural categories and systems of classification that structure and define sexual experience in different social and cultural contexts—with particular stress on the cross-cultural diversity that exists in the construction of same-sex interactions (Alonso & Koreck 1989; González Block & Liguori 1992; Carrier 1989; Carrier et al 1997; Carrillo 1999; Lichtenstein 2000; Ligouri & Aggleton 1999; Preston-Whyte et al 2000; Tan 1995, 1996). Indeed, it has become increasingly apparent that many of the key categories and classifications [not only "homosexuality," but also categories such as "prostitution," or "female sexual partner" (of male injecting drug users)] that have typically been used in biomedicine to describe sexual behaviors, or account for vectors of infection of interest to public health epidemiology, are in fact not relevant in all cultural contexts. Indeed, the meanings of these concepts are not stable even in those contexts in which these categories are in wide circulation (e.g., Alonso & Koreck 1989; Avila et al 1991; Carrier 1989, 1995, 1999; Carrier et al 1997; Carrillo 1999; Díaz 1998; Herdt 1997b,c; Herdt & Lindenbaum 1992; Irvine 1994; Jenkins 1996; Kane & Mason 1992; Larvie 1997, 1999; Law 1997; Lichtenstein 2000; Liguori & Aggleton 1999; Liguori et al 1996; Preston-Whyte 1995; Preston-Whyte et al 2000; Silva 1999; Tan 1995, 1996, 1999, 2000; Wright 1997; de Zalduondo 1991). By focusing more carefully on local categories and classifications, the cultural analysis of sexual meanings has thus sought to move from what, in other areas of anthropological or linguistic investigation, have been described as an "etic" or "outsider" perspective, to an "emic" or "insider" perspective—or, perhaps even more accurately, from the "experience-distant" concepts of biomedical science to the "experience-near" concepts and categories that the members of specific cultures use to understand and interpret their everyday lives (see Geertz 1973, 1983; Parker 1991).

This shift of emphasis from the study of individual behaviors to the investigation of cultural meanings has drawn attention to the socially constructed (and historically changing) identities and communities that structure sexual practice within the flow of collective life (see Bolton 1992; Carrillo 1999; Herdt & Boxer 1992; Klein 1999; Rubin 1997; Tan 1995; 1999; Terto 2000). On the basis of such work, an important reformulation of the very notion of intervention has begun to take place. It has become increasingly apparent that the idea of a behavioral intervention may in fact be a misnomer, since HIV/AIDS prevention interventions almost never function at the level of behavior but rather at the level of social or collective representations (Parker 1996a). New knowledge and information about perceived sexual risk will always be interpreted within the context of pre-existing systems of meaning—systems of meaning that necessarily mediate the ways in which such information must always be incorporated into action. Because action has increasingly come to be understood as socially constructed and fundamentally collective in nature, earlier notions of behavioral intervention have given way to ethnographically grounded AIDS education and prevention programs that are community-based and culturally sensitive—programs aimed at transforming social norms and cultural values, and thus at reconstituting collective meanings in ways that will ultimately promote safer sexual practices (see Altman 1994; Bolton & Singer 1992; Paiva 1995, 2000).

FROM CULTURAL MEANINGS TO STRUCTURAL VIOLENCE

Such ethnographically grounded descriptive and analytic research on the social and cultural construction of sexual meanings provides important insights to the representations shaping HIV-related risk and offers the basis for the development of culturally sensitive and culturally appropriate, community-based HIV/AIDS prevention programs. However, since the start of the 1990s it has also become increasingly evident that the range of factors influencing the construction of sexual realities is far more complex than previously perceived. It has become evident that not just cultural, but also structural, political, and economic factors shape sexual experience (and hence constrain the possibilities for sexual behavior change) to a far greater extent than had previously been understood (Singer et al 1990; Farmer 1992; Schoepf 1991). In particular, research has emphasized that political and economic factors have played a key role in determining the shape and spread of the epidemic and has emphasized that these same factors have been responsible for many of the most complex barriers to effective AIDS prevention programs (Baer et al 1997; González Block & Liguori 1992; Farmer 1992, 1999; Farmer et al 1996; Lindenbaum 1997, 1998; Schoepf 1991, 1995; Singer 1994, 1998; Singer et al 1990, 1992). By the early to mid-1990s, cultural analysis had emerged as an important corrective to the perceived limitations of earlier behavioral approaches. At the same time, a new focus on political and economic analysis of the structural factors associated with an increased risk for HIV infection, and with both the structural barriers and facilitators for risk reduction, emerged as central to the evolving anthropological response to the epidemic (Farmer et al 1996; Feldman 1994; Singer 1994, 1998).

Because this research on structural factors in relation to HIV/AIDS has emerged in a number of different social settings, ranging from deeply impoverished rural areas in developing countries to the marginalized inner cities in the United States, the language that it has used, the conceptual tools that it has employed, and the specific focus of analysis have often varied (e.g., Bond et al 1997b; Farmer 1992; Kreniske 1997; Schoepf 1991, 1992a,b,c, 1995; Singer 1994, 1998). In spite of the differences in terminology and at times in research emphasis, this work has consistently focused on what can be described as forms of "structural violence," which determine the social vulnerability of both groups and individuals. In developing these concepts, the work considers the interactive or synergistic effects of social factors such as poverty and economic exploitation, gender power, sexual oppression, racism, and social exclusion (Farmer et al 1996; Singer 1998; Parker & Camargo 2000; Parker et al 2000b). And the research has typically linked this vulnerability to a consideration of the ways in which such structural violence is itself situated in historically constituted political and economic systems—systems in which diverse political and economic processes and policies (whether related to economic development, housing, labor, migration or immigration, health, education, and welfare) create the dynamic of the epidemic and must be addressed in order to have any hope of reducing the spread of HIV infection (Bond et al 1997a; de Zalduondo & Bernard 1995; González Block & Liguori 1992; Farmer et al 1996; Kammerer et al 1995; Long 1997; Porter 1997; Romero-Daza 1994; Romero-Daza & Himmelgreen 1998; Susser & Kreniske 1997; Symonds 1998). To respond to this growing perception of the importance of structural factors and structural violence in shaping sexual experience and vulnerability to HIV infection, attention has increasingly focused on the ways in which societies and communities structure the possibilities of sexual interaction between social actors—the ways in which they define the available range of potential sexual partners and practices, as well as the ways in which they impose both the sexual possibilities and options that will be open to differentially situated actors. With whom one may have sex, in what ways, under what circumstances, and with what specific outcomes are never simply random questions (Akeroyd 1997; de Zalduondo & Bernard 1995; McGrath et al 1992, 1993; Parker et al 1991; Rwabukwali et al 1994).[1] Such possibilities are defined through the implicit and explicit rules and regulations imposed by the sexual cultures of specific communities as well as the economic and

political power relations that underpin these sexual cultures. They can never be fully understood without examining the importance of issues such as "class," "race" or "ethnicity" and the other multiple forms through which different societies organize systems of social inequality and structure the possibilities for social interaction along or across lines of social difference.

This awareness of the ways in which social orders structure the possibilities (and obligations) of sexual contact has drawn special attention to socially and culturally determined differentials in power—particularly between men and women (de Zalduondo & Bernard 1995; Gupta & Weiss 1993; Parker 1991; Schoepf 1992a,b; Sobo 1993, 1994, 1995a,b, 1998)—but also, in some instances, between different types of men (Carrillo 1999; González Block & Liguori 1992; Liguori et al 1996; Prieur 1998; Silva 1999; Tan 1995, 1999).

Because different societies organize sexual (as well as other forms of) inequality in specific ways, social and cultural rules and regulations place specific limitations on the potential for negotiation in sexual interactions. These rules and regulations, in turn, condition the possibilities for the occurrence of sexual violence, for patterns of contraceptive use, for sexual negotiation, for HIV/AIDS risk reduction strategies, and so on. The dynamics of gender power relations have thus become a major focus for contemporary research, particularly in relation to reproductive health and the rapid spread of HIV infection among women in many parts of the world (e.g., Farmer et al 1996; Ginsberg & Rapp 1995; Gupta & Weiss 1993; Schoepf 1992a,b, 1995; Ward 1991). Just as detailed cross-cultural and comparative investigation of the social construction of same-sex interactions provided perhaps the key test case for demonstrating the importance of cultural analysis in relation to sexuality and HIV/AIDS, issues related to gender and power have been central to a better understanding of the importance of structural factors in organizing sexual relations and HIV/AIDS-related vulnerability (Akeroyd 1997; de Zalduondo & Bernard 1995; de Zalduondo et al 1991; Farmer 1999; Farmer et al 1996; Farmer et al 1993; Gupta & Weiss 1993, Long 1997; Obbo 1995;

Paiva 1995; Romero-Daza 1994; Schoepf 1992b,c; Sobo 1993, 1995a,b).

As Farmer's work, in particular, has demonstrated, the political economic factors that drive the HIV/AIDS epidemic in virtually all social settings are intertwined with gender and sexuality, whose hierarchies make women, and low-income women in particular, especially vulnerable to HIV infection (Farmer 1992). In spite of this, there have still been relatively few ethnographically grounded studies on the ways in which gender and sexuality as structural (rather than behavioral) factors shape the AIDS epidemic. Farmer, Lindenbaum and Delvecchio-Good attribute this neglect to the initial predominance of AIDS cases among gay men in the industrialized Western countries, the fact that sexuality is a topic poorly understood by nearly all social scientists, and the fact that AIDS intervention programs often rely on superficial "rapid ethnographic assessment" procedures rather than on more detailed ethnographic description and analysis (Farmer et al 1993). The inappropriateness of many AIDS interventions directed toward women increasingly led a number of anthropologists to look more closely at gender and sexuality systems with the hopes of developing more realistic and effective HIV risk reduction options for women (Kammerer et al 1995; Schoepf 1991, 1992a,b; Symonds 1998).

Over the course of the 1990s, this growing interest in understanding the role of gender and sexuality structures in promoting HIV vulnerability, particularly among heterosexually active women and men, has increasingly generated a number of impressive ethnographic analyses that are attentive to both cultural and political economic factors. For example, Kammerer et al examine the ways in which the mountain tribes of the northern Thailand periphery are being exposed to the threat of HIV (Kammerer et al 1995). The vulnerability of these hillside tribes to HIV is in large measure generated by state and capitalist penetration, which has led to a breakdown of the material base rural life and has caused young people to migrate to valley towns in order to work not only as prostitutes but also as maids, waiters, and construction workers. These socioeconomic transformations have affected hillside sexuality, which until recently was structured around core values of "shame, name and blame." The authors provide ethnographic descriptions of these core values in relation to HIV/AIDS and how the gender power relations and customary prescriptions and prohibitions of hillside sexuality make talking about sex and taking precautions against HIV transmission difficult.

Similarly, Symonds, writing on the Hmong in Northern Thailand, has examined how the epidemic of HIV/AIDS in Thailand, and the place of Hmong within it, can be explained only by a combination of inter-related factors: the commercial sex industry, the prevalence of injection drug use, the political economic changes that have forced the Hmong living in the highlands to rely on lowland markets, racism and discrimination against the Hmong by the Thai majority, and sexual double standards, which permits polygyny among men yet controls the sexuality of young women (Symonds 1998). Finally, Schoepf has used vignettes from the life histories of women from various socioeconomic classes in Kinshasa, Zaire to demonstrate that HIV is spreading not through exotic cultural practices but because of many people's normal responses to situations of everyday life, such as dealing with substantial economic hardship and uncertainty (Schoepf 1992c). Like Kammerer et al and Symonds, Schoepf has promoted a participatory and collaborative form of action research with vulnerable women as a means to help redefine the gendered social roles and socioeconomic conditions that have contributed to the rapid spread of HIV in many parts of the world (Schoepf 1992a,b; Schoepf et al 1988).

In turning to issues of power, attention has focused not only on gender but also on poverty, both in the context of developing countries (see Farmer 1992, 1995, 1999; Farmer et al 1996; Farmer et al 1993; Kreniske 1997; Paiva 1995, 2000; Schoepf 1991) and in the impoverished inner-city ethnic communities of the United States (Farmer et al 1996; Singer 1994, 1998; Sobo 1993, 1994, 1995a), particularly as poverty interacts with gender power relations. Especially in the U.S.-based urban ethnography of HIV and AIDS, the impact of race and racism has necessarily been linked to issues of both poverty and gender, creating a kind of synergistic effect (Baer et al 1997; Farmer et al 1993; Singer 1994, 1998), involving multiple forms of oppression and shaping the nature of HIV/AIDS-related risk due to injecting drug use and voluntary as well as involuntary sexual practices (Singer 1998; Sobo 1995a). Although it has received less attention (perhaps because of the homophobia that affects anthropology as much as any other discipline), the extension of gender power inequalities together with pervasive heterosexism have also increasingly been understood as interacting with other forms of structural violence, including both poverty and racism, in creating situations of extreme vulnerability in relation to gender nonconformity, to transgender and male sex work, to gay men from ethnic minority groups, and among young men who have sex with men generally (see Díaz 1998; Carrier et al 1997; Khan 1996; Lichtenstein 2000; Parker et al 1998; Silva 1999; Tan 1995, 1999; Whitehead 1997; Wright 1993, 1997).

Ultimately, work casting the body as both a symbolic and a material product of social relations—a construct that is necessarily conditioned by a whole range of structural forces—has provided an especially important way of reframing recent research on sexuality in relation to HIV and AIDS (e.g., Bishop & Robinson 1998; Manderson & Jolly 1997; Parker 1999). The potential implications of this understanding for prevention interventions and strategies are far-reaching. In seeking to broaden the potential scope and impact of intervention strategies, a number of new approaches have been developed that have been heavily influenced by anthropologically and ethnographically grounded understandings of the political economy of HIV and AIDS. What have been described as structural interventions have come to the fore. For example, there are attempts to change the employment options for sex workers or improve the logistics of condom availability and distribution, with the ultimate goal of altering the structural conditions that may impede or facilitate the adoption of safer sex (Parker et al 2000a,b; Preston-Whyte et al 2000). Strategies aimed at "community mobilization" and the stimulation of activism or advocacy have also drawn attention, with a growing number of intervention studies now focusing on the dynamics of community organizing in different settings (Susser & Kreniske 1997). In some of the most innovative work currently being carried out, HIV/AIDS intervention research

has increasingly drawn on theories of "social transformation" and "collective empowerment" in order to examine issues related to power and oppression. The research has increasingly turned from the psychological theorists of reasoned decision-making to the work of community activists and popular educators in seeking the basis for a transformative or dialogical educational process in which participants explore and question their own lives and realities. Through this exploration and questioning, the participants begin to undergo a process of collective empowerment and transformation in order to respond to the forces that threaten and oppress them (see Paiva 2000, Parker 1996b).

All of this recent work has called attention to the need for structural changes aimed at transforming the broader forces that structure HIV/AIDS vulnerability and at enabling the members of affected communities to more adequately respond to these forces. Perhaps most important, it has focused on the extent to which HIV/AIDS prevention (and prevention research, in anthropology as in other disciplines) must be understood as part of a broader process of social transformation aimed not merely at the reduction of risk but at the redress of the social and economic inequality and injustice that has almost universally been found linked to increased vulnerability in the face of HIV and AIDS.

CONCLUSION

Anthropologists were rather slow to respond to the initial impact of the HIV/AIDS epidemic during the early and mid-1980s, allowing an essentially biomedical and highly individualistic model of AIDS research and intervention that has continued up to the present time as the dominant approach to the epidemic. Nevertheless anthropological perspectives have taken a leading role in defining what have been perhaps the most important alternative currents of social research in response to AIDS. Since the late 1980s, and increasingly over the course of the 1990s, anthropological research on the cultural meanings that shape and construct sexual experience, and on the political economy of structural forces that impinge upon sexual life, have provided alternative models and paradigms for responding to the epidemic both locally and cross-culturally (Parker et al 2000a; Treichler 1999). Although these two approaches for the most part emerged independently, inspired by distinct tendencies within the discipline more broadly, by the end of the 1990s both cultural and political economic or structural approaches increasingly merged in offering an important counterpoint to the more biomedical and behavioral perspectives that continue to dominate the field and to receive the lion's share of funding and prestige. Although it is impossible to fully predict the ways in which HIV/AIDS research will develop in the future, the fact that the epidemic continues to expand in large part independent of all of the efforts thus far to control it, and the fact that it continues to take its greatest toll in the so-called developing world and among the most impoverished and marginalized sectors of all societies, suggests that the kinds of approaches that anthropologists have offered for the study of sexuality and HIV/AIDS will continue to be important. The kind of response that anthropology continues to make in relation to the epidemic will be an important indicator of the relevance of the discipline as we enter the new millennium.

NOTE

1. These concerns have of course long been present in anthropological studies of sexuality in non-Western societies and, in particular, in the anthropological literature on kinship (e.g., Fortes 1967; Goody 1973; Leach 1961; Lévi-Straus 1969; Malinowski 1929, 1955).

REFERENCES

Aggleton P, ed. 1996. *Bisexualities and AIDS: International Perspectives.* London: Taylor Francis

Aggleton P, ed. 1999. *Men Who Sell Sex: International Perspectives on Male Prostitution and HIV/AIDS.* London: UCL Press

Akeroyd A. 1997. Sociocultural aspects of AIDS in Africa: occupational and gender issues. See Bond et al. 1997a, pp. 11–30

Alonso AM, Koreck MT. 1989. Silences: "Hispanics," AIDS and sexual practices. *Differences* 1:101–24

Altman D. 1994. *Power and Community: Organizational and Cultural Responses to AIDS.* London: Taylor Francis

Avila M, Zuñiga P, de Zalduondo B. 1991. Diversity in commercial sex work systems: preliminary findings from Mexico City and their implications for AIDS interventions. See Chen et al. 1991, pp. 179–94

Baer H, Singer M, Susser I. 1997. *Medical Anthropology and the World System.* Westport, CT/London: Bergin Garvey

Bibeau G. 1991. L'Afrique, terre imaginaire du SIDA: la subversion du discours scientifique par le jeu des fantasmes. *Anthropol. Soc.* 15(2–3):125–47

Bishop R, Robinson LS. 1998. *Night Market: Sexual Cultures and the Thai Economic Miracle.* New York/London: Routledge

Bolognone D. 1986. AIDS: a challenge to anthropologists. *Med. Anthropol. Q.* 17(2):36 (Abstr.)

Bolton R. 1992. Mapping terra incognita: sex research for AIDS prevention—an urgent agenda for the 1990s. See Herdt & Lindenbaum 1992, pp. 124–58

Bolton R, Lewis M, Orozco G. 1991. AIDS literature for anthropologists: a working bibliography. *J. Sex Res.* 28(2):307–46

Bolton R, Singer M, eds. 1992. *Rethinking AIDS Prevention: Cultural Approaches.* Philadelphia: Gordon Breach Sci.

Bond G, Kreniske J, Susser I. Vincent J, eds. 1997a. *AIDS in Africa and the Caribbean.* Boulder: Westview

Bond G, Kreniske J, Susser I. Vincent J. 1997b. The anthropology of AIDS in Africa and the Caribbean. See Bond et al. 1997a, pp. 3–9

Bond K, Celentano D, Phonsophakul S, Vaddhanaphuti C. 1997. Mobility and migration: female commercial sex work and the HIV epidemic in Northern Thailand. See Herdt 1997b, pp. 185–215

Carballo M, Cleland J, Caraël M, Albrecht G. 1989. A cross-national study of patterns of sexual behavior. *J. Sex Res.* 26:287–99

Carrier J. 1989. Sexual behavior and the spread of AIDS in Mexico. *Med. Anthropol.* 10:129–42

Carrier J. 1995. *De Los Otros: Intimacy and Homosexuality among Mexican Men.* New York: Columbia Univ. Press

Carrier J. 1999. Reflections on ethical problems encountered in field research on Mexican male homosexuality: 1968 to present. *Cult. Health Sex.* 1(3):207–21

Carrier J, Magaña R. 1991. Use of ethnosexual data on men of Mexican origin for HIV/AIDS prevention programs. *J. Sex Res.* 28(2):189–202

Carrier J, Ngyen B, Su S. 1997. Sexual relations between migrating populations (Vietnamese with Mexican and Anglo) and HIV/STD infections in Southern California. See Herdt 1997b, pp. 225–50

Carrillo H. 1999. Cultural change, hybridity and male homosexuality in Mexico. *Cult. Health Sex.* 1(3):223–38

Chen LC, Amor JS, Segal SJ, eds. 1991. *AIDS and Women's Reproductive Health.* New York/London: Plenum

Chouinard A, Albert J, eds. 1989. *Human Sexuality: Research Perspectives in a World Facing AIDS*. Ottawa: Int. Dev. Res. Cent.

Clatts M. 1989. Ethnography and AIDS intervention in New York City: life history as an ethnographic strategy. In *Community-Based AIDS Prevention, Studies of Intravenous Drug Users and their Sexual Partners*. Rockville, MD: Natl. Inst., Drug Abuse

Clatts M. 1994. "All the king's horses and all the king's men": some personal reflections on ten years of AIDS ethnography. *Hum. Organ.* 53:93–95

Clatts M. 1995. Disembodied acts: on the perverse use of sexual categories in the study of high-risk behaviour. See ten Brummelhuis & Herdt 1995, pp. 241–55

Cleland J, Ferry B, eds. 1995. *Sexual Behavior and AIDS in the Developing World*. London: Taylor Francis

Conant F. 1988a. Evaluating social science data relating to AIDS in Africa. In *AIDS in Africa: Social and Policy Impact*, ed. N Miller, R Rockwell, pp. 197–209. Lewiston, NY: Edwin Mellen

Conant F. 1988b. Using and rating cultural data on HIV transmission in Africa. See Kulstad 1988, pp. 198–204

Daniel H, Parker R. 1993. *Sexuality, Politics and AIDS in Brazil*. London: Falmer

de Zalduondo BO. 1991. Prostitution viewed cross-culturally: toward recontextualizing sex work in AIDS research. *J. Sex Res.* 22:223–48

de Zalduondo BO, Avila M, Zuñiga P. 1991. Intervention research needs for AIDS prevention among commercial sex workers and their clients. See Chen et al. 1991, pp. 165–78

de Zalduondo BO, Bernard J. 1995. Meanings and consequences of sexual-economic exchange. See Parker & Gagnon 1995, pp. 155–80

Díaz RM. 1998. *Latino Gay Men and HIV: Culture, Sexuality, and Risk Behavior*. New York/London: Routledge

Dyson T. 1992. *Sexual Behaviour and Networking: Anthropological and Socio-Cultural Studies on the Transmission of HIV*. Liège: Derouax-Ordina

Farmer P. 1992. *AIDS and Accusation: Haiti and the Geography of Blame*. Berkeley/Los Angeles: Univ. Calif. Press

Farmer P. 1995. Culture, poverty, and the dynamics of HIV transmission in rural Haiti. See ten Brummelhuis & Herdt 1995, pp. 3–28

Farmer P. 1999. *Infections and Inequalities: The Modern Plagues*. Berkeley/Los Angeles: Univ. Calif. Press

Farmer P, Connors M, Simmons J, eds. 1996. *Women, Poverty and AIDS: Sex, Drugs and Structural Violence*. Monroe, Maine: Common Courage

Farmer P, Lindenbaum S, Delvecchio-Good MJ. 1993. Women, poverty and AIDS: an introduction. *Cult. Med. Psychiatry* 17(4):387–97

Feldman D. 1985. AIDS and social change. *Hum. Organ.* 44(4):343–48

Feldman D, ed. 1994. *Global AIDS Policy*. Westport, Connecticut/London: Bergin Garvey

Feldman D, Johnson T, eds. 1986. *The Social Dimensions of AIDS: Method and Theory*. New York: Praeger

Feldman DA, Friedman SR, Des Jarlais DC. 1987. Public awareness of AIDS in Rwanda. *Soc. Sci. Med.* 24(2):97–100

Flowers N. 1988. The spread of AIDS in rural Brazil. See Kulstad 1988, pp. 159–73

Fortes M. 1967. *The Web of Kinship among the Tallensi*. London: Oxford Univ. Press

Gagnon JH, Parker RG. 1995. Conceiving sexuality. See Parker & Gagnon 1995, pp. 3–16

Geertz C. 1973. *The Interpretation of Cultures*. New York: Basic Books

Geertz C. 1983. *Local Knowledge*. New York: Basic Books

Ginsberg FD, Rapp R. 1995. *Conceiving the New World Order: The Global Politics of Reproduction*. Berkeley/Los Angeles: Univ. Calif. Press

González Block MA, Liguori AL. 1992. *El SIDA en los Estratos Socioeconómicos de México*. Cuernavaca, Mex.: Inst. Nac. Salud Pública

Goody J, ed. 1973. *The Character of Kinship*. Cambridge, UK: Cambridge Univ. Press

Gorman E. 1986. The AIDS epidemic in San Francisco: epidemiological and anthropological perspectives. In *Anthropology and Epidemiology: Interdisciplinary Approaches to the Study of Health and Disease*, ed. CR Janes, R Stall, SM Grifford, pp. 157–72. Dordrecht, Neth.: D. Reidel

Gorman E. 1991. Anthropological reflections on the HIV epidemic among gay men. *J. Sex Res.* 28(2):263–73

Gorman M. 1986. Introduction. *Med. Anthropol. Q.* 17(2): 31–32

Gupta GR, Weiss E. 1993. Women's lives and sex: implications for AIDS prevention. *Cult. Med. Psychiatry* 17(4):399–412

Henriksson B. 1995. *Risk Factor Love: Homosexuality, Sexual Interaction and HIV Prevention*. Göteborg, Swed.: Göteborgs Univ.

Henriksson B, Mansson S. 1995. Sexual negotiations: an ethnographic study of men who have sex with men. See ten Brummelhuis & Herdt 1995, pp. 157–82

Herdt G. 1987. AIDS and anthropology. *Anthropol. Today* 3(2):1–3

Herdt G. 1997a. Intergenerational relations and AIDS in the formation of gay culture in the United States. See Levine et al. 1997, pp. 245–81

Herdt G, ed. 1997b. *Sexual Cultures and Migration in the Era of AIDS: Anthropological and Demographic Perspectives*. London: Claredon

Herdt G. 1997c. Sexual culture and population movement: implications for AIDS/STDs. See Herdt 1997b, pp. 3–22

Herdt G, Boxer A. 1991. Ethnographic issues in the study of AIDS. *J. Sex Res.* 28(2):171–87

Herdt G, Boxer A. 1992. Sexual identity and risk for AIDS among gay youth in Chicago. See Dyson 1992, pp. 153–202

Herdt G, Leap WL, Sovine M. 1991. Anthropology, sexuality and AIDS. *J. Sex Res.* 28(2):167–69

Herdt G, Lindenbaum S, eds. 1992. *The Time of AIDS: Social Analysis, Theory, and Method.* Newbury Park, CA: Sage

Hogsborg M, Aaby P. 1992. Sexual relations, use of condoms and perceptions of AIDS in an urban area of Guinea-Bissau with a high prevalence of HIV-2. See Dyson 1992, pp. 203–32

Irvine JM, ed. 1994. *Sexual Cultures and the Construction of Adolescent Identities.* Philadelphia: Temple Univ. Press

Jenkins CL. 1996. Homosexual context, heterosexual practice in Papua New Guinea. See Aggleton 1996, pp. 191–206

Kammerer CA, Hutheesing OK, Maneeprasert R, Symonds PV. 1995. Vulnerability to HIV infection among three hilltribes in Northern Thailand. See ten Brummelhuis & Herdt 1995, pp. 53–78

Kane S, Mason T. 1992. "IV drug users" and "sex partners": the limits of epidemiological categories and the ethnography of risk. See Herdt & Lindenbaum 1992, pp. 199–222

Kendall C. 1995. The construction of risk in AIDS control programs. See Parker & Gagnon 1995, pp. 249–58

Khan S. 1996. Under the blanket: bisexualities and AIDS in India. See Aggleton 1996, pp. 161–77.

Klein C. 1999. "The ghetto is over, darling": emerging gay communities and gender and sexual politics in contemporary Brazil. *Cult. Health Sex.* 1(3):239–60

Kreniske J. 1997. AIDS in the Dominican Republic: anthropological reflections on the social nature of disease. See Bond et al. 1997a, pp. 33–50

Kulstad R, ed. 1988. *AIDS 1988: AAAS Symposia Papers.* Washington, DC: Am. Assoc. Adv. Sci. 478 pp.

Lang N. 1986. AIDS: biocultural issues and the role of medical anthropology. *Med. Anthropol. Q.* 17(2):35–36

Larvie P. 1997. Homophobia and ethnoscape of sex work in Rio de Janeiro. See Herdt 1997b, pp. 143–64

Larvie P. 1999. Natural born targets: male hustlers and AIDS prevention in urban Brazil. See Aggleton 1999, pp. 159–77

Law L. 1997. A matter of "choice": discourses on prostitution in the Philippines. See Manderson & Jolly 1997, pp. 233–61

Leach ER. 1961. *Rethinking Anthropology.* London: Athlone

Levi-Strauss C. 1969. *The Elementary Structures of Kinship.* Boston, MA: Beacon

Levine MP, Nardi PM, Gagnon JH, eds. 1997. *Changing Times: Gay Men and Lesbians Encounter HIV/AIDS.* Chicago/London: Univ. Chicago Press

Lichtenstein B. 2000. Sexual encounters: black men, bisexuality, and AIDS in Alabama. *Med. Anthropol. Q.* 14(3):374–93

Liguori AL, González Block MA, Aggleton P. 1996. Bisexuality and HIV/AIDS in Mexico. See Aggleton 1996, pp. 76–98

Liguori A, Aggleton P. 1999. Aspects of male sex work in Mexico City. See Aggleton 1999, pp. 103–25

Lindenbaum S. 1997. AIDS: body, mind, and history. See Bond et al. 1997a, pp. 191–94

Lindenbaum S. 1998. Images of catastrophe: the making of an epidemic. See Singer 1998, pp. 33–58

Long L. 1997. Refugee women, violence, and HIV. See Herdt 1997b, pp. 87–103

Lyttleton C. 2000. *Endangered Relations: Negotiating Sex and AIDS in Thailand.* Amsterdam: Harwood Acad.

Magaña JR. 1991. Sex, drugs and HIV: an ethnographic approach. *Soc. Sci. Med.* 33(1): 5–9

Malinowski B. 1929. *The Sexual Life of Savages in Northwestern Melanesia.* London: G. Routledge

Malinowski B. 1955. *Sex and Repression in Savage Society.* New York: Meridian Books

Manderson L, Jolly M, eds. 1997. *Sites of Desire/Economies of Pleasure: Sexualities in Asia and the Pacific.* Chicago: Univ. Chicago Press

McGrath JG, Rwabukwali CB, Schumann DA, Pearson-Marks J, Nakayiwa S, et al. 1993. Anthropology and AIDS: the cultural context of sexual risk behaviors among urban Baganda women in Kampala, Uganda. *Soc. Sci. Med.* 36(4):429–39

McGrath JG, Schumann DA, Rwabukwali CB, Pearson-Marks J, Mukasa R, et al. 1992. Cultural determinants of sexual risk behavior for AIDS among Baganda women. *Med. Anthropol. Q.* 6(2):153–61

Nachman SR, Dreyfuss G. 1986. Haitians and AIDS in South Florida. *Med. Anthropol. Q.* 17(2):32–33

Obbo C. 1988. Is AIDS just another disease? See Kulstad 1988, pp. 191–97

Obbo C. 1993. HIV transmission through social and geographic networks in Uganda. *Soc. Sci. Med.* 36:949–55

Obbo C. 1995. Gender, age and class: discourses on HIV transmission and control in Uganda. See ten Brummelhuis & Herdt 1995, pp. 79–95

Paiva V. 1995. Sexuality, AIDS and gender norms among Brazilian teenagers. See ten Brummelhuis & Herdt 1995, pp. 97–114

Paiva V. 2000. Gendered scripts and the sexual scene: promoting sexual subjects among Brazilian teenagers. See Parker et al. 2000a, pp. 216–39

Parker R. 1999. *Beneath the Equator: Cultures of Desire, Male Homosexuality and Emerging Gay Communities in Brazil.* New York/London: Routledge

Parker R, Aggleton P, eds. 1999. *Culture, Society and Sexuality: A Reader.* London: UCL Press

Parker R, Camargo Jr K. 2000. Pobreza e HIV/AIDS: aspectos antropológicos e sociológicos. *Cad. Saúde Pública* 16(Suppl. 1):89–102

Parker R, Khan S. Aggleton P. 1998. Conspicuous by their absence? Men who have sex with men (msm) in developing countries: implications for HIV prevention. *Crit. Public Health* 8(4):329–46

Parker RG. 1987. Acquired immunodeficiency syndrome in urban Brazil. *Med. Anthropol. Q.* (New Ser.) 1:155–72

Parker RG. 1988. Sexual culture and AIDS education in urban Brazil. See Kulstad 1988, pp. 269–89

Parker RG. 1991. *Bodies, Pleasures and Passions: Sexual Culture in Contemporary Brazil.* Boston: Beacon

Parker RG. 1994. Sexual cultures, HIV transmission, and AIDS prevention. *AIDS* 8(Suppl. 1):S309–14

Parker RG. 1996a. Behavior in Latin American men: implications for HIV/AIDS interventions. *Int. J. STD AIDS* 7(Suppl. 2):62–65

Parker RG. 1996b. Empowerment, community mobilization, and social change in the face of HIV/AIDS. *AIDS* 10(Suppl. 3):S27–31

Parker RG, Barbosa RM, Aggleton P, eds. 2000a. *Framing the Sexual Subject: The Politics of Gender, Sexuality, and Power.* Berkeley/Los Angeles/London: Univ. Calif. Press

Parker RG, Easton D, Klein C. 2000b. Structural barriers and facilitators in HIV prevention: a review of international research. *AIDS.* 14(Suppl. 1):S22–32

Parker RG, Gagnon JH, eds. 1995. *Conceiving Sexuality: Approaches to Sex Research in a Postmodern World.* New York/London: Routledge

Parker RG, Herdt G, Carballo M. 1991. Sexual culture, HIV transmission, and AIDS research. *J. Sex Res.* 28:77–98

Pollak M. 1988. Les homosexuels face au SIDA. Paris: A Métaillé

Porter D. 1997. A plague on the borders: HIV, development, and traveling identities in the Golden Triangle. See Manderson & Jolly 1997, pp. 212–32

Preston-Whyte E. 1995. Half-way there: anthropology and intervention-oriented AIDS research in KwaZulu/Natal, South Africa. See ten Brummelhuis & Herdt 1995, pp. 315–37

Preston-Whyte E, Varga C, Oosthuizen H, Roberts R, Blose F. 2000. Survival sex and HIV/AIDS in an African city. See Parker et al. 2000a, pp. 165–90

Prieur A. 1998. *Mema's House, Mexico City: On Transvestites, Queens and Machos.* Chicago: Univ. Chicago Press

Romero-Daza N. 1994. Multiple sexual partners, migrant labor and the makings for an epidemic: knowledge and beliefs about AIDS among women in highland Lesotho. *Hum. Organ.* 53:192–211

Romero-Daza N, Himmelgreen D. 1998. More than money for your labor: migration and the political economy of AIDS in Lesotho. See Singer 1998, pp. 185–204

Rubin G. 1997. Elegy for the Valley of Kings: AIDS and the leather community in San Francisco, 1981–1996. See Levine et al. 1997, pp. 101–44

Rwabukwali CB, Schumann DA, McGrath JG, Carroll-Pankhurst C, Mukasa R, et al. 1994. Culture, sexual behavior, and attitudes toward condom use among Baganda women. See Feldman 1994, pp. 70–89

Schoepf B. 1991. Ethical, methodological and political issues of AIDS research in central Africa. *Soc. Sci. Med.* 33:749–63

Schoepf B. 1992a. AIDS, sex and condoms: African healers and the reinvention of tradition in Zaire. *Med. Anthropol.* 14:225–42

Schoepf B. 1992b. Sex, gender and society in Zaire. See Dyson 1992, pp. 353–75

Schoepf B. 1992c. Women at risk: case studies from Zaire. See Herdt & Lindenbaum 1992, pp. 259–86

Schoepf B. 1995. Culture, sex research and AIDS prevention in Africa. See ten Brummelhuis & Herdt 1995, pp. 29–51

Schoepf B, Nkera R, Ntsomo P, Engundu W, Schoepf C. 1988. AIDS, women, and society in central Africa. See Kulstad 1988, pp. 176–81

Setel PW. 1999. *A Plague of Paradoxes: AIDS, Culture and Demography in Northern Tanzania.* Chicago: Univ. Chicago Press

Silva L. 1999. Travestis and gigolos: male sex work and HIV prevention in France. See Aggleton 1999, pp. 41–60

Sindzingré N, Jourdain G. 1987. Le SIDA: épidémiologie et anthropologie. *Polit. Afr.* 28:33–41

Singer M. 1994. AIDS and the health crisis of the U.S. urban poor: the perspective of critical medical anthropology. *Soc. Sci. Med.* 39:931–48

Singer M, ed. 1998. *The Political Economy of AIDS.* Amityville, NY: Baywood

Singer M, Flores C, Davidson L, Burke G, Castillo Z, et al. 1990. SIDA: the economic, social and cultural context of AIDS among Latinos. *Med. Anthropol. Q.* 4(1):72–114

Singer M, Jia Z, Schensul J, Weeks M, Page JB. 1992. AIDS and the IV drug user: the local context in prevention efforts. *Med. Anthropol.* 14:285–306

Sobo EJ. 1993. Inner-city women and AIDS: psychosocial benefits of unsafe sex. *Cult. Med. Psychiatry* 17:454–85

Sobo EJ. 1994. Attitudes toward HIV testing among impoverished urban African-American women. *Med. Anthropol.* 16:1–22

Sobo EJ. 1995a. *Choosing Unsafe Sex: AIDS-Risk Denial Among Disadvantaged Women.* Philadelphia, PA: Univ. Penn. Press

Sobo EJ. 1995b. Finance, romance, social support, and condom use among impoverished inner-city women. *Hum. Organ.* 54:115–28.

Sobo EJ. 1998. Love, jealousy and unsafe sex among inner-city women. See Singer 1998, pp. 75–103

Stall R. 1986. The behavioral epidemiology of AIDS: a call for anthropological contributions. *Med. Anthropol. Q.* 17(2): 36–37

Susser I, Kreniske J. 1997. Community organizing around HIV prevention in rural Puerto Rico. See Bond et al. 1997a, pp. 51–64

Symonds PV. 1998. Political economy and cultural logics of HIV/AIDS among the Hmong in Northern Thailand. See Singer 1998, pp. 205–26

Tan ML. 1995. From *bakla* to gay: shifting gender identities and sexual behaviors in the Philippines. See Parker & Gagnon 1995, pp. 85–96

Tan ML. 1996. *Silahis:* looking for the missing Filipino bisexual male. See Aggleton 1996, pp. 207–25

Tan ML. 1999. Walking the tightrope: sexual risk and male sex work in the Philippines. See Aggleton 1999, pp. 241–61

Tan ML. 2000. AIDS, medicine, and moral panic in the Philippines. See Parker et al. 2000a, pp. 143–64

ten Brummelhuis H, Herdt G, eds. 1995. *Culture and Sexual Risk: Anthropological Perspectives on AIDS.* Amsterdam: Gordon Breach

Terto V. 2000. Male homosexuality and seropositivity: the construction of social identities in Brazil. See Parker et al. 2000a, pp. 60–78

Treichler PA. 1999. *How to Have Theory in an Epidemic: Cultural Chronicles of AIDS.* Durham, NC/London: Duke Univ. Press

Turner CF, Miller HG, Moses LE, eds. 1989. *AIDS: Sexual Behavior and Intravenous Drug Use.* Washington, DC: Natl. Acad. Press

Ward M. 1991. Cupid's touch: the lessons of the family planning movement for the AIDS epidemic. *J. Sex Res.* 28(2):289–305

Whitehead T. 1997. Urban low-income African American men, HIV/AIDS, and gender identity. *Med. Anthropol. Q.* 11:411–47

Wilson C. 1995. *Hidden in the Blood: A Personal Investigation of AIDS in the Yucatan.* New York: Columbia Univ. Press

Wright JW. 1993. African-American male sexual behavior and the risk of HIV infection. *Hum. Organ.* 52:421–31

Wright JW. 1997. African American males and HIV: the challenge of the AIDS epidemic. *Med. Anthropol. Q.* 11:454–55

INDEX